MUSEUMS
ARCHITEKTUR

MUSÉES
ARCHITECTURE

MUSEOS
ARQUITECTURA

Original title: *Contemporary Museums | Architecture History Collections*
Original ISBN: 978-3-03768-067-4

Editorial coordination: Editorial office van Uffelen
Editorial staff: Jennifer Kozak, Lisa Rogers, Sarah Schkölziger
Graphic design: Michaela Prinz
Layout: Christine Maier, Sarah Schkölziger, Georgia van Uffelen

h.f.ullmann is an imprint of Tandem Verlag GmbH

Project coordination for h.f.ullmann: Lars Pietzschmann

Coordination of the translations: Alphagriese, Tom Griese
Copy-Editing German: Anja Breloh
Translation into French: Lucie Brevelet
Translation into Spanish: Fabio Descalzi

Coverdesign: Manuela Roth

Overall responsibility for production: h.f.ullmann publishing, Potsdam, Germany

Printed in Slovakia

ISBN 978-3-8331-6033-2
ISBN 978-3-8331-6057-8
ISBN 978-3-8331-6058-5

10 9 8 7 6 5 4 3 2 1
X IX VIII VII VI V IV III II I

If you would like to be informed about forthcoming h.f.ullmann titles, you can request our newsletter by visiting our website (**www.ullmann-publishing.com**) or by emailing us at: newsletter@ullmann-publishing.com.
h.f.ullmann, Birkenstraße 10, 14469 Potsdam, Germany

Chris van Uffelen

MUSEUMS
ARCHITEKTUR

MUSÉES
ARCHITECTURE

MUSEOS
ARQUITECTURA

h.f.ullmann

INHALT
SOMMAIRE
CONTENIDO

MUSEUMS ARCHITEKTUR
MUSÉES ARCHITECTURE
MUSEOS ARQUITECTURA

VORWORT

Das vorliegende Buch *MUSEUMSARCHITEKTUR* betrachtet, so die Bedeutung des griechischen Ursprungswortes „Museion", die Heiligtümer der Musen. Und wie in der Antike prachtvolle Tempel errichtet wurden, sind heutige Museumsbauten Tempel unseres bürgerlich aufgeklärten Kulturideals: Tempel für die Kunst, die Sprache, die Technik, die Seefahrt, die Literatur, die Geschichte und die Natur, aber auch Andachtsstätten für weniger erfreuliche Erinnerungen. Denn meistens beschäftigen sich Museen wissenschaftlich mit Vergangenem und bereiten es für ein gegenwärtiges Publikum auf. Indem sie aber archivieren, dokumentieren, analysieren und präsentieren, legen sie auch eine Spur von der Vergangenheit in die Zukunft und müssen schon heute – nach letztendlich noch nicht endgültig objektivierbaren Kriterien – Gegenwärtiges für die zukünftige Darstellung von Vergangenheit wählen.

Das umfangreichste „Exponat", mit dem Museen heute in ihre Zukunft investieren, ist der eigene Museumsbau, sei es ein Neu-, Aus- oder Umbau. Er sagt viel über das Selbstverständnis der Institution und die entsprechende wissenschaftliche Disziplin aus und kann selbstsicher, elegant, leger, experimentell oder spektakulär, introvertiert oder extrovertiert sein. Eine wichtige Rolle spielen zudem die Lage des Gebäudes im Stadtraum oder die Präsentation der Sammlung, wobei das Raumprogramm je nach Ausrichtung die wissenschaftliche Erforschung, die Darstellung von kanonisiertem Kulturgut oder die Entdeckung neuer Themen in den Mittelpunkt stellt. In der Nachfolge von Frank O. Gehrys Guggenheim Museum in Bilbao ist ein Museum heute auch eine touristische Attraktion. Diese Tendenz war zwar schon in den 1970er Jahren abzusehen, doch erst mit dem „Bilbao-Effekt" kam der Wendepunkt im modernen Museumsbau. Entsprechend der unterschiedlichen Selbstdefinitionen und der Vielzahl der Sammlungen zeigt sich auch die Baugattung vielseitig. Jede aktuelle stilistische Variante findet sich auch im Museumsbau, und der Entwurf und die Errichtung dieser Tempel aufgeklärter Gesellschaften gehören zu den beliebtesten Aufgaben bei Architekten. Das hat mehrere Gründe. So wollen sich die Träger – privat oder staatlich – kulturell interessiert präsentieren und sind somit bereit, in einen Repräsentationsbau zu investieren. Auf Architektenseite bietet ein Museumsbau ein viel größeres Spektrum an freier Gestaltung und Interpretation als beispielsweise ein Bürobau mit gleichem Kostenrahmen. Auch wenn die eigentliche Ausstellungsinszenierung oftmals Spezialisten überlassen wird, bestimmt der Architekt den übergreifenden Rahmen und die äußere Erscheinung der Sammlung.

In diesem Punkt zeigen Museumsbauten eine funktionale Ähnlichkeit mit mittelalterlichen Reliquiaren: Die eigentliche Reliquie konnte faktisch noch so unscheinbar sein, das kostbare Reliquiar, das sie umgab, bestimmte ihr Erscheinungsbild. Denn unscheinbar zu sein, bedeutete ja nicht, dass die Reliquie unbedeutend war, doch konnte man ihre Bedeutung nur durch das aufwändige Reliquiar um sie herum sichtbar machen. Ebenso weist ein Museumsbau im städtischen Kontext auf eine sehenswerte Sammlung hin und hebt sie aus ihrem Umfeld heraus, denn Kunstmuseen liegen oftmals in der historischen Innenstadt oder an der Grenze zum Stadtraum des 19. Jahrhunderts. So haben die Um- und Ausbauten dieser Museen oft mit beengten Grundstücken zu kämpfen. Aber auch für Museumsneubauten wird bevorzugt ein Bauplatz in der Innenstadt gesucht, wo sie sich in ein oft heterogenes Umfeld eingliedern und darin behaupten müssen.

MUSEUMSARCHITEKTUR zeigt Meisterwerke moderner Architektur von vielen renommierten Architekten, aber auch weniger bekannte Bauten, die sich durch außergewöhnliche Lösungen hervortun. Anhand von rund 170 Unikaten wird ein repräsentativer Querschnitt durch die möglicherweise interessanteste und vielfältigste Bauaufgabe unserer Zeit gezeigt.

PRÉFACE

Le présent livre *MUSÉES ARCHITECTURE* fait référence au terme grec d'origine « museion », sanctuaire consacré aux muses. A l'instar des splendides temples édifiés pendant l'Antiquité, les musées des temps modernes représentent notre idéal culturel éclairé sur la civilité actuelle : temples artistiques, linguistiques, techniques, ou consacrés à la navigation, à la littérature, à l'histoire ou la nature et conservent néanmoins leur rôle de sites consacrés aux souvenirs agréables. En effet, ces nouveaux musées sont notamment dédiés à l'étude scientifique du passé, désormais présentée au grand public. L'archivage, la documentation, l'analyse et la présentation retracent le passé dans l'avenir grâce à des critères non finalisés soigneusement sélectionnés parmi l'héritage culturel actuel afin de transmettre le passé au aux générations futures.

Les « œuvres exposées » volumineuses jaillissent du passé à l'avenir grâce aux musées construits, restaurés ou agrandis. Cette logique est très explicite sur l'idée muséale et la discipline scientifique qui se présente sous de multiples facettes : assurée, élégante, légère, expérimentale, introvertie ou extrovertie. Par ailleurs, le site du bâtiment dans le contexte urbain ainsi que la présentation de la collection jouent un rôle primordial, défini par la recherche scientifique, la représentation de biens culturels canonisés et la découverte de nouvelles thématiques centralisées. A l'instar du musée Guggenheim érigé par Frank O. Gehry à Bilbao, tout musée représente aujourd'hui une attraction touristique. En effet, cette tendance s'est profilée dès les années 1970, mais « l'effet Bilbao » a permis la percée vers la construction de musées moderne. Les types de construction complexes représentent les différentes nuances et la multiplicité des collections. Toute variante stylistique actuelle est représentée par la construction muséale, la conception et la construction de temples dédiés aux sociétés éclairées par les missions d'architectes. Les raisons sont nombreuses. Les maîtres d'œuvre au niveau privé ou public souhaitent présenter leur intérêt pour la culture et investissent dans les bâtiments représentatifs. Côté architectural, la construction de musées offre une marge de manœuvre et d'interprétation plus large que la construction de bureaux à un coût identique. Certes, la mise en scène de l'exposition est souvent remise à des spécialistes, mais l'architecte reste toujours maître du cadre global et de la présentation extérieure au niveau de la collection.

En effet, les musées se définissent grâce à leur fonctionnalité semblable aux reliques médiévales : même si les véritables vestiges sont de fait insignifiants, leur représentation brille grâce à la présentation. Insignifiance ne signifie pas manque d'importance des vestiges désormais présentés dans un contexte représentatif. Tout site de musée construit dans une zone urbaine offre une collection présentable qui se distingue des musées d'art, souvent situés dans le centre-ville historique ou à la périphérie de la zone urbaine définie au XIX siècle. Dans ce contexte, les reconstructions et extensions de musées se voient souvent confrontées aux contraintes liées aux terrains existant. En effet, les nouveaux musées privilégient également un emplacement en centre-ville et souhaitent s'intégrer dans un environnement hétérogène avec l'obligation de s'imposer.

MUSÉES ARCHITECTURE présente les œuvres d'art de maîtres en architecture moderne accompagnées d'un certain nombre moins connues qui se profilent grâce à leurs solutions extraordinaires. Les 170 exemplaires uniques représentent actuellement une panoplie des constructions les plus intéressantes de notre temps sous toutes leurs facettes.

PRÓLOGO

Este libro, *MUSEOS ARQUITECTURA*, toma el significado de la palabra griega museion, santuario de las musas. De la misma manera que en la Antigüedad se levantaban fastuosos templos, los edificios museísticos de hoy plasman nuestro ideal de cultura ciudadana: templos para el arte, la lengua, la tecnología, la navegación, la literatura, la historia y la naturaleza; y también, lugares de recogimiento que evocan recuerdos menos gratos. En general, los museos se ocupan de manera científica del pasado, y lo preparan para un público presente. Pero, a medida que archivan, documentan, analizan y presentan, también van dejando una huella del pasado para el futuro y, por tanto, deben escoger lo actual para presentarlo al futuro a modo de pasado, y esto, según criterios que todavía no han sido objetivados de forma definitiva.

La "muestra" más ambiciosa con la que los museos invierten en su futuro es la propia edificación museística, ya sea obra nueva, ampliación o reforma. Revela mucho sobre la identidad de la institución y su correspondiente disciplina científica; puede ser tímida o segura de sí misma, elegante o informal, experimental o espectacular, introvertida o extrovertida. Lo decisivo es la ubicación del edificio en el entorno urbano o la forma de presentación de la colección; según la organización, se focaliza la atención en la investigación científica, la presentación de bienes culturales emblemáticos o el descubrimiento de nuevas temáticas. La secuela del Museo Guggenheim de Bilbao de Frank O. Gehry es que los museos de hoy en día también constituyen atracciones turísticas. Esta tendencia ya se preveía en la década de 1970, pero recién con el "efecto Bilbao" se dio el punto de inflexión en las modernas edificaciones museísticas. Según las diferentes definiciones y la diversidad de las colecciones, hasta el linaje de las construcciones es muy variado. Cada variante estilística actual se manifiesta también en las edificaciones museísticas, y proyectar y concretar estos templos de las sociedades iluminadas es una de las tareas más soñadas por los arquitectos. Los motivos son diversos. Los actores, ya sean públicos o privados, quieren presentarse como interesados en la cultura y, por tanto, están dispuestos a invertir en un edificio representativo. Al arquitecto, un edificio de museo le ofrece un espectro de posibilidades de configuración e interpretación mucho más vasto que, por ejemplo, un edificio de oficinas con un nivel de precios similar. Aun cuando se suele dejar en manos de especialistas la escenificación de las propias exhibiciones, de todos modos el arquitecto define el marco genérico y la apariencia externa de la colección.

En este punto, las edificaciones museísticas constituyen símiles funcionales de los relicarios medievales: la propia reliquia podía ser, de hecho, muy discreta, no obstante lo cual el precioso relicario que la contenía determinaba su imagen. En realidad, el ser discreta no indicaba que la reliquia fuera insignificante, pero su significado solamente se captaba y se hacía visible gracias al costoso relicario. De manera análoga, un edificio de museo inserto en un contexto urbano señala una colección digna de verse y la destaca de su entorno, puesto que los museos de arte, a menudo, se levantan en los barrios históricos o en el límite con un barrio del siglo XIX. Así, las reformas y ampliaciones de estos museos suelen tener que lidiar con parcelas muy reducidas. Pero, también para las edificaciones museísticas completamente nuevas se prefiere un sitio en el casco urbano, con lo cual se deben insertar en un entorno a menudo heterogéneo y, por consiguiente, deben despegarse del mismo.

MUSEOS ARQUITECTURA es una colección de obras maestras de la arquitectura moderna, muchas firmadas por arquitectos afamados, y también otras menos conocidas que ostentan soluciones novedosas. Con unos 170 ejemplos se brinda una muestra representativa de la que tal vez sea la tarea arquitectónica más interesante y variada de nuestro tiempo.

america

ALERIA ADRIANA VAREJÃO_BRAZIL_BRUMADINHO_MUSEU DO PÃO_BRA
IL_ILÓPOLIS_FUNDAÇÃO IBERÊ CAMARGO_BRAZIL_PORTO ALEGRE_
USEÉ RODIN_BRAZIL_SALVADOR_ESTAÇÃO DA LUZ: MUSEU DA LÍNGUA
ORTUGUESA_BRAZIL_SÃO PAULO_MUSEU EXPLORATÓRIO DE CIÊNCIAS DA
NICAMP_BRAZIL_SÃO PAULO_ART GALLERY OF ALBERTA _CANADA_EDMON
ON_CANADIAN MUSEUM OF NATURE_CANADA_OTTAWA_MUSÉE NATIONAL DES
EAUX-ARTS IN QUEBEC_CANADA_QUÉBEC_GARDINER MUSEUM_CANADA_TO
ONTO_MUSEO DE LA MEMORIA Y LOS DERECHOS HUMANOS_CHILE_SANTIAGO_
USEO DEL CHOCOLATE NESTLÉ_MEXICO_MEXICO CITY_MUSEO TAMAYO_MEX
CO_MEXICO CITY_HORNO3: MUSEO DEL ACERO_MEXICO_MONTERREY_MU
EO CAO _PERU_EL BRUJO_AKRON ART MUSEUM_USA_AKRON (OH)_LIGHT
ATCHER AT THE WHATCOM MUSEUM _USA_BELLINGHAM (WA) _MUSEUM OF
INE ARTS_USA_BOSTON (MA)_BOSTON CHILDREN'S MUSEUM_USA_BOS
ON (MA)_ LEANOR AND WILSON GREATBATCH PAVILION_USA_BUFFALO (NY)

BRAZIL_BRUMADINHO **GALERIA ADRIANA VAREJÃO**

BRASILIEN_BRÉSIL_BRASIL
RODRIGO CERVIÑO LOPEZ
2008
KUNST- UND NATURKUNDEMUSEUM_MUSEE DE L'ART ET DE L'HISTOIRE NATURELLE_MUSEO DE ARTE Y DE HISTORIA NATURAL
558 M²
PHOTOS LEONARDO FINOTTI

Das Gebäude verändert das Gelände und fügt ein künstliches Element ein: einen regelmäßigen Block aus Stahlbeton. Das Gebäudevolumen wird von einer unregelmäßigen Stützmauer gebildet, die den Raum im Erdgeschoss definiert und die Lasten des Blocks im hinteren Teil mittels zweier Träger, in der Mitte mittels vier in die Wand eingelassener Säulen ableitet. Das Gebäude wurde zudem als spiralförmiger Weg konzipiert, der zwei verschiedene Ebenen des Parks miteinander verbindet, wobei Momente der Kontraktion/Passage und der Ausdehnung/Ausstellung alternieren: ein schmaler Spazierweg im Teich, der kleine quadratische Platz, das Erdgeschoss, das Treppenhaus, der erste Gehweg, die Rampe, die Terrasse, die Brücke und umgekehrt.

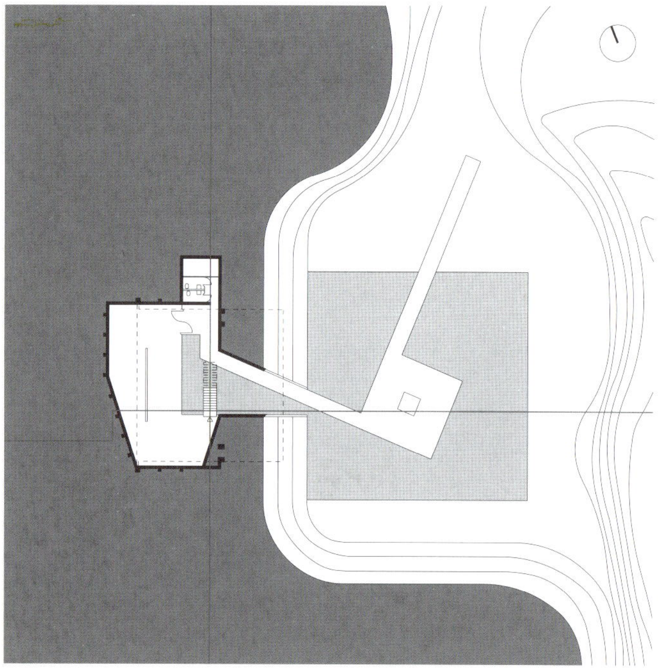

Le bâtiment transforme le terrain en intégrant un élément artistique : un bloc régulier en béton armé. Le volume du bâtiment est formé par un mur d'appui irrégulier qui définit l'espace au niveau du rez-de-chaussée et intègre les charges du bloc dans la partie arrière grâce à deux appuis et, au centre, grâce aux quatre colonnes encastrées dans le mur. Par ailleurs, le bâtiment fournit une voie communicante en forme de spirale entre les deux niveaux de hauteur différents du parc avec une alternance de moments de contraction / passage et d'extension / exposition : la promenade étroite à l'étang, la petite place carrée, le rez-de-chaussée, la cage d'escalier, le premier trottoir, la rampe, la terrasse, le pont et vice-versa.

El edificio modifica el predio y agrega un elemento artístico: un bloque regular de hormigón armado. El volumen edilicio está conformado por un muro de contención irregular que define el espacio en la planta baja y descarga la masa del bloque, en la parte trasera con dos vigas y en el medio con cuatro pilares incorporados en el muro. El edificio, como recorrido en espiral, conecta además entre dos niveles de altura diferentes del parque, de modo que se alternan momentos de contracción (pasaje) y de distensión (exhibición): un angosto sendero en el estanque, la pequeña plaza cuadrada, la planta baja, la caja de la escalera, el primer camino, la rampa, la terraza, el puente y viceversa.

links: Grundriss Erdgeschoss_Bank auf der Dachterrasse_Betonrampe_Ausstellungsraum Erdgeschoss. rechts: Fassade_Ausstellungsraum 1. Obergeschoss_Gläsernes Treppenhaus.
gauche: Plan du rez-de-chaussée_Banc sur la terrasse de toit_Rampe en béton_Espace d'exposition rez-de-chaussée. droite: Espace d'exposition du 1er étage_Cage d'escalier encastrée dans une boite en verre.
izquierda: Plano de planta baja_Vista de la azotea_Rampa de hormigón_Sala de exhibiciones en planta baja. derecha: Fachada_Sala de exhibiciones en el primer piso_Caja de la escalera acristalada.

BRAZIL_ILÓPOLIS **MUSEU DO PÃO**

BRASILIEN_BRÉSIL_BRASIL
BRASIL ARQUITETURA STUDIO WITH ANSELMO TURAZZI
2007
KULTURMUSEUM_MUSÉE DE LA CULTURE_MUSEO DE LA CULTURA
320 M²
PHOTOS NELSON KON, SÃO PAULO

Das Brotmuseum ist der Ausgangspunkt zu einer „Route der Mühlen im Taquari-Tal". Die 100-jährige Ilópolis-Mühle sollte nach dem Tod des Müllers verschwinden, wurde aber als Brotmuseum und Backatelier wiederbelebt. Die Neubauten sind vom Bestand inspiriert. Die rohen Fichtenbretter der Sichtbetonschalung hinterließen für alle Zeiten ihre Spuren auf den Neubauten. Museografie und Architektur gehen Hand in Hand. Die ersten Exponate sind demzufolge die alte Mühle selbst, die neuen Gebäude in städtischer Proportion, die Art und Weise, in der das Licht eintritt, die Materialien, die hölzernen Gehwege, die Präsentation und natürlich die aus der Region stammenden Exponate der Ausstellung.

Le musée du pain est le point de départ d'une « Route des moulins à Taquari-Tal ». Le moulin d'Ilópolis datant de 100 ans devait disparaitre après la mort du meunier, mais fût ranimé comme musée du pain et atelier de boulanger. Les nouveaux bâtiments sont inspirés comme les parties restantes. Le coffrage en béton visibles et planches d'épicéa brutes laisse ses traces pour l'éternité sur les nouveaux bâtiments. La muséographie et l'architecture allaient de pair. Par conséquent, les premiers objets exposés sont l'ancien moulin, les nouveaux bâtiments proportionnés à la ville, le mode et la manière de l'entrée de la lumière, les matériaux, les passerelles en bois, la présentation, et enfin, les objets de l'exposition provenant de la région.

El Museo del Pan es el punto de partida de una "Ruta de los molinos del valle del Taquarí". El centenario molino de Ilópolis debía desaparecer tras la muerte del molinero, pero se decidió preservarlo como museo del pan y taller de panadería. Las construcciones nuevas se inspiraron en lo preexistente. El encofrado de hormigón en tablas de abeto fue dejando sus huellas en las construcciones nuevas. Museografía y arquitectura van de la mano. Las primeras muestras en exposición son el propio molino, los nuevos edificios a escala urbana, la manera de penetrar de la luz, los materiales, las pasarelas de madera, la presentación y, por último, los objetos provenientes de la región que están en exposición.

links: Zeichnung_Innenraum alte Mühle_Neues Café im alten Getreidelager_Garten mit Mühlsteinen. rechts: Beton- und Holzstützen im Museum_Durchgehender Balkon vor der Backstube_Eingang_Neubau neben Altbau.
gauche: Dessin_Espace intérieur de l'ancien moulin_Nouveau bar dans l'ancien espace prévu pour l'entreposage des céréales_Jardin avec les pierres du moulin. droite: Appuis en bois et béton dans le musée_Balcon d'accès devant l'atelier de boulangerie_Entrée_Nouveau bâtiment à côté de l'ancien bâtiment.
izquierda: Ilustración_Interior del viejo molino_Nuevo café en el viejo depósito de cereales_Jardín con piedras de molino. derecha: Pilares de hormigón y madera en el museo_Balcón corrido en la panadería_Acceso_Nueva y antigua construcción.

si-nkhwa

BRAZIL_PORTO ALEGRE **FUNDAÇÃO IBERÊ CAMARGO**

BRASILIEN_BRÉSIL_BRASIL
ÁLVARO SIZA VIEIRA
2008
KUNSTMUSEUM_MUSÉE D'ART_MUSEO DE ARTE
11,834 M²
PHOTOS LEONARDO FINOTTI

Der erste Bau von Álvaro Siza in Brasilien ragt als viergeschossiges weißes Betongebäude über der Uferstraße auf und erstreckt sich mit einem eingeschossigen Flügel an ihr entlang. Der hohe Bauteil wird von Rampen gegliedert, die sich mit zunehmender Höhe vom eigentlichen Baukörper lösen. Im Inneren laufen sie weiter und erschließen die Emporen mit den Ausstellungsräumen. An den Schmalseiten, an denen die Rampen den Baukörper verlassen, befinden sich Aufzugsschächte. So umschließen die Rampen sowohl ein innen gelegenes wie auch ein äußeres Atrium. Der niedrige Flügel umfasst Rezeption, Museumsshop und Serviceeinrichtungen.

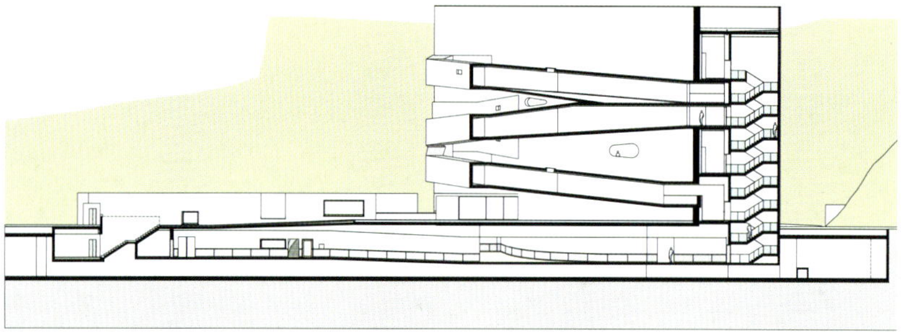

La première construction d'Álvaro Siza au Brésil se dresse comme un bâtiment blanc à quatre étages sur la route longeant la mer et évolue par une aile à un étage. La partie haute du bâtiment est structurée par des rampes qui se distinguent du corps de bâtiment en progressant en hauteur. Elles se poursuivent à l'intérieur afin de donner accès aux estrades servant de salles d'exposition. La cage d'ascenseur se situe sur le côté largeur du bâtiment qui mène aux rampes. Ainsi, les rampes entourent, et l'atrium situé à l'intérieur, et l'atrium extérieur. L'aile basse comprend la réception, la boutique du musée et les installations de service.

La primera construcción de Álvaro Siza Vieira en el Brasil es un edificio de hormigón que se levanta cuatro niveles sobre la avenida costera y se extiende a lo largo de esta con un ala de una planta. El volumen en altura está subdividido por rampas que se van despegando a medida que crece la altura. Se prolongan en el interior, donde se conectan con las salas de exhibiciones. En los lados angostos, donde las rampas se vinculan con el volumen edilicio, se encuentran los elevadores. Así, las rampas envuelven tanto un atrio interior como otro exterior. El ala de una planta comprende la recepción, la tienda del museo y las instalaciones de servicio.

links: Schnitt_Außenbau_Inneres Atrium. rechts: Gallerien_Äußeres Atrium_Skulpturale Form.
gauche: Coupe_Extérieur_Atrium intérieur. droite: Galeries_Atrium extérieur_Forme sculpturale.
izquierda: Corte_Vista exterior_Atrio interior. derecha: Galerías_Atrio exterior_Forma escultural.

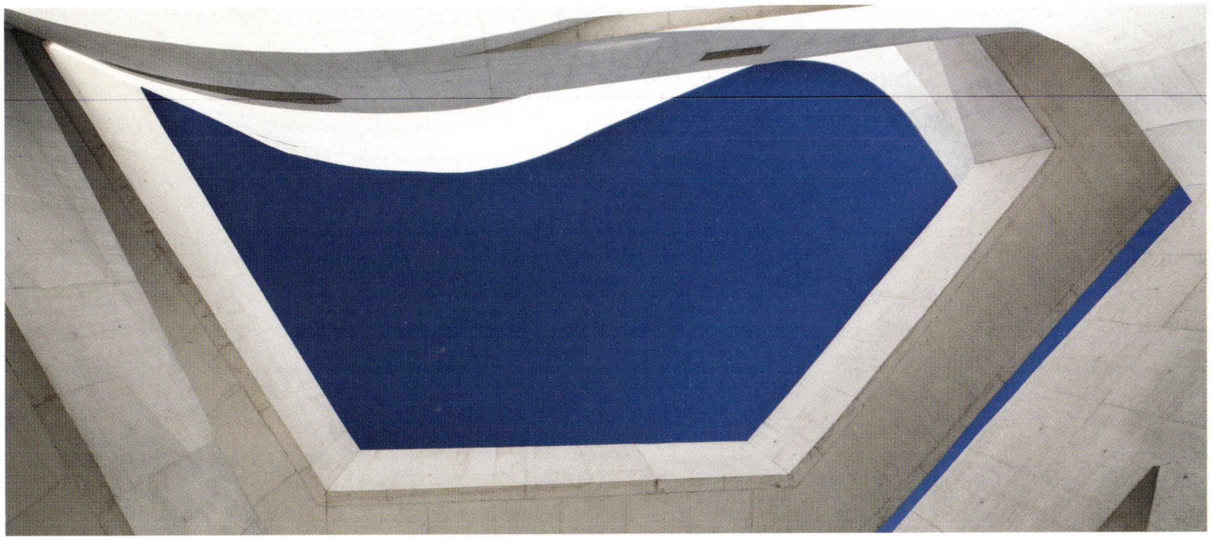

BRAZIL_SALVADOR **MUSÉE RODIN**

BRASILIEN_BRÉSIL_BRASIL
BRASIL ARQUITETURA STUDIO
2006
KUNSTMUSEUM_MUSÉE D'ART_MUSEO DE ARTE
3,055 M²
PHOTOS NELSON KON, SÃO PAULO

Das Museum ist die einzige Dependance des Pariser Rodin Museums. Es besteht aus einem alten Herrenhaus und einem zeitgenössischen Gebäudeteil aus Beton-, Glas- und Holzelementen. Dieser dient Wechselausstellungen, während die Säle des Palasts und der Garten Werke des bedeutenden französischen Bildhauers zeigen. Die ehemalige, 1912 erbaute Residenz wurde restauriert und der neuen Funktion angepasst. Das oberste Geschoss wurde mit einem kleinen Auditorium versehen. Der neue rückwärtige Bauteil aus Beton dient als vertikale Erschließung, und Beton verbindet die beiden Gebäude. Ein subtiler Dialog zwischen den beiden zeitlich 100 Jahre auseinanderliegenden Architekturen entsteht dadurch, dass beiden eigener Raum und eine eigene Aussage zugestanden wird.

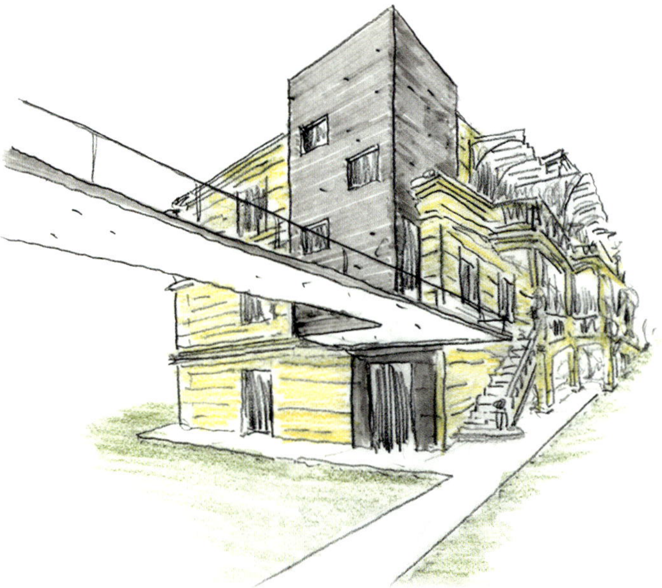

Le musée, unique dépendance du musée Rodin à Paris, est composé d'un ancien manoir et d'une partie contemporaine constituée d'éléments en béton, verre et bois au service des expositions en alternance, tandis que les salles du palais et le jardin exposent les œuvres du sculpteur français renommé. L'ancienne résidence construite en 1912 a été restaurée et adaptée à sa nouvelle fonction. L'étage supérieur a été aménagé avec un petit auditorium. La nouvelle partie arrière en béton sert à marquer un accès vertical grâce au béton qui lie les deux bâtiments afin d'aboutir à un dialogue subtil des deux éléments architecturaux séparés de 100 ans tout en conservant leur espace propre et individualité.

Este museo es la única sucursal del Museo Rodin de París. Comprende una antigua villa señorial y una edificación contemporánea hecha de elementos de hormigón, vidrio y madera. La misma alberga exhibiciones temporarias, mientras que las salas del palacio y el jardín exhiben obras del famoso escultor francés. La antigua residencia, levantada en 1912, fue restaurada y adaptada a la nueva función. El nivel superior fue dotado de un pequeño auditorio. La nueva edificación posterior de hormigón sirve como conexión vertical, y ambos edificios están unidos por elementos de hormigón. Se ha logrado así un diálogo sutil entre las dos arquitecturas, separadas por un siglo, pues a ambas les corresponde un espacio propio y una expresión propia.

links: Skizze neue Treppe und Fahrzugschacht_Neuer Zugang Altbau_Neue Erschließung bei Nacht Betonbrücke Alt und Neu verbindend. rechts: Neubau_Skulpturengarten_Hauptausstellungsraum.
gauche: Esquisse du nouvel escalier et de la cage d'ascenseur_Nouvel accès à l'ancien bâtiment Nouvel accès de nuit_Pont en béton harmonisant le nouveau à l'ancien. droite: Nouveau bâtiment Jardin orné de sculptures_Espace d'exposition principal.
izquierda: Esbozo de nueva escalera y torre del elevador_Nuevo acceso del edificio antiguo_Nueva conexión por la noche_Puente de hormigón entre lo antiguo y lo nuevo. derecha: Edificación nueva Jardín de esculturas_Sala principal de exhibiciones.

BRAZIL_SÃO PAULO

ESTAÇÃO DA LUZ: MUSEU DA LÍNGUA PORTUGUESA

BRASILIEN_BRÉSIL_BRASIL
PAULO A. MENDES DA ROCHA ARQUITETOS ASSOCIADOS,
PEDRO MENDES DA ROCHA ARQUITETOS ASSOCIADOS
2005
SPRACHENMUSEUM_MUSÉE DES LANGUES_MUSEO LINGÜÍSTICO
7,088 M²
PHOTOS LEONARDO FINOTTI

Der Eingriff in dieses eigenartige Gebäude setzte sich von Anfang an mit der Organisation eines umfangreichen Rundgangs für Besucher auseinander. Da dieser von dem existierenden Zugang zum öffentlichen Nahverkehr in der Hauptlobby separiert werden sollte, dienen die symmetrisch angelegten West- und Ostpatios dem Museum als überdachte Lobbys und Haupteingänge. Die dekorativen Türme an den vier Ecken des Gebäudes beherbergen Aufzüge. Sie bringen die Besuchergruppen in den dritten Stock, wo der Rundgang beginnt (Auditorium, Sprach-Plaza, Terrasse). Im zweiten Stock wird er fortgesetzt (Große Galerie, Galerie der Einflüsse, Zeitachse) und endet im ersten Stock (Wechselausstellungen, Forschung, Verwaltung).

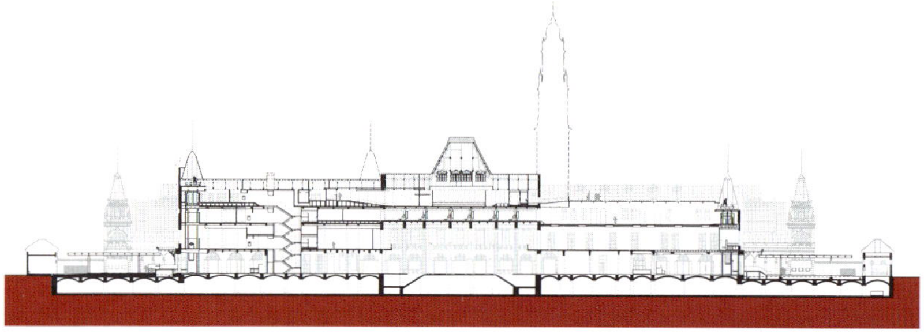

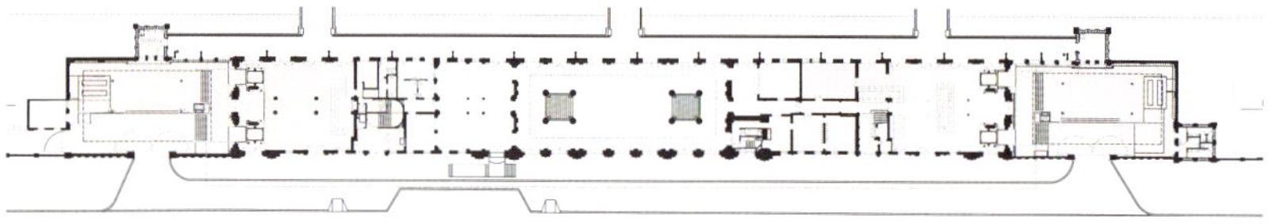

Dès le début, toute intervention dans ce bâtiment intrigant interpelle grâce à l'organisation d'une rotonde exhaustive offerte aux visiteurs. L'objectif fût la séparation de l'accès existant aux transports publics de proximité dans le hall central. L'objectif est atteint grâce au patio ouest et est du musée servant d'entrée couverte. Les tours décoratives positionnées aux quatre coins du bâtiment comportent les ascenseurs. Ils permettent aux groupes de visiteurs d'atteindre le troisième étage, point de départ du circuit (auditorium, Plaza d'échanges et terrasse). La logique se poursuit au deuxième étage (grande galerie, galerie des influences et axe temporel) pour finir au premier étage (expositions alternantes, recherche et administration).

La intervención en este edificio de características únicas comprendió desde el inicio la organización de un ambicioso recorrido para los visitantes. Como este debía separarse del pasaje existente al transporte público de cercanías en el vestíbulo principal, los patios este y oeste sirven al museo como vestíbulos techados. Las torres decorativas en los cuatro rincones del edificio contienen elevadores. Transportan a los grupos de visitantes hacia el tercer nivel, donde comienza el recorrido: auditorio, Plaza de la Lengua, terraza. Continúa en el segundo nivel con la Gran Galería, Galería de las Influencias, Línea del Tiempo, para finalizar en el primer nivel con las exhibiciones temporarias y las áreas de investigación y administración.

links: Schnitt und Grundriss Erdgeschoss_Turm durch neue Überdachung gesehen_Hof_Eingang. rechts: Ausstellung_Medienwand_Interaktive Ausstellung.
gauche: Coupe et plan du rez-de-chaussée_Tour vue de la nouvelle toiture_Cour_Entrée. droite: Exposition_Mur de médias_Exposition interactive.
izquierda: Corte y plano de planta baja_Torre vista a través de la nueva cubierta_Patio_Acceso. derecha: Exposición_Pared multimedia_Muestra interactiva.

REQUERIAM
ERA SARAR,
NÃO DESEJAVAM
CÉU NENHUM.
PÁG. 49

CARNAVAIS

O PORTUGUÊS NO MUNDO

BRAZIL_SÃO PAULO

MUSEU EXPLORATÓRIO DE CIÊNCIAS DA UNICAMP

BRASILIEN_BRÉSIL_BRASIL
CORSI HIRANO ARQUITETOS
ONGOING
WISSENSCHAFTSMUSEUM_MUSÉE DE LA SCIENCE
MUSEO DE CIENCIAS
5,370 M^2
PHOTOS COURTESY OF THE ARCHITECTS

Aufgabe der Institution und Hauptziel des Projekts ist es, die Beziehung zwischen Mensch und Natur aufzuzeigen. Während sich die Wissenschaft in diesem Zusammenhang mit der Realität beschäftigt, ergänzt die Architektur das noch nicht Vorhandene. Sie präsentiert sich als eine Möglichkeit des menschlichen Ausdrucks und als Schöpfung der Menschheit, als autarkes Phänomen. Davon ausgehend werden zwei absolute Bedingungen präsentiert: der singuläre Ort des Gebäudes und die universelle Institution. Der Ort bedingt die Beziehung zwischen dem neuen Museum und der Landschaft, kreiert aber auch einen Bau, der selbst territoriale Bedeutung entfaltet. Ein Museum, das beobachtet und beobachtet wird.

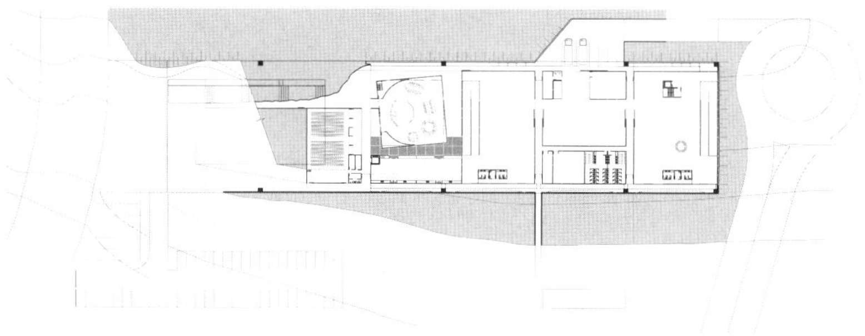

La mission de l'institution et l'objectif principal du projet consistent à dévoiler la relation entre l'homme et la nature. Alors que la science se consacre dans ce contexte à la réalité, l'architecture sert de complément à l'irréel. Ce concept se présente comme possibilité de l'expression humaine et comme création de l'humanité en tant que phénomène autarcique. Sur cette base, deux conditions absolues sont démontrées : le lieu singulier du bâtiment et l'institution universelle. Le lieu conditionne la relation entre le nouveau musée et le paysage et crée également une construction qui fait ressortir la signification territoriale. Un musée qui observe sous observation.

Poner en evidencia la relación entre el hombre y la naturaleza es la tarea de la institución y la finalidad principal del proyecto. En este contexto, en tanto la ciencia se ocupa de la realidad, la arquitectura se encarga de completar lo que todavía no existe. Se presenta como la posibilidad de expresión humana y como creación de la humanidad, como fenómeno autárquico. A partir de esto, manifiesta dos condiciones absolutas: la ubicación singular del edificio y la institución universal. El sitio condiciona la relación entre el nuevo museo por un lado y el paisaje por el otro, pero crea también una construcción que despliega su propio significado territorial. Un museo que observa y es observado.

links: Grundriss_Eingangsbereich. rechts: Empfang_Zeit und Raum-Platz.
gauche: Plan du rez-de-chaussée. droite: Réception_Place du temps et de l'espace.
izquierda: Plano_Planta baja. derecha: Recepción_Plaza del Espacio y el Tiempo.

nano
aventura

14 bis

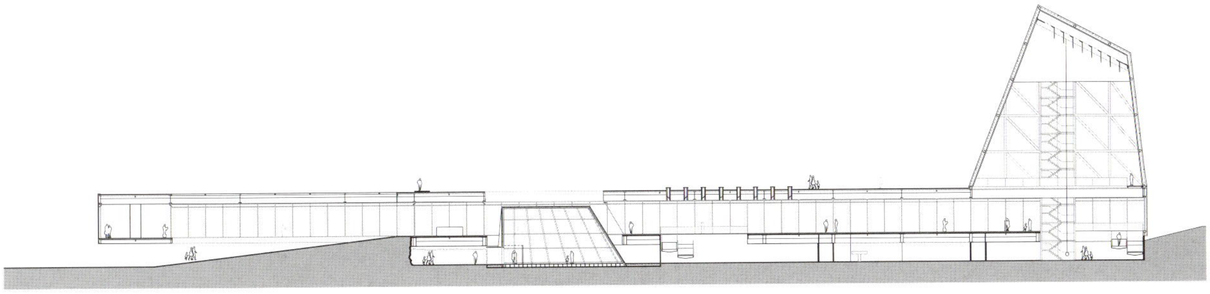

links: Ständige Ausstellung. rechts: Schnitt_Wechselausstellung_Nächtliche Vogelperspektive.
gauche: Exposition permanente. droite: Coupe_Expositions tournantes_Perspective à vol d'oiseau de nuit.
izquierda: Muestra permanente. derecha: Corte_Muestra temporaria_Perspectiva nocturna a vuelo de pájaro.

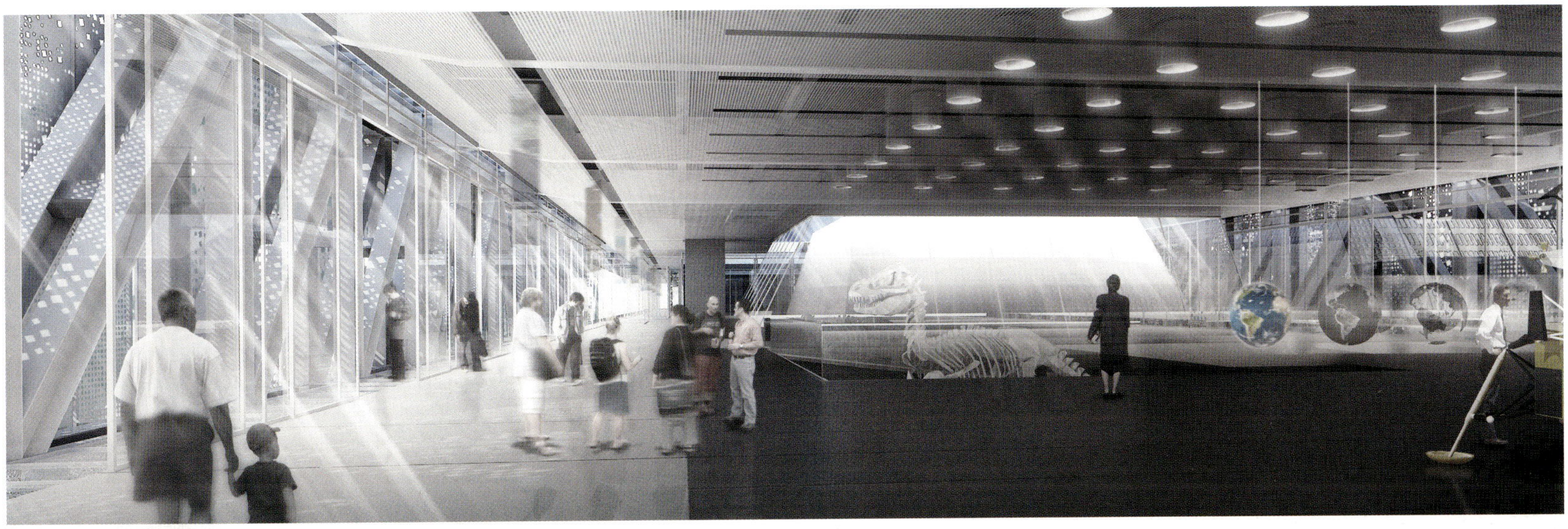

CANADA_EDMONTON **ART GALLERY OF ALBERTA**

KANADA_CANADA_CANADÁ
RANDALL STOUT ARCHITECTS, INC
2010
KUNSTMUSEUM_MUSÉE D'ART_MUSEO DE ARTE
7,800 M²
PHOTOS RANDALL STOUT, LOS ANGELES (26 B. L., B. R.),
ROBERT LEMERMEYER, CALGARY (27, 28, 29)

Die neue Art Gallery of Alberta feiert ihre kulturell prominente Lage auf dem Sir Winston Churchill Square. Der Ursprungsbau der 1960er Jahre wurde durch den Anbau neuer öffentlicher Räume und Galerien, eines einheitlichen Pädagogikflügels, eines Cafés und von Büros verwandelt. Grundriss und vertikale Organisation der fünf Ebenen lösen die verschiedenen Ströme zu Kunst und Gastronomie, des Personals und der Besucher mit großer Klarheit auf, und Verbindungen zur U-Bahn und Fußgängerzone verbessern die Anbindung an die Stadt. Die sorgfältige Fertigung aus lackiertem Zink, Hochleistungsverglasung und Edelstahl verleiht dem Gebäude eine außergewöhnliche Beständigkeit im nördlichen Klima. Geschwungene Formen sowie eine dramatische Beleuchtung helfen, intuitiv den Weg in den Galerien und öffentlichen Räumen zu finden.

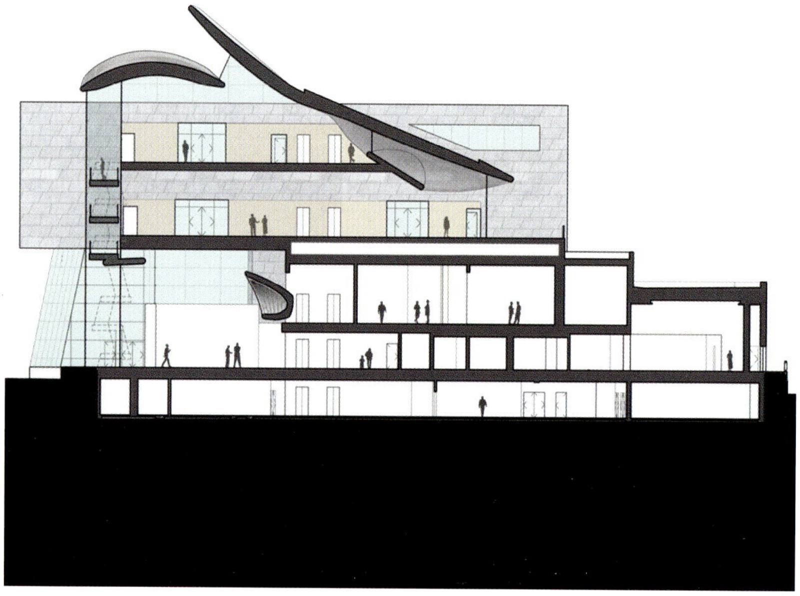

La nouvelle galerie d'Art Alberta fête sa situation phare au niveau culturel sur le Sir Winston Churchill Square. La construction d'origine datant des années 1960 accueille une extension avec de nouveaux espaces et galeries publics, une aile homogène dédiée à la pédagogie, un café et des bureaux. Le plan et l'organisation verticale des cinq niveaux se présentent comme des espaces clairs dédiés aux différentes orientations : art, gastronomie, visiteurs et collaborateurs en offrant une nouvelle jonction urbaine au métro et à la zone piétonnière. Le recours artisanal au zinc laqué, les vitrages de haute performance et l'acier fin assurent une résistance inhabituelle du bâtiment au climat septentrional. Les courbes et l'éclairage généreux servent à un guidage intuitif dans les galeries et les espaces publics.

La nueva Galería de Arte de Alberta celebra su destacada ubicación cultural sobre la plaza Sir Winston Churchill. La edificación original de los años sesenta ha sido ampliada con nuevas salas para público y galerías, un ala pedagógica, un café y oficinas. La planta y la organización vertical de los cinco niveles resuelven los múltiples desplazamientos del personal y de los visitantes hacia el arte y la gastronomía con gran claridad, y logran una nueva vinculación urbana con la zona peatonal y la estación del metro. El tratamiento artesanal del cinc esmaltado, el acristalamiento de alta resistencia y acero garantizan una resistencia formidable de la edificación frente al adverso clima boreal. Fantásticas formas contorsionadas y una iluminación de efecto espectacular colaboran con el recorrido intuitivo por las galerías y las salas para público.

links: Schnitt_Hauptatrium_Hauptatrium. rechts: Blick vom Sir Winston Churchill Square.
gauche: Coupe_Atrium principal_Atrium principal. droite: Vue de Sir Winston Churchill Square.
izquierda: Corte_Atrio principal_Atrio principal. derecha: Vista desde Sir Winston Churchill Square.

art gallery of alberta

links: Detail Innenraum. rechts: Skizze_Große Ausstellungshalle_Atrium, 2. Obergeschoss.
gauche: Coupe_Espace intérieur en détail. droite: Esquisse_Grand hall d'exposition_Atrium, 2ème étage.
izquierda: Detalle del interior. derecha: Esbozo_Gran sala de exhibiciones_Atrio en el segundo piso.

CANADA_OTTAWA **CANADIAN MUSEUM OF NATURE**

KANADA_CANADA_CANADÁ
PADOLSKY, KUWABARA, GAGNON JOINT VENTURE ARCHITECTS
2010
NATURKUNDEMUSEUM_MUSEE DE L'HISTOIRE NATURELLE
MUSEO DE HISTORIA NATURAL
23,225 M^2
PHOTOS TOM ARBAN PHOTOGRAPHY, TORONTO

Das Museum war der erste Museumbau des Landes. Die Revitalisierung präsentiert das ursprüngliche Gebäude mittels moderner Architektur in einem Dialog von Vergangenheit und Gegenwart. Die gläserne Laterne stellt die ursprüngliche Proportion des Haupteingangs wieder her und bildet eine überdimensionale Vitrine. Innerhalb der Laterne ermöglicht die neue zweiflügelige Treppe einen durchgängigen Bewegungskreislauf um das Atrium herum und durch alle vier Ebenen des Museums hindurch. Die Galerieräume wurden so umgestaltet, dass ein Gleichgewicht zwischen dunkleren Räumen und Tageslichtgalerien entstand. Die Südterrasse schafft einen kombinierten Innen- und Außenbereich für zwanglose und formelle Veranstaltungen.

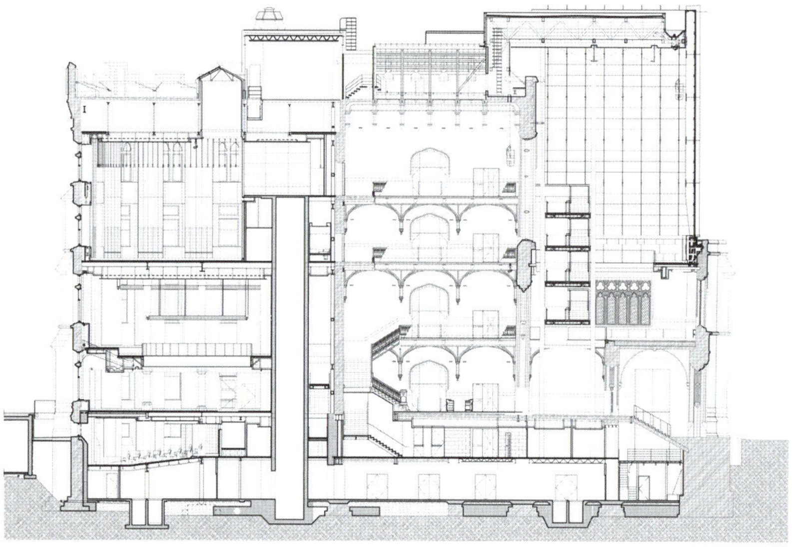

Le musée était le premier du pays. La rénovation présente le bâtiment d'origine sous le signe d'un dialogue entre passé et présent grâce à l'architecture moderne. Le lanternon en verre reproduit les proportions d'origine de l'entrée principale et forme une vitrine surdimensionnée. En dessous du lanternon, le nouvel escalier papillon d'une longueur interminable favorise le mouvement vers l'atrium et les quatre niveaux du musée. L'espace de galeries fut reconfiguré afin de produire un équilibre entre les espaces sombres et les galeries éclairées par la lumière naturelle. La terrasse Sud crée un espace intérieur et extérieur combiné pour les manifestations informelles et formelles.

Este edificio museístico ha sido el primero del país. La revitalización del edificio original implicó lograr un diálogo entre el pasado y el presente con arquitectura moderna. La linterna acristalada reproduce las proporciones originales del acceso principal y constituye una vitrina sobredimensionada. Bajo la linterna, la nueva escalinata de dos ramas posibilita una sensación de bucle sin fin de movimiento alrededor del atrio y en todos los cuatro niveles del museo. Las áreas de exhibición han sido reconfiguradas para lograr un equilibrio entre ambientes oscuros y galerías iluminadas por luz diurna. La terraza sur logra un espacio interior-exterior combinado para actividades formales e informales.

links: Schnitt_Blick aus der Metcalfe Street_Decke des Lichthofs. rechts: Nachtansicht Oberlicht.
gauche: Coupe_Vue sur Metcalfe Street_Plafond de la cour lumineuse. droite: Vue de nuit éclairage en hauteur.
izquierda: Corte_Vista desde Metcalfe Street_Cubierta del patio de luz. derecha: Vista nocturna del lucernario.

VICTORIA MEMORIAL MUSEUM
NATURE
Main Entrance
Entrée principale
Group Entrance
Entrée des groupes

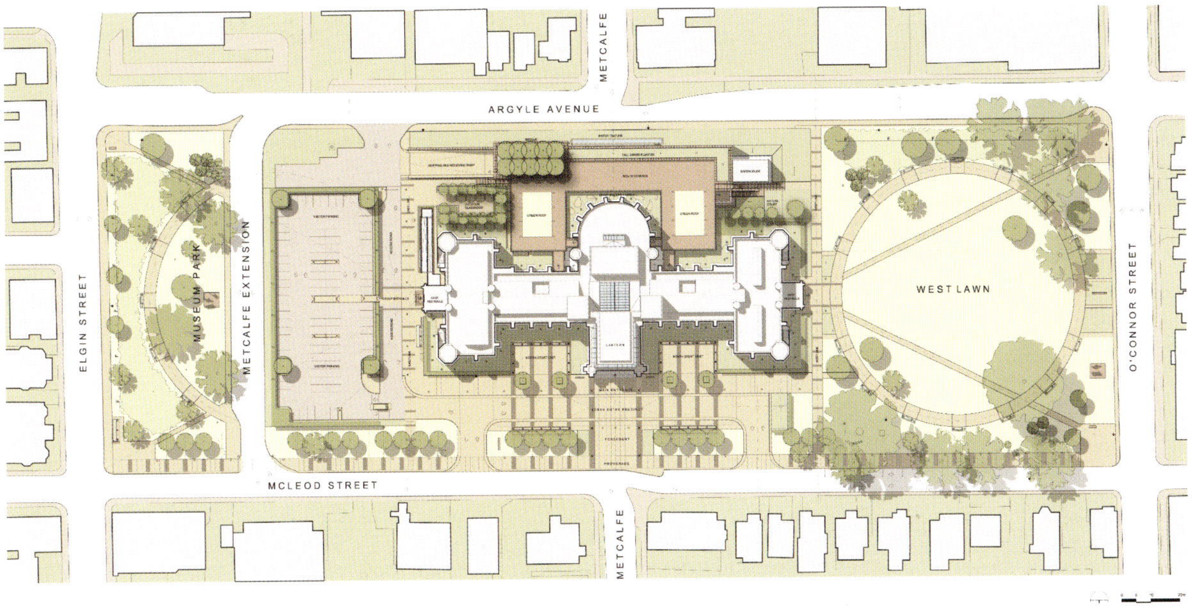

links: Doppelläufiges Treppenhaus. rechts: Lageplan_Blick von der Haupttreppe durch den Glaskubus_Atrium mit deckmalgeschütztem Fenster_Decke des Atriums mit Haupttreppe.
gauche: Cage d'escalier double. droite: Plan de site_Vue sur l'escalier principal à travers le cube en verre_Atrium avec une fenêtre protégée au titre de monument historique_Plafond de l'atrium avec l'escalier principal.
izquierda: Escalera doble. derecha: Plano de ubicación_Vista desde la escalera principal a través del cubo de cristal_Atrio con ventana histórica_Techo del atrio con escalera principal.

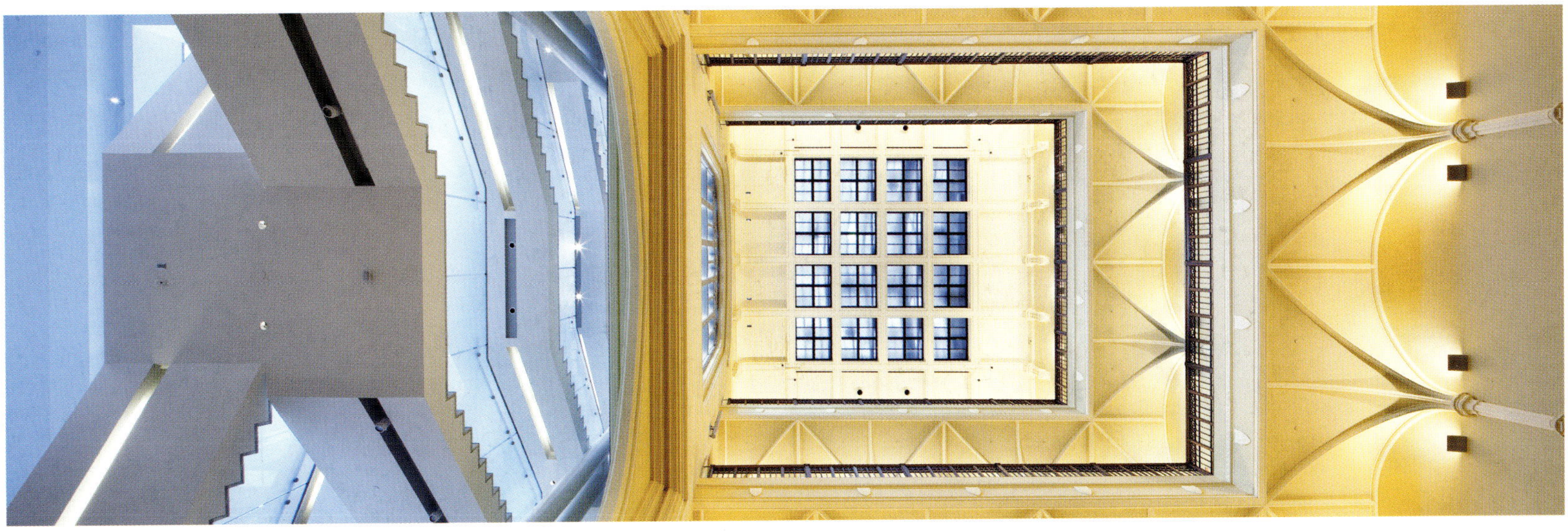

CANADA_QUEBEC **MUSÉE NATIONAL DES BEAUX-ARTS DU QUÉBEC**

KANADA_CANADA_CANADÁ
OFFICE FOR METROPOLITAN ARCHITECTURE (OMA)
2013
KUNSTMUSEUM_MUSÉE D'ART_MUSEO DE ARTE
15,000 M²
PHOTOS OFFICE FOR METROPOLITAN ARCHITECTURE (OMA)
(34 B. L.), COPYRIGHT OMA; IMAGE BY LUXIGON (34 B. R., 35 A., B.)

Die Architekten stapeln die neuen Galerien in drei Volumen von abnehmender Größe und erreichen so eine Stufung vom Park in die Stadt hinab. Der Entwurf möchte auf diese Weise Stadt, Park und Museum miteinander verbinden. Die Stapelung erzeugt eine 14 Meter hohe, von einem dramatischen Überstand überfangene Haupthalle. Sie dient als Schnittstelle zur Grande-allée, einem städtischen Platz für die öffentlichen Funktionen des Museums, und bietet Zugänge, die in die Galerien, den Hof und das Auditorium führen. Das neue Gebäude stellt die Verbindung zum Charles-Baillairge-Pavillon, einem ehemaligen Gefängnis von 1867, durch einen Tunnel her. Es schafft eine Mischung aus Galerieräumen, die den Besucher anscheinend zufällig in den Rest des Museumskomplexes führt.

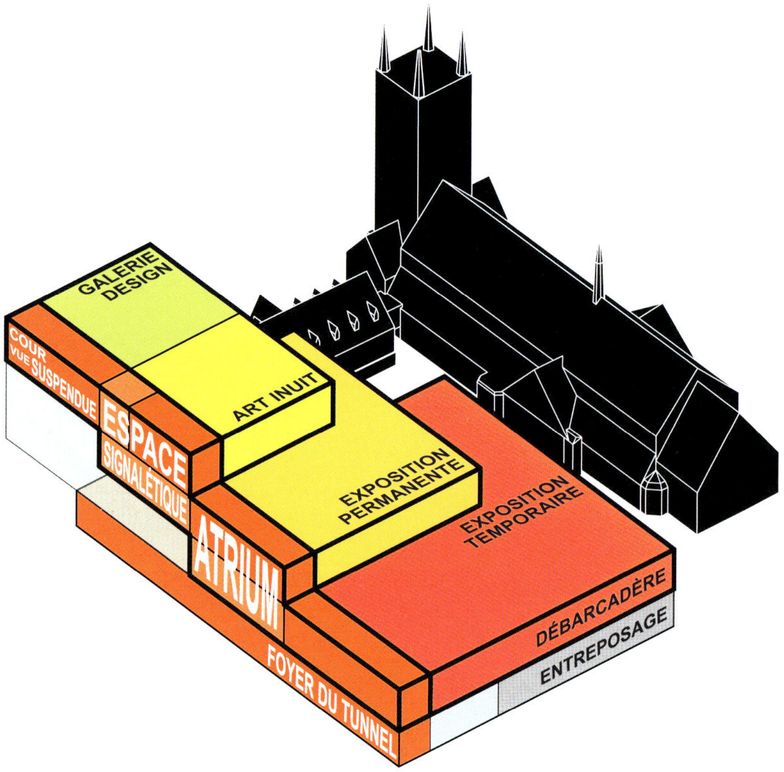

Les architectes ont superposés les nouvelles galeries en trois volumes de grosseur décroissante afin d'obtenir un aménagement en gradins donnant sur le parc de la ville en contrebas. Le projet aspirait ainsi à réunir la ville, le parc et le musée. La partie superposée est formée par un porte-à-faux impressionnant du hall principal, de 14 mètres de hauteur, servant d'interface à la grande-allée, une place municipale prévue pour les fonctions publiques du musée avec des portes desservant les galeries, la cour et l'auditorium. Le nouveau bâtiment est contigu au pavillon Charles-Baillairge, une ancienne prison de 1867 accessible par un tunnel. Ainsi, l'ensemble offre une variété de galeries qui accompagne les visiteurs d'une manière apparemment fortuite dans les autres espaces du musée.

Los arquitectos han definido las nuevas galerías como tres volúmenes apilados de tamaño decreciente y logran así una sensación de escalonamiento entre el parque y la ciudad. De esta manera, el proyecto vincula entre sí la ciudad, el parque y el museo. El escalonamiento genera una sala principal con un espectacular saliente de 14 metros de altura. Sirve como nexo con la Grande-Allée, una plaza urbana para las funciones públicas del museo, con portones que conducen a las galerías, el patio y el auditorio. El nuevo edificio conecta por un túnel con el pabellón Charles-Baillairge, una antigua penitenciaría de 1867. Se obtiene una combinación de espacios galerísticos, que conducen al visitante hacia el resto del complejo museístico, dando una sensación de casualidad.

links: Axonometrie und Raumprogramm_Transluzentes Modell_Außenbau bei Nacht. rechts: Vogelperspektive_Atrium.
gauche: Axométrie programmée_Modèle translucide_Extérieur de nuit. droite: Perspective à vol d'oiseau_Atrium.
izquierda: Axonometría y programa_Maqueta translúcida_Vista exterior nocturna. derecha: Perspectiva a vuelo de pájaro_Atrio.

CANADA_TORONTO **GARDINER MUSEUM**

KANADA_CANADA_CANADÁ
KUWABARA PAYNE MCKENNA BLUMBERG ARCHITECTS
2006
KUNSTMUSEUM_MUSÉE D'ART_MUSEO DE ARTE
4,300 M²
PHOTOS EDUARD HUEBER / ARCHPHOTO INC., NEW YORK (36 B.L., B. R., 37 B. L.), SHAI GIL PHOTOGRAPHY, TORONTO (37 A.), TOM ARBAN PHOTOGRAPHY, TORONTO (37 B. R.)

Das Museum ist das einzige auf keramische Kunst spezialisierte in Kanada. Die Erneuerung ist eines der Projekte im Rahmen der kulturellen Renaissance Torontos und erfüllt den Wunsch des Auftraggebers, Raum für die ständig wachsenden Sammlungen sowie für Bildungs- und Forschungsprogramme bereitzustellen. Unter anderem wurden Eingangsbereich und vertikale Zirkulation völlig umgestaltet und ein drittes Stockwerk, das einen stützenfreien Raum für Wechselausstellungen bietet sowie ein Restaurant und ein Mehrzweckraum mit Zugang zur Südterrasse hinzugefügt. Die frühere rosa Granitverkleidung wurde durch polierten, grau-bräunlichen Indiana-Kalkstein und schwarzen Granit ersetzt.

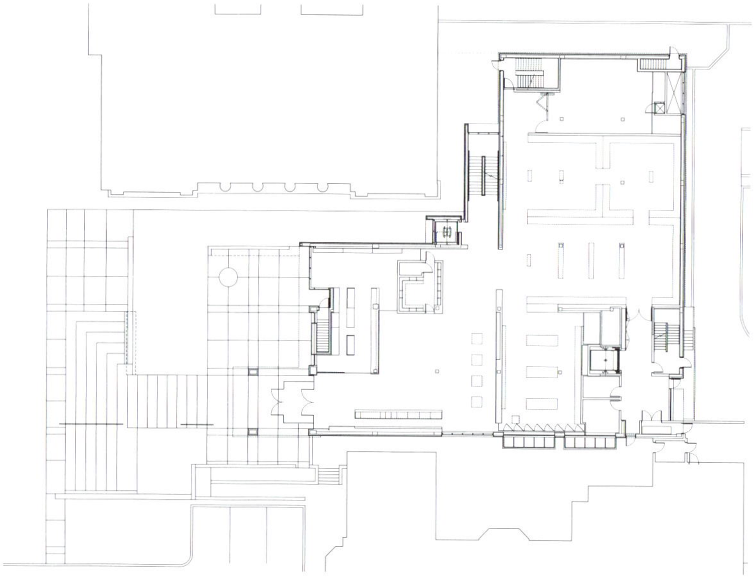

C'est l'unique musée spécialisé dans l'art de la céramique au Canada. La rénovation compte parmi l'un des projets les plus importants de la renaissance culturelle de Toronto. Le maître d'ouvrage souhaitait proposer un espace dédié aux collections toujours plus nombreuses et accueillir des programmes de formation et de recherche. Le projet prévoyait également la transformation intégrale de la zone d'entrée et l'amélioration de la circulation verticale grâce à l'ajout d'un troisième étage offrant un espace sans appui aux expositions tournantes ainsi qu'un restaurant comme destination et un espace polyvalent avec un accès sur la terrasse Sud. Le revêtement en granit rose fut remplacé par de la pierre calcaire d'Indiana polie d'un brun grisâtre et du granit noir.

El museo es el único en todo Canadá que se especializa en arte cerámico. Esta revitalización es uno de los proyectos que se enmarca en el renacimiento cultural de Toronto y cumple el deseo del comitente de lograr espacio para las colecciones que no cesan de crecer y, al mismo tiempo, facilitar programas de educación e investigación. También fue necesario reconfigurar por completo el área del acceso y la circulación vertical, como además incorporar un tercer nivel con una sala sin apoyos intermedios para exhibiciones temporarias, un restaurante para relajarse y un salón multifuncional con acceso a la terraza sur. El revestimiento en granito rosado fue sustituido por granito negro y piedra caliza pardusca de Indiana.

links: Grundriss Erdgeschoss_Hauptlobby und Museumsshop_Flexible Ausstellungsfläche im 2. Obergeschoss. rechts: Hauptfassade_Ständige Sammlung_Töpferatelier.
Gauche: Plan du rez-de-chaussée_Entrée principale et boutique du musée_Surface d'exposition flexible au deuxième étage. droite: Façade principale_Collection permanente_Atelier de poterie.
izquierda: Plano de planta baja_Vestíbulo principal y tienda del museo_Área flexible para exhibiciones en el segundo piso. derecha: Fachada principal_Colección permanente_Taller de cerámica.

Gardiner Museum

CHILE_SANTIAGO

MUSEO DE LA MEMORIA Y LOS DERECHOS HUMANOS

CHILE_CHILI_CHILE
ESTUDIO AMERICA DE ARQUITETURA – CARLOS DIAS, LUCAS FEHR AND MARIO FIGUEROA
2010
GESCHICHTSMUSEUM_MUSÉE D'HISTOIRE_MUSEO HISTÓRICO
10,900 M²
PHOTOS CRISTÓBAL PALMA, SANTIAGO

Der Entwurf versucht unter Berücksichtigung der Tradition der Santiagoer Innenstadt die Möglichkeiten der Bebauung eines neuen Geländes auszuloten und dabei die Vielfalt der Bürger und der Demokratie zu berücksichtigen: Ein großzügiger Raum voller Möglichkeiten und Wege entstand. Zwei konzeptionelle Komponenten bilden den Ausgangspunkt: der Ausstellungsriegel und die Basis. Ersterer erhebt sich über dem Boden und ist auf beiden Seiten offen: für Geschichte, Information und lebendige Erinnerung. Der Sockel ist zunächst tief wie ein Bergwerk, in dem Studium, Produktion und Wissen ihre Räumlichkeiten haben. Die Glaskästen im Inneren bieten die notwendige Transparenz und Lebendigkeit, um die in Fragmenten erhaltene Erinnerung, die sich zur Schatzkiste nationaler Eigenart zusammenfügt, zu präsentieren.

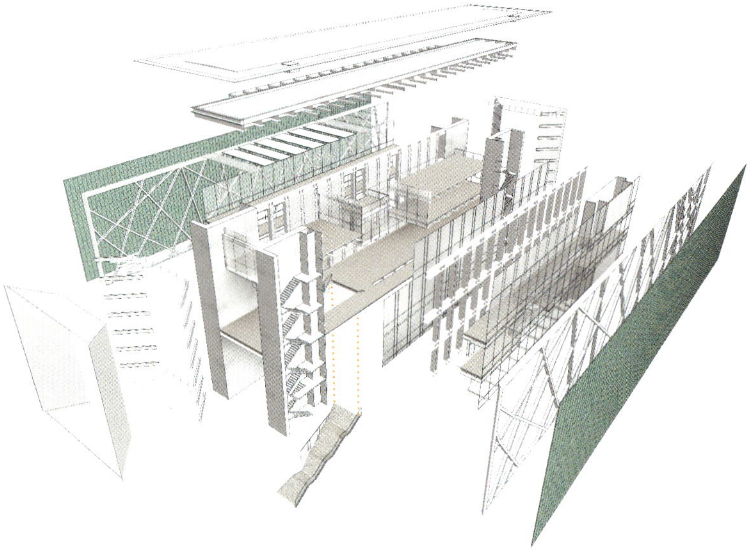

La conception tient compte de la tradition du centre-ville de Santiago concernant les possibilités d'une nouvelle urbanisation pour la diversité des citoyens et la démocratie afin de créer un espace généreux doté de possibilités variées et de voies multiples. Deux conceptions de base forment le point de départ du projet. D'une part, les poutres d'exposition ouvertes élevées sur le sol et sur les deux côtés rappellent historiquement : l'information et le souvenir vivant. D'autre part, la base initiée en profondeur dans une mine offre des espaces dédiés à l'étude, la production et au savoir. Les boites vitrifiées situées à l'intérieur offrent la transparence requise et l'animation autour de la conservation du souvenir fragmentaire présentée dans le coffre à trésor des caractéristiques d'une nation.

Respetando las tradiciones del casco antiguo de Santiago de Chile, el proyecto intenta aprovechar las posibilidades de una obra nueva bajo observancia de la diversidad ciudadana y de la democracia: así surge un espacio grandioso lleno de posibilidades y caminos. Dos componentes conceptuales constituyen el punto de partida. Por un lado, la gigantesca barra de exhibición elevada por sobre el suelo y abierta de ambos lados sirve como memoria viva, información e historia. Por otro lado, la base, que arranca desde lo profundo, en la cual tienen cabida el estudio, la producción y el saber. Cajas de cristal interiores ofrecen la necesaria transparencia y la vitalidad para presentar los recuerdos preservados en fragmentos, que reunidos constituyen la particularidad de una nación.

links: Explosionszeichnung_Brücke des Ausstellungstraktes_Stadtansicht aus dem Inneren. rechts: Zugangsrampe_Plaza de la Memoria.
gauche: Vue éclatée_Passerelle de l'aile d'exposition_Vue sur la ville de l'intérieur. droite: Rampe d'accès_Plaza de la memoria.
izquierda: Perspectiva de despiece_Puente de la sección de exhibiciones_Vista de la ciudad desde el interior. derecha: Rampa de acceso_Plaza de la Memoria.

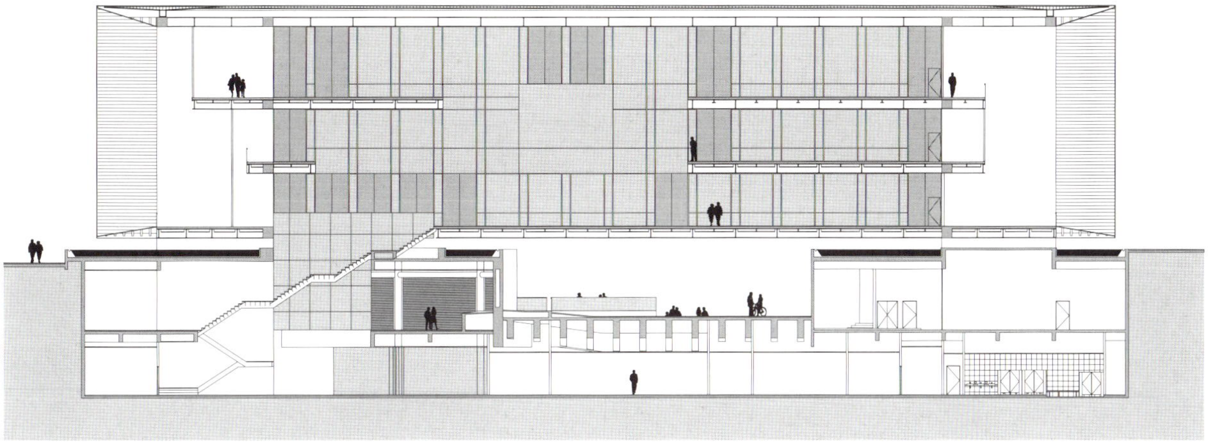

links: Ausstellungs-Brückentrakt und Plaza de la Memoria. rechts: Schnitt_Zugang zur Ausstellung_Hauptraum Ausstellung.
gauche: Aile d'exposition servant de passerelle et plaza de la memoria. droite: Coupe_Accès à l'exposition_Espace principal de l'exposition.
izquierda: Sección de puente de exhibiciones y Plaza de la Memoria. derecha: Corte_Acceso a la exhibición_Sala principal de exhibiciones.

MEXICO_MEXICO CITY **MUSEO DEL CHOCOLATE NESTLÉ**

MEXIKO_MEXIQUE_MÉXICO
ROJKIND ARQUITECTOS
2007
FIRMENMUSEUM_MUSÉE D'ENTREPRISE_MUSEO DE EMPRESA
634 M^2
PHOTOS © PAÚL RIVERA / ARCHPHOTO.COM

Die Nestlé-Schokoladenfabrik in Mexiko-Stadt in der Nähe von Toluca benötigte einen Rundgang, um den Besuchern die Herstellung von Pralinen zeigen zu können. Die Architekten schufen Mexikos erstes Schokoladen-Museum mit einer 300 Meter langen Fassade an der Autobahn, die nun das Erscheinungsbild der Fabrik prägt. In dieser ersten Phase entstanden Raum für den Haupteingang, der den Kindern einen spielerischen und doch markanten Auftakt zur großen Vergnügungsreise durch den Bau bietet, Platz für den Eingangsbereich, für den Theatersaal, der auf die Schokoladen-Erfahrung vorbereitet, für den Museumsshop, und für den Zugang zum Tunnel, der in die alte bestehende Fabrik führt.

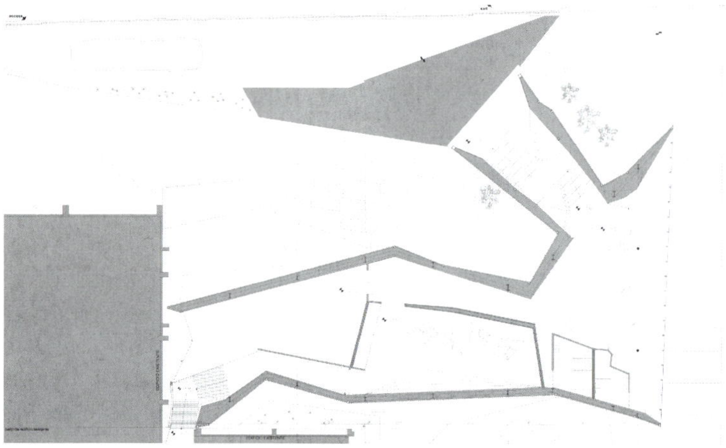

L'usine de chocolat Nestlé dans la ville de Mexico à proximité de Toluca nécessitait une galerie afin de montrer aux visiteurs la fabrication des pralines. Les architectes ont créé le premier musée du chocolat de Mexico doté d'une façade de 300 mètres de longueur au bord de l'autoroute qui symbolise désormais cette usine. Tout d'abord, un espace a été érigé à l'entrée principale offrant aux enfants le départ ludique et marquant d'un grand voyage de plaisir dans l'édifice, de la réception, à la salle de théâtre qui prépare à l'expérience Nestlé, en passant par le magasin du musée jusqu'au tunnel menant à l'ancienne usine.

La fábrica de chocolate Nestlé de Ciudad de México, cerca de Toluca, necesitaba un recorrido que permitiera mostrarles a los visitantes la elaboración de los bombones. Los arquitectos plasmaron así el primer museo del chocolate en toda la historia de México, con una fachada de 300 metros de longitud que define la imagen de la fábrica. En esta primera fase se obtuvo espacio para el acceso principal que les ofrece a los niños, de manera juguetona pero elocuente, el preludio a un gran viaje placentero por la edificación; la recepción; la sala de teatro que prepara la experiencia Nestlé; el comercio que sirve como tienda del museo; y el túnel que conduce hacia la antigua fábrica.

links: Grundriss Erdgeschoss_Außenansicht. rechts: Eingang_Außenansicht_Treppe.
gauche: Plan du rez-de-chaussée_Vue extérieure. droite: Entrée_Vue extérieure_Escalier.
izquierda: Plano de planta baja_Vista exterior. derecha: Acceso_Vista exterior_Escalera.

Nestlé

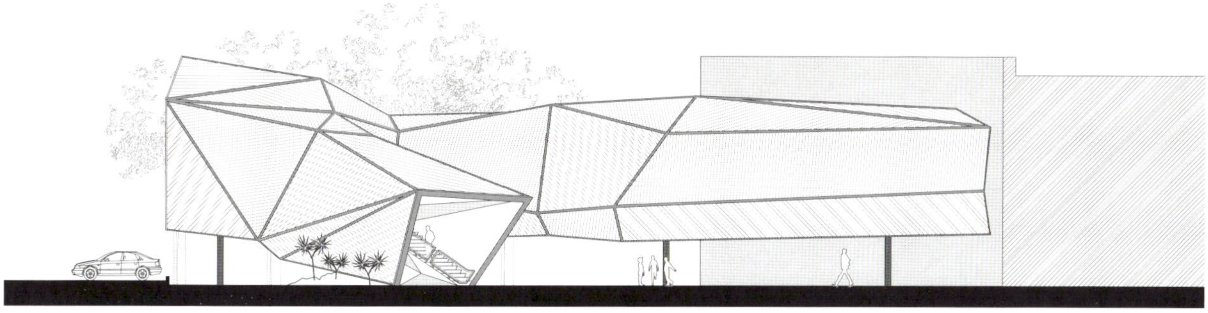

links: Treppe. rechts: Ostfassade_Detail Außenbau_Innenraum_Sitzgelegenheiten.
gauche: Escalier. droite: Façade est_Détail de l'extérieur_Espace intérieur_Places assises.
izquierda: Escalera. derecha: Fachada este_Detalle del exterior_Espacio interior_Zona de asientos.

MEXICO_MEXICO CITY **MUSEO TAMAYO**

MEXIKO_MEXIQUE_MÉXICO
BIG AND MICHEL ROJKIND
ONGOING
KUNST- UND KULTURMUSEUM_MUSÉE DE CULTURE ET DE L'ART
MUSEO DE ARTE Y CULTURA
2,250 M^2
PHOTOS COURTESY OF THE ARCHITECTS

Das auf einem steilen Hang in Atizapan gelegene Museum soll lokal, regional und international der Bildung und Kultur dienen. Benannt ist es nach dem in Oaxaca geborenen Künstler Rufino Tamayo. Die symbolische und sehr ausdrucksstarke Form des Kreuzes ist direkt auf die vorausgegangenen Studien zur optimalen Funktionalität des Museums zurückzuführen. Kernpunkt des Konzepts ist die Idee der „offenen Kiste", die weit geöffnet die Besucher ins Innere einlädt. Außen- und Innenräume verschneiden sich, um so die bestmöglichen Räumlichkeiten für die verschiedenen Aufgaben und eine optimale Klimanutzung bieten zu können. Die durchlässige und verschattende Backsteinfassade gewährleistet Tageslicht ohne direkte Sonneneinstrahlung und eine natürliche Belüftung.

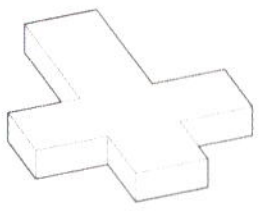

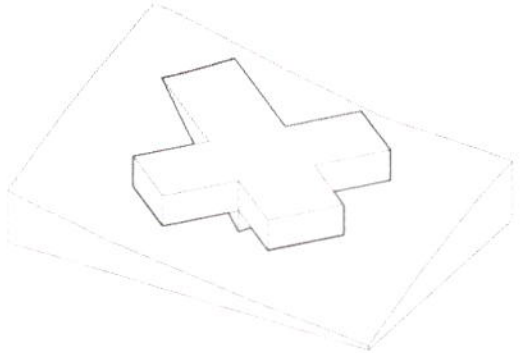

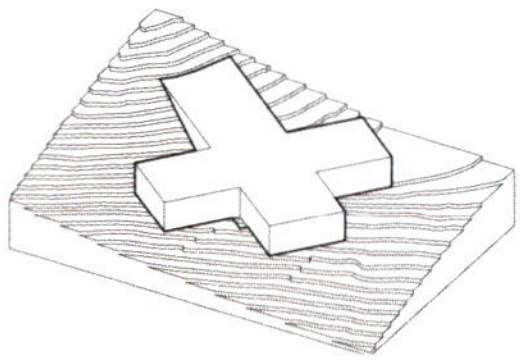

Le musée situé sur une pente abrupte à Atizapan se voue à la formation et à la culture au niveau local, régional et international. Baptisé en l'honneur de l'artiste Rufino Tamayo, né à Oaxaca, la forme de la croix symbolique et très expressive remonte directement aux études précédentes consacrées à l'optimisation des fonctionnalités du musée. Le facteur clé du concept est la perception de soi en tant que « boite ouverte » en grand afin d'inciter les visiteurs à entrer à l'intérieur. Les espaces intérieurs et extérieurs se séparent afin d'optimiser au maximum les espaces dédiés aux différentes missions ainsi que la climatisation. La façade en brique perméable et ombrageant garantit une lumière naturelle sans rayonnement direct du soleil et une aération naturelle.

El museo, que se erigirá en una empinada pendiente en Atizapán, debe servir a la educación y la cultura a nivel local, regional e internacional. Lleva el nombre del artista Rufino Tamayo, nacido en Oaxaca. La simbólica forma de cruz, tan intensamente expresiva, remite directamente a los estudios realizados para dotar al museo de una funcionalidad óptima. El concepto enfatiza la idea de "cajón abierto", que invita a los visitantes a ingresar en él. Los espacios exteriores e interiores se entrecruzan y, de esta manera, se ofrece la mejor espacialidad para las diversas tareas, además de un aprovechamiento climático optimizado. La fachada de ladrillo, al mismo tiempo transparente y sombreada, garantiza la penetración de luz diurna sin radiación solar directa, y también ventilación natural.

links: Einbettung in die Landschaft_Auskragung_Ausstellungsraum. rechts: Treppenanlage und Fassaden_Aussichtsplattform auf dem Dach.
gauche: Encastré dans le paysage_Porte-à-faux_Espace d'exposition. droite: Escaliers et façades Plate-forme panoramique sur le toit.
izquierda: Inserción en el paisaje_Saliente_Sala de exhibiciones. derecha: Escalinatas y fachadas Plataforma de observación sobre el techo.

MEXICO_MONTERREY **HORNO 3: MUSEO DEL ACERO**

MEXIKO_MEXIQUE_MÉXICO
GRIMSHAW WITH OFICINA DE ARQUITECTURA
AND WERNER SOBEK ENGINEERS
2007
INDUSTRIEMUSEUM_MUSÉE D'INDUSTRIE
MUSEO DE LA INDUSTRIA
9,000 M²
PHOTOS CHRISTIAN HOENIGSCHMID-GROSSICH / GRIMSHAW (48 L.),
PAÚL RIVERA / ARCHPHOTO (48 R., 49)

Für das „Museum des Stahls" Horno 3 wurde eine heruntergekommene Hochofenanlage der 1960er Jahre wiederhergestellt und der 70 Meter hohe Hochofen in nutzbare Räume umgewandelt. Es entstanden 9.000 Quadratmeter Museumsfläche im Innenraum und Außenbereich. Das eigentliche Museum wurde durch die Umnutzung des Ofens, seiner Plattformen, der Tanklager und Schaltstellen sowie als Anbau an den Bestand errichtet. Der stillgelegte Hochofen und die Gießhalle sind das Herzstück und beherbergen eine interaktive Ausstellung, die den alten Ofen zum Leben erweckt. So wird dem Besucher die einzigartige Erfahrung geboten, sich in einem Relikt der Industriegeschichte zu bewegen.

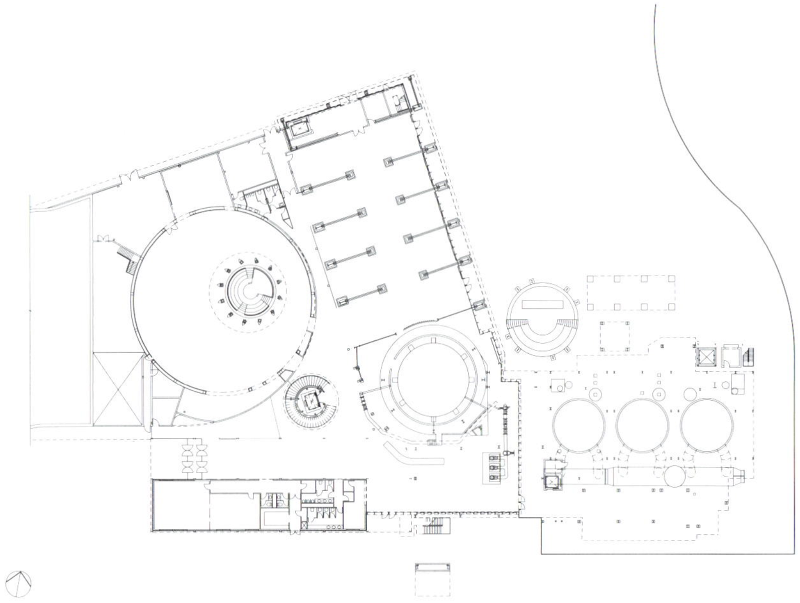

Un site de haut fourneau complètement délabré datant des années 1960 a été reconstruit et transformé en musée de l'acier Horno 3. Ce musée haut de 70 mètres s'étend vers le haut fourneau transformé en 9 000 mètres carrés d'espaces utiles comprenant l'espace intérieur et extérieur. En effet, le véritable musée a été créé grâce à la reconstruction du four, des plateformes, des sites de stockages et de commutation ainsi que par l'annexe associée au site existant. Le haut fourneau désormais désaffecté et la salle de fonderie se trouvent au cœur du musée afin d'héberger une exposition interactive qui réveille l'ancien four et offre aux visiteurs l'expérience unique de s'aventurer dans l'histoire industrielle présentée.

Para el Museo del Acero Horno 3 se aprovecharon las instalaciones abandonadas de una industria metalúrgica de la década de 1960 y se transformó el alto horno de 70 metros de alto en salas aprovechables. Se obtuvieron 9.000 metros cuadrados de espacio museístico en el interior y en el exterior. El museo propiamente dicho se logró gracias a la reutilización del horno, las plataformas, el depósito y los puntos de conmutación, y también se realizó una ampliación de las construcciones existentes. El alto horno fuera de servicio y la nave de fundición son el corazón del museo, y albergan una muestra interactiva que hace revivir los viejos hornos y le ofrece al visitante la experiencia original de desplazarse por una reliquia de la historia industrial.

links: Grundriss Erdgeschoss_Treppenspirale_Aufzug in Tragwerk_Auskrakende Treppenstufen. rechts: Hochofen zwischen Rohrleitungen und der neu verkleideten Gießhalle Begrüntes Dach Außenbau.
gauche: Plan du rez-de-chaussée_Escalier en colimaçon_Ascenseur au sein de son ossature_Marches d'escalier saillantes. droite: Haut-fourneau entre les canalisations et nouveau revêtement du hall de la fonderie_Toit de verdure_Extérieur.
izquierda: Plano de planta baja_Escalera en espiral_Elevador_Escalones en saliente. derecha: Alto horno entre tuberías y nave de fundición_Techo ajardinado_Vista exterior.

PERU_EL BRUJO **MUSEO CAO**

PERU_PÉROU_PERÚ
CLAUDIA UCCELLI
2008
ARCHÄOLOGIEMUSEUM_MUSÉE DE L'ARCHÉOLOGIE
MUSEO ARQUEOLÓGICO
1,420 M²
PHOTOS EDUARDO HIROSE

Das Cao-Museum befindet sich innerhalb der archäologischen Fundstätte „El Brujo" an der nördlichen Pazifikküste Perus, 70 Kilometer nördlich der Stadt Trujillo. Die archäologische Stätte umfasst eine Fläche von 100 Hektar, die seit mehr als 5000 Jahren bewohnt wird. In ihr liegen drei Huacas, heilige Pyramiden, mit der Huaca Prieta als einer der ältesten in Südamerika. Das von diesen drei Lehmbauten gebildete imaginäre Dreieck bestimmte die Lage des Museo Cao. Ästhetik und formale Merkmale des Museums ergaben sich aus den Blickachsen, aus der vorherrschenden Windrichtung und dem Meer. Die Architektur des Museums erscheint fast topografisch, indem sie sich der Umgebung anpasst.

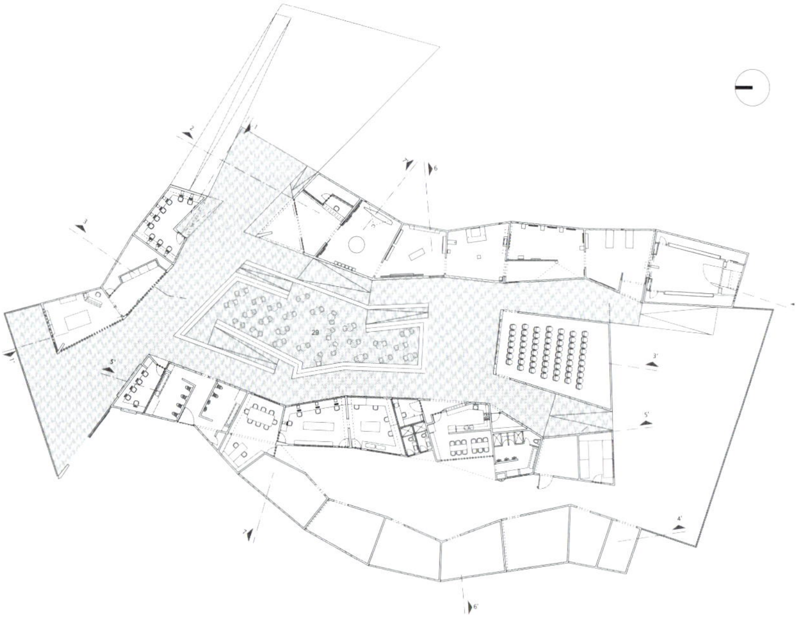

Le musée Cao se situe à l'intérieur du site archéologique « El Brujo » sur la côte pacifique du Pérou, à 70 kilomètres au Nord de la ville de Trujillo. Le site archéologique comprend une superficie de 100 hectares peuplée depuis plus de 5 000 ans. Sur ce site, il existe trois Huacas - pyramides saintes - dont la Huaca Prieta comptant parmi l'une des plus anciennes d'Amérique du Sud. L'imaginaire formé par ces trois constructions en argile a conditionné la situation du Museo Cao. L'esthétique et les caractéristiques formelles du musée résultent de ces axes de vue, de l'orientation du vent prédominant et de la mer. L'architecture du musée semble quasiment topographique et s'adapte parfaitement à l'environnement.

El Museo Cao se encuentra dentro del yacimiento arqueológico El Brujo sobre la costa norte del Pacífico peruano, 70 kilómetros al norte de la ciudad de Trujillo. El sitio arqueológico abarca una superficie de 100 hectáreas que han estado habitadas desde hace más de 5.000 años. En el mismo se hallaron tres huacas o pirámides sagradas, de las que la Huaca Prieta constituye una de las más antiguas de Sudamérica. El imaginario constituido por estas tres construcciones de arcilla fue lo que dio origen a la actual ubicación del Museo Cao. La estética y las características formales de este museo resultaron de estos ejes visuales, de los vientos predominantes y del mar. La arquitectura del museo aparece casi topográfica y se adapta al entorno.

links: Grundriss_Panoramaansicht mit Huaca Cao und Zeltbau. rechts: Eingang_Museum Cao und Huaca Cao.
gauche: Plan_Vue panoramique sur Huaca Cao et la structure suspendue. droite: Entrée_Musée Cao et Huaca Cao.
izquierda: Plano_Vista panorámica con huaca Cao y construcción de toldo. derecha: Acceso_Museo Cao y huaca Cao.

MUSEO
CAO

MUSEO
CAO
FUNDACIÓN
WIESE

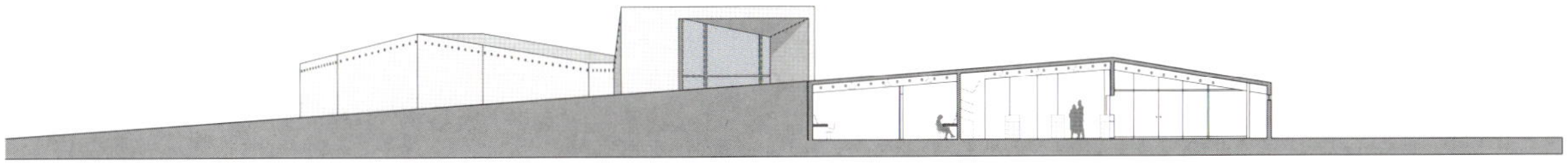

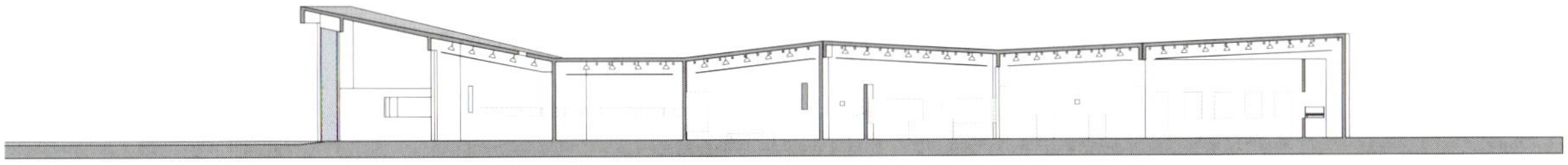

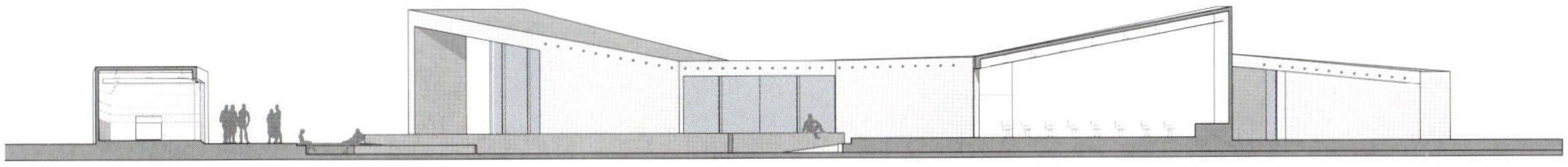

links: Raum 5 Bestattungsrituale. rechts: Schnitte: Raum 3 Moche Idole_Raum 4 Totenrituale Innenraum.
gauche: Salle 5 - rituels funéraires. droite: Coupe: Salle 3 - idole moche_Salle 4 - rituels mortuaires_Intérieur.
izquierda: Sala 5 con ritual funerario. derecha: Cortes: Sala 3 ídolos moche_Sala 4 ritual de los muertos_Espacio interior.

USA_AKRON (OH) **AKRON ART MUSEUM**

USA_USA_EE.UU.
COOP HIMMELB(L)AU
2007
KUNSTMUSEUM_MUSÉE D'ART_MUSEO DE ARTE
8,370 M²
PHOTOS ROLAND HALBE / ARTURIMAGES

Das Museum von heute ist kein bloßer Ort des Wissens oder Schauraum mehr, sondern ein städtischer Erlebnisraum und ein dreidimensionales urbanes Zeichen, das die Inhalte unserer Bilderwelt kommuniziert. Die Kunst muss demnach aus dem Gebäude hinaus und die Stadt in das Gebäude hineinfließen können; das Museum wird hybrider Raum. Das Gebäude setzt sich aus drei Teilen zusammen: dem „Kristall" als Orientierungs- und Erschließungsbereich, der flexiblen „Galerienbox" und der schwebenden „Dachwolke", die den Innenraum umschließt, verschiedene Außenräume beschattet und ein horizontales Wahrzeichen in das Stadtbild setzt. Massen und Material der Elemente spielen in einem ausgeklügelten Klima- und Lichtkonzept miteinander.

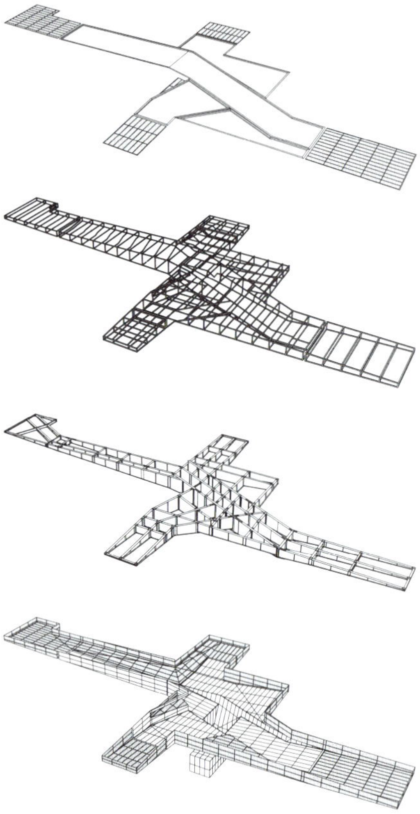

Le musée actuel n'est plus un simple lieu de connaissances ou une vitrine, mais un espace municipal expérimental et un symbole urbain tridimensionnel qui communiquent les valeurs intrinsèques de notre monde imagé. L'art aspire à sortir du bâtiment et, la ville, à rentrer dans le bâtiment afin de former un espace hybride. Le bâtiment se compose de trois parties : le « cristal » comme zone d'accès et d'orientation, la « boite de galeries » souple et le « toit de nuage » flottant entourant l'espace intérieur afin d'ombrager les différents espaces extérieurs et de représenter un emblème horizontal au sein de la ville. Les masses et matériaux des éléments jouent entre eux dans un climat et une conception lumineuse finement pensés.

El museo actual ya no es un mero sitio del saber o de exhibición, sino un espacio de vivencia ciudadana y un símbolo urbano tridimensional que comunica los contenidos de nuestro mundo pictórico. Por tanto, el arte debe poder fluir hacia fuera del edificio y la ciudad hacia dentro del mismo, constituyendo así un espacio híbrido. El edificio se compone de tres partes: el "cristal" como área de orientación y conexión, la flexible "caja de galería" y la flotante "nube de techo" que abarca el espacio interior, cubre diversos espacios exteriores y marca un sello horizontal en el paisaje urbano. La masa y el material de los elementos juegan entre sí en un concepto de luz y climatización sumamente elaborado.

links: Explosionszeichnung Dachelemente_Eingangshalle_Blick nach außen_Glaswand. rechts: Haupteingang_Außenbau_Außenbau Gegenseite.
gauche: Vues éclatées des éléments de la toiture_Hall d'entrée_Vue sur l'extérieur_Mur en verre. droite: Entrée principale_Extérieur_Extérieur - côté opposé.
izquierda: Vista de despiece de elementos del techo_Sala de acceso_Vista hacia el exterior_Muro acristalado. derecha: Acceso principal_Vista exterior_Fachada opuesta.

USA_BELLINGHAM (WA) LIGHTCATCHER AT THE WHATCOM MUSEUM

USA_USA_EE.UU.
OLSON KUNDIG ARCHITECTS
2009
KUNSTMUSEUM_MUSÉE D'ART_MUSEO DE ARTE
3,902 M²
PHOTOS BENJAMIN BENSCHNEIDER (56 B. R., 57, 58, 59 B. R.), TIM BIES / OLSON KUNDIG ARCHITECTS (56 B. L., 59 B. L.)

Lightcatcher ist ein Museum für regionale Kunst und Kinder. Der Name bezieht sich auf das auffälligste Merkmal, den „lightcatcher", eine mehr als 11 Meter hohe und 55 Meter lange Glaswand, die in einer sanften Kurve einen 2200 Quadratmeter großen Innenhof ausbildet. Bei Tag füllt diese lichtdurchlässige Wand das Innere mit Licht und wird so zu einer energiesparenden Leuchte, nachts verwandelt sich die Wand in ein Leuchtfeuer. Die doppelwandige Konstruktion des „lightcatcher" unterstützt die Klimatisierung des Gebäudes, indem sie während des Sommers heiße Luft herausleitet und es während des Winters isoliert. Das Bauprogramm umfasst Galerien, Unterrichtszimmer, Büros und Entspannungs- und Serviceräume. Das einstöckige Foyer wird von einem 915 Quadratmeter großen grünen Dach überfangen. Der Entwurf entspricht dem LEED Silver Standard.

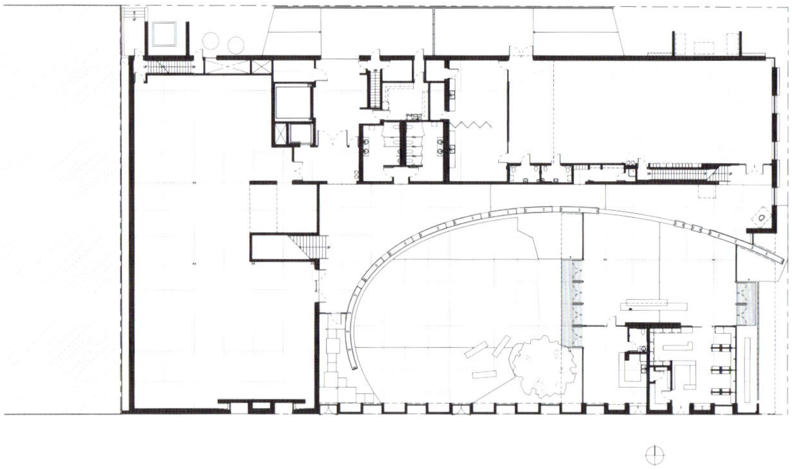

Lightcatcher est un musée de l'art régional dédié notamment aux enfants. En effet, Lightcatcher capte l'attention et la lumière grâce à sa principale caractéristique visible - le mur en verre haut de plus de 11 mètres et long d'environ de 55 mètres évoluant en courbe douce vers une cour intérieure spacieuse d'environ 2 200 mètres carrés. Le jour, la lumière jaillit de ce mur à l'intérieur en assurant un éclairage qui maitrise l'énergie et, la nuit, le mur se transforme en feu lumineux. La construction à double vitrage de lightcatcher sert de support à la climatisation du bâtiment : en effet, en été, l'air chaud est évacué alors que la chaleur est conservée en hiver. Le programme de construction comprend des galeries, salles de classe, bureaux et espaces de service et de détente. Le foyer à un étage est surplombé par un important toit vert de 915 mètres carrés. Le projet correspond à la norme LEED Silver.

El Lightcatcher es un museo de arte regional y para niños. El nombre se refiere a su característica más singular, el Lightcatcher (literalmente: "que atrapa la luz"), un muro acristalado de 37 pies de altura y 180 pies de longitud que, con su suave curva, configura un patio interior de 7000 pies cuadrados. Durante el día, la pared traslúcida llena de luz el interior y, de este modo, se transforma en una luminaria que ahorra energía; por la noche se transforma en un verdadero faro luminoso. La construcción de pared doble del Lightcatcher sirve de apoyo a la climatización del edificio; en verano extrae el aire caliente, y en invierno sirve de aislamiento. El programa arquitectónico comprende galerías, salas lectivas, oficinas y áreas de servicio y esparcimiento. El vestíbulo de una planta está cubierto por un techo verde de 3.000 pies cuadrados. El diseño cumple con el LEED nivel plata.

links: Grundriss Hauptgeschoss_Hof_Lichtfänger-Wand. rechts: Seitenansicht.
gauche: Plan de l'étage principal_Cour_Mur qui capte la lumière. droite: Vue latérale.
izquierda: Plano del piso principal_Patio_Muro Lightcatcher. derecha: Vista lateral.

OUT OF BOUNDS

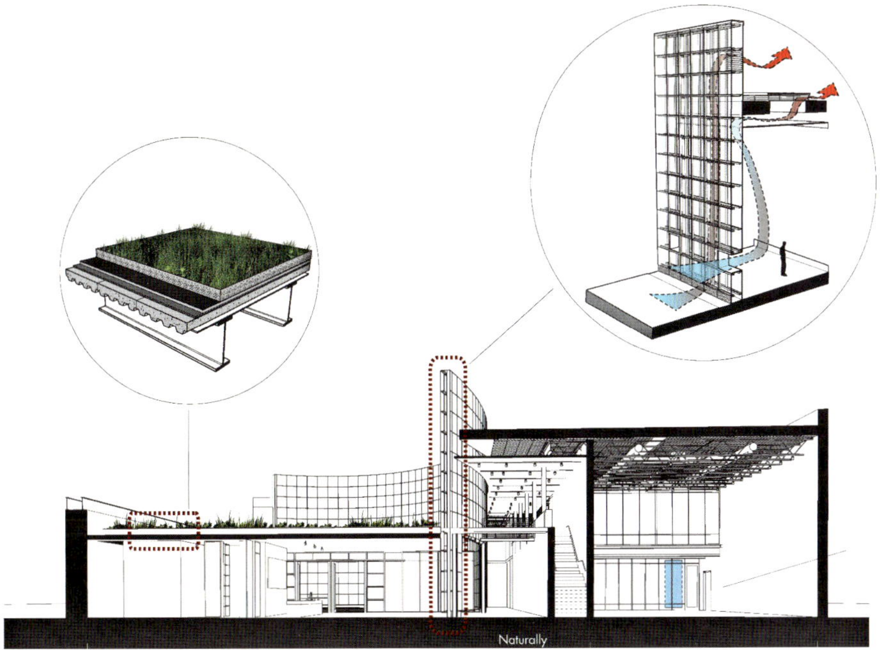

links: Ausstellungssaal. rechts: Schnitt_Lichtfängerwand_Umlauf.
gauche: Salle d'exposition. droite: Coupe_Mur qui capte la lumière_Cour.
izquierda: Sala de exhibiciones. derecha: Corte_Muro Lightcatcher_Pasillo.

USA_BOSTON (MA) **MUSEUM OF FINE ARTS**

USA_USA_EE.UU.
FOSTER + PARTNERS WITH CHILDS BERTMAN TSECKARES INC
2010
KUNSTMUSEUM_MUSÉE D'ART_MUSEO DE ARTE
12,415 M²
PHOTOS FOSTER + PARTNERS

Das Gebäude bietet Ausstellungen, Vorlesungen, Filmvorführungen und Lehrveranstaltungen Raum. Im Zentrum des Umbaus standen die Wiederherstellung der Symmetrie und Logik des ursprünglichen Beaux-Arts-Museumsplans. Die zentrale Achse des Hauptgebäudes wird durch die Wiederherstellung des Haupteingangs im Süden und eines Eingangs im Norden erneuert. Im Mittelpunkt dieser Achse befindet sich ein neues Informationszentrum. Eine verglaste Struktur, die „Kristallwirbelsäule", bietet neuen Raum und integriert Teile der beiden großen Innenhöfe im Zentrum des Museums in ein gläsernes „Schmuckkästchen". Rund um das Museum wurde eine umfangreiche neue Landschaftsgestaltung geplant, um den Zusammenhang mit der benachbarten Back Bay Fens auszubauen.

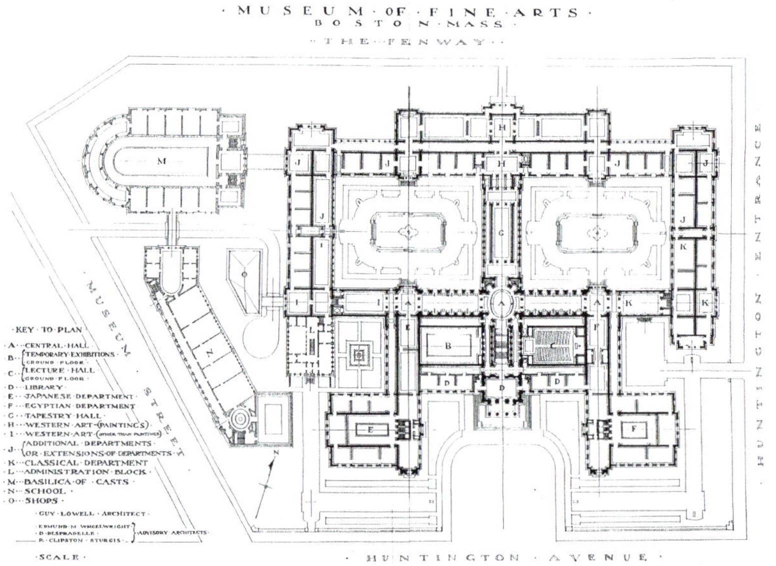

Le bâtiment offre des expositions, conférences, projections de films et activités éducatives. Au centre de la transformation, la reconstruction de la symétrie et de la logique du plan d'origine du Musée des Beaux-arts. L'axe central du bâtiment principal a été rénové par la reconstruction de l'entrée principale au Sud et une entrée au Nord. Au centre de cet axe se situe un nouveau centre d'information. Une structure vitrée, qui offre une « colonne vertébrale en cristal » au nouvel espace et intègre les parties des deux grandes cours intérieures au centre du musée comme une « boite à bijoux ». Autour du musée, la formation du paysage nouveau généreux est planifiée afin d'édifier le rapport au Back Bay Fens avoisinant.

El edificio sirve de espacio para exhibiciones, disertaciones, proyecciones cinematográficas y actividades educativas. Lo fundamental a lograr con la reforma era regenerar la simetría y la lógica de la planta original del edificio museístico estilo Beaux Arts. El eje central del edificio principal, ha sido renovado mediante una recreación del acceso principal al sur y un acceso al norte. En el centro de este eje se encuentra un nuevo centro de información. Una estructura acristalada, la "columna vertebral de cristal", ofrece nuevo espacio e integra partes de los dos grandes patios interiores en el centro del museo como "pequeño alhajero". Se ha planificado una amplia superficie paisajística alrededor del museo, para incrementar la vinculación con el vecino parque Back Bay Fens.

links: Grundriss_Erweiterung Außenbau bei Tag_Erweiterung Außenbau bei Nacht. rechts: Bestand Haupteingang_Bestand Fassade.
gauche: Plan_Extension du bâtiment extérieur prise de jour_Extension du bâtiment extérieur prise de nuit. droite: Partie restante de l'entrée principale_Partie restante de la façade.
izquierda: Plano_Vista exterior diurna de la ampliación_Vista exterior nocturna de la ampliación. derecha: Acceso principal en el edificio existente_Fachada del edificio existente.

ROBERT DAWSON EVANS
GALLERIES FOR PAINTINGS
MDCCCCXII — MDCCCCXIV
FENWAY ENTRANCE

links: Café. rechts: Skizze von Norman Foster_Visualisierung der Galerie_Visualisierung der Anbindung Neubau_Visualisierung des Atriums.
gauche: Cafétéria. droite: Esquisse de Norman Foster_Visualisation de la galerie_Visualisation de la jonction au nouveau bâtiment_Visualisation de l'atrium.
izquierda: Café. derecha: Esbozo de Norman Foster_Visualización de la galería_Visualización de la conexión con el nuevo edificio_Visualización del atrio.

USA_BOSTON (MA) **BOSTON CHILDREN'S MUSEUM**

USA_USA_EE.UU.
CAMBRIDGE SEVEN ASSOCIATES, INC.
2007
KINDERMUSEUM_MUSÉE POUR LES ENFANTS_MUSEO DE NIÑOS
2,137 M²
PHOTOS © ROBERT BENSON PHOTOGRAPHY

Der 2137 Quadratmeter große Anbau mit Fassaden aus Metall und Glas ist ein einfacher, geometrischer Skelettbau mit drei Ebenen, der über gläserne Brücken an den bestehenden Altbau angeschlossen wurde. Die Vorsprünge aus Holz sind mit leuchtend grünen Farbtupfern akzentuiert. Gelb und Grün tritt auch durch kreisförmige Perforationen in der Metallfassade in die Lobby. Innerhalb des Neubaus öffnet sich durch die großzügige Verglasung aus jedem Geschoss der Blick auf die Uferpromenade und den Fort Point Channel. Der Haupteingang des Museums wurde in den neuen Bauteil am Fort Point Channel verlegt. So ergeben sich auch Ausblicke über den Bostoner Hafen.

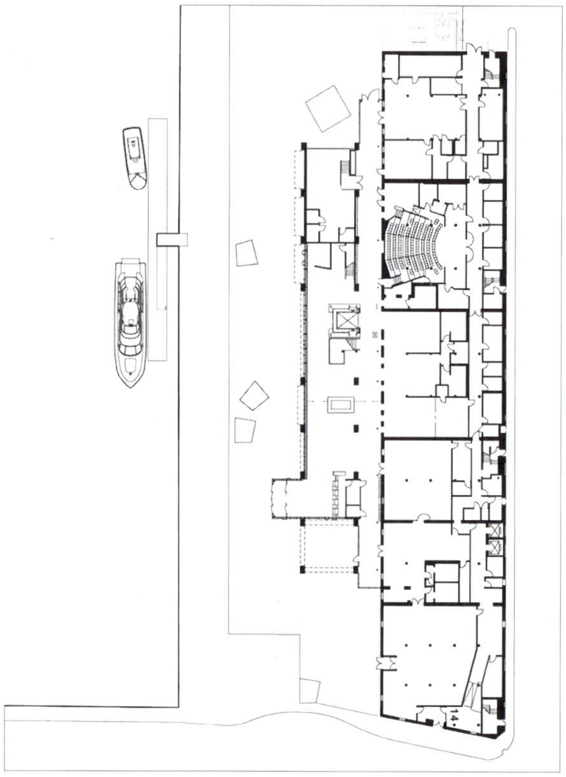

L'importante extension de 2137 mètres carrés avec ses façades en métal et verre est une simple ossature de construction géométrique à trois niveaux annexée sur le pont vitrifié de l'ancien bâtiment. Les éléments en porte-à-faux en bois sont accentués par des touches de couleur vert brillant. Le jaune et le vert apparaissent également par les verres circulaires situés dans la façade métallique au niveau du hall d'entrée. L'intérieur du nouveau bâtiment permet la vue sur la promenade maritime et le Fort Point Channel grâce à des vitrages généreux à chaque étage. L'entrée principale du musée a été déplacée dans le nouveau bâtiment au Fort Point Channel afin d'offrir une perspective fantastique sur le port de Boston.

La ampliación de 2137 metro cuadrados con fachadas de metal y cristal es una sencilla construcción geométrica con tres niveles; la misma ha sido conectada con la edificación existente mediante puentes acristalados. Los resaltes de madera han sido acentuados con luminosas manchas de color verde. El amarillo y el verde también aparecen en los acristalamientos circulares de la fachada de metal y del vestíbulo. Dentro de la nueva edificación se abren vistas desde cada nivel hacia la avenida costera y el canal Fort Point a través del magnífico acristalamiento. Se dispuso el acceso principal al museo en la nueva edificación junto al canal Fort Point. De este modo se tienen vistas del puerto de Boston.

links: Grundriss Erdgeschoss_Vorhangfassade mit durchbrochenen Paneelen und farbigem Glas Hauptfoyer mit Klettermöglichkeit. rechts: Eingang mit Hangartoren_Abendansicht von Congress Street Brücke.
gauche: Plan du rez-de-chaussée_Façade-rideau avec tôles perforées et verre de plusieurs couleurs_Entrée principale avec mur d'escalade pour les enfants. droite: Vue de l'entrée et portes du hangar surdimensionnées_Vue de nuit du pont de Congress Street.
izquierda: Plano de planta baja_Muro cortina con chapa perforada y vidrio multicolor_Vestíbulo principal con juego infantil para trepar. derecha: Vista del vestíbulo y portones sobredimensionados_Vista nocturna desde el puente Congress Street.

BOSTON CHILDREN'S MUSEUM
BOSTON CHILDREN'S MUSEUM

BOSTON CHILDREN'S MUSEUM

USA_BUFFALO (NY) **ELEANOR AND WILSON GREATBATCH PAVILION**

USA_USA_EE.UU.
TOSHIKO MORI ARCHITECT PLLC
2009
ARCHITEKTURMUSEUM_MUSÉE DE L'ARCHITECTURE
MUSEO DE ARQUITECTURA
530 M²
PHOTOS PAUL WARCHOL PHOTOGRAPHY, NEW YORK

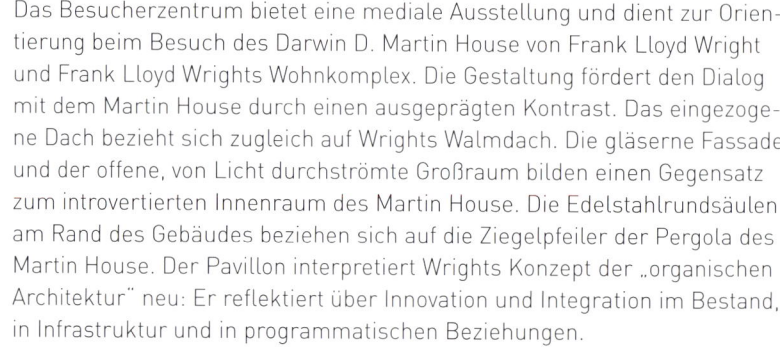

Das Besucherzentrum bietet eine mediale Ausstellung und dient zur Orientierung beim Besuch des Darwin D. Martin House von Frank Lloyd Wright und Frank Lloyd Wrights Wohnkomplex. Die Gestaltung fördert den Dialog mit dem Martin House durch einen ausgeprägten Kontrast. Das eingezogene Dach bezieht sich zugleich auf Wrights Walmdach. Die gläserne Fassade und der offene, von Licht durchströmte Großraum bilden einen Gegensatz zum introvertierten Innenraum des Martin House. Die Edelstahlrundsäulen am Rand des Gebäudes beziehen sich auf die Ziegelpfeiler der Pergola des Martin House. Der Pavillon interpretiert Wrights Konzept der „organischen Architektur" neu: Er reflektiert über Innovation und Integration im Bestand, in Infrastruktur und in programmatischen Beziehungen.

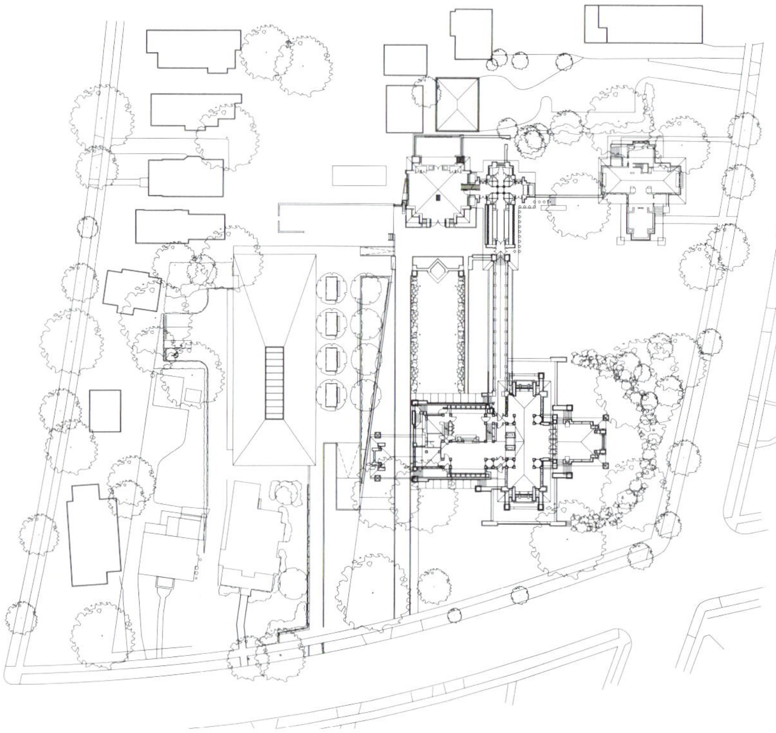

Ce centre des visiteurs offre une exposition multimédia et sert à l'orientation pour la visite de Darwin D. Martin House et à l'ensemble d'habitation de Frank Lloyd Wright. La conception favorise le dialogue avec la Martin House grâce à un contraste marqué. Le toit en retrait se réfère simultanément au toit en croupe de Wright. La façade vitrée et le grand espace ouvert pénétré par la lumière forment un contraste par rapport à l'intérieur introverti de la Martin House. Les colonnes rondes en acier noble au bord du bâtiment se réfèrent aux piliers en brique de la pergola de la Martin House. Le pavillon interprète d'une nouvelle manière le concept de Wright concernant « l'architecture organique »: en effet, ce pavillon reflète l'innovation et l'intégration dans les acquis, l'infrastructure et les relations programmatiques.

El centro de visitantes ofrece una exhibición multimedia y sirve como orientación para las visitas a la casa Darwin D. Martin y el conjunto habitacional, dos obras de Frank Lloyd Wright. El diseño propicia el diálogo con la Martin House gracias a un destacado contraste. El techo saliente se refiere claramente al techo a cuatro aguas, típico de Wright. La fachada acristalada y el gran ambiente inundado de luz contrastan con el introvertido interior de la Martin House. Las columnas de acero inoxidable al borde del edificio dialogan con los pilares de ladrillo de la pérgola de la Martin House. El pabellón reinterpreta el concepto wrightiano de "arquitectura orgánica": la misma se refleja en la integración de lo existente y la innovación, en la infraestructura y las relaciones programáticas.

links: Lageplan_Ostfassade. rechts: Transparente holografische Wand für animierte Präsentationen.
gauche: Plan de site_Façade est. droite: Mur holographique transparent pour des présentations animées.
izquierda: Plano de ubicación_Fachada este. derecha: Muro holográfico transparente para presentaciones animadas.

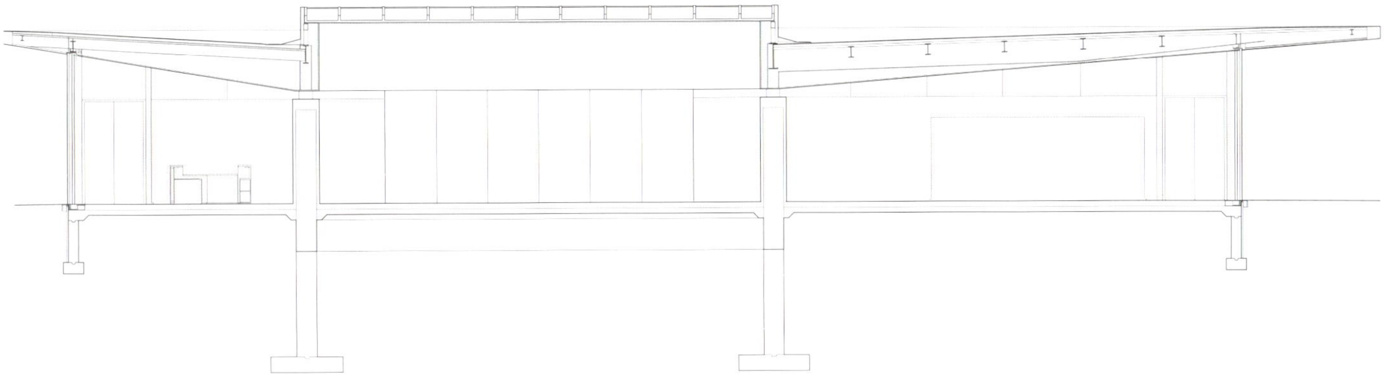

links: Südfassade. rechts: Längsschnitt_Eingang in den Pavillon_Interaktive Ausstellungsdisplays.
gauche: Façade sud. droite: Coupe longitudinale_Entrée dans le pavillon_écrans d'exposition interactifs.
izquierda: Fachada sur. derecha: Corte longitudinal_Acceso al pabellón_Pantallas con muestras interactivas.

USA_CHATTANOOGA (TN) **HUNTER MUSEUM OF AMERICAN ART**

USA_USA_EE.UU.
RANDALL STOUT ARCHITECTS, INC
2005
KUNSTMUSEUM_MUSÉE D'ART_MUSEO DE ARTE
6,290 M^2
PHOTOS TIM GRIFFITH, SAN FRANCISCO

Das Projekt verwandelt den zuvor isolierten Ort in einen leicht zugänglichen und prominenten öffentlichen Raum, indem es ein „Museum in einem Garten" schafft. Blühende Geometrien leiten den Besucher direkt in die multifunktionale Lobby mit ihren Ausblicken auf den Fluss, zu den Galerien und hinauf bis zu den Sonderausstellungen und Skulpturenterrassen. Der Entwurf führt die ständige Sammlung auf einem einzigen Stockwerk mit der Lobby, einem Auditorium, Seminarräumen, einem Café und einem Souvenirgeschäft zusammen. Eine Vorhangfassade aus Glas und Aluminium sowie Fassaden aus eloxiertem Zink und das Dach aus Edelstahl prägen kraftvoll das Äußere.

Le projet transforme le lieu auparavant isolé en un espace public célèbre et facilement accessible afin de créer un « Musée dans un jardin ». Les géométries splendides guident les visiteurs directement depuis le hall d'entrée polyvalent avec ses panoramas sur le fleuve, les galeries, vers le haut, dans les expositions particulières et les terrasses d'exposition de sculptures. Le projet propose un espace dédié à la collection permanente sur un seul étage qui comprend un hall d'entrée, un auditorium, des espaces de séminaires, un café et une boutique de souvenirs. Une façade-rideau en verre et aluminium ainsi que des façades en zinc anodisé et le toit en acier fin dominent majestueusement l'aspect extérieur.

El proyecto transforma un sitio aislado en un espacio público destacado y de fácil acceso; implica la creación de un "museo en un jardín". Floridas geometrías invitan al visitante a ingresar al vestíbulo multifuncional con sus vistas sobre el río, las galerías, las exhibiciones temporarias y las terrazas de esculturas. El proyecto reúne toda la colección permanente en un solo nivel con el vestíbulo, un auditorio, salas para seminarios, un café y una tienda de recuerdos. Un muro cortina en cristal y aluminio, fachadas de cinc anodizado y un techo en acero inoxidable caracterizan un exterior impactante.

links: Dachformen_Blick vom Tennessee River_Blick aus dem Skulpturengarten Richtung Eingang. rechts: Blick von der Walnut Street Fußgängerbrücke.
gauche: Formes de toiture_Vue du fleuve Tennessee_Vue depuis le jardin de sculptures orientation entrée. droite: Vue de la passerelle piétonnière Walnut Street.
izquierda: Formas del techo_Vista desde el río Tennessee Vista desde el jardín de esculturas hacia el acceso. derecha: Vista del puente peatonal de Walnut Street.

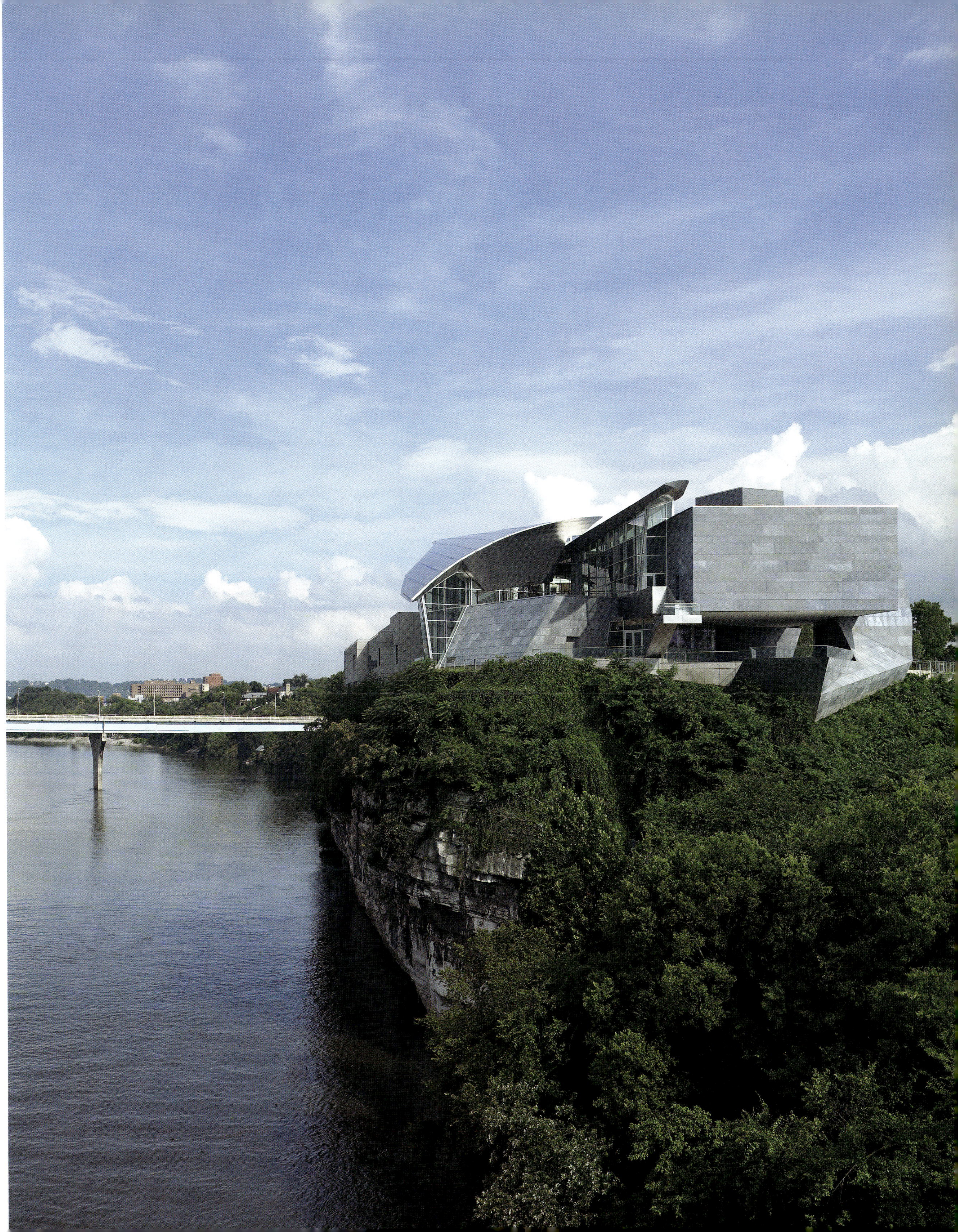

STUDIOS

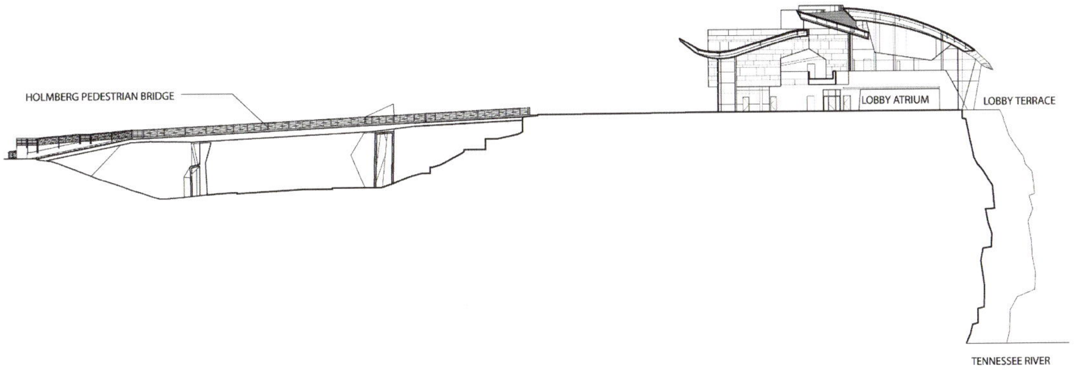

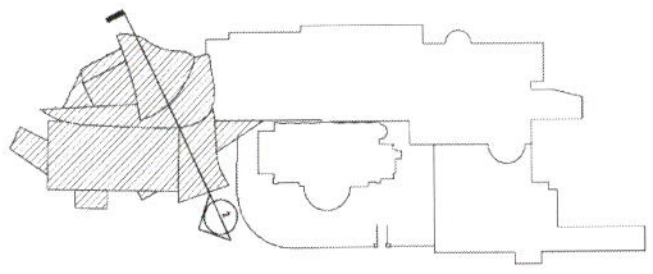

links: Lobby. rechts: Schnitt_Empfangstresen_Ständige Sammlung_Holmberg Fußgängerbrücke.
gauche: Hall d'entrée. droite: Coupe_Comptoir d'information_Collection permanente_Passerelle piétonnière Holmberg.
izquierda: Vestíbulo. derecha: Corte_Mostrador de recepción_Colección permanente_Puente peatonal Holmberg.

USA_CHICAGO (IL) CHICAGO ART INSTITUTE

USA_USA_EE.UU.
RENZO PIANO BUILDING WORKSHOP, ARCHITECT WITH INTERACTIVE DESIGN INC., ARCHITECTS
2009
KUNSTMUSEUM_MUSÉE D'ART_MUSEO DE ARTE
264,000 M²
PHOTOS NIC LEHOUX / RPBW

Der neue Flügel an der Nordostecke des Art Institute of Chicago verbindet den Millennium Park mit dem Zentrum des vorhandenen Museums mittels des neuen Griffin Court. Im Erdgeschoss wird der natürlich belichtete Hof von Bildungs- und öffentlichen Einrichtungen, Galerien und einem Garten flankiert. Das erste und zweite Geschoss sind der Kunst vorbehalten. Bei dem Schutzdach über dem Kunstpavillon handelt es sich um eine Art fliegenden Teppich aus Aluminium. Kalkstein prägt das Museum vom ursprünglichen Beaux-Arts-Palast bis zum aktuellen Anbau. Oberhalb des Steins erhebt sich der Neubau in Stahl und Glas leicht, transparent und durchlässig: Er ist solide und robust und gleichzeitig leicht und frisch.

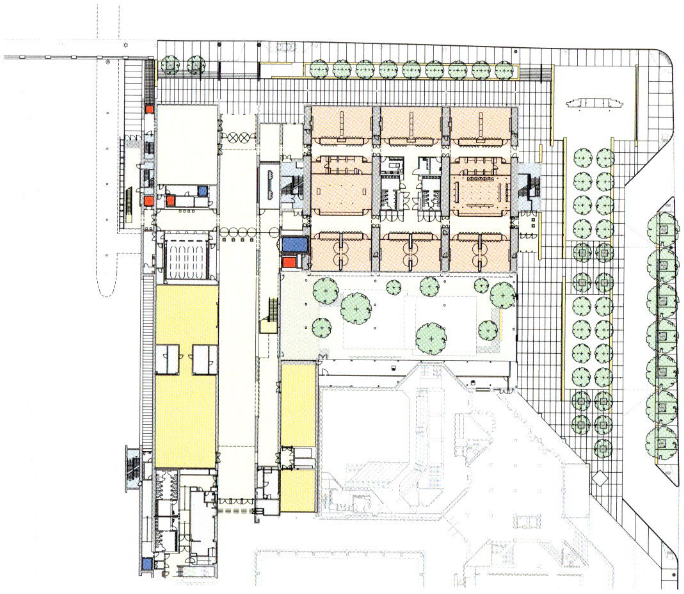

La nouvelle aile sur l'angle située au Nord-est du terrain de l'Art Institute de Chicago relie le Millennium Park au centre du musée actuel grâce à la nouvelle Griffin Court. Au premier étage au-dessus de cette cour éclairée naturellement, se situe des institutions publiques et éducatives, des galeries et un jardin. Le deuxième et troisième étage sont réservés à l'art. Une nuance de tapis volant en aluminium ferme le pavillon d'art vers le haut. La pierre calcaire caractérise l'ensemble du musée depuis le palais des Beaux-arts d'origine jusqu'à l'aménagement actuel. Au dessus du revêtement en pierre s'élève le nouveau bâtiment en verre et en acier, transparent et perméable, en toute légèreté : il reste solide et robuste tout en étant léger et représentatif de la modernité.

La nueva ala en el ángulo nordeste del terreno del Art Institute of Chicago conecta el Millennium Park con el centro del museo existente y con el nuevo Griffin Court. En el primer nivel por encima de este patio iluminado naturalmente se albergan las instalaciones educativas y públicas, las galerías y un jardín. El segundo y tercer nivel están dedicados al arte. Una especie de alfombra mágica de aluminio cierra el pabellón de arte por encima. La piedra caliza caracteriza el museo, desde el tradicional palacio estilo Beaux Arts hasta la construcción actual. Por encima de la piedra se levanta una edificación en acero y cristal, liviana, transparente y permeable: así, es al mismo tiempo sólida y robusta, liviana y fresca.

links: Grundriss Erdrgeschoss_Außenansicht_Obergeschoss mit Skyline. rechts: Fassade.
gauche: Plan du 1er étage_Vue extérieure_étage supérieur avec l'horizon. droite: Façade.
izquierda: Plano del primer piso_Vista exterior_Planta superior con silueta. derecha: Fachada.

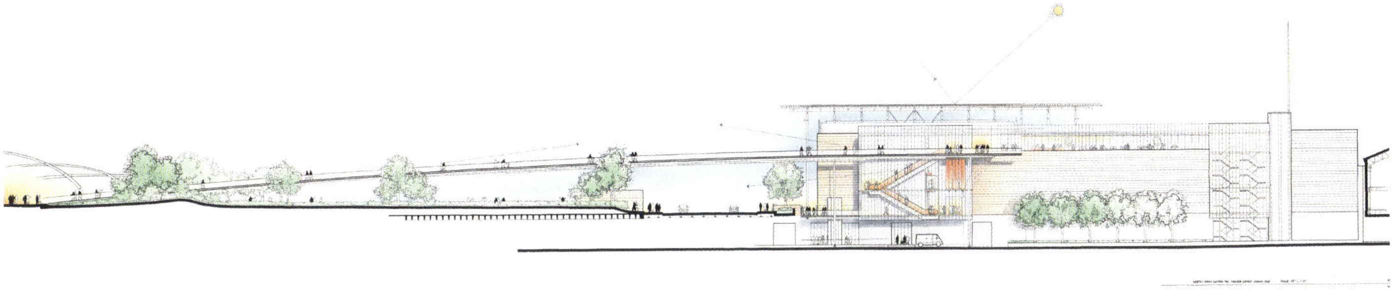

links: Foyer. rechts: Ansicht_Treppen_Ausstellungsräume.
gauche: Foyer. droite: Vue_Escalier_Espaces d'exposition.
izquierda: Vestíbulo. derecha: Vista_Escaleras_Salas de exhibiciones.

USA_CINCINNATI (OH) **ROSENTHAL CENTER FOR CONTEMPORARY ART**

USA_USA_EE.UU.
ZAHA HADID ARCHITECTS
2003
KUNSTMUSEUM_MUSÉE D'ART_MUSEO DE ARTE
8,500 M²
PHOTOS ROLAND HALBE / ARTURIMAGES

Um Besucher in die Wechselausstellungen zu locken und einen dynamischen öffentlichen Raum zu schaffen, sind Eingang, Lobby und der Anfang des Ausstellungsrundgangs als „städtischer Teppich" verstanden worden. Während er sich windet und aufsteigt, führt er zu einer abgehängten, zwischengeschossartigen Rampe, die durch die gesamte Lobby führt und tagsüber als offene, natürlich belichtete, landschaftsartige Erweiterung und künstlicher Park verstanden wird. Im Gegensatz zu diesen polierten, ondulierten Oberflächen, erscheinen die Galerien, als seien sie aus einem großen Betonklotz ausgehöhlt worden, der die Lobby überfängt. Teppich, Rampen und Galerien sind wie ein dreidimensionales, aus massiven Stücken und Leerräumen bestehendes Puzzle miteinander verwoben.

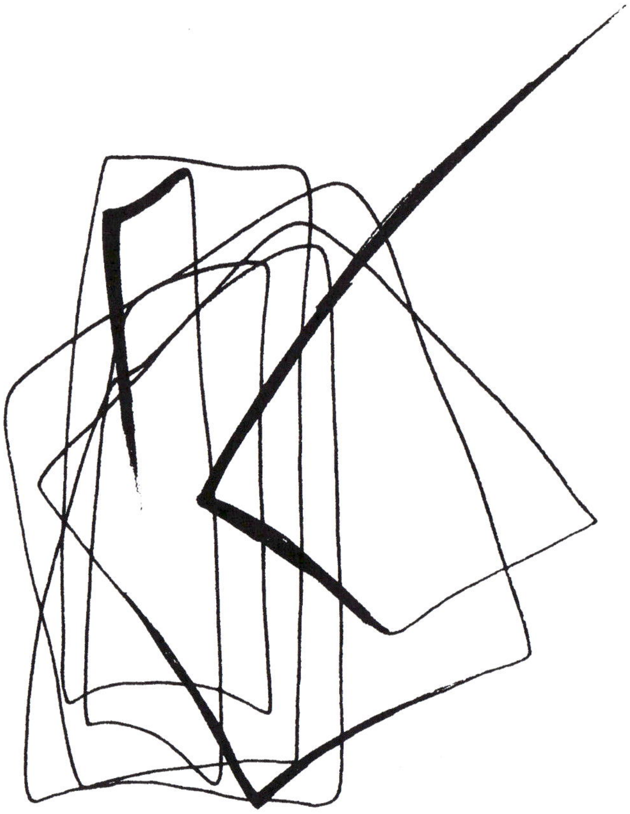

Afin de séduire les visiteurs dans les expositions tournantes et de créer un espace public dynamique, l'entrée, le hall central et le début de la galerie d'expositions sont assimilés à un « tapis urbain ». Alors que le centre serpente vers le haut pour rejoindre une rampe en forme de mezzanine suspendue conduisant au hall central, il est assimilé le jour à une extension paysagiste ouverte, éclairée par la lumière naturelle et à un parc artistique. En opposition aux surfaces ondulées polies, les galeries apparaissent comme si elles étaient creusées dans un grand cube en béton recouvrant le hall central. Le tapis, les rampes et les galeries sont étroitement liés comme un puzzle tridimensionnel consistant en pièces massives et espaces vides.

Con la finalidad de atraer los visitantes hacia las exhibiciones temporarias y lograr un espacio público dinámico, el acceso, el vestíbulo y el inicio de la recorrida por las muestras han sido entendidas como una "alfombra urbana". A medida que da vueltas y sube, conduce hacia una rampa suspendida que recorre todo el vestíbulo. Durante las horas diurnas se la puede apreciar como una ampliación paisajística abierta e iluminada naturalmente y, al mismo tiempo, como un parque artificial. En contraste con estas superficies pulidas y onduladas, las galerías parecen huecos cavados en un enorme macizo de hormigón que se cierne sobre el vestíbulo. La alfombra, las rampas y las galerías se asemejan a un rompecabezas tridimensional compuesto de piezas macizas y huecas entrelazadas entre sí.

links: Skizze_Rampe Zwischengeschoss in der Lobby_Treppenhaus_Fassade. rechts: Außenbau.
gauche: Esquisse_Rampe de la mezzanine dans le lobby_Cage d'escalier_Façade. droite: Extérieur.
izquierda: Esbozo_Rampa con nivel intermedio en el vestíbulo_Caja de la escalera_Fachada. derecha: Vista exterior.

CENTER FOR CONTEMPORARY ART
DO NOT BLOCK

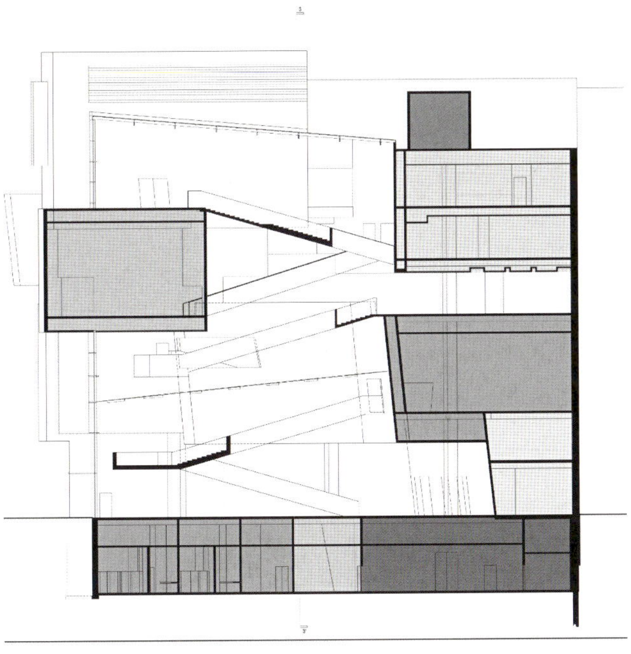

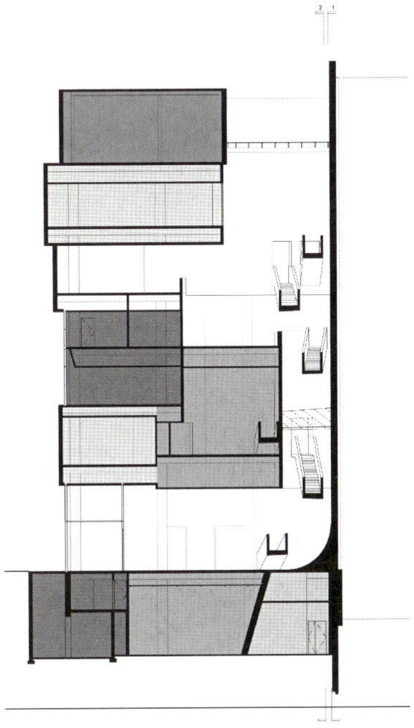

links: Blick ins Treppenhaus von oben. rechts: Schnitte_Treppenhaus_Ausstellungsraum_Café.
gauche: Vue descendante sur la cage d'escalier. droite: Coupe_Cage d'escalier_Espace d'exposition_Cafétéria.
izquierda: Vista escaleras abajo. derecha: Cortes_Caja de la escalera_Sala de exhibiciones_Café.

USA_CULVER CITY (CA) **SPF:A HEADQUARTERS**

USA_USA_EE.UU.
SPF:A
2006
DESIGN-, KUNST- UND ARCHITEKTURMUSEUM
MUSÉE DE DESIGN, D'ART ET D'ARCHITECTURE
MUSEO DE DISEÑO, ARTE Y ARQUITECTURA
2,604 M²
PHOTOS JOHN EDWARD LINDEN

Das Gebäude bietet einer öffentlichen Galerie, einem Architektur-Studio und einem Restaurant im Erdgeschoss Raum und umfasst sieben Atelierwohnungen für verschiedene Künstler und kreative Unternehmen in der zweiten Etage. Die Galerie widmet sich in Ausstellungen, Vorträgen und kulturellen Veranstaltungen der Wechselbeziehung zwischen Design, Kunst und Architektur. Betonfaserplatten am Außenbau brechen den Straßenlärm des geschäftigen Washington Boulevards und schirmen das Innere von der konstanten Sonneneinstrahlung ab. Die Variation der Platten in Breite und Tiefe ist als visuelle „Musik" gedacht und bildet kompositorische Varianten mit 20, 40 und 80 Zentimeter breiten Paneelen und in drei verschiedenen, zufällig auf die Oberfläche des Gebäudes verteilten Farben aus.

Le bâtiment offre une galerie publique, un cabinet d'architecture, un restaurant au rez-de-chaussée et comprend sept appartements d'atelier pour les différents artistes et entreprises de création au deuxième étage. La galerie est consacrée aux expositions, conférences et manifestations culturelles en corrélation entre conception, art et architecture. Les plaques en fibre de béton situées à l'extérieur protègent l'intérieur contre le bruit de la route provenant de la zone commerçante du Washington Boulevard et contre les rayons du soleil constants. La variation des plaques en largeur et profondeur rappellent la « musique » visuelle et forment des variantes de composition avec des largeurs de panneaux d'environ 20, 40 et 80 centimètres dans trois différentes teintes réparties aléatoirement sur la surface du bâtiment.

El edificio comprende una galería pública, un estudio de arquitectura y un restaurante en la planta baja, y en el segundo nivel dispone de siete estudios para diversos artistas y empresas de creativos. La galería está dedicada a exhibiciones, conferencias y acontecimientos culturales en los que se presenta la cambiante relación entre el diseño, el arte y la arquitectura. Las placas de fibrocemento del exterior amortiguan el mundanal ruido del ajetreado Washington Boulevard y protegen el interior de las radiaciones solares. La variación de la anchura y la profundidad de las placas ha sido concebida a modo de "música visual", como si se tratase de variaciones: se trata de una composición con paneles de 20, 40 y 80 centímetros, de tres colores diferentes, distribuidos de manera aleatoria sobre la superficie del edificio.

links: Schnitt_Nachtaufnahme_Fassadendetail. rechts: Fassade_Ausstellungshalle_Blick ins Studio.
gauche: Coupe_Vue nocturne_Détail de la façade. droite: Façade_Hall d'exposition_Vue dans le studio.
izquierda: Corte_Vista nocturna_Detalle de fachada. derecha: Fachada_Sala de exhibiciones_Vista del estudio.

USA_DENVER (CO) **DENVER ART MUSEUM**

USA_USA_EE.UU.
STUDIO DANIEL LIBESKIND WITH DAVIS PARTNERSHIP
2006
KUNSTMUSEUM_MUSÉE D'ART_MUSEO DE ARTE
13,560 M²
PHOTOS BITTER BREDT FOTOGRAFIE, BERLIN

Der 146.000 Quadratmeter umfassende, im Oktober 2006 eröffnete Erweiterungsbau beherbergt derzeit neben den Sammlungen moderner und zeitgenössischer Kunst auch die ozeanische und afrikanische Kunst. Die Volumen des Hamilton Buildings erinnern an die Gipfel der Rocky Mountains und an geometrische Kristalle, die in deren Ausläufern in der Nähe von Denver gefunden werden. Die Auswahl der Materialien für das Gebäude steht in enger Beziehung zu diesem Kontext, greift aber auch auf innovative neue Materialien zurück. So wurden 9000 Titanplatten verwendet, die das Gebäude bedecken und das helle Sonnenlicht Colorados spiegeln. Das Projekt entstand in einem sich entwickelnden Gebiet der Stadt als Teil einer übergreifenden Komposition aus öffentlichen Räumen, Denkmälern und Zufahrten.

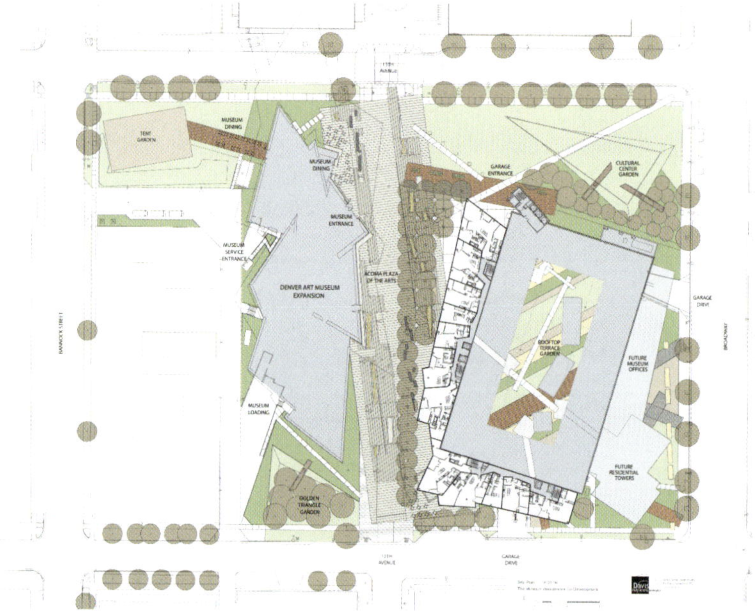

L'extension de 146 000 mètres carrés inaugurée au mois d'octobre 2006 abrite actuellement à proximité des collections d'art modernes et contemporaines, l'art africain et océanien. Les volumes des Hamilton Buildings rappellent les sommets de Rocky Mountains et les cristaux géométriques retrouvés dans les contreforts à proximité de Denver. La sélection des matériaux du bâtiment est en relation étroite au contexte existant qui introduit également de nouveaux matériaux innovants. 9000 plaques de titane recouvrent le bâtiment et jouent avec la lumière brillante du soleil du Colorado. Le projet fut développé dans une zone urbaine en plein essor en tant que partie d'une composition expansive d'espaces publics, monuments et portes architectoniques de la ville.

Esta ampliación, que cubre 146.000 metros cuadrados, fue inaugurada en octubre de 2006. Además de las colecciones de arte moderno y contemporáneo, alberga también las de arte oceánico y africano. Los volúmenes del edificio Hamilton evocan las cumbres de las Montañas Rocosas, y también se asemejan a los cristales geométricos que se pueden apreciar en las cercanías de Denver. Los materiales seleccionados para el edificio se relacionan estrechamente con el contexto existente; pero también se han introducido materiales innovadores. Tal es el caso de las 9.000 placas de titanio que cubren el edificio y reflejan la brillante luz del sol de Colorado. El proyecto se realizó en un sector de la ciudad en pleno desarrollo, como parte de una composición que abarca espacios públicos y monumentos.

links: Übersichtsplan_Auskragung_Titanverkleideter Eingang. rechts: Detail_Gesamtansicht.
gauche: Plan général_Porte-à-faux sur la rue_Entrée revêtue en titane. droite: Détail_Vue générale.
izquierda: Plano del conjunto_Volumen que cuelga sobre la calle_Acceso recubierto en titanio.
derecha: Detalle_Vista del conjunto.

Adam's
Mark
HOTEL

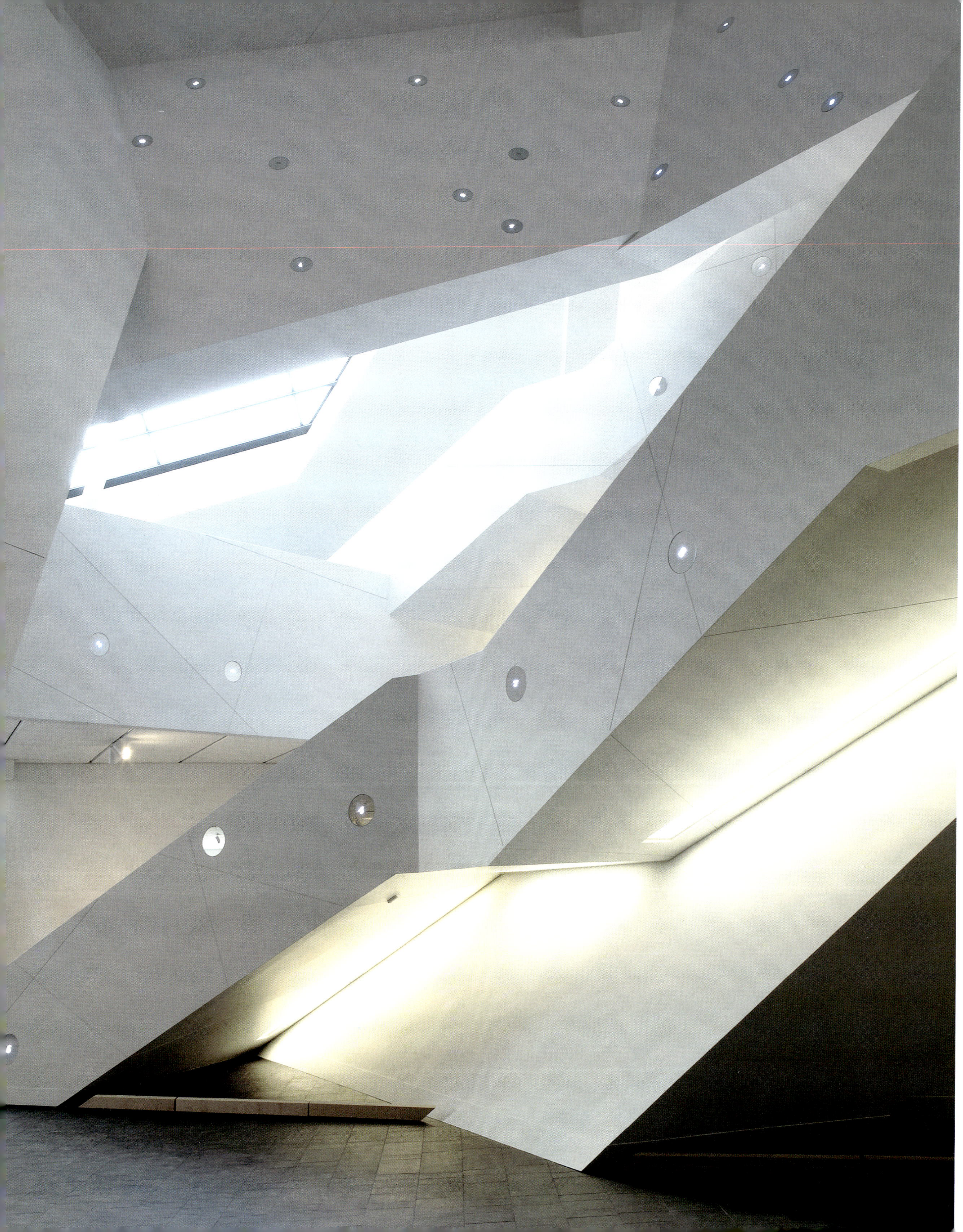

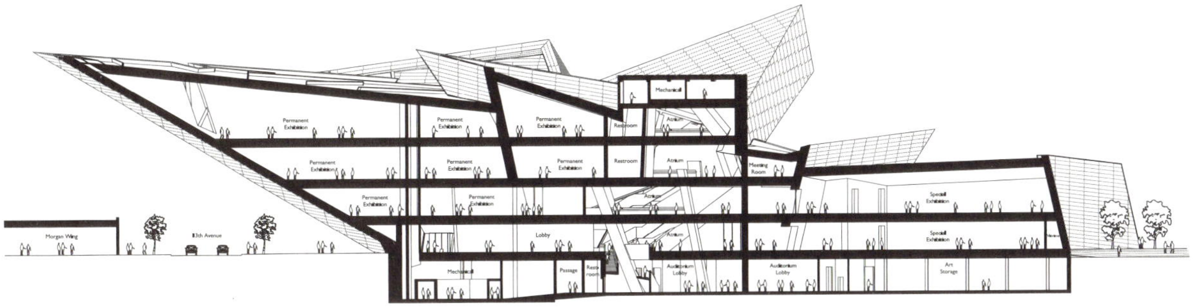

links: Treppenhausatrium mit digitaler Engi-Installation. rechts: Schnitt Richtung Osten_Ansicht Treppen, Atrium vom Erdgeschoss_Galerie zeitgenössischer Kunst_Galerie zeitgenössischer Kunst mit Treppe.
gauche: Cage d'escalier de l'atrium avec une installation numérique Engi. droite: Coupe vers l'est_Vue des escaliers de l'atrium du rez-de-chaussée_Galerie d'art contemporanéen_Galerie d'art contemporanéen avec l'escalier.
izquierda: Atrio de escaleras con instalación Engi digital. derecha: Corte mirando al este_Atrio de escaleras visto desde la planta baja_Galería de arte contemporáneo_Galería de arte contemporáneo con escalera.

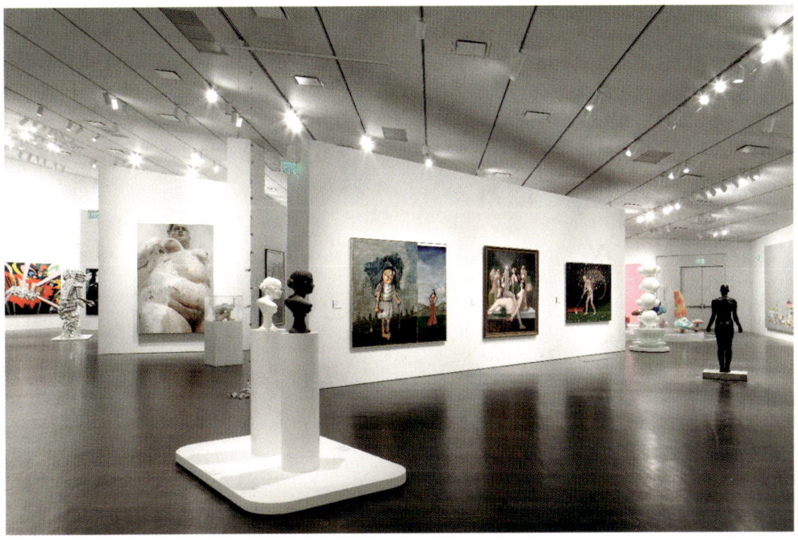

USA_FORT WORTH (TX) MODERN ART MUSEUM OF FORT WORTH

USA_USA_EE.UU.
TADAO ANDO ARCHITECT & ASSOCIATES
2002
KUNSTMUSEUM_MUSÉE D'ART_MUSEO DE ARTE
14,820 M²
PHOTOS MITSUO MATSUOKA

Der Architekt schuf ein sehr subtiles und klares räumliches Konzentrat, das als „Kunstwald" ohne Trennung von Innen- und Außenraum gedacht ist. Eine Reihe von fünf rechteckigen, festen Körpern, die jeweils aus einem Sichtbetonkern und einer Glashülle bestehen, findet sich von Wasser und Grün umgeben in einem Wald. Natur und Licht sind von innen ebenso zu erfahren, wie von außen die Gestaltung der Ausstellungsräume durch das Glas zu erfassen ist. Während man sich der an diesem Ort präsentierten Kunstwerke ständig bewusst ist, können Konzerte, Feste im Freien oder ähnliche Veranstaltungen auf dem Rasenplatz und im Wassergarten genossen werden.

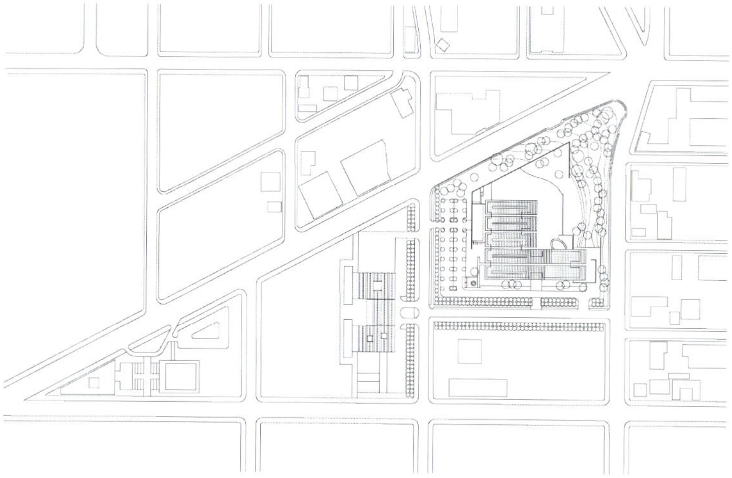

L'architecte a créé un concentré spatial très subtil et clair, pensé comme une « forêt de l'art », sans séparation entre la structure intérieure et extérieure. Une série de cinq corps de bâtiments fixes, respectivement en béton apparent, enveloppée de verre et à double cloison, est entourée par l'eau et par une zone de verdure située dans une forêt. L'expérience relative à la nature et à la lumière est à vivre de l'intérieur comme il faut vivre l'expérience de la formation des espaces d'exposition par le verre de l'extérieur. La prise de conscience des œuvres d'art sur le terrain rend l'organisation de concerts, fêtes en plein air ou autres manifestations similaires, idéale sur la place gazonnée ou dans le jardin aquatique.

El arquitecto concibió una espacialidad bien concentrada, clara y sutil, que se percibe como un "bosque artificial", sin separaciones entre interior y exterior. En una zona verde rodeada de agua y un bosque, se encuentra una hilera de cinco cuerpos rectangulares, cada uno de ellos constituido por un núcleo de hormigón y una envolvente de cristal. También desde el interior se aprecian la naturaleza y la luz; y desde fuera, el cristal permite apreciar la configuración de las salas de exhibición. Mientras se contempla las obras de arte presentadas en este lugar, se pueden disfrutar conciertos, fiestas al aire libre u otras actividades que se llevan a cabo en la plaza de césped y en el jardín acuático.

links: Lageplan_Dächer verschatten den Außenbau_Außenansicht. rechts: Ausstellungsfläche Großer reflektierender Teich.
gauche: Plan de site_Toits ombrageant l'extérieur du bâtiment. droite: Surface d'exposition_Reflet sur le grand bassin.
izquierda: Ubicación_Los techos arrojan sombra sobre las fachadas_Vista exterior. derecha: Área de exhibiciones_Gran estanque reflejante.

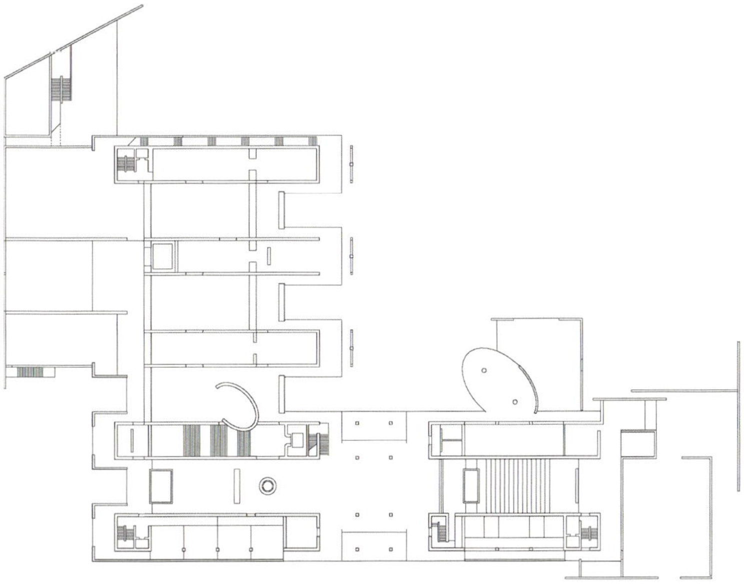

links: Treppenhaus. rechts: Grundriss 1. Obergeschoss_Y-Stütze aus Beton_Kabinett für Anselm Kiefers „Buch mit Flügeln"_Museumsshop.
gauche: Cage d'escalier. droite: Plan du 1er étage_Appuis Y en béton_Cabinet dédié au « livre avec des ailes » d'Anselm Kiefer_Boutique du musée.
izquierda: Caja de la escalera. derecha: Plano del primer piso_Pilares de hormigón en forma de Y_Gabinete del "Libro con alas" de Anselm Kiefer_Tienda del museo.

USA_GRAND RAPIDS (MI) **GRAND RAPIDS ART MUSEUM**

USA_USA_EE.UU.
WHY ARCHITECTURE WITH DESIGN PLUS, INC.
2007
KUNSTMUSEUM_MUSÉE D'ART_MUSEO DE ARTE
11,600 M^2
PHOTOS STEVE HALL (92, 93 A., 94), COURTESY OF THE ARCHITECTS (93 B.), SCOTT MCDONALD (95)

Das neue Gebäude liegt direkt neben einem Park, der als urbane Oase, umgeben von hohen Gebäuden, dient. Die vorspringenden Vordächer greifen wie Baumkronen aus und bilden einen Rahmen zwischen Park und Stadt, ähnlich dem japanischen Konzept der „geborgten Landschaft". Museumslobby, Restaurant und Bildungszentrum sind in Richtung Park vorgesetzte Pavillons mit Grünbereichen dazwischen. Bauliches Zentrum ist der dreigeschossige Galerieturm dahinter, dessen Galerien im obersten Stockwerk durch Oberlichter beleuchtet werden. Da dieses Museum als erstes Kunstmuseum der Welt die LEED-Zertifizierung in Gold erhalten soll, ist die Nutzung natürlichen Lichts im Gebäude eingeplant worden.

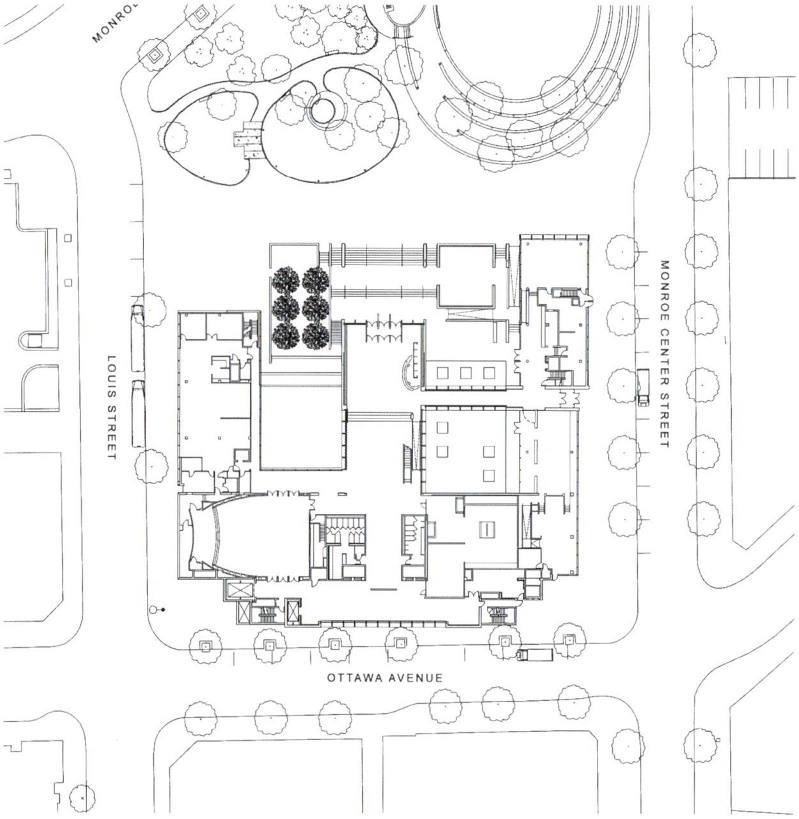

Le nouveau bâtiment se situe directement à proximité d'un parc servant d'oasis urbain entouré de bâtiments de grande taille. Les avant-toits en saillie s'élèvent comme des arbres et forment un cadre entre le parc et la ville qui s'assimile au concept japonais du « paysage emprunté ». Le hall d'entrée, le restaurant et le centre de formation du musée sont abrités dans le pavillon situé en direction du parc avec les zones de verdure intermédiaires. Le centre architectural est formé par la tour de galeries à trois étages située à l'arrière dont les galeries sont éclairées à l'étage supérieur par des lumières situées en hauteur. L'utilisation de la lumière naturelle dans le bâtiment fait partie des planifications. C'est le premier musée d'art au monde à avoir obtenu la certification LEED.

El nuevo edificio se ubica junto a un parque rodeado de altos edificios que oficia de oasis urbano. Los prominentes pórticos sobresalen como copas de árboles y configuran un marco entre el parque y la ciudad, acorde con el concepto japonés de "paisaje prestado". El vestíbulo del museo, el restaurante y el centro educativo se albergan en pabellones orientados en dirección al parque, separados entre sí por áreas verdes. El centro edilicio lo constituye la torre de galerías de tres niveles detrás de estos pabellones; estas galerías se iluminan cenitalmente en el último nivel. Este museo se perfila como uno de los primeros museos de arte en el mundo en recibir la certificación LEED nivel oro, por ende se planea el aprovechamiento de la luz natural en el edificio.

links: Grundriss_Haupteingang_Eingang Monroe Avenue. rechts: Fassade bei Nacht_Eingangshalle_Außenbereich.
gauche: Plan_Entrée principale_Entrée Monroe Avenue. droite: Façade de nuit_Hall d'entrée_Zone extérieure.
izquierda: Plano_Acceso principal_Acceso por la avenida Monroe. derecha: Fachada por la noche Vestíbulo_Vista exterior por la noche.

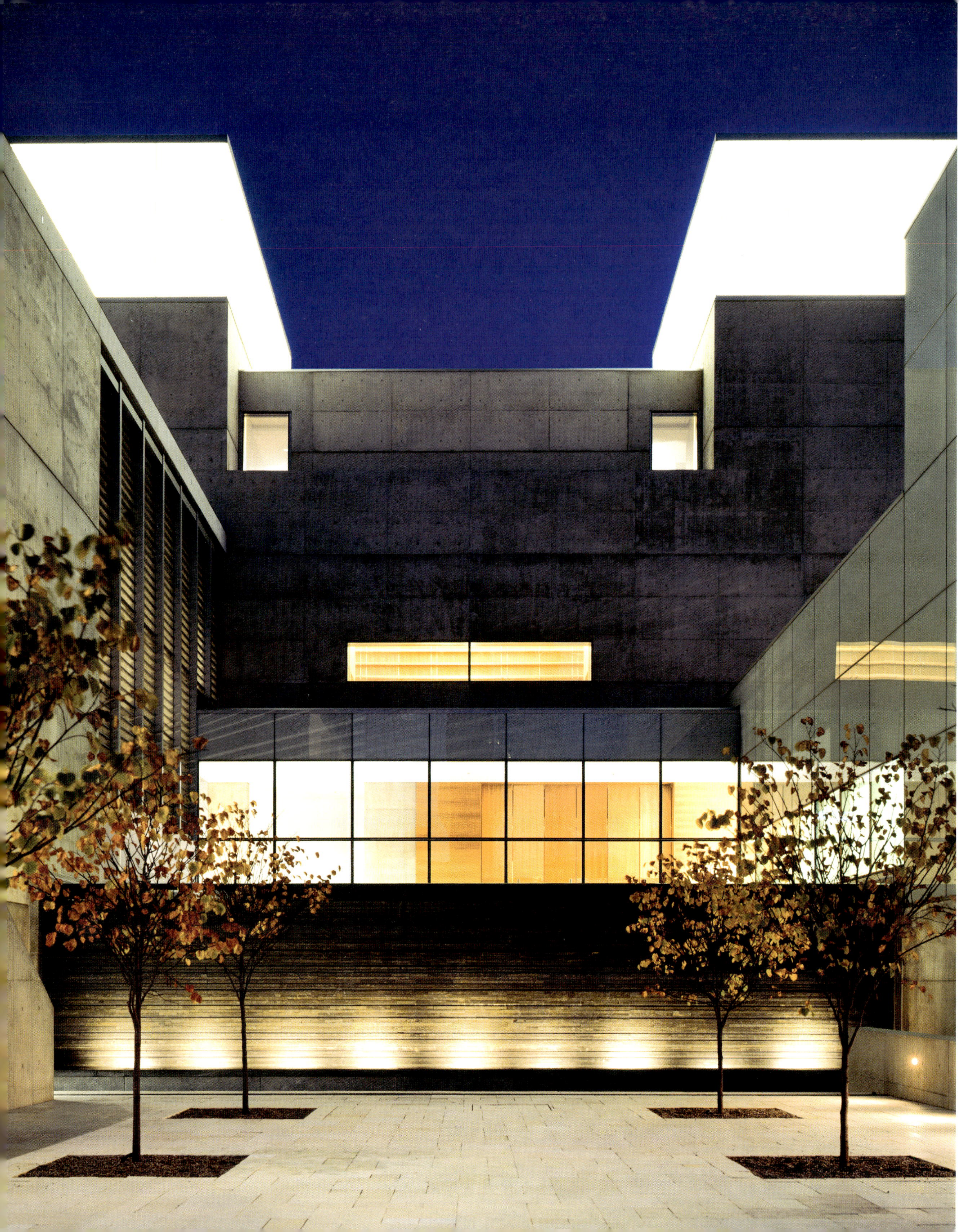

links: Fassade Pocket Park. rechts: Hauptfassade_Galerie_Ostbau.
gauche: Façade Pocket Park. droite: Façade principale_Galerie_Bâtiment à l'est.
izquierda: Fachada sobre el Pocket Park. derecha: Fachada principal_Galería_Ala este.

USA_KANSAS CITY (MO) **NELSON-ATKINS MUSEUM OF ART**

USA_USA_EE.UU.
STEVEN HOLL ARCHITECTS
2007
KUNSTMUSEUM_MUSÉE D'ART_MUSEO DE ARTE
15,300 M^2
PHOTOS ANDY RYAN

Der Erweiterungsbau Bloch Building mit 15.300 Quadratmetern entwickelt sich, abgesehen von fünf gläsernen Galerien am östlichen Ende des Campus, die „Linsen" genannt werden, gänzlich unterirdisch. Der Ausbau umfasst den bestehenden Skulpturengarten und verwandelt das gesamte Museumsgelände in eine Besucherzone. Es gibt sieben Zugänge zu dem Gebäude. Die erste der fünf „Linsen" bietet eine helle und transparente Lobby, lädt in das Museum ein und ermutigt die Besucher, über Rampen die Galerien in Richtung Garten hinab zu beschreiten. Die Zusammenarbeit mit Kuratoren und Künstlern führte zur Verschmelzung von Landschaft, Architektur und Kunst.

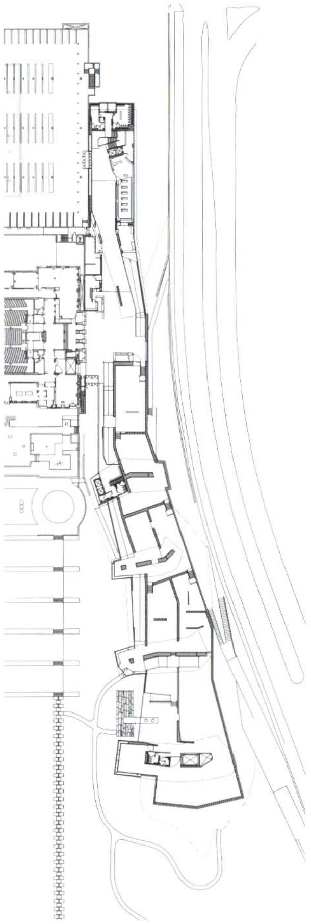

L'extension du Bloch Building s'étend sur 15 300 mètres carrés intégralement en espaces souterrains à l'exception des cinq galeries en verre situées à l'extrémité occidentale du campus baptisées « lentilles ». L'aménagement comprend les jardins de sculptures présents et transforme l'ensemble du terrain du musée en une cour dédiée aux visiteurs. Le bâtiment a sept accès. Le premier des cinq « lentilles» dispose d'un hall d'entrée clair et transparent qui invite dans le musée et incite les visiteurs à descendre par des rampes dans les galeries situées dans le jardin. La coopération entre la direction de musée et artistes a abouti à une fusion entre le paysage, l'architecture et l'art.

Con sus 15.300 metros cuadrados, la ampliación conocida como Bloch Building se desarrolla bajo tierra e incluye además cinco galerías acristaladas en el extremo este del campus, conocidas como "lentes". La reforma incluye el jardín de esculturas existente y transforma todo el predio del museo en un área de visita. Hay siete accesos al edificio. La primera de las cinco "lentes" ofrece un vestíbulo claro y transparente que invita al museo y anima a los visitantes a recorrer las rampas y las galerías para volver en dirección al jardín. La colaboración con curadores y artistas permitió la fusión del arte, la arquitectura y el paisaje.

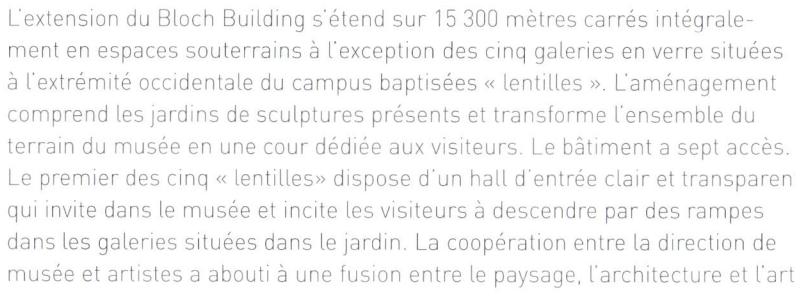

links: Grundriss Erdgeschoss_Nachtaufnahme Außenbau_Panoramaansicht. rechts: Außenbau Wanddetail_Treppenhaus_Treppen und Emporen.
gauche: Plan du rez-de-chaussée_Perspective de nuit de la construction extérieure_Vue panoramique. droite: Construction extérieure_Particularité du mur_Cage d'escalier_Escalier et matroneum.
izquierda: Plano de planta baja_Vista nocturna del exterior_Vista panorámica. derecha: Vista exterior_Detalle del muro_Caja de la escalera_Escaleras y galerías.

USA_MANCHESTER (NH) **CURRIER MUSEUM OF ART**

USA_USA_EE.UU.
ANN BEHA ARCHITECTS
2008
KUNSTMUSEUM_MUSÉE D'ART_MUSEO DE ARTE
6,781 M²
PHOTOS JONATHAN HILLYER, ATLANTA (98, 99 B.),
BRUCE T. MARTIN, NATICK (99 A.)

Durch die Sanierung und Erweiterung des historischen Museums verdoppelt sich der Raum für Ausstellungen, Programme und Dienstleistungen. Ein Anbau im Norden bietet den Besuchern ein neues Foyer und verschiedene Dienstleistungen. Im Süden umschließen drei neue Galerien einen Wintergarten, der ganzjährig Raum für ein Café, Empfänge und Aufführungen zur Verfügung stellt. Eine Treppe führt aus dem Wintergarten zum neuen Hörsaal, zu Unterrichtsräumen und Verwaltungsbüros. Durch die neuen Räume und eine Überprüfung der vorhandenen konnte ein neuer Rundgang durch die Galerien angelegt werden, der sich die Symmetrie des ursprünglichen Beaux-Arts-Entwurfs zunutze macht.

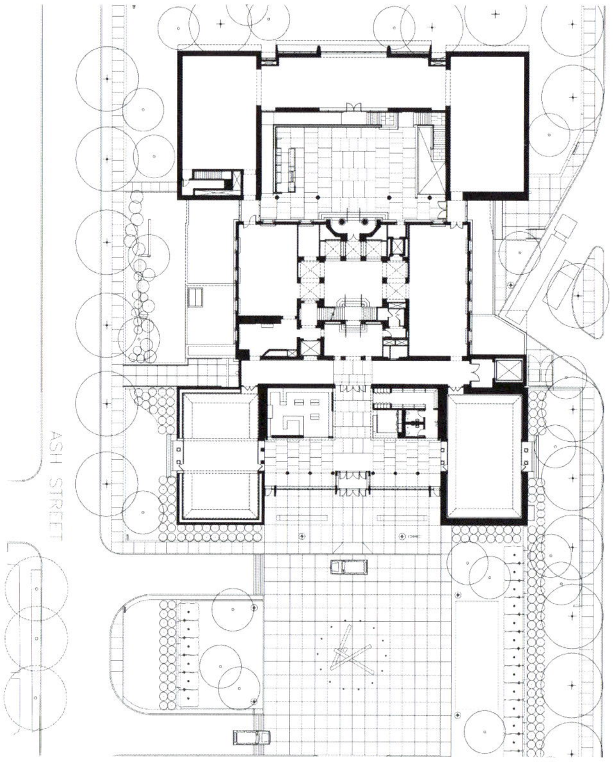

La rénovation et l'extension du musée historique doublent l'espace prévu aux expositions, programmes et prestations. Une annexe située au Nord offre aux visiteurs un nouveau foyer et différentes prestations de service. Au Sud, trois nouvelles galeries entourent un jardin d'hiver disponible toute l'année qui sert de cafétéria ou lieu de réceptions et de manifestations. Un escalier s'élevant du jardin d'hiver conduit à la nouvelle salle de conférence, aux salles de cours et aux bureaux réservés à l'administration. La création des nouveaux espaces et la vérification des espaces existant ont permis l'installation d'un nouveau circuit à travers les galeries qui bénéficie de la symétrie du plan d'origine des Beaux Arts.

La reforma y ampliación del museo histórico duplica el espacio disponible para las exhibiciones, los programas y los servicios. Una edificación nueva al norte les ofrece a los visitantes un nuevo vestíbulo y diversas áreas de servicios. En el sur, tres nuevas galerías encierran un jardín de invierno, que proporciona espacio todo el año para un café, recepciones y actividades. Una escalinata desde el jardín de invierno conduce hacia la nueva sala de audiciones, los salones lectivos y las oficinas administrativas. Gracias a las nuevas salas y una reconfiguración de las preexistentes se pudo disponer de un recorrido por las galerías que valoriza la simetría original de la antigua planta estilo Beaux Arts.

links: Grundriss Hauptgeschoss_Eingang Neubau_Süderweiterung. rechts: Verbindung Neubau und Bestand_Blick aus der Südgalerie in den Wintergarten_Hauptlobby.
gauche: Plan de l'étage principal_Entrée du nouveau bâtiment_Extension sud. droite: Connexion entre le nouveau et l'ancien bâtiment_Vue depuis la galerie sud dans les jardins d'hiver_Hall d'entrée principal.
izquierda: Plano del piso principal_Acceso al nuevo edificio_Ampliación sur. derecha: Vinculación entre el antiguo edificio y el nuevo_Vista desde la galería sur hacia el jardín de invierno_Vestíbulo principal.

BYZANTINE

USA_MILWAUKEE (WI) **MILWAUKEE ART MUSEUM**

USA_USA_EE.UU.
SANTIAGO CALATRAVA ARCHITECT & ENGINEER
2001
KUNSTMUSEUM_MUSÉE D'ART_MUSEO DE ARTE
13,200 M²
PHOTOS ALAN KARCHMER

Das Museum war bislang teilweise in einem 1957 von Eero Saarinen als Kriegsdenkmal errichteten Gebäude untergebracht, das durch einen pavillonartigen Aufbau in der Achse der Wisconsin Avenue erweitert wurde. Als unabhängige Einheit von Calatrava konzipiert, bildet die weiße, an ein Schiff erinnernde Stahl- und Betonform des Pavillons sowohl in Geometrie als auch in Material einen Kontrast zum bestehenden Ensemble. Der Neubau fügt dem Bestand 13.200 Quadratmeter hinzu. Ein linearer Flügel aus Glas und rostfreiem Stahl mit Lamellendach steht im rechten Winkel zu Saarinens Gebäude. Das Konzept ermöglicht die künftige Erweiterung. Der Pavillon besitzt eine kinetische Struktur: einen Sonnenschutz mit Lamellen, der sich wie die Flügel eines großen Vogels hebt und senkt.

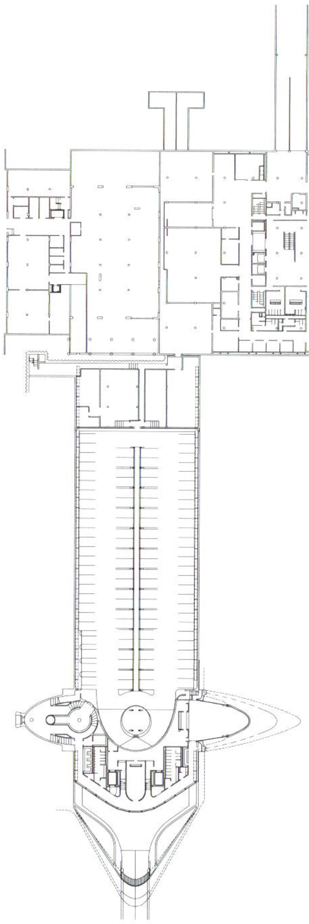

Jusqu'à présent, le musée était partiellement abrité dans un bâtiment créé en 1957 par Eero Saarinen en tant que monument de guerre qui fut élargi par un bâtiment en forme de pavillon dans l'axe de la Wisconsin Avenue. Conçu comme une unité indépendante de Calatrava, le pavillon en acier et béton de couleur blanche rappelant la forme d'un navire par sa géométrie et le choix des matériaux, contraste avec l'ensemble existant. Le nouveau bâtiment ajoute 3 200 mètres carrés à la construction existante. Une aile linéaire en verre et acier inoxydable recouverte d'un toit de lamelles se situe à l'angle droit du bâtiment Saarinen. Le concept favorise l'extension future. Le pavillon comprend également une structure cinétique : une protection contre les rayons solaires grâce aux lamelles qui s'élèvent et s'abaissent comme les ailes d'un grand oiseau.

Hasta hace poco, el museo se albergaba parcialmente en un edificio diseñado por Eero Saarinen en 1957 como monumento conmemorativo de guerra, y que había sido ampliado con un pabellón en el eje de la avenida Wisconsin. Concebido por Calatrava como unidad independiente, la forma blanca del pabellón de acero y cristal recuerda un barco, tanto en geometría como en material, y constituye un contraste con el conjunto existente. La nueva edificación agrega 13.200 metros cuadrados a los existentes. Un ala lineal en cristal y acero inoxidable con techo de láminas está en el ángulo derecho respecto del edificio de Saarinen. El concepto posibilita una futura ampliación. El pabellón cuenta con una estructura cinética: un parasol hecho con láminas, que se levantan y se bajan como las alas de un gran pájaro.

links: Grundriss_Sequenz Öffnung. rechts: Ansicht Dämmerung_Ansicht im Kontext.
gauche: Plan_Séquence ouverture. droite: Vue au crépuscule_Vue dans son contexte.
izquierda: Plano_Secuencia de apertura. derecha: Vista al atardecer_Vista del museo en su contexto

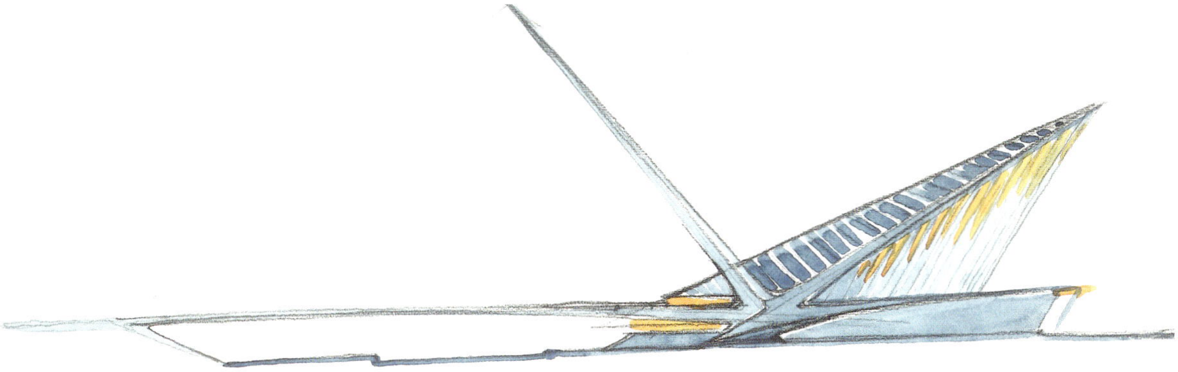

links: Detail Außenbau. rechts: Skizze_Oberlicht und Ausblick_Einhüftiger Bogengang_Innenraum.
gauche: Détail de l'extérieur. droite: Esquisse_Lumière du plafond et perspective_Arc rampant_Intérieur.
izquierda: Detalle del exterior. derecha: Esbozo_Lucernario y vista_Pasaje con arcadas_Espacio interior.

USA_NATCHITOCHES (LA) LOUISIANA STATE SPORTS HALL OF FAME AND REGIONAL HISTORY MUSEUM

USA_USA_EE.UU.
TRAHAN ARCHITECTS
2011
SPORT- UND GESCHICHTSMUSEUM_MUSÉE DE SPORTS ET D'HISTOIRE_MUSEO DEL DEPORTE E HISTÓRICO
2,600 M²
PHOTOS COURTESY OF THE ARCHITECTS

Louisianas Geschichte und den Einfluss des Sports auf diese feiernd, wird das regionalhistorische Museum mit Sportruhmeshalle eine Sammlung präsentieren, die sowohl Sportmemorabilien als auch historische Exponate umfasst. Der Entwurf vereint diese beiden scheinbar so unterschiedlichen Programme in einem modernen Ambiente, in dem beide Kollektionen als Teil einer Kulturgeschichte gezeigt werden. Der Entwurf greift das Landschaftsmuster fließender Kanalformen und eingeflochtener Landmassen auf. Diese Idee liegt auch der Organisationsstruktur von Besucherstrom und Galerieanordnung zugrunde. Das Atrium bildet das Zentrum im Inneren. Es dient der allgemeinen räumlichen Orientierung und fungiert auch als Veranstaltungsort.

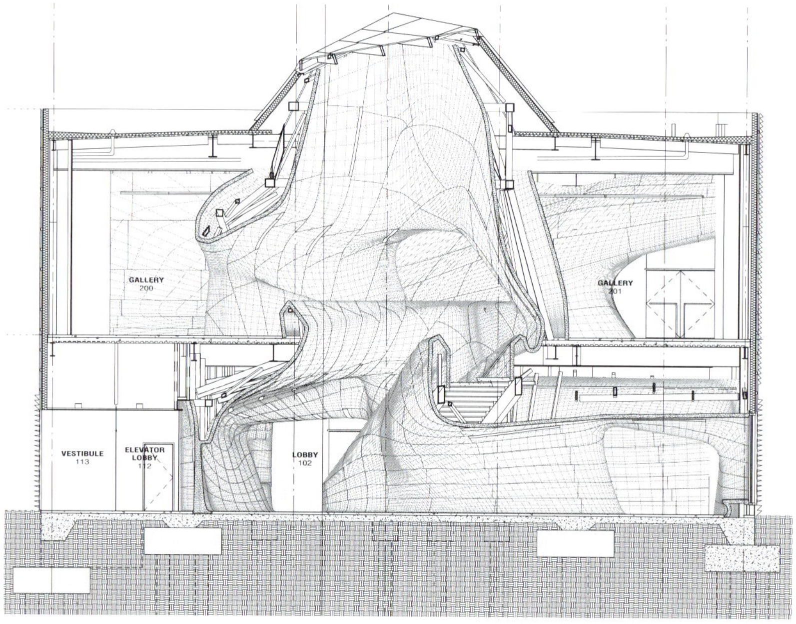

Afin de célébrer l'histoire de la Louisiane et l'influence du sport, le musée historique régional présente une collection grâce à une nouvelle salle de sport présentant des objets à la mémoire du sport et de l'histoire. Le projet réunit ces deux programmes si différents à première vue dans une ambiance moderne où ils seront montrés comme une collection de l'histoire de la culture. Le concept du projet reprend le modèle de paysage sous les formes d'un canal qui s'écoule et de paysages massifs imbriqués. Cette idée se fonde également sur la structure organisationnelle du flux de visiteurs et de l'agencement des galeries. L'atrium est au centre pour permettre l'orientation spatiale générale et servir également de lieu dédié aux manifestations.

El museo histórico regional, con su nuevo gimnasio deportivo, presenta una colección que celebra la historia de Luisiana y la influencia del deporte en ella; con tal motivo, se incluyen recuerdos notables del deporte y también objetos históricos. El diseño aúna estos dos programas aparentemente tan dispares en un moderno ambiente; la unión se logra presentando las dos colecciones como parte de una misma historia cultural. El concepto proyectual captura el modelo paisajístico de formas de canales que fluyen y masas de tierra que se entrecruzan. Esta idea también se aprecia en la estructura organizativa del flujo de visitantes y en la disposición de la galería. El atrio configura el centro del interior; sirve para la orientación espacial en general y sirve también como sitio de actividades comunitarias.

links: Schnitt_Treppe im Foyer. rechts: Atrium_Eingangsbereich_Foyerdetail.
gauche: Coupe_Escalier dans le foyer. droite: Atrium_Zone d'entrée_Détail du foyer.
izquierda: Corte_Escalera en el vestíbulo. derecha: Atrio_Zona del acceso_Detalle del vestíbulo.

USA_NEW YORK CITY (NY) **THE BRONX MUSEUM OF THE ARTS**

USA_USA_EE.UU.
ARQUITECTONICA
2006
KUNSTMUSEUM_MUSÉE D'ART_MUSEO DE ARTE
1,551 M²
PHOTOS NORMAN MCGRATH, NEW YORK CITY

Das neue Gebäude befindet sich auf dem Grand Concourse in der Bronx. Es steigt als unregelmäßig gefalteter Schirm aus gesinterten Glasscheiben im Wechsel mit Metallpaneelen vom Bürgersteig auf. Die diagonale Stellung der Paneele betont die Tiefe der Faltung. Die vertikalen Metall- und Glaszonen verkanten und verknicken sich wie ein architektonisches Origami, so dass die Straßenwand durchlässig erscheint. Im Erdgeschoss bietet sich dem nahenden Fußgänger in der Diagonalen der Blick durch die semitransparenten Glassplitter in die Galerie. Diese vorhangähnliche Gestaltung dramatisiert die Vertikalität des ansonsten bescheidenen Gebäudes und verleiht ihm eine unerwartet monumentale Erscheinung.

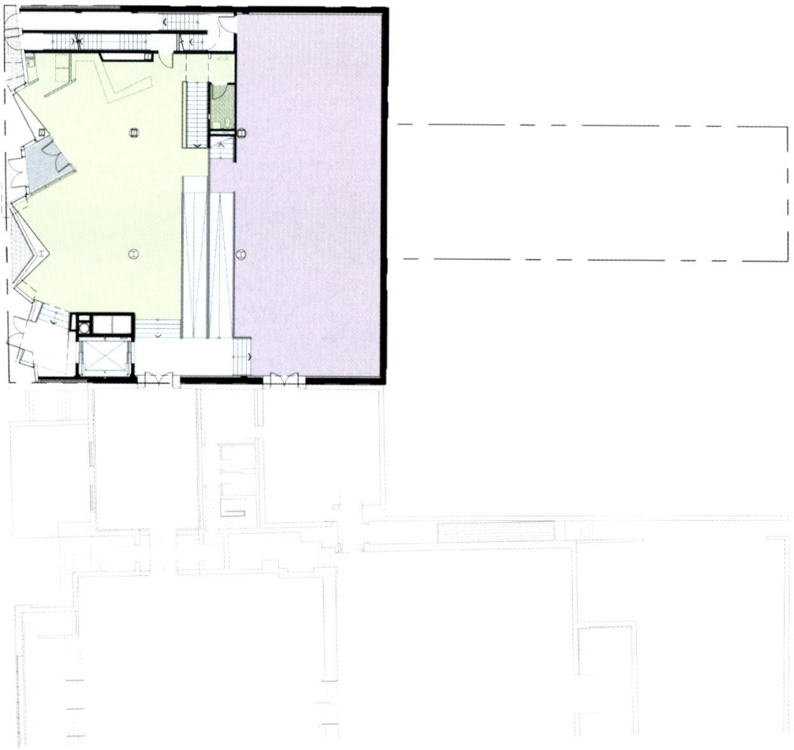

Le nouveau bâtiment se situe sur le Grand Concourse dans le Bronx. Il s'élève au dessus du trottoir à l'instar d'un parapluie irrégulièrement replié en vitres constituées de verre poreux en alternance avec des panneaux métalliques. La position diagonale des panneaux accentue les profondeurs des plis. L'alternance entre métal et verre au niveau horizontal forme des arêtes et bords repliés tel un origami architectonique qui donne une impression de transparence au mur côté rue. Au rez-de-chaussée, le piéton voit, à l'approche, la vue oblique à travers les éclats de verre semi-transparents dans la galerie. Cette géométrie semblable à un rideau souligne la verticalité du bâtiment, modeste par ailleurs, et lui confère un aspect monumental inattendu.

El nuevo edificio se levanta sobre el Grand Concourse en el Bronx. Se yergue desde la acera como una pantalla plegada de manera irregular, formada por láminas de cristal poroso alternadas con paneles de metal. La posición diagonal de los paneles recalca la profundidad de los pliegues. La alternancia de metal y cristal en horizontal, se pliega y quiebra como un origami arquitectónico y, de este modo, el muro de fachada parece ser permeable. En la planta baja se invita al peatón a que se acerque a mirar hacia la galería a través de los elementos de cristal semitransparente. Esta geometría que semeja un cortinado dramatiza la verticalidad de un edificio de por sí discreto, dándole una apariencia inesperadamente monumental.

links: Grundriss Erdgeschoss_Fassadendetail_Ansicht nachts von Nordwesten. rechts: Westseite_Lobby_Treppenaufgänge.
gauche: Plan du rez-de-chaussée_Façade en détail_Vue de nuit du nord-ouest. droite: Côté ouest-hall d'entrée_Cages d'escalier.
izquierda: Plano de planta baja_Detalle de fachada_Vista nocturna desde el noroeste. derecha: Fachada oeste_Vestíbulo_Ascenso por escaleras.

THE BRONX MUSEUM OF THE

USA_NEW YORK CITY (NY) **THE SKYSCRAPER MUSEUM**

USA_USA_EE.UU.
SKIDMORE, OWINGS & MERRILL LLP
2004
ARCHITEKTURMUSEUM_MUSÉE DE L'ARCHITECTURE
MUSEO DE ARQUITECTURA
560 M²
PHOTOS ROBERT POLIDORI

Trotz seines begrenzten Raums vermittelt das Museum die Großartigkeit eines Wolkenkratzers, indem es Wert auf Materialien, Sichtachsen und Details legt. Es belegt im Erdgeschoss des Battery Park Ritz-Carlton 560 Quadratmeter. Böden und Decken sind mit vollkommen ebenen, hochglanzpolierten Edelstahlplatten verkleidet. Die ungebrochenen Reflexionen lassen den Ausstellungsraum größer wirken als er ist, und scheinen ihn in vertikaler Erstreckung endlos zu verlängern. Zusammen mit hohen, von innen beleuchteten Ausstellungsvitrinen, die Neuanordnungen für verschiedene Ausstellungen und Veranstaltungen ermöglichen, erzeugen die reflektierenden Oberflächen ein Umfeld, das das Bild von Wolkenkratzern evoziert.

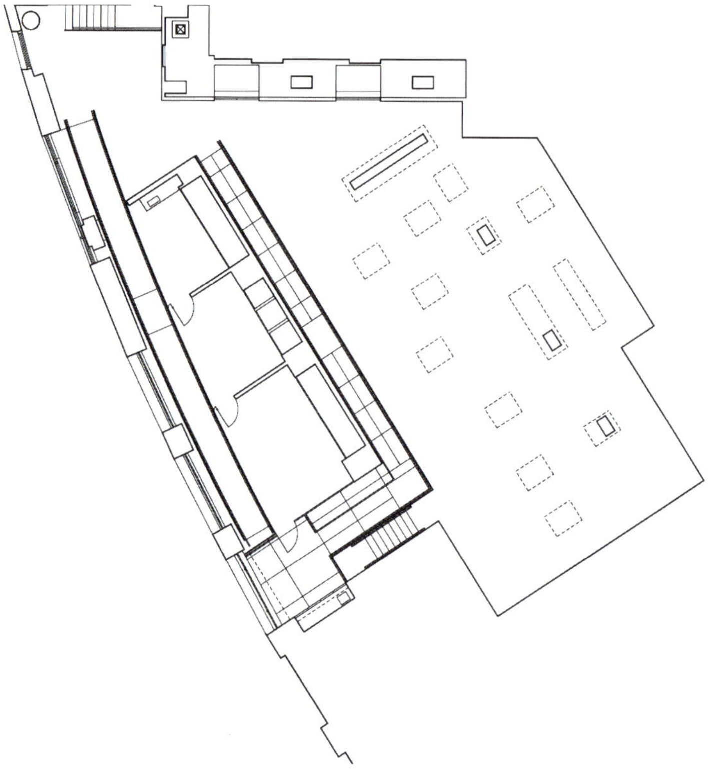

Le musée transmet l'idée généreuse d'un gratte-ciel malgré l'espace limité où l'accent est mis sur les matériaux, les angles de vue et les détails. Il est situé au premier étage du Battery Park Ritz-Carlton, une fondation de 560 mètres carrés. Les sols et les plafonds sont revêtus d'acier noble poli intégralement plat. Les réflexions immuables assurent son apparence plus grande que nature de l'espace d'exposition et contribue à son allongement illimité au niveau vertical. Les hautes vitrines d'exposition éclairées de l'intérieur permettent une nouvelle disposition dédiée aux différentes expositions et manifestations et les surfaces réfléchissantes produisent un environnement qui évoque l'image de gratte-ciels.

El museo logra comunicar la grandiosidad del rascacielos a pesar de lo escueto del espacio propio, gracias al esmero que se puso al elegir los materiales, los ejes visuales y los detalles. Alojado en el primer nivel del Battery Park Ritz-Carlton, dispone de 560 metros cuadrados de espacio dedicado. Los suelos y los cielorrasos están recubiertos de acero inoxidable pulido completamente liso. Los reflejos francos y brillantes hacen que el espacio de exposiciones parezca mucho mayor, hace el efecto de prolongarse indefinidamente en dirección vertical. Las elevadas vitrinas de exhibición, iluminadas desde dentro, permiten novedosas distribuciones de objetos en las diversas exposiciones y actividades y, de esta manera, las superficies reflectantes generan un entorno que evoca la imagen de los rascacielos.

links: Grundriss Mezzanin_Ansicht bewegliche Vitrinen_Ansicht Zugangsrampen. rechts: Ansicht der Galerie_Ansicht Zugangsrampe im unteren Geschoss.
gauche: Plan de la mezzanine_Vue des vitrines amovibles_Vue des rampes d'accès. droite: Vue de la galerie_Vue de la rampe d'accès à l'étage inférieur
izquierda: Plano del entrepiso_Vista de las vitrinas móviles_Vista de las rampas de acceso. derecha: Vista de la galería_Vista de la rampa de acceso en el nivel inferior.

MUSEUM

USA_OVERLAND PARK (KS) **NERMAN MUSEUM OF CONTEMPORARY ART**

USA_USA_EE.UU.
KYU SUNG WOO ARCHITECTS INC. WITH
GOULD EVANS ARCHITECTS
2007
KUNSTMUSEUM_MUSÉE D'ART_MUSEO DE ARTE
3,865 M²
PHOTOS TIMOTHY HURSLEY, LITTLE ROCK

Das Museum in einem Vorort von Kansas City ist ein bedeutendes Zentrum für den Austausch zwischen Kunst, Kultur und Bildung. Es schafft Raum für die herausragende Kunstsammlung und integriert die Kunst in das universitäre Umfeld und den Alltag der Studenten, Dozenten und Besucher. Formal setzt sich das Museum von dem bestehenden Kontext ab, betont seine Präsenz auf dem Campus und in der angrenzenden Landschaft. Durch eine umfangreiche Verglasung des Foyers im Erdgeschoss besteht eine Verbindung zum Außenraum; strategisch platzierte Fenster im Obergeschoss bieten atemberaubende Ausblicke auf die weite Landschaft.

Le musée se situe dans la périphérie de Kansas City et constitue un important centre d'échange entre l'art, la culture et l'enseignement. Cet espace permet d'exposer une extraordinaire collection d'œuvres d'art et d'intégrer l'art dans l'environnement universitaire et dans le quotidien des étudiants, des professeurs et des visiteurs. Au niveau des formes, le musée se distingue du contexte existant en affirmant sa présence sur le campus et dans le paysage environnant. Le vaste vitrage du foyer au rez-de-chaussée crée une connexion entre le musée et l'espace extérieur, tandis que les fenêtres situées à l'étage offrent des vues époustouflantes sur l'étendue du paysage.

El museo, ubicado en un suburbio de Kansas City, es un centro significativo para el intercambio entre el arte, la cultura y la educación. Logra un espacio para una formidable colección de obras de arte. También integra el arte en el entorno universitario y en la rutina de los estudiantes, los docentes y los visitantes. Formalmente, el museo se desprende del contexto existente, marca su presencia en el campus y en el paisaje circundante. Con un generoso acristalamiento del vestíbulo en la planta baja surge una vinculación con el espacio exterior. Ventanas estratégicamente ubicadas en la planta superior ofrecen arrobadoras vistas del amplio paisaje que se pierde en la lejanía.

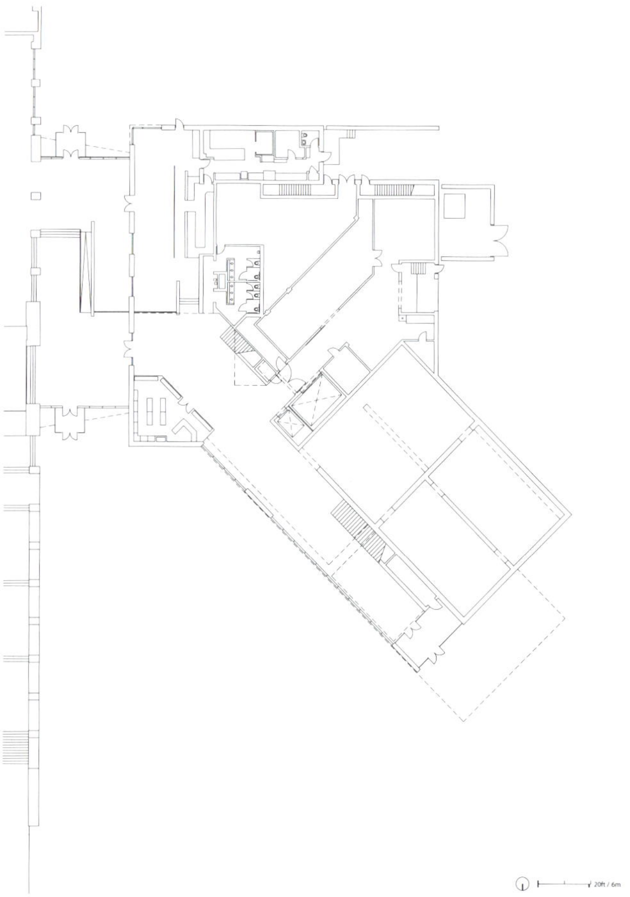

links: Grundriss Erdgeschoss_Ausstellungshalle_Innenansicht. rechts: Außenbau_Blick ins Innere_Glasfassade.
gauche: Plan du rez-de-chaussée_Hall d'exposition_Vue intérieure. droite: Construction extérieure Vue à l'intérieur_Façade de verre.
izquierda: Plano de planta baja_Sala de exhibiciones_Vista interior. derecha: Vista exterior_Vista hacia el interior_Fachada acristalada.

USA_ROCHESTER (NY) **STRONG NATIONAL MUSEUM OF PLAY**

USA_USA_EE.UU.
CJS ARCHITECTS
2006
GESCHICHTSMUSEUM_MUSÉE D'HISTOIRE_MUSEO HISTÓRICO
15,340 M²
PHOTOS COURTESY OF STRONG NATIONAL MUSEUM OF PLAY (112, 113 B.), DON COCHRAN PHOTOGRAPHY / ROCHESTER, NEW YORK (113 A., 114, 115)

Mit skurriler Architektur, die sowohl den Charakter des Strong als auch seine Aufgabe, das Spielen zu erforschen, widerspiegelt, wird der Umfang des Museums von 15.600 auf 26.200 Quadratmeter nahezu verdoppelt. Die architektonische Umgestaltung macht das Museum zu einem markanten Tor zur südöstlichen Stadt. Ein gigantisches, bronzefarbenes, raupenförmiges Atrium organisiert und verbindet Galerien und Geschosse. Eine Ansammlung aus Stahlblöcken, die mit bunten Kunstharzplatten verkleidet sind, erscheint wie ein riesiger Haufen aus bunten Bauklötzen, und ein hoch aufragender, roter Turm nimmt Heizung, Lüftung und Klimaanlage auf. Der Schmetterlingsgarten ist mit einer Gewebestruktur überspannt, die leuchtenden, ausgebreiteten Flügeln gleicht.

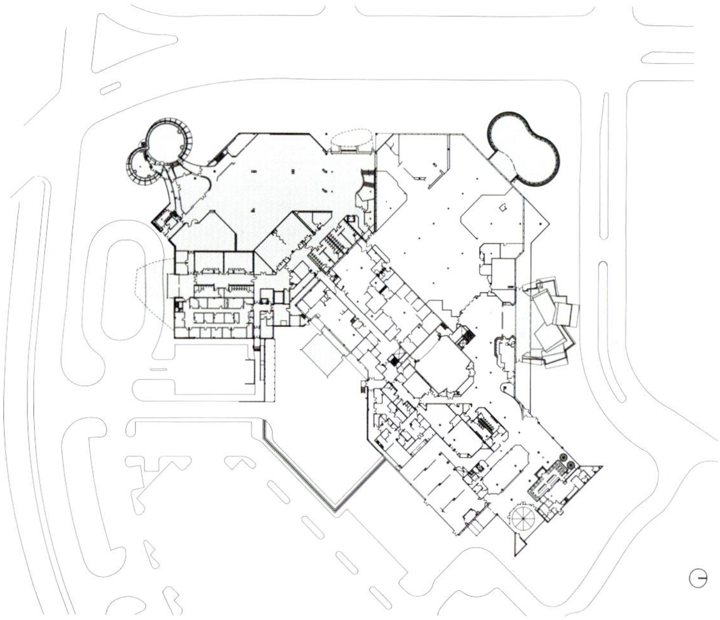

L'architecture bizarre se reflète dans la mission et le caractère de Strong d'explorer le jeu : la taille du musée a été quasiment doublée de 15 600 à 26 200 mètres carrés. La transformation architectonique présente le musée comme un accès emblématique au Sud-est de la ville. Un gigantesque atrium en forme de chenille couleur bronze organise et relie les galeries et les étages. Un montage en acier angulaire revêtu de plaques en résine synthétique de couleur apparait comme un énorme amas de cubes de construction en couleur pour enfants et une haute tour rouge qui se dresse abrite le chauffage, l'aération et la climatisation. Le jardin aux papillons est couvert par une structure en tissu ressemblant à des ailes lumineuses déployées.

Una juguetona arquitectura procura reflejar el carácter y la finalidad de este museo de explorar los juegos; el área del Museo Strong casi se duplica, pasando de 15.600 a 26.200 metros cuadrados. La configuración arquitectónica convierte a esta edificación museística en una especie de puerta de acceso al sudeste de la ciudad. Un gigantesco atrio color bronce en forma de oruga organiza galerías y niveles y los conecta entre sí. Un montaje de perfiles de acero recubiertos con coloridas placas de resina sintética parece un enorme montón de cubos para armar; una elevada torre roja alberga las instalaciones de calefacción, aire acondicionado y ventilación. En el Jardín de las Mariposas se extiende una estructura de tejido que semeja alas extendidas.

links: Grundriss_Eingang in die Spiele-Ausstellung_Gesamtansicht Ausstellung. rechts: Spiele Galerie_Kleinkinder-„Aquarium"_Theaterbereich_Musikbereich.
gauche: Plan_Entrée dans l'exposition des jeux_Vue générale de l'exposition. droite: Galerie de jeux_« aquarium » pour les petits enfants_Zone du théâtre_Espace musique.
izquierda: Plano_Acceso a la exhibición de juegos_Vista de conjunto de la exhibición. derecha: Galería de juegos_"Acuario" para niños pequeños_Área de teatro_Área de música.

Strong
NATIONAL
MUSEUM of PLAY

Understanding

LEARN
DISCOVER

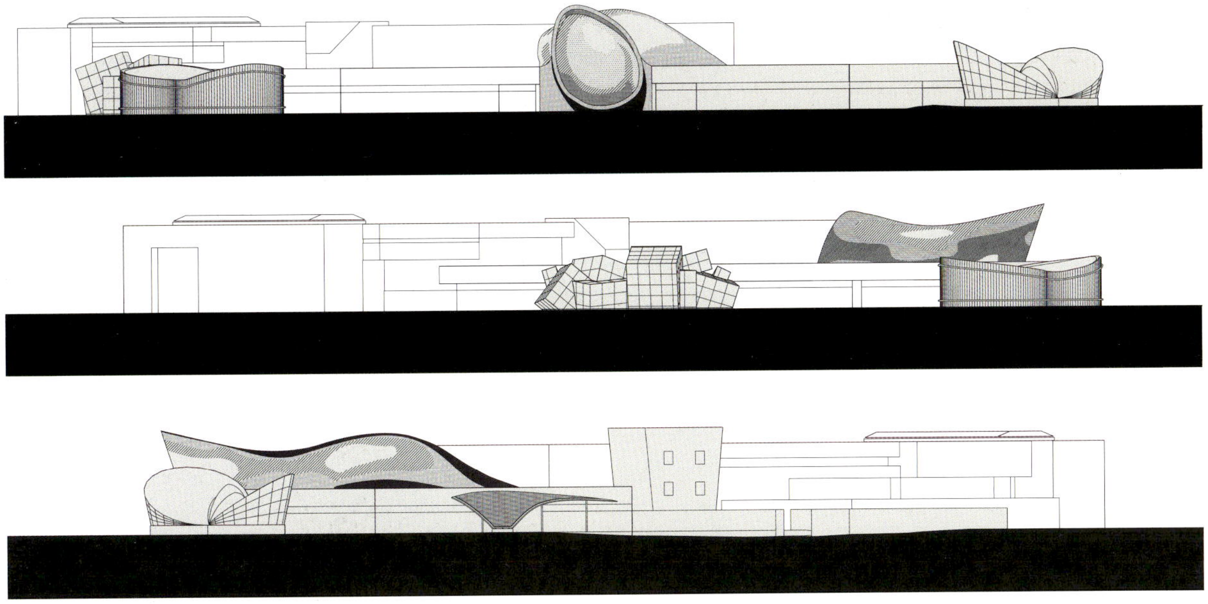

links: Atrium Auge. rechts: West-, Nord- und Südansicht_Blaues Taschentuch-Vordach_Pavillon Schmetterlingsgarten_Außenansicht.
gauche: Œil de l'atrium. droite: Vue à l'ouest, au nord et au sud_Avant-toit bleu en forme de mouchoir_Pavillon du jardin papillon_Vue extérieure.
izquierda: Ojo en el atrio. derecha: Fachadas oeste, norte y sur_Alero en forma de pañuelo azul Pabellón del Jardín de las Mariposas_Vista exterior.

USA_SAN FRANCISCO (CA) **CONTEMPORARY JEWISH MUSEUM**

USA_USA_EE.UU.
STUDIO DANIEL LIBESKIND
2008
GESCHICHTSMUSEUM_MUSEE D'HISTOIRE_MUSEO HISTÓRICO
5,850 M^2
PHOTOS BITTER BREDT FOTOGRAFIE, BERLIN
(116, 117 A., 118, 119 A. R., B. R.),
MARK DARLEY, MILL VALLEY (117 B., 119 L.)

Das 63.000 Quadratmeter große Museum liegt in der Mission Street in der Innenstadt von San Francisco. Seit der Eröffnung im Juni 2008 bietet es nicht nur Wechselausstellungen sowie öffentlichen und pädagogischen Veranstaltungen Raum – es wurde auch zum Symbol der Geschichte und Wiederbelebung des jüdischen Lebens in San Francisco. Das Museum befindet sich in den seit 1976 unter Denkmalschutz stehenden, ehemaligen Jessie Street-Umspannwerken, die aus dem Ende des 19. Jahrhunderts stammen und im ersten Jahrzehnt des 20. Jahrhunderts von Willis Polk renoviert wurden. Mit Bausubstanz aus dem 19., 20. und 21. Jahrhundert macht es die Beziehungen zwischen Neu und Alt, Tradition und Innovation, Vergangenheit, Gegenwart und Zukunft offensichtlich.

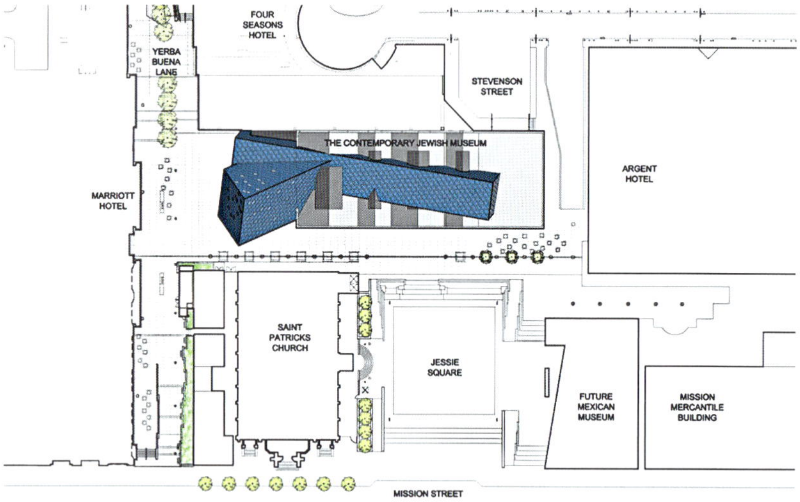

Le musée de 63 000 mètres carrés se situe à Mission Street dans le centre-ville de San Francisco. Depuis l'inauguration en juin 2008, il ne propose plus uniquement des expositions tournantes ou des manifestations pédagogiques et publiques, mais symbolise également l'histoire et le renouveau de la vie des juifs à San Francisco. Le musée se situe dans l'ancienne centrale de transformation à Jessie Street datant de la fin du XIX siècle, rénovée vers 1910 par Willis Polk, et protégée monument historique depuis 1976. Les relations entre ancien et nouveau, tradition et innovation, passé, présent et futur sont évidentes dans l'essence même de la construction datant du XIX, XX et XXI siècle.

Este museo cubre una superficie de 63.000 metros cuadrados sobre Mission Street, en pleno centro de San Francisco. Desde su inauguración en junio de 2008 ofrece no solo exhibiciones temporarias, sino también actividades pedagógicas y públicas. Se ha convertido así en un símbolo de la historia y renacimiento de la vida de los judíos en San Francisco. Este museo está ubicado en estaciones de transformación eléctrica que datan de fines del siglo XIX y fueron renovadas en la primera década del siglo XX por Willis Polk; desde 1976 están protegidas con el carácter de monumento histórico. Las edificaciones de los siglos XIX, XX y XXI evidencian la vinculación entre lo viejo y lo nuevo, entre la tradición e la innovación, entre el pasado, el presente y el futuro.

links: Situation_CJM-Platz_Yud-Galerie und Platz. rechts: Abendansicht_Foyer_Aufsteigender Chet-Raum und Oberlichter des Kraftwerks_Yud-Raum mit 36 diamantförmigen Fenstern.
gauche: Plan de site_Place CJM_Galerie Yud et place. droite: Vue en soirée_Foyer_Espace chet ascendant et éclairage naturel de la centrale_Espace Yud avec ses 36 fenêtres en forme de diamant.
izquierda: Ubicación_Plaza del CJM_Galería Yud y plaza. derecha: Vista al anochecer_Vestíbulo_Sala Chet de múltiple altura, lucernarios de la usina_Sala Yud con 36 ventanas en forma de diamante.

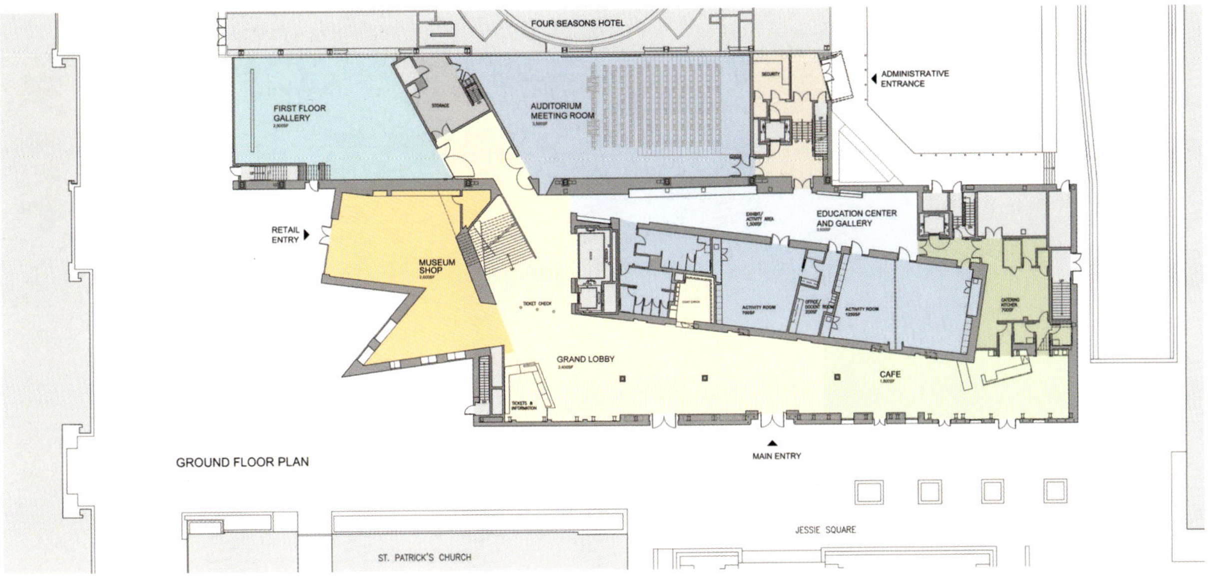

links: Treppenhaus. rechts: Grundriss Erdgeschoss_3000 strahlend blaue Diamanten erscheinen am Himmel_Detail der blauen Stahlverkleidung_Galerie.

gauche: Cage d'escalier. droite: Plan du rez-de-chaussée_3000 diamants bleus brillants apparaissent dans le ciel_Détail du revêtement en cier bleu_Galerie.

izquierda: Caja de la escalera. derecha: Plano de planta baja_3000 diamantes azules parecen brillar en el cielo_Detalle del recubrimiento de acero azul_Galería.

USA_SAN FRANCISCO (CA) **MH DE YOUNG MUSEUM**

USA_USA_EE.UU.
HERZOG & DE MEURON WITH FONG & CHAN
2005
KUNSTMUSEUM_MUSÉE D'ART_MUSEO DE ARTE
27,000 M^2
PHOTOS FINE ARTS MUSEUMS OF SAN FRANCISCO

Das neue Museum an einem umstrittenen Standort in der Bay Area wurde zum neuen Wahrzeichen des Gebiets. Der flache Baukörper besteht aus hintereinander gestaffelten und ziehharmonikaartig verkanteten, ineinander geschobenen Trakten sowie einem Turm, dessen Umriss der Silhouette eines Trichters gleicht. Zwischen den Trakten befinden sich Schlitze und Höfe, die eine Verbindung zwischen Sammlung und umgebendem Park entstehen lassen. Die 7200 Kupferplatten der Außenhaut sind mit einem Raster aus fünf Kreisen verschiedener Größe perforiert und mit Auswölbungen und Eindellungen strukturiert, was von weitem einen gleichmäßigen, aus der Nähe einen natürlich vielfältigen und sich verändernden Eindruck ergibt.

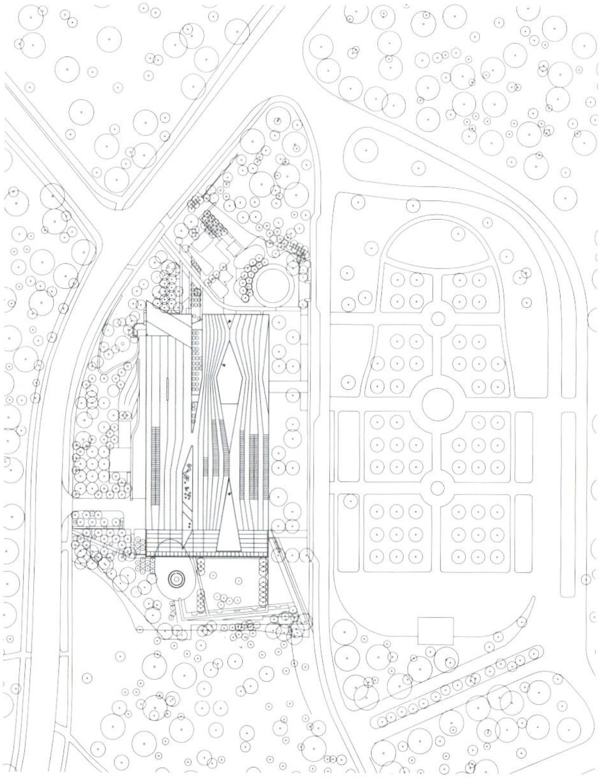

Le nouveau musée situé sur un site contesté dans la Bay Area est devenu le nouveau monument de la région. Le corps du bâtiment plat se compose d'ailes imbriquées les unes dans les autres par rangées successives et se présente à l'instar d'un accordéon en raison de ses angles vifs et d'une tour dont le contour de la silhouette est comparable à un entonnoir. Entre les ailes se situent des fentes et des cours permettant la jonction entre la collection et le parc environnant. Les 7 200 plaques en cuivre du revêtement extérieur sont perforées par une trame constituée de cinq cercles de taille différente, structurées par des saillies et enfoncements qui se présente de loin de manière uniforme et offre à proximité une impression riche en facettes et complexe.

El nuevo museo en una discutida ubicación en el Área de la Bahía se convirtió en un nuevo símbolo de la región. El edificio achatado comprende secciones dispuestas una tras otra, similares a un acordeón, plegadas e insertas entre sí, y también una torre cuyo contorno recuerda la silueta de un embudo. Entre las secciones se aprecian rendijas y patios; los mismos constituyen una conexión entre la colección y el parque circundante. Las 7200 placas de cobre de la piel exterior están perforadas según una cuadrícula de cinco círculos de diversos tamaños y se estructuran con partes convexas y cóncavas, lo que confiere un aspecto uniforme cuando se ve de lejos, aunque desde cerca resulta naturalmente polifacético y cambiante.

links: Lageplan_Ausstellungsraum und Sitzgelegenheiten_Eingang. rechts: Außenbau_Museum bei Nacht_Reflektion auf der Glaswand.
gauche: Plan de site_Espace d'exposition avec coin salon_Entrée. droite: Extérieur_Musée de nuit_Réflexion sur le mur en verre.
izquierda: Plano de situación_Sala de exhibiciones con asientos_Acceso. derecha: Vista exterior Museo por la noche_Reflejos en la pared de vidrio.

USA_SEATTLE (WA) **OLYMPIC SCULPTURE PARK**

USA_USA_EE.UU.
WEISS/MANFREDI
2007
KUNSTMUSEUM_MUSÉE D'ART_MUSEO DE ARTE
1,116 M²
PHOTOS BENJAMIN BENSCHNEIDER

Das neue Modell eines städtischen Skulpturenparks verbindet drei durch Bahngleise und eine Hauptverkehrsstraße getrennte Standorte durch eine durchgehende z-förmige, begrünte Plattform. Sie führt zwölf Meter von der Innenstadt aus zum Wasser hinab und verbindet über die vorhandene In-frastruktur hinweg Stadtkern und zu revitalisierendes Hafengebiet, so dass die ursprüngliche Topografie des Geländes wiederhergestellt wird. An der höchsten Stelle des Parks befindet sich der 18.000 Quadratmeter große Ausstellungspavillon, der oberhalb seines als Basis dienenden Parkhauses zu schweben scheint. Er bietet unter seiner freitragenden Dachkonstruktion Raum für Kunstinstallationen, Performances und Bildungsprogramme.

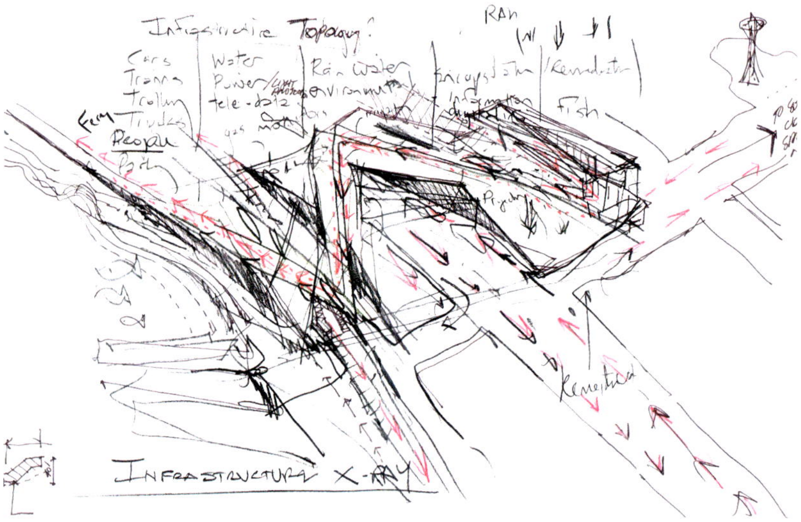

Le nouveau modèle consiste en un parc municipal de sculptures reliant trois sites séparés par des rails et une voie de circulation principale grâce à une plateforme de verdure ininterrompue en forme de Z qui mène à 12 mètres en contrebas du centre-ville vers le niveau de l'eau. Ainsi, l'infrastructure existante est intégrée au cœur de la ville et à la zone portuaire revitalisée afin de faire revivre la topographie originale du terrain. Le parc est dominé par un pavillon d'exposition de 18 000 mètres carrés qui semble être installé en suspension de sa base comme un parking couvert. Au dessous de sa construction porteuse libre au niveau de la toiture, cet espace offre des espaces dédiés aux œuvres artistiques, représentations et programmes de formation.

El novedoso modelo de parque urbano de esculturas vincula entre sí tres barrios que estaban separados por vías férreas y una autopista, mediante una plataforma verde ininterrumpida en forma de Z. La misma desciende cuarenta pies desde la ciudad hacia el agua, y conecta el casco urbano por encima de la infraestructura existente con el barrio portuario revitalizado, de modo que se regenera la topografía original del territorio. En el punto más alto del parque se encuentra el pabellón de exposiciones de 18.000 metros cuadrados, que parece flotar por encima del aparcamiento que simula ser su base. Su estructura de techo brinda un amplio espacio para instalaciones artísticas, teatro, música y programas educativos muy variados.

links: Skizze Durchsicht mit Infrastruktur_Innenraum Pavillon. rechts: Pavillon bei Dämmerung Pavillondetail, Spiegelglas_Elliot Avenue Brücke.
gauche: Esquisse de l'infrastructure_Espace intérieur du pavillon. droite: Pavillon au crépuscule Détail du pavillon_Pont Elliot Avenue.
izquierda: Esbozo de la infraestructura_Interior del pabellón. derecha: Pabellón al atardecer Detalle del pabellón_Puente sobre Elliot Avenue.

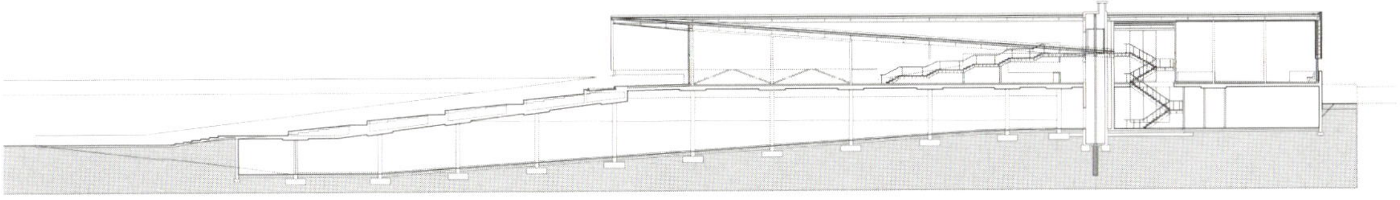

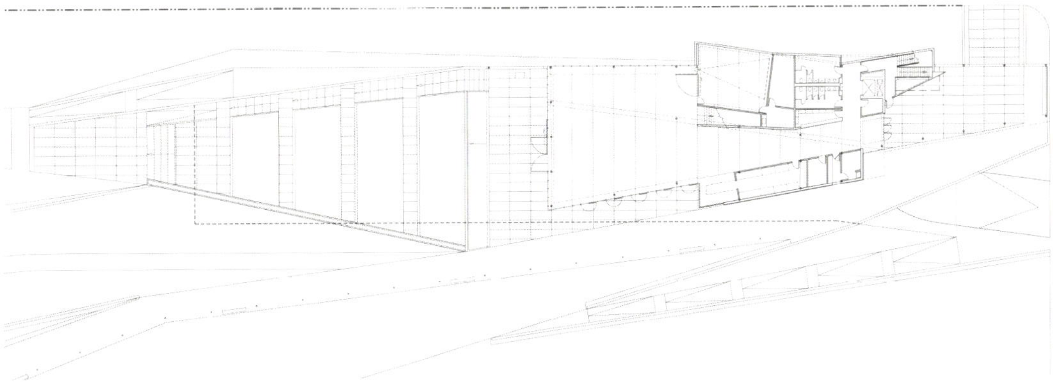

links: Luftaufnahme. rechts: Schnitt und Grundriss Pavillon_Innenraum Pavillon_Städtischer Kontext_Aufsteigender Weg vom Park zum Pavillon.
gauche: Vue aérienne. droite: Coupe du pavillon_Espace intérieur_Contexte urbain_Chemin piétonnier.
izquierda: Fotografía de conjunto. derecha: Corte del pabellón_Interior del pabellón_Contexto urbano_Sendero con transeúntes.

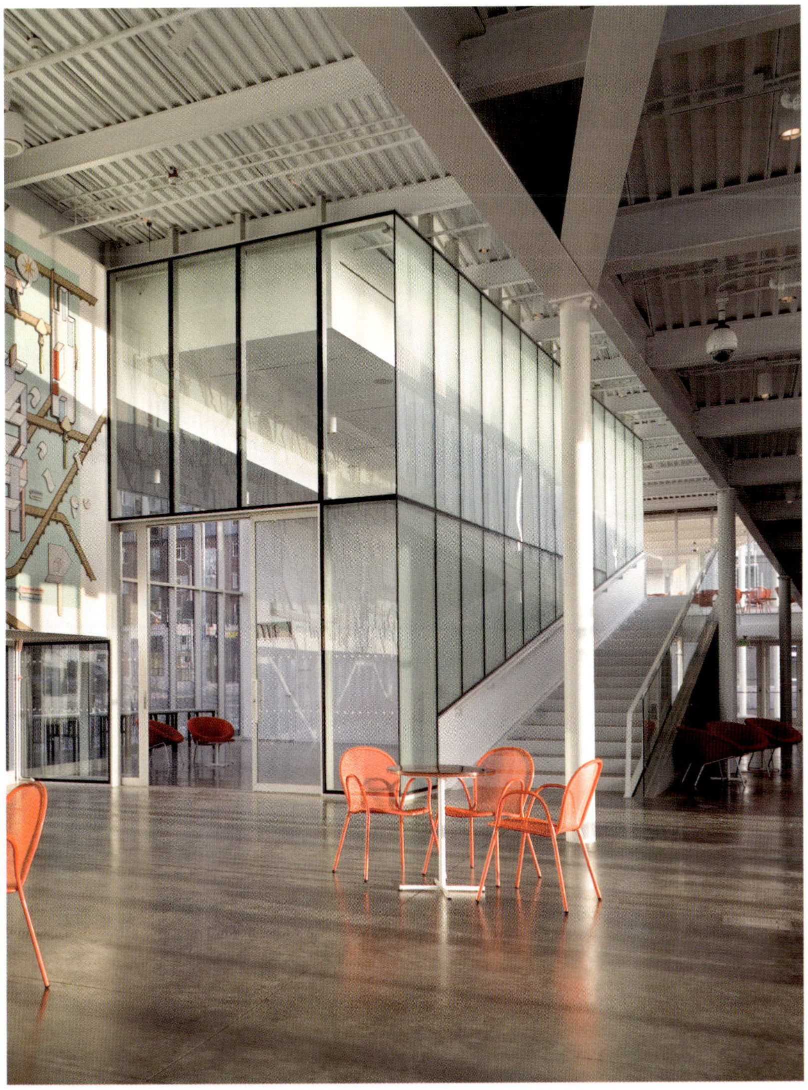

europe

CHÄOLOGISCHES MUSEUM AGUNTUM_AUSTRIA_DÖLSACH_LAPIDA
JM EGGENBERG_AUSTRIA_GRAZ_ARCHÄOLOGISCHES MUSEUM EGGEN
RG_AUSTRIA_GRAZ_VOLKSKUNDEMUSEUMGRAZ_AUSTRIA_GRAZ_KUNSTHAUS
AZ_AUSTRIA_GRAZ_AUT – ARCHITEKTURFORUM TIROL ARCHIV FÜR BAU
NST_AUSTRIA_INNSBRUCK_ARS ELECTRONICA CENTER_AUSTRIA_LINZ_
NTOS KUNSTMUSEUM_AUSTRIA_LINZ_BESUCHERZENTRUM MAUTHAUSEN
MORIAL_AUSTRIA_MAUTHAUSEN_ML MUSEUM LIAUNIG_AUSTRIA_NEU-
US_MUSEUM DER MODERNE_AUSTRIA_SALZBURG_GIRONCOLI MUSE-
_AUSTRIA_ST JOHANN / HERBERSTEIN_MUSEUMSQUARTIER_AUSTRIA_VI
NA_GROENINGEMUSEUM_BELGIUM_BRUGES_MAC'S – MUSEE DES ARTS
NTEMPOTAINS_BELGIUM_HORNUMONS_DOX-CENTRUMSOUˇCASNÉHOUMˇEN
ECHREPUBLIC_PRAGUE_DANSKJØDISKMUSEUM_DENMARK_COPENHAGEN_
NDELS- OG SØFARTSMUSEET_DENMARK_HELSINGØR_RANDERS KUNSTMU-
JM DENMAR_RANDERS_FUGLSANG_KUNSTMUSEUM_DENMARK_TOREBY

AUSTRIA_DÖLSACH **ARCHÄOLOGISCHES MUSEUM AGUNTUM**

ÖSTERREICH_AUTRICHE_AUSTRIA
MOSER KLEON ARCHITEKTEN
2005
ARCHÄOLOGIEMUSEUM_MUSÉE DE L'ARCHÉOLOGIE
MUSEO ARQUEOLÓGICO
1,200 M²
PHOTOS NIKOLAUS SCHLETTERER, INNSBRUCK (128, 129, 130, 131 R.), BARTH, BRIXEN (131 L.)

Das Gebäude lässt durch seine einfache Geometrie noch die eigene Frühgeschichte als schützende Hülle erahnen, wobei die gläserne Südseite Blicke auf den angrenzenden Wald ermöglicht. Die Nordseite wird von einer Cortenstahl-Fassade geprägt, die den Ort gegen den Verkehr abschirmt. Das Museum bietet in seinem durch Oberlichtbänder rhythmisierten Inneren von Ausblicken und Licht gefärbte Raumsituationen. Gussasphalt und gelochte Birkensperrholzplatten dominieren als innere Raumoberflächen. Schwarze und rote MDF-Platten sind das prägende Material der Einbauten und Einrichtung. Nur die Vitrinen sind durch einen farbigen Anstrich akzentuiert.

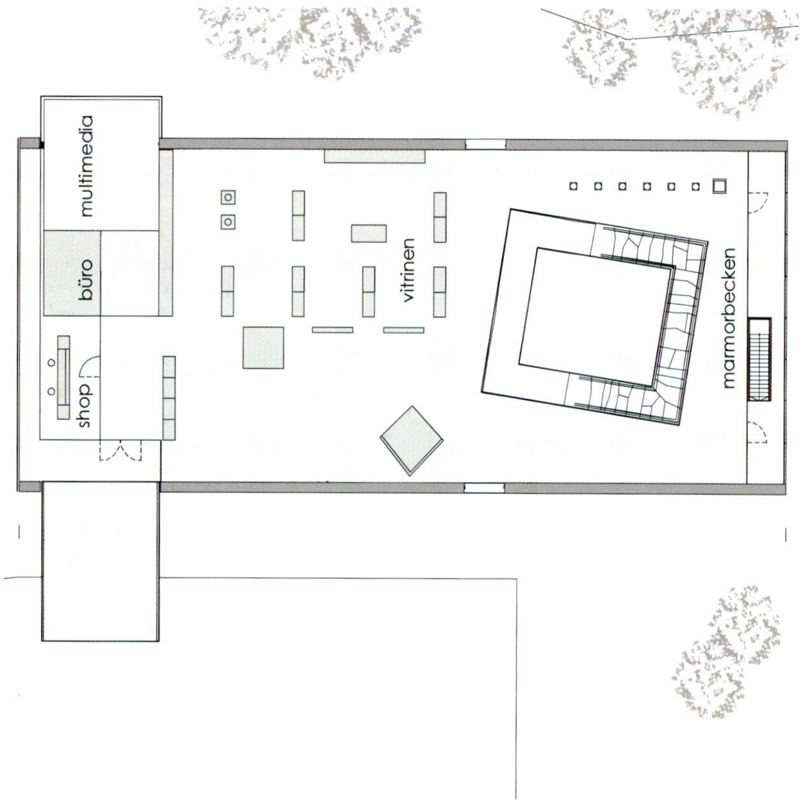

Le bâtiment laisse deviner, par sa géométrie simple, les origines de sa propre histoire comme écran de protection qui favorise simultanément avec ses parties vitrifiées au Sud, un panorama sur la forêt limitrophe. Le côté Nord se caractérise par une façade en acier corten afin de protéger le site du bruit de la circulation. Ainsi, le musée offre des vues et situations spatiales colorées de lumière dans son intérieur rythmé par des bordures lumineuses situées en hauteur. L'asphalte coulé et les plaques de contreplaqué en bouleau percées caractérisent l'aménagement et la structure intérieurs. Les plaques MDF noires et rouges sont des matériaux caractéristiques du montage et de l'installation. Seules les vitrines sont accentuées par une couche de peinture de couleur.

Con su sencilla geometría, el edificio permite vislumbrar la historia antigua como envoltura protectora y, al mismo tiempo, con su fachada sur acristalada posibilita vistas hacia el bosque cercano. La fachada norte está caracterizada por el acero cortén que la recubre para protegerla del tráfico. El museo ofrece diversas situaciones espaciales en sus interiores marcados por ritmos de franjas de iluminación cenital, con visuales y coloraciones luminosas. El asfalto y las placas de madera de abedul contrachapada dominan las superficies interiores. Las placas de MDF rojo y negro son el material más característico del equipamiento y de las subdivisiones. Solo se acentúan las vitrinas con una pintura coloreada.

links: Grundriss Erdgeschoss_Nordfassade_Eingang. rechts: Nordfassade_Eingangsbereich.
gauche: Plan du rez-de chaussé_Façade nord_Entrée. droite: Façade nord_Zone d'entrée.
izquierda: Plano de planta baja_Fachada norte_Acceso. derecha: Fachada norte_Zona del acceso.

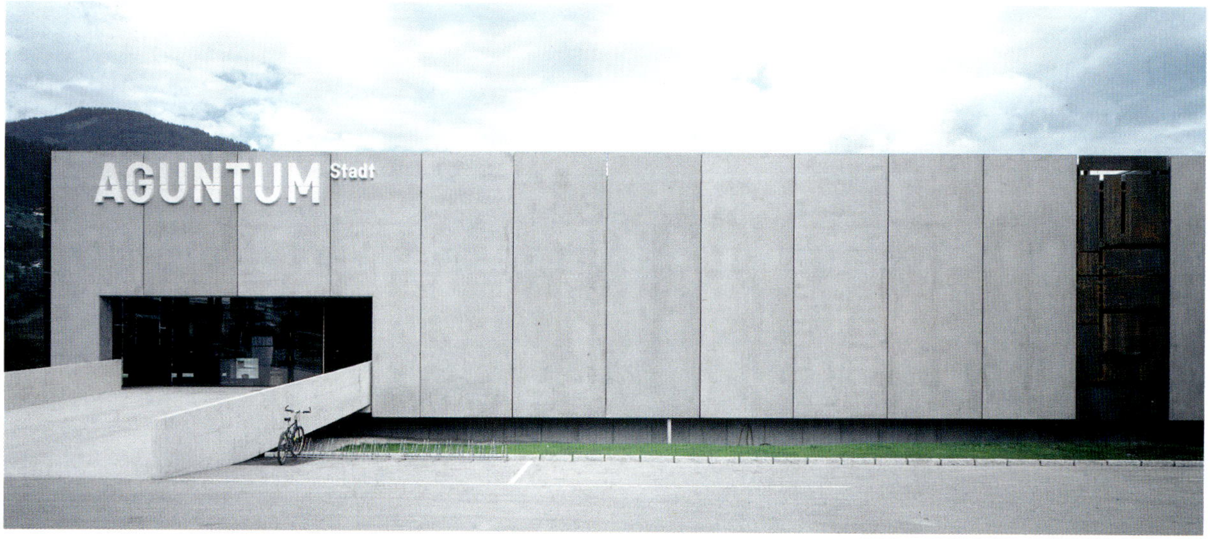

AGUNTUM Stadt

AGUNTUM Stadt

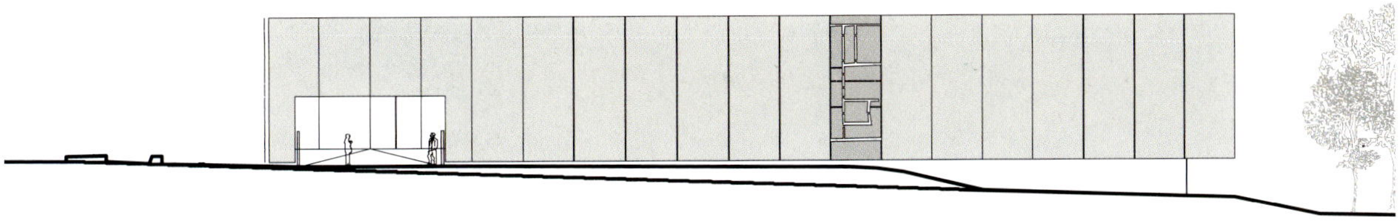

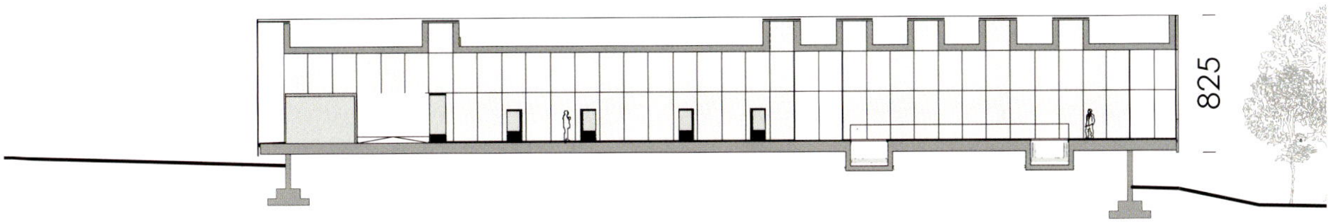

links: Ausstellungshalle. rechts: Aufrisse_Museumsshop_Ausstellungssaal, südlicher Teil Ausstellungssaal_Blick nach Norden.
gauche: Hall d'exposition. droite: Vues en élévation_Boutique du musée_Salle d'exposition, partie sud_Salle d'exposition, vue au nord.
izquierda: Sala de exhibiciones. derecha: Alzados_Tienda del museo_Sala de exhibiciones, parte sur_Sala de exhibiciones, vista al norte.

AUSTRIA_GRAZ **LAPIDARIUM EGGENBERG**

ÖSTERREICH_AUTRICHE_AUSTRIA
PURPUR. ARCHITEKTUR ZT GMBH
2009
ARCHÄOLOGIEMUSEUM_MUSÉE DE L'ARCHÉOLOGIE
MUSEO ARQUEOLÓGICO
1,500 M^2
PHOTOS ANGELO KAUNAT, SALZBURG

Am nördlichen Ende des neu errichteten Planetengartens am Schloss Eggenberg befindet sich neben der historischen Orangerie aus dem 18. Jahrhundert das neue Lapidarium. Es versteht sich als ein „Bauzustand" des Jetzt, als Fragment eines stetig anhaltenden Prozesses, und ist aufgespannt zwischen den Flügelmauern mit den kapitellbestückten Frontsäulen, Restbeständen der Orangerie und der nördlichen Begrenzungsmauer des Schlosses. Dieses „Zwischen" spiegelt sich auch in der Les- und Erlebbarkeit des musealen Konzepts wider: Der Kern des Ausstellungskonzepts liegt in der Ambivalenz zwischen objektiven und subjektiven Bildern und der dieser Polarität innewohnenden Spannung.

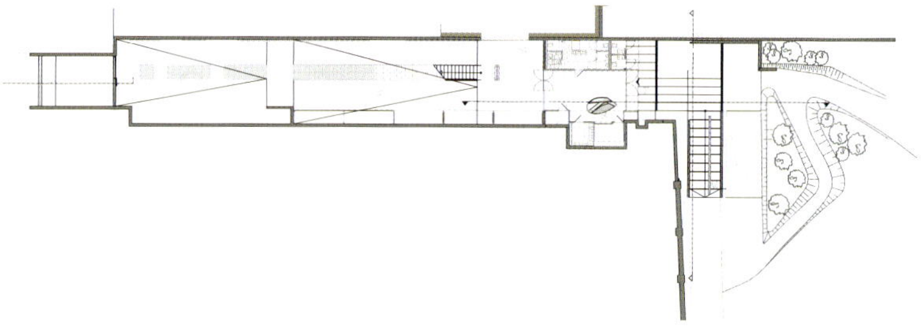

Le nouveau lapidarium se situe au Nord du jardin dédié aux planètes, créé récemment au Château d'Eggenberg, à côté de l'Orangerie historique datant du XVII siècle. Il s'intègre comme un « état de construction » du présent, un fragment d'un processus toujours durable, tendu entre les murs de l'aile aux piliers frontaux des chapiteaux décorés, les restes de l'Orangerie et le mur Nord de délimitation du château. Cet « entre-temps » reflète également la lisibilité et l'expérience vécue du concept dédié au musée : en effet, le centre de la conception des expositions consiste dans l'ambigüité entre les images objectives et subjectives et la tension inhérente de cette bipolarisation.

En el extremo norte del novedoso Jardín de los Planetas junto al castillo de Eggenberg, se encuentra el nuevo lapidario, al lado de la histórica orangerie del siglo XVIII. Se comprende como un "estado constructivo" del ahora, un fragmento de un proceso que se detiene de manera constante, con tensiones entre los muros dispuestos como alas con las columnas coronadas con capiteles, restos de la orangerie y del muro que limitaba el castillo por el lado norte. Este "intermedio" se refleja también en la legibilidad y en lo disfrutable de este concepto museístico. El núcleo del concepto de exhibición yace en la ambivalencia entre las imágenes objetivas y subjetivas y en la tensión intrínseca de esta bipolaridad.

links: Grundriss Erdgeschoss mit umgebautem neuem Eingangsbereich_Lapidarium im Planetengarten_Zwischenraum. rechts: Ausstellungsraum_Ausstellungsraum.
gauche: Plan du rez-de-chaussée avec une nouvelle zone d'entrée aménagée_Lapidarium dans le jardin des planètes_Espace intermédiaire. droite: Espace d'exposition_Espace d'exposition.
izquierda: Plano de planta baja con la nueva zona de acceso reformada_Lapidarium en el Jardín de los Planetas_Espacio de transición. derecha: Sala de exhibiciones_Sala de exhibiciones.

AUSTRIA_GRAZ **ARCHÄOLOGISCHES MUSEUM EGGENBERG**

ÖSTERREICH_AUTRICHE_AUSTRIA
BWM ARCHITEKTEN UND PARTNER – BERNARD WALTEN MOSER ZIVILTECHNIKER GMBH
2009
ARCHÄOLOGIEMUSEUM_MUSÉE DE L'ARCHÉOLOGIE
MUSEO ARQUEOLÓGICO
650 M²
PHOTOS RUPERT STEINER, VIENNA (134 B. R., 135, 136, 137 A., B. R.), PAUL OTT, GRAZ (134 B. L., 137 B. L.)

Zweck des Museumsneubaus war die unterirdische Erweiterung des bestehenden Lapidariums sowie die Neupräsentation der archäologischen Sammlung des Joanneums. Die Zonen der zweischiffigen Ausstellungshalle mit mittig durchlaufendem Oberlicht sind durch unterschiedliche Bodenniveaus definiert. Sichtbetonwände und Estrich bilden den dezenten Hintergrund für die kleinformatigen Exponate, die gleichsam im Raum schwebend in gänzlich gläsernen Vitrinen präsentiert werden. Architektur und Vitrinen verbinden sich zu einem zeitgemäßen und eleganten Raumgefüge, das Leichtigkeit und Helligkeit ausstrahlt.

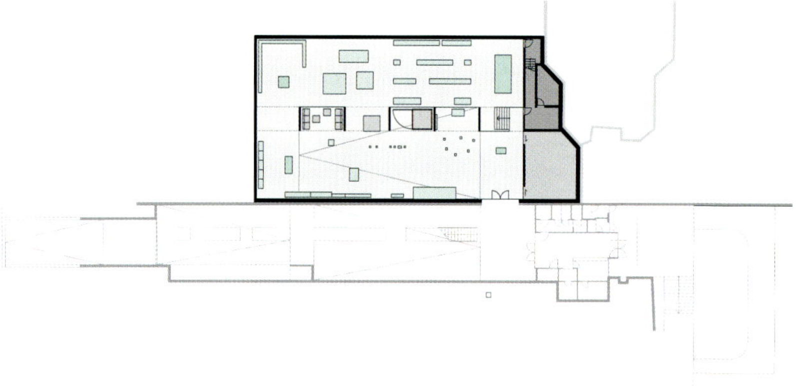

L'objectif du nouveau bâtiment du musée consistait en l'extension souterraine du lapidarium existant ainsi que la nouvelle exposition de la collection archéologique du Joanneum. Les zones du hall d'exposition à deux nefs avec la lumière pénétrant au centre sont définies par différents niveaux du sol. Les murs en béton apparent et le plâtre forment l'arrière-plan discret pour les objets exposés de petit format qui planent quasiment dans l'espace où ils sont présentés dans des vitrines en verre totalement transparentes. L'architecture et les vitrines se réunissent en une structure spatiale moderne et élégante qui irradie la légèreté et la luminosité.

La finalidad de este edificio museístico era la ampliación subterránea del lapidario existente y, además, albergar la colección arqueológica del Joanneum. Las zonas de la sala de exhibiciones de dos naves, con luz cenital central, están definidas por los diferentes niveles del suelo. Muros de hormigón visto y contrapiso constituyen un trasfondo digno para las muestras de pequeño formato, que son presentadas en este ambiente como si flotaran en vitrinas acristaladas de alta transparencia. Arquitectura y vitrinas se combinan en una espacialidad contemporánea y elegante, que irradia ligereza y claridad.

links: Grundriss mit Möblierung_Ausstellungsraum vor Möblierung_Grabungscontainer als Kinderzone. rechts: Ausstellungsbereich Götter_Ausstellungsbereich Waffen.
gauche: Plan avec le mobilier_Espace d'exposition avant l'ameublement_Conteneur enterré prévu comme zone destinée aux enfants. droite: Zone d'exposition des dieux_Zone d'exposition de l'armement.
izquierda: Planta equipada_Sala de exhibición sin equipar_Contenedor para excavaciones como área infantil. derecha: Área de exhibiciones sobre dioses_Área de exhibición de armas.

Brauchen

Tragen wir
Schmuck,
um begehrt
zu werden?

Dürfen
wir töten?

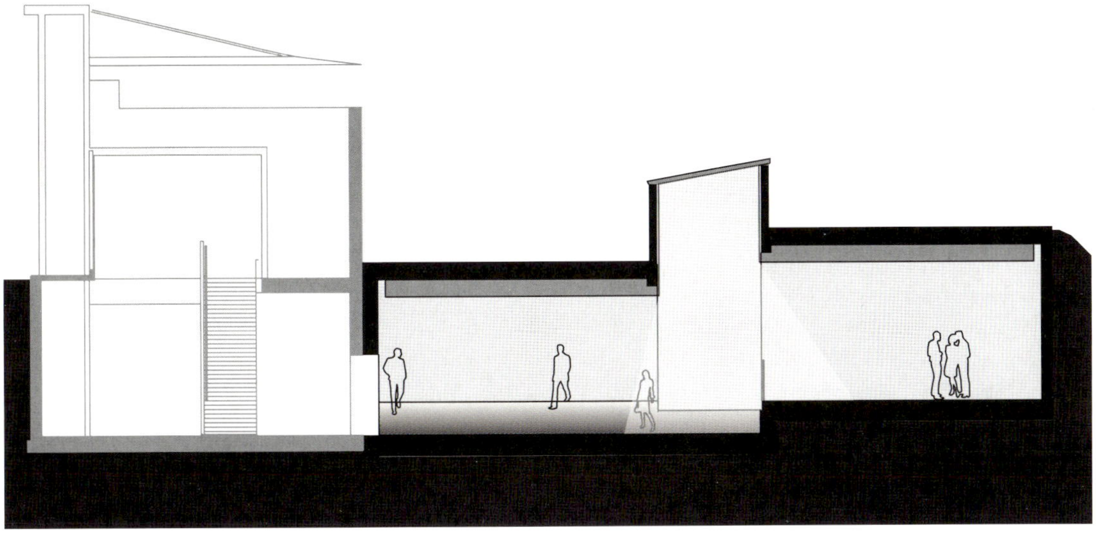

links: Info- und Ruhezone. rechts: Schnitt mit Belichtungsstudie_Ausstellungsbereich Gefäße_Ausstellungsbereich Kult_Ausstellungsbereich Schmuck_Ausstellungsbereich Gefäße.
gauche: Zone d'information et de détente. droite: Coupe avec étude de lumière_Zone d'exposition des pots_Zone d'exposition du culte_Zone d'exposition des bijoux_Zone d'exposition des pots.
izquierda: Zona de información y descanso. derecha: Corte con estudio de iluminación natural_Área de exhibición de vasijas_Área de exhibiciones sobre culto_Área de exhibición de joyería_Área de exhibición de vasijas.

AUSTRIA_GRAZ **VOLKSKUNDEMUSEUM GRAZ**

ÖSTERREICH_AUTRICHE_AUSTRIA
BWM ARCHITEKTEN UND PARTNER – BERNARD WALTEN MOSER ZIVILTECHNIKER GMBH
2003
KULTURMUSEUM_MUSÉE DE LA CULTURE_MUSEO DE LA CULTURA
1,500 M²
PHOTOS ALEXANDER KOLLER, VIENNA

Die Architekten waren für Sanierung, Umbau und Neuadaption des bestehenden Volkskundemuseums sowie eine Neupräsentation der Schausammlung, verantwortlich die den ländlichen Alltag des 19. und 20. Jahrhunderts zeigt. Die architektonische Konzeption intendiert die Trennung des neuen Raumgefüges von der historischen Substanz. Die Außenwände der ehemaligen Klosteranlage blieben unberührt. Die Interventionen sind anhand des verwendeten Materials erkennbar: Glas, Metall, Licht. Architektonisches Wahrzeichen der Neugestaltung ist eine gläserne Brückenverbindung zwischen Hauptgebäude und historischem Trachtensaal. Hinterleuchtete Glasvitrinen präsentieren die volkskundlichen Objekte wirkungsvoll auf Leuchttischen.

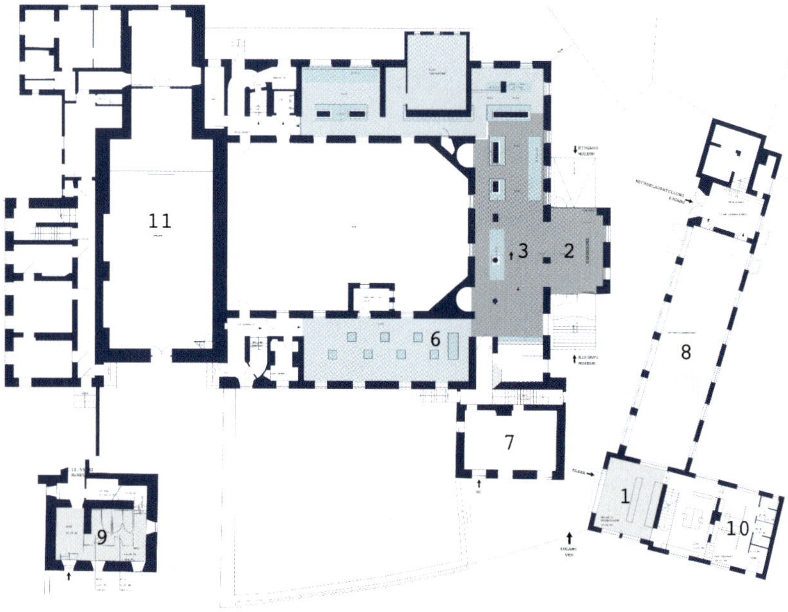

Les architectes étaient responsables de la rénovation, transformation et nouvelle adaptation du Musée de l'Art populaire ainsi qu'une nouvelle exposition de la collection représentative dédiée au quotidien rural aux XIX et XX siècles. La conception architectonique est prévue pour la séparation des nouvelles structures spatiales de la substance historique. Les murs extérieurs de l'ancien cloitre sont restés intacts. Les interventions sont reconnaissables grâce aux matériaux utilisés : verre, métal et lumière. Les symboles architectoniques de la nouvelle conception sont composés par une passerelle vitrifiée entre le bâtiment principal et la salle folklorique dédiée à l'histoire. Des vitrines en verre rétro-éclairées exposent de manière représentative des objets relatifs à la culture populaire sur des tables d'éclairage.

Los arquitectos tuvieron la responsabilidad de renovar, ampliar y adaptar el museo de folclore preexistente, y también de reconfigurar la colección que muestra la vida cotidiana de los siglos XIX y XX. La concepción arquitectónica procuró separar la nueva espacialidad de la sustancia histórica. Los muros exteriores del antiguo monasterio han permanecido inalterados. Se reconocen las intervencionespor los materiales utilizados: cristal, metal, luz. El símbolo arquitectónico del nuevo diseño es una conexión vidriada en forma de puente entre el edificio central y la histórica sala de indumentaria. Vitrinas acristaladas con iluminación trasera presentan los objetos folclóricos en mesas iluminadas, logrando un efecto llamativo.

links: Grundriss Erdgeschoss_Eingang bei Nacht_Brücke, Wechselausstellungsraum. rechts: Schlafstube_Schausammlung_Rauchstube.
gauche: Plan du rez-de-chaussée_Entrée de nuit_Passerelle, espace d'expositions alternantes. droite: Coin chambre_Coin collection_Fumoir.
izquierda: Plano de planta baja_Acceso por la noche_Puente y sala de exhibiciones temporarias. derecha: Dormitorio_Colección en exhibición_Cuarto del humo.

AUSTRIA_GRAZ **KUNSTHAUS GRAZ**

ÖSTERREICH_AUTRICHE_AUSTRIA
SPACELAB COOK / FOURNIER WITH ARCHITEKTUR CONSULT
2003
KUNSTMUSEUM_MUSÉE D'ART_MUSEO DE ARTE
13,100 M²
PHOTOS NICOLAS LACKNER / UMJ (140, 141 B. R.),
PETER GRADISCHNIGG, GRAZ (141 A.),
GEORG WALLNER (141 B. L.)

Der „Friendly Alien", wie das Kunsthaus Graz von seinen Architekten Peter Cook und Colin Fournier liebevoll genannt wird, belebt die Grazer Altstadt nicht nur durch sein außergewöhnliches Erscheinungsbild. Seit 2003 bereichert das Ausstellungsprogramm das kulturelle Leben der steirischen Landeshauptstadt mit nationaler und internationaler Kunst von den 1960er Jahren bis in die Gegenwart. Eine gläserne Galerie – die sogenannte „Needle"– bietet einen fantastischen Blick über die Mur zur Stadt. Ein reduziertes gläsernes Erdgeschoss trägt die biomorphe Struktur mit einer Acrylglashaut, die sich zwischen die Dächer der Altstadt schmiegt. Die Multimediafassade kann mit digitalen Kunstwerken bespielt werden.

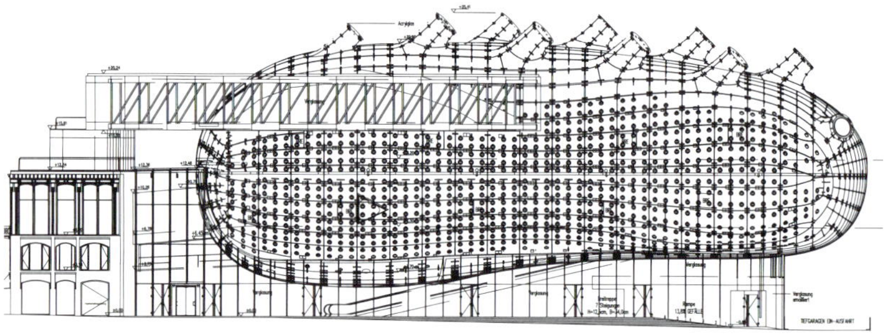

Le « Friendly Alien », nom affectueux donné au Kunsthaus Graz par ses architectes, Peter Cook et Colin Fournier, n'anime pas la vieille ville de Graz uniquement par son apparence extraordinaire. Depuis 2003, le programme d'expositions enrichit la vie culturelle de la capitale régionale de Styrie par l'Art au niveau national et international des années 1960 jusqu'à nos jours. Une galerie vitrifiée– « Needle »– offre une vue fantastique sur le fleuve avec une perspective sur la ville. Un rez-de-chaussée en verre de taille réduite supporte la structure biomorphe avec un revêtement vitrifié en acrylique forgé entre les toits de la vieille ville. La façade multimédia joue avec les œuvres d'art digitales.

Los arquitectos Peter Cook y Colin Fournier le pusieron el sobrenombre de "Friendly Alien" a su obra, la Casa de Arte, que revitalizó el casco histórico de la ciudad de Graz, y no solo por su inusual imagen. Desde el año 2003 un nutrido programa de exhibiciones enriquece la vida cultural de la capital estatal de Estiria con obras de arte nacionales e internacionales de los últimos cincuenta años. Una galería acristalada, la llamada "Needle", ofrece una fantástica vista panorámica del río y la ciudad. Una reducida planta baja acristalada soporta la estructura biomórfica con una piel de cristal acrílico que se acurruca entre los tejados del casco histórico. En la fachada multimedia se proyectan fascinantes obras de arte digitales.

links: Ansicht Ostseite_BIX-Medienfassade und Needle_Space01. rechts: Außenansicht_Brücke zum Space03_BIX-Medienfassade und Needle.
gauche: Vue côté est_Façade média BIX et Needle_Espace 01. droite: Vue extérieure_Passerelle à l'espace 03_Façade média BIX et Needle.
izquierda: Fachada este_Fachada multimedia BIX y Needle_Space01. derecha: Vista exterior_Puente al Space03_Fachada multimedia BIX y Needle.

AUSTRIA_INNSBRUCK

AUT – ARCHITEKTURFORUM TIROL ARCHIV FÜR BAUKUNST

ÖSTERREICH_AUTRICHE_AUSTRIA
ARCHITEKTEN ARGE KÖBERL & GINER+WUCHERER, PFEIFER
2004
ARCHITEKTURMUSEUM_MUSÉE DE L'ARCHITECTURE
MUSEO DE ARQUITECTURA
1,410 M^2
PHOTOS LUKAS SCHALLER

Das ehemalige Brauhaus entstand als „Hülle" um die Produktionsanlage, die hier ungewöhnlich vertikal organisiert war. Für das Museum wurde die gesamte technische Anlage entfernt und der darauf zugeschnittene Baukörper zum Architekturforum umgestaltet: Aus „form follows function" wurde „function follows form". Der obere Bereich der Silos wurde zum Archiv, der untere des Kochens und Siedens zum Architekturforum, so dass die Organisation von oben nach unten erhalten blieb. Durch die Integration der Silos entsteht auf den minimalen Grundmaßen von 12 x 18 Metern ein „Raumplan" nicht im Loos'schen Sinne, sondern komplexen Strukturen wie Koolhaas' ZKM-Projekt für Karlsruhe ähnelnd.

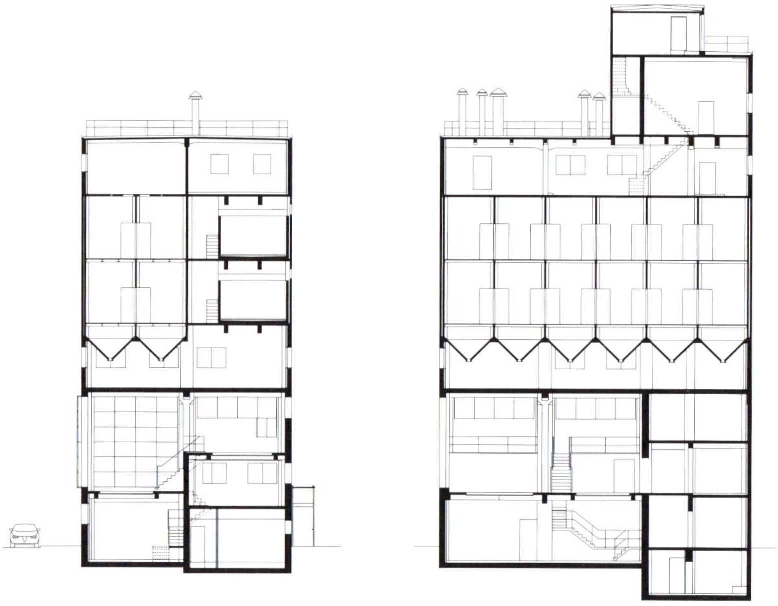

L'ancienne brasserie a été construite comme « façade » autour du site de production, installé de manière inhabituelle à la verticale. Désormais, l'installation technique a été enlevée dans sa totalité afin de transformer le volume bâti en forum d'architecture : la « forme suit la fonction » est devenue la « fonction suit la forme ». La partie supérieure du silo s'est convertie en archive, la partie inférieure prévue pour l'élaboration et le brassage s'est transformée en forum d'architecture et conserve, par conséquent, sa structure de haut en bas. Ainsi, l'intégration du silo permet de créer un « plan spatial » sur des dimensions minimales de 12x18 mètres -contrairement au style de Loos, mais présente des ressemblances au projet complexe ZKM de Koolhaas à Karlsruhe.

La antigua fábrica de cerveza se transformó en "envolvente" alrededor de las instalaciones de elaboración que aquí, de manera inusual, estaban organizadas en vertical. Posteriormente se retiraron todas las instalaciones tecnológicas y se recicló el volumen edilicio como foro arquitectónico: la consigna "la forma sigue a la función" se transformó en "la función sigue a la forma". La zona superior de los silos se transformó en archivo, la parte inferior —donde se hacía la cocción y el hervor— en foro de arquitectura, de modo que se mantuvo la organización de arriba hacia abajo. Con la integración de los silos se logra un "plano espacial" con unas dimensiones mínimas de 12x18 metros, no en el sentido de Loos, sino como estructuras complejas similares a las del proyecto ZKM de Koolhaas para Karlsruhe.

links: Schnitte_Archivebene_Außenbau_Archivebene. rechts: Sudraum_Seminarraum_Untere Ausstellungsebene.
gauche: Coupes_Archives_Extérieur_Archives. droite: Espace au sud_Espace dédié aux séminaires_Niveau d'exposition inférieur.
izquierda: Cortes_Nivel de archivos_Vista exterior_Nivel de archivos. derecha: Sala sur_Sala para seminarios_Nivel de exhibiciones inferior.

AUSTRIA_LINZ **ARS ELECTRONICA CENTER**

ÖSTERREICH_AUTRICHE_AUSTRIA
TREUSCH ARCHITECTURE ZT GMBH
2008
KUNST- UND MEDIENMUSEUM_MUSÉE D'ART ET DES MEDIAS
MUSEO DE ARTE Y DE LOS MEDIOS
4,620 M²
PHOTOS RUPERT STEINER (144, 145 B. R.),
ANDREA EHRENREICH (145 A., B. L.)

Leitgedanke des Entwurfs ist die Ausbildung eines skulpturalen Gebäudevolumens, dessen Struktur begehbar und somit erlebbar ist. Das bestehende Ars Electronica Center und die Erweiterung werden zu einer Einheit verknüpft und als Ganzes wahrgenommen. Die Ausbildung eines Glaskubus mit doppelschaliger Fassade vermittelt einen homogenen Eindruck. Städtebaulich beruht das Konzept auf einem Dialog mit der Umgebung, das eine freie Sicht auf die Donau gewährt, das historische Ensemble bewahrt und zeitgemäß ergänzt. Die Ausstellungsflächen können flexibel in kleinere, beziehungsweise größere Ausstellungsbereiche unterteilt werden.

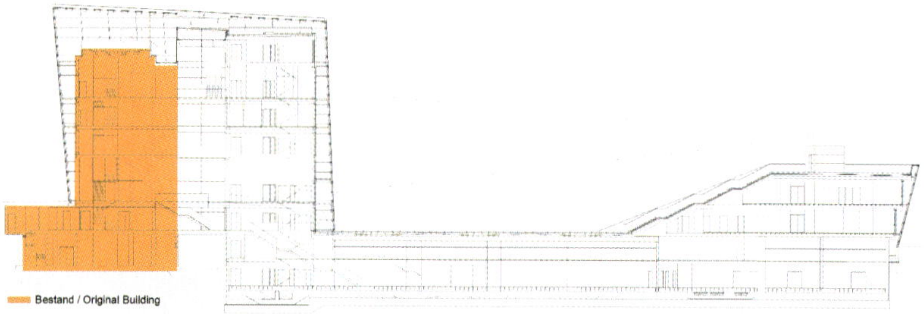

L'idée conductrice du projet est la formation d'un volume de construction sculpturale dont la structure est accessible afin d'offrir une expérience unique. L'Ars Electronica Center existant et l'extension sont reliés afin de former une unité et donner une perception d'ensemble. La formation d'un cube en verre avec une façade à double coffrage transmet une impression homogène. Dans le contexte de l'urbanisme, le concept repose sur un dialogue avec l'environnement : offrir une vue dégagée sur le Danube et conserver en soulignant l'harmonie moderne avec l'ensemble historique. Les surfaces d'exposition privilégient la souplesse de la répartition en petites et/ou grandes zones d'exposition.

El motivo central del proyecto fue la constitución de un volumen edilicio escultural, cuya estructura fuese transitable y, de este modo, plenamente disfrutable. El resultado es el Ars Electronica Center y su ampliación, que se vinculan como una unidad y se perciben como un todo. La configuración de un cubo de cristal con fachada doble transmite una impresión homogénea. Desde el punto de vista urbanístico, el concepto se basa en un diálogo con el entorno, que garantiza una vista amplia y franca sobre el Danubio; se respeta, y, al mismo tiempo, se complementa el contexto histórico. Las superficies de exhibición se pueden subdividir en zonas más grandes o más pequeñas, en función de lo que requieran las muestras.

links: Schnitt_Nachtansicht mit Kirche_Westfassade. rechts: Ansicht von der Donau_Ansicht von der Donau in Blau-Grün_Treppenhaus.
gauche: Coupe_Vue nocturne sur l'église_Façade ouest. droite: Vue sur le Danube_Vue sur le Danube en teinte bleu/vert_Cage d'escalier.
izquierda: Corte_Vista nocturna con la iglesia_Fachada occidental. derecha: Vista desde el Danubio_Vista desde el Danubio en verde y azul_Caja de la escalera.

Oberbank

AUSTRIA_LINZ **LENTOS KUNSTMUSEUM**

ÖSTERREICH_AUTRICHE_AUSTRIA
WEBER HOFER PARTNER AG
2003
KUNSTMUSEUM_MUSÉE D'ART_MUSEO DE ARTE
7,700 M²
PHOTOS DIETMAR TOLLERIAN, LINZ

Das Museum markiert den westlichen Abschluss des Donauparks und folgt in seiner Ausrichtung und Lage dem Hochwasserdamm. Wie ein Schiff liegt es am Ufer der Donau, auf der einen Seite von Wasser umspült, auf der anderen Seite vom Park umschlossen. Die offene, vom Gebäudekörper überspannte Skulpturenhalle ist ein stützenloser Raum von 60 x 24 Metern. Sie ist sowohl städtischer Platz als auch Eingangshalle des Museums und darüber hinaus Fenster zur Donau. Die raumhaltige Glasfassade mit verspiegelter Aufschrift reflektiert das Licht der Umgebung. Bei Dunkelheit verwandelt sich das Museum in einen Leuchtkörper, der sich in der Donau spiegelt.

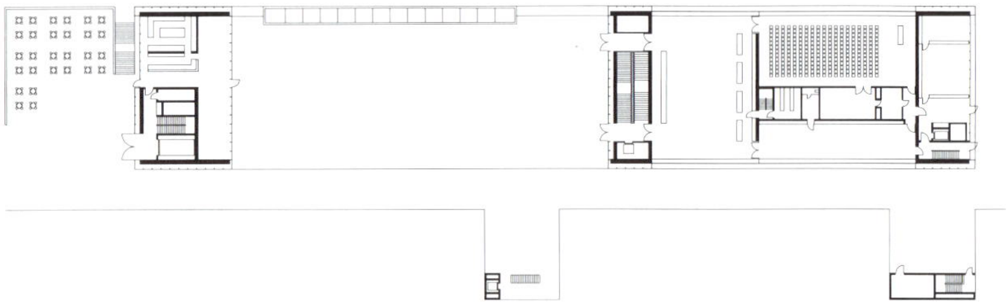

Le musée marque les confins de Donaupark à l'Ouest en suivant la digue grâce à son orientation et sa situation. A l'instar d'un bateau, il se situe sur la rive du Danube, entouré d'un côté par l'eau et, de l'autre, par le parc. La « salle des sculptures » ouverte, située dans le corps du bâtiment, consiste en un espace sans appui de 60 x 24 mètres. Elle constitue une partie intégrante à la ville, un hall d'entrée au musée et une fenêtre sur le Danube. La façade vitrifiée spacieuse avec inscription miroitante reflète la lumière environnante. La nuit, le musée se transforme en un corps lumineux qui se reflète dans le Danube.

El museo marca el remate occidental del parque sobre el Danubio y acompaña con su orientación y ubicación al dique de contención. Como si se tratase de un barco, se levanta junto a la orilla del Danubio, cuyas aguas lo bañan por un lado, mientras por el otro lo circunda un parque. La "sala de esculturas", sin apoyos intermedios, abarca todo el ancho del edificio y mide 60 por 24 metros. Es al mismo tiempo una plaza urbana y una sala de acceso al museo y, además, constituye una vidriera hacia el Danubio. La fachada acristalada, con efecto espejado, refleja la luz del entorno. Por la noche, el museo se transforma en un volumen luminoso que se refleja majestuosamente en las aguas del Danubio.

links: Grundriss Erdgeschoss_Stadtsilhouette_Skulpturenhalle bei Nacht. rechts: Spiegelung und Durchblick_Großer Ausstellungssaal.
gauche: Plan du rez-de-chaussée_Silhouette de la ville_Hall des sculptures de nuit. droite: Reflets et perspective_Grande salle d'exposition.
izquierda: Plano de planta baja_Panorama urbano_Sala de esculturas por la noche. derecha: Reflejo y vista a lo lejos_Gran sala de exhibiciones.

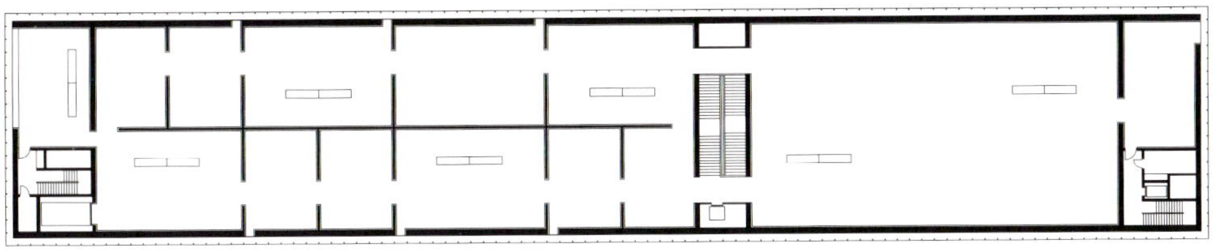

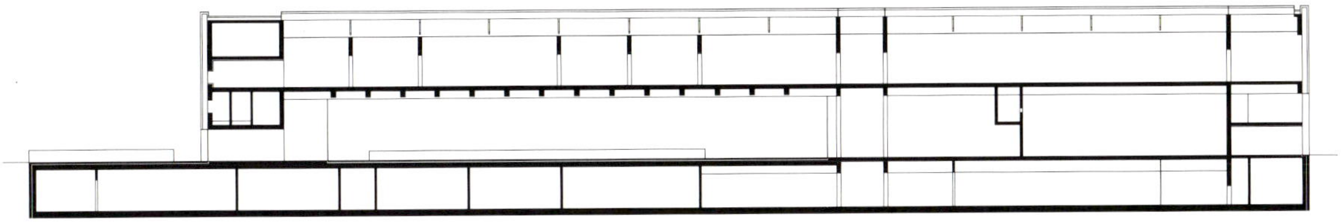

links: Kleiner Ausstellungssaal. rechts: Obergeschoss und Längsschnitt_Ausstellungsräume.
gauche: Petite salle d'exposition. droite: Étage supérieur et coupe longitudinale_Espaces d'exposition.
izquierda: Pequeña sala de exhibiciones. derecha: Corte longitudinal_Salas de exhibiciones.

AUSTRIA_MAUTHAUSEN

BESUCHERZENTRUM MAUTHAUSEN MEMORIAL

ÖSTERREICH_AUSTRIE_AUSTRIA
HERWIG MAYER / CHRISTOPH SCHWARZ / KARL PEYRER-HEIMSTÄTT
2003
GESCHICHTSMUSEUM_MUSÉE D'HISTOIRE_MUSEO HISTÓRICO
2,845 M²
PHOTOS JORK WEISSMANN

Ziel war es, die Besuchereinrichtungen klar von der eigentlichen Gedenkstätte abzugrenzen. Das Besucherzentrum wurde als kompakte, nach innen orientierte Anlage auf zwei Ebenen errichtet, zusammengefasst in einem fast zur Gänze unterirdisch situierten Baukörper von prismatischer Form, dessen begrüntes Flachdach mit dem angrenzenden Gelände auf einer Ebene liegt. Ein zentraler Innenhof und ein angrenzender zweigeschossiger Ausstellungsraum mit daran anschließenden Erschließungszonen in Rasterform bilden den Kern der Anlage. Die vorrangige Verwendung von Sichtbeton, Verputz und Glas kennzeichnet eine minimalistische Materialsprache, die mit dem Granit aus der Nazizeit kontrastiert.

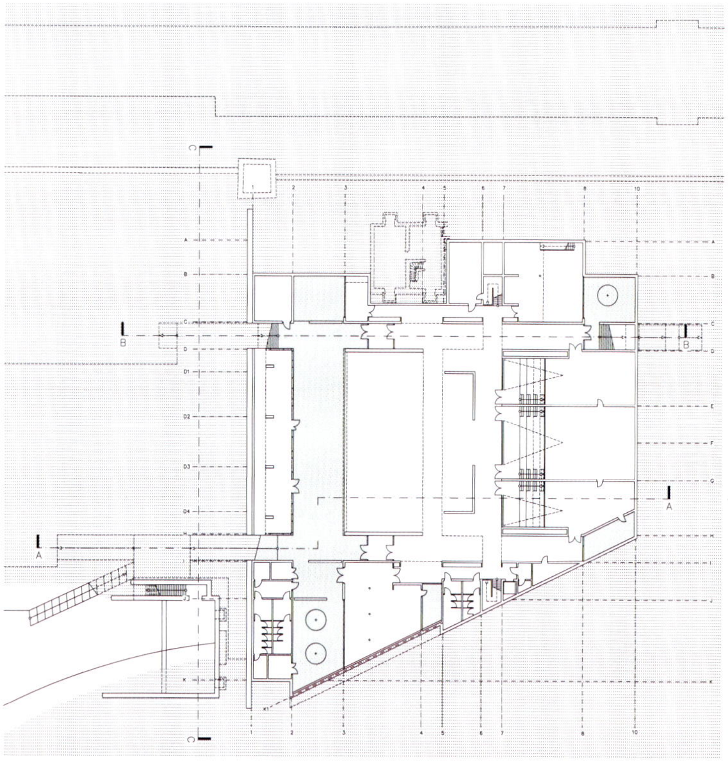

L'objectif était de limiter visiblement les installations du véritable lieu commémoratif pour les visiteurs. Un site compact orienté vers l'intérieur sur deux niveaux fut créé selon la conception architectonique d'un espace visiteurs qui se réduit presque entièrement à un corps de bâtiment de forme prismatique situé sous le niveau de la terre, dont le toit plat verdoyant, se situe sur un même niveau que le terrain limitrophe. Une cour intérieure centrale et un espace d'exposition à deux étages avoisinant les zones d'accès juxtaposées en forme de trame, forment le centre du site. L'utilisation prépondérante du béton apparent, crépi et verre caractérise un langage de matériaux minimaliste en contraste avec l'utilisation du granit au temps du nazisme.

Se procuró diferenciar claramente las instalaciones para visitantes del sitio conmemorativo propiamente dicho. El concepto arquitectónico del centro de visitantes es el de una edificación compacta, orientada hacia dentro, en dos niveles, ubicada en un volumen prismático que se encuentra casi en su totalidad bajo tierra y cuyo techo plano cubierto de verde coincide con el nivel del suelo adyacente. Un patio interior central y una sala de exhibiciones adjunta de dos niveles, con zonas de conexión distribuidas en retícula, constituyen el núcleo de las instalaciones. La utilización prevalente de hormigón visto, enlucido y cristal subraya un lenguaje minimalista que contrasta con la utilización de granito en la época nazi.

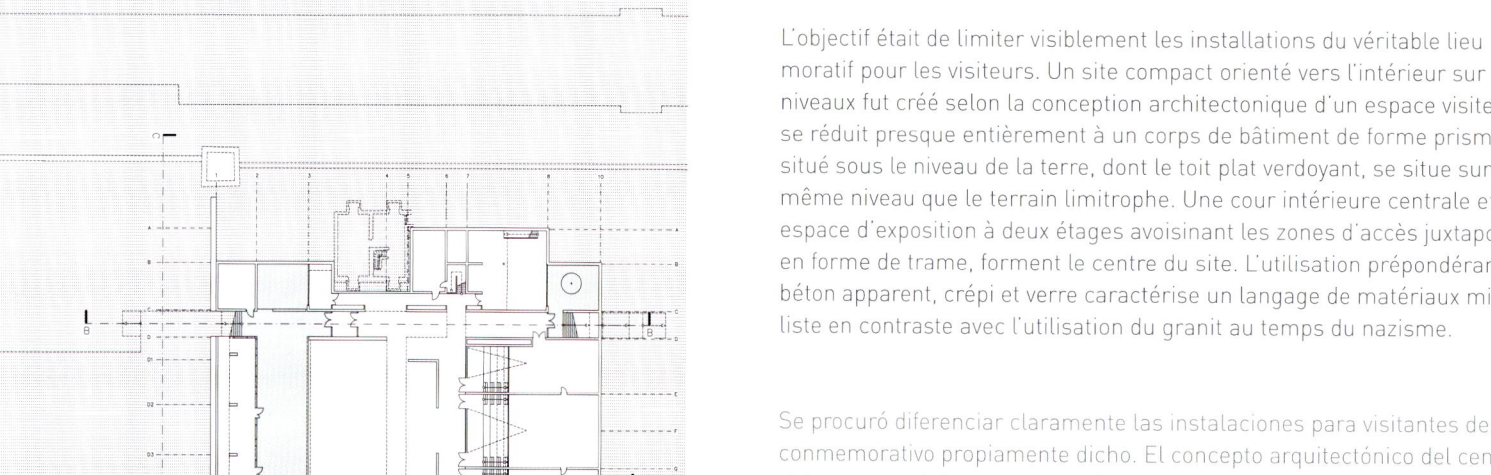

links: Grundriss Erdgeschoss_Zugang_Blick zwischen die Kuben. rechts: Innenraum_Glasfassade_Ausstellung_Blick nach außen.
gauche: Plan du rez-de-chaussée_Accés_Vue entre les cubes. droite: Espace intérieur_Façade en verre_Exposition_Vue vers l'extérieur.
izquierda: Plano de planta baja_Acceso_Vista entre los cubos. derecha: Espacio interior_Fachada acristalada_Exposición_Vista hacia el exterior.

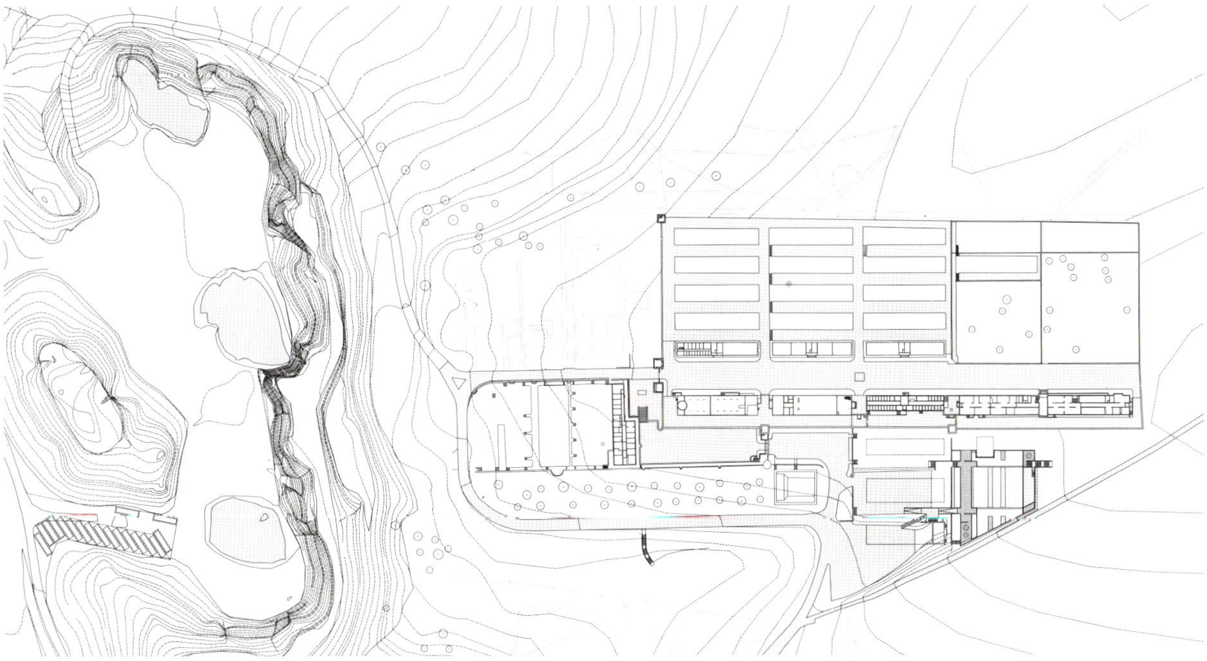

links: Ausblick von den Kuben. rechts: Situation_Details_Außenansicht.
gauche: Vue sur les cubes. droite: Situation_Détails_Vue extérieure.
izquierda: Vista desde los cubos. derecha: Ubicación_Detalles_Vista exterior.

AUSTRIA_NEUHAUS **ML MUSEUM LIAUNIG**

ÖSTERREICH_AUTRICHE_AUSTRIA
QUERKRAFT ARCHITEKTEN ZT GMBH
2008
KUNSTMUSEUM_MUSÉE D'ART_MUSEO DE ARTE
4,810 M²
PHOTOS QUERKRAFT / LISA RASTL

Das Museum für die umfangreiche private Kunstsammlung Herbert Liaunigs sollte bei minimalem Budget und niedrigsten Betriebskosten fernab aller urbanen Zentren Besucher anziehen und kontemplativen Kunstgenuss ermöglichen. Aus Kostengründen und zur Optimierung des Energiekonzepts liegen 95 Prozent der Kubatur unterhalb der Erde. Man betritt das Museum über das großzügige Schaudepot, den „Weinkeller der Kunst" und erreicht die helle Haupthalle an zentraler Stelle. Durch die intensive Fokussierung des Gebäudes auf die Landschaft treffen die Besucher als Gegenpol zur kontemplativen Kunstbetrachtung immer wieder auf Ausblicke, die gleichsam dramaturgische Höhepunkte darstellen. Dadurch entsteht niemals der Eindruck, sich unter der Erde zu befinden.

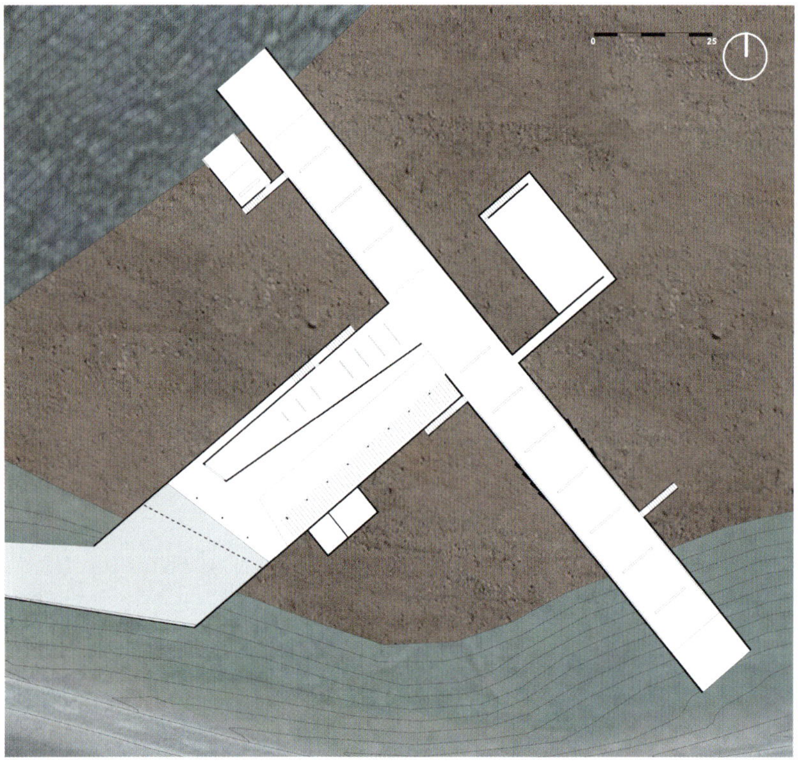

L'objectif du musée consacré à la collection privée importante d'art d'Herbert Liaunig vise à attirer des visiteurs de toutes les villes pour un budget minimal et des coûts d'exploitation réduits afin d'offrir le plaisir de l'art contemplatif. 95 pour cent du volume bâti est sous le niveau de la terre pour des raisons de coûts et d'optimisation énergétique. L'accès du musée s'effectue par un dépôt d'exposition généreux, la « Cave de l'Art » afin d'atteindre la salle principale lumineuse au centre. Outre la considération artistique contemplative, les visiteurs font l'expérience d'une apogée dramaturgique grâce à une concentration intensive sur le paysage. Cette contribution unique permet à personne d'avoir l'impression de se trouver sous le niveau de la terre.

El diseño del museo destinado a albergar la vasta colección privada de arte de Herbert Liaunig estaba condicionado por un presupuesto acotado y la exigencia de costes operativos ínfimos; además debía atraer visitantes de centros urbanos lejanos y permitirles el disfrute contemplativo del arte. Por motivos económicos y buscando optimizar el uso de la energía, el 95 por ciento del volumen se ubicó bajo tierra. Se accede al museo por un fabuloso muestrario, la "bodega del arte", y se llega a la luminosa nave principal en el centro del edificio. Como polo contrario de la contemplación artística, los visitantes descubren puntos culminantes dramáticos, intensamente focalizados en el paisaje, que contribuyen a hacerles imposible imaginar que se encuentran bajo tierra.

links: Lageplan_Eingangsbereich. rechts: Terrasse_Kunsthalle mit Tageslicht_Außenhaut aus industriell gefertigten Blechschalen.
gauche: Plan de site_Zone d'entrée. droite: Terrasse_Kunsthalle à la lumière naturelle_Revêtement extérieur en coques de tôle fabriquées industriellement.
izquierda: Plano de ubicación_Zona del acceso. derecha: Terraza_Sala de arte con luz diurna_Piel exterior elaborada en chapas industrializadas.

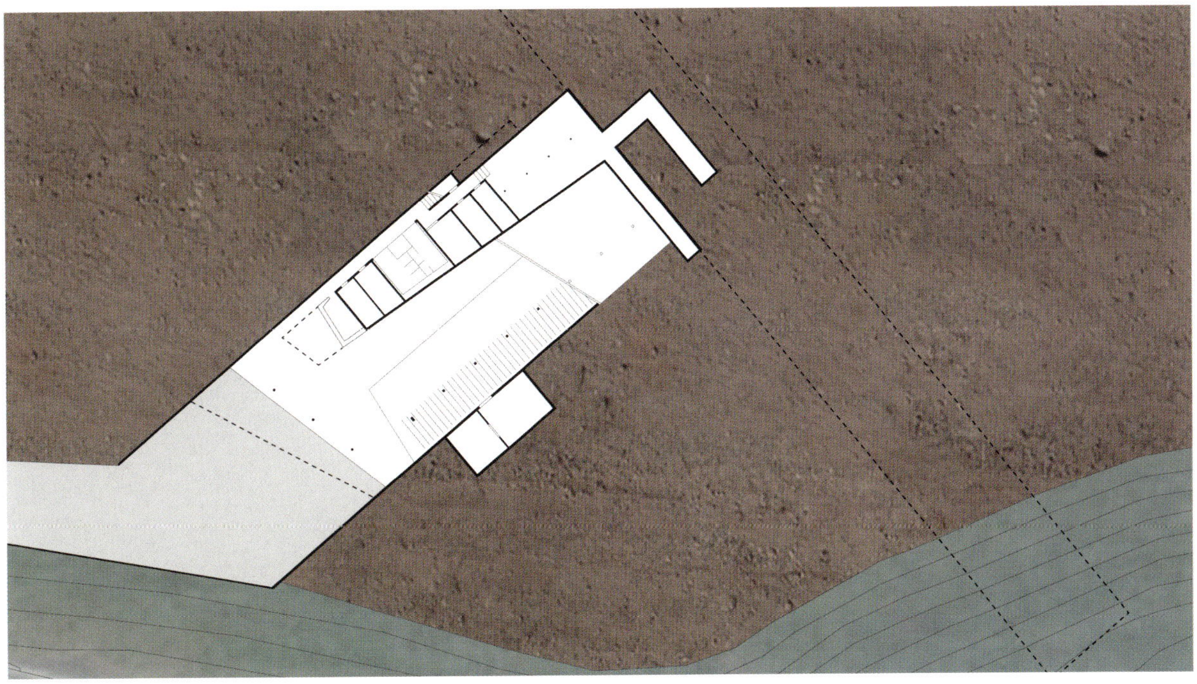

links: Außenansicht von der Strasse. rechts: Entwurf_Blick Richtung Terrasse_Verbindungsgang zur Goldsammlung mit Lichtkunst von Brigitte Kowanz.
gauche: Vue extérieure de la rue. droite: Projet_Vue en direction de la terrasse_Corridor de jonction à la collection en or, éclairé par la composition artistique lumineuse de Brigitte Kowanz.
izquierda: Vista exterior desde la calle. derecha: Proyecto_Vista en dirección a la terraza_Pasaje hacia la colección de oro con iluminación artística de Brigitte Kowanz.

AUSTRIA_SALZBURG **MUSEUM DER MODERNE**

ÖSTERREICH_AUTRICHE_AUSTRIA
FRIEDRICH HOFF ZWINK ARCHITEKTEN
2004
KUNSTMUSEUM_MUSÉE D'ART_MUSEO DE ARTE
6,550 M²
PHOTOS SIMONE ROSENBERG

Wichtigster Teil der Bauaufgabe war es, das Museum in die Besonderheiten des Bauplatzes einzubetten. Der Mönchsberg bietet einen atemberaubenden Blick auf die Salzburger Altstadt, weshalb schon 1892 der Wasserturm mit einer Aussichtsplattform versehen wurde. Er wurde nun von späterer Umbauung im Sockelbereich befreit, während das Restaurant an seiner ursprünglichen Stelle belassen wurde. Das Museum als monolithischer Block greift die horizontale Grundausrichtung des Berges ebenso auf, wie die vertikalen Einschnitte in die Bausubstanz die vertikalen Felsklüfte reflektieren. In Analogie zur serpentinenförmigen Landschaftsbewegung ist der Weg im Inneren des Hauses als Spirale angelegt.

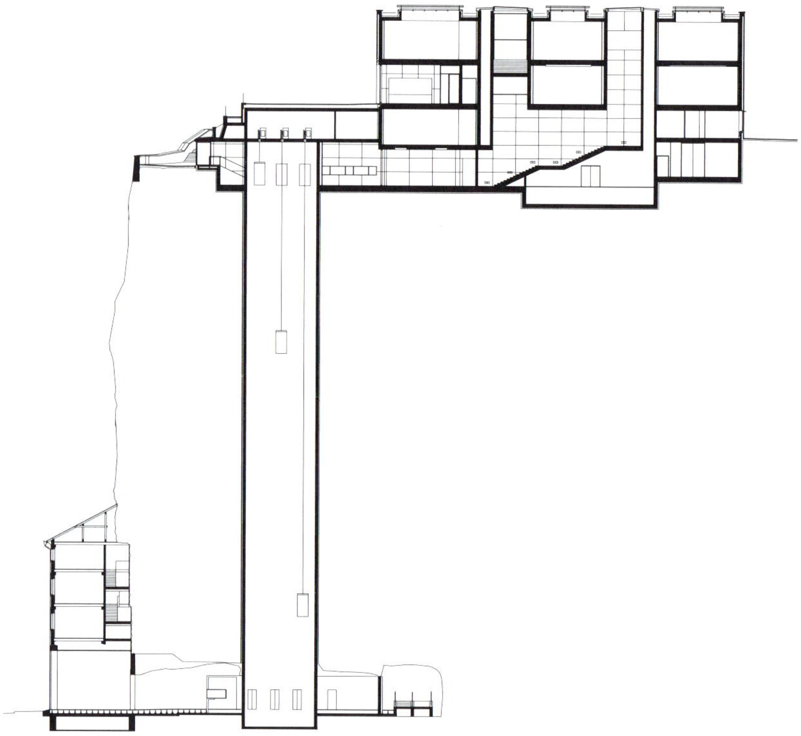

Intégrer le musée dans les caractéristiques du site : telle était la mission principale du projet. En effet, Mönchsberg offre une vue époustouflante sur la vieille ville de Salzbourg. Dès 1892, le château d'eau a été muni d'une plate-forme offrant cette perspective. Par la suite, le château d'eau a été dépourvu de transformations successives au niveau du socle alors que le restaurant a conservé sa place d'origine. Le musée constitue un bloc monolithique qui s'adapte à l'orientation horizontale de la montagne et reflète également les inclusions verticales par le volume bâti dans les clivages verticaux. Par analogie au paysage en serpentins, le chemin est construit en spirale à l'intérieur de la maison.

Lo más importante de esta tarea proyectual era lograr un anclaje del museo en las particularidades del sitio. La montaña Mönchsberg ofrece una visual arrobadora sobre el casco histórico de Salzburgo, por lo cual ya desde 1892 la torre de agua estaba provista de una plataforma de observación. Más tarde se la liberó en el área del basamento, al tiempo que el restaurante fue dejado en su sitio original. El museo como bloque monolítico capta la orientación básica horizontal de la montaña, del mismo modo que las incisiones verticales reflejan en la esencia arquitectónica las brechas verticales de los acantilados. Como analogía con el movimiento serpenteante del paisaje, el camino en el interior de esta casa se distribuye en espiral.

links: Schnitt_Südfassade_Ostfassade mit Restaurantterrasse. rechts: Verbindungssteg Tageslichtebene_Ausblick nach Süden_Ausstellungsbereich.
gauche: Coupe_Façade sud_Façade est avec terrasse de restaurant. droite: Passerelle de jonction – niveau de la lumière naturelle_Vue vers le sud_Zone d'exposition.
izquierda: Corte_Fachada sur_Fachada este con la terraza del restaurante. derecha: Pasaje de conexión, nivel con luz diurna_Vista al sur_Área de exhibiciones.

AUSTRIA_ST. JOHANN / HERBERSTEIN **GIRONCOLI MUSEUM**

ÖSTERREICH_AUTRICHE_AUSTRIA
ARCHITEKT DI HERMANN EISENKÖCK
2004
KUNSTMUSEUM_MUSÉE D'ART_MUSEO DE ARTE
2,183 M^2
PHOTOS PAUL OTT, GRAZ

Das Projekt umfasst einen Neu- und einen Anbau an eine historische Scheune im Schlosspark Herberstein. Erstmals in Österreich verwob das Museum für die Plastiken von Bruno Gironcoli repräsentative Werke zeitgenössischer Kunst mit ausgedehnten Natur- und historischen Baustrukturen im Sinne eines künstlerisch und landschaftlich geprägten Entertainmentparks. Die minimalistisch lapidare architektonische Hülle bietet mittels durchscheinender Haut aus Rodalux-Fassadenelementen auf Stahlskelettrahmen einen würdigen Kunstrahmen für die Exponate.

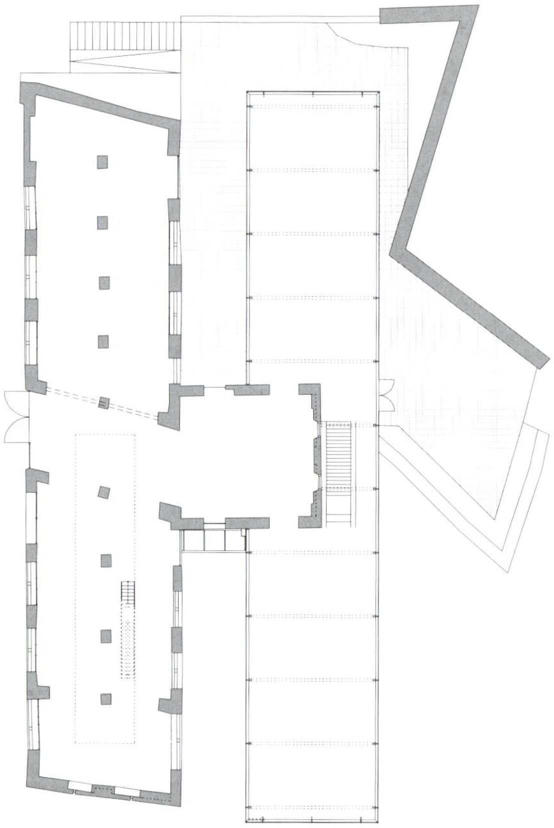

Le projet comprend un nouveau bâtiment et une annexe à une grange historique dans le parc du château d'Herberstein. Le musée dédié aux œuvres plastiques de Gironcoli veille principalement à l'effet artistique, architectonique et touristique étant donné que c'est la première fois en Autriche que des œuvres représentatives de l'art contemporain sont intégrées dans un style majestueux à des structures de construction allongées, inspirées de l'histoire et de la nature, dans la symbolique d'un parc d'attractions artistique et pittoresque. La couverture architectonique génère un minimalisme lapidaire et une aura qui produit un cadre artistique digne de ce nom grâce au revêtement transparent composé d'éléments de façade Rodalux sur un cadre d'ossature en acier.

El proyecto comprende la obra nueva y la ampliación de un histórico granero en el parque del castillo de Herberstein. El proyecto del museo que alberga las obras de arte de Gironcoli fue estudiado a fondo en sus aspectos artísticos, arquitectónicos y turísticos. Es la primera vez en la historia de Austria que se combinan obras representativas del arte contemporáneo de estilo grandioso con estructuras edilicias históricas y la amplitud de la naturaleza, con la concepción de un parque temático artístico caracterizado paisajísticamente. La envolvente arquitectónica es sumamente minimalista, concebida como una piel translúcida con elementos de fachada Rodalux sobre un esqueleto de acero, con lo cual se genera una especie de aura, un marco artístico dignificante.

links: Grundriss Obergeschoss_Südansicht mit Haupteingang_Galerie. rechts: Treppenaufgang und Ausstellungsraum_Museumsansicht Ost.
gauche: Plan de l'étage supérieur_Vue au sud avec l'entrée principale_Galerie. droite: Escaliers d'entrée et espace d'exposition_Vue à l'est du musée.
izquierda: Plano de planta alta_Fachada sur con acceso principal_Galería. derecha: Escalera y sala de exhibiciones_Vista este del museo.

AUSTRIA_VIENNA **MUSEUMSQUARTIER**

ÖSTERREICH_AUTRICHE_AUSTRIA
ORTNER&ORTNER BAUKUNST
2001
KUNSTMUSEUM_MUSÉE D'ART_MUSEO DE ARTE
53,000 M²
PHOTOS RUPERT STEINER, VIENNA (162 B. R., 163 B),
COURTESY OF THE ARCHITECTS (162 B. L., 163 A.)

Das Museumsquartier als Zentrum der Gegenwartskunst ist mit verschiedenen kulturellen Einrichtungen ausgestattet: dem Museum für Moderne Kunst, dem Leopold Museum, der Kunsthalle Wien, den Veranstaltungshallen E+G, dem Architekturzentrum, dem Kindermuseum mit Kindertheater, Produktionsräumen für neue Medien, Künstlerateliers, Restaurants, Cafés und Themenshops. Die Lage im Areal der ehemaligen Hofstallungen, die 1723 von Johann Fischer von Erlach erbaut wurden, ermöglicht eine ideale Anknüpfung der zeitgenössischen Kultur an die historische Tradition, die sich mit Hofburg und Hofmuseen in direkter Nachbarschaft befindet.

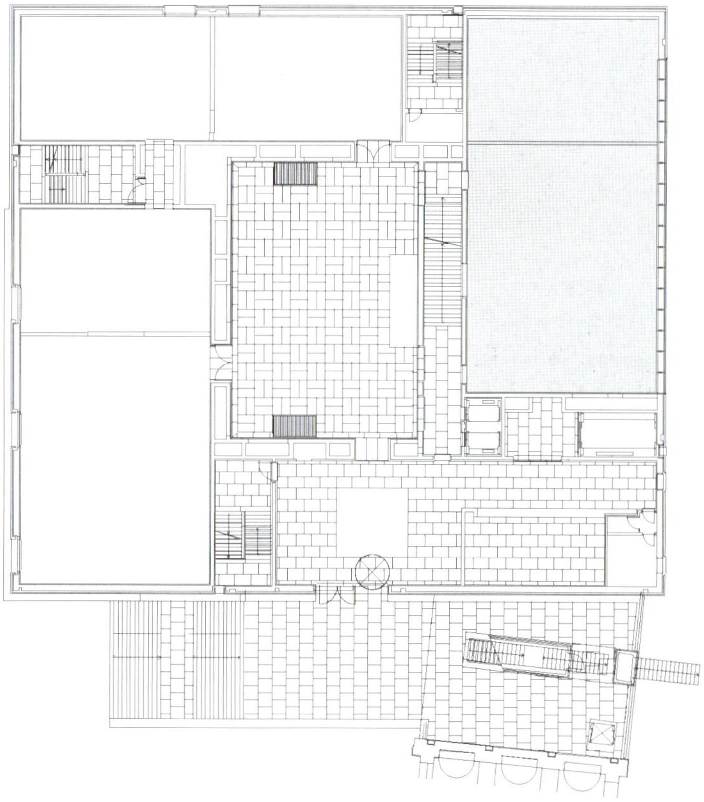

Le quartier des musées de Vienne est un lieu incontournable de l'art contemporain. En effet, il comprend de nombreux équipements et institutions dédiés à la culture : le musée d'art moderne, le musée Leopold, le Kunsthalle Wien, les salles d'événements E+G, le centre d'architecture, le musée et théâtre pour enfants, les espaces de production consacrés aux nouveaux médias, ateliers d'artistes, restaurants, cafés et boutiques à thème. Ce quartier est situé dans les anciennes écuries de la Cour impériale (construites en 1723 par J. Fischer von Erlach), site qui constitue un lien idéal entre la culture contemporaine et la tradition historique qui règne dans le château et dans les musées impériaux à proximité immédiate.

El Barrio de los Museos, en su carácter de centro del arte contemporáneo, comprende múltiples instituciones culturales: el Museo de Arte Moderno, el Museo Leopold, la Sala de Arte de Viena, las Salas de Actividades E+G, el Centro de Arquitectura, el Museo y Teatro Infantil, espacios de producción multimedia, talleres de artistas, restaurantes, cafés y tiendas temáticas. El sitio, en la antigua ubicación de los antiguos establos reales (concebidos por Johann Bernhard Fischer von Erlach en 1723), ofrece la vinculación ideal entre la cultura contemporánea y la tradición histórica, ineludible por la presencia vecina del Hofburg y los Museos Imperiales.

links: Plan Leopoldmuseum_Außenbau Museum für moderne Kunst_Fassade Kunsthalle. rechts: Luftaufnahme_Fassade Leopoldmuseum_Innenraum Leopoldmuseum.
gauche: Plan du musée Léopold_Extérieur du musée d'art moderne_Façade de Kunsthalle. droite: Vue aérienne_Façade du musée Léopold_Intérieur du Musée Léopold.
izquierda: Plano del Museo Leopold_Exterior del Museo de Arte Moderno_Fachada del Museo de Arte Moderno_Fachada de la Sala de Arte. derecha: Vista aérea_Fachada del Museo Leopold_Interior del Museo Leopold.

BELGIUM_BRUGES **GROENINGEMUSEUM**

BELGIEN_BELGIQUE_BÉLGICA
51N4E
2003
KUNSTMUSEUM_MUSÉE D'ART_MUSEO DE ARTE
1,170 M²
PHOTOS 51N4E (164 B. R., 165 B. R.),
HANS WERLEMANN / 51N4E (164 B. L., 165 A., B. L.)

Beim Groeningemuseum handelt es sich weniger um ein Gebäude als vielmehr um eine Sammlung miteinander verbundener Objekte in einer Gartenanlage. Der Garten macht das Groeningemuseum zum potenziellen öffentlichen Bereich, doch ist dieser im Laufe der Jahre organisch so gewachsen, dass der Gesamteindruck für die Museumsbesucher nicht mehr nachvollziehbar ist. Die schrittweise Sanierung des in den 1930er Jahren erbauten Groe-ningemuseums konzentriert sich nicht allein auf die Schaffung einer neuen Innenausstattung, sondern ist vielmehr eine eingehende Untersuchung zur Funktion eines Museums als öffentlichem Innenraum im Gefüge der Stadt. Das neue Konzept des Groeningemuseums vereint zweierlei: ein herkömmliches Museum mit einer „Expo-Route" und einen kokonartigen öffentlichen Bereich mit einer „öffentlichen Route".

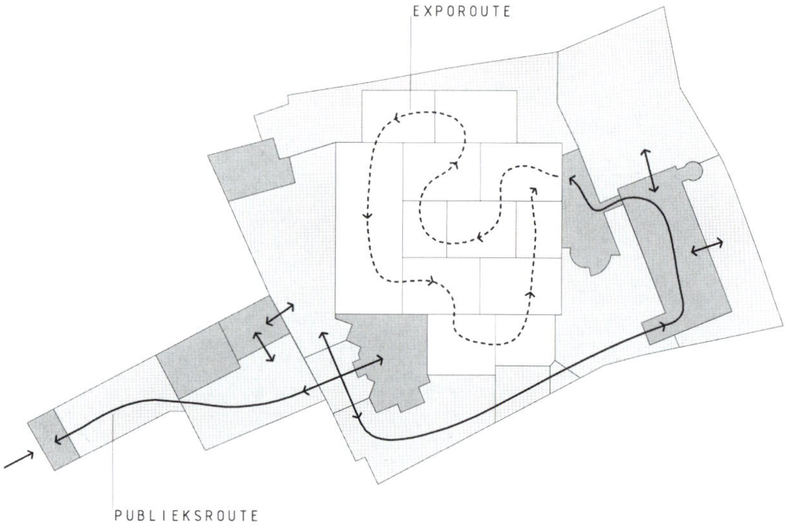

Le Groeningemuseum ressemble moins à un bâtiment qu'à une collection d'objets reliés disposée comme dans un parc. En effet, le parc confère au Groeningemuseum le statut potentiel de bien commun. Cependant, au cours des années, son évolution ne permet plus aux visiteurs du musée de distinguer tous les objets en raison de l'impression générale. La rénovation successive du Groeningemuseum depuis les années 1930 se concentre sur la création d'un intérieur renouvelé, et notamment sur l'intégration approfondie du musée comme un espace public intégré à la ville. Le nouveau concept du Groeningemuseum conjugue deux objectifs : un musée traditionnel avec « Expo-Route » et un espace public en forme de cocon avec une « route tout public ».

El Groeningemuseum no es tanto un edificio, sino más bien una colección de objetos vinculados entre sí, distribuidos por un jardín. Este jardín transforma al Groeningemuseum en un espacio público potencial, si bien en el correr de los años ha crecido orgánicamente de modo tal que la impresión de conjunto ya no es perceptible para los visitantes. La renovación paulatina de este museo, que data de la década de 1930, se concentra no solo en lograr un nuevo interior, sino que además implica la exploración a fondo del propio museo en tanto espacio interior en el tejido urbano. Por tanto, el nuevo concepto del Groeningemuseum reúne dos en uno: un museo convencional con un recorrido de muestras, y un espacio público similar a un capullo con un recorrido para el público.

links: Zusammenhang von Ausstellungs- und öffentlichem Rundgang_Barockraum_Renaissanceraum. rechts: Klassizismusraum_Abstrakte Kunst-Raum_Raum der Landschaftsmalerei.
gauche: Combinaison de parcours exposition et itinéraire public_Salle baroque_Salle renaissance. droite: Espace du classicisme_Espace d'art abstrait_Espace dédiée à la peinture paysagiste.
izquierda: Contexto del recorrido público y museístico_Sala del Barroco_Sala del Renacimiento. derecha: Sala del Clasicismo_Sala del arte abstracto_Sala de pintura paisajística.

BELGIUM_HORNU MONS **MAC'S – MUSÉE DES ARTS CONTEMPORAINS**

BELGIEN_BELGIQUE_BÉLGICA
ATELIER D'ARCHITECTURE PIERRE HEBBELINCK & PIERRE DE WIT
2002
KUNSTMUSEUM_MUSÉE D'ART_MUSEO DE ARTE
7,000 M²
PHOTOS HÉLÈNE BINET, LONDON

Die Architekten errichteten für das Museum in der ehemaligen Kohlebergbauanlage einen Neubau, der die Altbauten einerseits zur Geltung kommen lässt, ihre Monumentalität andererseits aber bricht. Die zurückhaltende, moderne und überaus präzise Architektur konterkariert das neoklassizistische Pathos der historischen Gebäude und schafft neue Raumgefüge sowie einen Dialog der Räumlichkeiten. Ähnlichkeiten und Unterschiede zeigen sich aber nicht nur in der Komposition der Anlage und einzelner Volumen, sie sind bis zum kleinsten architektonischen Element – etwa den unterschiedlichen Backsteinen aus beiden Epochen – zu verfolgen.

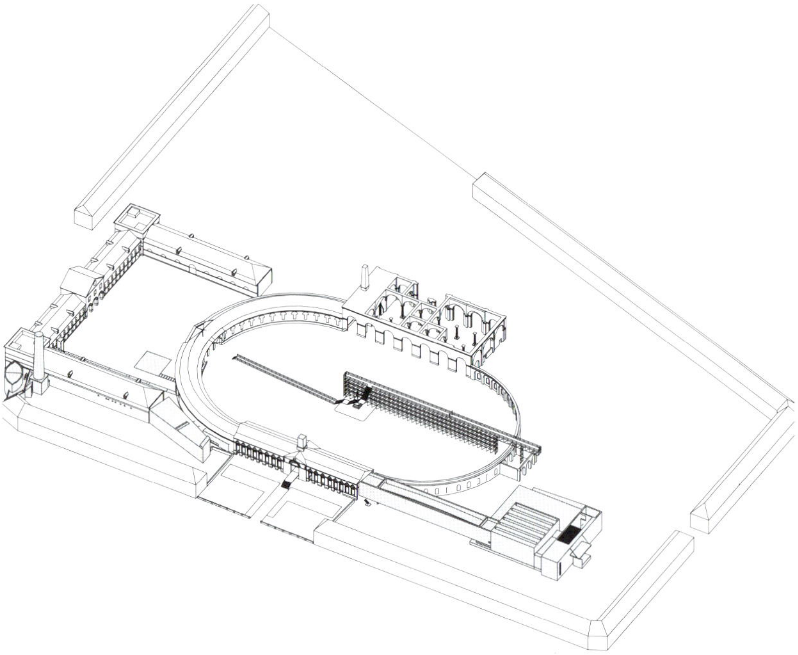

L'architecte érigea un nouveau bâtiment pour le musée sur un ancien charbonnage qui valorise à nouveau l'ancien site, d'une part, et brise son caractère monumental, d'autre part. L'architecture discrète, moderne et extrêmement précise altère l'impression symétrique néoclassique en créant une nouvelle structure spatiale au sein du site et un dialogue entre les espaces. Cependant, les similitudes et les différences ne se reflètent pas uniquement dans la composition du site et les volumes individuels. Elles se poursuivent jusqu'au plus petit élément architectonique : le contraste entre les briques des deux époques.

Para albergar el museo en las antiguas instalaciones de las minas de carbón, el arquitecto levantó una nueva edificación que revaloriza las antiguas construcciones existentes y, al mismo tiempo, logra una ruptura con su monumentalidad original. La arquitectura sumamente precisa, moderna y discreta se contrapone a la retórica de la simetría característica del estilo neoclásico y logra una nueva espacialidad en las instalaciones, además de un diálogo entre las salas. Las similitudes y las diferencias no solo se muestran en la composición del conjunto y de cada uno de los diversos volúmenes, sino que también se pueden apreciar hasta en los más mínimos detalles arquitectónicos, como los ladrillos de diferentes épocas.

links: Axonometrie_Alt- und Neubau_Fassadendetails_Detail. rechts: Fassade_Ausstellungsraum Treppenflucht_Eingang.
gauche: Axionométrie_Ancien et nouveau bâtiment_Détails de la façade_Détail. droite: Façade_Espace d'exposition_Escalier_Entrée.
izquierda: Axonométrica_Construcciones antigua y nueva_Detalles de fachada_Detalle. derecha: Fachada_Sala de exhibiciones_Pasaje con escalera_Acceso.

CZECH REPUBLIC_PRAGUE **DOX – CENTRUM SOUČASNÉHO UMĚNÍ**

TSCHECHISCHE REPUBLIK_TCHÉQUIE_REPÚBLICA CHECA
IVAN KROUPA ARCHITEKTI
2008
KUNSTMUSEUM_MUSÉE D'ART_MUSEO DE ARTE
6,250 M²
PHOTOS COURTESY OF THE ARCHITECTS (168, 171 R.),
JAN KUDEJ, PRAGUE (168 B., 169, 170, 171 L.)

Die Architektur ist ein integraler Bestandteil dieses spezifischen Stadtviertels, einem Industriegebiet aus der Wende vom 19. zum 20. Jahrhundert, das derzeit intensiv restrukturiert wird. Das Projekt nutzt nicht das gesamte Grundstück maximal aus, sondern lässt Freiräume über dem ursprünglichen Bestand, wo sich die dichte städtische Struktur auflockert. Das Konzept versteht sich als sensible Annäherung an Ort und Atmosphäre. Das Gebäude wurde seit 2004 schrittweise in privater Initiative errichtet. Bauverlauf und Baudauer waren stark von dem geringen Budget abhängig. Heute umfasst der Komplex zwölf Ausstellungsräume, ein Café mit Terrasse, eine Buchhandlung und weitere Einrichtungen.

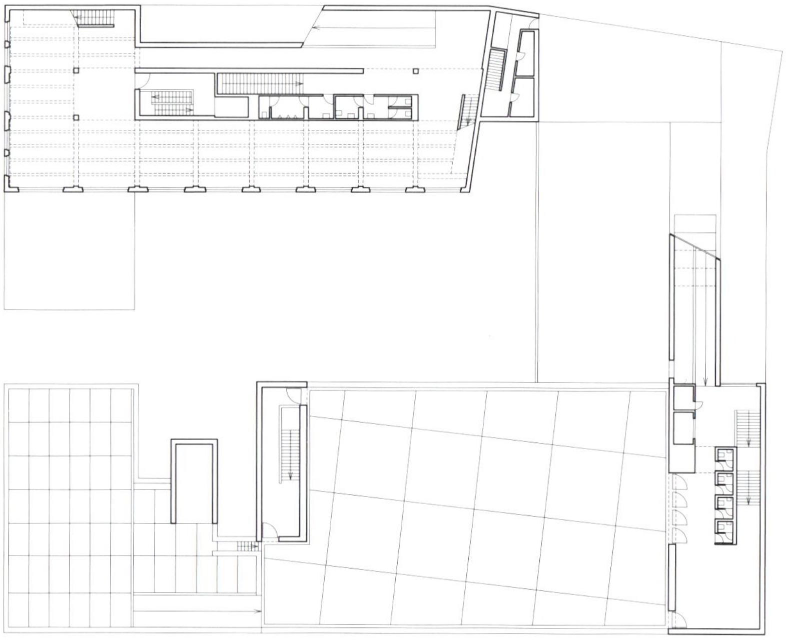

L'architecture est une composante intégrale spécifique du quartier de la ville, un domaine industriel au tournant entre le XIX et le XX siècle qui est actuellement en restructuration intensive. Le projet n'optimise pas l'intégralité du terrain, mais laisse néanmoins des espaces libres dans l'espace d'origine afin d'éviter la densité en milieu urbain. La conception repose sur le rapprochement sensible du lieu et de l'atmosphère. Depuis 2004, la construction du bâtiment s'est poursuivie successivement sur des initiatives privées. Le processus et la durée de construction furent fortement dépendants du budget restreint. Actuellement, le complexe comprend douze espaces d'exposition, un café avec terrasse, une librairie et d'autres installations.

La arquitectura es parte integral de un barrio específico, antigua zona industrial de fines del siglo XIX y principios del XX, que en la actualidad está siendo sometida a una intensa reestructuración. El proyecto no aprovecha todo el predio al máximo, sino que deja espacios libres en la edificación original, y permite así que la densa estructura urbana se afloje. El concepto se comprende como un acercamiento sensible al sitio y a su atmósfera. El edificio se construyó a partir de 2004 por iniciativa privada. El proceso y duración de la construcción dependieron mucho del acotado presupuesto. Hoy en día, el complejo abarca doce salas de exposiciones, un café con terraza, una librería y otros servicios.

links: Grundriss 3. Obergeschoss_Dachterrasse. rechts: Rampe Haupteingang.
gauche: Plan 3ème étage_Terrasse de toiture. droite: Rampe entrée principale.
izquierda: Plano del tercer piso_Terraza en el techo. derecha: Rampa del acceso principal.

Kavárna
Café
Knihy
Bookstore
Šatna
Cloakroom

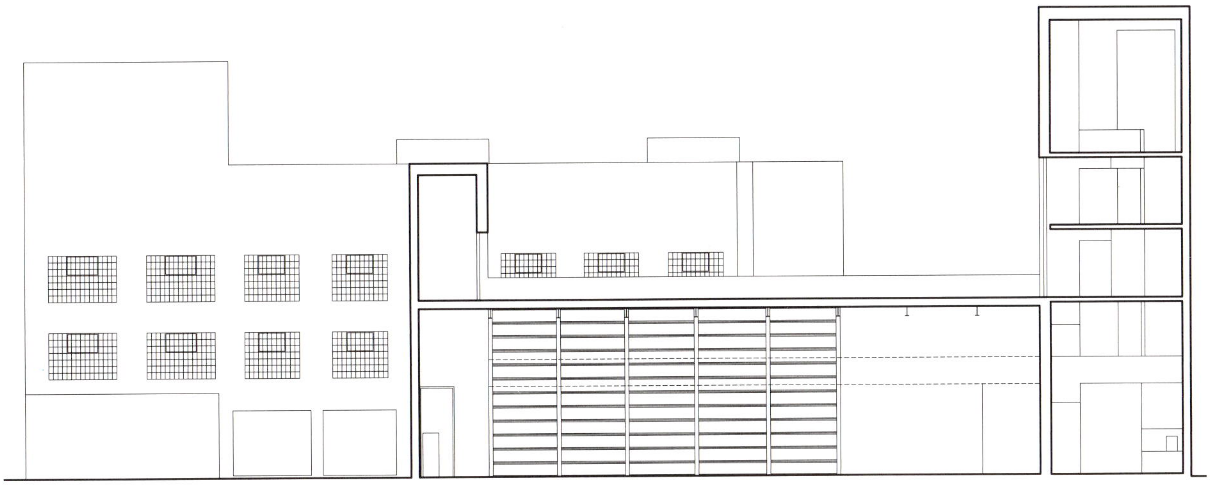

links: Turmgebäude. rechts: Schnitt_Blick aus dem Inneren auf den Turm_Raum mit Oberlicht Treppenaufgang.

gauche: Tour. droite: Coupe_Vue sur l'intérieur de la tour principale_Espace avec éclairage en hauteur_Cage d'escalier.

izquierda: Edificación en torre. derecha: Corte_Vista desde el interior hacia la torre principal_Sala con lucernario_Ascenso por escalera.

DENMARK_COPENHAGEN **DANSK JØDISK MUSEUM**

DÄNEMARK_DANEMARK_DINAMARCA
STUDIO DANIEL LIBESKIND
2003
GESCHICHTSMUSEUM_MUSÉE D'HISTOIRE_MUSEO HISTÓRICO
450 M²
PHOTOS BITTER BREDT FOTOGRAFIE, BERLIN

Das Museum ist der Geschichte des jüdischen Lebens in Dänemark seit dem 17. Jahrhundert gewidmet. In einem der ältesten Stadtteile von Kopenhagen gelegen, befindet sich das Museum in einem Gebäude, das König Christian IV. im 17. Jahrhundert erbauen ließ. Die Architekten gestalteten das Innere des Museums unter Beibehaltung der ursprünglichen Gebäudesubstanz. Dennoch bietet die architektonische Struktur dem Besucher eine nahtlose Anordnung der Artefakte. Das gesamte Gebäude ist als sowohl physisches als auch geistiges Abenteuer konzipiert und verfolgt das Ziel, die Schnittmengen und -punkte unterschiedlicher Geschichten und Aspekte der jüdischen Kultur offenzulegen.

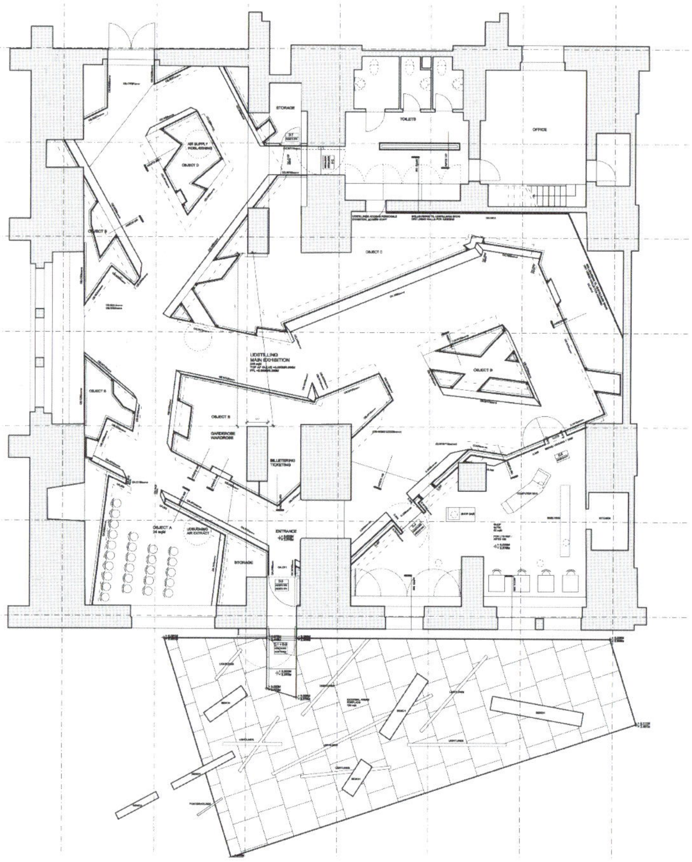

Le musée se consacre à l'histoire de la vie des juifs au Danemark depuis le XVII siècle. Situé dans l'une des plus anciennes parties de la ville de Copenhague, le musée se situe dans un bâtiment construit sous l'égide du roi Christian IV au XVII siècle. Les architectes aménagèrent l'intérieur du musée dans le respect de la structure d'origine du bâtiment. Cependant, la structure architectonique offre aux visiteurs une organisation lissée sans aucune fioriture. L'ensemble du bâtiment est conçu comme une aventure physique et spirituelle qui poursuit l'objectif de présenter les croisements et intersections des différentes histoires et aspects de la culture juive.

El museo está dedicado a la historia de los judíos en Dinamarca a partir del siglo XVII. Situado en uno de los barrios más antiguos de Copenhague, el museo está ubicado en un edificio que fue mandado construir por el rey Cristián IV en el siglo XVII. Los arquitectos organizaron el interior del museo respetando la sustancia edilicia original. No obstante, la estructuración arquitectónica le ofrece al visitante una organización de los objetos expuestos que no presenta fisuras. El edificio en su conjunto está concebido al mismo tiempo como aventura material y espiritual, y persigue el objetivo de transmitirle al público los más diversos aspectos de la historia y la cultura judías.

links: Grundriss Erdgeschoss_Museumsbau_Vier sich verschneidende Ebenen bilden die Innenlandschaft_Ausstellungsraum_Vitrinen. rechts: Alte Ziegelmauern, Lichtstrahlen, Bruchstücke der Erinnerung.
gauche: Plan du rez-de-chaussée_Construction du musée_Quatre plans d'intersection forment le paysage intérieur_Espace d'exposition_Vitrines. droite: Anciens murs en brique, rayons lumineux, fragments de la mémoire.
izquierda: Plano de planta baja_Edificio del museo_Cuatro planos que se entrecruzan conforman el paisaje interior_Sala de exhibiciones_Vitrinas. derecha: Viejos muros de ladrillo, rayos de luz, fragmentos para el recuerdo.

DENMARK_HELSINGØR **HANDELS- OG SØFARTSMUSEET**

DÄNEMARK_DANEMARK_DINAMARCA
BIG
2013
MARITIMMUSEUM_MUSÉE MARITIME_MUSEO MARÍTIMO
7,200 M²
PHOTOS COURTESY OF THE ARCHITECTS

Das Museum muss sich seinen Platz in dem einmaligen historischen und räumlichen Umfeld zwischen dem Schloss Kronborg und einem neuen ambitionierten Kulturzentrum suchen und sich zugleich als eigenständige Institution behaupten. Der Bau zieht sich als unterirdisches Museum um ein ehemaliges, imposantes Trockendock, das als Freiluftausstellungsfläche dient und das Zentrum des Maritimen Museums bildet. Hiervon ausgehend entstand der Grundriss des gesamten Museums. Brücken und Rampen durchschneiden den Freiraum strukturell und skulptural und lassen den Besucher in die Raumtiefe vordringen.

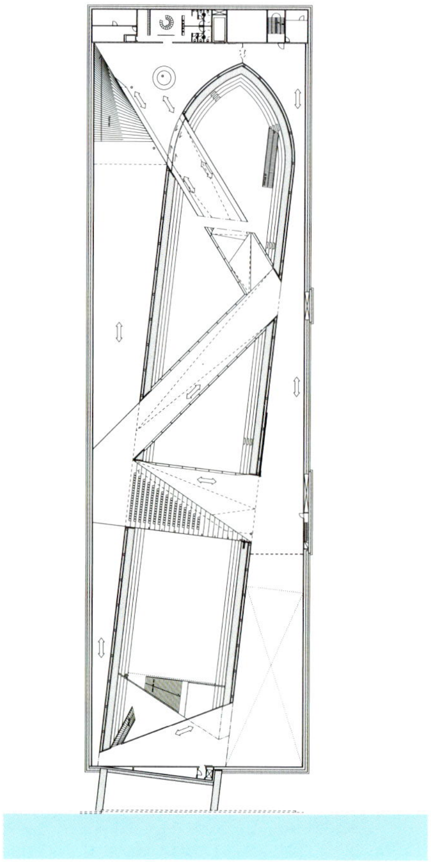

Le musée doit se trouver sa place appropriée dans un environnement spatial et historique unique entre le château de Kronborg et un nouveau centre culturel ambitieux afin de s'affirmer en tant qu'institution individualisée. La construction du musée souterrain est intégrée dans un ancien dock asséché servant de surfaces d'exposition en plein air grâce à son apparence imposante afin de former le centre du musée maritime. Sur cette base évolue le plan d'ensemble du musée. Les ponts et rampes découpent au niveau structurel et sculptural l'espace aérien en permettant aux visiteurs l'accès dans les profondeurs de l'espace.

El museo debió ubicarse en un entorno único por sus características históricas y espaciales: entre el castillo de Kronborg y un nuevo centro cultural que se planeaba construir y, al mismo tiempo, debía imponerse como institución por derecho propio. La construcción se concibió como museo subterráneo en un antiguo dique seco que, con su imponente imagen, sirve de superficie de exposiciones al aire libre y constituye el centro del Museo Marítimo. La planta de todo el museo se configuró tomando eso como centro. Puentes y rampas entrecruzan el espacio de manera estructural y escultural, y permiten al visitante penetrar en la profundidad de ese espacio.

links: Situation im Dock_Abgesenkter Hof_Treppen und Stufen im Hof. rechts: Blick über den Hof Ausstellungsraum_Blick aus dem Museum in den Hof.
gauche: Situation sur le dock_Cour en soubassement_Escaliers et marches dans la cour. droite: Vue sur la cour_Espace d'exposition_Vue depuis le musée sur la cour.
izquierda: Ubicación en el dique_Patio hundido_Escalinatas y escalones en el patio. derecha: Vista sobre el patio_Sala de exhibiciones_Vista desde el museo hacia el patio.

DENMARK_RANDERS **RANDERS KUNSTMUSEUM**

DÄNEMARK_DANEMARK_DINAMARCA
3XN
2013
KUNSTMUSEUM_MUSÉE D'ART_MUSEO DE ARTE
7,550 M²
PHOTOS COURTESY OF THE ARCHITECTS

Das neue Randers Kunstmuseum basiert auf der Grundannahme, dass sich ein gutes Museum einerseits extrovertiert zur Umgebung öffnet und sich andererseits introvertiert ganz auf das Erleben von Kunstwerken konzentriert. Das eingeschossige Museumsgebäude steigt an den Enden auf und wird im Ausstellungstrakt in voller Länge von einer Diagonalen mit Halbgeschoss durchzogen. Diese Diagonale bildet eine Brücke zwischen der ständigen Sammlung und dem Bereich der temporären Ausstellungen. Sie greift zugleich das Umfeld außerhalb des Baus auf, das sich von der Stadt Randers bis zum neuen Skulpturenpark am Fluss erstreckt.

Le nouveau musée de l'Art Randers repose sur l'hypothèse de base qu'un excellent musée extraverti à l'environnement est complètement introverti sur l'expérience des œuvres d'art. Le bâtiment du musée composé d'un étage avec extension aux extrémités est traversé par une diagonale comprenant une mezzanine sur l'ensemble de l'espace d'exposition. Cette diagonale forme un pont entre la collection permanente et la zone d'expositions tournantes. Ce tracé intérieur reprend l'environnement extérieur de la construction qui s'étend de la ville de Randers au nouveau parc de sculptures au bord de la rivière.

El novedoso Museo de Arte de Randers parte de la premisa de que un buen museo debe, por una parte, abrirse extrovertido hacia el entorno y, por la otra, concentrarse introvertido en la vivencia de las obras de arte. Este edificio museístico de una sola planta se eleva en los extremos y está surcado por una diagonal con medio nivel en toda la longitud de la exhibición. Esta diagonal constituye un puente entre la colección permanente y el área de exhibiciones temporarias. Este recorrido interior acaricia el entorno exterior que se extiende desde la ciudad de Randers hacia el nuevo parque de esculturas junto al río.

links: Skizze_Seitlicher Gang der Ausstellung_Innenraum. rechts: Außenbau_Museumsbau im Kontext.
gauche: Esquisse_Corridor latéral de l'exposition_Espace intérieur. droite: Extérieur_Musée dans son contexte.
izquierda: Esbozo_Pasillo lateral de la exhibición_Espacio interior. derecha: Vista exterior_El museo en su contexto.

DENMARK_TOREBY L. **FUGLSANG KUNSTMUSEUM**

DÄNEMARK_DANEMARK_DINAMARCA
TONY FRETTON ARCHITECTS
2008
KUNSTMUSEUM_MUSÉE D'ART_MUSEO DE ARTE
2,500 M^2
PHOTOS PETER COOK

Das niedrige Gebäude des neuen Museums fügt sich in die lose Folge ländlicher Gebäude ein. Wie die rote Scheune und Schmiede sich in die umliegende Landschaft erstrecken, dehnt sich auch das Museum in die Felder aus. Gleichzeitig steht es in axialem, wenn auch versetztem Bezug zum wichtigsten Gebäude, dem Herrenhaus, und seiner formalen Umgebung. Auch das Profil des Museums mit der Anordnung dreier diagonaler Oberlichter stellt eine Beziehung zwischen diesen beiden Bauten her. Die Fassaden des Museums sind aus Backstein errichtet. Wie in der Scheune an der Westseite des Hofes sind sie weiß gestrichen, während die Dachlichter, die die Farbe der Dächer der umliegenden Gebäude aufgreifen, aus grauem Stein bestehen.

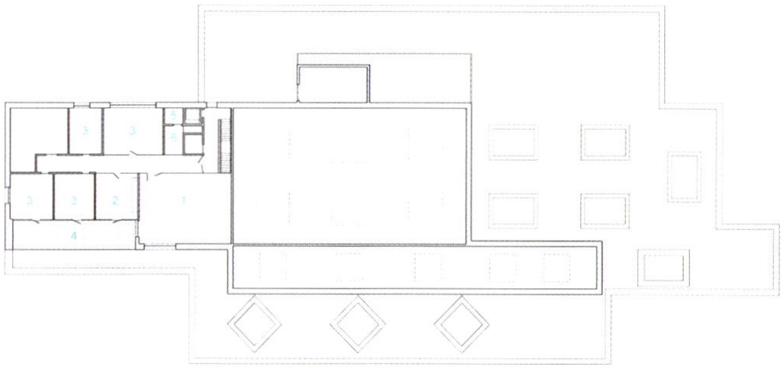

Le petit bâtiment du nouveau musée s'encastre dans la suite sans contrainte d'un bâtiment rural. A l'instar de la grange et de la forge de couleur rouge qui s'avancent dans le paysage environnant, le musée s'étend dans les champs. Il se situe simultanément dans le bâtiment axial décalé par rapport au bâtiment principal, la maison seigneuriale et son environnement formel. Le profil du musée avec la disposition de trois lumières diagonales supérieures établit un rapport entre ces deux constructions. Les façades du musée sont réalisées en brique. A l'instar de la grange située sur le côté occidental de la cour, elles sont peintes en blanc et contrastent avec la couleur des toits des bâtiments environnants en pierre grise.

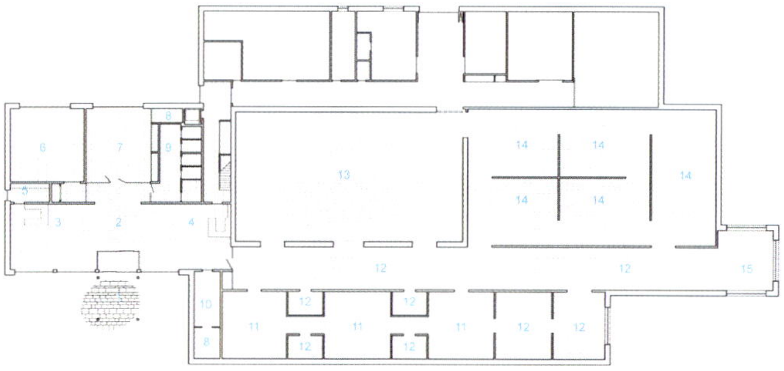

El edificio de baja altura del nuevo museo se inserta en la interminable secuencia de construcciones rurales. Del mismo modo que las viviendas y los graneros rojos se extienden por el paisaje circundante, también el museo se extiende hacia las praderas. Al mismo tiempo está vinculado de manera axial, si bien un poco desfasada, respecto de la casa solariega y su entorno formal. También el perfil del museo, con su disposición de tres lucernarios diagonales, constituye una conexión entre ambas edificaciones. Las fachadas del museo están elaboradas en ladrillo. Como en el granero del lado oeste, estas fachadas están pintadas de blanco, mientras que el techo de piedra gris evoca el color de los techos de las edificaciones circundantes.

links: Grundrisse_Südfassade. rechts: Ansicht aus Südwesten mit Eingangsbereich_Ansicht aus Südosten.
gauche: Plan_Façade sud. droite: Vue du sud-ouest avec la zone d'entrée_Vue du sud-est.
izquierda: Planos_Fachada sur. derecha: Vista desde el sudoeste con el área del acceso_Vista desde el sudeste.

FUGLSANG

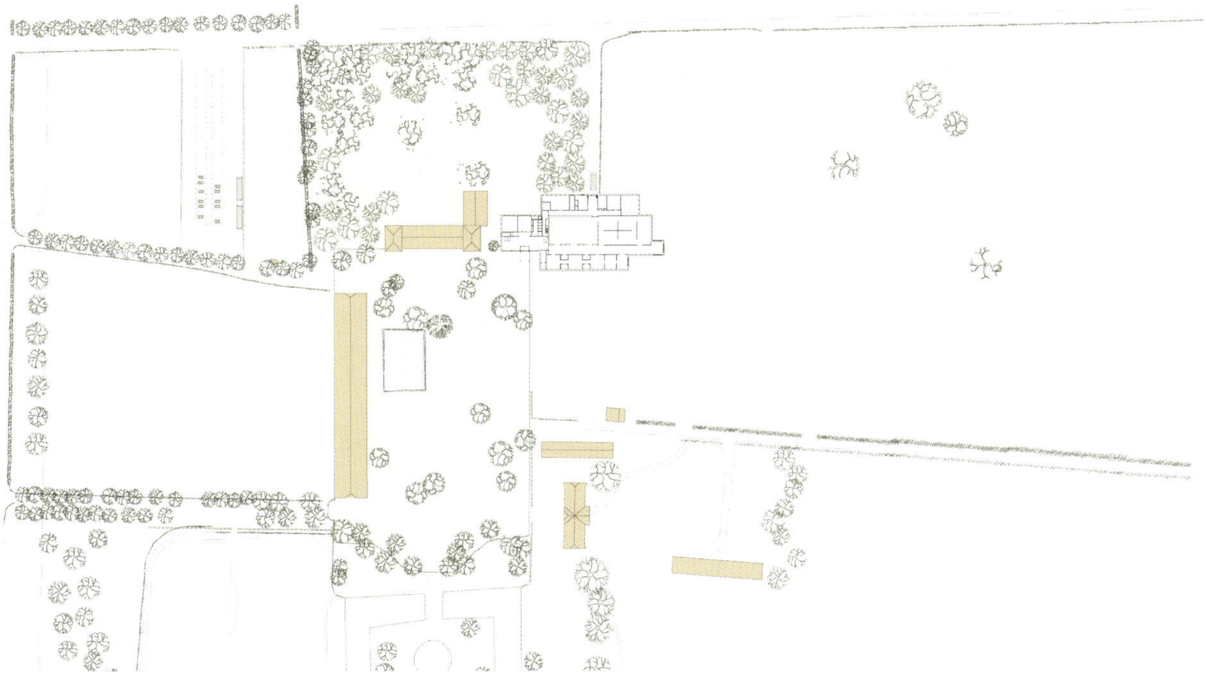

links: Natürliche Belichtung durch die Decke. rechts: Lageplan_Galerie mit strukturierter Decke und Schräge des Oberlichts_Ausstellungsraum_Hauptgalerie.
gauche: Éclairage naturel par le plafond. droite: Situation_Galerie avec le plafond décoré et les inclinaisons de la lumière en hauteur_Espace d'exposition_Galerie principale.
izquierda: Iluminación natural a través del techo. derecha: Ubicación_Galería con cielorraso decorado y lucernario oblicuo_Sala de exhibiciones_Galería principal.

ESTONIA_TALLINN **KUMU**

ESTLAND_ESTONIE_ESTONIA
VAPAAVUORI ARCHITECTS
2006
KUNSTMUSEUM_MUSÉE D'ART_MUSEO DE ARTE
23,900 M^2
PHOTOS JUSSI TIAINEN, HELSINKI

Das Grundstück mit einem 20 Meter hohen Kalksteinabhang befindet sich am südlichen Ende des Kadriorg-Park, drei Kilometer vom Zentrum von Tallinn entfernt. Das Museum wurde in diesen Abhang hinein teilweise unterirdisch errichtet, um den Park so wenig wie möglich anzutasten und die Auswirkungen eines derart großen Gebäudes auf die Umgebung zu reduzieren. Eine gebogene Mauer dient der Vereinheitlichung des Entwurfs: Außen fasst sie den Hof ein, im Inneren teilt sie die Funktionen voneinander ab. Die Ausstellungsräume sind einfach und bescheiden, sie lassen die Kunstwerke im Mittelpunkt stehen. Die Askese des Interieurs setzt sich auch am Außenbau fort, der ganz der Ausdruckskraft klarer geometrischer Formen vertraut. An der Hauptfassade dominieren Kalkstein, grün patiniertes Kupfer und Glas.

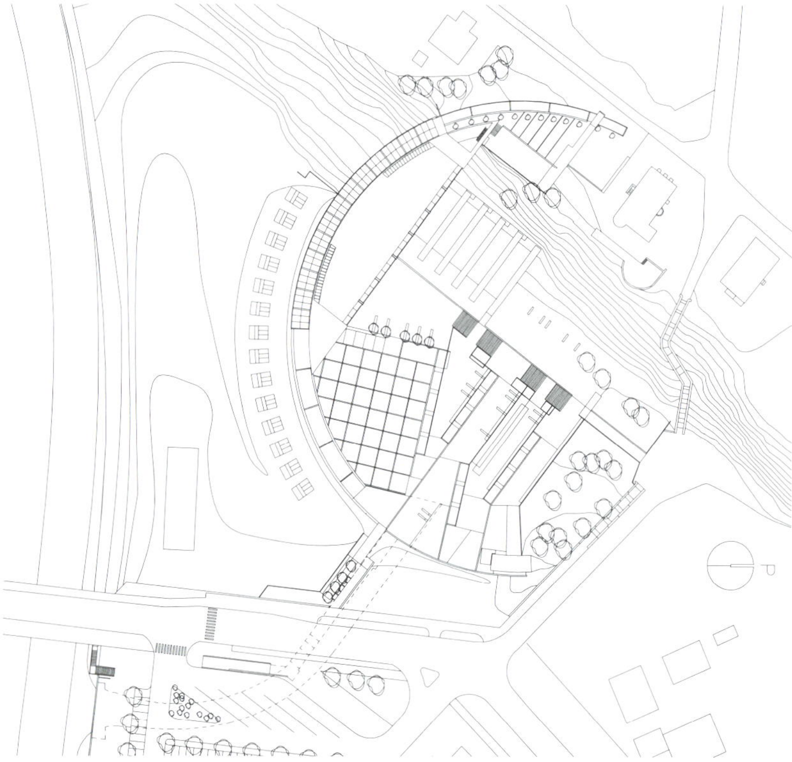

Le terrain caractérisé par une pente en pierre calcaire de 20 mètres de haut se situe aux confins Sud du parc Kadriorg, à trois kilomètres du centre de Tallinn. Le musée a été créé sur cette pente au-dessus et au-dessous du niveau de la terre afin de conserver au mieux l'aspect d'origine du parc et de réduire l'effet impact d'un bâtiment sur l'environnement. Un mur vouté contourne le musée autour d'une cour extérieure et nuance les fonctionnalités intérieures de l'espace. Les espaces d'exposition sont simples et modestes en présentant des œuvres d'art en premier plan. La simplicité ascétique adaptée à l'intérieur évolue à l'extérieur afin de traduire complètement la force d'expression claire des formes géométriques. Les matériaux dominant la façade principale sont la pierre calcaire, le cuivre patiné vert et le verre.

El terreno, con una escarpa de piedra caliza de 20 metros de alto, se encuentra en el extremo sur del parque Kadriorg, a tres kilómetros del centro de Tallinn. El museo fue levantado sobre esta escarpa y parcialmente bajo tierra, para tocar el parque lo menos posible y reducir los efectos en el entorno de un edificio tan grande. Un muro curvo envuelve el museo formando un patio exterior, y subdivide funciones en el interior. Las salas de exhibición son sencillas y discretas, y permiten apreciar las obras de arte en toda su relevancia. El ascetismo del interior se prolonga también en el exterior, que se juega a la fuerza expresiva de formas geométricas claras. En la fachada principal predominan como materiales la piedra caliza, el cobre patinado verde y el cristal.

links: Lageplan_Haupteingang_Eingang vom Hof. rechts: Haupteingang_Gestufter Hof mit Skulpturengarten_Durchgang.
gauche: Plan de site_Entrée principale_Entrée de la cour. droite: Entrée principale_Cour étagée avec son jardin de sculptures_Passage.
izquierda: Ubicación_Acceso principal_Acceso desde el patio. derecha: Acceso principal_Patio escalonado con jardín de esculturas_Pasaje.

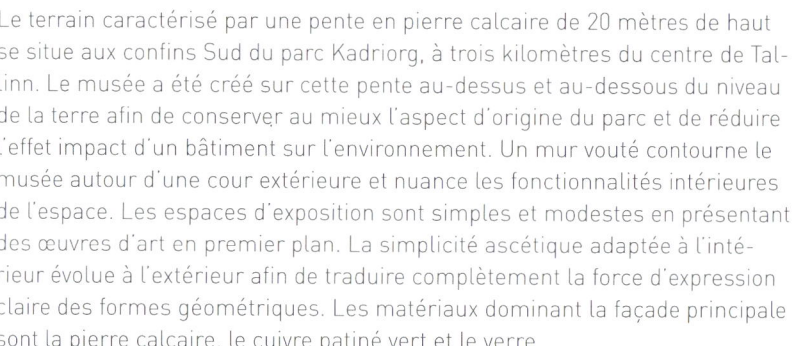

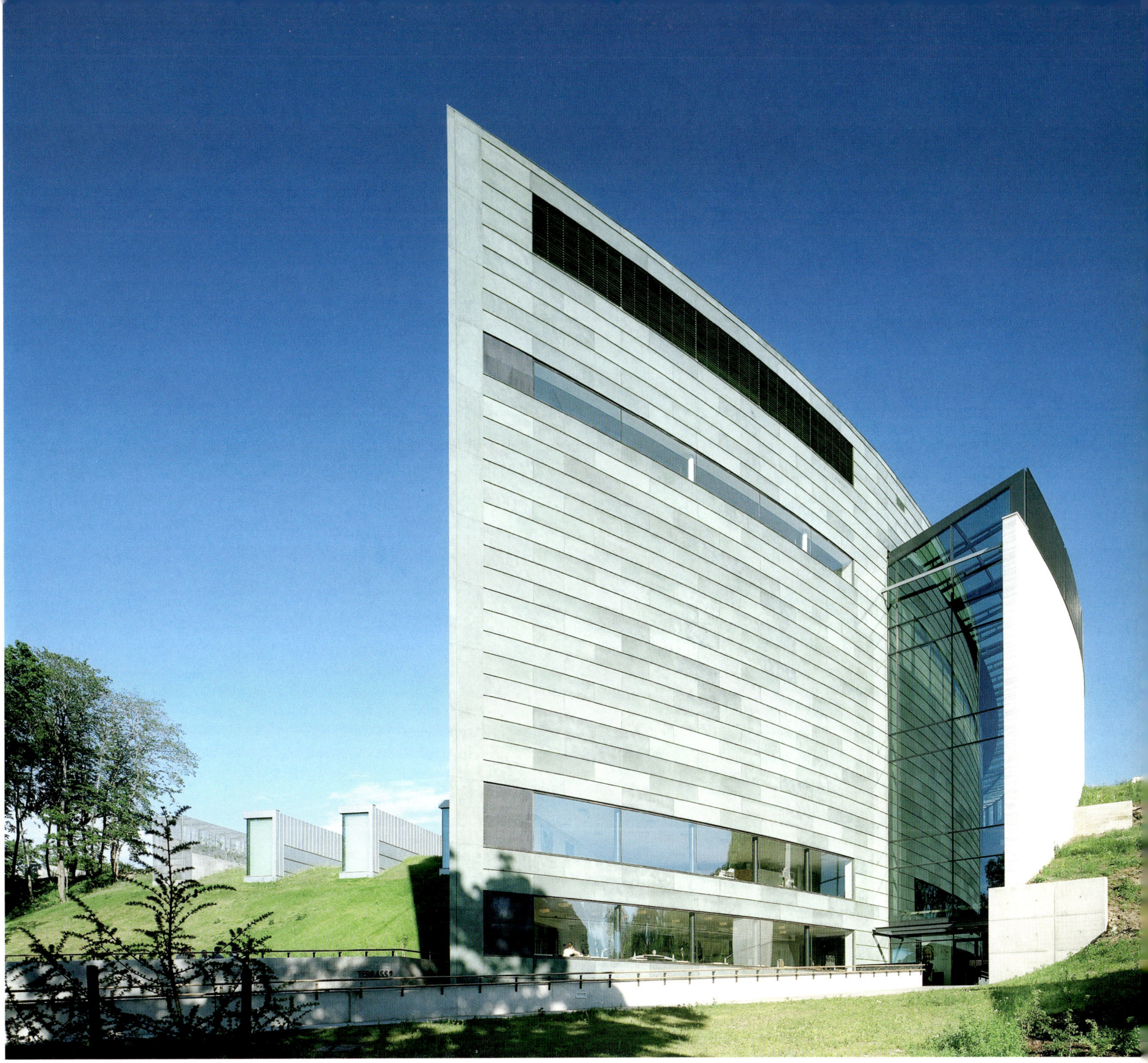

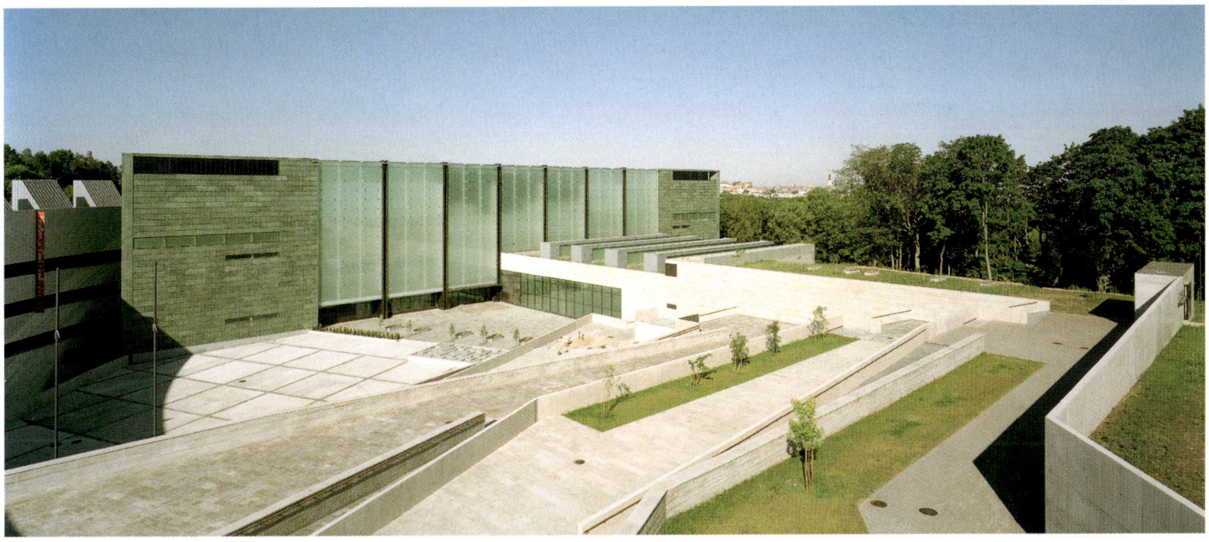

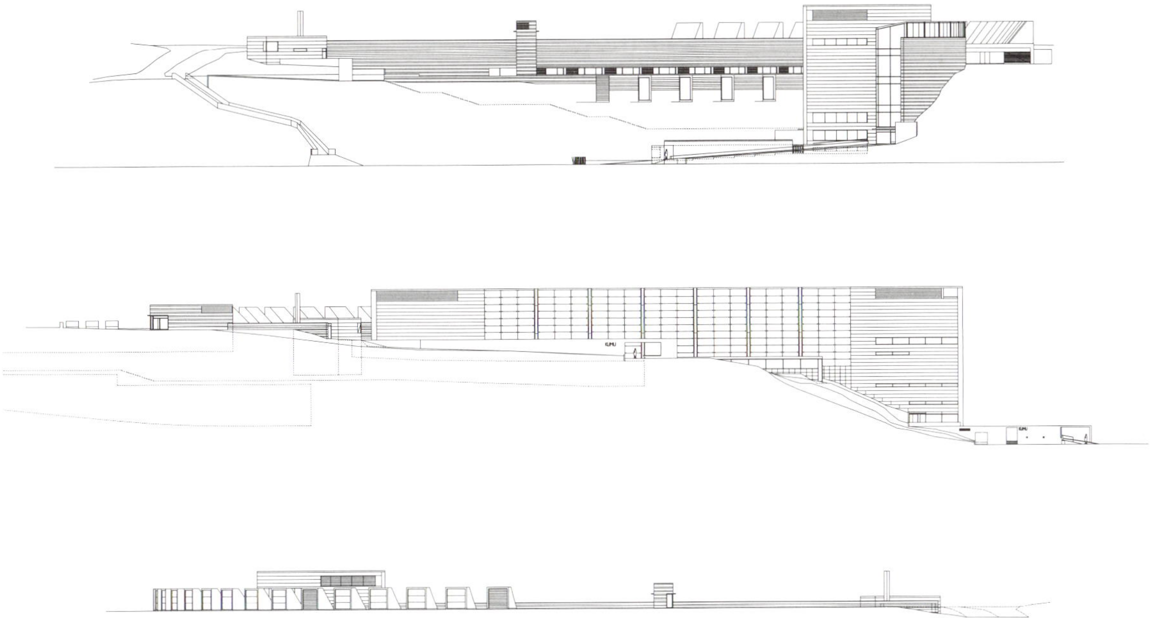

links: Ausstellungsraum. rechts: Aufrisse_Foyer_Wechselausstellungsraum_Detail Wechselausstellungsraum.
gauche: Espace d'exposition. droite: Vue en élévation_Foyer_Espace d'expositions alternantes_Détail de l'espace d'expositions alternantes.
izquierda: Sala de exhibiciones. derecha: Alzados_Vestíbulo_Sala de muestras temporarias_Detalle de la sala de muestras temporarias.

FRANCE_CALAIS

CITÉ INTERNATIONALE DE LA DENTELLE ET DE LA MODE DE CALAIS

FRANKREICH_FRANCE_FRANCIA
AGENCE MOATTI ET RIVIÈRE WITH FLINT
2009
MODEMUSEUM_MUSÉE DE LA MODE_MUSEO DE LA MODA
7,500 M²
PHOTOS MICHEL DENANCÉ, PARIS (186 B. L., 187 B.), AGENCE MOATTI ET RIVIÈRE, PARIS (186 B. R., 187 A.)

Das Projekt regt die Fantasie an und weist auf eine jahrhundertealte Tradition hin. Die neue Fassade der „Stadt der Spitzen und Mode" macht neugierig. Vom Kanal aus überformt sie die alte Mühle, füllt den Raum und reflektiert Bilder des Kanals und der Straßen anamorphotisch auf der konvexen und konkaven Fassade, als seien es Bilder sich wandelnder Zeiten. Die feinen Siebdruckmuster in metallischem Schmelzglas orientieren sich an der Perforation der Lochkarten für die Jacquardweberei, wie sie bei britischen Leaver-Webstühlen gebräuchlich waren. Im Laufe der Zeit wurden diese Hightech-Karten zu Artefakten.

Le projet permet d'éveiller l'imagination et renvoie à une tradition séculaire. La nouvelle façade de la « ville de la dentelle et de la mode » éveille la curiosité. A partir du canal, elle transcende l'ancien moulin, remplit l'espace et reflète des images du canal et des rues comme anamorphose sur la façade convexe et concave en donnant l'impression de représenter des images datant d'autres époques. Les motifs de sérigraphie sur le verre soufflé métallisé s'inspirent des perforations existantes dans les cartes perforées des tissages Jacquard utilisées dans les métiers à tisser britanniques Leaver. Au fil du temps, ces anciennes cartes de haute technologie devinrent désuètes.

El proyecto estimula la fantasía y evoca una tradición centenaria. La nueva fachada de la "Ciudad del encaje y la moda" despierta curiosidad. Vista desde el canal, transforma el antiguo molino, llena el espacio y refleja imágenes del canal y de las calles como anamorfismo en la fachada convexa y cóncava, como si se tratase de imágenes de otras épocas. La delicada textura serigrafiada en esmalte metálico evoca los orificios de las antiguas tarjetas perforadas para el tejido Jacquard, que se apreciaban en los telares británicos Leaver. Con el correr del tiempo, las tarjetas de alta tecnología se convirtieron en artefactos.

links: Masterplan_Fassade im Innenbereich_Detail der Glasfassade_Blick ins Innere. rechts: Detail der Fassade_Neue Glasfassade.
gauche: Plan de masse_Façade dans la zone intérieure_Détail de la façade en verre_Vue sur l'intérieur. droite: Détail de la façade_Nouvelle façade en verre.
izquierda: Plan maestro_Fachada en el área interior_Detalle de la fachada acristalada_Vista hacia el interior. derecha: Detalle de la fachada_Nueva fachada de cristal.

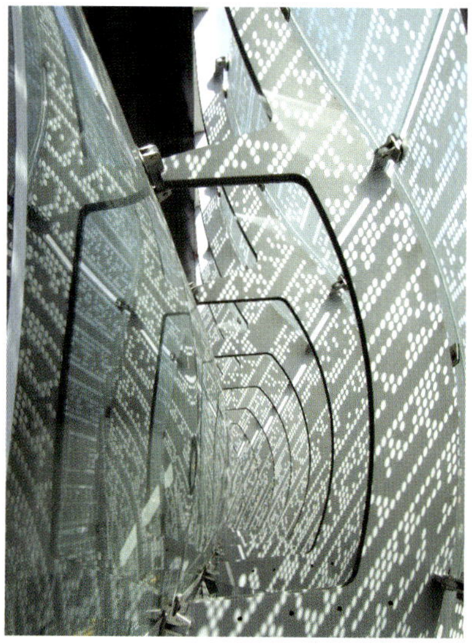

FRANCE_ERSTEIN **MUSÉE WÜRTH**

FRANKREICH_FRANCE_FRANCIA
JACQUES ET CLÉMENT VERGÉLY
2008
KUNSTMUSEUM_MUSÉE D'ART_MUSEO DE ARTE
3,416 M²
PHOTOS COURTESY OF THE ARCHITECTS

Das Museum ist ein zweistöckiger, rechteckiger Neubau aus glattem Rohbeton. Der Eingang zu den beiden 70 Meter langen Quadern befindet sich auf der Mittellinie des Gebäudes. Seitlich sind die Ausstellungssäle, die durch zwei Reihen Deckenfenster beleuchtet werden, angeordnet. Im „blinden" Mittelpunkt befindet sich ein Auditorium mit 224 Plätzen. Der Rohbeton und der schlichte weiße Putz stehen im Kontrast zu den Kunstobjekten. Durch zwei Lichtkästen auf dem Flachdach dringt Tageslicht in die Räume ein. Je nach Wetterbedingungen und Bedarf kann dieses Licht geregelt und dosiert werden. Mit Rollläden und eingebauter künstlicher Beleuchtung lassen sich kalte und warme Farbtöne erzeugen.

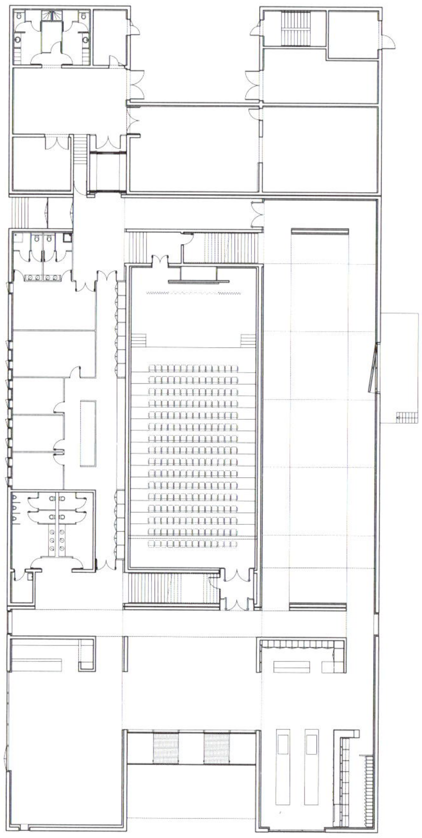

Le musée est un nouveau bâtiment rectangulaire à deux étages en béton brut et lisse. L'entrée des deux rectangles, longue de 70 mètres, se situe à la médiane du bâtiment. Les salles d'exposition sont disposées de chaque côté et éclairées grâce à deux rangées de fenêtres de toit. Au centre « aveugle » se situe un auditorium de 224 places. Le béton brut et le crépi blanc et simple contrastent avec les objets artistiques. Deux caissons de lumière installés sur le toit plat permettent à la lumière naturelle de pénétrer dans les espaces. Le réglage et le dosage de cette lumière sont possibles en fonction des conditions d'éclairage et des conditions climatiques. Les stores et l'éclairage artificiel intégré permettent de créer des teintes chaudes ou froides.

El museo es una edificación rectangular en dos niveles, construida en hormigón visto liso. El acceso al volumen de 70 metros de longitud se encuentra en la línea central de la construcción. A los lados se encuentran las salas de exhibiciones; las mismas están iluminadas por dos hileras de lucernarios. En el punto medio, "ciego", se alberga un auditorio con 224 butacas. El hormigón visto y el sobrio revoco blanco contrastan con las obras de arte expuestas. Dos lucernarios en el techo plano permiten que la luz natural penetre en las salas. Según las condiciones climáticas y las necesidades, se puede regular y dosificar la iluminación. Con persianas e iluminación artificial incorporada se pueden lograr coloraciones cálidas y frías, a discreción.

links: Grundriss Erdgeschoss_Haupteingang_Skulpturenhof. rechts: Dämmerung_Ausstellungssaal_Ausstellungssaal.
gauche: Plan du rez-de-chaussée_Entrée principale_Cour des sculptures. droite: Crépuscule_Salle d'exposition_Salle d'exposition.
izquierda: Plano de planta baja_Acceso principal_Patio de esculturas. derecha: Crepúsculo_Sala de exhibiciones_Sala de exhibiciones.

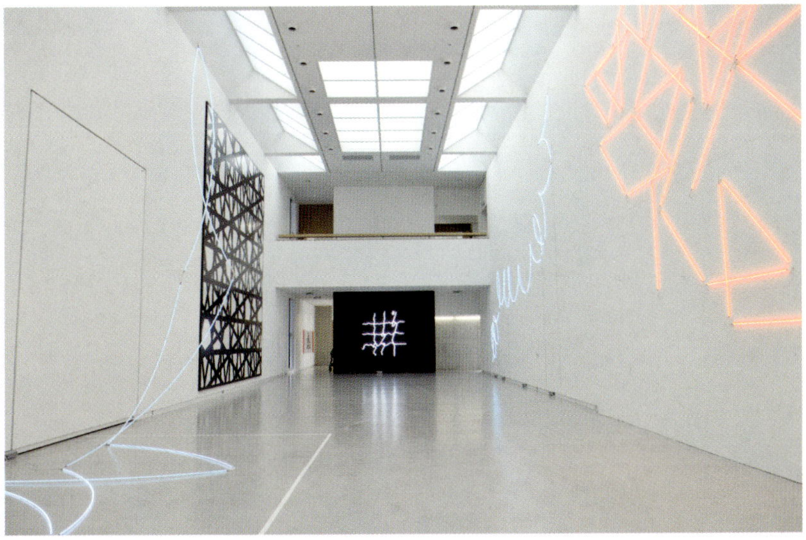

FRANCE_FIGEAC **MUSÉE CHAMPOLLION**

FRANKREICH_FRANCE_FRANCIA
AGENCE MOATTI ET RIVIÈRE
2007
ARCHÄOLOGIEMUSEUM_MUSÉE DE L'ARCHÉOLOGIE
MUSEO DE ARQUEOLOGÍA
1,300 M²
PHOTOS LUC BOEGLY, PARIS (190 B., 191, 192, 193 L. A., R.),
AGENCE MOATTI ET RIVIÈRE, PARIS (193 L. B.)

Das Museum ist auf drei Gebäude in der historischen Altstadt verteilt. Die Schirmfassade am Platz Champollion macht das Museum kenntlich: Sie zeigt mittels animierter Alphabete eine Metapher auf Schrift und Entschlüsselung. Dieses „vielsprachige typografische Fenstergitter" ist ein poetischer, von vibrierendem Licht inspirierter Ausdruck der Modernität. Die alte Steinfassade führt das städtische Gefüge fort, während die Schirmfassade als Komposition aus Glas und Kupfer dahinterliegt. Die Loggien zwischen diesen beiden Fassaden sind der Öffentlichkeit zugänglich, und oben befindet sich ein aus der ländlichen Architektur der Region entlehntes „Soleilo". Der Raum zwischen den Fassaden bildet einen Übergang vom öffentlichen Raum des Marktplatzes zum Museum.

Le musée se situe dans trois bâtiments appartenant à l'ancienne ville historique. La façade en écran donne sur la place Champollion et signale le musée : en effet, grâce à des alphabets animés, elle affiche une métaphore d'écriture et de décodage. Cette grille de fenêtres polyglotte sous forme typographique est une expression de la modernité poétique et inspirée par les vibrations de lumière animées. L'ancienne façade en pierre se poursuit dans la continuité de la structure citadine devant la façade en écran composée de verre et cuivre. Entre les deux façades, les loggias sont accessibles au public et sont surplombées par un « Soleilo » emprunté à l'architecture rurale de la région. L'espace intermédiaire des façades forme une transition entre l'espace public de la place du marché et le musée.

El museo ocupa tres edificaciones del casco histórico. La fachada —una pantalla sobre la plaza Champollion— lo hace inconfundible: sus alfabetos animados son una metáfora de la escritura y su decodificación. Esta especie de reja tipográfica políglota es una expresión luminosa, poética, vívida y vibrante de la modernidad. La antigua fachada de piedra es una prolongación del tejido urbano, mientras que la fachada-pantalla es una composición de cristal y cobre ubicada detrás. Entre ambas fachadas hay arcadas accesibles al público, y por encima se encuentra el "soleilo", tomado de las referencias arquitectónicas regionales. El espacio intermedio de las fachadas constituye una transición entre espacio público de la plaza del mercado y el museo.

links: Gesamtplan_Ausstellung, Mittelmeerraum. rechts: Nachtansicht Fassade.
gauche: Plan de site_Exposition dans la salle méditerranée. droite: Vue de nuit de la façade.
izquierda: Plano de conjunto_Exhibición, sala del Mediterráneo. derecha: Vista nocturna de la fachada.

FNAIM

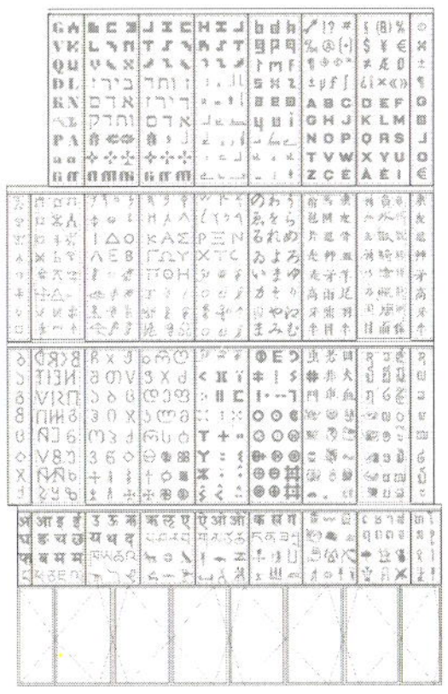

links: Fassadendetail. rechts: Aufrisse_Detail zwischen den Fassaden_Das Museum in seiner Umgebung bei Nacht_Fassade.
gauche: Détail de la façade. droite: Vues en élévation_Détail entre les façades_Le musée dans son environnement la nuit_Façade.
izquierda: Detalle de fachada. derecha: Alzados_Detalle entre las fachadas_El museo y su entorno por la noche_Fachada.

FRANCE_LENS **LOUVRE-LENS**

FRANKREICH_FRANCE_FRANCIA
SANAA
2012
KUNSTMUSEUM_MUSÉE D'ART_MUSEO DE ARTE
33,000 M²
PHOTOS FRANCIS BOCQUET (194 A.), KAZUYO SEJIMA + RYUE NISHIZAWA / SANAA, TIM CULBERT + CELIA IMREY / IMREY CULBERT, CATHERINE MOSBACH

Das Gebäudevolumen wird in kleine Einheiten aufgebrochen, um einerseits das Grundstück nicht zu verstellen und andererseits das umfangreiche Bauprogramm in übersichtlichere Bereiche aufzuspalten. In Dimension und Anordnung greift es die umliegenden Bastionen auf dem sanften Hang auf. Der zentrale Gebäudeteil aus Glas, zugleich Eingangsbereich und großer öffentlicher Raum, konstituiert einen Leerraum zwischen den Baukörpern, der es ermöglicht, das Museum zu queren, ohne es zu betreten. Um Natur und Gebäude zu verschmelzen, wurde die Fassade mit stark reflektierendem, poliertem und eloxiertem Aluminium verkleidet. Den ruhigen Kurven der Volumina folgend, spiegelt sie die Umgebung verschwommen wider und verändert sich entsprechend der Landschaft, dem Wetter und der Position des Besuchers ständig.

Le volume du bâtiment est réparti en petites unités afin de ne pas cacher le terrain et de scinder le vaste programme de construction en zones dégagées. La dimension et disposition rappellent les bastions environnants situés sur la pente douce. La partie centrale du bâtiment vitrifiée servant simultanément de zone d'entrée et de grand espace public, constitue un espace vide entre les corps de construction qui permet de traverser le musée sans y accéder. La nature et le bâtiment fusionnent au niveau de la façade en aluminium poli et anodisé, très réflectrice, réfléchissant les courbes tranquilles du volume et les reflets de l'environnement qui évoluent en fonction du paysage, du temps et de la position du visiteur.

El volumen edilicio se desagrega en pequeñas unidades. Por un lado, se evita mover terreno, por otro, se puede subdividir el vasto programa arquitectónico en ámbitos más nítidos. Dimensión y disposición caracterizan a los bastiones distribuidos por la suave pendiente. La edificación central acristalada, que reúne el ámbito de acceso y un gran espacio público, constituye un vacío entre los volúmenes que posibilita atravesar el museo pero sin ingresar propiamente al mismo. Naturaleza y edificación se funden en la fachada de aluminio pulido y anodizado altamente reflectante, que acompaña las suaves curvas de los volúmenes, refleja el difuso entorno y cambia continuamente el paisaje y el clima a los ojos del visitante que pasea.

links: Luftaufnahme_Außenbau_Innenraum. rechts: Außenbereich_Panoramaansicht der Halle.
gauche: Vue aérienne_Extérieur_Espace intérieur. droite: Espace extérieur_Vue panoramique du hall.
izquierda: Vista aérea_Exterior_Espacio interior. derecha: Área exterior_Vista panorámica de la sala.

FRANCE_MOUANS-SARTOUX **ESPACE DE L'ART CONCRET (EAC)**

FRANKREICH_FRANCE_FRANCIA
ANNETTE GIGON / MIKE GUYER, ARCHITEKTEN
2003
KUNSTMUSEUM_MUSEÉE D'ART_MUSEO DE ARTE
1,829 M²
PHOTOS SERGE DEMAILLY

Der Neubau befindet sich in unmittelbarer Nachbarschaft des kleinen Schlosses von Mouans-Sartoux an der steilen Waldböschung des umgebenden Parks. Auskragungen des turmartigen Gebäudes mit kleiner Standfläche vergrößern die Ausstellungsfläche und bilden am Hang verschiedene ebenerdige Zugänge aus. Spiralförmig aufsteigende Treppen verbinden die halbgeschossig versetzten Ausstellungsräume miteinander. Das Licht tritt durch seitlich angeordnete Fenster in den Raum, beleuchtet die Werke und ermöglicht den Blick auf die Baumkronen und die Stadt. Den Moos- und Algenbefall durch die nahe stehenden Bäume antizipierend, ist die tragende Betonstruktur mit gelbgrüner Mineralfarbe gestrichen.

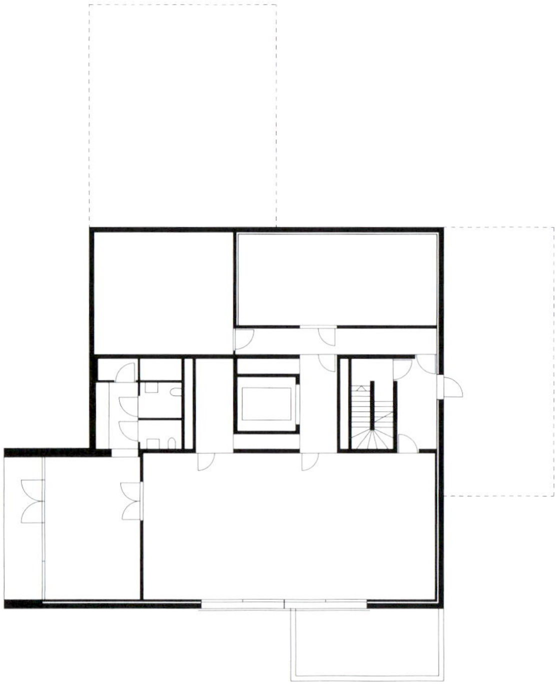

Ce nouveau bâtiment se situe à proximité immédiate du petit château de Mouans-Sartoux sur la pente boisée abrupte du parc environnant. Les saillies du bâtiment en forme de tour avec ses petits miradors agrandissent la surface d'exposition. Différents accès sont intégrés en terre-plein au niveau de la pente. Les escaliers en colimaçon relient les espaces d'exposition supérieurs, décalés à chaque demi-étage. La lumière pénètre par les fenêtres rangées latéralement dans l'espace et éclaire les œuvres d'art. A ce niveau, la vue sur les couronnes d'arbres et sur la ville est fantastique. La structure porteuse en béton est réalisée dans une teinte minérale vert-jaune afin d'anticiper le recouvrement prévisible par la mousse et les autres végétaux en raison des arbres situés à proximité.

La construcción nueva se yergue en las inmediaciones del pequeño castillo de Mouans-Sartoux, en una escarpadísima cuesta del parque circundante. La superficie de exhibición se ve incrementada gracias a volúmenes que sobresalen de este edificio en forma de torre y conforman diversos accesos a nivel en la ladera. Escalinatas que suben en espiral conectan las salas de exhibición dispuestas a medios niveles. La luz penetra a las salas por ventanas laterales, ilumina las obras y posibilita una hermosa vista de las copas de los árboles y, a lo lejos, la ciudad. Anticipándose a la formación de musgo y algas que tarde o temprano ocasionarán los árboles vecinos, la estructura portante de hormigón ha sido recubierta con pintura mineral amarillo-verdosa.

links: Grundriss 1. Obergeschoss_Haupteingang in der Dämmerung_Gebäude am Hang. rechts: Haupteingang_Ausstellungsraum_Bezug zum Außenraum.
gauche: Plan 1er étage_Entrée principale au crépuscule_Bâtiment situé sur la pente. droite: Entrée principale_Espace d'exposition_Vue depuis l'espace extérieur.
izquierda: Plano del primer piso_Acceso principal al atardecer_Edificio en la ladera. derecha: Acceso principal_Sala de exhibiciones_Vinculación con el exterior.

FRANCE_PARIS **PALAIS DE TOKYO**

FRANKREICH_FRANCE_FRANCIA
LACATON & VASSAL
2001
KUNSTMUSEUM_MUSÉE D'ART_MUSEO DE ARTE
7,800 M²
PHOTOS CHRIS VAN UFFELEN (198 B. L., 199 B. L., B. R.),
PHILIPPE RUAULT (198 B. R., 199 A.)

Bei dem Umbau sollte kein in sich abgeschlossenes Museum, sondern ein offener Veranstaltungsort entstehen. Es wurde ein großer Freiraum ohne Begrenzungen, Einbauten und Zwänge geschaffen, der einer Platzanlage entspricht. Der sehr lang gestreckte Betonbau von 1937 wurde im Inneren entkleidet und erscheint nun roh und industriell. Am Außenbau wurden leicht wirkende Bauteile wie Treppen und Stege hinzugefügt. Sie reduzieren die Monumentalität des Ursprungsbaus und entsprechen dem temporären Charakter der zeitgenössischen Kunstinstallationen im Inneren. Hinter den monumentalen Fassaden erinnert das Innere an eine imposante Industriebrache. Durch die großen Atrien und Fenster flutet das Tageslicht gleichmäßig in den Ausstellungsraum.

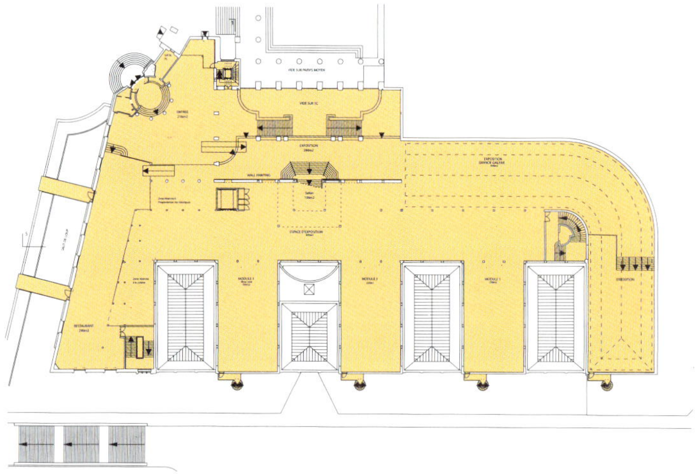

Lors de la transformation, le musée ambitionnait à devenir un centre de manifestations ouvert à tous, doté d'un grand espace libre sans démarcations, cloisonnements, mobiliers ou contraintes. Le lieu doit ressembler à une place. La structure en béton très élancée de 1937 fut mise à nu à l'intérieur, dans un aspect paraissant désormais brut et industriel. A l'extérieur, il fut ajouté des éléments architecturaux légers, notamment des escaliers et passerelles qui permettent d'atténuer la monumentalité de l'édifice d'origine, à l'intérieur, dans l'esprit du caractère provisoire de l'installation du site d'art contemporain. Derrière les façades monumentales, l'intérieur du bâtiment ressemble à une friche industrielle magnifique et la lumière naturelle permanente et généreuse jaillit dans l'espace d'exposition grâce aux grandes verrières et larges baies disposées sur les façades.

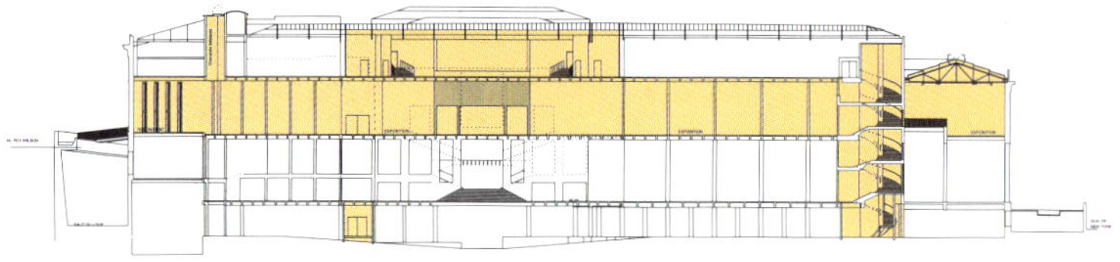

Esta reforma no podía dar lugar a un museo cerrado, sino a un centro de actividades abierto. Se logró un gran espacio libre sin limitaciones ni obstáculos, que equivale a una plaza pública. El alargado edificio en hormigón de 1937 fue despojado en sus interiores y aparece ahora crudo e industrial. En los exteriores se agregaron algunos componentes como escaleras y pasarelas. Reducen la monumentalidad de la construcción original y corresponden al carácter temporario de las instalaciones artísticas contemporáneas en el interior. Detrás de las monumentales fachadas, el interior del edificio recuerda una imponente factoría; a través de los grandes atrios y ventanas de las fachadas la luz diurna penetra hacia el espacio de exhibición de manera pareja y grandiosa.

links: Grundriss 2. Obergeschoss und Schnitt der Ausstellungsebene_Außenbau_Ausstellungshalle. rechts: Ausstellungsebene_Ausstellungshalle_Buchshop.
gauche: Plan et coupe du niveau exposition_Extérieur_Salle d'exposition. droite: Niveau d'exposition_Hall d'exposition_Librairie.
izquierda: Planos y cortes del nivel de exhibiciones_Vista exterior_Sala de exhibiciones. derecha: Nivel de exhibiciones_Sala de exhibiciones_Librería.

BY
AN
orman Inc.
PARTICIPEZ À L'AVENIR DE L'ART

FRANCE_PARIS **MUSÉE DU QUAI BRANLY**

FRANKREICH_FRANCE_FRANCIA
ATELIERS JEAN NOUVEL
2006
KULTURMUSEUM_MUSÉE DE LA CULTURE_MUSEO DE LA CULTURA
76,500 M²
PHOTOS PHILIPPE RUAULT

Das Gebäude befindet sich in einer 18.000 Quadratmeter großen Gartenanlage. Diese erstreckt sich auch unter dem ersten Stockwerk, da das Erdgeschossniveau zu großen Teilen unbebaut bleibt. Eine 12 Meter hohe und 200 Meter lange gläserne Wand schirmt die Anlage zum Quai Branly ab und greift die Straßenflucht auf. Über einen komplexen Weg gelangt man in die Ausstellungsräume und Kabinette des Hauptgebäudes. Diese sind an der gläsernen Nordfassade als farbige Kuben im Außenbereich sichtbar. Horizontale Fensterreihen prägen die rot-braune Südfassade des Museums. Das zentrale Element dieser Fassade bildet ein gerundetes Bauteil mit drei Fensterreihen.

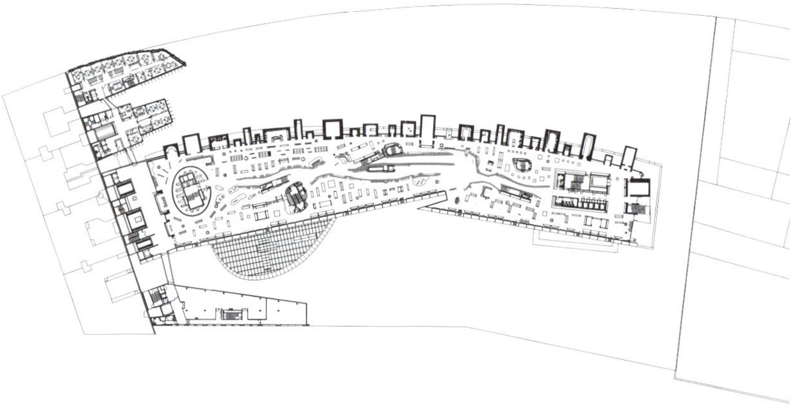

Le bâtiment se situe dans un vaste parc de 18 000 mètres carrés qui s'étend également sous le rez-de-chaussée, resté majoritairement non aménagé. Un mur vitré de 12 mètres de haut sur 200 mètres de long protège le site du Quai Branly et accompagne l'avenue. Les espaces d'exposition et les cabinets du bâtiment principal sont accessibles par un chemin complexe. Ils se présentent à travers la façade Nord vitrifiée comme des cubes colorés dans l'espace extérieur. Les rangées horizontales de fenêtres caractérisent la façade Sud du musée de couleur marron/rouge. L'élément central de cette façade forme un composant arrondi marqué par les trois rangées de fenêtres.

El edificio se levanta dentro de una superficie ajardinada de 18.000 metros cuadrados. La misma se extiende también por debajo de la planta baja, que en gran parte permanece sin edificar. Un muro acristalado de 12 metros de alto y 200 metros de longitud protege las instalaciones que se vuelcan hacia el Quai Branly. Por un complejo camino se llega hacia las salas de exhibiciones y los gabinetes del edificio principal. Los mismos son visibles desde fuera, a través de la acristalada fachada norte, en forma de cubos coloridos. Hileras de ventanas horizontales caracterizan la fachada sur del museo, roja y marrón. El elemento central de esta fachada lo constituye un componente constructivo redondeado con tres hileras de ventanas.

links: Grundriss 1. Obergeschoss_Fassade. rechts: Hauptfassade und Glasschirm_Ausstellung Ausstellungsraum.
gauche: Plan du premier étage_Façade. droite: Façade principale et écran de verre_Exposition Espace d'exposition.
izquierda: Plano del primer piso_Fachada. derecha: Fachada principal y pantalla de vidrio_Exposición_Sala de exhibiciones.

19/06/07-16/09/07
Ideqqi
Art de femmes berbères
03/04/07 - 08/07/07
Jardin d'amour
Installation de Yinka Shonibare, MBE

FRANCE_RENNES **ÉCOMUSÉE DU PAYS DE RENNES**

FRANKREICH_FRANCE_FRANCIA
GUINEE*POTIN ARCHITECTS
2010
NATURKUNDEMUSEUM_MUSÉE DE L'HISTOIRE NATURELLE
MUSEO DE HISTORIA NATURAL
990 M²
PHOTOS S CHALMEAU, NANTES

Das Museum stimmt mit seiner Fassade aus Holz auf das Thema „Öko-Museum" ein und macht das Gebäude zu einem Wahrzeichen. Die Erweiterung des bestehenden Gebäudes umfasst eine neue Eingangshalle und den Wechselausstellungsbereich in Holzfachwerk und mit Holzverkleidung. An der Südseite setzt sich das Fachwerk von einer Sockelzone aus ökologischem, mit natürlichen Pigmenten durchgefärbten Beton ab. Die Holzverkleidung darüber besteht aus Naturholzschindeln (Kastanie), die ein grafisches Muster bilden. Die Rundpfeiler sind aus unbearbeiteten Baumstämmen gefertigt, während möglichst viele Bäume auf dem Gelände erhalten blieben.

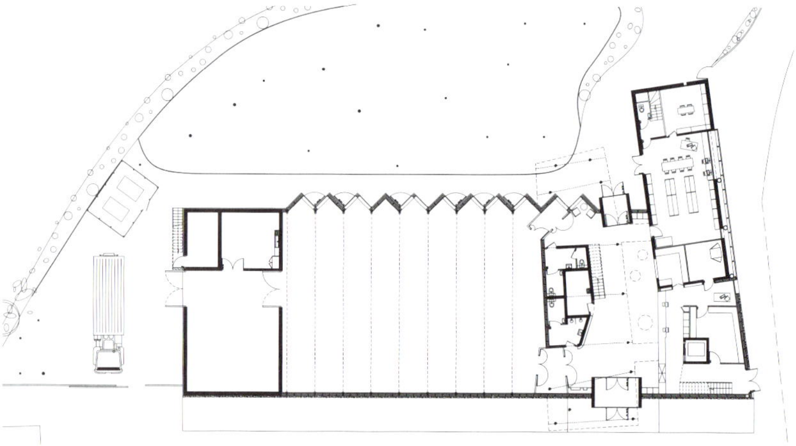

Le musée sensibilise à « l'écologie » grâce à sa façade en bois qui rend le site emblématique. L'extension du bâtiment existant comprend un nouveau hall d'entrée et des zones d'expositions alternantes caractérisées par une charpente en bois et son boisage. Sur la partie Sud, la charpente contraste avec la partie du socle en béton écologique colorée par des pigments naturels. Le boisage est constitué de barbeaux en bois naturel (châtaignier) positionnés selon un modèle graphique particulier. Les colonnes rondes sont réalisées en troncs d'arbres non usinés qui optimisent cependant la conservation de nombreux arbres sur le terrain avoisinant.

Con su fachada de madera, el museo está a tono con el tema "ecomuseo" y convierte el edificio en un verdadero símbolo. La ampliación del edificio existente comprende una nueva sala de acceso y el área de exhibiciones temporarias con estructura de entramado y recubrimiento de madera. En la fachada sur, el entramado se compone de una zona de basamento de hormigón ecológico coloreado con pigmentos naturales. El recubrimiento de madera encima del mismo consiste en ripias de madera de castaño natural con un diseño gráfico. Los pilares redondos se elaboraron a partir de troncos sin pulir, y se procuró conservar la mayor cantidad posible de los árboles existentes en el terreno.

links: Grundriss Erdgeschoss_Hauptansicht_Umfeld. rechts: Eingang_Ausstellungsraum_Nordfassade.
gauche: Plan du rez-de-chaussée_Vue générale_Contexte. droite: Entrée_Espace d'exposition_Façade nord.
izquierda: Plano de planta baja_Fachada principal_Entorno. derecha: Acceso_Sala de exhibiciones_Fachada norte.

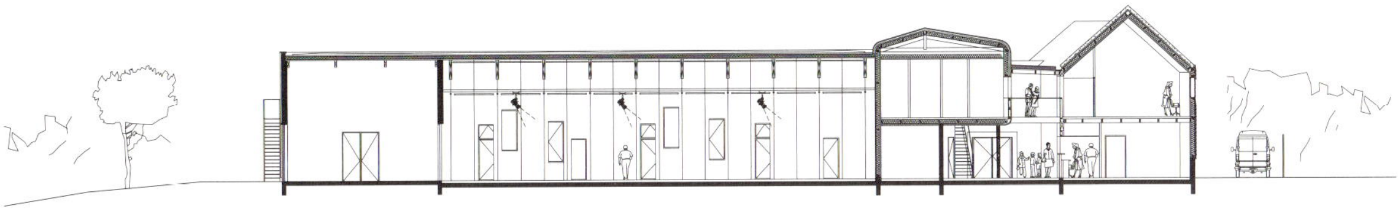

links: Eingangsbereich und Treppe. rechts: Schnitt_Eingangshalle.
gauche: Zone d'entrée et escalier. droite: Coupe_Hall d'entrée.
izquierda: Área de acceso y escalera. derecha: Corte_Sala de acceso.

FRANCE_SABRES **ÉCOMUSÉE DE LA GRANDE LANDE**

FRANKREICH_FRANCE_FRANCIA
BRUNO MADER ARCHITECTE
2008
NATURKUNDEMUSEUM_MUSEE DE L'HISTOIRE NATURELLE
MUSEO DE HISTORIA NATURAL
2,860 M²
PHOTOS GASTON F. BERGERET, PARIS

Als wichtigster Bau des Gesamtprojekts entwickelt der Pavillon der „Landes de Gascogne" eine moderne Architektur, die auf den lokalen Kontext Bezug nimmt. Trotz der Größe und einer amorphen architektonischen Form integriert er sich reibungslos in die Umgebung, indem er die Linearität der Gleise, das Volumen der einzeln stehenden Häuser und die Bretterfassaden der traditionellen Schuppen aufgreift. Je nach Blickwinkel kann er als ein Gebäude mit geschmeidigen, breit lagernden Formen oder als Verbindung mehrerer Bauten gelesen werden, das die Massenverteilung des Bahnhofs und der Stadt Sabres aufgreift.

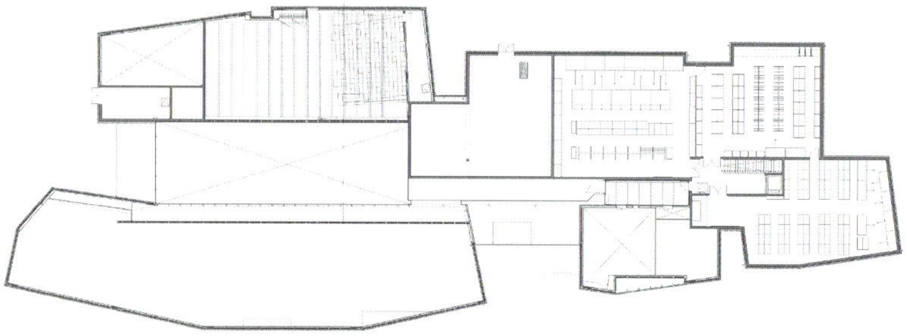

Le pavillon du « Pays de Gascogne » développe une architecture moderne reprise sur le contexte de la région afin de réaliser la plus importante construction du projet principal. Malgré la dimension et la forme architectonique amorphe, il s'intègre sans heurts dans l'environnement grâce à sa composition basée sur la linéarité des rails qui rappelle les volumes des pavillons individuels et les façades en planches des hangars. A partir des perspectives différentes, il peut s'assimiler à un bâtiment grâce à ses formes souples largement supportées ou à une jonction de plusieurs constructions qui fait référence à la répartition des masses de la gare et de la ville de Sabres.

El pabellón de las "Landas de Gascuña" presenta una moderna arquitectura que capta el contexto local; el mismo constituye la construcción más importante del conjunto proyectual. A pesar del tamaño y del lenguaje arquitectónico amorfo, se integra sin conflictos en el entorno, en tanto su composición adopta la linealidad de las vías, el volumen de las casas de familia y las fachadas de tablas de madera de los graneros. Desde diferentes ángulos visuales se puede apreciar un edificio de formas muy amplias y flexibles, o bien se puede interpretar como una conexión visual entre varias edificaciones que comprenden la distribución de volúmenes de la estación de trenes y de la ciudad de Sabres.

links: 1. Obergeschoss_Anblick von Westen_Wechselausstellungsraum_Blick aus dem Wechselausstellungsraum. rechts: Außenansicht von Westen_Ansicht von Süden.
gauche: Premier étage_Vue à l'ouest_Espace des expositions tournantes_Vue de l'espace des expositions tournantes. droite: Vue extérieure à l'ouest_Vue au sud.
izquierda: Primer piso_Vista desde el oeste_Sala de muestras temporarias_Vista desde la sala de exhibiciones temporarias. derecha: Vista exterior desde el oeste_Vista desde el sur.

FRANCE_SAINT-OURS-LES-ROCHES **VULCANIA**

FRANKREICH_FRANCE_FRANCIA
HANS HOLLEIN
2002
NATURKUNDEMUSEUM_MUSEE DE L'HISTOIRE NATURELLE
MUSEO DE HISTORIA NATURAL
4,700 M^2
PHOTOS ATELIER HOLLEIN / SINA BANIAHMAT
(208, 209, 210, 211 A . R., B. R.),
VUCANIA /JOEL DAMASE (211 B. L.)

Vulcania ist das weltweit erste moderne vulkanologische Zentrum. In der Auvergne zwischen erloschenen Vulkanen gelegen, dient es der Information, Forschung und Lehre sowie dem direkten Erlebnis der ursprünglichen Gewalten der Natur und der Entstehung unseres Planeten. Die vorwiegend unterirdischen Räume betritt man über eine lange Rampe, die hinab in einen metaphorischen Vulkankrater führt. Der Konus ist außen mit dunklem Lavagestein gedeckt und innen mit goldfarben schimmernden Metallplatten ausgekleidet. Vulcania dient auch der professionellen Erforschung von Vulkanen und verfügt über Einrichtungen für wissenschaftliche Untersuchungen und Konferenzen sowie über ein IMAX-Theater und Gewächshäuser.

Vulcania est le premier centre moderne au monde consacré à la vulcanologie. Situé en Auvergne parmi les volcans éteints, ce centre est une plateforme pour l'information, la recherche et l'enseignement ainsi qu'une expérience directe vécue de la violence originaire de la nature et de la genèse de notre planète. Les espaces principalement souterrains sont accessibles par une longue rampe qui descend dans un cratère volcanique métaphorique. Le cône est recouvert de pierre de lave foncée à l'extérieur et d'un revêtement en plaques métalliques dorées et miroitantes à l'intérieur. Vulcania sert également à étudier de manière professionnelle les volcans et dispose d'espaces dédiés à la recherche et aux conférences ainsi qu'un théâtre IMAX et des serres.

Vulcania es el primer centro vulcanológico moderno a nivel mundial. Situado en Auvernia, en medio de volcanes extintos, este centro sirve para la información, la investigación y la enseñanza, y también para facilitar la vivencia directa de las fuerzas primigenias de la naturaleza y del nacimiento de nuestro planeta. Se accede a las salas, predominantemente subterráneas, por una larga rampa que conduce hacia un cráter volcánico metafórico. El cono está recubierto por fuera con rocas de lava oscuras y por dentro con placas de metal de refulgente coloración dorada. Vulcania también sirve para la investigación profesional de los volcanes y dispone de instalaciones para investigación y conferencias, además de un teatro IMAX e invernaderos.

links: Skizze_Goldverkleidetes Inneres des Konus_Ansicht von außen. rechts: Konus_Außenbau bei Nacht_Ausstellungsbereich.
gauche: Esquisse_Intérieur revêtu d'or d'un segment du cône_Vue extérieure. droite: Segment du cône_Extérieur de nuit_Espace d'exposition.
izquierda: Esbozo_Interior del cono con recubrimiento dorado_Vista exterior. derecha: Cono_Vista exterior por la noche_Área de exhibiciones.

Volcans-boucliers :

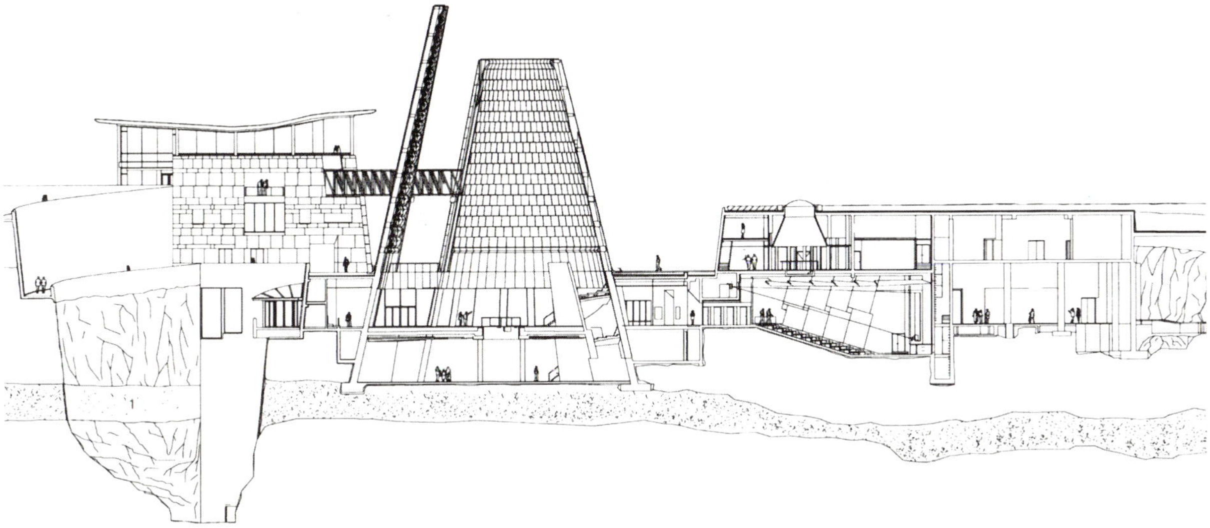

links: Konus aus dunklem Vulkangestein, akzentuiert mit goldfarbenem Metall. rechts: Schnitt
Luftaufnahme_Innenliegender Garten_Außenansicht.
gauche: Le cône est revêtu d'une pierre noire volcanique rehaussé à l'intérieur d'un métal doré.
droite: Section_Vue aérienne_Jardin intérieur_Vue extérieure.
izquierda: Cono en lava volcánica oscura, acentuado con metal dorado. derecha: Corte_Vista aérea
Jardín interior_Vista exterior.

FRANCE_VILLENEUVE D'ASCQ

LAM – MUSÉE D'ART MODERNE D'ART CONTEMPORAIN ET D'ART BRUT

FRANKREICH_FRANCE_FRANCIA
MANUELLE GAUTRAND ARCHITECTURE
2010
KUNSTMUSEUM_MUSÉE D'ART_MUSEO DE ARTE
9,000 M²
PHOTOS MAX LEROUGE

Die Architekten errichteten den neuen Bauteil nicht in „gebührendem" Abstand zum Altbau, sondern wickelten ihn um dessen Ecke. Das Projekt für die Communauté Urbaine de Lille zielt darauf ab, das Museum als ein durchgehendes Ensemble wiederherzustellen, die neuen Galerien, die eine Sammlung Art Brut aufnehmen, in den Rundgang einzugliedern und vorhandene Räume zu erschließen. Der Erweiterungsbau umfasst das nördliche und östliche Ende des eckigen Backsteinbaus als doppelte Auffächerung langer, organisch fließender Volumina. Am einen Ende entwickelt sich der neue Flügel in engen Falten zu einem Restaurant mit einem zentralen Innenhof, am anderen nimmt er in größeren Falten je eine der fünf Art-Brut-Galerien auf.

Les architectes ont créé une nouvelle extension à une distance non « respectueuse » de l'ancien bâtiment qui s'imbrique cependant sur son côté. Le projet destiné à la Communauté Urbaine de Lille aspirait à reproduire le musée comme un ensemble continu et les nouvelles galeries accueillant une collection d'art brut sont intégrées dans la partie du circuit visiteur afin de valoriser les espaces présents. L'extension du bâtiment comprend à l'extrémité septentrionale et orientale de la construction angulaire en brique, une disposition en éventail double de volumes longs, aérés, cohérents et organiques. A l'autre extrémité, la nouvelle aile caractérisée par des plis étroits évolue vers un restaurant dotée d'une cour intérieure centrale et accueille respectivement les cinq galeries consacrées à l'Art Brut dans ses larges plis.

Los arquitectos no quisieron alzar una construcción nueva a distancia de la existente, por el contrario, apostaron a envolver una en otra. El proyecto para la Comunidad Urbana de Lille apunta a reconfigurar el museo como un conjunto transparente y a integrar las nuevas galerías con una colección de Art Brut en el recorrido y con las salas existentes. La ampliación abarca las alas norte y este del anguloso edificio de ladrillo en forma de volúmenes orgánicos que fluyen y se alargan. En un extremo se despliega la nueva ala, que con apretados pliegues lleva a un restaurante con patio interior central; en otro extremo y con pliegues más amplios abarca cinco galerías de Art Brut.

links: Modell (1/200)_Blick in den Innenhof. rechts: Nachtansicht des Außenbaus_Innenansicht des Ausbaus_Außenbau.
gauche: Modèle (1/200)_Vue sur la cour intérieure. droite: Extérieur de nuit_Vue intérieure de l'extension_Vue panoramique extérieure.
izquierda: Maqueta (1/200)_Vista del patio interior. derecha: Vista nocturna del exterior_Vista interior de la ampliación_Exterior.

GERMANY_BERLIN **JÜDISCHES MUSEUM BERLIN**

DEUTSCHLAND_ALLEMAGNE_ALEMANIA
STUDIO DANIEL LIBESKIND
1999, EXTENSION 2007
GESCHICHTSMUSEUM_MUSÉE D'HISTOIRE_MUSEO HISTÓRICO
15,500 M²
PHOTOS BITTER BREDT FOTOGRAFIE, BERLIN
(214, 215 B. L., B. R., 217 L., A. R.),
GUENTER SCHNEIDER, BERLIN (215 A.),
MICHELE NASTASI, MILAN (216, 217 B. R.)

Das 2001 eröffnete Museum zeigt die soziale, politische und kulturelle Geschichte des Judentums in Deutschland vom 4. Jahrhundert bis in die Gegenwart. Das Museum integriert und präsentiert erstmals in Deutschland explizit auch die Auswirkungen des Holocausts in der Nachkriegszeit. Der Anbau befindet sich auf dem Gelände des ehemaligen preußischen Gerichtshofs, der 1735 fertig gestellt, in den 1960er Jahren renoviert und als Museum der Stadt Berlin genutzt wurde. Der Entwurf, der ein Jahr vor dem Fall der Berliner Mauer entstand, basiert auf einer Ost- und Westberlin verbindenden Eigenschaft: auf dem Verhältnis der Deutschen zu den Juden.

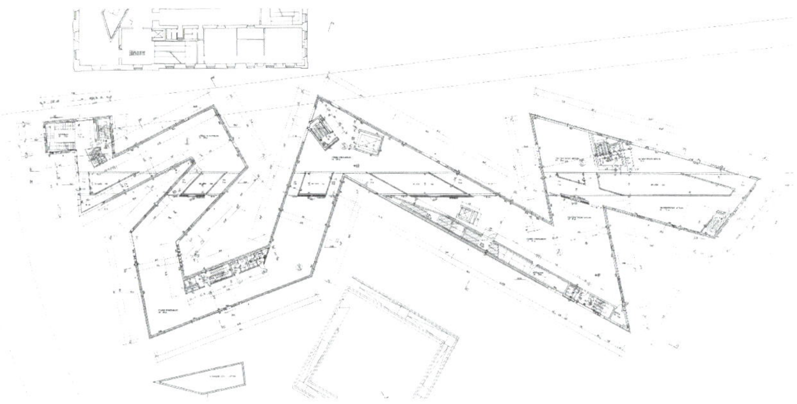

Le musée inauguré en 2001 témoigne de l'histoire sociale, politique et culturelle du judaïsme en Allemagne depuis le IV siècle jusqu'à nos jours. Pour la première fois en Allemagne, le musée présente explicitement les effets de l'holocauste pendant l'Après-guerre. L'annexe est située sur le terrain de l'ancienne cour de justice de la Prusse, achevée en 1735 et rénovée en musée de la ville de Berlin dans les années 1960. Le projet réalisé un an avant la chute du Mur de Berlin repose sur une caractéristique commune entre Berlin-Est et Berlin-Ouest : la relation entre allemands et juifs.

El museo, inaugurado en 2001, expone la historia social, política y cultural del judaísmo en Alemania desde el siglo IV hasta la actualidad. El museo también abarca y presenta de manera explícita, por primera vez en la historia de Alemania, los efectos del holocausto en la época de posguerra. La construcción se levanta sobre el terreno del antiguo tribunal judicial prusiano, edificado en 1735 y renovado en la década de 1960 como museo de la ciudad de Berlín. El proyecto, concebido un año antes de la caída del Muro de Berlín, se basa en un elemento común de los berlineses occidentales con los orientales: la relación de los alemanes con los judíos.

links: Lageplan_JMB neben dem barocken Altbau_Der „Leerraum"_Holocaustturm. rechts: Luftaufnahme_Haupttreppe_Übersicht.
gauche: Plan de site_JMB à proximité de l'ancien bâtiment baroque_Espace vide_Tour de l'holocauste. droite: Prise aérienne escalier principal_Vue générale.
izquierda: Ubicación_El nuevo museo judío junto al edificio barroco_Espacio vacío_La Torre del Holocausto. derecha: Vista aérea_Escalinata principal_Vista del conjunto.

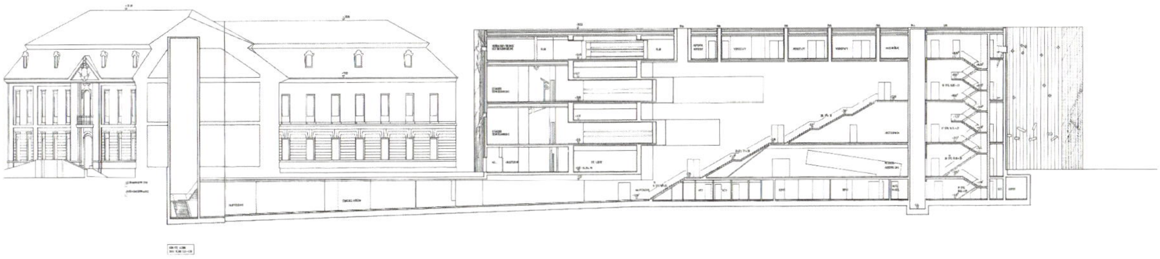

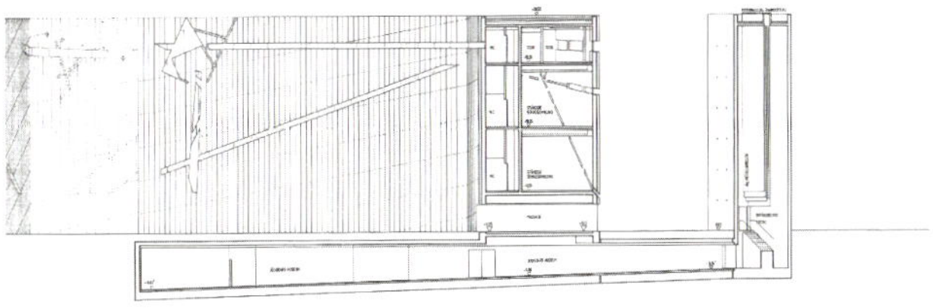

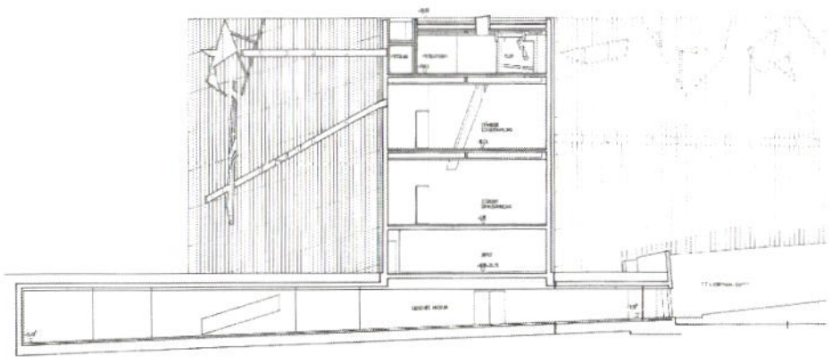

links: Garten des Exils. rechts: Schnitt mit Treppe_Paul Celan Hof_Holocaustturm und Garten des Exils_Fenster als Teil der Davidsstern-Matrix.
gauche: Jardin de l'exil. droite: Coupe avec l'escalier_Cour Paul Celan_Tour de l'holocauste et jardin de l'exil_Fenêtres comme partie de la matrice de l'étoile de David.
izquierda: Jardín del Exilio. derecha: Corte con escalera_Patio Paul Celan_Torre del Holocausto y Jardín del Exilio_Ventanas dibujan parte de la estrella de David.

GERMANY_BERLIN **NEUES MUSEUM**

DEUTSCHLAND_ALLEMAGNE_ALEMANIA
DAVID CHIPPERFIELD ARCHITECTS
2009
KUNSTMUSEUM_MUSÉE D'ART_MUSEO DE ARTE
20,500 M²
PHOTOS SPK / DAVID CHIPPERFIELD ARCHITECTS, PHOTOGRAPHER: UTE ZSCHARNT (218, 221 L., A. R.), SPK / DAVID CHIPPERFIELD ARCHITECTS, PHOTOGRAPHER: JÖRG VON BRUCHHAUSEN (219 A., B. M.), SPK / DAVID CHIPPERFIELD ARCHITECTS, PHOTOGRAPHER: CHRISTIAN RICHTERS (219 B. L., B. R., 220, 221 B. R.)

Die Rekonstruktion des Museums nach den Zerstörungen im Zweiten Weltkrieg umfasst neue Bereiche aus Betonfertigteilen, die aus weißem Zement mit sächsischem Marmor als Zuschlagstoff bestehen. Die neue Haupttreppe greift die Grunddisposition der Ursprungstreppe auf, ohne diese zu replizieren. Ihre Halle ist lediglich als Volumen aus Backstein ohne die ursprüngliche Ornamentik konserviert. Weitere neue Gebäudeteile – der Nordwestflügel mit dem ägyptischen Hof und der Apollo Risalit, die Apsis im griechischen Hof und die Südkuppel – wurden aus wiederverwendeten, handgestrichenen Ziegeln erbaut. Durch die Wiederherstellung und Vollendung der am besten erhaltenen Kolonnade auf der Ost- und Südseite des Museums wird die städtebauliche Situation der Vorkriegszeit rekonstruiert.

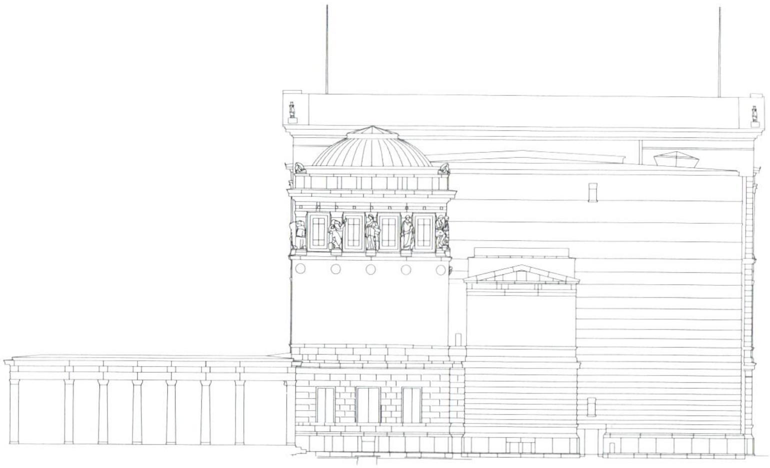

La reconstruction du musée après sa destruction au cours de la Deuxième Guerre Mondiale comprend de nouveaux espaces en pièces préfabriquées en béton et en ciment blanc avec du marbre de Saxe, comme matériaux complémentaires. Le nouvel escalier principal reprend la disposition de base de l'escalier d'origine sans le répliquer. Son hall se limite à un volume en brique qui ne conserve pas les ornements d'origine. Toutes les autres parties nouvelles du bâtiment, l'aile au Nord-Ouest avec la cour égyptienne et l'Apollo Risalit, l'abside de la cour grecque et la coupole Sud furent construites en brique recyclée, recuite à la main. La situation de l'urbanisation de l'avant-guerre fut restaurée grâce à la reproduction et à la finition de la colonnade la mieux préservée de la partie Sud-est du musée.

La reconstrucción del museo tras los daños sufridos en el curso de la Segunda Guerra Mundial abarcó nuevas áreas hechas con elementos prefabricados de hormigón; estos constan de cemento blanco con mármol de Sajonia. La nueva escalinata principal retoma la disposición original de la antigua escalinata, pero sin replicarla. Su salón es meramente un volumen de ladrillo, que no conserva la ornamentación original. Otras nuevas secciones edilicias, como el ala noroeste con el patio egipcio y el Apollo risalit, el ábside en el patio griego y la cúpula sur, fueron construidas con ladrillos reciclados hechos a mano. Reproduciendo y completando la columnata mejor preservada en el este y sur del museo, se recreó la situación urbanística de la época anterior a la guerra.

links: Ansicht Nord_Westfassade. rechts: Treppenhalle_Treppenhalle, Blick in den Griechischen Saal_Treppenhalle_Saal hinter der Treppe, Blick in den Ethnografischen Saal.
gauche: Vue au nord_Façade ouest. droite: Hall d'escaliers_Hall d'escaliers, vue sur la salle grecque_Hall d'escalier_Salle à l'arrière de l'escalier, vue sur la salle d'ethnographie.
izquierda: Fachada norte_Fachada occidental. derecha: Escaleras_Vista desde la escalera hacia la Sala Griega_Escaleras_Sala detrás de la escalera, vista hacia la Sala Etnográfica.

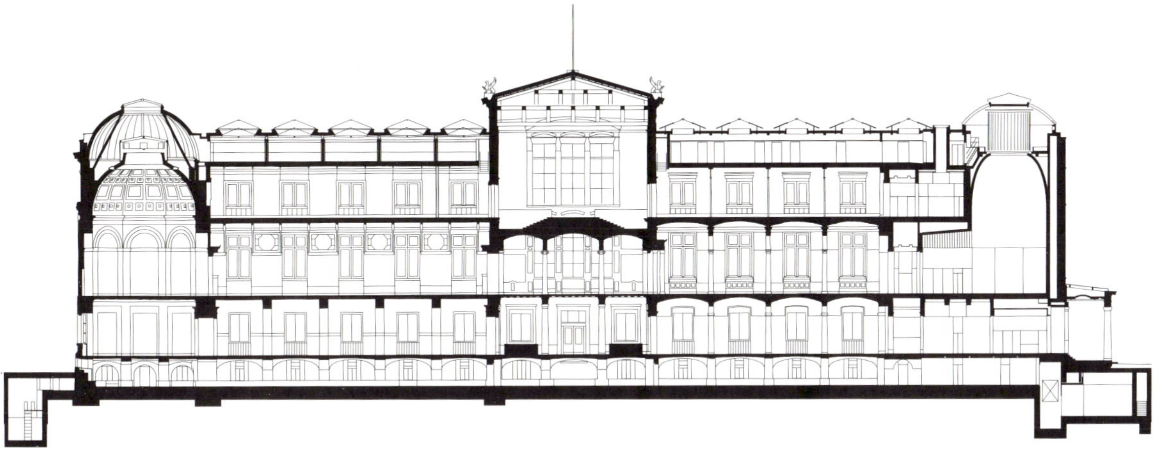

links: Griechischer Hof. rechts: Schnitt durch Ostflügel_Enfilade Ebene 2 Ostflügel_Detail Ägyptischer Hof_Sternensaal, Blick in den Westlichen Kunstkammersaal.
gauche: Cour grecque. droite: Coupe de l'aile Est_Enfilade au niveau 2, aile Est_Détail de la cour égyptienne_Salle des étoiles, vue sur la salle d'art « Kunstkammersaal » à l'Ouest.
izquierda: Patio Griego. derecha: Corte por el ala oriental_Secuencia de puertas en el nivel 2 del ala oriental_Detalle del Patio Egipcio_Sala de las Estrellas, vista hacia la sala de arte occidental.

GERMANY_BERLIN **BERLINISCHE GALERIE**

DEUTSCHLAND_ALLEMAGNE_ALEMANIA
DIPL.-ING. JÖRG FRICKE, ARCHITEKT
2004
KUNST-, FOTOGRAFIE- UND ARCHITEKTURMUSEUM
MUSÉE D'ART, DE PHOTOGRAPHIE ET D'ARCHITECTURE
MUSEO DE ARTE, FOTOGRAFÍA Y ARQUITECTURA
14,055 M²
PHOTOS HANS PRAEFKE, BERLIN

Innerhalb eines knappen Jahres wurden eine ehemalige Industriehalle und ein Verwaltungsgebäude mit begrenztem Budget zum Museum umgebaut. Im Vordergrund standen dabei die Optimierung und funktionale Gestaltung der Ausstellungsflächen. Unterschiedliche Raumhöhen, fließende Übergänge und Raumfolgen sowie vielfältige Blickbeziehungen charakterisieren das Gebäude im Inneren. Planungskriterien waren neben den Nutzeranforderungen ein nachhaltiges Betreiben sowie günstige Unterhaltskosten. Mit durchdachten Detaillösungen, dem Einsatz von wenigen Materialien und einer zurückhaltenden Architektursprache wird eine vornehme Sachlichkeit erzeugt, die nur eines in den Mittelpunkt stellt: die Kunst.

Un ancien hall industriel et un bâtiment administratif ont été reconvertis en musée grâce à un budget limité en l'espace d'une année. Pour réaliser ce projet, le budget était limité et les travaux devaient se réaliser en moins d'un an. Les priorités étaient l'optimisation et la fonctionnalité des surfaces d'exposition. Les différentes hauteurs d'espace, les transitions sans heurts, les suites d'espaces et la richesse des perspectives donnent son caractère au bâtiment. En plus des exigences d'ordre utilitaire, les critères de planification reposaient sur une exploitation durable et sur une optimisation des coûts d'entretien. Les solutions détaillées, mûrement réfléchies, l'utilisation de matériaux peu abondants et un langage architectural discret créent une objectivité noble centrée sur un objectif : l'art.

En tan solo un año y con un acotado presupuesto, una antigua nave industrial y un edificio administrativo se transformaron en museo. Lo fundamental era lograr la optimización y funcionalidad de las áreas de exhibición. Diversas alturas de salas, transiciones fluidas y secuencias de espacios, además de múltiples vinculaciones visuales, caracterizan a la edificación. Además de las exigencias utilitarias, los criterios de planificación incluían una operación sostenible y costes de mantenimiento accesibles. Con soluciones detallistas muy bien pensadas, la aplicación de pocos materiales y un lenguaje arquitectónico discreto, se logró una neutralidad agradable que se centra en una sola cosa: el arte.

links: Grundriss Erdgeschoss_Südansicht mit Plastik „Dreiheit" von Brigitte und Martin Matschinsky-Denninghoff_Raum in Raum. rechts: Großer Ausstellungsraum mit Kunstwerken von Gerold Miller, Stefan Beck, Ronald de Bloeme, Tim Trantenroth und Fritz Balthaus_Blick vom Seitenraum_Zentrale Treppe.
gauche: Plan du rez-de-chaussée_Vue au sud avec l'œuvre plastique « trinité » de Brigitte et Martin Matschinsky-Denninghoff_L'espace dans l'espace. droite: Grand espace d'exposition des œuvres d'art de Gerold Miller, Stefan Beck, Ronald de Bloeme, Tim Trantenroth et Fritz Balthaus_Vue depuis l'espace latéral_Escalier central.
izquierda: Plano de planta baja_Fachada sur con obra "Trinidad" de Brigitte y Martin Matschinsky-Denninghoff_Sala dentro de otra sala. derecha: Gran sala de exhibiciones con obras de Gerold Miller, Stefan Beck, Ronald de Bloeme, Tim Trantenroth y Fritz Balthaus_Vista de sala lateral_Escalera central.

GERMANY_BRÜHL **MAX ERNST MUSEUM**

DEUTSCHLAND_ALLEMAGNE_ALEMANIA
ARGE VAN DEN VALENTYN ARCHITEKTUR, SMO ARCHITEKTUR
2004
KUNSTMUSEUM_MUSÉE D'ART_MUSEO DE ARTE
5,400 M²
PHOTOS RAINER MADER

Die klassizistische, um 1844 errichtete Dreiflügelanlage wurde in ihrem Charakter bewahrt, von allen Anbauten befreit und in ihrer Urform mit dem zum Park geöffneten Innenhof wiederhergestellt. Ergänzt wurde sie um einen halb unterirdischen Neubau, dessen Dachfläche als leicht erhöhtes Natursteinplateau im Park sichtbar ist. Ein in den Innenhof geschobener Eingangspavillon bildet das verbindende Element zwischen Alt und Neu. Der Raum für Wechselausstellungen wird über begehbare Oberlichter mit Tageslicht versorgt. Ein daneben liegender Konzertsaal lässt sich autark nutzen. Die Kunst von Max Ernst ist vor allem im Altbau untergebracht, in dessen Haupttrakt die ständige Sammlung ihren festen Platz hat.

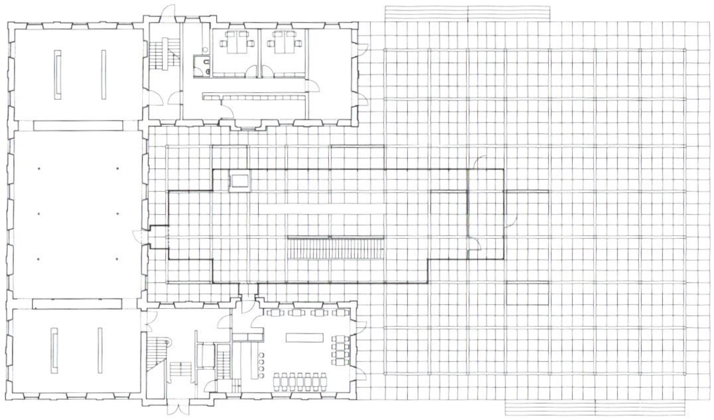

L'installation classique à trois ailes créée autour de 1844 a conservé son caractère après avoir été dépourvue de toute annexe afin de retrouver sa forme initiale avec la cour intérieure ouverte sur le parc. Elle fut complétée par un nouveau bâtiment à moitié souterrain dont la toiture se reflète sur le parc comme un plateau en pierre naturelle légèrement surélevé. Un pavillon d'entrée en retrait dans la cour intérieure forme l'élément de liaison entre l'ancien et le nouveau. L'espace consacré à l'exposition alternante est éclairé par l'éclairage en hauteur et la lumière du jour. Une salle de concert située à proximité est utilisée de manière autonome. La collection d'art de Max Ernst est exposée dans l'ancien bâtiment dans sa majorité où l'aile principale est dédiée à la collection permanente.

Se respetó el carácter de la edificación clásica de tres alas, construida en 1844, se eliminaron las construcciones accesorias y se reconstituyó su forma original con el patio interior abierto al parque. Se complementó con una edificación nueva semienterrada, cuya superficie de techo se inserta en el parque a modo de meseta de piedra natural. Un pabellón de acceso incorporado al patio interior constituye el elemento vinculante entre lo nuevo y lo antiguo. La sala de las exposiciones temporarias se ilumina con luz natural a través de lucernarios transitables. La sala para conciertos, adjunta, puede utilizarse en forma autónoma. El arte de Max Ernst está principalmente en la edificación antigua, en cuyo cuerpo central se alberga la colección permanente.

links: Grundriss Erdgeschoss_Südansicht. rechts: Galerie_Ansicht von der Commesstraße_Säulenhalle.
gauche: Plan du rez-de-chaussée_Vue au sud. droite: Galerie_Vue de la Commesstraße_Salle des piliers.
izquierda: Plano de planta baja_Fachada sur. derecha: Galería_Vista desde la Commesstrasse_Sala con columnas.

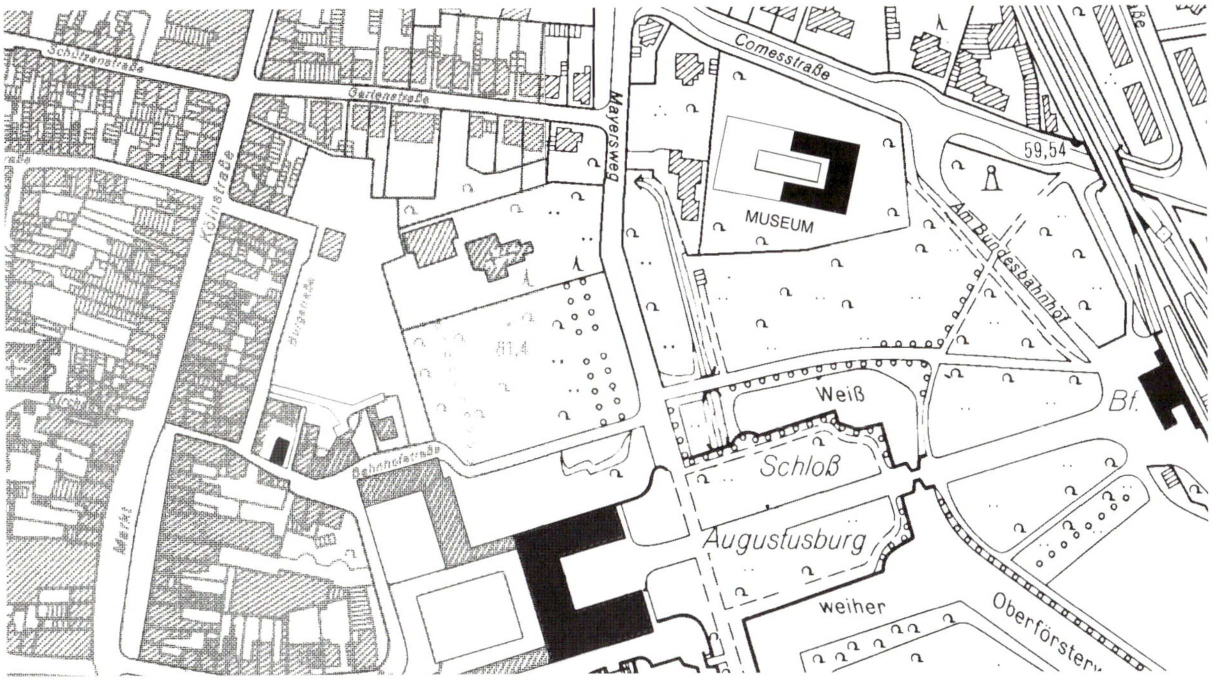

links: Pavillondetail. rechts: Lageplan_Eingangspavillon.
gauche: Détail du pavillon. droite: Plan de situation_Pavillon d'entrée.
izquierda: Detalle del pabellón. derecha: Plano de ubicación_Pabellón de acceso.

GERMANY_CELLE **KUNSTMUSEUM CELLE**

DEUTSCHLAND_ALLEMAGNE_ALEMANIA
AHRENS GRABENHORST ARCHITEKTEN BDA
2006
KUNSTMUSEUM_MUSÉE D'ART_MUSEO DE ARTE
1,200 M²
PHOTOS ROLAND HALBE / ARTURIMAGES

Der zirka 10 x 10 x 10 Meter große Glaskubus nimmt die Traufhöhen und Gebäudefluchten des Bomann-Museums und der vorhandenen Erweiterung von 1992 auf. In der Nacht leuchtet der zweigeschossige Bau farbig. Die Dachterrasse ermöglicht einen Blick auf das gegenüberliegende Residenzschloss. Die Fassadengestaltung schafft durch die Reduktion des eingesetzten Materials einen Dialog zwischen Altem und Neuem. Gleichmäßig reflektierende Oberflächen aus Klar- und weißen Mattgläsern, die ohne Glashalteleisten, sichtbare Befestigungen oder Blechabdeckungen in einer Ebene gefügt wurden, spiegeln die Umgebung wider. Die Komposition des Gebäudes setzt sich aus Fläche, Linie und Volumen zusammen.

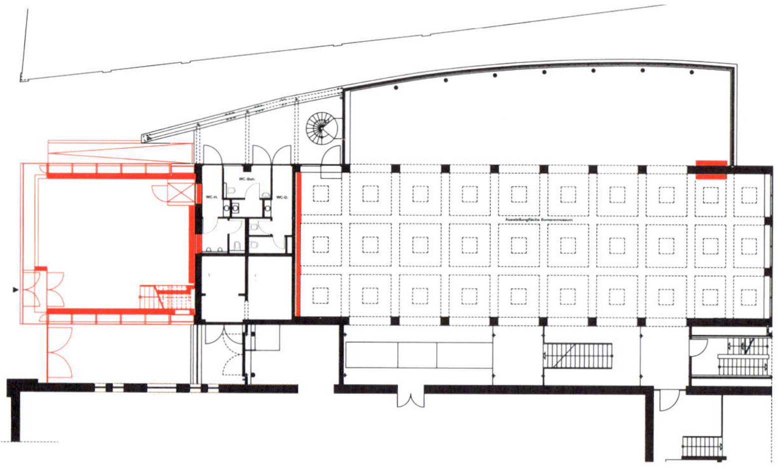

Le cube en verre d'une dimension d'environ 10x10x10 mètres abrite les façades alignées et hauteurs de corniche du musée Bomann ainsi que l'extension datant de 1992. La nuit, cette construction à deux étages brille en couleur. La terrasse située sur le toit offre une vue sur le château résidentiel situé en face. La disposition de la façade crée un dialogue entre l'ancien et le nouveau par la réduction des matériaux utilisés. L'environnement se reflète sur les surfaces réfléchissant régulièrement, en verre mat, blanc et clair, dépourvues de listels retenant le verre ou de fixations visibles, voire de revêtements en tôle. La structure de la composition conceptuelle repose sur les surfaces, lignes et volumes.

El cubo geométrico de vidrio de unos diez metros de arista adopta las alturas de cumbrera y la alineación del museo Bomann y de la ampliación de 1992. Por la noche, este edificio de dos niveles se ilumina de colores. La terraza sobre el techo permite una vista del vecino castillo de la Residencia. Gracias a lo despojado del material empleado, la configuración de la fachada logra un diálogo entre lo nuevo y lo antiguo. El entorno se refleja en las superficies uniformemente reflectantes elaboradas con cristales mate, blancos y claros, se han montado en un solo plano y carecen de listones de sujeción, fijaciones visibles o recubrimientos de chapa. La sobria composición consta de superficies, líneas y volumen.

links: Grundriss Sockelgeschoss_Alt- und Neubau_Im Satteldach. rechts: Fassade in der Dämmerung_Beleuchtungsvarianten.
gauche: Plan du soubassement_Ancien et nouveau_Toiture à deux versants. droite: Façade dans le crépuscule_Variantes d'éclairage.
izquierda: Plano del piso del basamento_Construcciones antigua y nueva_En el techo a dos aguas. derecha: Fachada al atardecer_Variantes de iluminación.

KUNSTMUSEUM CELLE MIT SAMMLUNG ROBERT SIMON

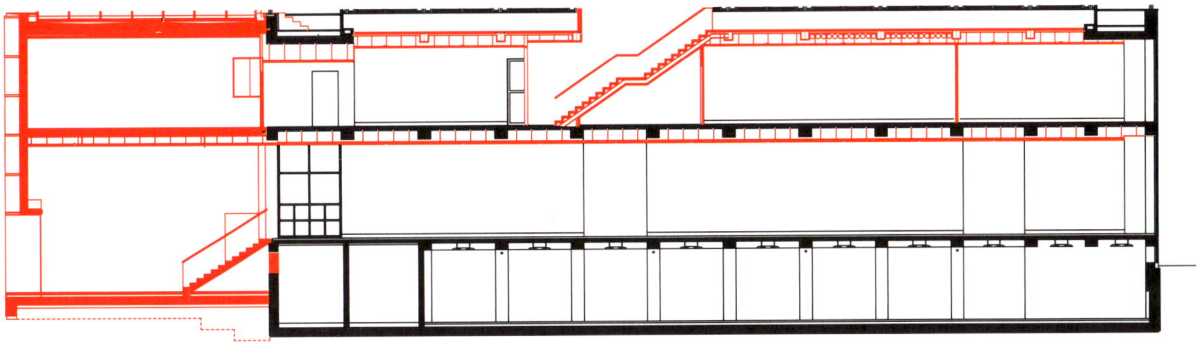

links: Fassade. rechts: Schnitt_Blick nach Außen und Fensterladen_Dachterrasse Ausstellungssaal.
gauche: Façade. droite: Coupe_Vue de l'extérieur et des contrevents_Terrasse de toit_Salle d'exposition.
izquierda: Fachada. derecha: Corte_Vista del exterior y postigos de ventana_Terraza en el techo Sala de exhibiciones.

GERMANY_DRESDEN MILITÄRHISTORISCHES MUSEUM DER BUNDESWEHR

DEUTSCHLAND_ALLEMAGNE_ALEMANIA
STUDIO DANIEL LIBESKIND WITH
ARCHITEKT DANIEL LIBESKIND AG
2011
GESCHICHTSMUSEUM_MUSÉE D'HISTOIRE_MUSEO HISTÓRICO
20,000 M²
PHOTOS COURTESY OF THE ARCHITECTS (233),
BITTER BREDT FOTOGRAFIE, BERLIN (232 B. L., B. M., B. R.)

Das Museum ist das offizielle Militärhistorische Museum der Bundeswehr. Der neue Erweiterungsbau entstand, indem ein keilförmiges Stück aus der alten Struktur des Arsenals herausgeschnitten wurde. Ein 140 Tonnen schwerer Keil aus Glas, Stahl und Beton zerteilt nun das 130 Jahre alte ursprüngliche Museumsgebäude und dient als Ort des Nachdenkens über organisierte Gewalt. Eine Aussichtsplattform in 30 Metern Höhe an der Spitze bietet einen Ausblick auf Dresden. Der Erweiterungsbau gibt dem Gebäude dadurch eine neue Ausrichtung, dass er die Aussicht auf die historische Innenstadt erlaubt. Darüber hinaus ist der über dem Dach des Originalbaus in den Himmel aufragende Teil auch ein von außen sichtbares, deutliches Zeichen für die Modernisierung des Museums.

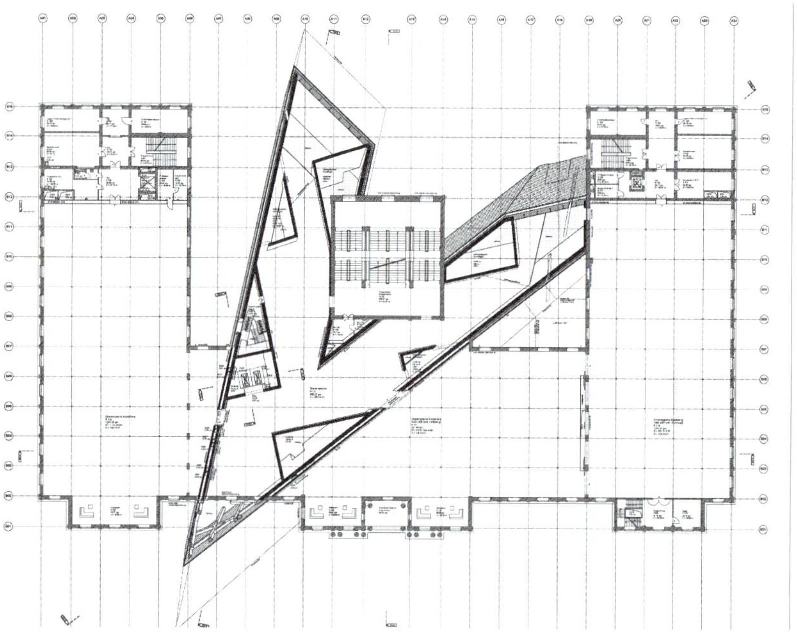

Le bâtiment abrite le musée central officiel de l'armée allemande. L'extension se compose d'une pièce cunéiforme découpée provenant de l'ancienne structure de l'arsenal. Cette pièce de 140 tonnes en verre, acier et béton découpe désormais les bâtiments d'origine, anciens de 130 ans, et sert de lieu de réflexion contre la violence organisée. Une plateforme panoramique de 30 mètres de hauteur à la pointe, offre une vue sur Dresde. Les travaux ont permis d'orienter le bâtiment sous une nouvelle perspective afin d'offrir un panorama sur le centre historique de la ville. Par ailleurs, la partie s'élevant sur le toit de la construction d'origine vers la voute céleste représente également un signe caractéristique de la modernisation du musée de l'extérieur.

Este es el museo central oficial del Ejército Alemán. La construcción surge de extraerle una sección en forma de cuña a la antigua estructura del arsenal. Esa cuña de cristal, acero y hormigón de 140 toneladas corta el antiguo edificio, que ya cumplió 130 años, y sirve como lugar de reflexión sobre la violencia organizada. Una plataforma de observación a 30 metros de altura ofrece impresionantes vistas de Dresde. La reforma reorienta el edificio, permitiendo ver el casco antiguo de la ciudad. Además, la parte de la edificación original que apunta hacia el cielo también constituye un elocuente símbolo exterior de la modernización del museo.

links: Lageplan_Alt- und Neubau_Innenaufname Bau_Bau. rechts: Transparenz der neuen gegen die Undurchsichtigkeit der alten Fassade_Ansicht Café.
gauche: Plan de site_Ancien et nouveau_Prise intérieure de la construction_Construction. droite: La transparence de la nouvelle façade s'oppose à l'opacité de l'ancienne façade_Vue du café.
izquierda: Ubicación_Construcciones antigua y nueva_Vista interior de la obra_Construcción. derecha: La transparencia de lo nuevo frente a la impenetrabilidad de la antigua fachada_Vista del café.

GERMANY_DRESDEN AUSSTELLUNGSGEBÄUDE BRÜHLSCHE TERRASSE

DEUTSCHLAND_ALLEMAGNE_ALEMANIA
AUER+WEBER+ASSOZIIERTE
2005
KUNSTMUSEUM_MUSÉE D'ART_MUSEO DE ARTE
3,350 M²
PHOTOS ROLAND HALBE / ARTURIMAGES

Das Ausstellungsgebäude liegt im Ostflügel der 1894 durch Constantin Lipsius fertiggestellten Dresdner Kunstakademie. Der „Kunsttempel an der Brühlschen Terrasse" wurde im Zweiten Weltkrieg schwer zerstört und der Außenbau erst nach 1990 wieder saniert. Die Ausstellungsflächen wurden nach funktionalen und architektonischen Gesichtspunkten für Wechselausstellungen wieder nutzbar gemacht und durch eine Galerieebene ergänzt, doch blieben die Spuren der Geschichte gereinigt und restauriert erhalten. Die neuen Einbauten respektieren die Qualitäten der historischen Räume, bilden jedoch durch die Auswahl der Materialien und Farben einen Kontrast zur Substanz des Gebäudes.

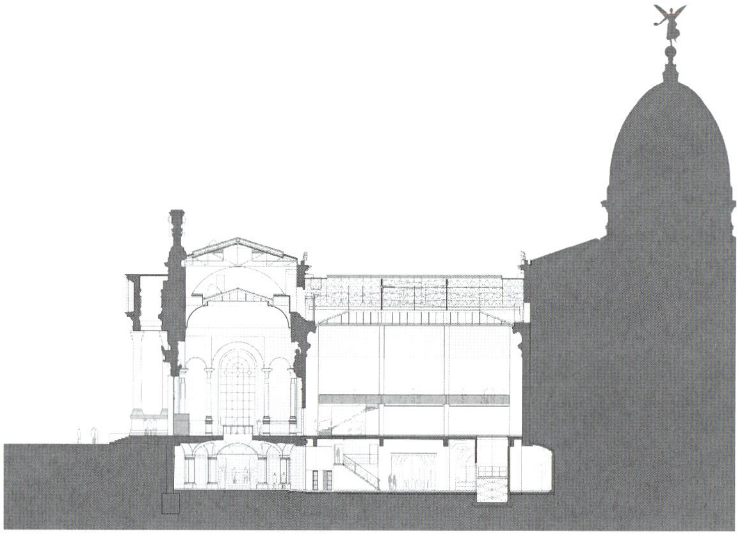

Le bâtiment d'exposition se situe dans l'aile Est de l'académie des arts de Dresde, construit par Constantin Lipsius en 1894. Le « temple de l'Art à la terrasse de Brühl » fut détruit dans sa majorité pendant la Deuxième Guerre Mondiale et la structure extérieure, rénovée seulement après 1990. Les surfaces d'exposition ont été remises en état d'un point de vue fonctionnel et architectonique pour les expositions tournantes et remplacées par un niveau de galeries. Les traces de l'histoire on été effacées et restaurées. Les nouveaux éléments intégrés respectent les qualités des espaces historiques et restent cependant en contraste avec la substance du bâtiment par le choix des matériaux et des couleurs.

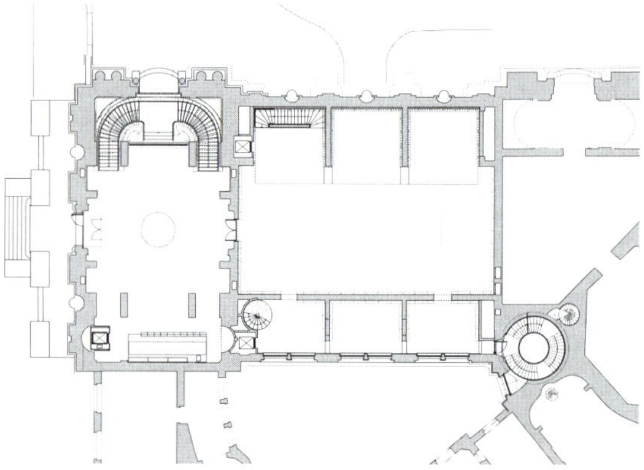

El edificio de exposiciones se levanta en el ala oriental de la Academia de Arte de Dresde y fue construido por Constantin Lipsius en 1894. El "Templo de Arte en la Terraza de Brühl" fue severamente dañado en la segunda guerra mundial y la construcción exterior recién fue restaurada después de 1990. Las áreas de exhibición fueron reconfiguradas según puntos de vista arquitectónicos y funcionales para muestras temporarias. Una galería completa el conjunto. Sin embargo, se preservaron y restauraron los testimonios del pasado. La nueva edificación respeta la calidad de los espacios interiores históricos; no obstante, los materiales y coloraciones escogidos contrastan con la sustancia de la edificación.

links: Grundriss Erdgeschoss_Blick durch Gewölbeöffnung zum Oberlicht. rechts: Ergänzter Bestand und Gewölbeöffnung ins Untergeschoss_Ergänzung Gesims_Ausstellungssaal_Gewölbe im Untergeschoss mit Occulus.
gauche: Plan du rez-de-chaussée_Vue à travers l'ouverture de la voute vers l'éclairage supérieur. droite: Partie restante complétée et ouverture de la voute vers le sous-sol_Complément de corniches_Salle d'exposition_Voute dans le sous-sol avec oculus.
izquierda: Plano de planta baja_Vista por orificio en la bóveda hacia el lucernario. derecha: Edificación antigua y orificio en la bóveda en la planta inferior_Complemento de cornisa_Sala de exhibiciones_Bóveda en el nivel inferior con óculo.

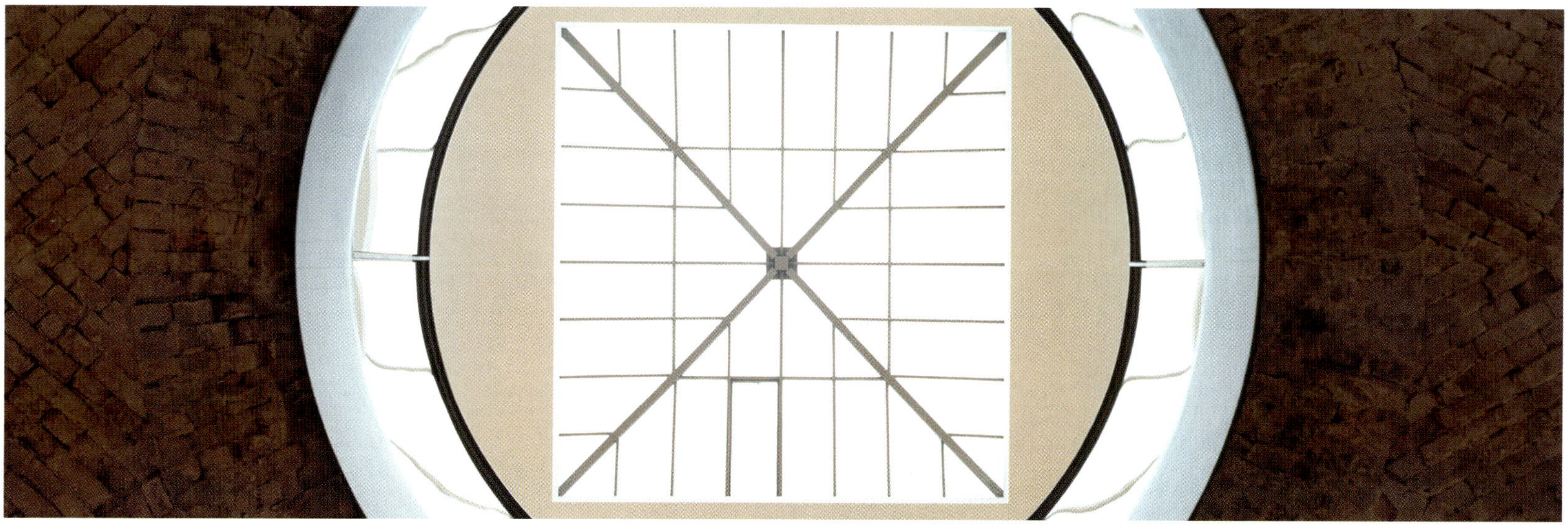

GERMANY_DÜSSELDORF K21 KUNSTSAMMLUNG STÄNDEHAUS

DEUTSCHLAND_ALLEMAGNE_ALEMANIA
KIESSLER + PARTNER ARCHITEKTEN
2002
KUNSTMUSEUM_MUSÉE D'ART_MUSEO DE ARTE
13,600 M²
PHOTOS RALPH RICHTER, DÜSSELDORF
(236 B. L., B. R., 237 B. L., B. R),
WOLFGANG SCHWAGER, AACHEN (237 A.)

Im Zuge des Umbaus erhielt das Gebäude eine neue Kuppel und eine große unterirdische Ausstellungshalle. Die Kuppel aus Glas und Stahl überwölbt den gesamten Bau. Der Kuppelraum gewährt einen Panoramablick über die Stadt. In der neuen Ausstellungshalle finden Wechselausstellungen statt. Sie befindet sich unter dem Ständehaus, ist über sechs Meter hoch und reicht im Norden bis zum Kaiserteich. Durch Bullaugenfenster eröffnet sich der Blick auf und unter die Wasseroberfläche des Teichs. Die historische Außenfassade blieb bestehen. Weitere historische Elemente, wie die Treppenanlage und die Doppelsäulen, werden durch die weißen Decken und Wände hervorgehoben.

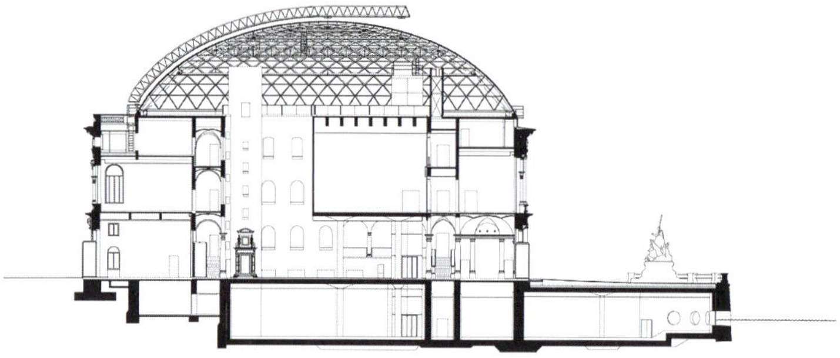

Au cours de la transformation, le bâtiment a obtenu une nouvelle coupole et un grand hall d'exposition souterrain. La coupole en verre et acier offre une voute à l'ensemble du bâtiment. La salle de la coupole présente une vue panoramique sur la ville. Le nouveau hall d'exposition sert aux expositions tournantes. Il se situe sous la maison de l'armurerie, mesure plus de six mètres de hauteur et rejoint au Nord la Kaiserteich. Grâce aux hublots, la vue donne sur et sous le niveau du lac. Les façades extérieures historiques furent conservées. D'autres éléments liés à l'histoire, notamment les escaliers et les colonnes géminées, sont valorisés grâce aux murs et plafonds blancs.

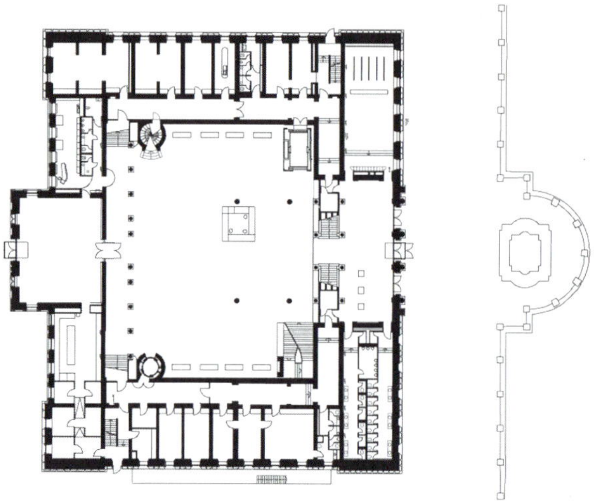

En el curso de la reforma, el edificio fue dotado de una nueva cúpula y de una gran sala de exposiciones subterránea. La cúpula de cristal y acero en forma abovedada recubre todo el edificio. El espacio bajo la cúpula permite una vista panorámica de la ciudad. En la nueva sala de exposiciones se realizan muestras temporarias. Ubicada bajo la Ständehaus, tiene más de seis metros de altura y al norte llega hasta la laguna Kaiserteich. Ventanas de ojo de buey abren una visual sobre la superficie del agua y debajo de la misma. Se respetó la histórica fachada exterior. Otros elementos históricos como las escalinatas y las dobles columnas han sido resaltados por los muros y los cielorrasos blancos.

links: Schnitt und Grundriss Erdgeschoss_Nachtaufnahme_Café, gestaltet von Jorge Pardo. rechts: Nordansicht mit Kaiserteich_Ausstellungsraum unter der Kuppel_Piazza, nachts.
gauche: Coupe et plan du rez-de-chaussée_Vue de nuit_Café aménagé par Jorge Pardo. droite: Perspective nord avec la Kaiserteich_Espace d'exposition sous la coupole_Piazza, de nuit.
izquierda: Corte y plano de planta baja_Vista nocturna_Café diseñado por Jorge Pardo. derecha: Fachada norte y Kaiserteich_Sala de exhibiciones bajo la cúpula_Plaza por la noche.

GERMANY_DÜSSELDORF **JULIA STOSCHEK COLLECTION**

DEUTSCHLAND_ALLEMAGNE_ALEMANIA
KUEHN MALVEZZI
2007
KUNSTMUSEUM_MUSÉE D'ART_MUSEO DE ARTE
4,350 M²
PHOTOS ULRICH SCHWARZ, BERLIN

Das Gebäude, eine Fabrik aus dem letzten Jahrhundert, sollte am Außenbau seine ursprüngliche Erscheinung beibehalten, während das Innere entsprechend den neuen Anforderungen zu reorganisieren war. Die Stapelung der Innenräume beginnt mit einem Kinoraum im Keller und endet in einer Panoramaterrasse oben auf einer Glasbox, die wiederum auf dem Dach der ehemaligen Fabrik platziert wurde. Schwerpunkt der Sammlung sind Werke der Videokunst, die der Öffentlichkeit in jährlich wechselnden Themenausstellungen präsentiert werden. So waren flexible und leicht zu verändernde Ausstellungsräume erforderlich. Die Videoräume sind von schalldichten Wänden umgeben. Räume zwischen den einzelnen Videoinstallationen bilden Ruhepunkte zwischen den Exponaten.

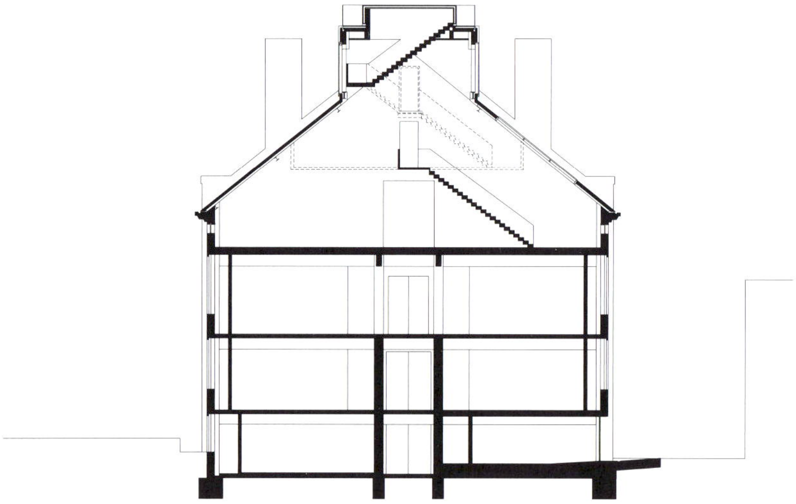

Le bâtiment, une usine datant du siècle dernier, était censé conserver sa présentation d'origine au niveau de la structure extérieure et offrir néanmoins les avantages de la nouvelle réorganisation intérieure. La superposition des espaces intérieurs commence par une salle de cinéma dans la cave et se termine par une terrasse panoramique sur une boite vitrifiée placée sur le toit de l'ancienne usine. Les éléments phare de la collection sont des œuvres d'art vidéo présentées au public dans le cadre d'expositions thématiques renouvelées annuellement. Ce mode d'exposition exigeait une souplesse d'espaces facilement variables. Les salles vidéo sont cloisonnées par des murs insonorisés. Les espaces intermédiaires des installations vidéo individuelles forment des points de repos entre les objets exposés.

El edificio, una fábrica del siglo pasado, debía conservar su apariencia exterior original, en tanto se debía reorganizar el interior en función de los nuevos requisitos espaciales. Los ambientes interiores, de abajo hacia arriba, comienzan por un cine para niños en el subsuelo y terminan con una terraza panorámica en una caja de cristal que fue ubicada sobre el techo de la antigua fábrica. El énfasis de la colección está puesto en obras audiovisuales que se presentan al público en exhibiciones temáticas rotativas a lo largo del año. Por consiguiente, se requerían salas de exhibición flexibles y sencillas de modificar. Las salas de vídeo están encerradas por muros con aislamiento acústico. Los espacios entre las instalaciones de vídeo constituyen lugares de reposo entre las exposiciones.

links: Schnitt_Ausstellungsraum mit Videoinstallation von Doug Aitken_Eingang zur Ausstellung Ausstellungsraum mit Kunstwerken von Tony Oursler und Jeppe Hein. rechts: Wegführung im Dachraum_Dachterrasse.
gauche: Coupe_Espace d'exposition avec l'installation vidéo de Doug Aitken_Entrée à l'exposition_Espace d'exposition consacré aux œuvres d'art de Tony Oursler et Jeppe Hein. droite: Passage dans l'espace toiture_Terrasse de toit.
izquierda: Corte_Sala de exhibición con instalación de vídeo de Doug Aitken_Acceso a la exhibición Muestra de obras de Tony Oursler y Jeppe Hein. derecha: Pasaje en el ático_Terraza en el techo.

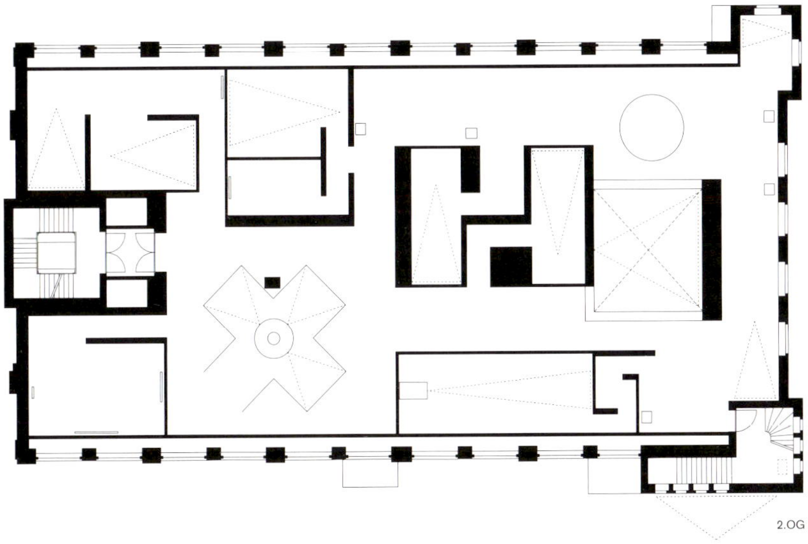

links: Außenbau und Dachterrasse. rechts: Grundriss_Videogalerie, Ausstellung: DISTROY, SHE SAID (Juni 07 - August 08)_Dachterrasse mit Kunstwerk von Dan Graham_Treppe zur Dachterrasse.
gauche: Bâtiment extérieur et terrasse de toit. droite: Plan_Galerie vidéo_Exposition: DISTROY, SHE SAID (juin 07 – août 08)_Terrasse de toit avec œuvre d'art de Dan Graham_Escalier menant à la terrasse de toiture.
izquierda: Vista exterior con terraza. derecha: Plano_Galería de vídeos, exhibición: DISTROY, SHE SAID (junio 07 - agosto 08)_Terraza superior con obra de arte de Dan Graham_Escalera a la terraza superior.

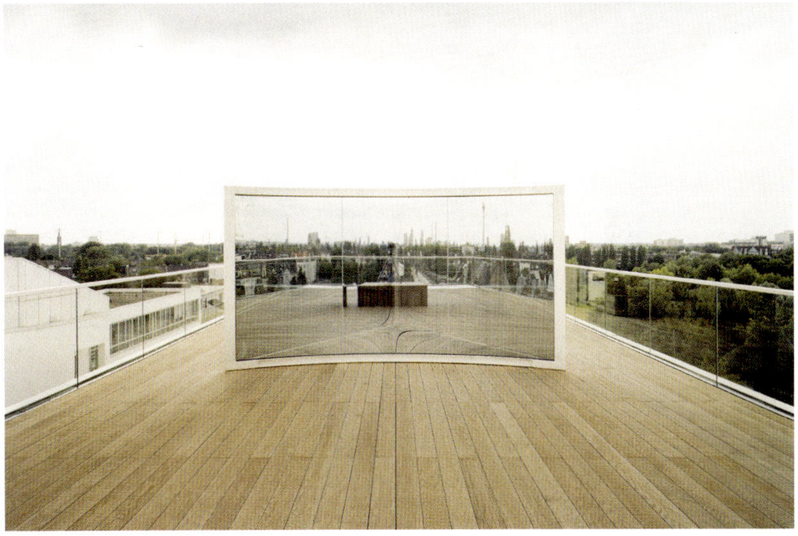

GERMANY_EISLEBEN **MARTIN LUTHER GEBURTSHAUS**

DEUTSCHLAND_ALLEMAGNE_ALEMANIA
SPRINGER ARCHITEKTEN GESELLSCHAFT VON ARCHITEKTEN MBH
2007
GESCHICHTSMUSEUM_MUSÉE D'HISTOIRE_MUSEO HISTÓRICO
1,700 M²
PHOTOS BERND HIEPE, BERLIN

Das Geburtshaus Martin Luthers unterlag seit seiner Erbauung mehreren Veränderungen. Die beiden daneben errichteten Neubauten ermöglichen nun eine umfassende museale Aufbereitung zum Leben und Wirken des Reformators. Das Ausstellungsgebäude bietet einen zentralen Zutritt über den Hof und gestattet erstmals einen musealen Rundgang. Das Besucherzentrum mit Nebenräumen verweist auf das im Stadtraum nur ansatzweise sichtbare Geburtshaus. Trotz der eigenständigen, modernen Gestalt verfügen die neuen Gebäude über zurückhaltende Fassaden aus grau-braunem Sichtmauerwerk. Die Backsteinstruktur setzt sich im Inneren fort. Die Wandflächen sind hier ebenfalls steinsichtig und nur leicht grau geschlämmt.

La maison natale de Martin Luther a connu plusieurs réaménagements depuis sa construction en 1693. Les deux constructions récentes ont permis la transformation globale en musée. Le bâtiment d'exposition dispose désormais d'un accès central à la cour qui permet de faire le tour intégrale du musée. L'espace visiteurs et les annexes orientent sur la maison natale en filigrane dans l'espace urbain. Malgré la forme moderne individualisée, les nouveaux bâtiments sont dotés de façades discrètes en maçonnerie transparente de couleur marron-gris. La structure en brique se poursuit à l'intérieur. A ce niveau, les nouvelles surfaces murales font également transparaitre la pierre grise légèrement délavée.

Desde su apertura al público en 1693, la casa natal de Martín Lutero fue sometida a sucesivas alteraciones. Las últimas dos ampliaciones posibilitaron un concepto museístico amplio. El edificio de exhibiciones hace posible un acceso central por el patio y permite por primera vez un recorrido por el museo. El centro de visitantes con sus salas anexas remite a la casa natal, que apenas se aprecia en el panorama urbano. A pesar de su imagen moderna y autónoma, los nuevos edificios están dotados de fachadas discretas en ladrillo visto de coloración parda. La estructura de ladrillo se prolonga hacia el interior. Las nuevas superficies de muros también muestran ladrillos y apenas están coloreadas en gris.

links: Grundriss Erdgeschoss_Haupttreppe Ausstellungsgebäude_Ausstellungsraum_Historisches Portal, Zugang zum Ensemble. rechts: Hof des Ensembles_Putzbau und Ziegelmauerwerk Fachwerk und Ziegelmauerwerk.
gauche: Plan du rez-de-chaussée_Escalier principal du bâtiment d'exposition_Espace d'exposition Portail historique, accès à l'ensemble. droite: Cour de l'ensemble_Bâtiment en crépi et maçonnerie en brique_Charpente et maçonnerie en brique.
izquierda: Plano de planta baja_Escalera principal del edificio de exhibiciones_Sala de exhibiciones_Portal histórico de acceso al conjunto. derecha: Patio del conjunto_Construcción revocada y albañilería_Entramado y albañilería.

GERMANY_FRANKFURT / MAIN **KUNSTHALLE PORTIKUS**

DEUTSCHLAND_ALLEMAGNE_ALEMANIA
PROF. CHRISTOPH MÄCKLER ARCHITEKTEN
2006
KUNSTMUSEUM_MUSÉE D'ART_MUSEO DE ARTE
770 M²
PHOTOS CHRISTOPH LISON (244 B. L., 245),
WOLFGANG GUENZEL (244 B. R., 246, 247)

Die Ausstellungshalle für zeitgenössische Kunst steht auf der Maininsel an der Alten Brücke. Die Bebauung der Insel vollzieht sich im Zusammenhang mit der Sanierung und Verbreiterung der Brücke. Die architektonische Form des neuen Bauwerks orientiert sich an der Geschichte des Ortes und geht typologisch auf die mittelalterlichen Häuser Frankfurts zurück. Die ochsenblutrote Farbgebung der Fassaden lehnt sich an den traditionellen Farbton des Frankfurter Römers an. Sie harmoniert mit dem roten Mainsandstein der Alten Brücke und hebt sich gleichzeitig von ihr ab. Das Gebäude besteht aus einem klaren und wohlproportionierten Ausstellungsraum, der durch eine umlaufende Galerie gegliedert wird.

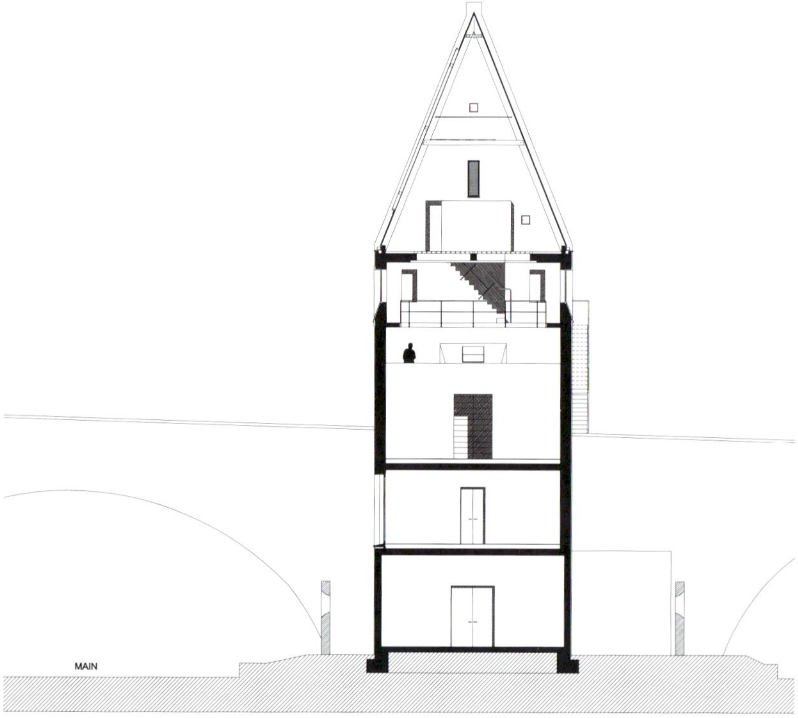

La salle d'exposition de l'art contemporain se situe sur l'île de la rivière Main sur le vieux pont. L'aménagement de l'île s'effectue dans le cadre de l'assainissement et de l'élargissement du pont. La forme architectonique du nouveau bâtiment s'oriente sur l'histoire du lieu et remonte au niveau typologique aux maisons médiévales de Francfort. La teinte rouge-brun des façades s'inspire de la coloration traditionnelle du Frankfurter Römer. Elle s'harmonise avec le grès rouge du Main des vieux ponts tout en contrastant simultanément avec cette teinte. Le bâtiment est constitué d'un espace d'exposition clair et bien proportionné, séparé par une galerie circulaire.

La sala de exhibiciones de arte contemporáneo se levanta sobre la isla Maininsel junto al Puente Viejo. La edificación de la isla se aprecia en el contexto de la renovación y ensanche del puente. La forma arquitectónica de la nueva construcción se orienta a la historia del sitio y tipológicamente evoca las viviendas del Fráncfort medieval. La coloración sangre de buey de las fachadas se refiere a la tonalidad tradicional del Römer. Armoniza con la arenisca roja del Meno presente en el Puente Viejo y al mismo tiempo se destaca de la misma. El edificio comprende una sala de exhibiciones clara y bien proporcionada, subdividida por una galería circundante.

links: Schnitt_Fassadendetail_Luftaufnahme. rechts: Fassade.
gauche: Coupe_Détail de la façade_Vue aérienne. droite : Façade.
izquierda: Corte_Detalle de fachada_Vista aérea. derecha: Fachada.

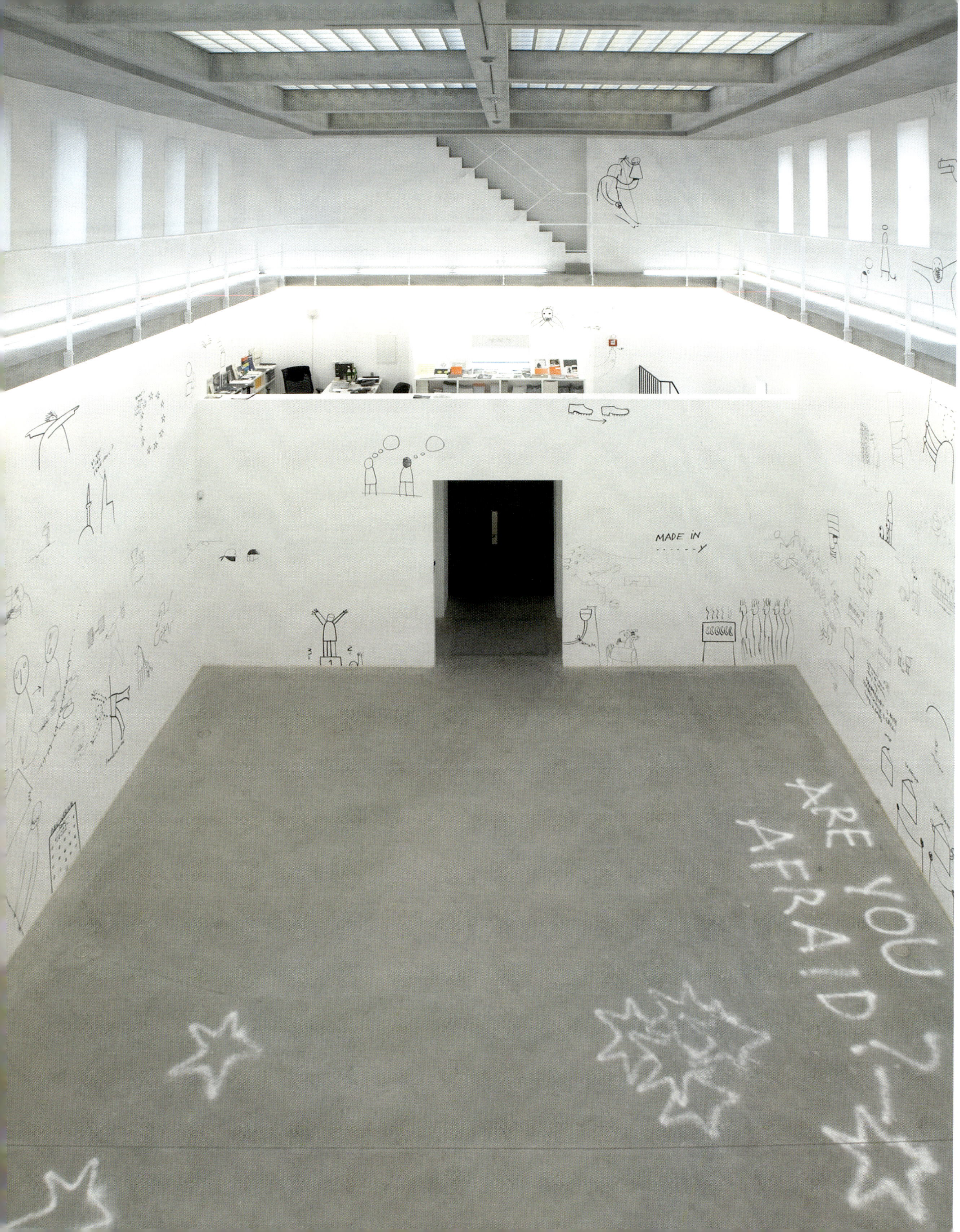
MADE IN
ARE YOU
AFRAID?

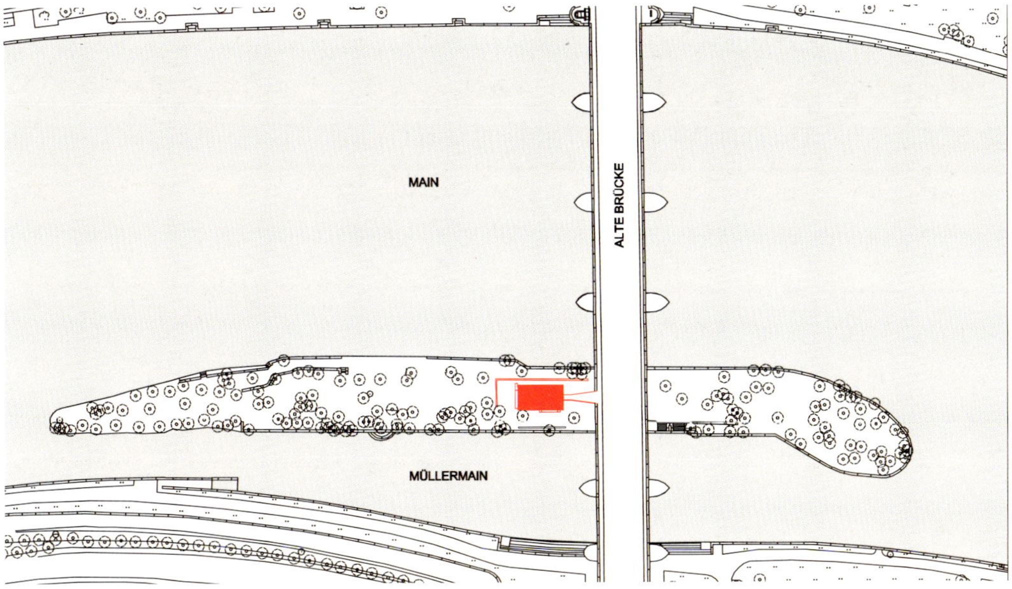

links: Dan Perjovschi, "On the other hand", 2007. rechts: Lageplan_Olafur Eliasson, erste Lichtinstallation in der Reihe "Light Lab", 2006/07_Ausstellungsraum – Lichtsituation mit der ersten Lichtinstallation im Dachraum von Olafur Eliasson_Paola Pivi, "It's a cocktail party", 2008.
gauche: Dan Perkovschin « on the other hand », 2007. droite: Plan de site_Olafur Eliasson, première installation lumineuse de la série « Light Lab », 2006/07_Espace d'exposition – avec la première installation lumineuse dans l'espace de la toiture par Olafur Eliasson_Paola Pivi, « It's a cocktail party », 2008.
izquierda: Dan Perjovschi, "On the other hand", 2007. derecha: Plano de ubicación_Olafur Eliasson, primera instalación de luz en la serie "Light Lab", 2006/07_Sala de exhibiciones – instalación de luz de Olafur Eliasson en el ático_Paola Pivi, "It's a cocktail party", 2008.

GERMANY_FREIBURG **AUGUSTINERMUSEUM**

DEUTSCHLAND_ALLEMAGNE_ALEMANIA
PROF. CHRISTOPH MÄCKLER ARCHITEKTEN
2010
KUNSTMUSEUM_MUSÉE D'ART_MUSEO DE ARTE
4,095 M^2
PHOTOS CHRISTIAN RICHTERS

Kernidee des Umbaus war es, die Raumwirkung durch eine ins Kirchenschiff eingestellte zweite Raumschale wieder erlebbar zu machen. Es wurden adäquate Räume für die Sammlung kirchlicher Kunst geschaffen. So präsentieren sich insbesondere die Münsterfiguren aus dem 13. und 14. Jahrhundert im Mittelraum der Skulpturenhalle. Ein neuer großzügig verglaster Vorbau an der Westfassade öffnet diese für die Besucher, und das große repräsentative Portal am Augustinerplatz lädt zum Eintritt in das Foyer ein. Als sichtbares Zeichen nach außen werden die originalen „Kaiserfenster" aus dem Freiburger Münster in den Vorbau integriert und wieder voll zur Geltung gebracht.

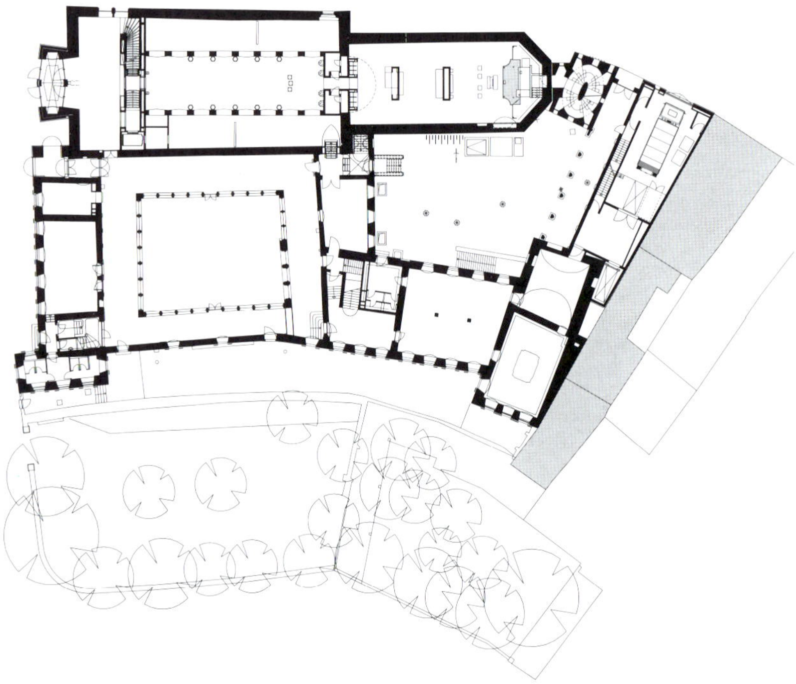

L'idée centrale de la transformation était la revitalisation de l'effet spatial par un deuxième mur d'enceinte installé dans la nef. Ainsi, des espaces adaptés à la collection de l'art ecclésiastique ont été créés. L'espace central du hall de sculptures présente notamment des figures de la cathédrale datant du XIII et XIV siècle. Une nouvelle partie saillante généreuse vitrée sur la façade Ouest ouvre cet espace aux visiteurs et le grand portail représentatif sur la Augustinerplatz invite à l'accès au foyer. Les grands vitraux d'origine de la Cathédrale de Fribourg consacrés à l'empereur, bien visibles de l'extérieur, sont intégrés dans la partie saillante et ont retrouvé toute leur splendeur.

La idea fundamental de esta reforma era lograr una espacialidad revitalizada con una segunda envolvente espacial dentro de la nave del templo. Se lograron así salas adecuadas para la colección de arte eclesiástico. De este modo, se muestran las figuras catedralicias de los siglos XIII y XIV en el espacio central de la sala de esculturas. Una nueva y grandiosa construcción acristalada en la fachada occidental las abre al visitante, y el gran portal representativo sobre la plaza Augustinerplatz invita a acceder al vestíbulo. Como símbolo visible desde el exterior, las "vidrieras imperiales" originales de la catedral de Friburgo se integran en esta construcción y son revalorizadas en toda su dimensión.

links: Grundriss Erdgeschoss_Treppe. rechts: Blick vom Kirchenschiff Richtung Kaiserfenster im Foyer.
gauche: Plan du rez-de-chaussée_Escalier. droite: Vue sur la nef de l'église en direction des vitraux consacrés à l'empereur dans le foyer.
izquierda: Plano de planta baja_Escalera. derecha: Vista desde la nave en dirección a la vidriera imperial en el vestíbulo.

es of Freiburg Cathedral
es de la cathédrale de Fribourg
urger Münsterfiguren
–1380

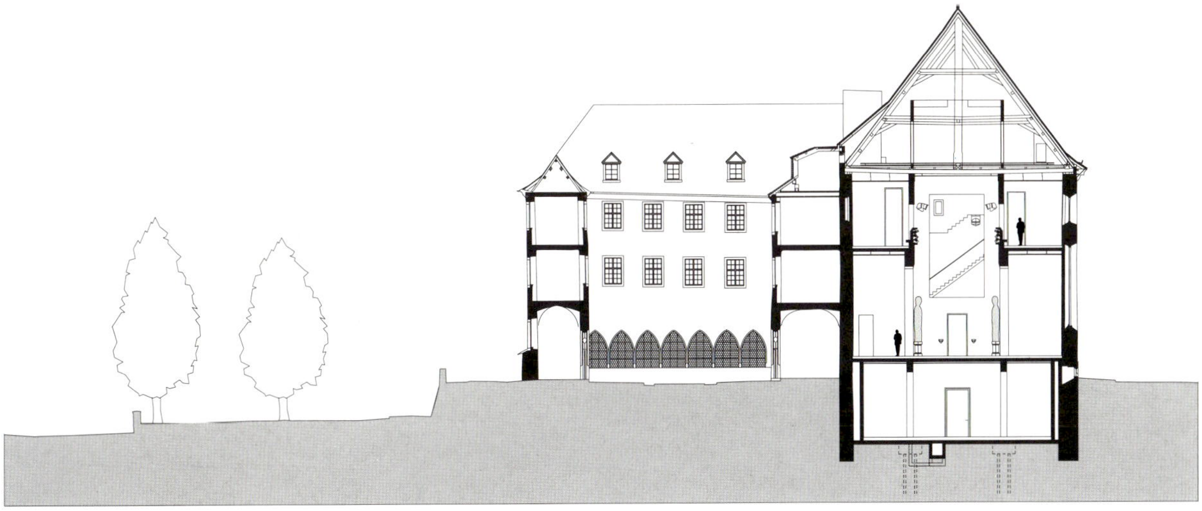

links: Kirchenschiff. rechts: Querschnitt_Galerie_Detail.
gauche: Nef. droite: Coupe longitudinale_Galerie_Détail.
izquierda: Nave de la iglesia. derecha: Corte_Galería_Detalle.

GERMANY_GIENGEN **MARGARETE STEIFF MUSEUM**

DEUTSCHLAND_ALLEMAGNE_ALEMANIA
RAMSEIER & ASSOCIATES LTD.
2005
FIRMENMUSEUM_MUSÉE D'ENTREPRISE_MUSEO DE EMPRESA
2,400 M²
PHOTOS COURTESY OF THE ARCHITECTS

Der Gebäudekomplex besteht aus zwei unterschiedlichen Baukörpern: dem Hauptbau und dem Annexbau. In dem ellipsenförmigen Hauptbau ist das eigentliche Museum untergebracht. Er besitzt einen Längsdurchmesser von 33 Metern und ist als stützenfreie Stahlkonstruktion errichtet. Die Außenhaut der Ellipse wurde mit großflächigen, radialen Messingpaneelen verkleidet. Der rechteckige, langgezogene Annexbau bildet mit einer Länge von 85 Metern den Abschluss zu den bestehenden Fabrikbauten. Er ist zurückhaltend und farbneutral in Sichtbeton und Glas gehalten, steht aber im Kontrast zu den grünlich wirkenden Doppelglasfassaden des Altbestandes. Das Innere des Museumsbaus ist komplett in Weiß gehalten.

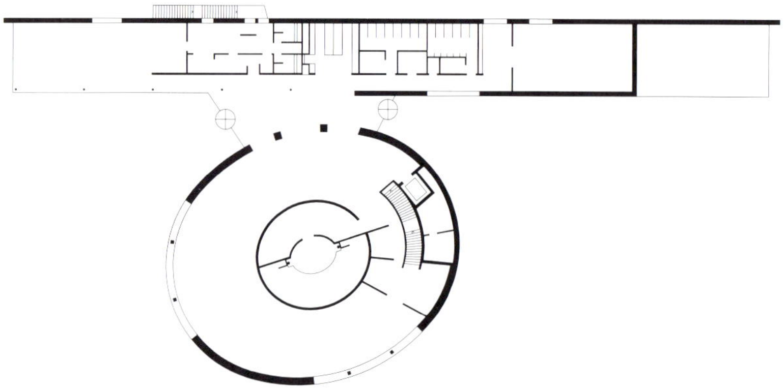

Le complexe du bâtiment se compose de deux différents volumes bâtis : le bâtiment principal et l'annexe. Le bâtiment principal en forme d'ellipse abrite le véritable musée. Il a un diamètre longitudinal de 33 mètres. L'édifice est réalisé en construction d'acier sans pilier. Le revêtement extérieur de l'ellipse est constitué d'importants panneaux en laiton en position radiale. L'annexe allongée rectangulaire de 85 mètres de longueur forme la liaison aux bâtiments industriels existant. Elle reste discrète dans une couleur neutre en béton apparent et en verre qui contraste cependant avec les façades à double vitrage à effet verdoyant des anciens bâtiments. L'intérieur du musée est intégralement en blanc.

El complejo edilicio consta de dos volúmenes diferentes: la construcción principal y el anexo. El cuerpo principal en forma de elipse alberga el museo propiamente dicho. Tiene un eje mayor de 33 metros y ha sido concebido como construcción de acero sin pilares. La piel exterior de la elipse está recubierta de paneles de latón radiales de gran superficie. El edificio anexo, rectangular y alargado, con 85 metros de longitud, constituye el remate de las construcciones fabriles preexistentes. Es discreto y de colores neutros, elaborado en hormigón visto y cristal, pero contrasta con las fachadas de cristal doble de la edificación existente que tienen un efecto de coloración verdoso. El interior del museo es completamente blanco.

links: Grundriss Erdgeschoss_Südfassade mit Haupteingang_Fassadendetail. rechts: Nachtaufnahme Nordfassade_Zugang Parkplatz_Blick vom großen Fenster zum Eingangsbereich.
gauche: Plan du rez-de-chaussée_Façade sud avec entrée principale_Façade en détail. droite: Prise de vue de nuit, façade nord_Accès parking_Vue de la grande fenêtre sur la zone d'entrée.
izquierda: Plano de planta baja_Fachada sur con acceso principal_Detalle de fachada. derecha: Vista nocturna de la fachada norte_Acceso al estacionamiento_Vista desde la gran ventana hacia el área de acceso.

GERMANY_GREVESMÜHLEN MUSEUM UND VEREINSHAUS

DEUTSCHLAND_ALLEMAGNE_ALEMANIA
ARCHITEKT ROLAND SCHULZ
2005
GESCHICHTSMUSEUM_MUSÉE D'HISTOIRE_MUSEO HISTÓRICO
1,378 M²
PHOTOS JÖRN LEHMANN, SCHWERIN

Das Museum befindet sich im Erdgeschoss des Gebäudes und ist über den Haupteingang vom Kirchplatz aus zugänglich. Die Vertikalerschließung wurde bei dem Umbau aus dem historischen Gebäude herausgenommen und hinter das Gebäude gestellt. Auf diese Weise entstand ein Treppenturm, der mit seiner besonderen Grundrissgeometrie gleichzeitig eine Gelenkfunktion zwischen dem alten Schulhaus und dem neuen Veranstaltungssaal übernimmt. Die Fassaden des alten Schulgebäudes aus Ziegelsichtmauerwerk sind erhalten geblieben und kontrastieren mit dem Sichtbeton des Treppenturms.

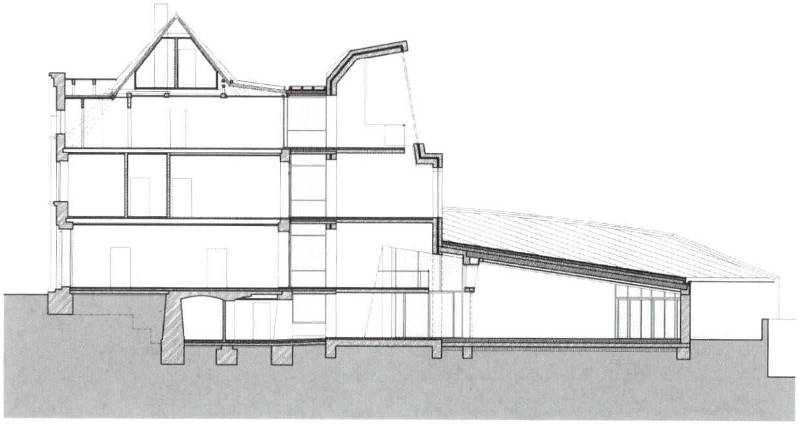

Le musée se situe au rez-de-chaussée du bâtiment avec un accès à l'entrée principale au niveau de la place de l'église. L'élément vertical fut retiré du bâtiment historique lors des travaux de transformation afin d'être aménagé à l'arrière du bâtiment pour servir simultanément de tour d'escalier et d'articulation entre l'ancien édifice d'école et la nouvelle salle dédiée aux manifestations grâce à la géométrie particulière de son plan. Les façades de l'ancien édifice d'école maçonnées de briques se sont conservées correctement et contrastent avec le béton apparent de la tour d'escalier.

El museo se encuentra en la planta baja de la edificación. Se ingresa a través el acceso principal desde la Plaza de la Iglesia. Durante la reforma, las circulaciones verticales preexistentes fueron eliminadas del interior del edificio histórico y ubicadas detrás del mismo. De este modo cobró vida una torre de escaleras que, con su sofisticada geometría volumétrica, oficia al mismo tiempo como articulación entre la antigua escuela y la nueva sala de actividades y exhibiciones. Las fachadas de ladrillo visto originales de la antigua edificación escolar se pudieron conservar, y constituyen un contraste con el liso hormigón visto de la torre de escaleras.

links: Schnitt_Westansicht_Veranstaltungssaal_Ostansicht Gebäudeensemble. rechts: Südostansicht_Treppenturm mit Aufzug_Veranstaltungssaal_Eingangshalle mit Treppenturm.
gauche: Coupe_Vue à l'ouest_Salle de manifestation_Vue à l'est de l'ensemble du bâtiment. droite: Vue au sud-est_Tour d'escalier avec ascenseur_Salle de manifestation_Hall d'entrée avec la tour d'escalier.
izquierda: Corte_Vista oeste_Sala de actividades_Vista este del conjunto edilicio. derecha: Vista sudeste_Torre de escaleras con ascensor_Sala de actividades_Sala de acceso con torre de escaleras.

GERMANY_HALLE **LANDESMUSEUM FÜR VORGESCHICHTE**

DEUTSCHLAND_ALLEMAGNE_ALEMANIA
DIETZSCH & WEBER ARCHITEKTEN
2008
ARCHÄOLOGIEMUSEUM_MUSÉE DE L'ARCHÉOLOGIE
MUSEO ARQUEOLÓGICO
7,580 M^2
PHOTOS N. BLEUL, A. WEBER / HALLE

Mit dem Aus- und Umbau wurden historische Raumstrukturen und -proportionen wiederhergestellt und durch eine moderne Ausstattung ergänzt. Shop, Café und Vortragssaal wurden als variabel nutzbare Raumachse neu in das Erdgeschoss eingefügt. Der Neubau für die Restaurierungswerkstätten, die bis dahin auf verschiedene Standorte verteilt waren, entstand gleichzeitig in der Nachbarschaft des Museums. Drei Werkstattbereiche (Stein, Metall und Holz) mit dazugehörigen Laboratorien, Büros und Lagerflächen besetzen je eine Etage. Der Stahlbetonbau mit vorgehängter Profilglasfassade interpretiert mit vertikaler Fassadenstruktur und horizontaler, gesimsartiger Bänderung die Formensprache des Museums mit Mitteln des Industriebaus.

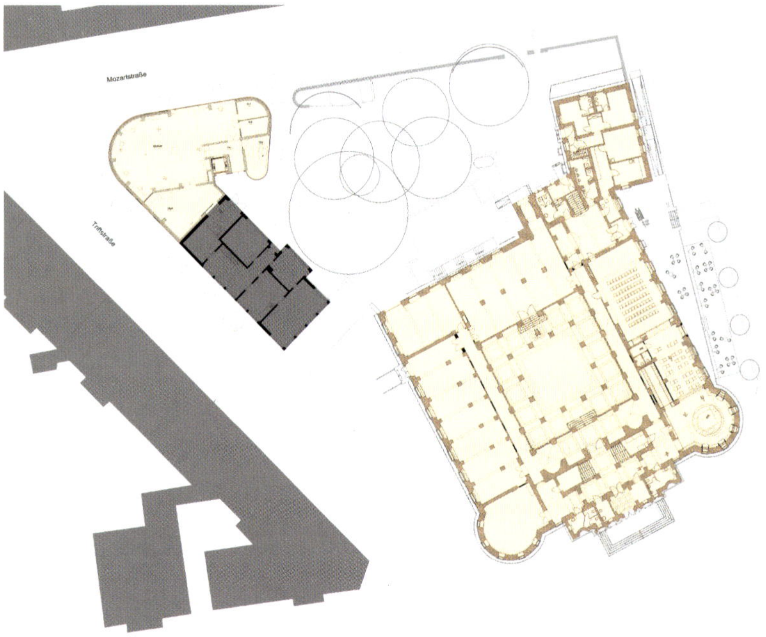

Lors de la construction et de la transformation, les structures et proportions de l'espace historiques ont été reprises et complétées par un équipement moderne. La boutique, le café et la salle de conférence furent intégrés au rez-de-chaussée comme espaces utiles variables. Le nouveau bâtiment consacré aux ateliers de restauration qui étaient répartis sur différents sites, est situé désormais à proximité du musée. Trois zones d'atelier (pierre, métal et bois) avec leurs laboratoires, bureaux et entrepôts occupent respectivement un étage. La structure en béton armé avec sa façade en verre suspendue profilée interprète grâce aux moyens de construction industrielle et la structure verticale de sa façade ornée de bandes horizontales au niveau de la corniche, le langage des formes du musée.

Con la reforma y ampliación se reconfiguraron las estructuras y proporciones históricas de los espacios museísticos, que se completaron con moderno equipamiento. En la planta baja se incorporaron la tienda, el café y la sala de conferencias como un eje espacial de usos múltiples. En la inmediata vecindad del museo nació el edificio nuevo para albergar los talleres de restauración, que antes se hallaban dispersos en varias ubicaciones. Tres áreas de talleres para piedra, metal y madera, con sus respectivos laboratorios, oficinas y zonas de depósito, ocupan un nivel cada una. La construcción en hormigón armado con fachada suspendida de cristal y perfiles se expresa mediante una estructura vertical y elementos horizontales similares a cornisas, y reinterpreta el lenguaje formal del museo con elementos de la construcción industrial.

links: Lageplan_Hauptansicht_Treppenhaus Werkstatt. rechts: Hofansicht Werkstatt_Neubau Restaurierungswerkstätten_Zugang Café.
gauche: Plan de site_Vue principale_Cage d'escalier de l'atelier. droite: Vue de la cour de l'atelier Nouveau bâtiment des ateliers de restauration_Accès au café.
izquierda: Plano de ubicación_Fachada principal_Caja de escaleras de los talleres. derecha: Vista de los talleres desde el patio_Talleres de reparaciones en nueva edificación_Acceso al café.

GERMANY_HAMBURG **LOKI SCHMIDT HAUS**

DEUTSCHLAND_ALLEMAGNE_ALEMANIA
PROF. BERNHARD WINKING ARCHITEKTEN BDA,
FRANK WEITENDORF
2006
NATURKUNDEMUSEUM_MUSEE DE L'HISTOIRE NATURELLE
MUSEO DE HISTORIA NATURAL
460 M²
PHOTOS TOBIAS WILLE (258 B. L., B. M. R., B. R., 259, 260)
CHRISTIAN WOLTER (258 B. M. L.,261)

Die 1870 gegründete Botanische Sammlung erhielt ein eigenes Museum im Botanischen Garten. Das gestalterische Konzept sieht einen Solitärbau als Kubus vor, der mit seiner Außenhaut aus blauer, prismatisch gebrochener Keramik im übertragenen Sinne den blauen Planeten, unsere Erde, darstellt. Er birgt die Schätze der Erde: die Vielfalt der Nutzpflanzen. Das Museum verfügt über zwei große schaufensterartige Öffnungen sowie wenige kleine Fenster, die ausgesuchte Blicke in den Garten erlauben. Die Ausstellungsfläche erstreckt sich über drei Ebenen. Ein großer exzentrischer Luftraum verbindet alle Ebenen miteinander und präsentiert das wohl spektakulärste Ausstellungsstück, die haushohe Würgefeige.

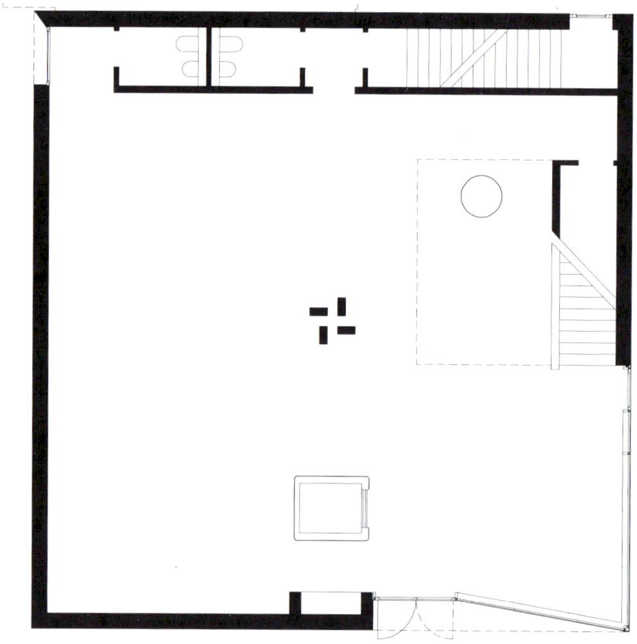

Un musée dédié accueille la collection botanique fondée en 1870 dans le jardin botanique. La conception d'origine prévoit un concept cubique avec son revêtement extérieur recouvert de morceaux de céramique bleu prismatiques qui représente au sens figuré la planète bleue, notre terre. Il abrite les trésors de la terre et la diversité des plantes utiles. Le musée comprend deux grandes ouvertures comparables à des vitrines et quelques fenêtres de petite taille qui offrent une vue exquise sur le jardin. Les surfaces d'exposition s'étendent sur trois niveaux. Un grand espace aérien excentré relie tous les niveaux et présente la pièce d'exposition la plus spectaculaire : un figuier des banyans de la hauteur d'une maison.

La colección de botánica, existente desde 1870, dispone de museo propio en el Jardín Botánico. El concepto de diseño prevé un volumen solitario en forma de cubo que, con su recortada piel exterior de cerámica azul, representa en sentido literal al planeta azul, nuestra Tierra. Encierra los tesoros de la Tierra, la diversidad de las plantas útiles. El museo comprende dos grandes aberturas que semejan vitrinas y algunas ventanas más pequeñas que permiten vistas selectas del jardín. La superficie de exhibiciones se extiende por tres niveles. Un gran espacio excéntrico de altura múltiple conecta los tres niveles entre sí y alberga el ejemplar más espectacular de la colección: una especie de higuera que llega hasta el techo.

links: Grundriss Erdgeschoss_Eingang_Ausstellung im 1. Obergeschoss_Außenansicht von Nordosten_Treppenhaus. rechts: Eingangsansicht.
gauche: Plan du rez-de-chaussée_Entrée_Exposition au 1er étage_Vue extérieure du nord-est_Cage d'escalier. droite: Vue de l'entrée.
izquierda: Plano de planta baja_Acceso_Exhibición en el primer piso_Vista exterior desde el nordeste_Caja de la escalera. derecha: Vista del acceso.

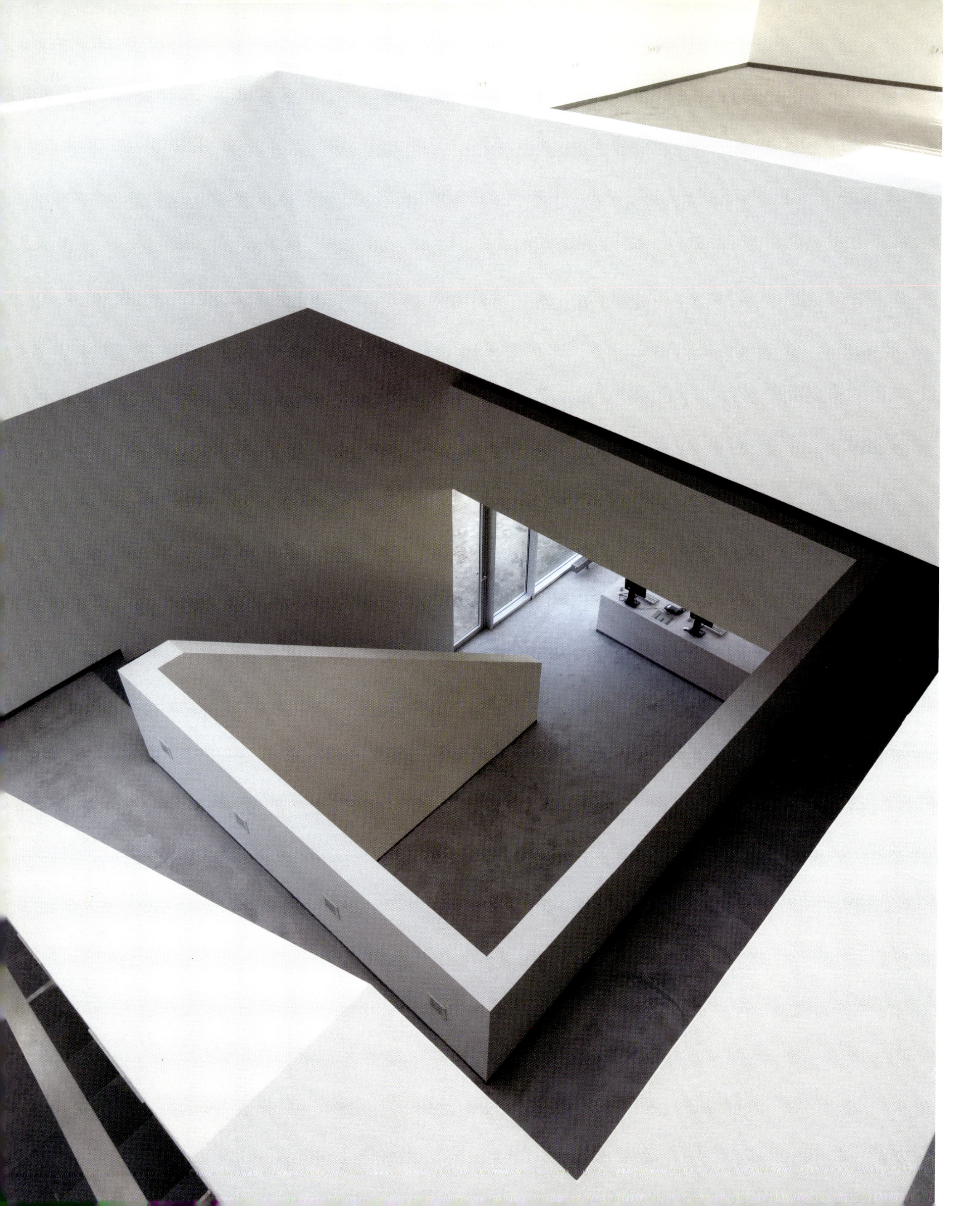

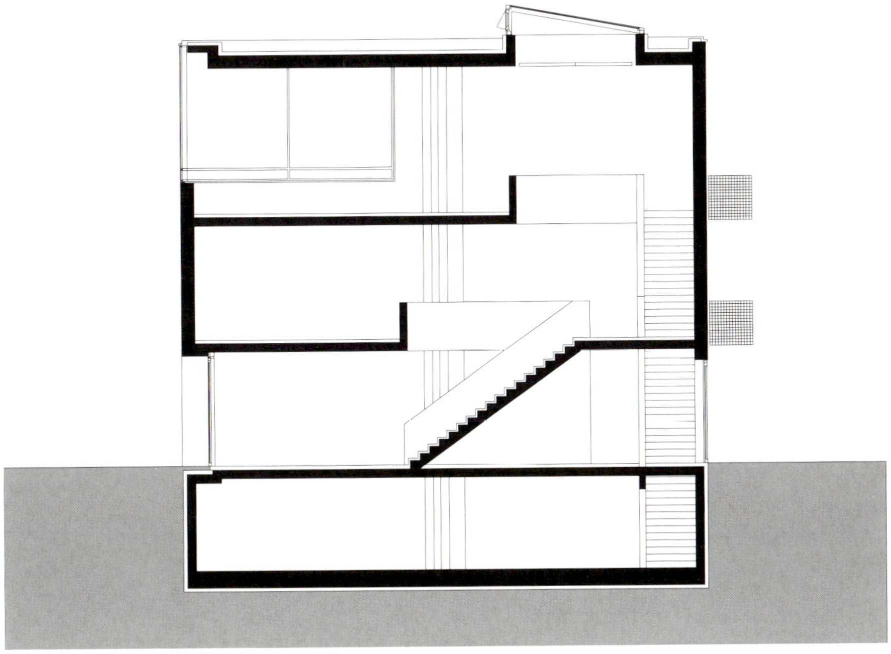

links: Blick hinab zum Eingangsbereich. rechts: Schnitt_Schaumagazin im 1. Obergeschoss.
gauche: Vue vers le bas sur la zone d'entrée. droite: Coupe_Showroom au 1er étage.
izquierda: Vista desde arriba hacia el área de acceso. derecha: Corte_Gabinete de exhibición en el primer piso.

GERMANY_HINZERT **GEDENKSTÄTTE HINZERT**

DEUTSCHLAND_ALLEMAGNE_ALEMANIA
WANDEL HOEFER LORCH + HIRSCH
2005
GESCHICHTSMUSEUM_MUSÉE D'HISTOIRE_MUSEO HISTÓRICO
471 M²
PHOTOS NORBERT MIGULETZ, FRANKFURT / MAIN

Mit dem neuen Dokumentationszentrum und Begegnungshaus legt sich eine Schicht von historischen Orten über die Landschaft und erklärt die Systematik des ehemaligen SS-Lagers. Aus der Zweidimensionalität der Landschaft entwickelt sich das Haus als dreidimensionales Faltwerk, das auf einfache Art Grenzen sichtbar werden lässt. Aus der Topografie entstand ein Gebäude, das als Verwerfung der Landschaft deutlich macht, dass die Idylle an diesem Ort trügt. Information, Lernen und Auseinandersetzung mit der Geschichte werden neben dem Gedenken aufgrund des allmählichen Verschwindens der Generation der Zeitzeugen immer wichtiger und sind Aufgabe dieses Hauses.

Le nouveau centre de documentation et la maison communale créent un réseau de lieux historiques dans le paysage qui explique la systématique de l'ancien camp SS. A partir du paysage bidimensionnel, la maison s'épanouit au niveau tridimensionnel pour manifester les frontières simplement par opposition au paysage. La topographie a permis de créer un bâtiment qui contraste avec le paysage et montre que ce lieu est faussement idyllique uniquement grâce à son apparence. Informer, apprendre et interpeler l'histoire, se consacrer à la mémoire des générations de témoins de l'époque qui disparaissent au fil du temps : telle est la mission de plus en plus importante de cette maison.

Con el nuevo centro de documentación y casa de reuniones se descubre una red de localidades históricas en el paisaje, y se aclara la sistemática del antiguo campo de las S.S. En las dos dimensiones del paisaje se despliega esta casa como obra tridimensional y, en su interacción con el paisaje, se hacen claramente visibles sus límites. De la topografía surge un edificio que, cual recusación del paisaje, muestra que lo idílico de ese lugar es engañoso. Información, aprendizaje y discrepancia con la historia se van haciendo cada vez más importantes, al igual que la reflexión sobre la desaparición paulatina de la generación de testigos presenciales: esa es la tarea de esta casa.

links: Lageplan_Außenansicht_Faltwerk. rechts: Fassade_Blick aus der Ausstellung_Ausstellung.
gauche: Plan de site_Vue extérieure_Ossature plissée. droite: Façade_Vue à partir de l'exposition_Exposition.
izquierda: Plano de ubicación_Vista exterior_Plegado. derecha: Fachada_Vista desde la exhibición_Exposición.

GERMANY_HOMBROICH **LANGEN FOUNDATION**

DEUTSCHLAND_ALLEMAGNE_ALEMANIA
TADAO ANDO ARCHITECT & ASSOCIATES
2004
KUNSTMUSEUM_MUSÉE D'ART_MUSEO DE ARTE
3,050 M²
PHOTOS TOMAS RIEHLE / ARTURIMAGES

Das Museum Insel Hombroich befindet sich in der Nähe der Erft. Das gesamte Grundstück ist eine in einer ausgedehnten Auenlandschaft schwimmende Insel, ein „Park"-Museum. Auf 200.000 Quadratmetern bewaldetem Park verteilt finden sich Außenskulpturen neben zahlreichen schicken Ausstellungspavillons, die ebenfalls wie Skulpturen wirken. Das Museum umfasst orientalische und moderne Kunst, so dass Räume zweierlei verschiedenen Charakters vonnöten waren. Jener für die orientalische Kunst ist ein Raum der „Ruhe", der von weichem Licht erfüllt ist, und der andere für die moderne Kunst ist ein Raum mit pochender „Bewegung" und gemischter Beleuchtung. Durch die verschachtelte Beton- und Glasbauweise ist der ruhige Raum der ständigen Ausstellung von einem Puffer umgeben.

Le musée de l'île Hombroich se situe à proximité de la rivière Erft. L'ensemble du terrain est formé par une île située sur une vaste terre basse riche en limon à l'image d'un musée dans un parc. La forêt répartie sur 200 000 mètres carrés est parsemée de sculptures à l'aire libre à proximité de nombreux pavillons d'exposition chics qui séduisent également par les sculptures. Le musée abrite l'art oriental et l'art moderne. Par conséquent, la création d'espaces à deux caractères distincts fut requise. L'espace dédié à l'art oriental fut créé comme un espace de tranquillité rempli de lumière et l'espace dédié à l'art moderne animé par un éclairage mixte. Grâce à la construction enchevêtrée en béton et verre, l'espace de tranquillité de l'exposition permanente est entouré d'un tampon qui consolide l'ensemble.

El museo de la isla de Hombroich se encuentra en las cercanías del río Erft. El terreno parece una isla que flota en un gigantesco pantanal, y se pretende ofrecer un museo como parque. Sobre 200.000 metros cuadrados de bosque se distribuyen esculturas al aire libre junto a numerosos pabellones de exhibición muy vistosos que también parecen esculturas. El museo comprende arte oriental y moderno, con lo que aparecen salas con dos caracteres diferenciados. Las salas de arte oriental son espacios de tranquilidad llenos de luz, mientras que las salas de arte moderno presentan iluminación mixta y movimiento palpitante. El método constructivo en hormigón y cristal logra que las salas silenciosas de la exhibición permanente estén rodeadas de un efecto amortiguador.

links: Zeichnung_Außenbereich mit Wasserbecken_Wasserspiegelung. rechts: Glasfassade_Gang Ausstellungsgebäude_Ausstellungsraum.
gauche: Dessin_Surface d'exposition_Reflet sur le grand bassin. droite: Façade de verre_Corridor du bâtiment d'exposition_Espace d'exposition.
izquierda: Ilustración_Exterior con estanque de agua_Reflejo en el agua. derecha: Fachada acristalada_Pasaje del edificio de exhibiciones_Sala de exhibiciones.

GERMANY_KOCHEL AM SEE **FRANZ MARC MUSEUM**

DEUTSCHLAND_ALLEMAGNE_ALEMANIA
DIETHELM & SPILLMANN
2008
KUNSTMUSEUM_MUSÉE D'ART_MUSEO DE ARTE
1,550 M²
PHOTOS ROGER FREI, ZURICH

In einem dreigeschossigen Neubau sind neben den Werken Franz Marcs auch Exponate aus der Sammlung Stangl zu sehen, während der Altbau Restaurant, Verwaltung und Museumspädagogik aufnimmt. In einer Waldlichtung gelegen, gruppieren sich die beiden Gebäude unter Einschluss eines Vorhofs zu einem kompakten Ensemble, das sich je nach Blickwinkel unterschiedlich präsentiert. Mit Ausnahme des Foyers basieren die Grundrisse auf einer kammerartigen Raumstruktur. Aufgrund der vielen lichtempfindlichen Arbeiten der Sammlung wurde von einem Tageslichtkonzept abgesehen. Der Hauptzweck der wenigen Fenster besteht deshalb in erster Linie darin, einen Ausblick auf die schöne Umgebung zu bieten.

Le nouveau bâtiment à trois étages abrite, outre les œuvres de Franz Marc, également des objets exposés provenant de la collection de Stangl. L'ancien bâtiment accueille le restaurant ainsi que la partie administrative et pédagogique du musée. Situés au cœur d'une clairière, les deux bâtiments sont regroupés avec une cour d'entrée en un ensemble compact qui se présente différemment selon l'angle de vue. A l'exception du foyer, les plans se basent sur une structure spatiale rectangulaire. En raison de la sensibilité à la lumière de nombreuses œuvres de la collection, une conception d'éclairage est prévue afin d'éviter un excès de la lumière naturelle. Par conséquent, le nombre réduit de fenêtres vise principalement à admirer l'environnement magnifique.

En una nueva construcción de tres niveles se reúnen las obras de Marc y muestras de la colección Stangl, mientras que el edificio antiguo alberga un restaurante, la administración e instalaciones pedagógicas. Emplazados en un claro del bosque, los dos edificios se agrupan sobre un patio delantero para configurar un conjunto compacto que se presenta con diferentes vistas según el ángulo desde el que se lo mire. Con excepción del vestíbulo, las plantas se basan en una estructura espacial en cámaras. Debido a la cantidad de obras sensibles a la luz que hay en la colección, se renunció a un concepto de luz diurna. Por lo tanto, la finalidad de las escasas ventanas es, en primer término, ofrecer una hermosa vista de los alrededores.

links: Lageplan_Altbau und neues Museum_Fassade aus diamantgesägtem Crailsheimer Muschelkalk. rechts: Außenansicht Neubau_Ausblick im Aussichtsraum_Blick vom unteren Foyer Richtung Treppenhaus.
gauche: Plan de site_Ancien bâtiment et nouveau musée_Façade en calcaire coquillier de Crailsheim découpé au diamant. droite: Vue extérieure de nouveau bâtiment_Vue dans l'espace d'exposition_Vue du foyer inférieur en direction de la cage d'escalier.
izquierda: Plano de ubicación_Edificios antiguo y nuevo del museo_Fachada en piedra caliza de Crailsheim aserrada. derecha: Vista exterior del nuevo edificio_Vista hacia el exterior_Vista desde el vestíbulo inferior hacia la escalera.

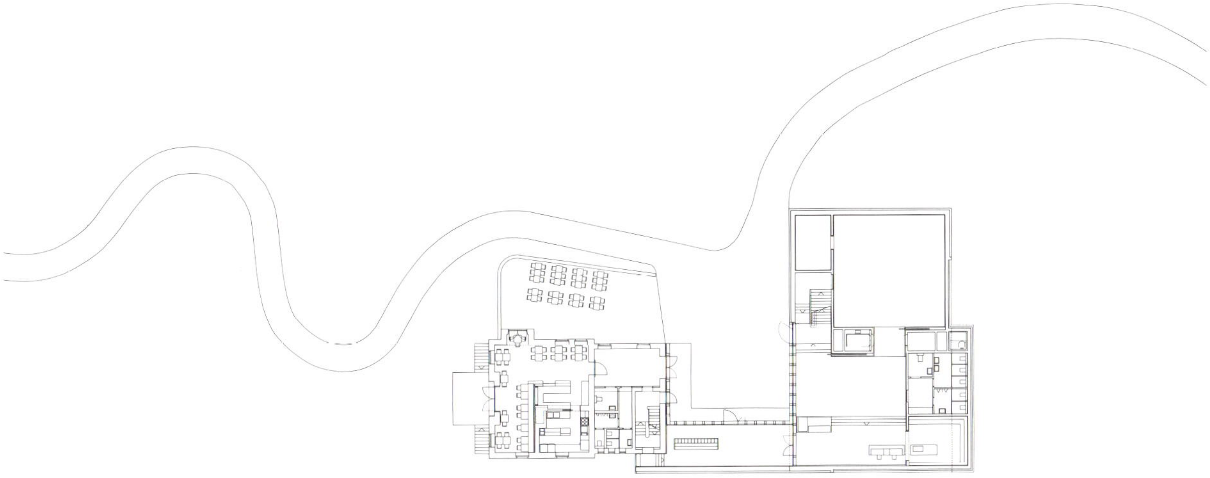

links: Fassadenausschnitt mit Kastenfenster. rechts: Grundriss_Farbige Wände in den Kabinetten 1. Obergeschoss_Das lange Kabinett im 2. Obergeschoss_Diele im 2. Obergeschoss.
gauche: Coupe de la façade avec fenêtres à caisson. droite: Plan_Murs de couleur dans les cabinets au 1er étage_Le long cabinet au 2ème étage_Entrée au 2ème étage.
izquierda: Sector de fachada con ventana tipo cajón. derecha: Plano_Muros coloridos en los gabinetes del primer piso_El gabinete alargado del segundo piso_Salón en el segundo piso.

GERMANY_LEIPZIG MUSEUM DER BILDENDEN KÜNSTE

DEUTSCHLAND_ALLEMAGNE_ALEMANIA
HUFNAGEL PÜTZ RAFAELIAN ARCHITEKTEN
2004
KUNSTMUSEUM_MUSÉE D'ART_MUSEO DE ARTE
16,732 M²
PHOTOS WERNER HUTHMACHER, BERLIN (270 B. M., B. R., 271), AZIZI NAMINI (270 B. L.)

Im Vordergrund des Entwurfs stand das Anliegen, eine „Stadtreparatur" eines kleinteiligen Umfeldes mittels eines repräsentativen und großen Museumsbaus durchzuführen. Der die umliegenden Häuser überragende Museumsbau zieht sich in den Block zurück und ist von einem Ring städtischer Bebauung umgeben. Der quaderförmige Neubau sucht ein Gleichgewicht zwischen autonomer Architektur und Verankerung am Ort. Die Autonomie der den skulpturalen Baukörper umfassenden gläsernen Hülle steht im Kontrast zur steinernen Stadt und thematisiert mit großmaßstäblichen, urbanen Innenräumen die für Leipzig typischen gläsernen Passagen und Höfe.

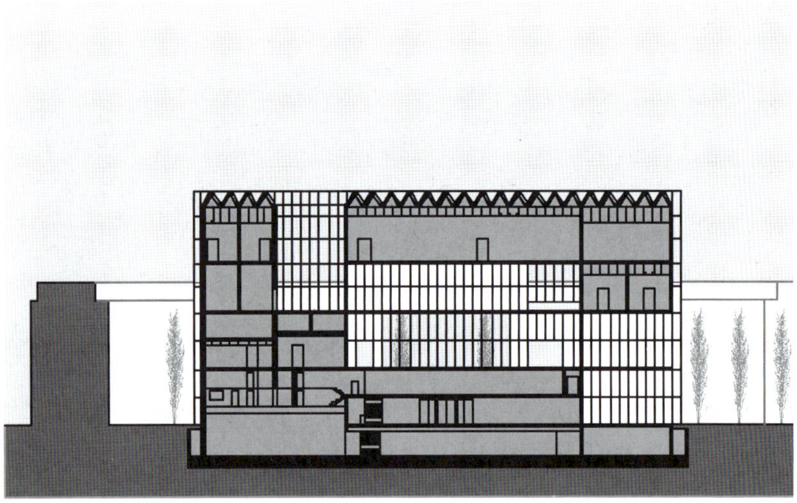

L'idée première du projet visait un assainissement de la ville réalisé à petite échelle grâce à une construction représentative et majestueuse d'un musée. La construction du musée dominant les maisons environnantes se situe en retrait dans le bloc entouré par un cercle de petits bâtiments de la ville. Le nouveau bâtiment rectangulaire cherche un équilibre entre architecture autonome et ancrage au site. L'autonomie de la couverture en verre englobant le corps sculptural du bâtiment contraste avec la pierre présente en ville et fait référence aux passages et cours vitrés spécifiques à Leipzig avec des espaces urbains intérieurs de grande taille.

Al encarar el proyecto, en primer término era necesario considerar una intervención urbana a pequeña escala con un gran edificio museístico representativo. El museo, que descolla entre las casas circundantes, se repliega en la manzana y está rodeado por un anillo de edificaciones urbanas más bien pequeñas. Este edificio con forma de paralelepípedo busca un equilibrio entre la arquitectura autónoma y el anclaje al sitio. La autonomía de la envolvente acristalada que contiene a la estructura escultural contrasta con la pétrea ciudad; con sus espacios interiores urbanos de gran escala tematiza las galerías y los patios tan característicos de Leipzig.

links: Schnitt_Zeichnung bei Nacht_Horizontale Durchsicht_Diagonale Durchsicht. rechts: Museumshalle_Tageslichtsaal im 3. Obergeschoss.
gauche: Coupe_Dessin de nuit_Transparence horizontale_Transparence diagonale. droite: Hall du musée_Salle éclairée par la lumière naturelle au 3ème étage
izquierda: Corte_Ilustración nocturna_Visuales horizontales_Visuales en diagonal. derecha: Salón del museo_Sala con luz diurna en el tercer piso.

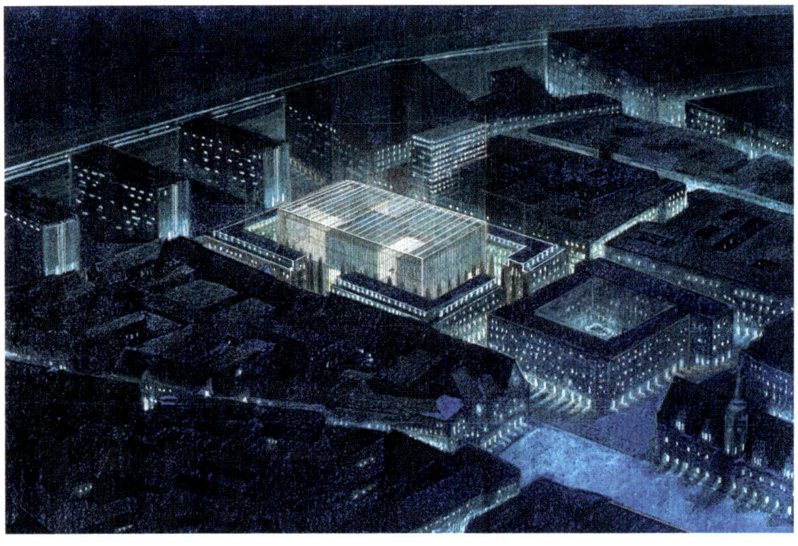

GERMANY_LEIPZIG

GFZK-2 – GALERIE FÜR ZEITGENÖSSISCHE KUNST

DEUTSCHLAND_ALLEMAGNE_ALEMANIA
AS-IF BERLINWIEN
2005
KUNSTMUSEUM_MUSÉE D'ART_MUSEO DE ARTE
1,020 M²
PHOTOS WOLFGANG THALER, VIENNA

Mit dem neuen Ausstellungsgebäude wurde das bestehende Ensemble aus Museum und Nebengebäuden um zirka 1000 Quadratmeter ergänzt. Das Gebäude ist an der Schnittstelle zwischen Museumsarchitektur und spezifischer Ausstellungsarchitektur positioniert. Die Konzeption basiert auf der Frage nach einer räumlichen Entsprechung für die vielschichtige Arbeitsweise einer Galerie, mit variablen Verbindungen dieser Arbeitsebenen. Das polygonale Raumgefüge bietet eine veränderbare architektonische Infrastruktur für eine zeitgenössische Ausstellungspraxis, die die Grundbedingungen der Institution und des Ausstellens zu einem zentralen Thema der Gestaltung macht.

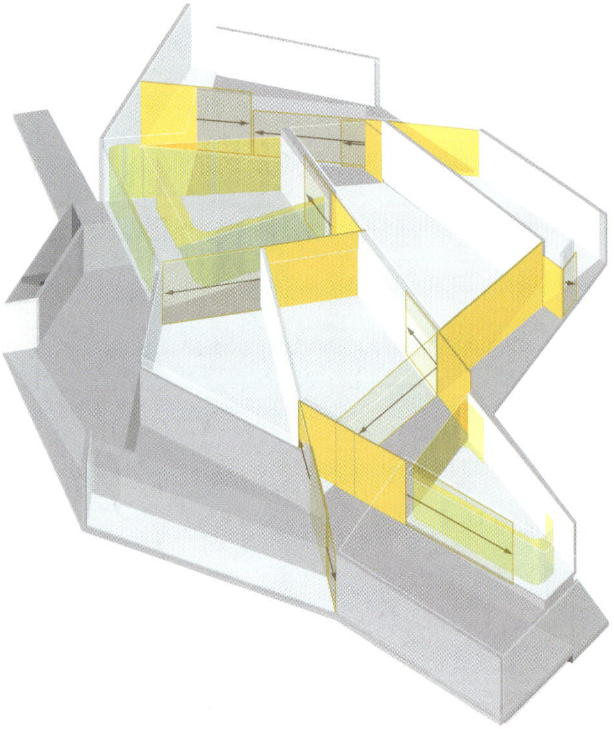

L'ensemble existant du musée et des bâtiments annexes fut complété par un nouveau bâtiment d'exposition d'environ 1 000 mètres carrés. Le bâtiment est localisé à l'interface entre l'architecture du musée et l'architecture d'exposition spécifique. La conception repose sur l'adéquation spatiale et la forme travaillée à plusieurs niveaux d'une galerie avec leurs correspondances variables au niveau des structures. La structure spatiale polygonale est une infrastructure architectonique modifiable dans la pratique contemporaine liée aux expositions qui constitue les conditions de base d'une thématique centrale de formation de l'institution et de l'exposition.

Con el nuevo edificio de exhibiciones se logró ampliar en mil metros cuadrados el conjunto existente del museo y sus edificaciones anexas. El edificio en sí constituye una encrucijada entre la arquitectura museística y la arquitectura para muestras específicas. El concepto básico es la cuestión de la espacialidad correspondiente a la forma de trabajo estratificada de una galería, con las conexiones variables de sus niveles de trabajo. La espacialidad poligonal constituye una infraestructura arquitectónica variable para la práctica contemporánea de las muestras, que pone las condiciones de la institución y de las exhibiciones como tema central del diseño.

links: Axonometrie mit Schiebewänden und Vorhängen_Außenansicht. rechts: Fassade_Variables Raumkonzept.
gauche: Axonométrie avec des cloisons amovibles et rideaux_Vue extérieure. droite: Façade Concept de l'espace variable.
izquierda: Axonometría con muros corredizos y cortinas_Vista exterior. derecha: Fachada_Concepto de interior variable.

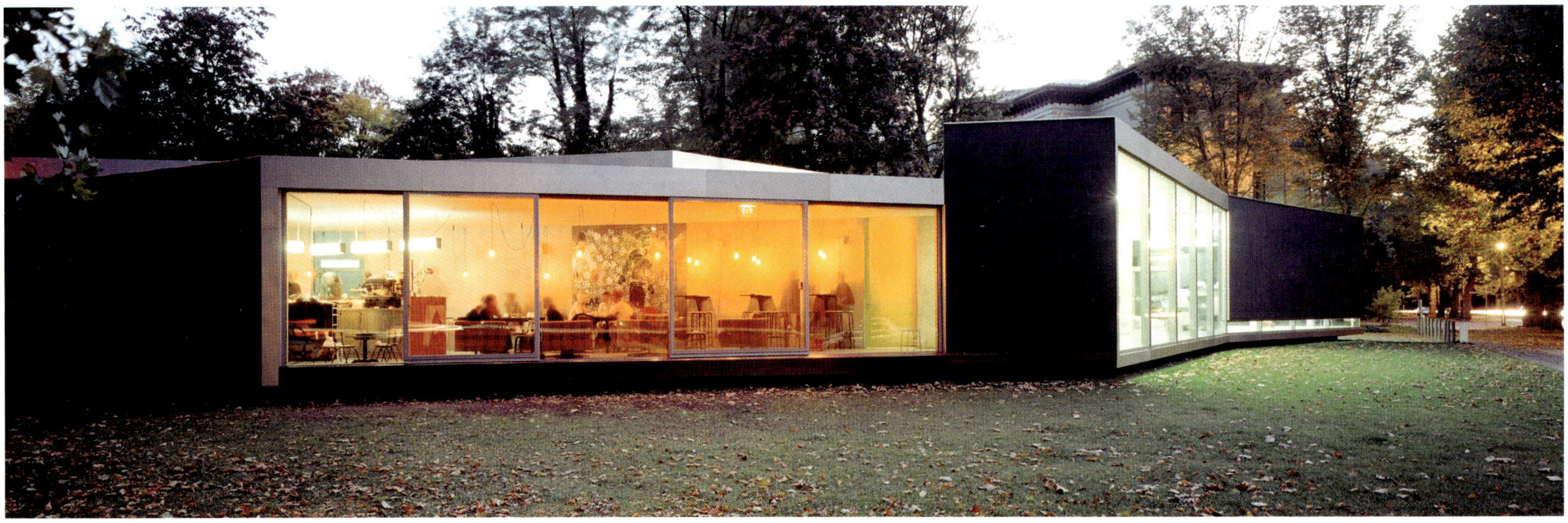

GERMANY_MANCHING **KELTEN RÖMER MUSEUM**

DEUTSCHLAND_ALLEMAGNE_ALEMANIA
FISCHER ARCHITEKTEN, MUNICH – PROF. FLORIAN FISCHER
ARCHITEKT BDA DWB, ALEXANDRA ZEILHOFER ARCHITEKTIN
2006
ARCHÄOLOGIEMUSEUM_MUSÉE D'ARCHÉOLOGIE
MUSEO ARQUEOLÓGICO
1,895 M^2
PHOTOS MICHAEL HEINRICH, MUNICH

Der Besucher nähert sich dem Museum auf unkonventionelle Weise. Ein fast 100 Meter langer, sanft ansteigender Steg führt zu Eingang und Foyer, so dass sich auf dem Weg in eine andere Zeit Distanz zum Hier und Jetzt aufbaut. Wie eine überdimensionale Vitrine liegt das Ausstellungsgeschoss auf einem fast gänzlich geschlossenen, monolithischen Geschoss und einem transparenten Sockel. Die Öffnung der Ausstellungsräume nach außen steigt mit der Dichte der überlieferten Relikte. Das große, nach Norden orientierte Panoramafenster in der Keltenausstellung fängt als bildhaften Hintergrund die wilde Vegetation am Flussufer der Paar ein. Die zweigeschossige Halle, in der die römischen Militärschiffe präsentiert werden, öffnet sich zum Museumspark.

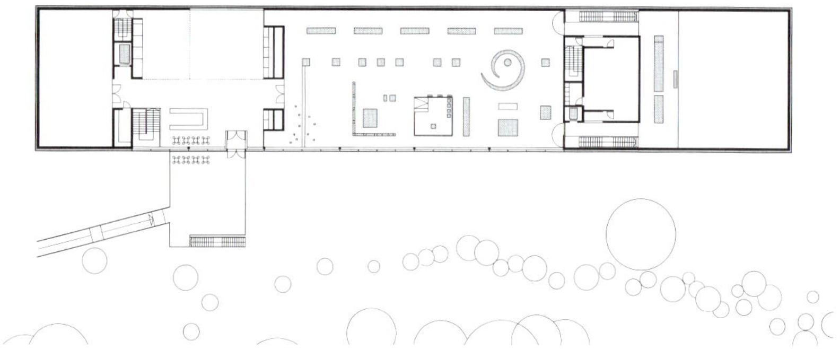

Le visiteur s'approche du musée de manière peu conventionnelle. Un sentier en pente douce, long de quasiment 100 mètres, conduit à l'accès et au foyer afin de prendre conscience au cours du chemin de la distance entre le temps passé et présent. L'étage consacré aux expositions se présente telle une vitrine surdimensionnée sur l'étage monolithique quasiment totalement fermé, muni d'un socle transparent. L'ouverture des espaces d'exposition vers l'extérieur s'accroit avec la densité des reliques exposées. La grande fenêtre panoramique orientée Nord au niveau de l'exposition celtique capte l'arrière plan imagé de la végétation sauvage située sur les rives de la Paar. Le hall à deux étages consacré aux navires de guerre romains s'ouvre sur le parc du musée.

El visitante se acerca al museo de manera nada convencional. Una pasarela de casi 100 metros de longitud conduce al acceso y al vestíbulo, de modo que en el camino se va generando una distancia respecto del aquí y ahora. Como una vitrina sobredimensionada, la planta de exhibiciones está elevada sobre un nivel casi totalmente cerrado y monolítico, con un basamento transparente. La apertura de las salas de exhibición hacia fuera crece a la par de la densidad de las reliquias ancestrales. La ventana panorámica orientada hacia el norte de la exhibición sobre los celtas adopta como fondo colorido la vegetación silvestre de la orilla. La sala de dos niveles donde se exponen las naves militares romanas se abre hacia el parque del museo.

links: Eingangsgeschoss_Steg zum Eingang_Keltenausstellung_Ansicht Nord. rechts: Römerausstellung_Ansicht Süd-West bei Tag_Ansicht Süd-West bei Nacht.
gauche: Niveau d'accès_Passerelle vers l'entrée_Exposition consacrée aux celtes_Vue du nord. droite: Exposition consacrée aux romains_Vue de jour au sud-ouest_Vue de nuit au sud-ouest.
izquierda: Nivel de acceso_Pasaje hacia el acceso_Exhibición sobre los celtas_Fachada norte. derecha: Exhibición sobre los romanos_Vista sudoeste de día_Vista sudoeste de noche.

römer
kelten

römer
kelten

GERMANY_MARBACH / NECKAR **LITERATURMUSEUM DER MODERNE**

DEUTSCHLAND_ALLEMAGNE_ALEMANIA
DAVID CHIPPERFIELD ARCHITECTS
2006
LITERATURMUSEUM_MUSÉE DE LA LITTÉRATURE
MUSEO LITERARIO
3,800 M^2
PHOTOS CHRIS VAN UFFELEN (276 B. L., B. R., 277 B. L.),
JÖRG VON BRUCHHAUSEN (277 A.), CHRISTIAN RICHTERS (277 B. R.)

Das Museum befindet sich auf einem Felsplateau in einem Park über dem Neckar. Das Sichtbetongebäude wurde aus sandgestrahltem Betonwerkstein mit Kalkstein, Holz, Filz und Glas als Zuschlagsstoffen errichtet. Das Innere erschließt sich, wenn man durch Loggia, Foyer und Treppenhaus hinabsteigt und schließlich die mit dunklem Holz vertäfelten Ausstellungsräume erreicht, in denen die fragilen und empfindlichen Exponate ausschließlich durch Kunstlicht beleuchtet werden. Jeder der klimatisch streng kontrollierten Ausstellungsräume grenzt aber auch an eine natürlich belichtete Galerie, so dass sich der introvertierte Blick auf die Welt der Texte und Manuskripte mit Ausblicken auf das grüne Tal jenseits der Fensterscheiben die Waage hält.

Ce musée se situe sur un plateau rocheux dans un parc surplombant la rivière Neckar. Le bâtiment en béton apparent fut créé en blocs en béton décapés au sable agrémentés de calcaire, bois, feutre et verre comme matériaux auxiliaires. L'accès à l'intérieur s'effectue par la loggia, le foyer et l'escalier afin d'accéder en descendant vers les espaces d'exposition revêtus de panneaux en bois foncé. Dans ces espaces, les objets exposés, fragiles et sensibles, sont éclairés uniquement par la lumière artificielle. Chaque salle d'exposition est strictement climatisée et également reliée à une galerie éclairée par la lumière naturelle afin d'assurer l'équilibre entre la vue introvertie sur le monde des textes et des manuscrits et les perspectives sur la vallée verdoyante de l'autre côté à travers les vitres.

El museo se yergue sobre una elevación pedregosa en un parque sobre el río Neckar. El edificio en hormigón visto fue arenado, e incorpora piedra caliza, madera, textiles y cristales como materiales adicionales. El interior se empieza a ver a medida que se transita por la columnata, el vestíbulo y la escalinata, para llegar finalmente a las salas de exhibiciones revestidas en paneles de madera. En ellas, los delicados y frágiles objetos expuestos están iluminados exclusivamente por luz artificial. Cada una de las salas de exhibición también tiene una climatización estrictamente controlada, no obstante lo cual se acerca a una galería con iluminación natural, de modo que una mirada introvertida hacia el mundo de los textos y los manuscritos se compensa con una panorámica del valle verde más allá de las ventanas de cristal.

links: Lageplan_Unteres Foyer_Ausstellungsebene. rechts: Ausstellungsebene im Sockelgeschoss Offene Loggia, Eingangsebene_Ansicht West, Blick Richtung Haupteingang.
gauche: Plan de site_Foyer inférieur_Niveau d'exposition. droite: Zone d'exposition située dans le piédestal_Loggia ouverte, niveau entrée_Vue à l'Ouest_Vue en direction de l'entrée principale.
izquierda: Plano de ubicación_Vestíbulo inferior_Nivel de exhibiciones. derecha: Nivel de exhibiciones en el basamento_Loggia abierta, nivel de acceso_Fachada oeste, vista en dirección al acceso principal.

GERMANY_MUNICH **BMW MUSEUM**

DEUTSCHLAND_ALLEMAGNE_ALEMANIA
ATELIER BRÜCKNER
2008
FIRMENMUSEUM_MUSÉE D'ENTREPRISE_MUSEO DE EMPRESA
12,200 M^2
PHOTOS MARCUS MEYER, BREMEN

Das BMW Museum spricht die zeitgemäße, dynamische Sprache der automobilen Welt. Analog zur Marke, die für innovative Technik und zukunftsweisendes Design steht, geht das Museum bei der integrativen Verbindung von Architektur, Ausstellungsgestaltung und kommunikativen Medien neue Wege. Am historischen Ort innerhalb der denkmalgeschützten Konzernzentrale taucht der Besucher in ein urbanes Ambiente ein. Über asphaltierte Straßen und Plätze erreicht er hell erleuchtete Ausstellungshäuser, die jeweils einem Thema gewidmet sind. Neue Medien tragen zur Dynamisierung bei. Rund um den zentralen BMW Platz setzt eine Symbiose aus Medien und Architektur Raum und Exponate in Bewegung. Ein bewegter und bewegender Eindruck entsteht.

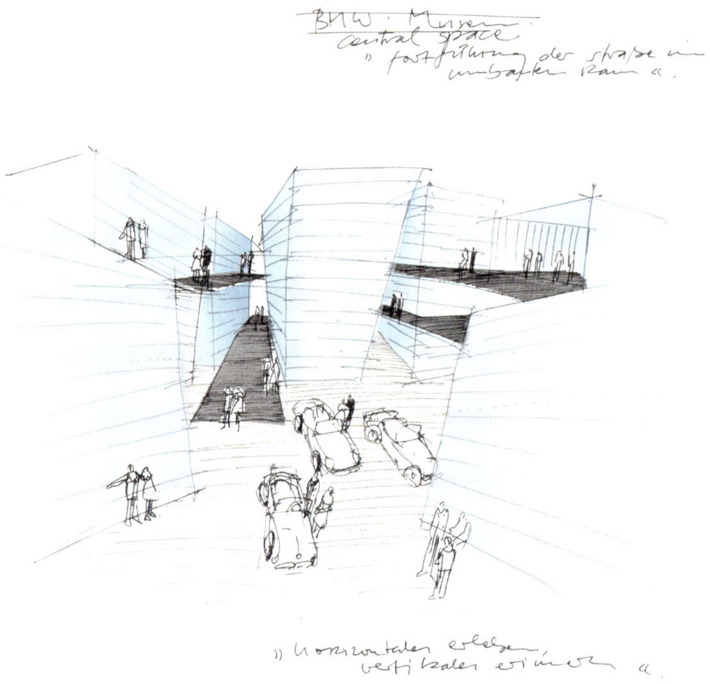

Le musée BMW dynamise la langue contemporaine du monde de l'automobile. En analogie à la marque, reconnue pour sa technique innovatrice et sa conception futuriste, le musée ouvre de nouvelles voies de liaison exhaustives entre l'architecture, la conception d'exposition et les médias. Au centre historique situé au siège du groupe, protégé monument historique, le visiteur plonge dans une ambiance urbaine. Des routes et places en asphalte l'accompagnent aux espaces d'exposition bien éclairés qui sont tous consacrés à une thématique particulière. Les nouveaux médias contribuent à la dynamique. Autour de la BMW Platz centrale, une symbiose s'anime entre les médias, l'espace consacré à l'architecture et les objets exposés en produisant une impression animée et mouvementée.

El Museo BMW expresa el dinámico lenguaje contemporáneo del mundo del automovilismo. De la misma manera que la marca, que representa la tecnología innovadora y el diseño futurista, el museo recorre nuevos caminos en la vinculación integradora de arquitectura, diseño de exhibiciones y medios comunicativos. En el sitio histórico de la sede central de la empresa, declarada monumento histórico, el visitante ingresa en un ambiente de impronta urbana. Atravesando calles y plazas asfaltadas, accede a las claras y luminosas salas de exhibición, que están dedicadas cada una a un tema diferente. Medios nuevos colaboran con la dinamización. En torno a la central BMW Platz, una simbiosis de arquitectura y multimedia pone en movimiento el espacio y las muestras. Se genera una impresión de movimiento y movilizadora.

links: Skizze_Haus des Motorsports, Tourenwagen_Haus des Unternehmens, Begegnungen. rechts: Aufgang in die Museumsschüssel.
gauche: Esquisse_Maison des sports automobiles_Voiture touring, maison de la société_Rencontres. droite: Accès dans les Museumschüssel « les boules du musée ».
izquierda: Esbozo_Casa del Deporte de Motor – automóviles de turismo_Casa de la Empresa, encuentros. derecha: Bol del museo.

BMW Motorsport
1956
BMW 507

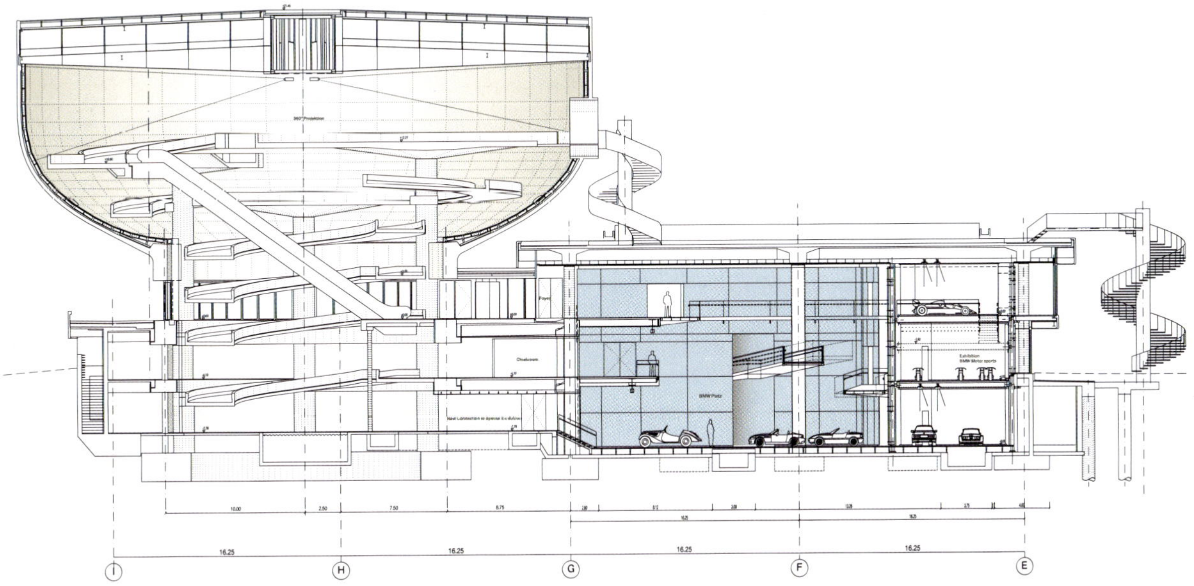

links: BMW Platz. rechts: Querschnitt_Haus der Technik, Leichtbau_Haus des Unternehmens, Aspekte_BMW Platz.
gauche: BMW Platz. droite: Coupe longitudinale_Maison de la technique, construction légère Maison de l'entreprise, aspects_BMW Platz.
izquierda: BMW Platz. derecha: Corte_Casa de la Tecnología, construcción liviana_Casa de la Empresa, aspectos_BMW Platz.

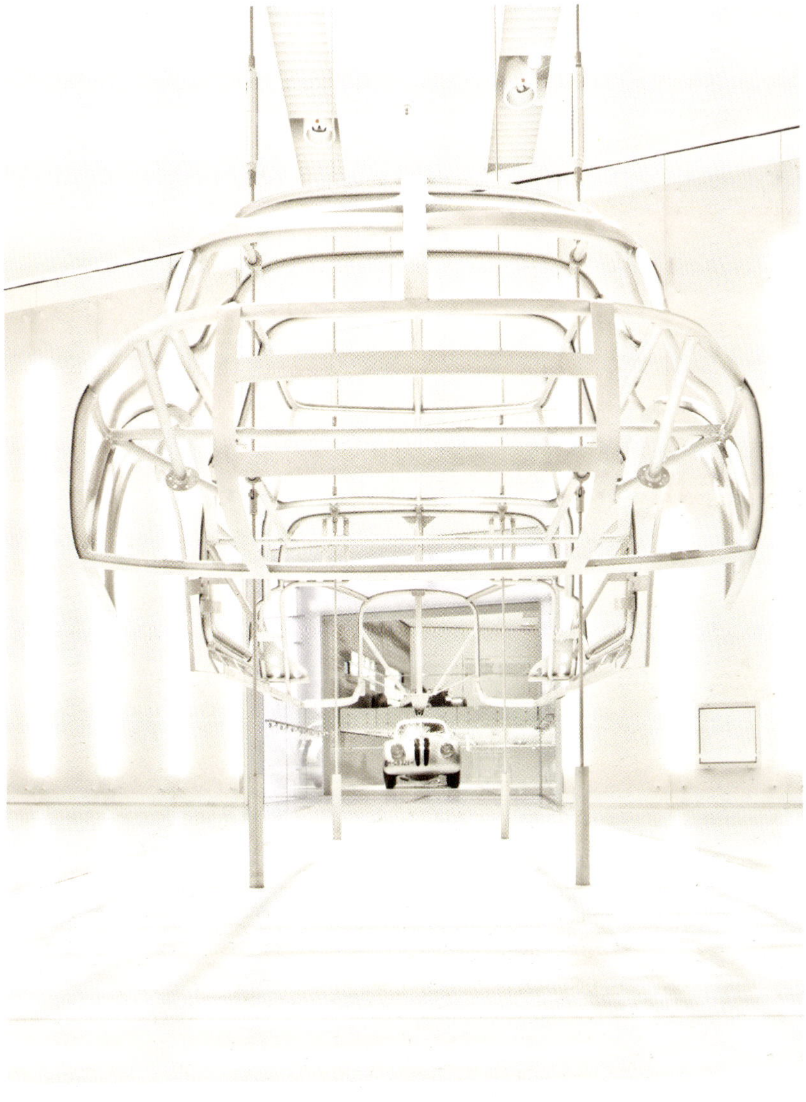

GERMANY_MUNICH **MUSEUM BRANDHORST**

DEUTSCHLAND_ALLEMAGNE_ALEMANIA
SAUERBRUCH HUTTON
2008
KUNSTMUSEUM_MUSÉE D'ART_MUSEO DE ARTE
12,000 M²
PHOTOS ANNETTE KISLING, BERLIN

In dem dreigeschossigen Gebäude an der Nordostecke des Münchner Museumsquartiers sind nahezu alle Ausstellungsräume natürlich belichtet – das Erdgeschoss über ein komplexes System von Reflektoren, die Tageslicht gleichmäßig in die Galerien bringen. Die bewusste Variation von Belichtung, Abfolge, Größe und Proportion lässt eine subtile Differenzierung der Räume entstehen. Die schillernde Erscheinung der polychromen Außenhaut aus vertikalen, in 23 Farbtönen glasierten Keramikstäben sowie einer horizontal gefalteten Blechfassade verändert sich je nach Standort des Betrachters. Das innovative Energiekonzept des Museums schont Ressourcen und schafft hervorragende Bedingungen für die ausgestellten Werke.

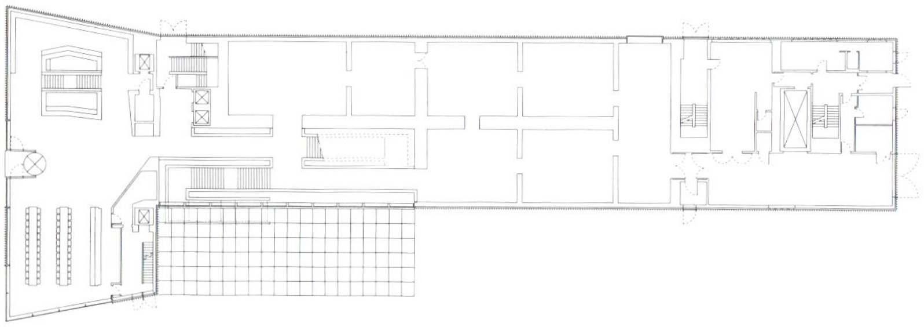

Dans le bâtiment à trois étages situé à l'angle Nord-Est du quartier du musée à Munich, quasiment tous les espaces d'exposition sont éclairés par la lumière naturelle. Par contre, l'éclairage du rez-de-chaussée bénéficie d'un système complexe de réflecteurs amenant la lumière régulièrement du zénith dans les galeries. La variation consciente de l'éclairage, la logique, la grandeur et la proportion permettent d'introduire une différenciation subtile dans les espaces. L'apparence scintillante de la couche extérieure en polychrome provenant des barres verticales de céramique vernies en 23 teintes, ainsi que la façade de tôle ondulée à l'horizontale, modifient la perception selon l'endroit de l'observateur sur le site. La conception énergétique innovante du musée préserve les ressources et crée des conditions optimisées pour les œuvres exposées.

El edificio de tres niveles se ubica en el ángulo nororiental del barrio de los museos de Múnich. Casi todas sus salas de exhibición se iluminan naturalmente; en la planta baja, un complejo sistema de reflectores distribuye de manera uniforme la luz cenital por las galerías. La variación consciente de iluminación, secuencia, tamaño y proporción permite que se aprecie una sutil diferencia entre las salas. La multifacética apariencia de la piel exterior polícroma, elaborada con barras cerámicas verticales vitrificadas en 23 tonalidades y una fachada de chapa plegada horizontalmente, va cambiando según la ubicación del observador. El innovador concepto energético del museo ahorra recursos y logra condiciones sensacionales para las obras expuestas.

links: Grundriss Erdgeschoss_Fassade Hofseite_Museumseingang. rechts: Fassade Türkenstraße Ausstellungssaal Obergeschoss_Ausstellungsräume Erdgeschoss_Museumscafé.
gauche: Plan du rez-de-chaussée_Façade côté cour_Entrée du musée. droite: Façade côté Türkenstrasse Salle d'exposition à l'étage supérieur_Espaces d'exposition au rez-de-chaussée_Cafétéria du musée.
izquierda: Plano de planta baja_Fachada sobre el patio_Acceso al museo. derecha: Fachada sobre la Türkenstrasse_Sala de exhibiciones en planta alta_Salas de exhibiciones en planta baja_Café del museo.

GERMANY_MUNICH **PINAKOTHEK DER MODERNE**

DEUTSCHLAND_ALLEMAGNE_ALEMANIA
STEPHAN BRAUNFELS ARCHITEKTEN BDA
2002
KUNST-, ARCHITEKTUR- UND DESIGNMUSEUM_MUSÉE DE L'ART, ARCHITECTURE ET DESIGN_MUSEO DE ARTE, ARQUITECTURA Y DISEÑO
33,500 M²
PHOTOS JENS WEBER

Die vier Museen des Hauses – Sammlung Moderne Kunst, Neue Sammlung, Architekturmuseum und Staatliche Graphische Sammlung – liegen auf drei Ausstellungsebenen und werden durch die große, sich trichterförmig nach oben und nach unten erweiternde Treppenanlage vertikal miteinander verknüpft. Mit einer Länge von 100 Metern und einem Höhenunterschied von zwölf Metern bildet sie eine Innenraumskulptur, die alle Teile des Hauses zusammenführt und im Zentrum mit einer durch eine Lichtkuppel überwölbten Rotunde vereint. Dadurch entstehen abwechslungsreiche Räume und vielfältige Durchblicke. In den Ausstellungsräumen tritt die Architektur in den Hintergrund. Einfache, klare Oberlichtsäle lenken die Konzentration auf die Exponate.

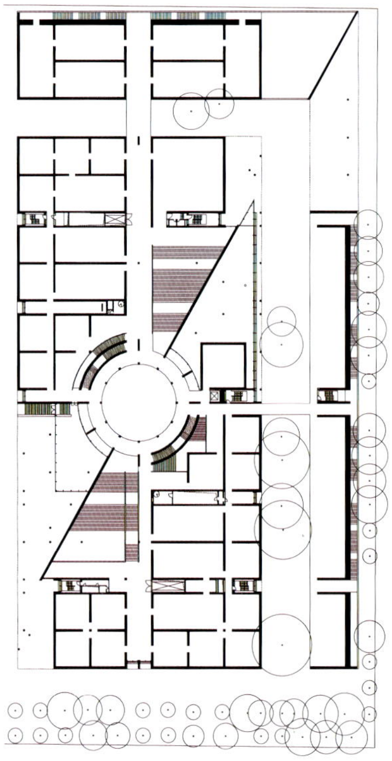

Les quatre musées de la maison – la galerie nationale d'art moderne, la nouvelle collection, le musée d'architecture et la collection graphique fédérale – se situent sur trois niveaux dédiés aux expositions, reliés verticalement par des escaliers en forme d'entonnoir qui s'élargissent vers le bas et le haut. Ces escaliers de 100 mètres de longueur et d'une dénivellation de douze mètres sculptent l'espace intérieur en reliant toutes les parties de l'édifice qui se rejoignent sous la voute d'une coupole centrale lumineuse dans la rotonde. Cet effet crée la richesse des facettes et perspectives variées. Dans les espaces d'exposition, l'architecture se situe en arrière-plan : les salles des combles claires et simples dirigent la concentration sur les œuvres exposées.

Los cuatro museos de esta casa de arte (la Galería Estatal de Arte Moderno, la Nueva Colección, el Museo de Arquitectura y la Colección Gráfica Estatal) se encuentran en tres niveles de exhibición y se vinculan entre sí como por un embudo, gracias a la amplia caja de la escalera. Con una longitud de 100 metros y una diferencia de alturas de 12 metros, constituye una escultura interior que conecta entre sí a todas las partes del edificio y las une en el centro con una rotonda recubierta por un lucernario. De este modo se generan salas variadas y perspectivas polifacéticas. En las salas de exhibición, la arquitectura queda en segundo plano: la iluminación cenital clara y sencilla orienta la concentración directamente hacia las muestras.

links: Grundriss Erdgeschoss_Eingang_Halle in der Rotunde. rechts: Eingang und alte Pinakothek Ausstellung_Treppenanlage.
gauche: Coupe du rez-de-chaussée_Entrée_Hall dans la rotonde. droite: Entrée et ancienne pinacothèque_Exposition_Escaliers
izquierda: Plano de planta baja_Exhibición de colección de sillas_Exposición. derecha: Acceso y Antigua Pinacoteca_Vista desde la exhibición hacia la rotonda_Sala en la rotonda_Sala de acceso.

GERMANY_MUNICH JÜDISCHES MUSEUM MÜNCHEN

DEUTSCHLAND_ALLEMAGNE_ALEMANIA
WANDEL HOEFER LORCH
2007
GESCHICHTSMUSEUM_MUSÉE D'HISTOIRE_MUSEO HISTÓRICO
1,520 M²
PHOTOS ROLAND HALBE / ARTURIMAGES

Das Jüdische Zentrum am St.-Jakobs-Platz ist mit der Stadtstruktur verwoben, seine Öffentlichkeit und Offenheit ist in Plätzen, Wegen und Passagen im Stadtraum erlebbar. Synagoge, Museum und Gemeindehaus sind als ausbalanciertes Ensemble in ihrer jeweiligen Eigenständigkeit formuliert und über die Zwischenräume hinweg zueinander in Beziehung gesetzt. Das Museum als kleinster Kubus am Jakobsplatz vermittelt zwischen Synagoge und Gemeindezentrum und spiegelt Offenheit und Geschlossenheit entsprechend den eigenen Bedürfnissen: Über einem offenen, mit der Platzfläche zum Kommunikationsraum verschmelzenden Foyer liegen die geschlossenen, Konzentration ermöglichenden Ausstellungsräume.

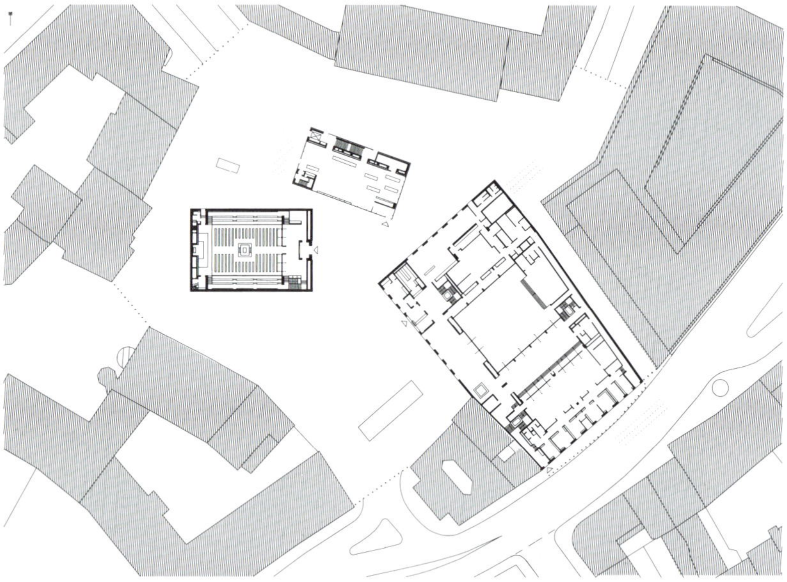

Le centre juif est intégré dans la structure urbaine au niveau de St.-Jakobs-Platz et offre son expérience au public grâce à l'ouverture de places, chemins et passages dans l'espace urbain. La synagogue, le musée et la maison communale sont un ensemble équilibré qui reste individualisé et relié par des espaces intermédiaires. Le musée forme le plus petit cube situé sur Jakobsplatz et sert d'intermédiaire entre la synagogue et le centre communal pour refléter l'ouverture et la fermeture en fonction des exigences : les salles d'exposition se situent au-dessus du foyer qui fusionne avec l'espace ouvert de la place afin d'offrir un lieu de communication en liaison avec le foyer et de favoriser l'isolation et la concentration.

El Centro Judío sobre la St.-Jakobs-Platz se entreteje con la estructura urbana; su apertura y su carácter público se perciben en plazas, caminos y pasajes del espacio urbano. La sinagoga, el museo y la casa comunitaria son un conjunto equilibrado, formulado en su correspondiente independencia, y puesto en relación con los espacios intermedios. El museo, como cubo mínimo en la Jakobsplatz, es un intermediario entre la sinagoga y el centro comunitario, y refleja apertura y circunspección según las necesidades propias. Encima del vestíbulo que conecta con la plaza a modo de espacio comunicativo se encuentran las salas de exhibición cerradas que posibilitan la concentración.

links: Lageplan_Außenansicht_Blick in die Synagoge. rechts: Fassade des Museums_Synagoge am Abend_Museumsbau.
gauche: Plan de site_Vue extérieure_Vue dans la synagogue. droite: Façade du musée_Synagogue prise en soirée_Bâtiment du musée.
izquierda: Plano de ubicación_Vista exterior_Vista de la sinagoga. derecha: Fachada del museo_Sinagoga por la noche_Edificio del museo.

 GERMANY_NEUMARKT IN DER OBERPFALZ

MUSEUM LOTHAR FISCHER

DEUTSCHLAND_ALLEMAGNE_ALEMANIA
BERSCHNEIDER + BERSCHNEIDER
2004
KUNSTMUSEUM_MUSÉE D'ART_MUSEO DE ARTE
1,559 M²
PHOTOS COURTESY OF THE ARCHITECTS

Der kubische Baukörper, am Stadtpark Neumarkts gelegen, zeigt sich als schlichtes, streng geometrisches Gebäude. Das quadratische rote Eingangstor und der transparente Treppenturm mit rotem Aufzugskern kontrastieren mit dem sonst weißen Bau. Die Architekten arbeiteten eng mit dem Künstler zusammen, so dass die Einwirkung des Tageslichts auf die verschiedenen Materialien der Kunstwerke abgestimmt werden konnte. Dazu wurden indirekte Lichtführungen, Wandschlitze und Vitrinen in die Fassade eingebaut. Die Vitrinen und Glasflächen der beiden Etagen lassen das Grün des Parks selbst wie Bilder in den Wandflächen erscheinen. Gleichzeitig gewähren sie von außen Einblicke in das Gebäude.

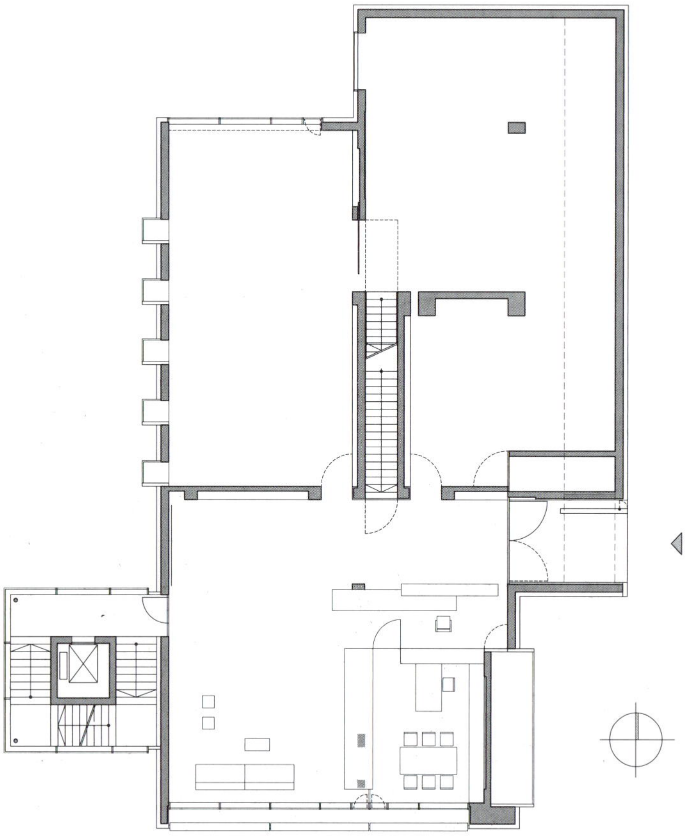

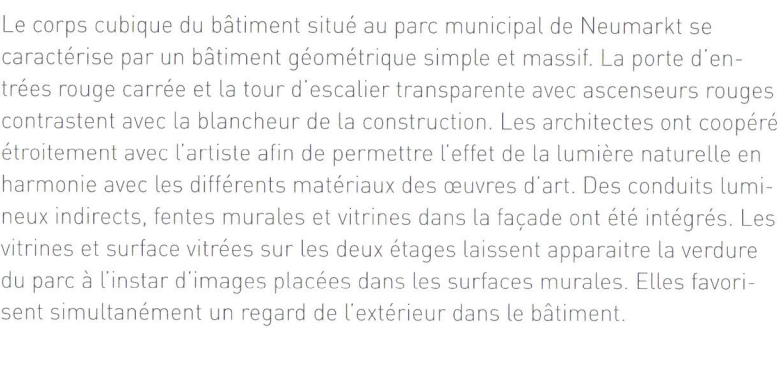

Le corps cubique du bâtiment situé au parc municipal de Neumarkt se caractérise par un bâtiment géométrique simple et massif. La porte d'entrées rouge carrée et la tour d'escalier transparente avec ascenseurs rouges contrastent avec la blancheur de la construction. Les architectes ont coopéré étroitement avec l'artiste afin de permettre l'effet de la lumière naturelle en harmonie avec les différents matériaux des œuvres d'art. Des conduits lumineux indirects, fentes murales et vitrines dans la façade ont été intégrés. Les vitrines et surface vitrées sur les deux étages laissent apparaitre la verdure du parc à l'instar d'images placées dans les surfaces murales. Elles favorisent simultanément un regard de l'extérieur dans le bâtiment.

El edificio cúbico se yergue al borde del parque urbano de Neumarkt como un sobrio volumen estrictamente geométrico. El cuadrado portón de acceso rojo y la transparente caja de la escalera con ascensor rojo contrastan con la construcción blanca. Los arquitectos colaboraron estrechamente con el artista para determinar con precisión el efecto de la luz diurna sobre los diversos materiales de las obras de arte. Por tanto, se incorporaron dispositivos de iluminación indirecta, ranuras en los muros y vitrinas en la fachada. Las vitrinas y superficies acristaladas de los dos niveles permiten que el verde del parque aparezca como cuadros en la superficie de los muros. Al mismo tiempo, posibilitan vistas hacia el interior del edificio.

links: Grundriss Erdgeschoss_Schaufenster_Skulpturensaal. rechts: Fassade_Gestaffelte Bauvolumina_Treppenturm in der Dämmerung.
gauche: Plan du rez-de-chaussée_Vitrines_Salle des sculptures. droite: Façade_Volume de construction échelonné_Tour d'escalier au crépuscule.
izquierda: Plano de planta baja_Vidriera_Sala de esculturas. derecha: Fachada_Volúmenes escalonados_Torre de escaleras al atardecer.

MUSEUM LOTHAR FISCHER

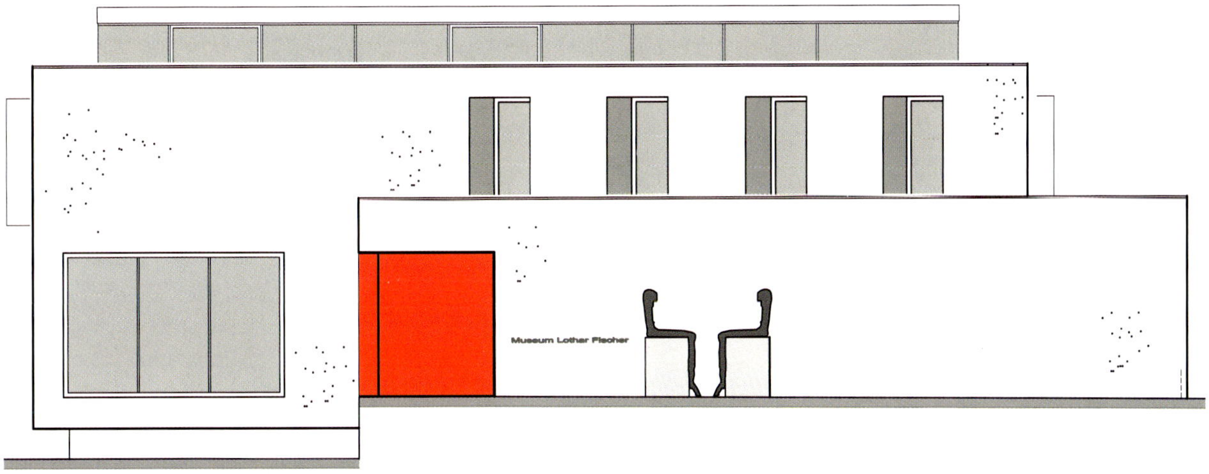

links: Eingang. rechts: Ostansicht_Treppe_Ausstellungskabinette_Empfang.
gauche: Entrée. droite: Vue à l'est_Escalier_Cabinet d'exposition_Réception.
izquierda: Acceso. derecha: Fachada este_Escalera_Gabinetes de exhibiciones_Recepción.

 GERMANY_NEUMARKT IN DER OBERPFALZ

MUSEUM FÜR HISTORISCHE MAYBACH-FAHRZEUGE

DEUTSCHLAND_ALLEMAGNE_ALEMANIA
BERSCHNEIDER + BERSCHNEIDER
2009
TECHNIKMUSEUM_MUSÉE DE LA TECHNIQUE
MUSEO TECNOLÓGICO
6,710 M^2
PHOTOS COURTESY OF THE ARCHITECTS

Das Museum nutzt die historische Bausubstanz der ehemaligen Fabrik und verbindet sie mit moderner Architektur. Kantige Rahmen aus Stahlblech kennzeichnen neue Öffnungen und Durchgänge in den historischen Fassaden und Wänden. Der neue Foyerbau in Sichtbeton verbindet die Gebäude als zentrale Erschließungsplattform. Vitrinen und Durchgänge scheinen scharfkantig aus den Betonflächen geschnitten. In die Hallen dringt sowohl Tages- als auch Kunstlicht, während hinter die Ausstellungsmodelle bewusst dunkle Grafitflächen gesetzt wurden. Der Boden aus alten Asphaltplatten wurde mitsamt den Abnutzungsspuren früherer Tage konserviert.

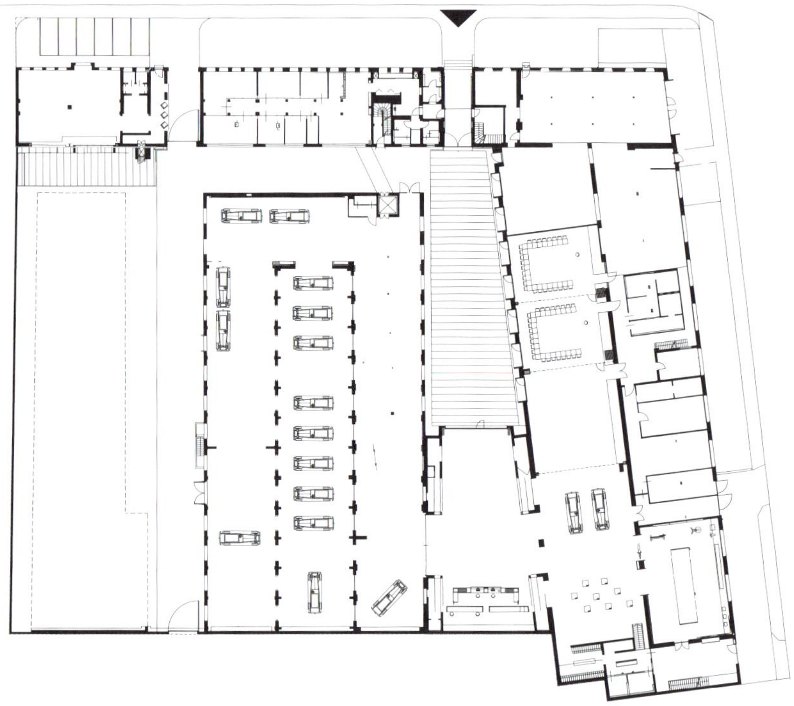

Le musée utilise la substance initiale de la construction historique de l'ancienne usine et l'harmonise à l'architecture moderne. La tôle en acier typique des nouveaux passages et ouvertures utilisés comme des cadres à arêtes vives dans les façades et les murs historiques. La nouvelle construction du foyer en béton apparent relie le bâtiment comme une plateforme d'accès centrale. Les vitrines et passages semblent découpés à bords vifs dans la surface du béton. La lumière naturelle et artificielle pénètre dans les halls tandis que des surfaces graphites foncées ont été placées à dessein derrière les modèles d'exposition. Le sol revêtu d'anciennes plaques d'asphalte a été conservé avec ses traces d'usure du passé.

El museo aprovecha la histórica sustancia edilicia de la antigua fábrica y la vincula con la arquitectura moderna. La chapa de acero identifica a las nuevas aberturas y pasadizos a modo de marco anguloso en los históricos muros y las fachadas. El moderno vestíbulo de hormigón visto constituye un nodo de conexión central entre los edificios. Las vitrinas y los pasajes parecen recortarse como aristas filosas en las superficies de hormigón. En las salas penetra la luz diurna al igual que la artificial, al tiempo que superficies oscuras de grafito sirven de fondo a los modelos en exhibición. Se ha respetado el suelo, con sus antiguas placas de asfalto que muestran huellas del desgaste de otras épocas.

links: Grundriss Erdgeschoss_Haupteingang_Turmbau. rechts: Hof in der Dämmerung_Ausstellungshalle_Umbau.
gauche: Plan du rez-de-chaussée_Entrée principale_Construction en tour. droite: Cour au crépuscule_Hall d'exposition_Transformation.
izquierda: Plano de planta baja_Acceso principal_Construcción en torre. derecha: Patio al atardecer_Sala de exhibiciones_Reforma.

MAYBACH

AUSSTELLUNG
EXPRESS-WERKE

bulthaup

1938 Maybach SW 38
Maybach

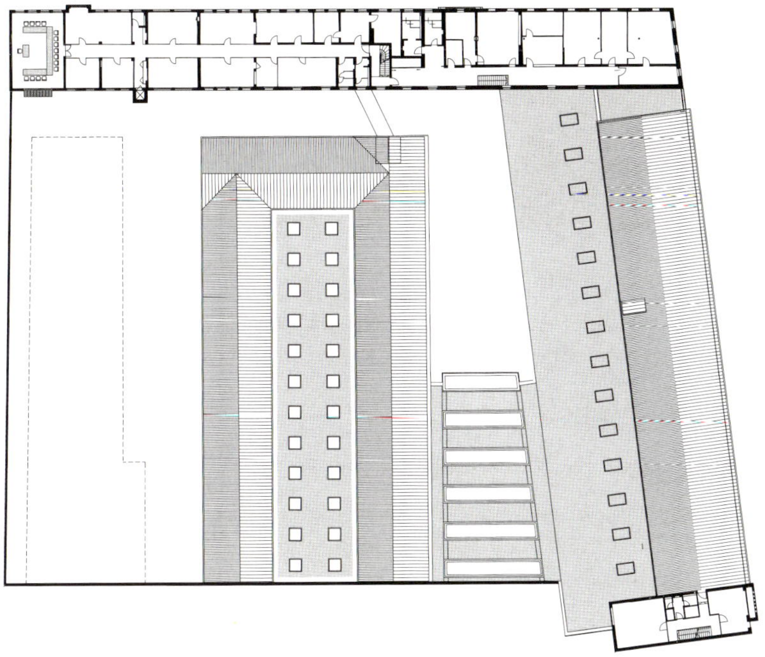

links: Blick in die Ausstellungshalle. rechts: Grundriss 1. Obergeschoss_Ausstellungsbereich_Autohalle_Ausstellung mit Durchgängen_Treppe.
gauche: Vue sur le hall d'exposition. droite: Plan du 1er étage supérieur_Zone d'exposition_Salle des automobiles_Zone d'exposition_Escalier.
izquierda: Vista de la sala de exhibición. derecha: Plano del primer piso_Área de exhibiciones_Sala de automóviles_Exhibición con pasajes_Escalera.

GERMANY_STRALSUND **OZEANEUM**

DEUTSCHLAND_ALLEMAGNE_ALEMANIA
BEHNISCH ARCHITEKTEN,
ATELIER LOHRER
2008
MARITIMMUSEUM_MUSÉE MARITIME_MUSEO MARÍTIMO
17,400 M²
PHOTOS ROLAND HALBE / ARTURIMAGES

Das Ozeaneum ist ein offenes Haus, in das von allen Seiten Besucher eintreten können. Die Fassade ist aus großformatigen, vorgebogenen Stahlblechen zusammengesetzt. Die Oberflächen der Bleche sind in einem weißen Farbton dauerhaft beschichtet und stellen eine Verbindung des Gebäudes zur maritimen Umgebung her. Das Gebäude ist in vier einzelne Baukörper gegliedert, die den Themen des Ausstellungskonzepts zugeordnet sind. Die Aquarien sind so gruppiert, dass sie über einen Rundgang besichtigt werden können. Die räumlichen Gegebenheiten der Besucherbereiche im Gebäude und auch die raumklimatischen Anforderungen sind sehr unterschiedlich und reichen von dunklen Ausstellungsbereichen bis hin zum verglasten Atrium.

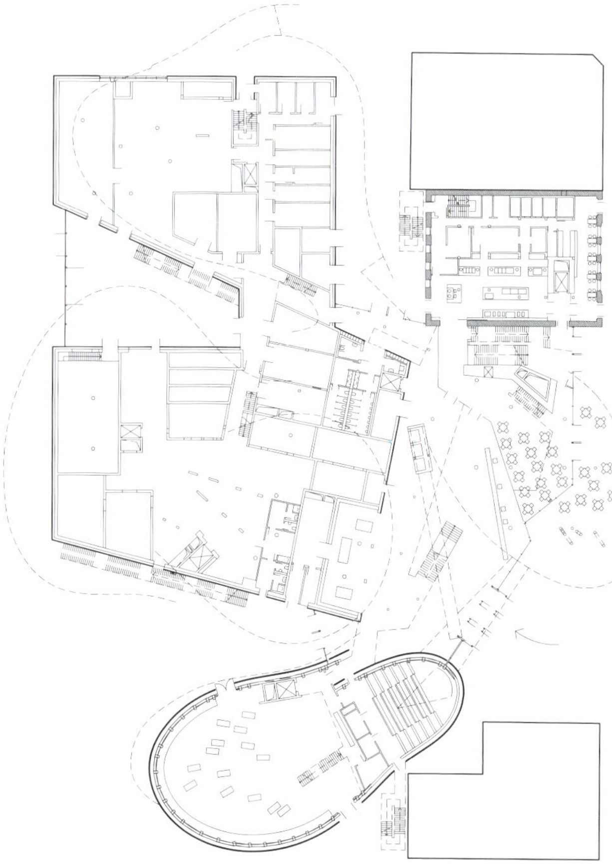

Le musée Ozeaneum est un édifice ouvert, accessible de tous les côtés par les visiteurs. La façade est assemblée en tôles d'acier pliées de grand format. Les superficies de tôles sont enduites d'une teinte blanche durable qui produit un rappel du bâtiment à l'environnement maritime. Le musée est composé de quatre corps de bâtiment individuels classés selon les thématiques relatives à la conception des expositions. Les aquariums sont regroupés afin de faciliter les visites via une galerie. Les effets spatiaux des zones de visite dans le bâtiment et les exigences climatiques sont très diversifiés et couvrent les zones d'exposition sombres et l'atrium en verre.

El Ozeaneum es una casa abierta que recibe visitantes por sus cuatro lados. La fachada se compone de chapas de acero precurvadas de gran formato. Las superficies de las chapas tienen un recubrimiento muy duradero de tonalidad blancuzca y constituyen una vinculación del edificio con el entorno marítimo. El edificio se subdivide en cuatro volúmenes; a cada uno se le asignan los temas del concepto museístico. Los acuarios se agrupan de tal forma que se pueden visitar en un recorrido. Las comodidades espaciales de las áreas para visitantes del edificio son muy variadas, y también los requisitos de climatización; la variedad abarca desde el acristalado atrio transparente hasta zonas de exhibición a oscuras.

links: Grundriss Erdgeschoss_Walaustellung_Tunnel durch das Aquarium_Foyer mit Treppe. rechts: Außenbau_Panorama.
gauche: Plan du rez-de-chaussée_Exposition consacrée aux baleines_Tunnel à travers l'acquarium Foyer avec escalier. droite: Extérieur_Panorama.
izquierda: Plano de planta baja_Exhibición de ballenas_Túnel por el acuario_Vestíbulo con escalera. derecha: Vista exterior_Panorama.

GERMANY_STUTTGART **KUNSTMUSEUM STUTTGART**

DEUTSCHLAND_ALLEMAGNE_ALEMANIA
HASCHER JEHLE ARCHITEKTUR
2004
KUNSTMUSEUM_MUSÉE D'ART_MUSEO DE ARTE
13,000 M^2
PHOTOS ROLAND HALBE, STUTTGART (298, 299, 300, 301 A. R.),
SVENJA BOCKHOP, BERLIN (301 L., B. R.)

Das Museum präsentiert sich im Stadtraum als glasumhüllter, steinerner Würfel. Die transparente, durchlässige Eingangsebene schafft einen fließenden Übergang vom öffentlichen Raum der angrenzenden Einkaufsstraße in das Museum. Von hier aus führt eine großzügige Treppenanlage entweder ins Innere des mehrgeschossigen, steinernen Kerns, in dem die Wechselausstellungen stattfinden, oder in die zweigeschossigen unterirdischen Ausstellungsräume, die sich unter dem gesamten Kleinen Schlossplatz und in einem ehemaligen Verkehrstunnel ausbreiten und der ständigen Sammlung dienen. Ein in den Platz eingelassenes Lichtband verweist auf die unterirdisch verborgene Kunst.

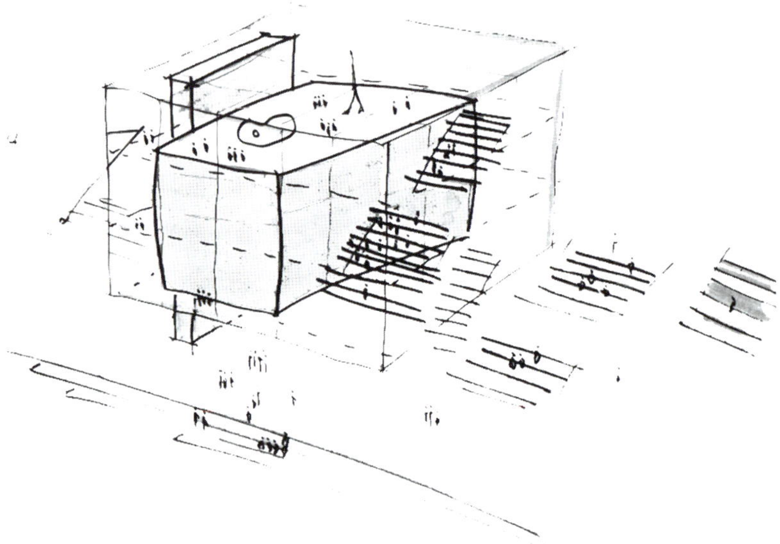

Le musée se présente dans l'environnement urbain comme un dé en pierre enveloppé de verre. Le niveau d'entrée transparent et perméable crée une transition sans heurts sur l'espace public des rues commerçantes limitrophes au musée. A ce niveau, des escaliers généreux accompagnent, soit à l'intérieur du centre en pierre construit sur plusieurs étages où se situent des expositions tournantes, soit dans les espaces d'exposition situés sur deux étages sous le niveau de la terre qui s'élargissent sous l'ancienne petite place du château et dans l'ancien tunnel routier pour présenter la collection permanente. Une bande lumineuse encastrée dans la place signale l'art abrité en souterrain.

El museo se presenta en el espacio urbano como un dado pétreo revestido de cristal. El nivel de acceso, transparente y permeable, logra una transición fluida desde el espacio público en la arteria comercial hacia el interior del museo. Desde aquí, un grandioso conjunto de escaleras conduce hacia el interior del núcleo pétreo de varios niveles en el que tienen lugar las exhibiciones temporarias, o bien hacia los dos niveles de salas de exhibición subterráneas, que se ubican debajo de la plaza Kleiner Schlossplatz y se extienden por un antiguo túnel de tráfico; estas sirven para albergar la colección permanente. Una franja de lucernario en la plaza remite al arte "escondido" bajo tierra.

links: Skizze Entwurf_Blick vom Schlossplatz auf das Kunstmuseum. rechts: Fassade_Eingangshalle.
gauche: Projet d'esquisse_Vue de la Schlossplatz sur le musée d'art. droite: Façade_Hall d'entrée.
izquierda: Esbozo del proyecto_Vista desde la Schlossplatz hacia el museo. derecha: Fachada_Sala de acceso.

SCALA
ADRESSE

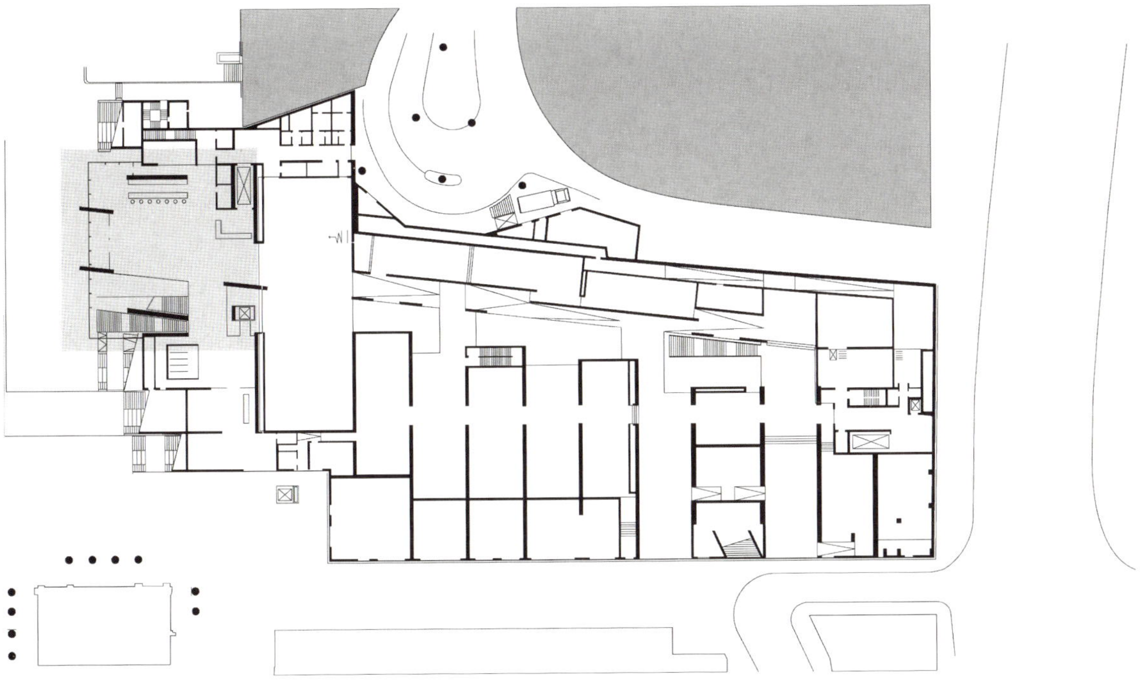

links: Gläserner Kubus um steinernen Kern. rechts: Grundriss Eingangsebene_Oberlichter der unterirdischen Ausstellungsräume_Innenraum_Sammlungsbereich.
gauche: Cube en verre autour d'un cœur en pierre. droite: Zone d'entrée_Éclairage plafond des espaces d'exposition souterrains_Espace intérieur_Zone de la collection.
izquierda: Cubo acristalado con núcleo pétreo. derecha: Nivel de acceso_Lucernarios de las salas de exhibición subterráneas_Espacio interior_Área de las colecciones.

GERMANY_STUTTGART **MERCEDES-BENZ MUSEUM**

DEUTSCHLAND_ALLEMAGNE_ALEMANIA
UNSTUDIO – BEN VAN BERKEL
2006
FIRMENMUSEUM_MUSÉE D'ENTREPRISE_MUSEO DE EMPRESA
16,500 M^2
PHOTOS CHRISTIAN RICHTERS (302, 303 A., 304, 305),
CHRIS VAN UFFELEN (303 B.)

Das Museum liegt dem Thema entsprechend an einer der Schnellstraßen, die in die Stadt führen. Der Besucher beginnt nach einer multimedial begleiteten Aufzugfahrt auf der achten Ebene mit einem von zwei sich mehrfach kreuzenden Rundgängen, die sich auf den zwischen die Stränge eines DNA-Moleküls gespannten Geschossen abwärts winden. Aus einem Grat werden eine Wand, eine Decke und schließlich ein Raum. Die Räume lassen im Zentrum ein Atrium in Gebäudehöhe frei, das immer wieder neue Blicke quer durch den Bau ermöglicht. Die komplexe Geometrie machte herkömmliche Bauzeichnungen unmöglich, so dass ein digitales Computermodell, das im Bauverlauf weiter abgewandelt werden konnte, deren Platz einnahm.

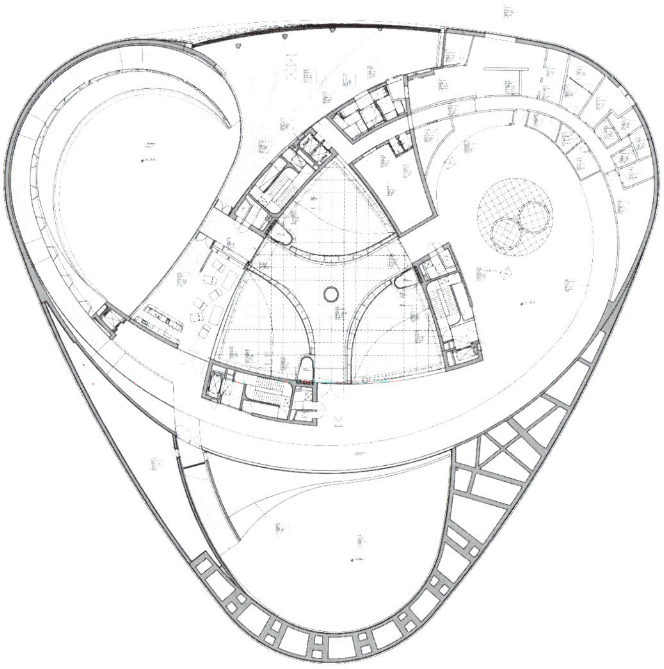

Le musée se situe au bord d'une voie rapide menant à la ville. Le visiteur commence sa visite guidée muni de moyens multimédias au huitième niveau dans l'une des deux galeries qui s'entrecroisent à plusieurs reprises et s'étire comme l'hélice d'une molécule d'ADN sur les étages vers le bas. Du point culminant apparaissent un mur, un plafond et un espace. Au centre des espaces se situe un atrium dans toute sa hauteur qui favorise continuellement les nouvelles perspectives sur la construction. La géométrie complexe fut impossible à reproduire sur les dessins d'étude classiques qui furent remplacés par un modèle assisté par ordinateur afin de permettre le suivi des modifications successives au cours de la construction.

Rindiendo honor a su temática, el museo se levanta junto a una de las vías rápidas que conducen hacia la ciudad. Tras un recorrido en elevador con acompañamiento multimedia, el visitante llega al octavo nivel y puede comenzar uno de los recorridos que se entrecruzan varias veces, como si se tratase de las ramas de una molécula de ADN. Una arista se transforma en pared, después en cielorraso y finalmente en ambiente. Las salas dejan al centro un atrio libre de la altura de todo el edificio, que posibilita visuales cruzadas por todo el interior. La compleja geometría hizo imposible el diseño mediante dibujos arquitectónicos convencionales; se hizo necesario un modelo digital informático, que se pudo ir transformando en el transcurso del avance de obra.

links: Grundriss_Fassade_Totale und Umfeld. rechts: Außenansicht bei Nacht_Präsentation der Rennwagen_Aufzug im Atrium_Oberlicht Atrium.
gauche: Plan_Façade_Présentation globale et situation. droite: Vue extérieure de nuit_Présentation des voitures de course_Ascenseur dans l'atrium_éclairage de l'atrium.
izquierda: Plano_Vista de fachada_Vista del conjunto. derecha: Vista exterior por la noche_Presentación de coches de carreras_Elevador en el atrio_Lucernario en el atrio.

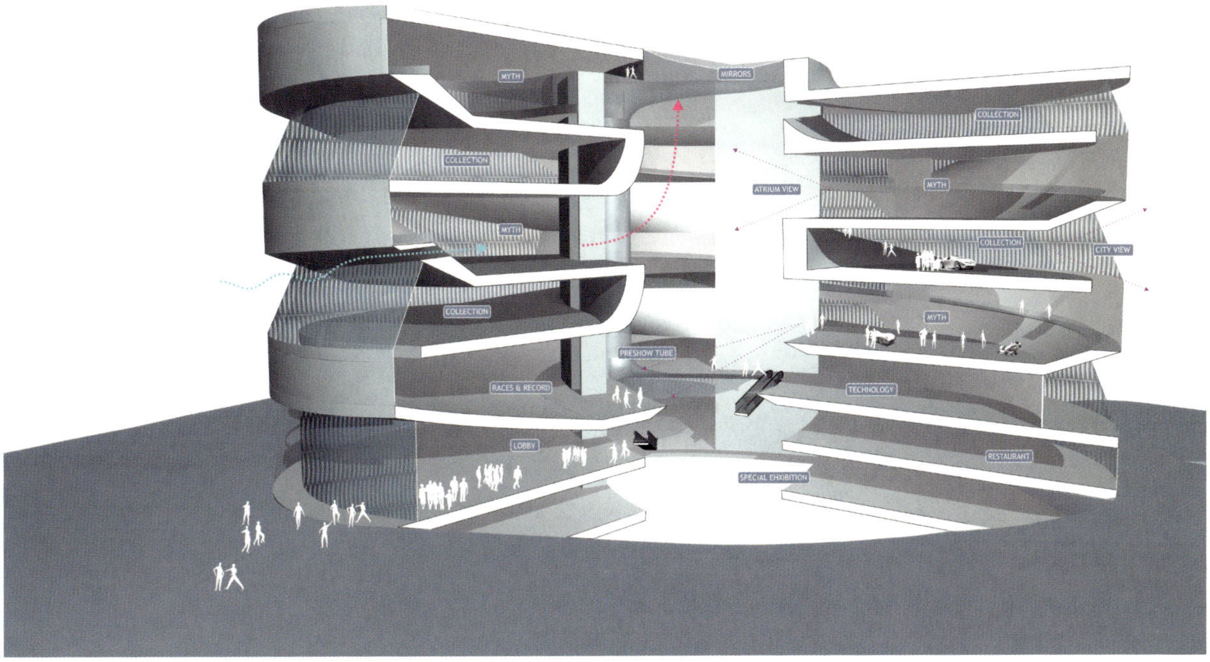

links: Atrium. rechts: Schnitt_Oberstes Geschoss_Ausstellungsfläche_Café.
gauche: Atrium. droite: Coupe_Espace supérieur_Surface d'exposition_Café.
izquierda: Atrio. derecha: Corte_Nivel superior_Área de exhibición Café.

GERMANY_STUTTGART **MAHLE INSIDE**

DEUTSCHLAND_ALLEMAGNE_ALEMANIA
HEINISCH.LEMBACH.HUBER ARCHITEKTEN BDA
2008
FIRMENMUSEUM_MUSÉE D'ENTREPRISE_MUSEO DE EMPRESA
1,970 M^2
PHOTOS ZOOEY BRAUN, STUTTGART

Dem Gebäudeentwurf liegt ein inhaltliches und räumliches Ausstellungskonzept zugrunde, welches die Architekten als Basis für ihre Formfindung entwickelten. Architektur und Ausstellung bilden somit eine untrennbare Einheit. Der schlichte Baukörper dient als Hülle für ein komplexes, durch Lufträume und Sichtbezüge verbundenes System von Räumen unterschiedlicher Proportion und Anmutung. Das räumliche Konzept des Hauses bildet so die vielfältigen Beziehungen der Ausstellungsthemen untereinander ab. Auf vier Etagen werden die Produktlinien der Firma präsentiert sowie deren Historie, Unternehmensphilosophie, Methoden und Ziele in Forschung und Entwicklung dargestellt.

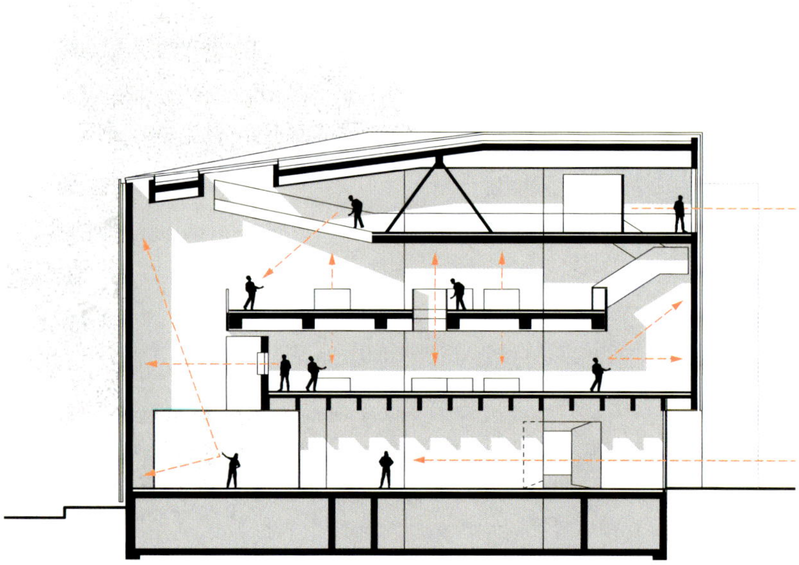

Le projet du bâtiment consiste en un concept d'expositions reposant sur l'espace et le contenu, développé par les architectes comme une base de découverte des formes. L'architecture et l'exposition forment ainsi une unité inséparable. Le corps du bâtiment simple sert d'enceinte à un système d'espaces de proportions et d'apparences diversifiées lié par des espaces aériens et relations visuelles complexes. La conception spatiale de la maison reproduit ainsi une série de références diversifiées aux thématiques consacrées aux expositions. Les quatre étages présentent des lignes de produits ainsi que l'histoire, la philosophie d'entreprise, les méthodes et objectifs requis pour la recherche et le développement social.

Un concepto espacial y de contenidos fue la base de la exploración formal que ocupó a los arquitectos a la hora de concebir este proyecto museístico. Arquitectura y exhibición constituyen así una unidad indisoluble. El discreto edificio sirve de cáscara para un complejo sistema de salas de diversas proporciones e impresiones, conectados por espacios de aire y vinculaciones visuales. El concepto espacial de la edificación ilustra así las múltiples relaciones entre los temas de las muestras en exhibición. En cuatro niveles se presentan las líneas de productos de la empresa, y también la historia y filosofía de la empresa, los métodos y objetivos de la investigación y desarrollo.

links: Schnitt_Südfassade bei Nacht_Westfassade bei Nacht. rechts: Ansicht Haldenstraße_Ausstellung Grundlagen der Motortechnik_Ausstellung Rennsport.
gauche: Coupe_Façade sud de nuit_Façade ouest de nuit. droite: Vue Haldenstrasse_Exposition sur les principes de la technique moteur_Exposition sur le sport de course.
izquierda: Corte_Fachada sur por la noche_Fachada oeste por la noche. derecha: Vista desde la Haldenstrasse_Exhibición de los fundamentos de la tecnología del motor_Exhibición sobre carreras.

INSIDE
MAHLE

MAHLE SYSTEME

GERMANY_WALDENBUCH **MUSEUM RITTER**

DEUTSCHLAND_ALLEMAGNE_ALEMANIA
MAX DUDLER
2005
KUNST- UND FIRMENMUSEUM_MUSEE D'ART ET D'ENTREPRISE
MUSEO DE ARTE Y DE EMPRESA
4,450 M²
PHOTOS STEFAN MÜLLER, BERLIN

Das Museum für die Sammlung Marli Hoppe-Ritter liegt am Rand einer weiten Wiese direkt neben dem Werksgelände des Schokoladenherstellers Ritter Sport. Der markante Kalksteinquader zeichnet sich durch ein abwechslungsreiches Spiel geometrischer Formen und den Gegensatz zwischen Offenheit und Geschlossenheit aus. Der Museumsbau fungiert als markanter Grenzposten zwischen Stadt und Land, Natur und Kunst. Er besteht aus zwei Teilen und einer sie verbindenden Passage. Das Betriebskonzept mit seiner Ausrichtung auf Energiegewinnung durch natürliche Ressourcen wie Solarenergie, Biomasse und Geothermie dient einer möglichst ausgeglichenen Umweltbilanz.

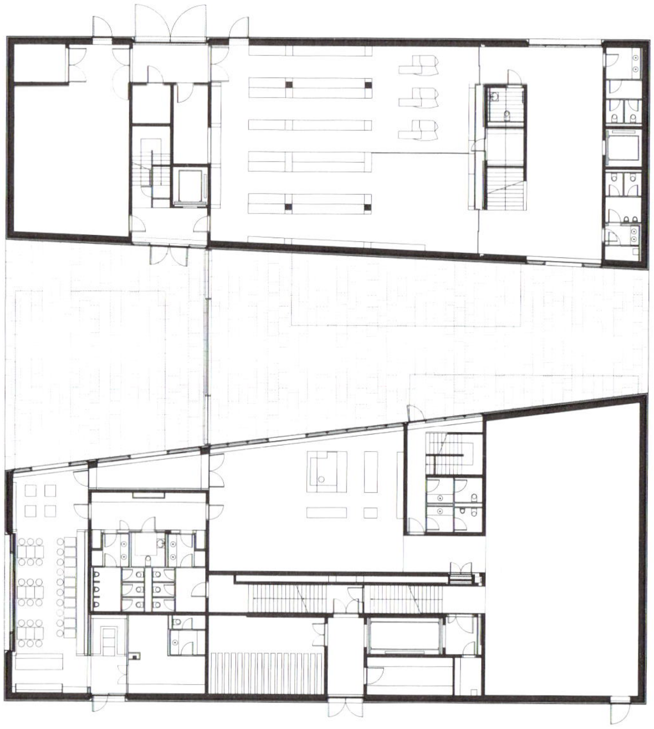

Le musée consacré à la collection Marli Hoppe-Ritter se situe en lisière d'une vaste prairie donnant directement sur l'enceinte de l'usine du chocolatier Ritter Sport. La pierre de taille calcaire remarquable se distingue grâce à son jeu de formes géométriques riche en facettes et à son opposition entre ouverture et fermeture. La construction du musée fait office de poste frontière entre la ville et la campagne, la nature et l'art. Le bâtiment se constitue de deux parties et d'un passage communiquant. La conception opérationnelle dédiée à la valorisation de l'énergie grâce aux ressources naturelles comme l'énergie solaire, la biomasse et la géothermie permet une amélioration marquée du bilan écologique.

El museo que alberga la colección Marli Hoppe-Ritter se encuentra al borde de una amplia pradera contigua a las instalaciones fabriles de la chocolatera Ritter Sport. El imponente volumen ortogonal de piedra caliza se destaca por su rico juego de formas geométricas y por el contraste entre apertura y encierro. El edificio del museo sirve a la vez como marcada frontera entre la ciudad y el campo, entre la naturaleza y el arte. La edificación comprende dos partes y un pasaje que las une. El concepto operativo se orienta a la obtención energética a partir de recursos naturales como la energía solar, la biomasa y la geotermia, y colabora así al equilibrio del medio ambiente.

links: Erdgeschoss_Passage_Ausstellungsräume_Landschaftsraum_Treppenaufgang 1. Obergeschoss. rechts: Außenbau von Südosten_Ausstellungsraum_Lounge und Museumsshop.
gauche: Plan du rez-de-chaussée_Passage_Espaces d'exposition_Espace paysage_Rampe d'escalier du 1er étage. droite: Vue extérieure du sud-est_Espace d'exposition_Salon et boutique du musée.
izquierda: Planta baja_Pasaje_Salas de exhibiciones_Panorama interior_Ascenso por escalera hacia la planta alta. derecha: Vista exterior desde el sudeste_Sala de exhibiciones_Salón y tienda del museo.

GERMANY_WANGEN **BESUCHERZENTRUM ARCHE NEBRA**

DEUTSCHLAND_ALLEMAGNE_ALEMANIA
HOLZER KOBLER ARCHITEKTUREN /
BARBARA HOLZER, TRISTAN KOBLER
2007
ARCHÄOLOGIEMUSEUM_MUSÉE DE L'ARCHÉOLOGIE
MUSEO ARQUEOLÓGICO
2,100 M²
PHOTOS JAN BITTER

Die zeichenhafte Architektur bettet die Geschichte der Himmelsscheibe von Nebra in die Umgebung ihres Fundorts ein und verweist auf die Themen Archäologie und Astronomie. Ein 60 Meter langer Baukörper greift das Bild der Barke vor dem Stapellauf auf und beherbergt Dauer- und Wechselausstellung sowie ein Planetarium. In der offenen Fuge befindet sich das transparente Eingangsgeschoss, darunter schiebt sich der Sockel aus dem Boden. Das Gebäude ist auf den 30 Meter hohen Aussichtsturm am Fundort der Himmelsscheibe ausgerichtet. Der geneigte Turm verweist auf die prähistorischen Orientierungspunkte in der Landschaft; er ist eine architektonische Interpretation des Messinstruments Himmelsscheibe.

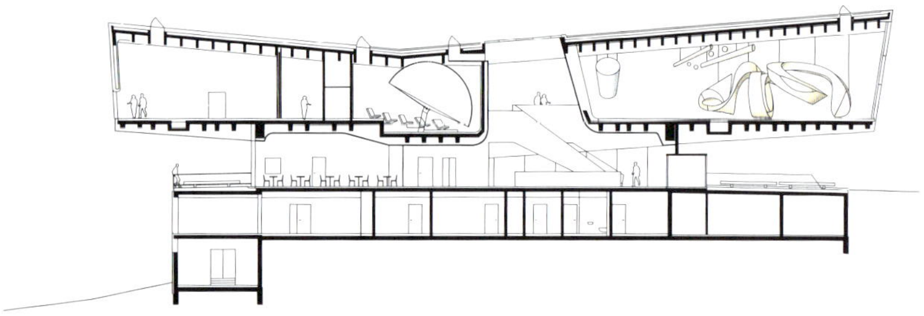

L'architecture symbolique intègre l'histoire du disque céleste de Nebra dans l'environnement de son site archéologique et renvoie aux thématiques concernant l'archéologie et l'astronomie. Un corps de bâtiment de 60 mètres de longueur reprend l'image de la barque avant la mise à la mer et abrite des expositions permanentes et tournantes ainsi qu'un planétarium. Dans la jointure ouverte se situe l'entrée transparente du rez-de-chaussée avant sa mise en placement sur le socle. Le bâtiment dispose d'un belvédère de 30 mètres de hauteur sur le site archéologique du disque céleste. La tour penchée renvoie aux points d'orientation préhistoriques dans le paysage et donne une interprétation architectonique de l'instrument de mesure du disque céleste.

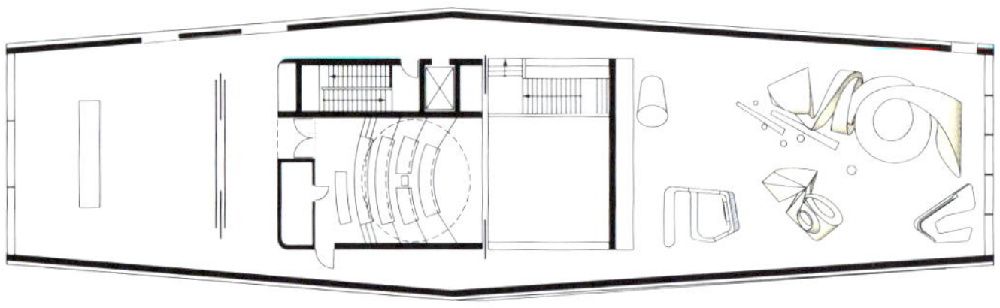

La emblemática arquitectura de este museo inserta la historia del disco celeste de Nebra en el entorno del sitio de su hallazgo y remite a las temáticas de la arqueología y la astronomía. Un volumen edilicio de 60 metros de longitud evoca la imagen de una barca antes de su botadura y alberga exhibiciones permanentes y temporarias, además de un planetario. En la rendija abierta se ubica el transparente nivel de acceso, por debajo del mismo, el basamento se eleva por encima del terreno. El edificio se orienta hacia la torre panorámica de 30 metros de altura en el sitio donde se descubrió el disco celeste. La torre inclinada remite a los puntos de orientación prehistóricos en el paisaje y constituye una interpretación arquitectónica de este singular instrumento de medición celeste.

links: Schnitt und Grundriss 1. Obergeschoss_Innenansicht. rechts: Eingang_Außenansicht.
gauche: Coupe et plan du 1er étage_Vue d'intérieur. droite: Accès_Vue d'extérieur.
izquierda: Corte y plano del primer piso_Vista interior. derecha: Acceso_Vista exterior.

GERMANY_WAREN **MÜRITZEUM**

DEUTSCHLAND_ALLEMAGNE_ALEMANIA
WINGÅRDH ARKITEKTKONTOR AB
2007
NATURKUNDEMUSEUM_MUSEE DE L'HISTOIRE NATURELLE
MUSEO DE HISTORIA NATURAL
3,137 M²
PHOTOS ÅKE E:SON LINDMAN, STOCKHOLM

Die Stadt Waren wünschte sich ein Gebäude, das sowohl als Besucherzentrum für die Altstadt als auch für den benachbarten Naturpark an der Müritz dienen konnte. Das Raumprogramm von 2985 Quadratmetern umfasst Flächen für Wechselausstellungen, ein Aquarium, ein Multimediatheater, Raum für Seminare, Geschäfte und einen Animationsbereich für Kinder. Das runde Volumen wird durch scharfe Einschnitte, am deutlichsten am Eingang, aufgebrochen. Eine dünne Glasscheibe trennt zwei verschiedene Holzschalen: einerseits abgeflammte, schwarze Bohlen an der Fassade, andererseits helle, glatte Paneele im Inneren. Der schiffsartige Charakter des Gebäudes entspricht seinem auf den See hinausgreifenden Standort, während die runde Form zur räumlichen Qualität im Inneren beiträgt.

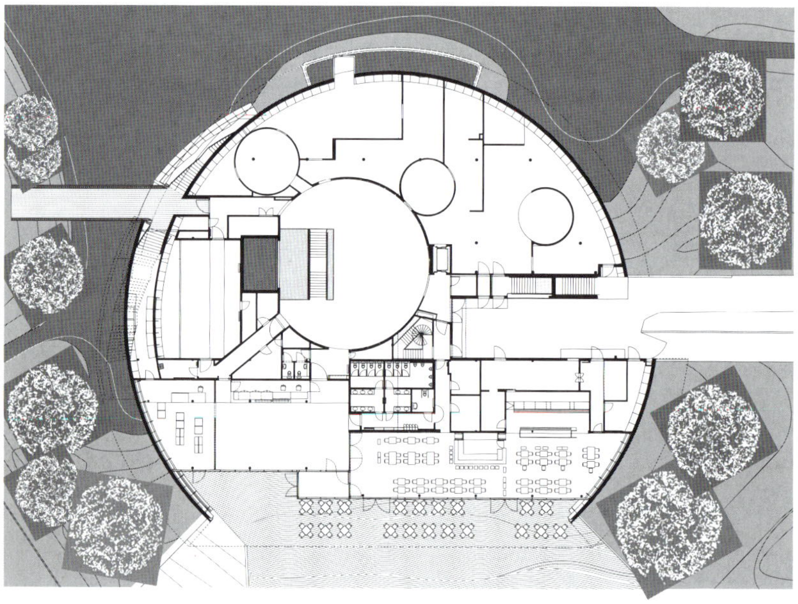

La ville de Waren souhaitait un bâtiment faisant office de centre dédié aux visiteurs de la vieille ville et également de parc naturel avoisinant la rivière Müritz. Le projet concernant un espace de 2 985 mètres carrés comprend une superficie pour les expositions tournantes, un aquarium, un théâtre multimédia, un espace dédié aux séminaires, des commerces et une zone d'animation pour les enfants. Le volume de forme arrondie est brisé par des entailles aigues situées notamment à l'entrée. Une plaque de verre fine sépare les deux coques différentes en bois: un panneau noir flammé sur la façade et un panneau en couleur jaune lisse à l'intérieur. Le caractère suspendu du bâtiment est dans l'esprit du site plongeant sur l'eau tandis que la forme ronde contribue à la qualité de l'espace intérieur.

La ciudad de Waren deseaba contar con un edificio que sirviera como centro para quienes visitan no solo el casco histórico, sino también del vecino parque natural junto al lago Müritz. El programa abarca 2.985 metros cuadrados de superficie para exposiciones temporarias, un acuario, un teatro multimedia, salas para seminarios y negocios, y animación para niños. El volumen redondeado es quebrado por filosos recortes, el más notorio de los cuales se encuentra en el acceso. Una delgada lámina de cristal separa dos tipos de paneles de madera: uno tostado oscuro en la fachada, y otro amarillento y liso en el interior. El carácter "flotante" del edificio dialoga con el entorno acuático, como si se tratara de una embarcación; la forma redondeada crea la calidad espacial del interior.

links: Grundriss_Detail Innenraum_Ausblick_Außentreppe_Außenbau und Brücke. rechts: Eingangsbereich_Blick über das Wasser_Wasseroberfläche.
gauche: Plan_Détail de l'espace intérieur_Vue_Escalier extérieur_Extérieur et passerelle. droite: Zone d'entrée_Vue sur l'eau_Surface de l'eau.
izquierda: Plano_Detalle del interior_Vista_Escalera exterior_Vista exterior con puente. derecha: Zona del acceso_Vista del lago_Superficie del agua.

MÜRITZEUM

GREECE_ATHENS **NEW MUSEION AKROPOLIS**

GRIECHENLAND_GRÈCE_GRECIA
BERNARD TSCHUMI ARCHITECTS WITH
MICHAEL PHOTIADIS, ARSY
2009
ARCHÄOLOGIEMUSEUM_MUSÉE DE L'ARCHÉOLOGIE
MUSEO ARQUEOLÓGICO
21,000 M²
PHOTOS CHRISTIAN RICHTERS (314, 315, 316),
PETER MAUSS / ESTO (317 L., B. R.), NIKOS DANIILIDIS (317 A. R.)

Beim Bau des Museums am Fuße der Akropolis mussten empfindliche archäologische Ausgrabungen, das zeitgenössische Straßenraster und der Parthenon selbst berücksichtigt werden. Das Museum erhebt sich auf Stützen über den bestehenden archäologischen Ausgrabungen, und ein Netzwerk aus Rundpfeilern dominiert den Bau. Eine Glasrampe gewährt den Blick auf die Ausgrabungen und führt zu den Galerien in doppelter Raumhöhe im mittleren Gebäudebereich. Der obere Bereich der rechteckigen Parthenon-Galerie ist gegenüber der übrigen Baumasse versetzt, so dass der Marmorfries genauso ausgerichtet werden konnte, wie er vor Jahrhunderten am Parthenon zu sehen war.

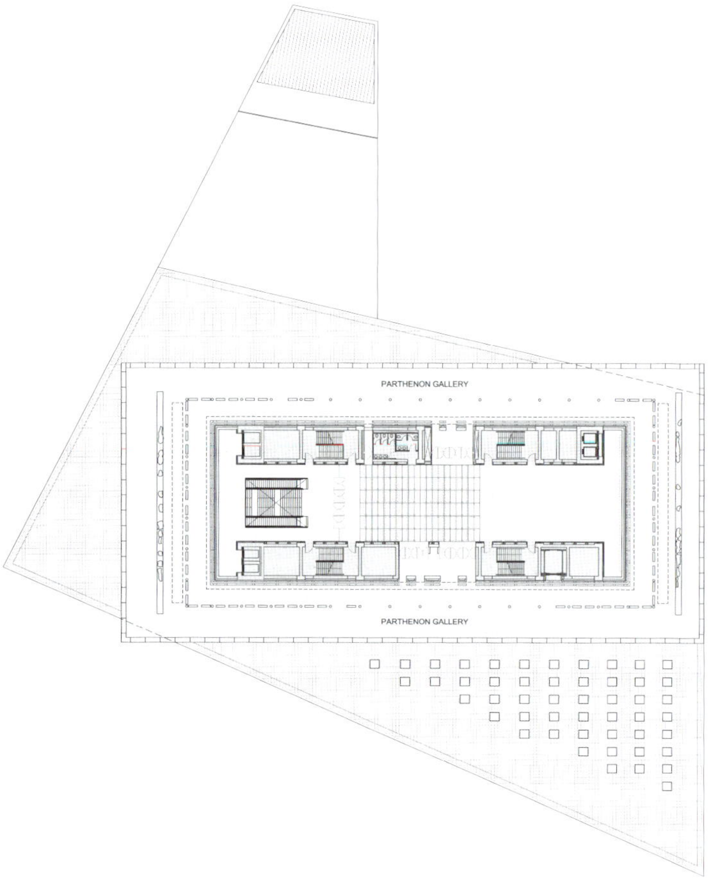

Situé au pied de l'acropole, le nouveau bâtiment tient compte des fouilles archéologiques délicates, du tracé routier contemporain et également du Parthénon. Le musée s'élève sur des appuis au-dessus des fouilles archéologiques existantes et un réseau de colonnes domine la construction. Une rampe en verre assure la vue sur les fouilles afin de mener aux galeries situées dans la hauteur de l'espace double dans la zone centrale du bâtiment. La zone supérieure de la galerie du Parthénon rectangulaire se tourne vers le volume bâti extérieur de telle manière que la frise est orientée à l'instar d'une exposition au Parthénon il y a des siècles.

Al pie de la Acrópolis, junto a la nueva edificación, se debieron respetar excavaciones arqueológicas muy delicadas, el trazado vial moderno y el propio Partenón. El museo se levanta sobre pilares por encima de las excavaciones arqueológicas existentes; una red de pilares redondos domina la obra. Una rampa acristalada permite una visual sobre las excavaciones y conduce a las galerías de doble altura en el área central del edificio. La zona superior de la galería rectangular del Partenón está girada respecto del resto del volumen edilicio, de modo que se pudo dar al friso la misma orientación que tuvo siglos atrás en el Partenón.

links: Grundriss Parthenongalerie_Überdachung Grabungen_Blick aus den Grabungen. rechts: Ostfassade_Parthenongalerie.
gauche: Plan de la galerie du Parthénon_Couverture des fouilles_Vue sur les fouilles. droite: Façade est_Galerie du Parthénon.
izquierda: Plano de la galería del Partenón_Cubierta sobre las excavaciones_Vista desde las excavaciones. derecha: Fachada este_Galería del Partenón.

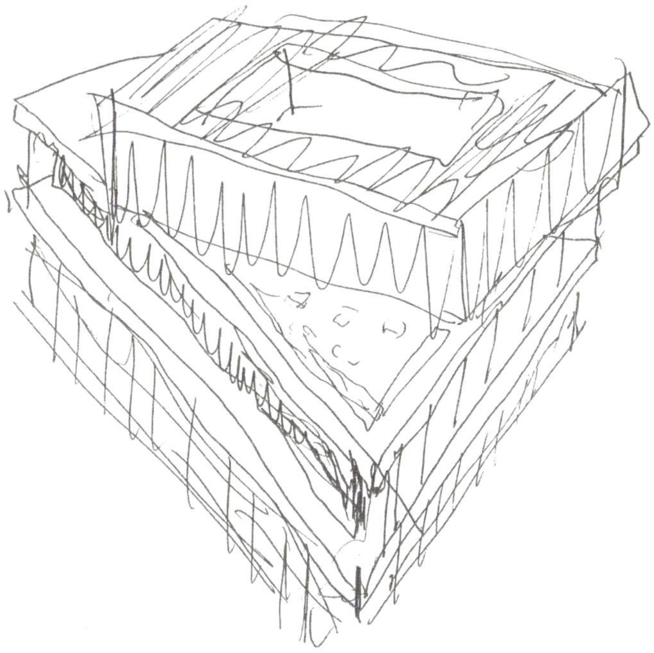

links: Nordfassade. rechts: Skizze_Neubau über Grabungen_Relieffries_Skulpturen zwischen Rundpfeilern.
gauche: Façade nord. droite: Esquisse_Nouveau bâtiment sur les fouilles_Frise en relief_Sculptures entre les colonnes.
izquierda: Fachada norte. derecha: Esbozo_Obra nueva sobre las excavaciones_Friso en relieve Esculturas entre pilares redondos.

GREECE_PATRA **MOUSEIO PATRAS**

GRIECHENLAND_GRÈCE_GRECIA
THEOFANIS BOBOTIS ARCHITECTS
2009
ARCHÄOLOGIEMUSEUM_MUSÉE DE L'ARCHÉOLOGIE
MUSEO ARQUEOLÓGICO
8,000 M²
PHOTOS CHARALAMBOS LOUIZIDIS

Eine Gruppe asymmetrischer prismatischer Volumen beherbergt die Funde aus einer alten Kultur. Eine moderne Komposition, die mit ihrer unregelmäßigen Anordnung versucht, die Harmonie der Volumen, Oberflächen und der Bewegung durch die Ausstellungsräume herzustellen – eine organische und funktionale Dekonstruktion, die von statischer Symmetrie befreit den Dialog mit der Umwelt, den Besuchern und Benutzern sucht. An der Nationalstraße von Athen nach Patras gelegen, macht der Entwurf diese zu einer wichtigen, städtischen Schnellstraße. Er erhebt das Museum zum Wahrzeichen der Region und sorgt für einfache und direkte Zugänglichkeit.

Un groupe de volumes prismatiques, asymétriques abrite les reliques récupérées provenant de cultures anciennes. Une composition moderne aspirant à créer l'harmonie des volumes, des surfaces et du mouvement dans l'espace d'exposition grâce à sa disposition irrégulière : une déconstruction organique et fonctionnelle qui libère le dialogue avec l'environnement au niveau de la symétrie statique à la recherche des visiteurs et des utilisateurs. Situé sur la route nationale reliant Athènes à Patras, le projet a fait connaitre cette importante voie rapide permettant un accès direct et simple au musée, l'emblème de la région.

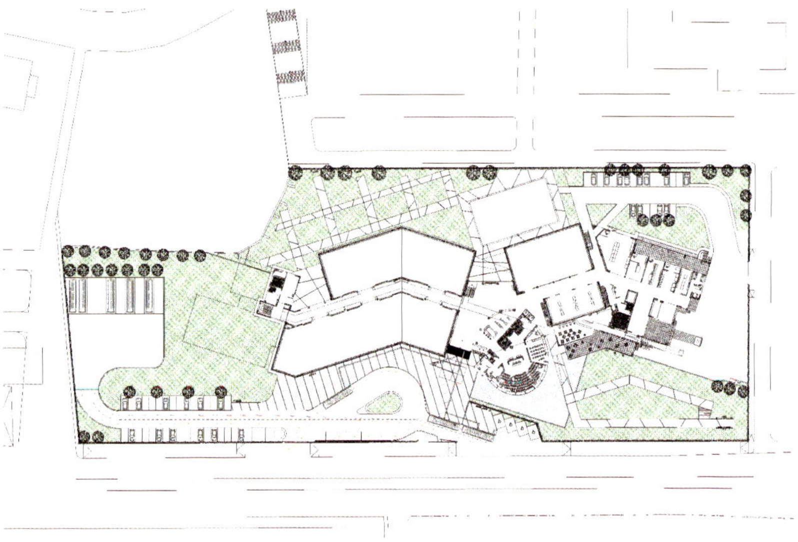

Un grupo de volúmenes prismáticos asimétricos alberga hallazgos de antiguas culturas. Se trata de una moderna composición que procura, con su disposición irregular, reproducir la armonía de los volúmenes, las superficies y el movimiento con la propia exhibición: una deconstrucción orgánica y funcional que procura un diálogo con el medio ambiente, los visitantes y los usuarios, liberada de la simetría estática. Ubicado en la carretera nacional que une Atenas con Patras, el proyecto la transforma en una importante arteria ciudadana; el museo se erige como símbolo de la región y procura una accesibilidad directa y sencilla.

links: Lageplan_Außenansicht. rechts: Eingangsbereich_Innenraum_Verknickte Wand.
gauche: Plan de site_Vue extérieure. droite: Entrée_Intérieur_Mur encliqueté.
izquierda: Ubicación_Vista exterior. derecha: Zona del acceso_Espacio interior_Muro torcido.

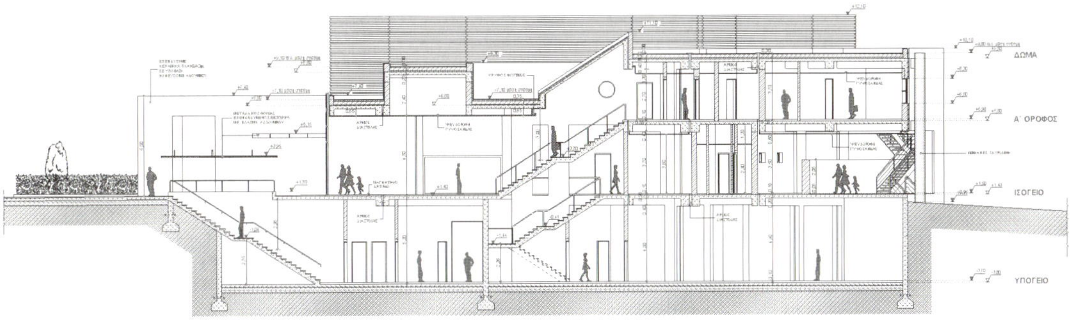

links: Erschließungsbrücke. rechts: Schnitt_Abgehängte Wegführung_Außenansicht_Eingangs- und Verteilungsbereich.

gauche: Pont d'entrée. droite: Coupe_Guide des passages suspendus_Vue extérieure_Zone d'entrée et de distribution.

izquierda: Puente de conexión. derecha: Corte_Pasadizo colgante_Vista exterior_Zona de acceso y distribución.

ITALY_ROME **ARA PACIS**

ITALIEN_ITALIE_ITALIA
RICHARD MEIER & PARTNERS
2006
ARCHÄOLOGIEMUSEUM_MUSÉE DE L'ARCHÉOLOGIE
MUSEO ARQUEOLÓGICO
4,250 M²
PHOTOS ROLAND HALBE / ARTURIMAGES

Das Museum am Ufer des Tiber wurde als Hülle für die Ara Pacis, einem auf das Jahr 9 v. Chr. datierten Opferaltar errichtet. Das Gebäude besteht aus einer langen, einstöckigen verglasten Loggia, die sich auf einem flachen Podium erhebt und eine transparente Barriere zwischen dem Ufer des Tiber und der runden Umfassungsmauer des um 28 v. Chr. erbauten Augustus-Mausoleums bildet. Dominantes Merkmal des Neubaus ist eine gläserne Vorhangfassade von 150 Metern Länge und 40 Metern Höhe. Die asymmetrische Eingangshalle, geprägt von sieben schlanken Stahlbetonrundpfeilern mit einer Oberfläche aus weißem gewachstem Stuckmarmor, führt zur Haupthalle. Das Dach über der Haupthalle ruht auf vier Rundpfeilern, Oberlichter maximieren den Tageslichteinfall.

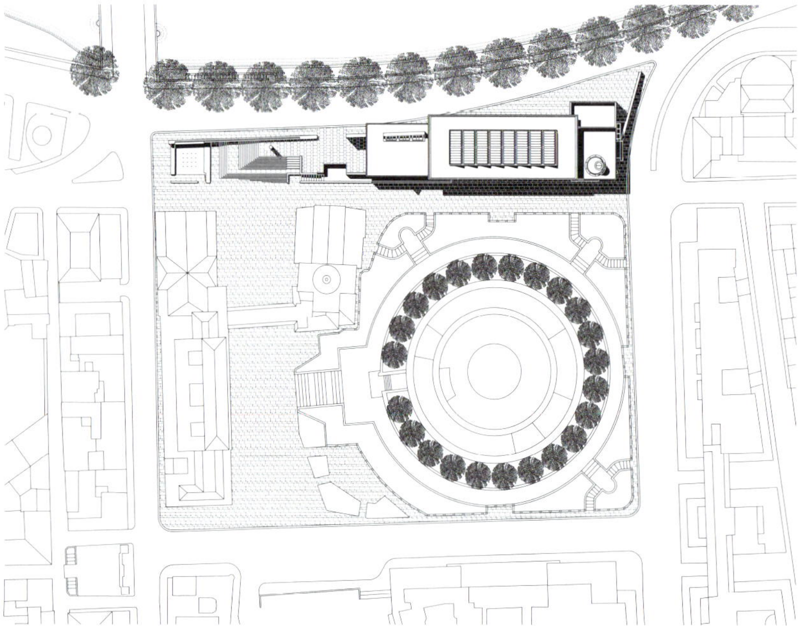

Le musée situé sur la rive du Tibre a été érigé en guise d'enveloppe pour Ara Pacis, un autel pour la paix en l'honneur de la victime au IXème siècle avant JC. Le bâtiment comprend une loggia vitrifiée, allongée, sur un étage reposant sur un podium plat qui forme une barrière transparente entre la rive du Tibre et le mur d'enceinte rond du mausolée d'Auguste construit environ au XXVIII siècle avant JC. La caractéristique dominante du nouveau bâtiment est une façade-rideau en verre de 150 mètres de long sur 40 mètres de hauteur. Le hall d'entrée asymétrique caractérisé par sept colonnes fines en béton armé avec une surface en marbre artificiel blanc naturel conduit au hall principal. Le toit du hall principal repose sur quatre colonnes et la lumière provenant du plafond accentue l'entrée de la lumière naturelle.

El museo a orillas del Tíber se levantó como envolvente para el Ara Pacis, un altar de sacrificios que data del año 9 antes de Cristo. El edificio consta de una alargada loggia acristalada de una planta, la misma se levanta sobre un podio plano y constituye una barrera transparente entre la orilla del Tíber y el muro circular que rodea el mausoleo de Augusto, erigido hacia el año 28 antes de Cristo. La característica predominante de la construcción nueva es su muro cortina acristalado, de 150 metros de longitud y 40 metros de altura. La sala de acceso asimétrica, sostenida por siete pilares redondos de hormigón armado con superficie de mármol estucado y encerado, conduce a la sala principal. El techo sobre la sala principal descansa sobre cuatro pilares redondos. Los lucernarios maximizan la incidencia de la luz solar.

links: Lageplan_Außenbau_Büsten. rechts: Tempelfassade_Museumsfassade_Tempel in Vitrine.
gauche: Plan de site_Extérieur_Bustes. droite: Façade du temple_Façade du musée_Temple en vitrine.
izquierda: Plano de ubicación_Vista exterior_Bustos. derecha: Fachada del templo_Fachada del museo_Templo en vitrina.

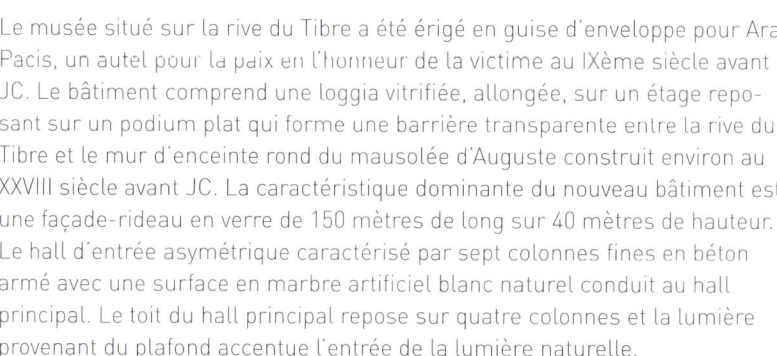

ITALY_ROME

MAXXI – MUSEO NAZIONALE DELLE ARTI DEL XXI SECOLO

ITALIEN_ITALIE_ITALIA
ZAHA HADID ARCHITECTS
2010
KUNSTMUSEUM_MUSÉE D'ART_MUSEO DE ARTE
29,000 M²
PHOTOS ROLAND HALBE / ARTURIMAGES

Aufgrund der Verflechtung des Besucherstroms mit dem städtebaulichen Kontext haben die Stadt und das Center auf den ehemaligen Kasernen eine gemeinsame öffentliche Dimension. Die Bewegung innerhalb und außerhalb des Gebäudes folgt der Gesamtdrift des Aufbaus. Vertikale und schräge Bewegungszonen sind als Bereiche des Zustroms, der Beeinflussung und Turbulenzen angelegt, Störung und Drift werden zur Form. Das Driften ist sowohl architektonisches Motiv als auch eine Möglichkeit, ein Museum experimentell zu erschließen. Einmal mehr wurde hier der Aspekt der Wiederkennung für eine bedeutende Institution in einen geschmeidigen und durchlässigen Organismus gebracht, der mehrere Formen der Identifikation anbietet.

En raison de la concentration des flux de visiteurs avec le contexte urbaniste, la ville et le centre ont une dimension publique générale sur l'ancienne caserne. Le mouvement à l'intérieur et à l'extérieur du bâtiment suit le processus géométrique. Les zones de mouvement verticales et obliques sont positionnées comme des zones d'afflux, d'inspiration et de turbulences afin de donner une forme à la perturbation et à la dérive. La dérive est un motif architectonique comme si l'art préférait mettre en valeur le musée. Une fois encore l'aspect de la reconnaissance pour une institution significative fut intégré à un organisme perméable et souple offrant plusieurs formes d'identification.

Debido a la estrecha vinculación del flujo de visitantes con el contexto urbano, la ciudad y el museo tienen una dimensión pública común en el antiguo cuartel. El movimiento dentro y fuera del edificio sigue las premisas geométricas. Las zonas de movimiento verticales y oblicuas están dispuestas como ámbitos de afluencia, de influencia y de turbulencias; las interferencias y desviaciones adoptan una forma. La desviación también se convierte en motivo arquitectónico, y además en el modo preferente de conectar un museo. Una vez más, en un organismo transparente y fluido, que ofrece múltiples formas de identificación, una institución significativa encuentra reconocimiento.

links: Studie Ölgemälde_Panoramaansicht. rechts: Fassade bei Nacht_Treppenhaus_Erdgeschoss.
gauche: Tableau à l'huile d'étude_Vue panoramique. droite: Façade de nuit_Cage d'escalier_Rez-de-chaussée.
izquierda: Estudio en pintura al óleo_Vista panorámica. derecha: Fachada por la noche_Caja de la escalera_Planta baja.

ITALY_ROVERETO

MART – MUSEO DI ARTE MODERNA E CONTEMPORANEA DI TRENTO E ROVERETO

ITALIEN_ITALIE_ITALIA
STUDIO ARCHITETTO MARIO BOTTA WITH GIULIO ANDREOLLI
2002
KUNSTMUSEUM_MUSÉE D'ART_MUSEO DE ARTE
29,000 M²
PHOTOS ENRICO CANO, COMO (326, 327, 329 L.), PINO MUSI, MILAN (328, 329 R.)

Das Museum wurde aus Rücksicht auf die beiden historischen Bauten der Palazzi Alberti und dell'Annona aus der Flucht des Corso Bettini zurückgesetzt. Der so entstandene Raum zwischen ihnen ist als Allee ausgebildet, die zu einem runden Platz führt, von dem verschiedene Zugänge Einlass zu Museum, Bibliothek, Auditorium und Café gewähren. Der von einer Glaskuppel überfangene Platz bildet das Herz des Gebäudes. Von hier erreichen die Besucher die Ausstellungsräume der beiden Obergeschosse sowie die Servicebereiche, die sich im Erdgeschoss am zentralen Atrium befinden. Das Atrium bietet unterschiedliche Ansichten und ermöglicht durch den Wechsel von Mezzaninen und großen Räumen vielfältige Nutzungen. Das Untergeschoss beherbergt die Bibliothek und die Archive des 20. Jahrhunderts.

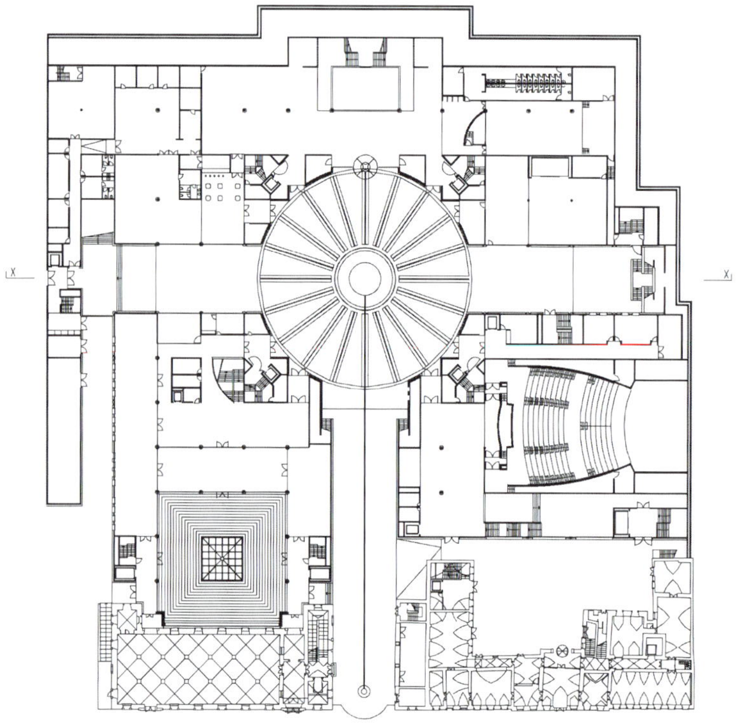

Après considération des deux sites historiques, le palais Alberti et Annona, le musée fut placé dans l'alignement de Corso Bettini. L'espace résultant fut utilisé comme allée menant à une place ronde qui garantit au musée l'accès à la bibliothèque, à l'auditorium et au café par plusieurs voies. La place dominée par une coupole en verre forme le cœur de la structure. A partir de cette place, les visiteurs peuvent atteindre les espaces d'exposition situés sur les deux étages supérieurs et les espaces de service situés au rez-de-chaussée dans l'atrium central. L'atrium offre des perspectives variées et une utilisation spatiale multiple grâce aux mezzanines aménageables et aux grands espaces. Le rez-de-chaussée abrite la bibliothèque et les archives du XX siècle.

El diseño de este museo sirve de fondo a las dos edificaciones históricas de los palacios Alberti y Annona, con frente al Corso Bettini. El espacio que surge entre ellos está tratado como una avenida, la que conduce a una plaza redonda; varias entradas permiten acceder al museo, la biblioteca, el auditorio y el café. La plaza cubierta por una cúpula de cristal constituye el corazón de la estructura. Desde aquí, los visitantes llegan hasta las salas de exhibiciones de ambos niveles superiores; al igual que las zonas de servicios que se encuentran en planta baja junto al atrio. Este ofrece vistas muy variadas y admite usos múltiples, gracias a la alternancia de grandes espacios y entrepisos. El subsuelo alberga la biblioteca y los archivos del siglo XX.

links: Grundriss Erdgeschoss_Blick vom Platz zum Corso Bettini_Wechselausstellungsraum. rechts: Platz und Glaskuppel_Ausstellungsraum.
gauche: Plan du rez-de-chaussée_Vue depuis la place vers Corso Bettini_Espace d'expositions tournantes. droite: Place et coupole en verre_Espace d'exposition.
izquierda: Plano de planta baja_Vista desde la plaza hacia el Corso Bettini_Sala de muestras temporarias. derecha: Plaza y cúpula de cristal_Sala de exhibiciones.

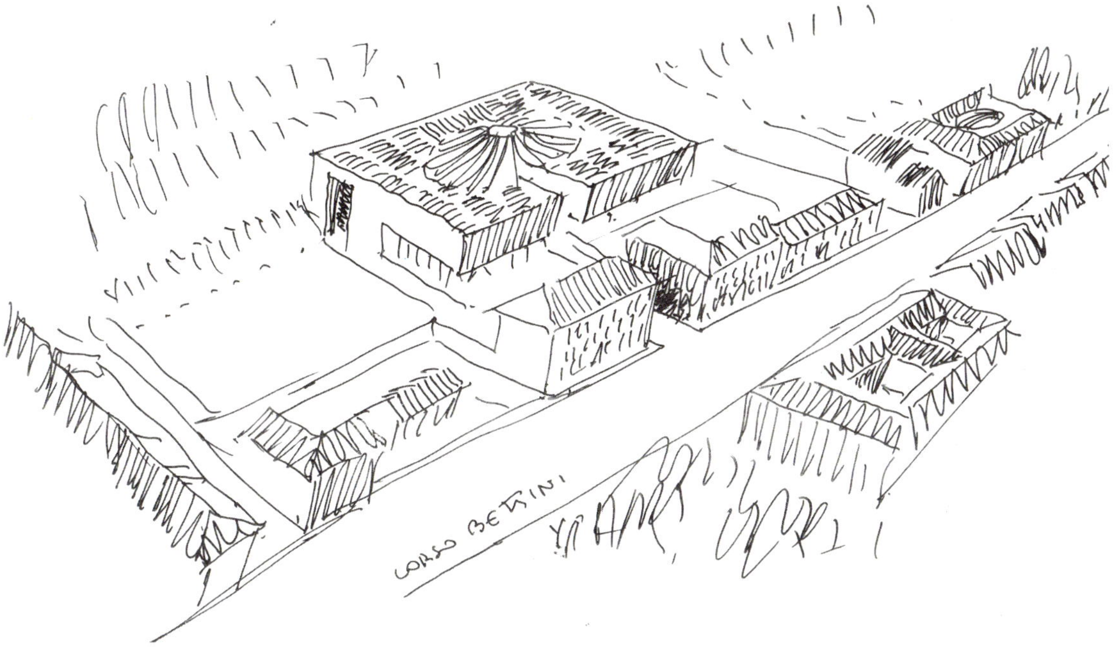

links: Detail von Platz und Glaskuppel. rechts: Skizze Gesamtanlage_Foyer_Brücke 2. Obergeschoss_Ausstellungsraum.
gauche: Vue de la place et coupole en verre. droite: Esquisse de l'installation totale_Réception_Passerelle du 2ème étage_Espace d'exposition.
izquierda: Vista de la plaza y la cúpula de cristal. derecha: Esbozo del conjunto_Recepción_Puente en el segundo piso_Sala de exhibiciones.

NORWAY_HAMARØY **HAMSUNSENTERET**

NORWEGEN_NORVÈGE_NORUEGA
STEVEN HOLL ARCHITECTS
2009
LITERATURMUSEUM_MUSÉE DE LA LITTÉRATURE
MUSEO LITERARIO
2,508 M²
PHOTOS STEVEN HOLL ARCHITECTS

Das dem Schriftsteller Knut Hamsun gewidmete Museum befindet sich jenseits des Polarkreises in der Nähe des Dorfes Presteid von Hamarøy unweit des Bauernhofs, auf dem der Schriftsteller aufwuchs. Es umfasst Ausstellungsräume, eine Bibliothek und einen Leseraum, ein Café und ein Auditorium mit einer Ausstattung für Filmprojektionen. Das Konzept versteht das Museum als „Gebäude wie einen Körper" und stellt ein Schlachtfeld für unsichtbare Kräfte zur Verfügung. Viele Formalia des Gebäudes greifen einheimische Elemente auf, so beispielsweise die charakteristischen, schwarz gebeizten Holzfassaden der großen hölzernen Stabkirchen Norwegens. Auch das hohe Gras auf dem Dachgarten bezieht sich in moderner Abwandlung auf die traditionellen norwegischen Grasdächer.

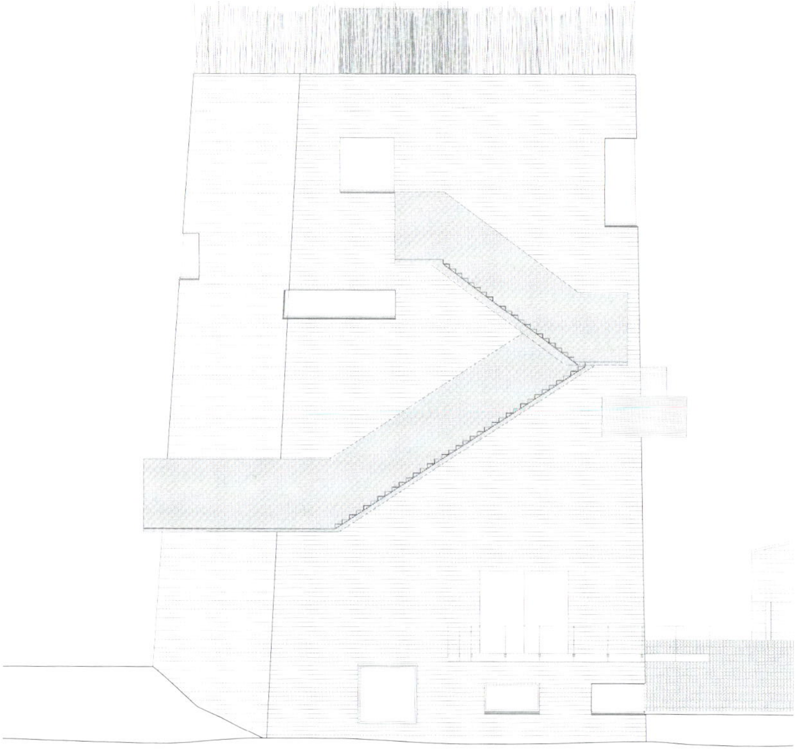

Le musée consacré à l'écrivain Knut Hamsun se situe au-dessus du cercle polaire auprès du village, Presteid de Hamarøy, à proximité de la ferme où l'écrivain a grandi. Il comprend des espaces d'exposition, une bibliothèque, une salle de lecture, un café et un auditorium avec l'équipement requis pour les projections de film. Le concept assimile le musée à un « bâtiment représenté comme un corps » mettant à disposition un champ de bataille pour les forces invisibles. Les nombreux éléments de style du bâtiment rappellent les éléments de la région, notamment les façades typiques en bois noires décapées des grandes églises en bois debout de Norvège. L'herbe haute placée sur le jardin de toit fait également référence aux toitures norvégiennes traditionnelles dans une conception modernisée.

El museo dedicado al escritor Knut Hamsun está más allá del Círculo Polar Ártico, cerca de la localidad de Presteid en la región de Hamarøy, no muy lejos de la granja donde creció el escritor. Comprende salas de exhibiciones, una biblioteca y una sala de lectura, un café y un auditorio con equipamiento para proyecciones cinematográficas. El concepto museístico es el de un "edificio que parece un cuerpo" y representa un campo de batalla para fuerzas invisibles. El edificio adopta elementos autóctonos como, por ejemplo, las características fachadas de madera barnizada oscura de las típicas iglesias noruegas llamadas "Stavkirken". También las gramíneas plantadas en el techo son una versión moderna de los tradicionales techos de césped de las casas noruegas.

links: Südfassade_Treppenhaus_Raumdurchblick_Innenraum. rechts: Gebäude im Umfeld_Ausbau_Balkon_Blick in die Landschaft_Bambus auf dem Dach.
gauche: Façade sud_Escalier_Vue horizontale_Intérieur. droite: Bâtiment aux alentours_Aménagement_Balcon_Vue sur le paysage_Bambous sur le toit.
izquierda: Fachada sur_La caja de la escalera_Vista interior_Interior. derecha: Edificio en su entorno_Construcción_Balcón_Vista del paisaje_Plataforma de observación sobre el techo.

POLAND_WARSAW **CHOPIN MUZEUM**

POLEN_POLOGNE_POLONIA
MIGLIORE + SERVETTO ARCHITETTI ASSOCIATI
2010
GESCHICHTSMUSEUM_MUSÉE D'HISTOIRE_MUSEO HISTÓRICO
1,200 M²
PHOTOS MARCIN CZECHOWICZ

Der Umbau des Ostrogski-Palastes zielt darauf ab, klassische Musik und die Person Chopins einem breiten Publikum näherzubringen, indem er die traditionelle Wahrnehmung in einem Museum in eine ganz individuelle Erfahrung von Wissen umwandelt. Zwar berücksichtigt der Umbau die architektonischen und konstruktiven Elemente des Palastes, das Projekt entwickelt aber analog zu den jeweiligen Exponaten elf unterschiedlich definierte emotionale Landschaften und Klangräume. Jedes Thema wird durch die Ausstellungsarchitektur spezifiziert, die im Hinblick auf die Musik, die besonderen Exponate der Sammlung sowie interaktive Multiplayer- und multimodale Systeme entworfen wurde.

La rénovation du palais Ostrogski vise à sensibiliser le grand public à la musique classique et à la personne de Chopin en transformant la perception traditionnelle d'un musée en une expérience très individualisée de connaissances. Certes, la rénovation respecte les éléments architectoniques et structurels du palais en s'adaptant néanmoins, par analogie, aux objets exposés, en onze paysages différents, définis au niveau émotionnel et acoustique. Chaque thème individuel spécifique au contexte de l'architecture de l'exposition intègre la musique et la conception des objets exposés accompagnées de systèmes multimédias et multimodaux dédiés et interactifs.

La reforma del palacio Ostrogski apuntó a atraer a un público amplio hacia la música clásica y la persona de Chopin. Para ello, se transformó la noción tradicional de museo en una experiencia muy individualizada del saber. El edificio respeta los elementos arquitectónicos y estructuradores del palacio, pero, de manera análoga a los objetos expuestos, se transforma en once paisajes emocionales y espacios sonoros definidos de diversas maneras. Cada uno de los diversos temas está especificado por la arquitectura museística, diseñada en el contexto de la música incorporada, los objetos de muestra particulares y los sistemas multimedia interactivos.

links: Schnitt_Fassade_Nohantraum. rechts: Warschauraum_Komponistenraum_Zelazowa Wola-Raum_Reiseraum.
gauche: Coupe_Façade_Espace Nohant. droite: Espace Varsovie_Espace compositeur_Espace Zelazowa Wola_Espace voyages.
izquierda: Corte_Fachada_Sala Nohant. derecha: Sala Varsovia_Sala del compositor_Sala Zelazowa Wola_Sala de viajes.

Krasinski Palace
Saxon Palace
Casimir P

Castle
Edinburgh

PORTUGAL_CASCAIS **PAULA RÊGO MUSEUM**

PORTUGAL_PORTUGAL_PORTUGAL
EDUARDO SOUTO DE MOURA
2008
KUNSTMUSEUM_MUSÉE D'ART_MUSEO DE ARTE
3,307 M²
PHOTOS LEONARDO FINOTTI

Nach dem Studium der umliegenden Bäume, insbesondere der Baumkronen, entwickelte der Architekt eine Reihe von Räumen mit unterschiedlichen Höhen. Die Verteilung dieser Boxen ist das steinerne Positiv zum Negativ des Umrisses der Baumkronen. Dieses Spiel von „Yang" und „Yin", von menschlicher Schöpfung und Natur, trug auch zur Materialwahl im Außenbereich bei: roter Beton im Gegensatz zum grünen Gehölz, dessen Bestand inzwischen jedoch prophylaktisch ausgedünnt wurde. Mit zwei großen Pyramiden - Oberlichtern für Bibliothek und Café - wurde eine Hierarchie entlang der Eingangsachse geschaffen. Ein Hauptanliegen des Architekten war es, jeden Ausstellungsraum nach außen zum Garten hin zu öffnen.

Après avoir étudié la nature des arbres environnants, notamment leurs couronnes, l'architecte a développé un programme nuancé composé d'une série d'espaces situés à différentes hauteurs. En effet, la répartition de ces boîtes représente un pôle positif en pierre vis-à-vis du pôle négatif formé par les couronnes des arbres. Ce jeu d'opposition - entre Yin et Yang, entre nature et création de l'homme - se reflète également dans le choix des matériaux : un béton rouge contrastant avec le bois vert élagué par anticipation à l'évolution. Les deux grandes pyramides qui permettent l'entrée de la lumière au-dessus de la bibliothèque et de la cafétéria ont été créées selon une hiérarchie le long de l'axe de l'entrée. Parmi les priorités de l'architecte, chaque salle d'exposition se devait d'avoir une ouverture vers le jardin extérieur.

El arquitecto llevó a cabo un estudio de los árboles circundantes, en particular de las copas de los árboles, y este estudio dio como resultado un programa arquitectónico de múltiples salas de diferentes alturas. La distribución de estas cajas equivale a un positivo pétreo, contrapuesto al negativo de las copas de los árboles. Este juego de "yang" y "yin", de creación humana y naturaleza, también se plasmó en la elección de los materiales: un hormigón rojo contrasta con la vegetación verde que, no obstante, fue reducida. Con dos grandes lucernarios en forma de pirámide para la biblioteca y el café, se logró una jerarquía a lo largo del eje del acceso. Otra preocupación del arquitecto fue lograr que cada sala de exhibiciones tuviera su propia abertura hacia el jardín.

links: Skizze_Gesamtansicht. rechts: Hof.
gauche: Esquisse_Vue d'ensemble. droite: Cour.
izquierda: Esbozo_Vista del conjunto. derecha: Patio.

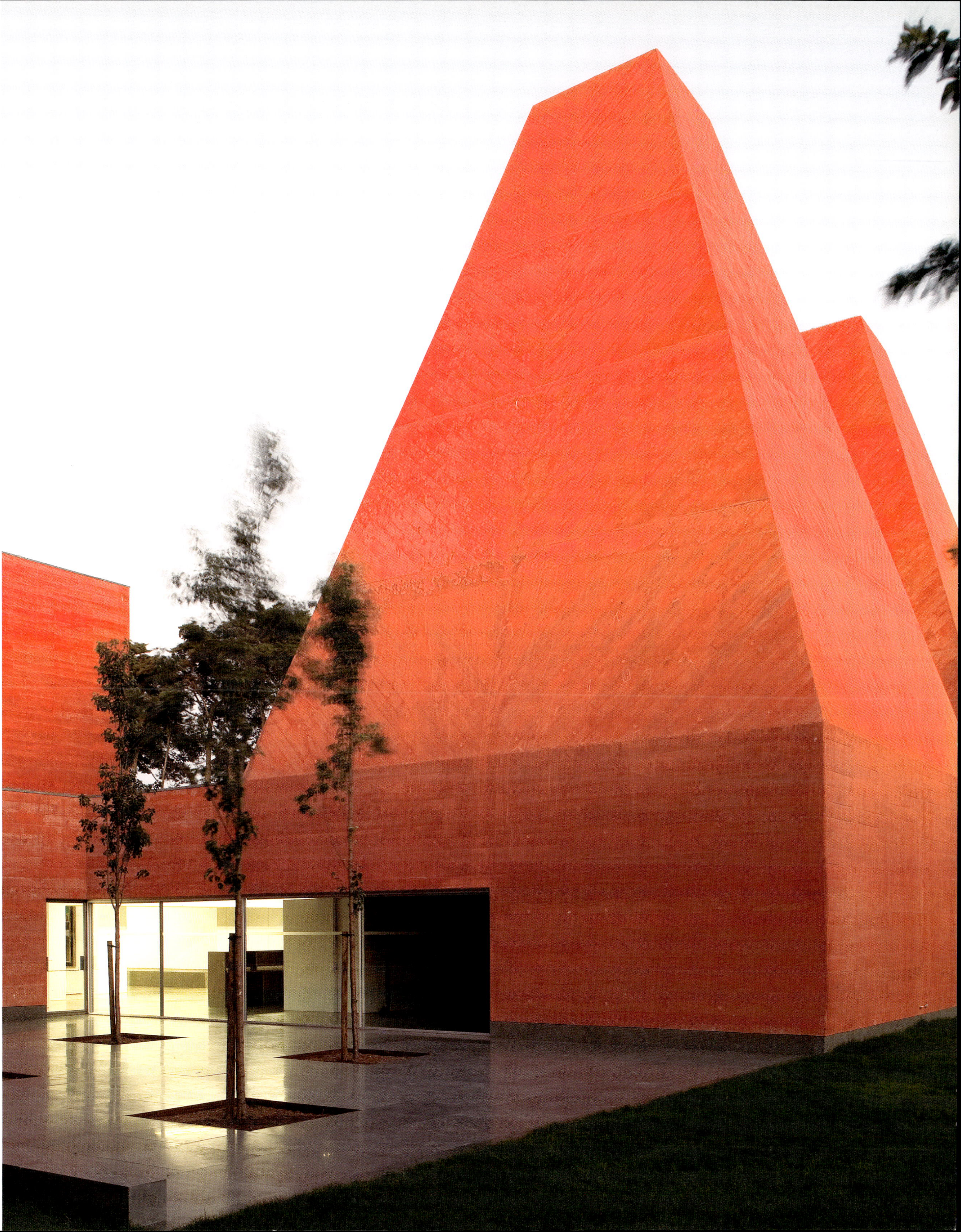

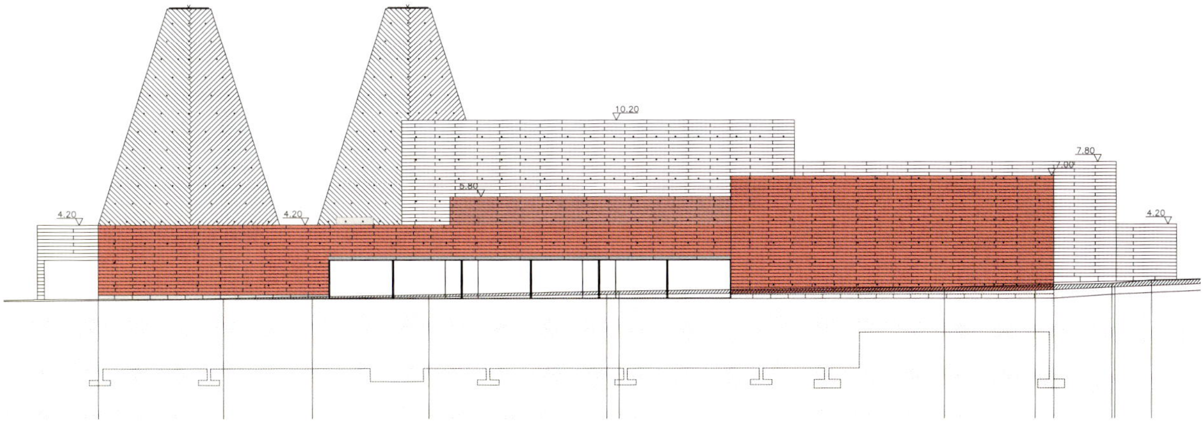

links: Ausstellungssaal. rechts: Schnitt_Ausstellungssaal_Shop.
gauche: Salle d'exposition. droite: Coupe_Salle d'exposition_Boutique.
izquierda: Sala de exhibiciones. derecha: Corte_Sala de exhibiciones_Tienda.

PORTUGAL_LISBON **MUSEU DO DESIGN E DA MODA**

PORTUGAL_PORTUGAL_PORTUGAL
RICARDO CARVALHO + JOANA VILHENA ARQUITECTOS
2009
DESIGN- UND MODEMUSEUM_MUSEE DU DESIGN ET DE LA MODE_MUSEO DE DISEÑO Y MODA
2,634 M^2
PHOTOS LEONARDO FINOTTI

Der Eingriff wurde hauptsächlich mit Licht vorgenommen. Das immaterielle Element Licht lenkt die Aufmerksamkeit sowohl auf den Sichtbeton als auch auf die Sammlung, und Kunstlicht hebt einzelne Elemente des Gebäudes hervor. Das Projekt zeichnet sich zudem durch die expressionistische Architektur in Sichtbeton und die Oberflächen aus industriellen Materialien aus. Sie verweisen auf die Straße und Paletten, die als Ausstellungsflächen dienen. Die Böden wurden teilweise mit reflektierender Farbe bemalt. Die Sammlung verteilt sich informell im Raum. Von der Cafeteria mit einem einzelnen langen Korktisch schaut man durch eine große Glasscheibe auf das Museum sowie die umliegenden Straßen der Baixa Pombalina.

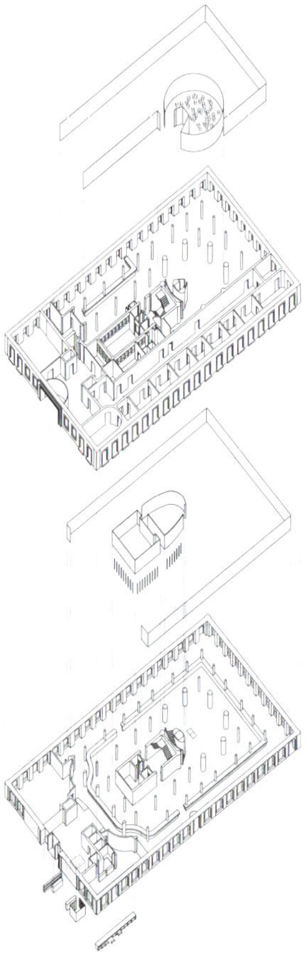

L'intervention résulte principalement de la lumière. La lumière, élément immatériel, projette l'attention, et sur le béton apparent, et sur la collection. En effet, la lumière artificielle fait ressortir les éléments individuels du bâtiment. Par ailleurs, le projet se caractérise par son architecture expressionniste en béton apparent et ses surfaces revêtues en matériaux industriels qui s'orientent sur la rue. Des palettes servent de surfaces d'exposition. Les revêtements de sol sont peints partiellement en couleur réfléchissante. La collection est répartie dans l'espace de manière informelle. De la cafétéria équipée d'une unique table longue en liège, la vue donne grâce à une grande baie vitrée sur le musée et les rues environnantes de Baixa Pombalina.

La intervención se comprende básicamente con la luz. Este elemento inmaterial, la luz, atrae la atención del visitante tanto hacia el hormigón visto como hacia la colección; la luz artificial destaca elementos de la edificación. El proyecto se destaca por la arquitectura expresionista de hormigón visto y por las superficies de materiales industriales. Remiten a la calle. Las paletas sirven como superficies de exhibición. Los suelos fueron pintados parcialmente con pintura reflectante. La colección se distribuye informalmente por el espacio. Desde la cafetería, caracterizada por una única mesa larga de corcho, se puede apreciar, a través de un gran cristal, el propio museo y las calles cercanas de la Baixa Pombalina.

links: Axonometrie_Ausstellungshalle_Fassade. rechts: Ausstellungssaal_Treppenhaus_Innenraum.
gauche: Axiométrie_Hall d'exposition_Façade. droite: Hall d'exposition_Cage d'escalier_Intérieur.
izquierda: Axonométrica_Sala de exhibiciones_Fachada. derecha: Sala de exhibiciones_Caja de la escalera_Espacio interior.

SPD

PORTUGAL_LUZ **MUSEU DA LUZ**

PORTUGAL_PORTUGAL_PORTUGAL
PEDRO PACHECO + MARIE CLÉMENT
2003
KULTURMUSEUM_MUSÉE DE LA CULTURE_MUSEO DE LA CULTURA
660 M^2
PHOTOS PAULO NUNO SILVA / ÉVORA, PORTUGAL (340, 343 L., R. B), LEONARDO FINOTTI, SÃO PAULO (341, 342, 343 R. A.)

Das Dorf Luz wurde durch den Bau des Alqueva-Staudamms komplett überflutet. Die Bewohner, ihre Kultur und ihre Traditionen mussten in ein neues Dorf umgesiedelt werden. Das Projekt umfasst die Neuerrichtung der Kirche, des Friedhofs und des Museums von Luz als wichtigem Erinnerungsort zwischen dem neuen und dem alten Dorf. Das Museum definiert die Topografie des Ortes als Neugründung, wo Wege, Mauern und Licht als eindeutige Elemente einer territorialen Definition dienen. Die Raumabfolge im Inneren legt Wert auf die Beachtung der Landschaft. Der Luz-Raum als zentraler Teil des Museums und die Lichtschächte sind die einzigen sichtbaren Spuren des Gebäudes in der Landschaft.

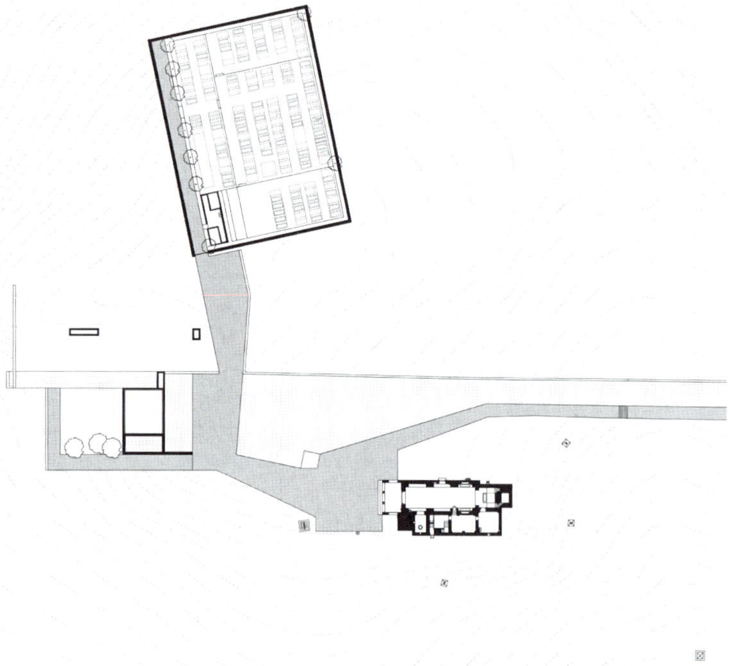

Le village Luz fut inondé dans sa totalité en raison de la construction du barrage d'Alqueva. Par conséquent, le transfert des habitants, de leur culture et traditions fut nécessaire dans un nouveau village. Le projet comprend la construction de l'église, du cimetière et d'un musée de Luz comme lieu de commémoration à l'ancien village dans le nouveau village. Le musée définit la topographie du lieu comme nouvelle fondation. Les chemins, murs et lumière sont des éléments bien définissables d'une culture du territoire. La succession des espaces met l'accent sur le respect du paysage. L'espace Luz, la partie centrale du musée et les puits de lumière sont les uniques éléments du bâtiment repérables dans le paysage.

El pueblo de Luz fue completamente anegado tras la construcción de la presa de Alqueva. Los habitantes, su cultura y sus tradiciones debieron ser trasladados a un pueblo nuevo. El proyecto comprende la edificación de la iglesia, el cementerio y un museo de Luz como sitio conmemorativo que sirve de conexión entre el antiguo pueblo y el nuevo. El museo define la topografía del sitio a modo de refundación. Senderos, muros y luz sirven como elementos inconfundibles de una cultura territorial. La secuencia espacial pone valor en el respeto por el paisaje. En este paisaje, solo la sala de Luz, corazón del museo, y los pozos de luz, se diferencian del edificio.

links: Lageplan_Ostansicht_Südansicht. rechts: Zugangsrampe und Dachfläche_Dachlandschaft und Aussichtspunkt über den See.
gauche: Plan de situation_Vue à l'est_Vue au sud. droite: Rampe d'accès et toit plat_Paysage de toitures et perspective sur le lac.
izquierda: Plano de ubicación_Fachada este_Fachada sur. derecha: Rampa de acceso y superficie de techos_Paisaje de techos y punto de observación sobre el lago.

MUSEUDALUZ

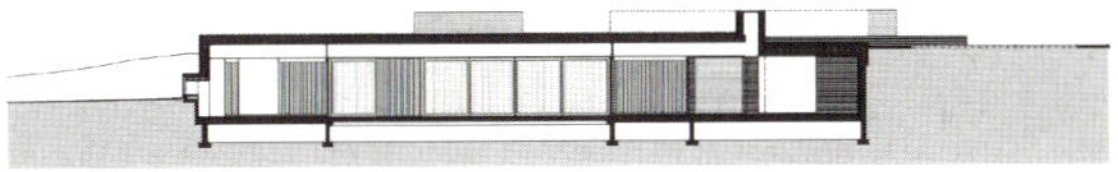

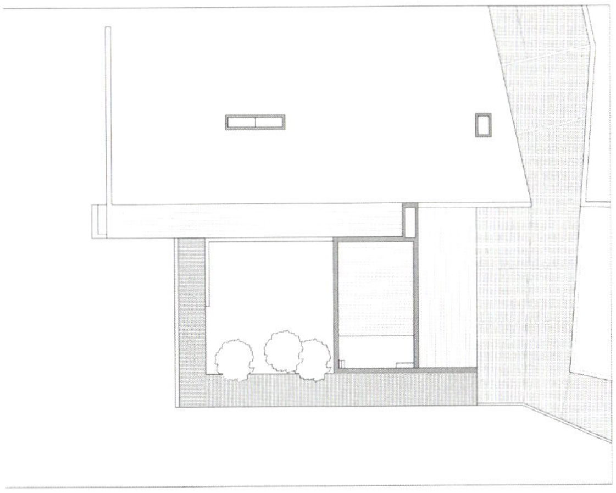

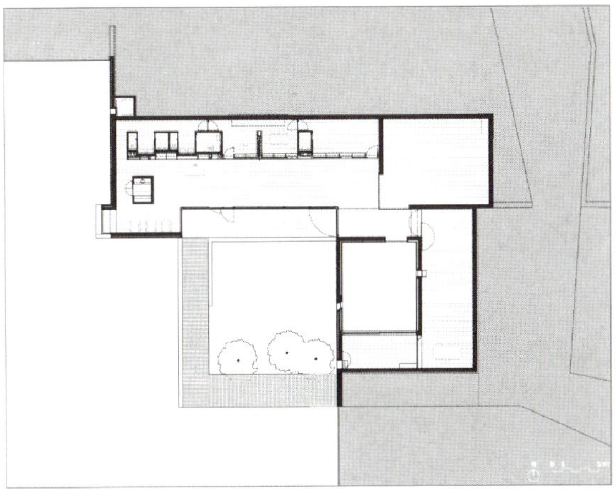

links: Ausstellungsraum. rechts: Schnitte und Pläne_Innenhof_Luz-Raum und Innenhof_Wechselausstellungs- und Gedenkraum.
gauche: Espace d'exposition. droite: Coupes et plans_Cour intérieure_Espace luz et cour intérieure Expositions alternantes et espace mémorial.
izquierda: Sala de exhibiciones. derecha: Cortes y plantas_Patio interior_Sala de Luz y patio interior_Sala de la memoria y exhibiciones temporarias.

SLOVENIA_LJUBLJANA **MESTNI MUZEJ LJUBLJANA**

SLOWENIEN_SLOVENIE_ESLOVENIA
OFIS ARHITEKTI/ROK OMAN, SPELA VIDECNIK
2004
KULTURMUSEUM_MUSÉE DE LA CULTURE_MUSEO DE LA CULTURA
3,250 M^2
PHOTOS TOMAZ GREGORIC

Das Projekt umfasst die Renovierung und Erweiterung des Palais' Auersperg im Herzen des historischen Stadtzentrums. Schloss und Neubaugrundstück blicken auf eine reiche Geschichte aus der Frühzeit, der römischen Antike und des Mittelalters zurück, und jede Epoche hinterließ Spuren im Bestand. Im Laufe seiner Geschichte änderte der Palast mehrfach seine Funktion, so dass die überlieferte Grundrissdisposition nicht geeignet war, ein Museumsprogramm aufzunehmen: Die Anlage war labyrinthisch, und die Räume waren separiert. Der Wettbewerbsbeitrag schlug eine spiralförmige Erschließung für den Besucher und einen ergänzenden Bauteil vor, der die Flügel des Schlosses miteinander verbindet.

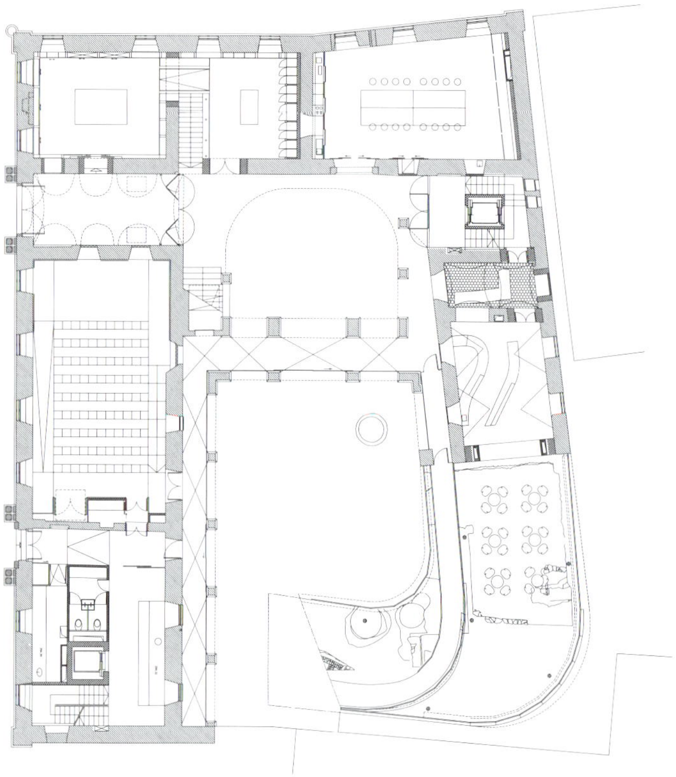

Le projet comprend la rénovation et l'extension du Palais Auersperg au cœur du centre historique de la ville. Le château et l'immeuble du bâtiment neuf font référence à une histoire riche remontant à la préhistoire, l'antiquité romaine et au Moyen-âge et chaque époque a laissé ses traces sur les bâtiments actuels. Au cours de son histoire, le palais a changé de fonction à plusieurs reprises et la disposition des plans livrés n'était pas adaptée à l'intégration d'un programme de musée : le site se présentait comme un labyrinthe et les espaces étaient séparés. La contribution à l'appel d'offres proposait pour les visiteurs un escalier hélicoïdal et une annexe permettant la jonction à l'aile du château.

El proyecto comprende la renovación y ampliación del Palais Auersperg en el corazón del casco histórico. El palacio y el sitio de la obra nueva tienen una rica historia que abarca el pasado reciente, la Antigüedad romana y la Edad Media; cada época ha dejado sus huellas características. A lo largo de su historia, el palacio cambió varias veces de destino; la distribución en planta no era la propicia para albergar un programa museístico moderno, puesto que el conjunto era más bien laberíntico y las salas estaban separadas. La propuesta arquitectónica incluye una circulación en forma de espiral para los visitantes y un moderno cuerpo adicional que conecta las alas del palacio entre sí.

links: Plan_Sitzbereich_Halle. rechts: Blick in den Innenraum_Ansicht Restaurant.
gauche: Plan_Coin salon_Hall. droite: Vue dans l'espace intérieur_Vue du restaurant.
izquierda: Planta_Zona para sentarse_Sala. derecha: Vista del interior_Vista del restaurante.

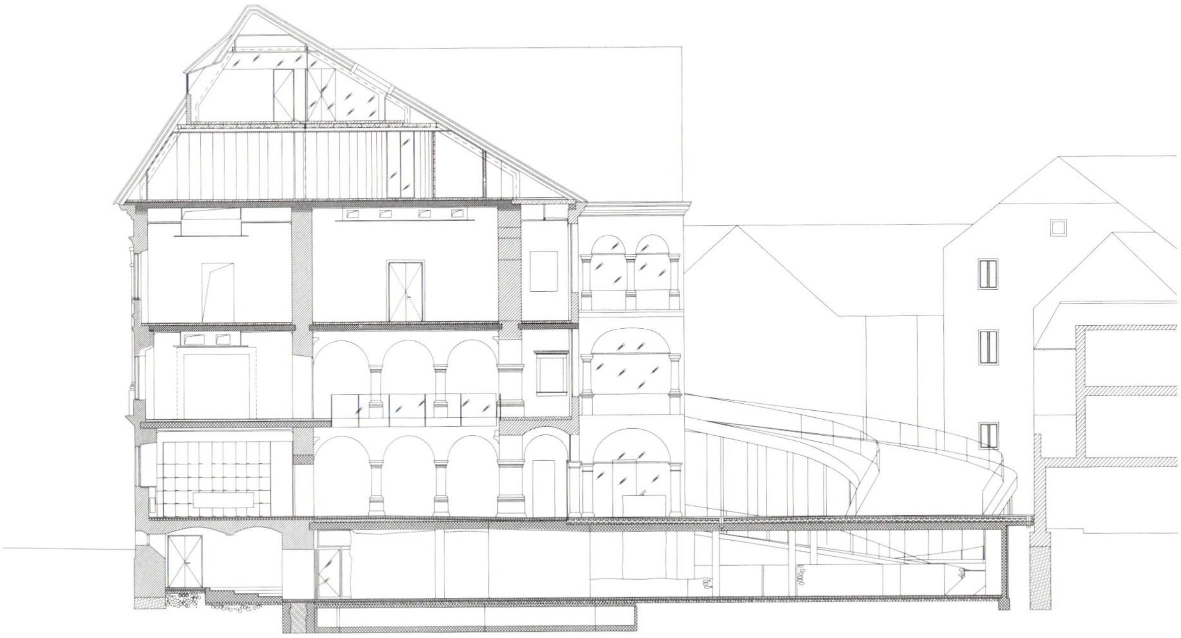

links: Licht und Spiegelungen. rechts: Schnitt_Kino_Modell_Außenbau.
gauche: Lumière et reflets. droite: Coupe_Cinéma_Modèle_Extérieur.
izquierda: Luz y reflejos. derecha: Corte_Cine_Maqueta_Vista exterior.

SPAIN_ALMERÍA **MUSEO ARQUEOLÓGICO DE ALMERÍA**

SPANIEN_ESPAGNE_ESPAÑA
PAREDES PEDROSA ARQUITECTOS
2003
ARCHÄOLOGIEMUSEUM_MUSÉE DE L'ARCHÉOLOGIE
MUSEO ARQUEOLÓGICO
6,284 M²
PHOTOS ROLAND HALBE / ARTURIMAGES

Der Eingang des Museums befindet sich am Ende eines Platzes, der sowohl öffentlicher Stadtraum als auch Freiluftlobby des Museums ist. Der bestehende Palmengarten an der Seite wurde beibehalten und erweitert, um ihn in die Ausstellungsfläche einzubeziehen. Das Museum beherbergt eine archäologische Sammlung. Eine Reihe verschiedenartiger Räume wird durch einen großen Leerraum verbunden. Er dient den Besuchern zur Orientierung und verknüpft die Räume der Dauerausstellung und verschiedene Bereiche mit anderer Funktion. An einigen Stellen sind die Außenwände als Aussichtspunkte auf die Stadt geöffnet, während die Belichtung vornehmlich durch Dachfenster in den Decken erfolgt. Das direkte Tageslicht wird durch lackierte, hölzerne Gitter über den Ausstellungsräumen gefiltert.

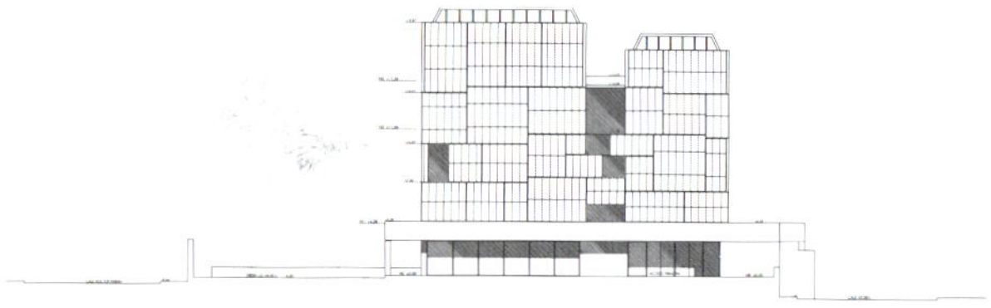

L'entrée du musée se situe aux confins d'une place qui permet d'accéder à l'espace public de la ville et au hall d'entrée en plein air du musée. Le jardin de palmiers existant sur le côté a été conservé et intégré comme extension à la surface d'exposition. L'objectif du musée est d'accueillir une collection d'archéologie. Une série d'espaces variés est accessible par un grand espace vide. Il sert à orienter les visiteurs et relie les espaces dédiés aux expositions permanentes et aux différentes zones fonctionnelles. A certains endroits, les murs extérieurs sont ouverts afin d'offrir des points panoramiques sur la ville. Par ailleurs, l'éclairage s'effectue surtout par les fenêtres de toit situées au plafond. La lumière naturelle directe est filtrée par les trames en bois laquées sur les espaces d'exposition.

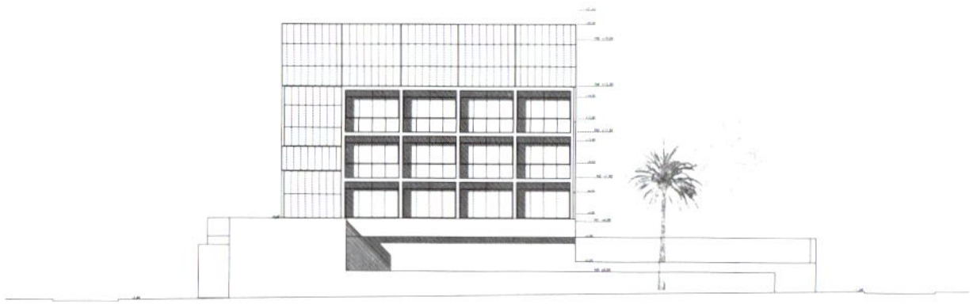

El acceso al museo se encuentra en un costado de una plaza; este espacio público urbano parece un vestíbulo al aire libre del museo. El jardín de palmeras existente a un lado fue respetado y se concibió como ampliación de la superficie para exhibiciones. El museo comprende una colección arqueológica. En el interior, una serie de salas muy variadas se conectan con un amplio espacio libre; el mismo sirve de orientación a los visitantes y vincula las salas de la exhibición permanente con otras áreas que cumplen diversas funciones. En algunos lugares, los muros exteriores se abren hacia la ciudad como puntos de observación, al tiempo que la iluminación natural penetra por lucernarios en el techo. Un enrejado enrejada en madera barnizada filtra la luz natural que penetra hacia las salas de exhibición.

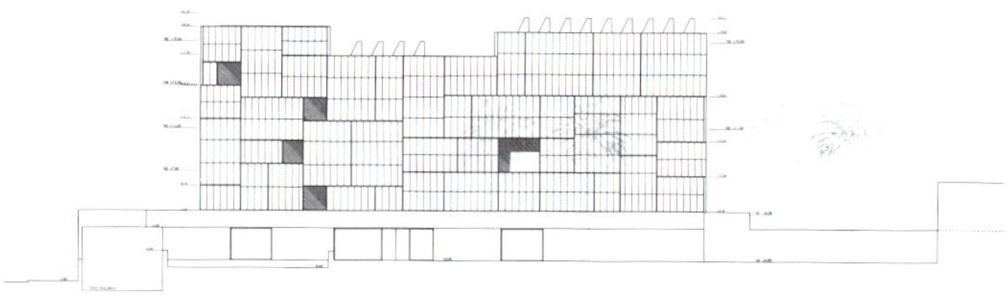

links: Aufrisse_Innenraum_Innenraum mit Deckendetail. rechts: Außenansicht_Treppenläufe_Fassade.
gauche: Vues en élévation_Intérieur_Espace intérieur avec le plafond détaillé. droite: Vue extérieure Système d'escalier_Façade.
izquierda: Alzados_Espacio interior_Interior con detalle del cielorraso. derecha: Vista exterior_Escaleras_Fachada.

MUSEO ARQUEOLÓGICO

SPAIN_BILBAO **GUGGENHEIM BILBAO MUSEOA**

SPANIEN_ESPAGNE_ESPAÑA
FRANK O. GEHRY – GEHRY PARTNERS
1997
KUNSTMUSEUM_MUSÉE D'ART_MUSEO DE ARTE
11,000 M^2
PHOTOS JOCHEN HELLE / ARTURIMAGES (350 B. L.),
KARIN HESSMANN / ARTURIMAGES (351 B. L.),
BARBARA STAUBACH / ARTURIMAGES (351 A., B. R.),
PAUL RAFTERY / ARTURIMAGES (350 B. R.)
© FMGB GUGGENHEIM BILBAO MUSEOA, FRANK O.GEHRY, 1997 (350 A. L.)

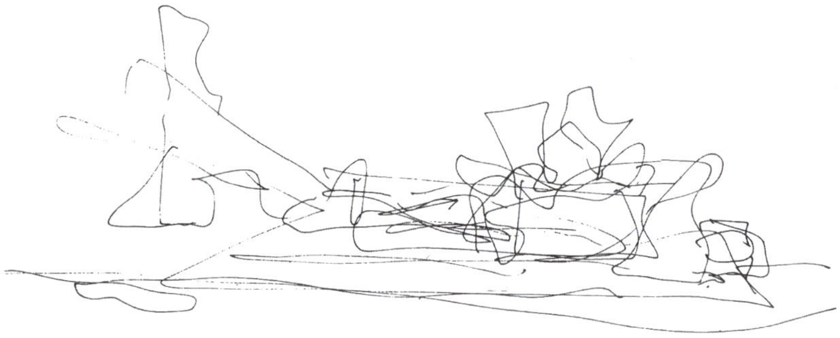

Nach dem Aufschwung und Niedergang der Stadt als Industriestandort sollte das Museum dem Wunsch der Stadt und des Wettbewerbsauslobers entsprechend ein Zeichen der Neuorientierung werden. Das in Höhe und Tiefe gestaffelte Gebäude entwickelt sich mit zahlreichen gekurvten Trakten asymmetrisch um ein Zentrum herum. Ein Flügel wird von einer Stadtautobahn gekreuzt, die Eingangsseite spiegelt sich im Nervíon. Die komplexe Geometrie der wogenden und gebrochenen Fassaden aus Titanplatten wurde mit dem für den Flugzeugbau entwickelten Computerprogramm CATIA berechnet. Die umfangreiche Presseberichterstattung und die touristische Anziehungs- und Symbolkraft des Gebäudes – der „Bilbao-Effekt" – läuteten für die Baugattung „Museum" eine neue Ära ein.

Après l'essor et le déclin de la ville comme site industriel, le musée était censé correspondre au souhait de la ville originaire de l'appel d'offre afin de symboliser la nouvelle orientation. Le bâtiment étagé vers le haut et le bas évolue en forme de nombreuses ailes asymétriques, courbées autour du centre. Une aile est croisée par une autoroute périphérique et la façade d'entrée se reflète dans le Nervíon. La géométrie complexe des façades caractérisées par des ondes et ruptures est composée de plaques en titane et doit sa structure à l'évolution grâce au logiciel CATIA, développé pour la construction aéronautique. L'importante médiatisation, l'effet d'attraction touristique et la force symbolique du bâtiment - « l'effet Bilbao » - inaugure une nouvelle ère pour le type de construction de « musée ».

En una ciudad que había vivido sus épocas de gloria industrial y posterior decadencia, este museo debía llenar los anhelos de la ciudad y de los organizadores del concurso, y conferirle un símbolo de una nueva orientación. El edificio, escalonado en altura y en profundidad, se despliega con secciones ricamente curvadas alrededor de un centro. Un ala está surcada por la autopista urbana; la fachada del acceso se refleja en las aguas del Nervión. La compleja geometría de las fachadas ondulantes y quebradas, construidas con placas de titanio, se calculó con el programa informático CATIA, concebido originalmente para la industria de la aviación. Los numerosos informes de prensa, el poder del atractivo turístico y la simbología del edificio, el "efecto Bilbao", significaron la llegada de una nueva era para la estirpe "museo".

links: Skizze von Frank O. Gehry_Panoramaansicht_Foyer. rechts: Haupteingang_Titanverkleidung Außenbau.
gauche: Esquisse de Frank O. Gehry_Vue panoramique_Foyer. droite: Entrée principale_Revêtement en titane Extérieur.
izquierda: Esbozo de Frank O. Gehry_Vista panorámica_Vestíbulo. derecha: Acceso principal_Recubrimiento de titanio_Vista exterior.

SPAIN_CARTAGENA **MUSEO DEL TEATRO ROMANO**

SPANIEN_ESPAGNE_ESPAÑA
RAFAEL MONEO
2008
ARCHÄOLOGIEMUSEUM_MUSÉE DE L'ARCHÉOLOGIE
MUSEO ARQUEOLÓGICO
17,000 M²
PHOTOS ROLAND HALBE / ARTURIMAGES

Ziel war es, das römische Theater durch die Verknüpfung mit bereits bestehenden Gebäuden und Leerräumen in den städtischen Rahmen einzubinden und dabei eine museale Wegführung vom tiefer gelegenen Hafen zum Cerro de la Concepción entstehen zu lassen. An dieser Route wurden das Zentrum römischer Studien und das Museum errichtet, das im Raum des Römischen Theaters seinen Höhepunkt findet. Die Promenade läuft durch die von Oberlichtern erhellten Ausstellungsräume. Der Komplex umfasst zwei durch einen Korridor verbundene Gebäude: das erste mit Zugang vom Riquelme-Palast hat einen Hof und beherbergt in den Geschossen Serviceräume. Das zweite Gebäude stellt an der Calle de General Ordoñez mit einer Terrasse die Verbindung zur alten Kathedrale her.

L'objectif consistait à intégrer le théâtre romain grâce à la liaison des bâtiments et des salles de lecture existant dans le cadre urbain et à créer un itinéraire reliant le musée au port situé vers le bas au Cerro de la Concepción. Le long de cette route, le centre des études romaines et le musée furent érigés afin d'atteindre leur point culminant dans l'espace du théâtre romain. La promenade passe par les espaces d'exposition éclairés par le haut. Le complexe comprend deux bâtiments reliés par un corridor : le premier accessible depuis le palais Riquelme comprend une cour qui abrite des espaces dédiés aux services aux étages. Le deuxième bâtiment établit la liaison à l'ancienne cathédrale au niveau de la Calle de General Ordoñez par une terrasse.

Se partió de la premisa de unir el Teatro Romano a los edificios preexistentes y los espacios vacíos del tejido urbano, y permitir que surgiera un recorrido museístico desde el puerto, ubicado más abajo, hasta el Cerro de la Concepción. En este camino se erigieron el centro de estudios romanos y el museo, que tiene en el espacio del Teatro Romano su punto más destacado. El paseo recorre salas de exhibición iluminadas cenitalmente. El complejo abarca dos edificios que se unen por un corredor: el primero de ellos con un acceso al palacio Riquelme, abarca un patio y alberga áreas de servicios. El segundo edificio, sobre la Calle del General Ordóñez, logra con su terraza la conexión con la antigua Catedral.

links: Schnitt und Ansicht_Harmonisches Nebeneinander von Alt und Neu_Luftaufnahme_Eingang. rechts: Fassade.
gauche: Coupe et vue_Ancien et nouveau en harmonie_Perspective à vol d'oiseau_Entrée. droite: Façade.
izquierda: Corte y fachada_Armonía entre antiguo y nuevo_Vista aérea_Acceso. derecha: Fachada.

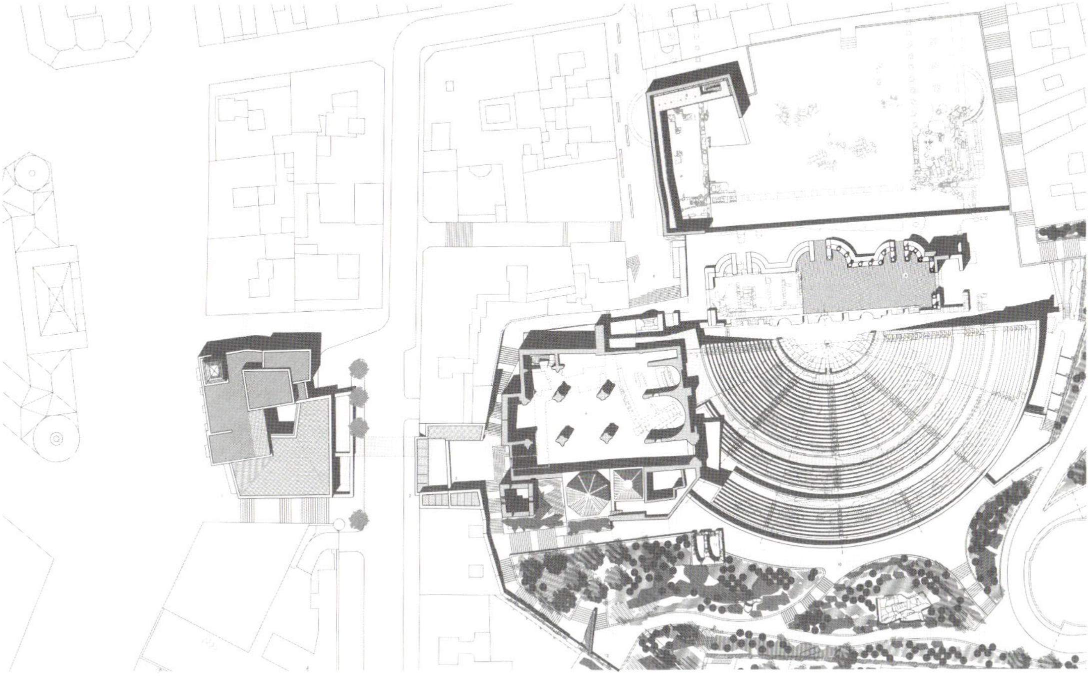

links: Museum beim römischen Theater. rechts: Lageplan_Gang_Foyer_Ausstellungsraum.
gauche: Musée près du théâtre romain. droite: Plan de site_Couloir_Foyer_Espace d'exposition.
izquierda: Museo junto al teatro romano. derecha: Plano de ubicación_Pasaje_Vestíbulo_Sala de exhibiciones.

SPAIN_CORDOBA **MADINAT AL ZAHRA**

SPANIEN_ESPAGNE_ESPAÑA
NIETO SOBEJANO ARQUITECTOS, S.L.P.
2008
ARCHÄOLOGIEMUSEUM_MUSÉE DE L'ARCHÉOLOGIE
MUSEO DE ARQUEOLOGÍA
9,125 M^2
PHOTOS ROLAND HALBE / ARTURIMAGES

Das Gebäude entfaltet seine Funktionen um eine Gruppe überdachter Räume und offener Patios, die teilweise leer, teilweise bepflanzt und möbliert sind. Vom Hauptvestibül aus dehnt sich ein breiter blauer Patio auf quadratischem Grundriss aus. Wie bei einem Kreuzgang liegen die wichtigsten öffentlichen Räume um ihn herum. Ein weiterer langer, tiefer und bepflanzter Patio nimmt die nicht öffentlichen Funktionen auf. Die Wände in den Ausgrabungen sind aus weiß gefasstem Beton, der in Holzschalungen gegossen wurde. Die auf ihnen aufliegenden Dächer sind als dünne Platten ausgebildet, die Patios mit Kalkstein ausgelegt. Das Gebäudekonzept antizipiert künftige Erweiterungen; insbesondere Museum und Werkstätten können durch Pavillons ergänzt werden.

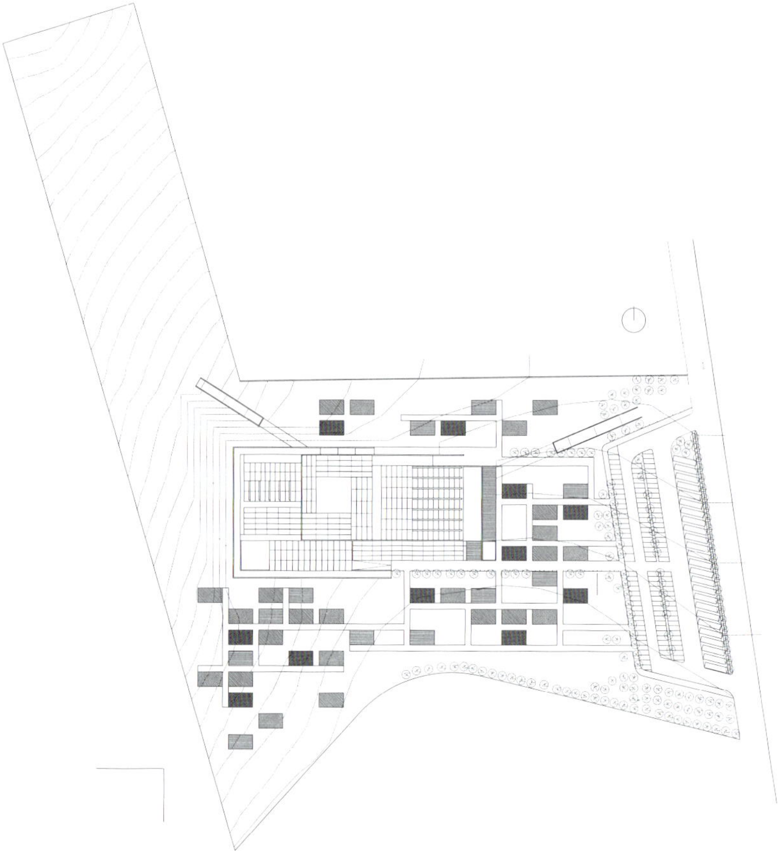

Le bâtiment déploie ses fonctions autour d'un groupe d'espaces couvert et de patios ouverts, partiellement vides et partiellement aménagés de plantes et de meubles. Un patio plus grand s'élargit sur le plan carré à partir du vestibule principal. Les espaces publics les plus importants se situent sur les côtés à l'instar d'un cloitre. Un autre patio profond tout en longueur et aménagé grâce à des plantes intègre des fonctions non publiques. Les murs sur le site archéologique sont en béton blanc coulé dans les lambrissages. Les toits reposant au niveau supérieur sont formés de fines plaques placées au niveau des patios en pierre calcaire. La conception du bâtiment anticipe sur les aménagements futurs, notamment l'extension du musée et les ateliers par les pavillons.

El edificio despliega sus funciones en un grupo de salas techadas y patios abiertos, en parte vacíos, en parte amueblados, y provistos de vegetación. Desde el vestíbulo principal se abre un amplio patio de planta cuadrada. Como si se tratase de un claustro, las salas para público más importantes se ubican a su alrededor. Otro patio —más largo, profundo y lleno de vegetación— absorbe las funciones no públicas. Las paredes de las excavaciones son de hormigón de color blanco, el que fue colado en encofrados de madera. Los techos que soporta se componen de delgadas placas; los patios están pavimentados en piedra caliza. El concepto edilicio anticipa futuras ampliaciones; en particular se pueden ampliar el museo y los talleres con más pabellones.

links: Lageplan_Gesamtansicht. rechts: Patio_Eingang_Das abgesenkte Museum.
gauche: Plan de site_Vue d'ensemble. droite: Patio_Entrée_Le musée abaissé.
izquierda: Plano de ubicación_Vista del conjunto. derecha: Patio_Acceso_El museo enterrado.

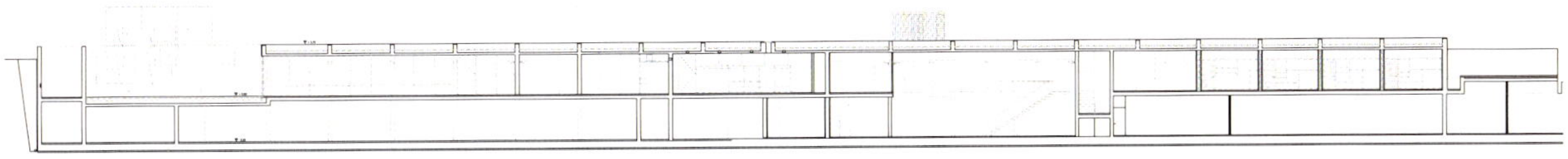

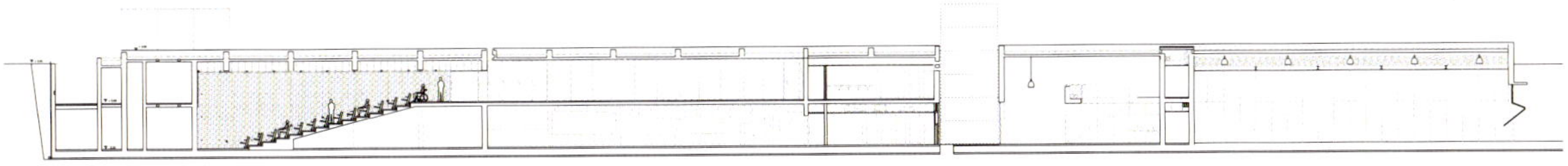

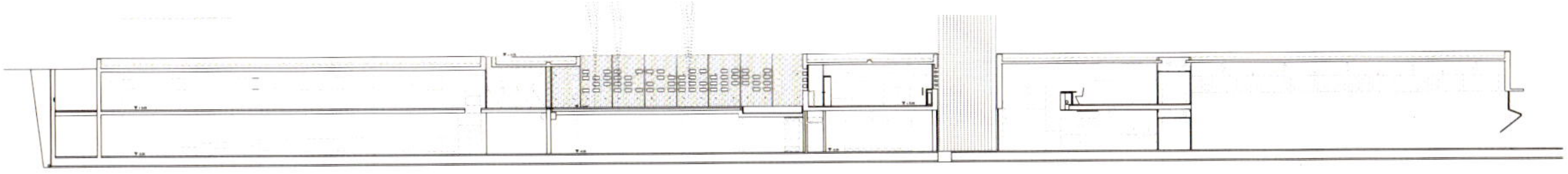

links: Blick über die Dächer. rechts: Schnitte_Foyer Richtung Patio_Ausstellungsraum_Wasserbecken im Patio.
gauche: Vue sur les toits. droite: Coupes_Foyer en direction du patio_Espace d'exposition_Bassin d'eau dans le patio.
izquierda: Vista de los techos. derecha: Cortes_Vestíbulo en dirección al patio_Sala de exhibiciones_Estanque en el patio.

SPAIN_CORUÑA **MUSEO NACIONAL DE CIENCIA Y TECNOLOGÍA**

SPANIEN_ESPAGNE_ESPAÑA
ACEBOXALONSO. ARCHITECTS
2010
WISSENSCHAFTSMUSEUM_MUSÉE DE LA SCIENCE
MUSEO DE CIENCIAS
6,000 M²
PHOTOS HECTOR SANTOS, CORUÑA (360 B. L., 361),
ANGEL ALONSO + VICTORIA ACEBO, MADRID (360 B. R.)

Dieses Projekt kombiniert zwei Bauaufgaben: eine Tanzschule und ein Museum, die die Architekten in einem Volumen zusammenführten, so dass einzelne Bereiche gemeinsam genutzt werden können. Der Betonkern dient der Schule, während der äußere Raum zwischen Kern und Außenhaut zum Museum wurde. Die Architekten modifizierten die Tanzschule so, dass diese zugleich als Servicebereich des Museums dient. Die Raumerfahrung im Museum umfasst gleichzeitig sechs verschiedene Ebenen. Der große, gestapelte Raum dient zugleich zahlreichen unterschiedlichen Aktivitäten. Unter dem Dach hängt, einem Schnürboden gleich, ein technisches Geschoss, von dem aus die Räume den Ausstellungen angepasst werden können.

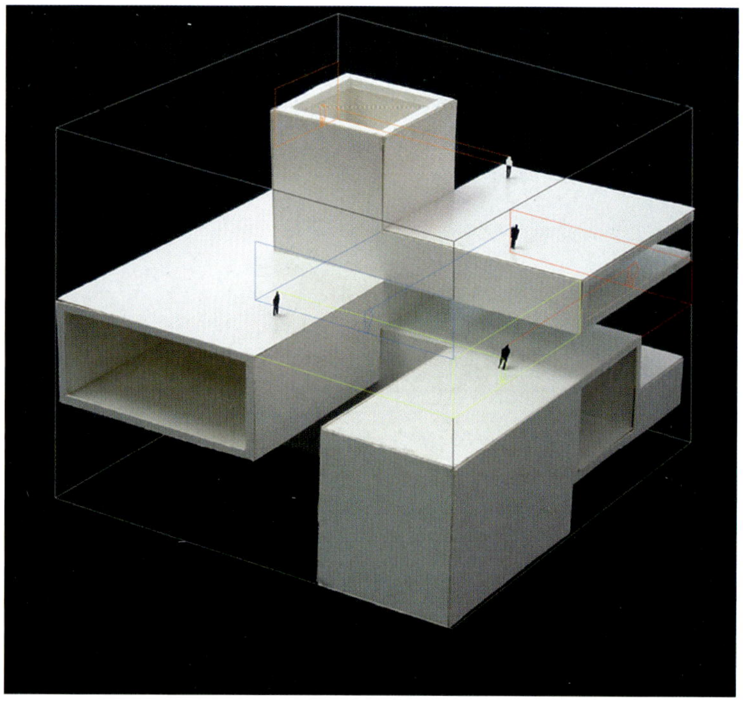

Ce projet combine deux chantiers de construction : création d'une école de danse et d'un musée réunis par les architectes dans un volume commun afin d'unir les espaces individuels. Le centre en béton sert à l'école et l'espace extérieur entre le centre et la partie extérieure sert au musée. Les architectes ont modifié l'école de danse afin de pouvoir servir simultanément de zone de service pour le musée. L'expérience spatiale du musée repose simultanément sur six niveaux différents. Le grand espace superposé sert à de nombreuses activités nuancées, notamment, grâce à son plafond technique qui permet l'adaptation des espaces aux expositions.

Este proyecto combina dos conceptos, una escuela de danza y un museo, que los arquitectos reunieron en un solo volumen para así poder compartir espacios en común. El núcleo en hormigón sirve a la escuela, mientras que el espacio comprendido entre este núcleo y la piel exterior del edificio está dedicado al museo. Los arquitectos adaptaron la escuela de danza de modo que sirva también como área de servicio para el museo. La experiencia del espacio museístico abarca al mismo tiempo seis niveles diferentes. El gran espacio "apilado" sirve simultáneamente a múltiples actividades. Bajo el techo cuelga un entrepiso técnico que evoca el telar de un teatro, de él se pueden colgar elementos para adaptar las salas para las exhibiciones.

links: Modell Konzept_Innenfassade_Außenansicht. rechts: Ausstellungsraum_Versorgungsgang Dachdetail.
gauche: Concept du modèle_Façade intérieure_Vue extérieure. droite: Espace d'exposition_Couloir d'approvisionnement_Toiture en détail.
izquierda: Maqueta conceptual_Fachada interior_Vista exterior. derecha: Sala de exhibiciones_Pasaje técnico_Detalle del cielorraso.

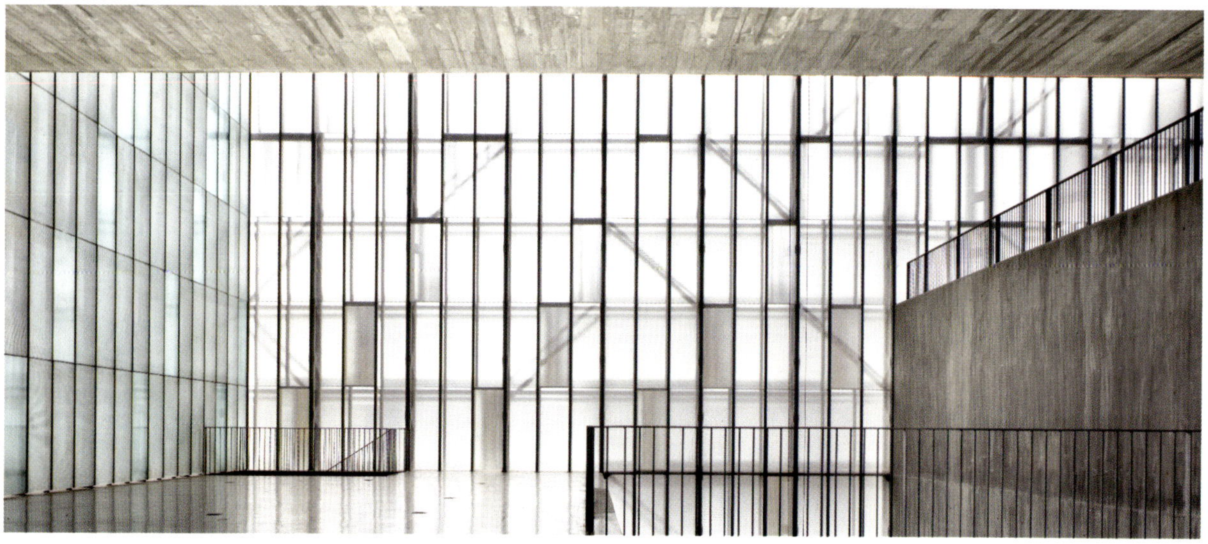

SPAIN_GRANADA **MUSEO MEMORIA DE ANDALUCÍA**

SPANIEN_ESPAGNE_ESPAÑA
ALBERTO CAMPO BAEZA
2009
GESCHICHTSMUSEUM_MUSÉE D'HISTOIRE_MUSEO HISTÓRICO
15,000 M^2
PHOTOS JAVIER CALLEJAS

Das Museum entstand im Kontext der Zentrale der Caja Granada Sparkasse, die die Architekten ebenfalls bis 2001 errichteten. Der obere Abschluss des dreigeschossigen Podiumsbaus mit einer Grundfläche von 60 x 120 Metern schließt zur Höhe des Podiumbaus der Caja Granada auf. Im Inneren befindet sich ein zentraler elliptischer Hof, in dem – zur Schaffung einer räumlichen Spannung – kreisrunde Rampen aufsteigen und die drei Ebenen erschließen. Mit einem vertikalen Bauteil in gleicher Höhe und Breite wie das Hauptgebäude der Caja Granada entsteht eine Art Stadttor. Den Abschluss der gesamten Maßnahme bildet eine große Plattform, die bis zum Fluss hinabführt und als öffentlicher Raum dient.

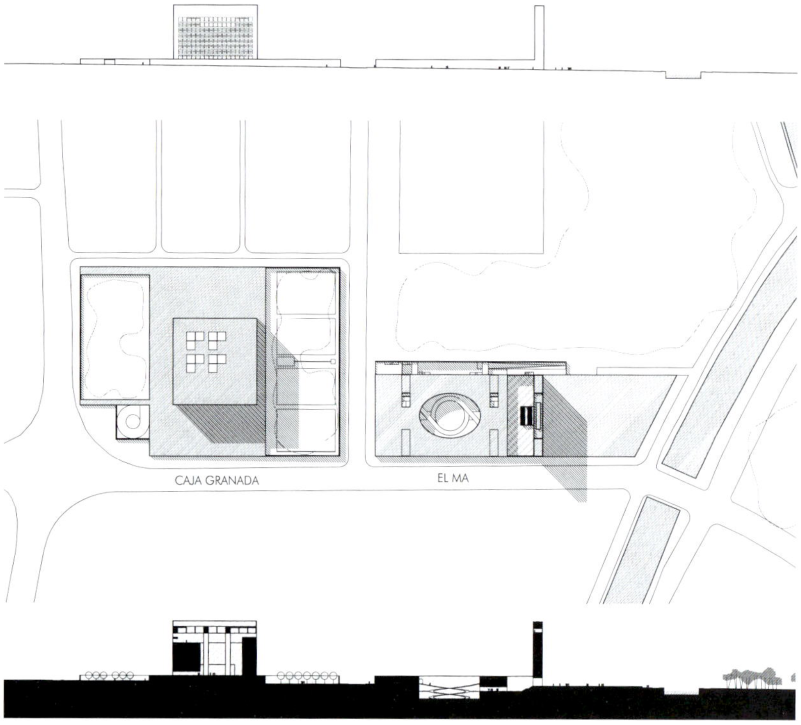

Ce musée se situe dans le cadre du projet de la centrale consacrée à la caisse d'épargne Caja Granada créée par les architectes jusqu'en 2001. La finition supérieure de la construction du podium à trois étages dotée d'une superficie de 60 x 120 mètres établit la liaison vers les hauteurs de la construction de la Caja Granada. Le podium comprend une cour centrale en forme d'ellipse présentant, dans l'objectif de créer un suspense spatial, des rampes circulaires qui permettent l'accès aux trois niveaux et à l'ensemble des espaces. La partie verticale du bâtiment édifiée à la même hauteur et largeur que le bâtiment principal de la Caja Granada constitue une sorte de porte de la ville. La fin de l'ensemble des mesures se compose d'une importante plateforme évoluant vers le bas jusqu'au fleuve qui offre un grand espace public à la ville.

El museo se aprecia en el contexto proyectual de la sede central del banco Caja Granada, que ocupó a los arquitectos hasta 2001. El remate superior de esta edificación de tres niveles, con una superficie de 60 x 120 metros, semeja un podio. En ella se ubica un patio central de forma elíptica; este patio está surcado por rampas helicoidales que generan una tensión espacial y conectan los tres niveles y todos los ambientes. Con un componente constructivo vertical de la misma altura y anchura que el edificio principal de la Caja Granada, surge una especie de puerta monumental. Como remate de esta intervención, una gran plataforma se extiende hasta el río y pone a disposición de la ciudad un gran espacio público.

links: Lageplan_Vogelperspektive_Frontalansicht. rechts: Elliptischer Innenhof.
gauche: Plan de site_Perspective à vol d'oiseau_Vue frontal. droite: Cour intérieure elliptique.
izquierda: Plano de ubicación_Vista a vuelo de pájaro_Vista frontal. derecha: Patio interior elíptico.

CAJAGRANADA

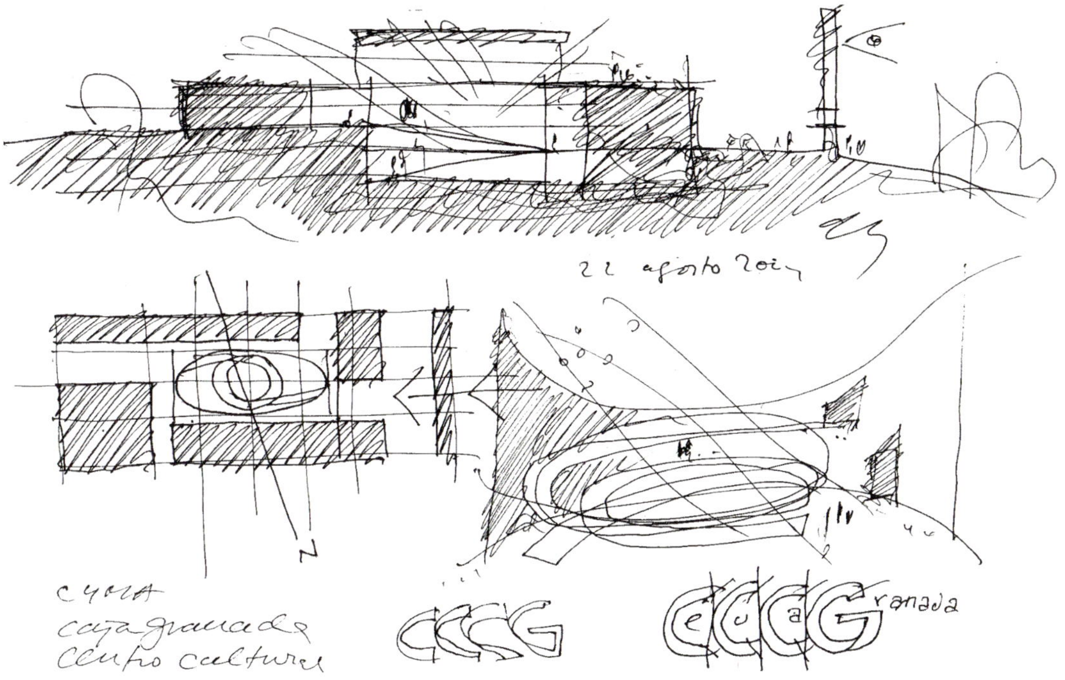

links: Gebäudescheibe. rechts: Skizze_Elliptischer Innenhof_Geschwungene Rampen_Überkreuzende Rampen.
gauche: Vitre du bâtiment. droite: Esquisse_Cour intérieure elliptique_Rampes élancées_Rampes entrecoupées.
izquierda: Edificio laminar. derecha: Esbozo_Patio interior elíptico_Rampas curvas_Rampas que se entrecruzan.

SPAIN_MADRID **MUSEO DEL PRADO**

SPANIEN_ESPAGNE_ESPAÑA
RAFAEL MONEO
2007
KUNSTMUSEUM_MUSÉE D'ART_MUSEO DE ARTE
22,040 M^2
PHOTOS ROLAND HALBE / ARTURIMAGES

Das Anwesen mit dem Jerónimo-Kloster wurde durch ein neues, auf den unteren Ebenen angebundenes Gebäude mit Raum für Wechselausstellungen, Restaurierungswerkstätten und technische Büros ergänzt. Das Programm setzt die maximale Raumnutzung auf zwei Ebenen voraus. Der restaurierte Kreuzgang behält seinen ursprünglichen Grundriss und Schnitt. Sein Quadermauerwerk wird durch eine Betonmauer geschützt und durch ein Glasdach bekrönt, das natürliches Licht in alle angrenzenden Räume lässt. Durch eine große zentrale Laterne fällt Licht in die Wechselausstellungsräume, die in den beiden Stockwerken unmittelbar unterhalb des Klosters liegen.

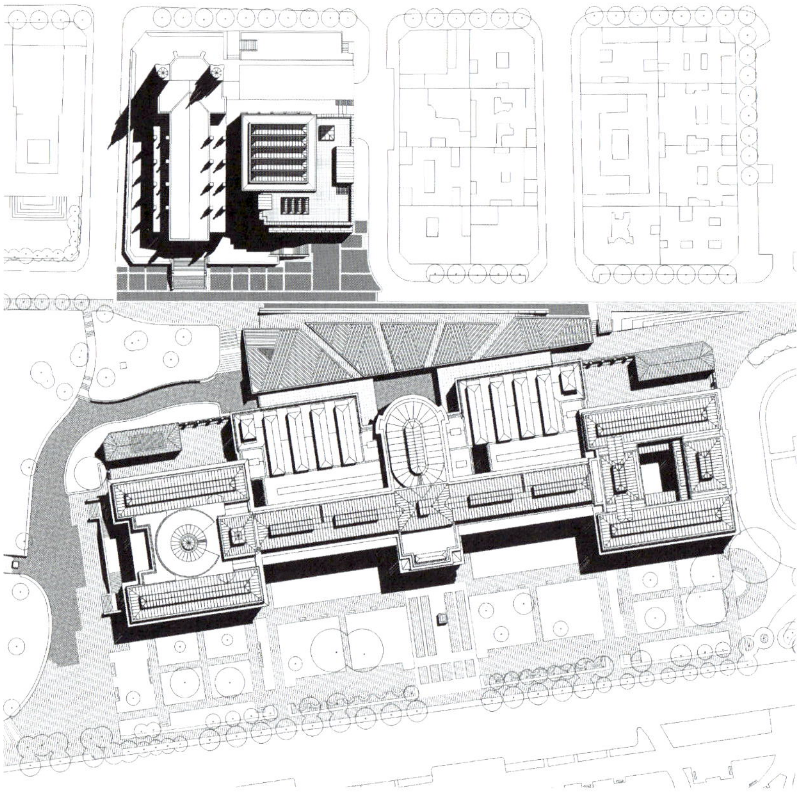

La propriété avec le cloître Jerónimo fut complétée par un nouveau bâtiment relié par les niveaux inférieurs avec l'espace consacré aux expositions tournantes, ateliers de restauration et bureaux techniques. Le programme prévoit l'optimisation de l'espace sur les deux niveaux. Le cloître restauré a conservé son plan et sa conception d'origine. Sa maçonnerie est protégée par un mur en béton et couronnée par un toit vitrifié permettant à la lumière naturelle de jaillir dans tous les espaces limitrophes. Par une grande lanterne centrale, la lumière plonge dans les espaces dédiées aux expositions alternantes au niveau des deux étages situés directement sous le cloître.

La presencia del claustro de los Jerónimos fue completada con un nuevo edificio que se conecta subterráneamente, con espacio para muestras temporarias, talleres de restauración y oficinas técnicas. El programa exigía una utilización óptima del espacio en dos niveles. El claustro restaurado preserva su planta y alzado originales. Sus antiguos muros de piedra están protegidos por una pared de hormigón; lo corona un techo de cristal que permite la penetración de luz natural en las salas. Gracias a una gran linterna central, la luz cae sobre las salas de exhibición en ambos niveles, que están inmediatamente debajo del claustro.

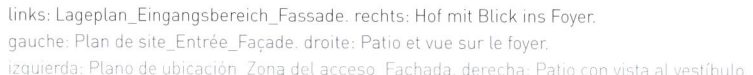

links: Lageplan_Eingangsbereich_Fassade. rechts: Hof mit Blick ins Foyer.
gauche: Plan de site_Entrée_Façade. droite: Patio et vue sur le foyer.
izquierda: Plano de ubicación_Zona del acceso_Fachada. derecha: Patio con vista al vestíbulo.

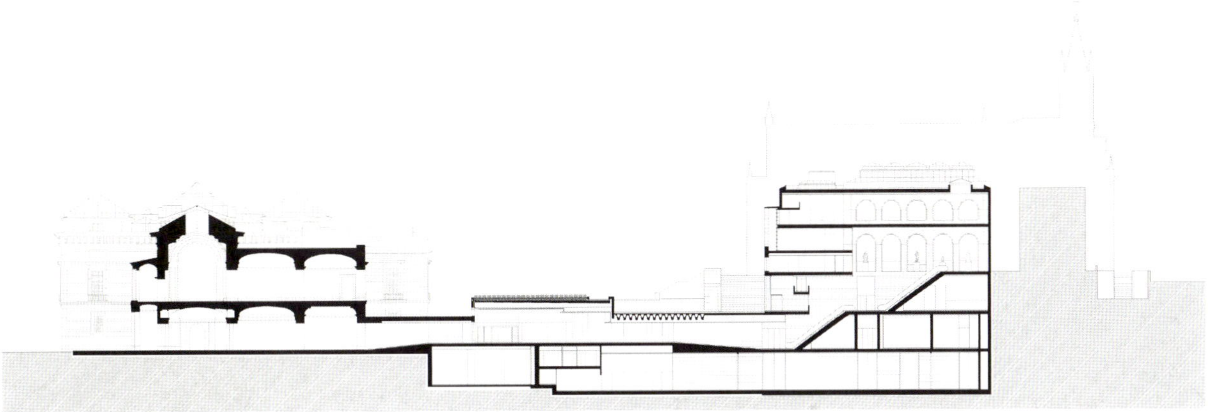

links: Blick auf den Kreuzgang mit Oberlicht. rechts: Längsschnitt_Im Kreuzgang_Musensaal Oberlicht im Ausstellungsraum.
gauche: Vue sur le cloître avec éclairage en hauteur. droite: Coupe longitudinale_Dans le cloître Salle des muses_Éclairage en hauteur dans l'espace d'exposition.
izquierda: Vista hacia el claustro con lucernario. derecha: Corte longitudinal_En el claustro_Sala de las musas_Lucernario en sala de exhibiciones.

SPAIN_MONTENMEDIO **NMAC – MUSEO MONTENMEDIO**

SPANIEN_ESPAGNE_ESPAÑA
ALBERTO CAMPO BAEZA
ONGOING
KUNSTMUSEUM_MUSÉE D'ART_MUSEO DE ARTE
2,000 M²
PHOTOS COURTESY OF THE ARCHITECTS

Die Architekten schlagen eine Architektur der weißen Wände mit akzentuierter Horizontalität vor. Die Wände folgen einer deutlich erkennbaren Nord-Süd-Achse und werden stellenweise durch Decken verbunden, so dass überdachte Räume für die kulturelle Nutzung entstehen: Ausstellungsräume, Bibliothek, Vortragssaal und Cafeteria können je nach Gefälle des Geländes einfache oder doppelte Raumhöhen haben. An Stellen, an denen eine größere lichte Höhe benötigt wird, wird die Erde ausgehoben. Die verschiedenen Bereiche umfassen zudem große Höfe mit Wasser und blühenden Kletterpflanzen.

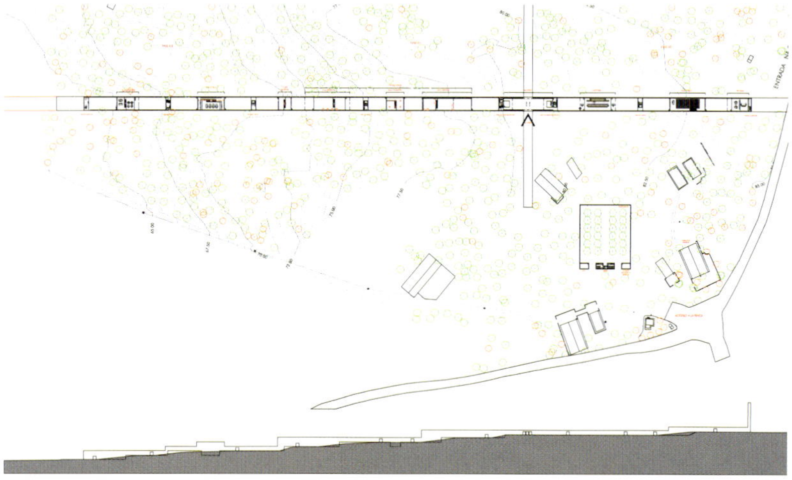

Les architectes proposent une architecture à base de murs blancs mettant l'accent sur l'horizontalité. Les murs suivent un axe Nord-Sud clairement perceptible comme base du projet et sont partiellement reliés par des plafonds qui permettent de créer des espaces couverts destinés à des utilisations culturelles : espaces d'exposition, bibliothèque, salle de conférence et cafétéria. Selon la déclivité du terrain, ils peuvent être installés à des hauteurs d'espaces simples ou doubles. Le terrain est évacué aux endroits nécessitant une hauteur sous plafond plus importante. En outre, les différents espaces comprennent des cours spacieuses agrémentées par l'eau et par une végétation en fleurs.

Los arquitectos proponen una arquitectura de muros blancos con acentuada horizontalidad. Los muros siguen un eje norte-sur claramente reconocible como base del proyecto, y cada tanto se conectan con techos, de modo que se logran ambientes techados para usos culturales: las salas de exhibiciones, la biblioteca, la sala de conferencias y la cafetería pueden adoptar diversas alturas, simples o dobles, según la pendiente del terreno. En los sitios en donde se necesita una mayor altura libre, se excava la tierra. Los diversos ámbitos abarcan además grandes patios con agua y vegetación florida.

links: Lageplan und Schnitt_Ausstellungssaal_Bibliothek. rechts: Innenhof_Außenbau_Café.
gauche: Plan de site et coupe_Salle d'exposition_Bibliothèque. droite: Cour intérieure_Extérieur Café.
izquierda: Plano de ubicación y corte_Sala de exhibiciones_Biblioteca. derecha: Patio interior_Vista exterior_Café.

SPAIN_PEDROSA DE LA VEGA **VILLA ROMANA LA OLMEDA**

SPANIEN_ESPAGNE_ESPAÑA
PAREDES PEDROSA ARQUITECTOS
2009
ARCHÄOLOGIEMUSEUM_MUSÉE DE L'ARCHÉOLOGIE
MUSEO ARQUEOLÓGICO
7,130 M^2
PHOTOS ROLAND HALBE / ARTURIMAGES

Die Maßnahmen umfassen eine Reihe von Interventionen, die Altes und Neues einander gegenüberstellen und die Fundstätte in die Landschaft einbeziehen. Es entstanden eine Überdachung der Ausgrabungen, Schutzvorrichtungen für die Mosaike sowie ein Ausstellungs- und Studienzentrum für Touristen und Archäologen. Diese Räume sind als Pavillons in die archäologische Siedlung eingestellt und bleiben unabhängig von dem breiten metallischen Dach, das die Funde überfängt. Die Mosaike sind durch ein Metallgeflecht eingegrenzt, das den ursprünglichen, sie umschließenden Raum andeutet. Ein angehobener Holzboden erschließt das Gelände und verbindet die Räume sowie die Mosaike.

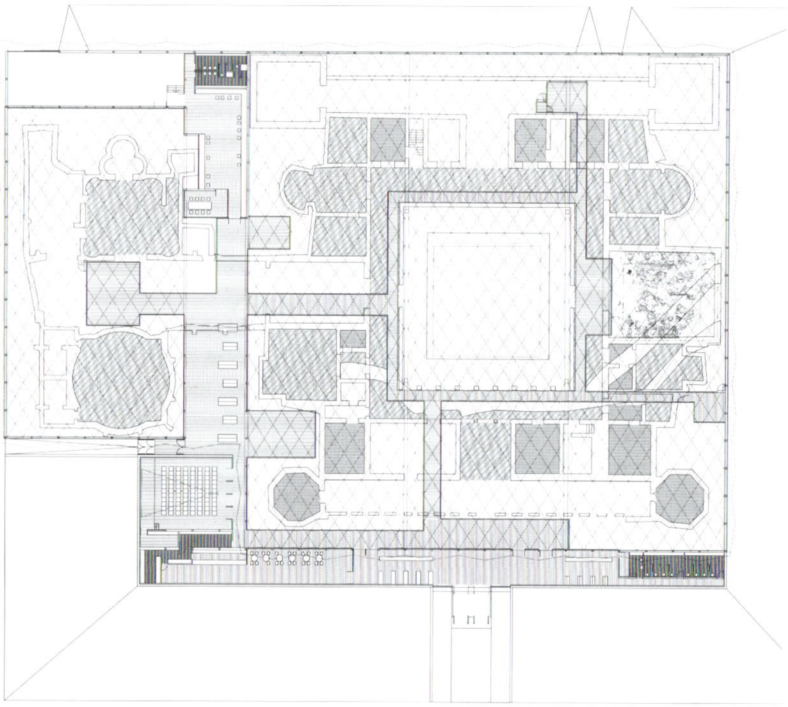

Les mesures englobent une série d'interventions opposant l'ancien et le nouveau et intégrent cependant les sites archéologiques au paysage. Ainsi, une couverture sur les fouilles, des dispositifs de protection des mosaïques et un centre d'exposition et d'étude furent créés pour les touristes et archéologues. Ces espaces se présentent comme des pavillons intégrés au site archéologique tout en restant indépendant du large toit métallique qui recouvre les fouilles. Les mosaïques sont entourées par un treillis métallique qui fait allusion, à l'origine, à l'espace fermé autour d'elles. Un plancher surélevé valorise le site et relie les espaces aux mosaïques.

Este proyecto implicó una serie de intervenciones que confrontan lo nuevo con lo antiguo y vinculan los hallazgos arqueológicos con el paisaje. En forma gradual, aparecieron un techado sobre las excavaciones, dispositivos de protección para los mosaicos y un centro de estudios y exhibiciones para arqueólogos y turistas. Estas salas se incorporaron al yacimiento arqueológico como pabellones y son independientes del amplio techado metálico que protege el conjunto. A su vez, los mosaicos están protegidos por mallas metálicas que insinúan el volumen de los antiguos ambientes donde antes se encontraban. Un suelo de madera sobreelevado se extiende por el sitio y vincula las salas y los mosaicos.

links: Grundriss_Eingang_Gebäudeecke. rechts: Fassadendetail_Außenansicht.
gauche: Plan_Entrée_Angle du bâtiment. droite: Façade en détail_Vue extérieure.
izquierda: Plano_Acceso_Rincón del edificio. derecha: Detalle de fachada_Vista exterior.

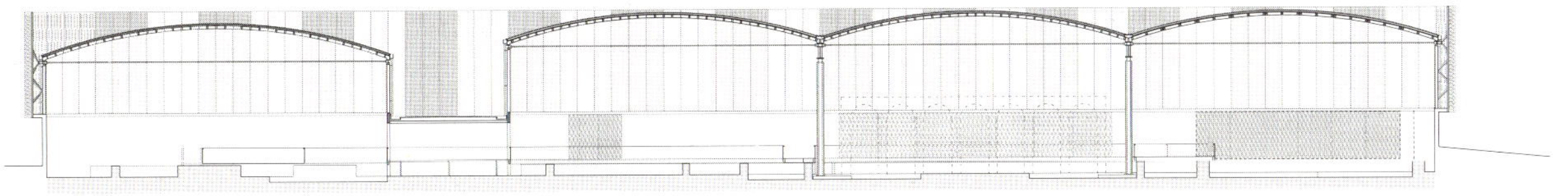

links: Vorhänge aus Metall als Raumteiler. rechts: Schnitt_Blick über das Ausgrabungsgelände Weitgespannte Deckenkonstruktion_Besucherstege.
gauche: Rideaux de métal comme séparateur d'espace. droite: Coupe_Vue sur le terrain de fouilles Structure au plafond tendue_Rampes des visiteurs.
izquierda: Cortinas de metal subdividen el espacio. derecha: Corte_Vista del sitio de las excavaciones_Construcción de techo de gran luz_Rampas para visitantes.

SPAIN_VALENCIA **CIUDAD DE LAS ARTES Y DE LAS CIENCIAS**

SPANIEN_ESPAGNE_ESPAÑA
SANTIAGO CALATRAVA ARCHITECT & ENGINEER
2004
KUNST- UND WISSENSCHAFTSMUSEUM
MUSÉE D'ART ET SCIENCES_MUSEO DE ARTE Y CIENCIA
42,000 M²
PHOTOS © OLIVER SCHUH / BARBARA BURG / WWW.PALLADIUM.DE

Im ausgetrockneten Flussbett des Turia reihen sich von Ost nach West das Opernhaus, das Planetarium mit hemisphärischem IMAX-Theater und das Príncipe Felipe Wissenschaftsmuseum aneinander. Als fünfter Bau bildet L'Umbracle, eine Promenade mit Parkhaus in einem offenen Bogengang, den Abschluss. Das Wissenschaftsmuseum ist 104 Meter breit und 241 Meter lang. Fünf aufgereihte „Betonbäume", groß genug, um Versorgungskerne und Aufzüge aufzunehmen, tragen auf ihren Ästen die Verbindung zwischen Fassade und Dach. Das weiße Betonskelett der Südfassade ist mit Glas ausgefacht, die Nordseite besitzt eine über die gesamte Gebäudelänge gehende Vorhangfassade aus Glas und Stahl.

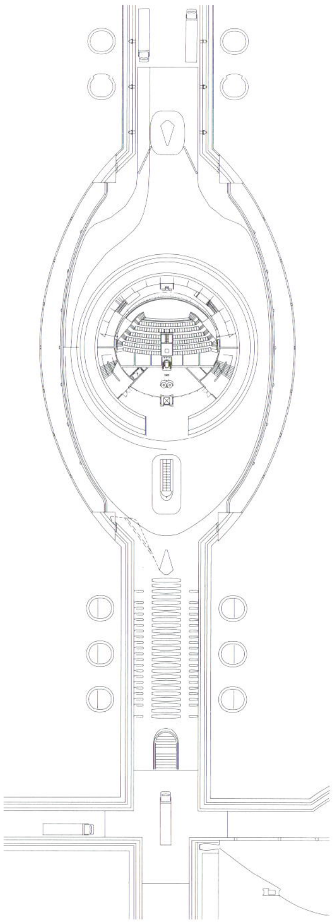

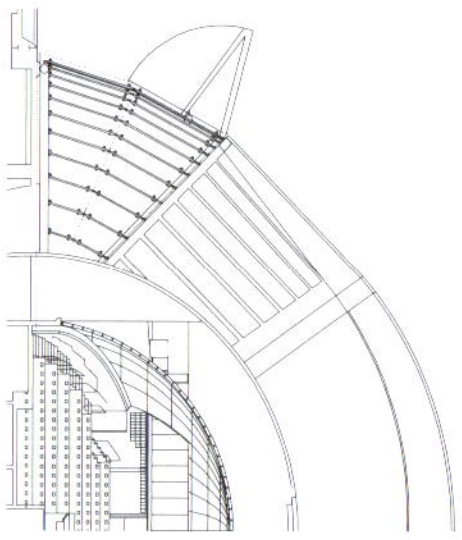

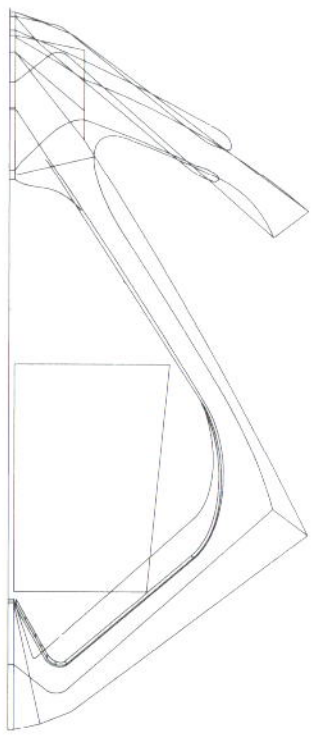

L'opéra, le planétarium avec le théâtre IMAX hémisphérique et le musée des sciences du Prince Philippe sont alignés d'Est en Ouest dans le lit asséché de la rivière Turia. Le dernier des cinq éléments de cet ensemble est formé par « L'Umbracle », une promenade avec parking à étages dans une arcade ouverte. Le musée des sciences a une largeur de 104 mètres et une longueur de 241 mètres. Les cinq « arbres en béton » suffisamment alignés pour accueillir un centre d'approvisionnement et des ascenseurs, ont un branchage servant de jonction entre la façade et le toit. L'ossature en béton blanc de la façade Sud est nuancée en verre, le côté Nord est orné sur la longueur totale du bâtiment d'une façade-rideau composée en verre et acier.

En el lecho del desecado río Turia se alinean de este a oeste: la Ópera, el planetario con teatro IMAX semiesférico, y el Museo de Ciencias Príncipe Felipe. Como quinta edificación aparece L'Umbracle, un paseo con estacionamiento en un recodo abierto; el mismo constituye un remate. El Museo de Ciencias tiene 241 metros de longitud y 104 de anchura. Cinco "árboles de hormigón" en hilera, lo suficientemente grandes como para albergar núcleos de circulaciones verticales y servicios, aguantan sobre sus "ramas" la conexión entre la fachada y el techo. El blanco esqueleto de hormigón de la fachada sur se alterna con el cristal. La fachada norte presenta un muro cortina de cristal y acero a lo largo de toda la longitud del edificio.

links: Grundriss Hemisphäre_Hemisphäre_Eingang Wissenschaftsmuseum. rechts: Wissenschaftsmuseum_Ausstellungsraum_Baumpfeiler.
gauche: Plan de l'hémisphère_Hémisphère_Entrée du musée des sciences. droite: Musée des sciences_Espace d'exposition_Piliers en forme d'arbre.
izquierda: Plano del Hemisferio_Hemisferio_Acceso al Museo de las Ciencias. derecha: Museo de las Ciencias_Sala de exhibiciones_Pilar en forma de árbol.

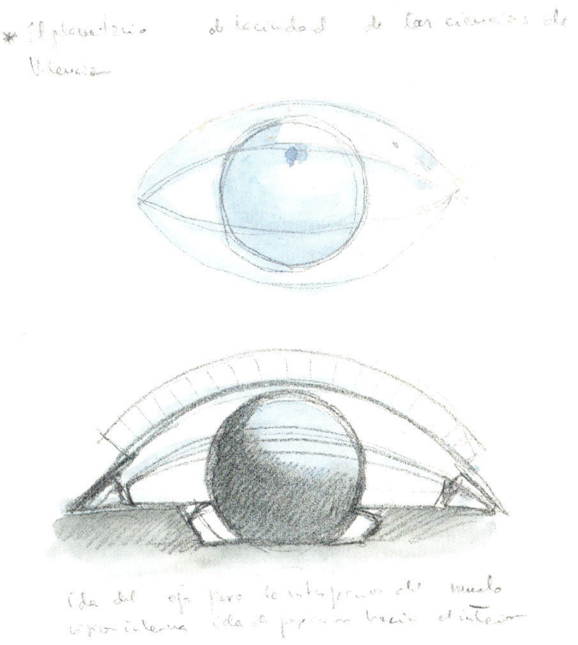

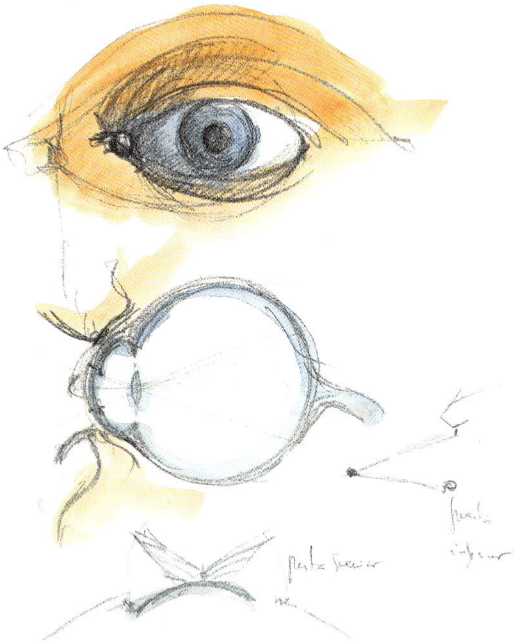

links: Fassade. rechts: Zeichnung_Hemisphäre_Luftaufnahme.
gauche: Façade. droite: Dessin_Hémisphère_Prise aérienne.
izquierda: Fachada. derecha: Ilustración_Hemisferio_Vista aérea.

SPAIN_VIGO **MUSEO DO MAR DE GALICIA**

SPANIEN_ESPAGNE_ESPAÑA
CESAR PORTELA
2002
MARITIMMUSEUM_MUSÉE MARITIME_MUSEO MARÍTIMO
10,463 M^2
PHOTOS EDUARDO MARTÍNEZ (380 B.),
HISAO SUZUKI (381)

Das Museum in Form einer Halbinsel oder eines Kaps ist zur Hälfte natürlich, zur Hälfte künstlich. Es liegt genau an der Küstenlinie, und der Entwurf bezieht die Meeresmündung mit ein. Das Museum wird zum Teil von einer Umfassungsmauer, aber zuweilen auch durch das Meer selbst definiert. Der Rundgang bietet Gärten, Gebäude, Terrassen, Innenhöfe, Gänge und Piere zwischen festem Boden und dem Saum des Wassers. Es ist eine kontinuierliche Bewegung vom Land zum Wasser. Das gesamte Projekt aus zwei Gruppen gewölbter, durch einen erhöhten Laufsteg verbundener Galerien kann als Aussichtsplattform verstanden werden. Von dem reflektierenden Granit, dem Stuck und den Fliesen wird das Licht in sich ständig verändernden, geometrischen Mustern auf die polierten Holzböden geworfen.

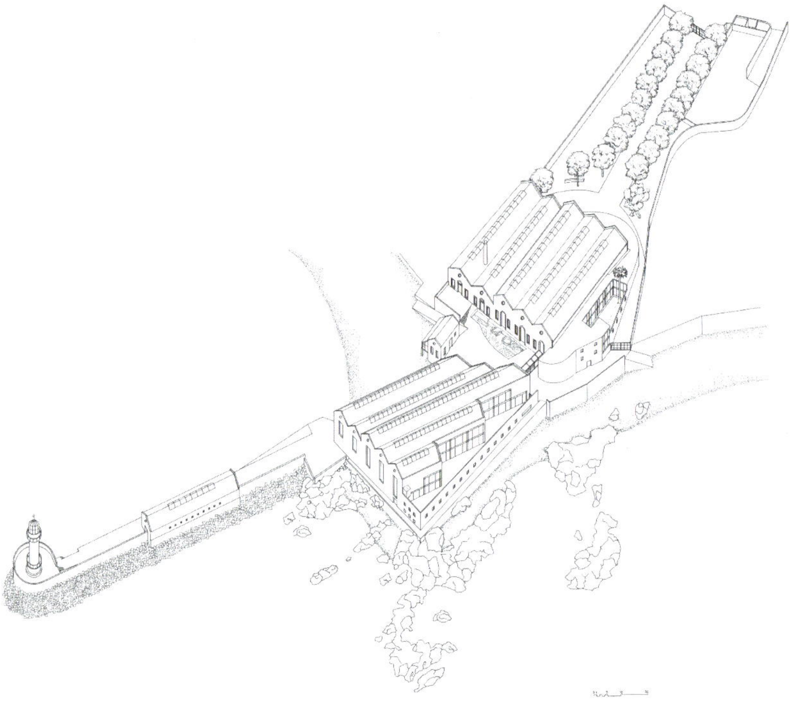

Le musée en forme d'une péninsule ou d'une enveloppe protectrice est constitué à 50% d'éléments naturels et à 50% d'éléments artificiels. Il se situe précisément sur le bord de la rive et le projet s'étend sur l'embouchure de la mer. Le bâtiment se caractérise en partie par un mur, mais également par la présence de la mer. La galerie à l'intérieur du musée présente des jardins, bâtiments, terrasses, cours intérieures, couloirs et appontements liant le sol dur au bord de l'eau. C'est un circuit continu reliant la terre à l'eau. Le projet d'ensemble basé sur deux groupes de galeries voutées, reliées par une passerelle surélevée, s'assimile à une plateforme panoramique. Grâce au granit, au stuc et à la faïence miroitants, la lumière est projetée dans des modèles géométriques se réfléchissant continuellement sur les planchers en bois poli.

Este museo con forma de península o capote es en parte natural y en parte artificial. Dispuesto sobre la línea de la costa, el diseño abarca la formación costera. El edificio está definido por un muro, y también por el propio mar. En una vuelta por el museo se aprecian jardines, edificaciones, terrazas, patios, pasajes y malecones que vinculan la tierra firme con la orilla del mar. Un diálogo constante entre la tierra y el agua. El conjunto de dos grupos de galerías abovedadas que se conectan por un pasaje elevado, se puede comprender como una plataforma de observación. El granito reflectante, el estuco y los azulejos arrojan luz sobre los suelos de madera pulida en cambiantes diseños geométricos.

links: Axonometrie_Gesamtansicht. rechts: Hof_Ausstellungsfläche_Aquarium.
gauche: Axonométrie_Vue principale. droite: Cour_Superficie d'exposition_Aquarium.
izquierda: Axonométrica Vista del conjunto. derecha: Patio_Área de exhibiciones_Acuario.

SPAIN_VITORIA-GASTEIZ **MUSEO DE ARQUEOLOGÍA DE ÁLAVA**

SPANIEN_ESPAGNE_ESPAÑA
FRANCISCO MANGADO
2009
ARCHÄOLOGIEMUSEUM_MUSÉE DE L'ARCHÉOLOGIE
MUSEO ARQUEOLÓGICO
6,000 M²
PHOTOS ROLAND HALBE / ARTURIMAGES

Das Gebäude grenzt an den Palast von Bendaña, das derzeitige Museum von Naipes Fournier. Der Zugang zum neuen Gebäude führt durch den gleichen Hof wie jener zum Palast. Aufgrund des abfallenden Geländes wird der Hof über eine Brücke betreten, die über einen Garten hinwegführt. Der abgesenkte Garten lässt Licht in die tiefer gelegenen Räume auf dieser Gebäudeseite fallen, die sonst keine natürliche Beleuchtung hätten. In der ständigen Ausstellung sind alle horizontalen Flächen dunkel, die Holzböden nahezu schwarz und die durchgehenden Decken ganz schwarz gehalten. Diesen dunklen Flächen stehen jedoch weiße Glasprismen gegenüber, um welche die Ausstellungsstücke arrangiert sind. Sie leiten tagsüber natürliches Licht durch die Decken in die Räume.

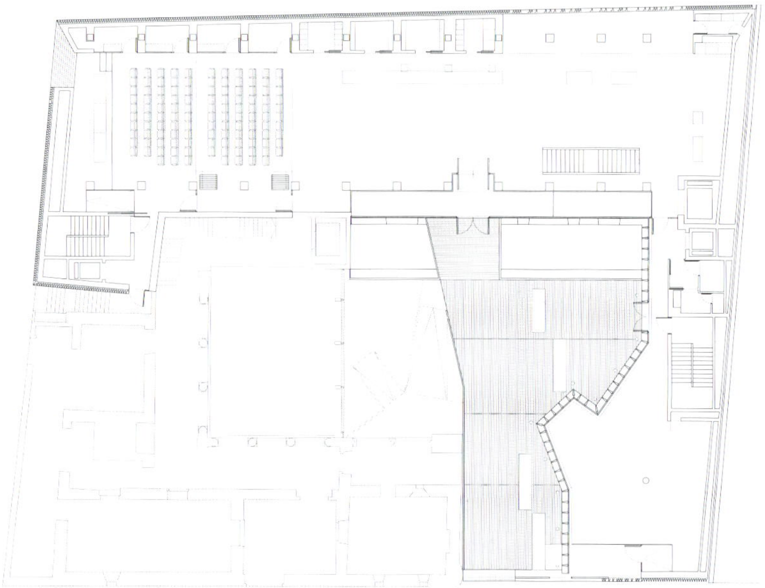

Le bâtiment se dresse à proximité du palais de Bendaña, le musée actuel de Naipes Fournier. L'accès du nouveau bâtiment s'effectue par la même cour que celle du palais. En raison du terrain en pente, la cour est accessible par une passerelle qui mène au jardin. Le jardin descendant en pente permet à la lumière de pénétrer dans les espaces situés en profondeur dans ce côté de la construction qui n'auraient sinon aucun éclairage naturel. Dans l'espace dédié à l'exposition permanente, toutes les surfaces horizontales sont en teintes foncées, les planchers en bois quasiment noirs et les plafonds continus entièrement noirs. Ces surfaces en teintes sombres se confrontent néanmoins à des prismes en verre blancs afin de mettre en valeur les pièces d'exposition. Pendant le jour, ils laissent la lumière naturelle pénétrer par les plafonds dans les espaces.

El edificio se levanta junto al Palacio de Bendaña, actualmente museo de Naipes Fournier. Un mismo patio permite acceder al nuevo edificio y también al Palacio. Debido a la pendiente del terreno, el patio está cruzado por un puente que conduce a un jardín. El jardín, hundido, permite que penetre la luz en las salas del subsuelo de este lado de la edificación, las que de lo contrario carecerían de iluminación natural. En la exhibición permanente todas las superficies horizontales son oscuras, los suelos de madera casi negros y los cielorrasos continuos totalmente negros. Sin embargo, prismas de vidrio blanco se contraponen a estas superficies oscuras; los objetos en exhibición se organizan en torno a ellos. Durante el día arrojan luz natural hacia las salas a través de los techos.

links: Grundriss Erdgeschoss_Fassaden, den Hof definierend_Nachtansicht Hof. rechts: Außenansicht.
gauche: Plan du rez-de-chaussée_Façades, accent sur la cour_Cour vue de nuit. droite: Vue extérieure.
izquierda: Plano de planta baja_Las fachadas definen el patio_Vista nocturna del patio. derecha: Vista exterior.

links: Treppen an der Hoffassade. rechts: Skizze_Bronzefassade_Verglaste Prismen in der Ausstellung_Überblick.
gauche: Espace d'exposition. droite: Esquisse_Façade en bronze_Prismes vitrifiés dans l'exposition_Vue générale.
izquierda: Escaleras en la fachada al patio. derecha: Esbozo_Fachada de bronce_Prismas acristalados en la exposición_Vista.

SWEDEN_GOTHENBURG **VÄRLDSKULTURMUSEET**

SCHWEDEN_SUEDE_SUECIA
BRISAC GONZALEZ
2004
KULTURMUSEUM_MUSÉE DE LA CULTURE_MUSEO DE LA CULTURA
10,950 M^2
PHOTOS HÉLÈNE BINET

Das Museum präsentiert die ethnografischen Sammlungen von Schweden der Öffentlichkeit und bietet zudem internationalen und lokalen Veranstaltungen ein Forum. Am Fuße eines Hügels im Zentrum der Stadt gelegen, verfügt es über ein Auditorium, ein Forschungszentrum, eine Bibliothek, Seminarräume, ein Restaurant und Verwaltungsbüros. Der Entwurf unterscheidet deutlich zwischen dem massiven Westflügel, in dem sich Galerieräume und Büros entlang der Straße befinden und einem zum Hügel offenen Ostflügel, der den öffentlichen Aktivitäten dient. Die schluchtartige Zone zwischen massivem West- und offenem Ostbereich nimmt die Haustechnik und den öffentlichen Rundgang zwischen den drei Funktionsbereichen auf.

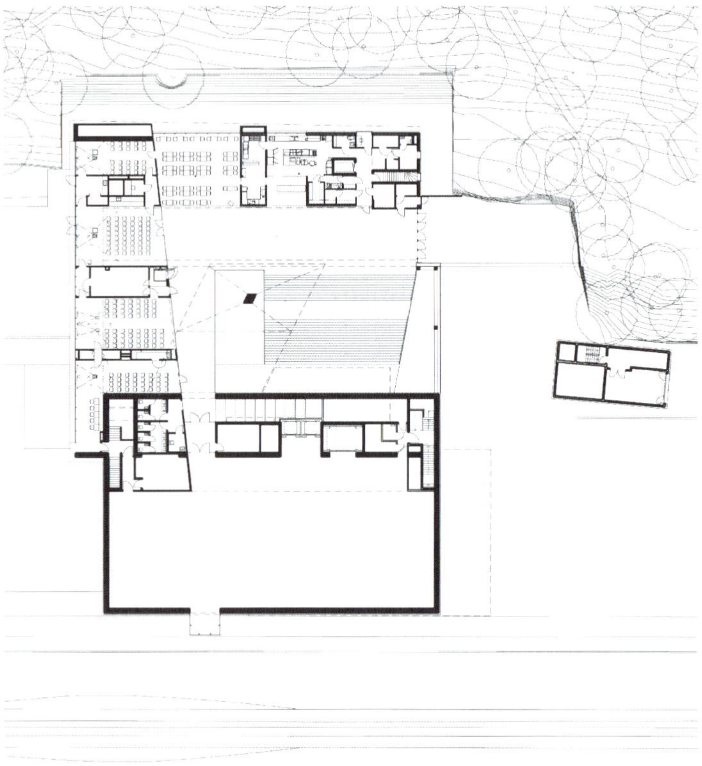

Le musée présente au public les collections ethnographiques de Suède et sert par ailleurs de forum aux manifestations locales et internationales. Situé au pied d'une colline au centre de la ville, le musée présente un auditorium, un centre de recherche, une bibliothèque, des espaces dédiés aux séminaires, un restaurant et des bureaux administratifs. La conception du projet se distingue principalement entre l'aile occidentale massive qui abrite les espaces de galeries et les bureaux longeant la route et l'aile orientale qui s'ouvre sur le côté de la colline servant aux activités publiques. La séparation entre la zone occidentale massive et la zone orientale ouverte accueillant l'ingénierie du bâtiment et la galerie publique se distinguent en trois zones fonctionnelles séparées.

El museo presenta al público las colecciones etnográficas de Suecia y sirve además de foro para acontecimientos locales e internacionales. Ubicado al pie de una colina en el centro de la ciudad, el museo dispone de auditorio, centro de investigaciones, biblioteca, salas para seminarios, restaurante y oficinas administrativas. El concepto proyectual diferencia claramente entre la maciza ala occidental, que aloja galerías y oficinas a lo largo de la calle, y un ala oriental, abierta, junto a la colina, que sirve de escenario para actividades públicas. La brecha entre las alas está ocupada por los equipos de climatización y las zonas para tránsito de público entre los tres ámbitos funcionales.

links: Grundriss 1. Obergeschoss_Haupthalle_Atriumwand. rechts: Eingang_Außenbau_Ostfassade.
gauche: Plan du premier étage_Hall principal_Mur de l'atrium. droite: Entrée_Extérieur_Façade est.
izquierda: Primer piso_Sala principal_Pared del atrio. derecha: Acceso_Vista exterior_Fachada este.

CITYRÖSTER
URBAN VOICES

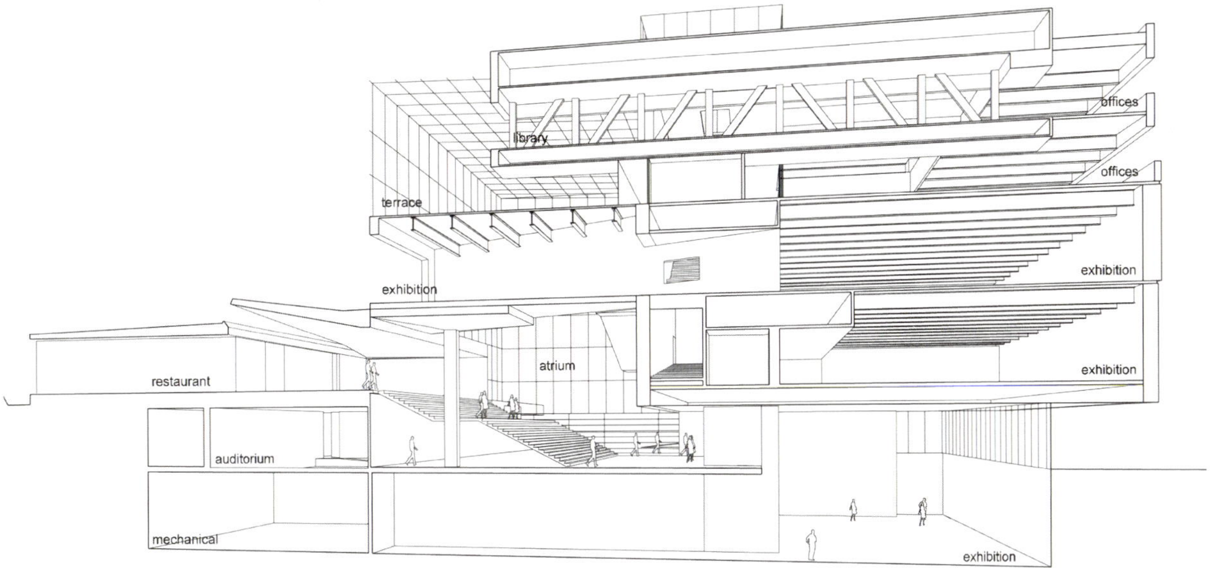

links: Abgesenkter Ausstellungsbereich. rechts: Schnitt_Terrasse_Galerie_Restaurant.
gauche: Zone d'exposition dénivelée. droite: Coupe_Terrasse_Galerie_Restaurant.
izquierda: Zona de exhibiciones hundida. derecha: Corte_Terraza_Galería_Restaurante.

SWEDEN_KALMAR **KALMAR KONSTMUSEUM**

SCHWEDEN_SUEDE_SUECIA
THAM & VIDEGÅRD ARKITEKTER
2008
KUNSTMUSEUM_MUSÉE D'ART_MUSEO DE ARTE
1,600 M²
PHOTOS ÅKE E:SON LINDMAN

Das Kunstmuseum liegt neben einem Restaurant aus den 1930er Jahren im Stadtpark der Renaissancestadt. Der Wettbewerb stand unter dem Motto „Plattform", und der Bau umfasst eine Folge offener Ebenen für kunstbezogene Aktivitäten. Mit großen Spannweiten auf allen Ebenen wurde eine maximale Flexibilität erreicht, und Licht und Raum können ausstellungsspezifisch modelliert und angepasst werden. Die vier jeweils unterschiedlich gestalteten Geschosse sind einerseits übereinander gestapelt und bilden andererseits einen vertikalen Weg hinauf in die Kronen der umliegenden Bäume aus, der verschiedene Raumerlebnisse und Aussichten auf die Umgebung, das Kalmarer Schloss, den See und das Stadtzentrum bietet.

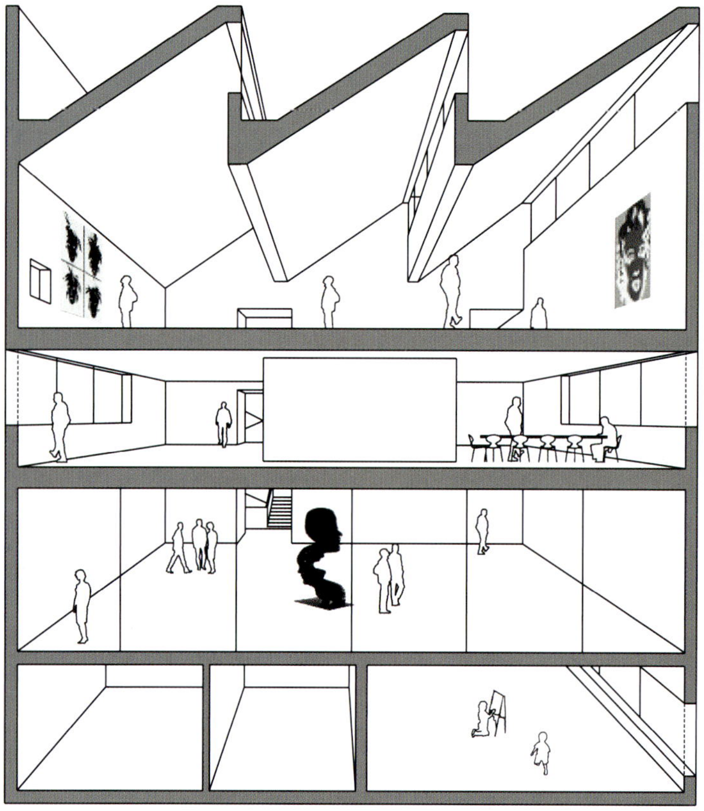

Le musée des beaux-arts se situe à proximité d'un restaurant datant des années 1930 dans le parc municipal de la Renaissance. Le leitmotiv de l'appel d'offres consistait en une « plateforme ». Ainsi, le bâtiment comprend une série de niveaux ouverts consacrés aux activités de l'art. Grâce à d'importantes ouvertures à tous les niveaux, une flexibilité maximale fut atteinte pour modeler et adapter la lumière et l'espace à un centre d'exposition. Les quatre étages, conçus de manière différente, sont superposés et offrent également des vues verticales sur les cimes des arbres environnants et favorisent ainsi des expériences variées au niveau de l'espace et de belles perspectives sur les environs : le château de Kalmar, le lac et le centre-ville.

El Museo de Arte se levanta junto a un restaurante de la década de 1930, en el parque urbano de la ciudad renacentista. La consigna del concurso de proyectos fue "Plataforma", y la construcción comprende una serie de plantas libres para actividades relacionadas con el arte. Con grandes luces libres en todos los niveles se logró un máximo de flexibilidad; la luz y el espacio se pueden moldear y adaptar de esa manera a los requisitos específicos de cada muestra. Los cuatro niveles, cada uno de ellos con una configuración diferente, se apilan uno encima del otro, pero, al mismo tiempo, conforman un recorrido vertical que permite apreciar las copas de los árboles del parque. Así, el visitante disfruta vivencias espaciales y vistas del entorno, el castillo de Kalmar, el mar y el centro de la ciudad.

links: Schnitt_Hauptfassade_Treppenhaus_Museum im Kontext. rechts: Gartenfassade_Blick nach außen.
gauche: Section_Façade principale_Cage d'escalier_Musée dans son contexte. droite: Façade jardin_Vue sur l'extérieur.
izquierda: Corte_Fachada principal_Caja de la escalera_El museo en su contexto. derecha: Fachada al jardín_Vista hacia el exterior.

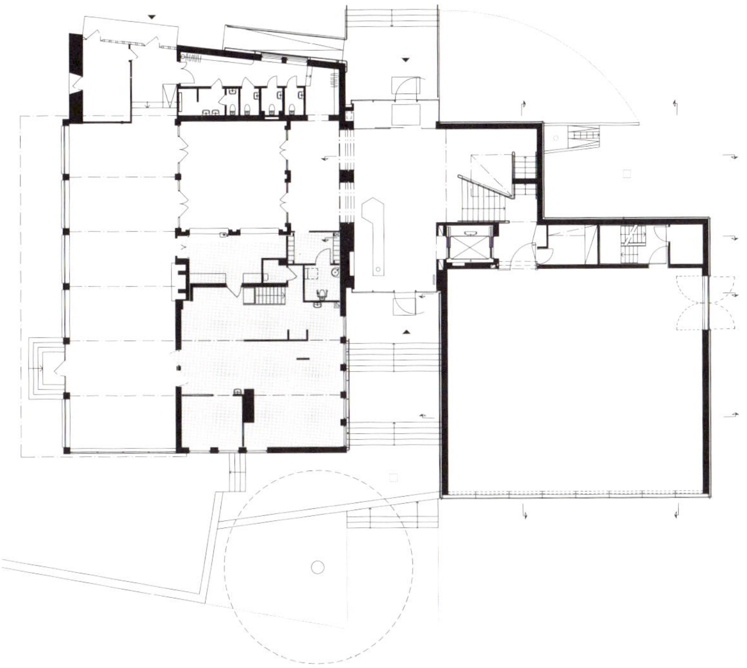

links: Außenbau über Eck. rechts: Plan_Treppenhaus_Sheddach_Blick aus dem Treppenhaus.
gauche: Construction extérieure sur l'angle. droite: Plan_Cage d'escalier_Toit d'abri_Vue de la cage d'escalier.
izquierda: Vista exterior en escorzo. derecha: Planta_Caja de la escalera_Techo en diente de sierra Vista desde la caja de la escalera.

SWEDEN_MALMO **MODERNA MUSEET**

SCHWEDEN_SUEDE_SUECIA
THAM & VIDEGÅRD ARKITEKTER
2009
KUNSTMUSEUM_MUSÉE D'ART_MUSEO DE ARTE
2,650 M²
PHOTOS ÅKE E:SON LINDMAN, STOCKHOLM

Der Entwurf ging davon aus, dass ein neues Kunstmuseum, ein öffentliches und kulturelles Gebäude, die seltene Gelegenheit bietet, einen neuen Knotenpunkt im Stadtgefüge zu schaffen. Das Museum befindet sich in einem ehemaligen Kraftwerk und dessen Erweiterungsbau. Das neue Gebäude markiert die Ankunft eines neuen Museums in der Stadt und umfasst Haupteingang, Eingangsbereich, Cafeteria und eine Galerie im Obergeschoss. Das Innere des Museums wurde räumlich rekonstruiert. Zwei neue Treppenhäuser ermöglichen dem Besucher den Rundgang durch die große Turbinenhalle und die Ausstellungsräume im Obergeschoss.

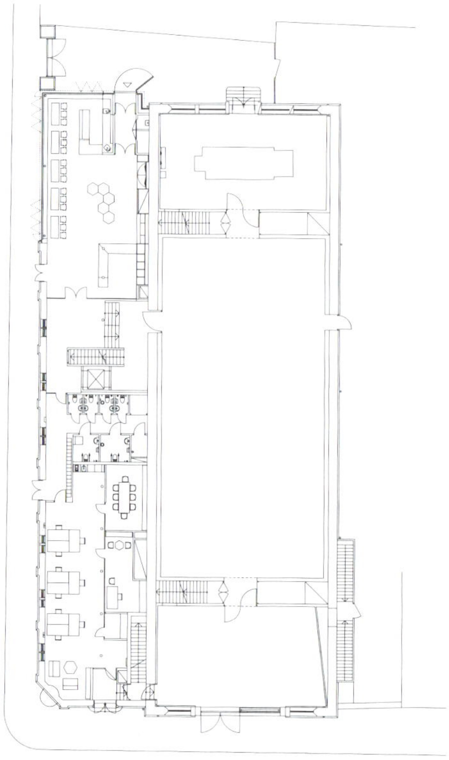

Le point de départ du projet était la création d'un musée de l'art dans un bâtiment dédié à la culture et au public offrant une opportunité rare de créer un nouveau carrefour dans le tissu urbain. Le musée se situe dans une ancienne centrale électrique et dans sa nouvelle annexe. Le nouveau bâtiment souligne la venue d'un nouveau musée en ville qui comprend une entrée principale, la réception, la cafétéria et une nouvelle galerie à l'étage supérieur. L'intérieur du musée a été reconstruit en tenant compte de l'espace. Les deux nouvelles cages d'escalier permettent aux visiteurs d'accéder à la galerie par la grande salle des turbines pour se rendre aux espaces d'exposition à l'étage supérieur.

El punto de partida del proyecto fue el concepto de museo de arte como edificio cultural y público al mismo tiempo, y esto ofreció la rara oportunidad de concretar un nuevo punto nodal en el tejido urbano. El museo se alberga en una antigua usina eléctrica y en una ampliación de la misma. El nuevo edificio marca la llegada de un novedoso museo a la ciudad y comprende el acceso principal, la recepción, la cafetería y una nueva galería en la planta alta. El interior del museo ha sido reconstruido desde el punto de vista espacial. Dos nuevas cajas de escaleras permiten a los visitantes un recorrido por la gran sala de turbinas y las salas de exhibición en la planta alta.

links: Grundriss Erdgeschoss_Ausstellungsraum_Ausstellungsraum, Deckendetail. rechts: Fassade_Schriftzug Museumsname.
gauche: Plan du rez-de-chaussée_Espace d'exposition_Plafond en détail de l'espace d'exposition. droite: Façade_Inscription nom du musée.
izquierda: Plano de planta baja_Sala de exhibiciones_Detalle del cielorraso. derecha: Fachada_Inscripción con el nombre del museo.

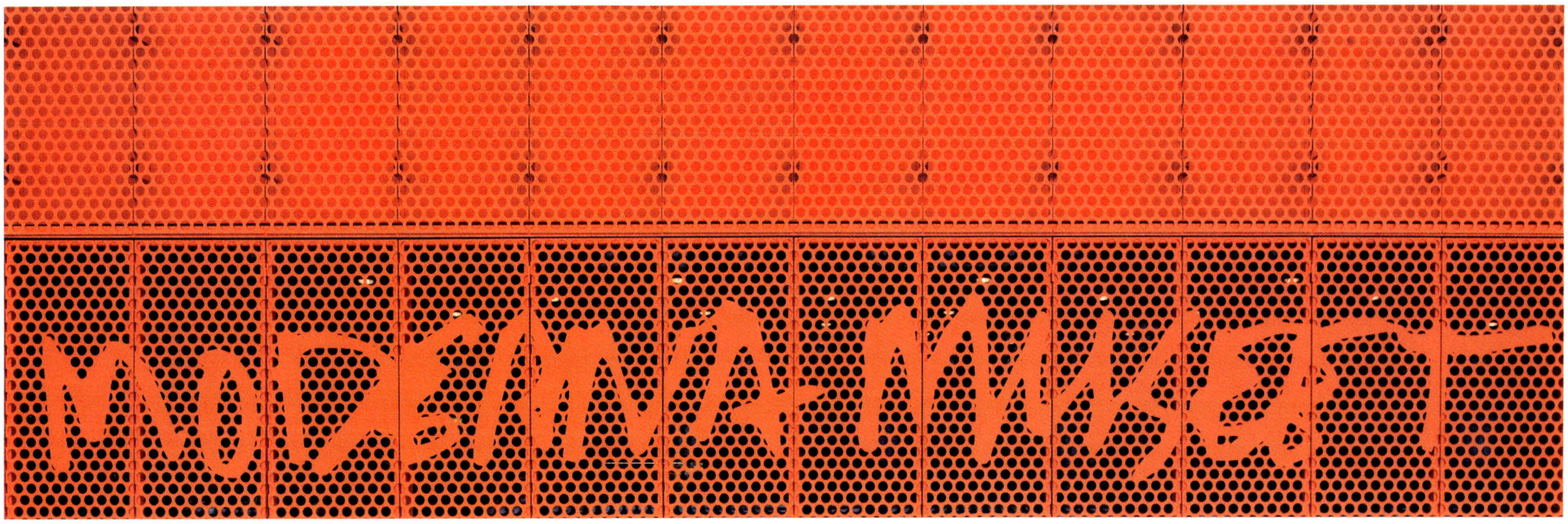

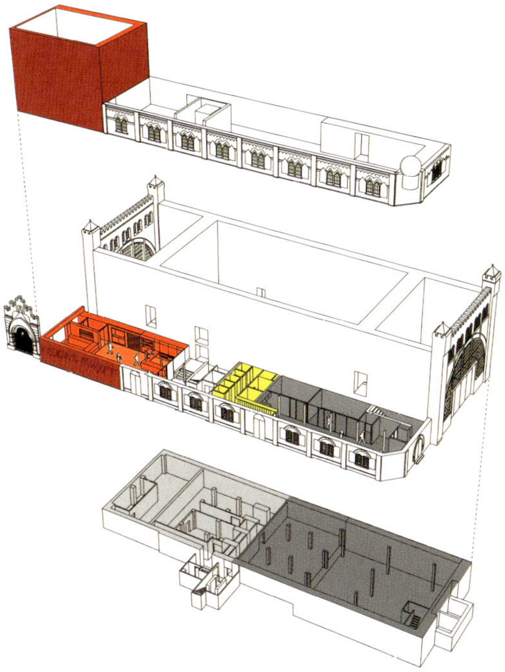

links: Maschinenhalle. rechts: Explosionszeichnung_Café_Zugang Café_Schriftzug Museumsname aus Café.
gauche: Salle des machines. droite: Dessin d'étude_Café_Accès au café_Inscription nom du musée.
izquierda: Sala de máquinas. derecha: Dibujo proyectual_Café_Acceso al café_Inscripción con el nombre del museo.

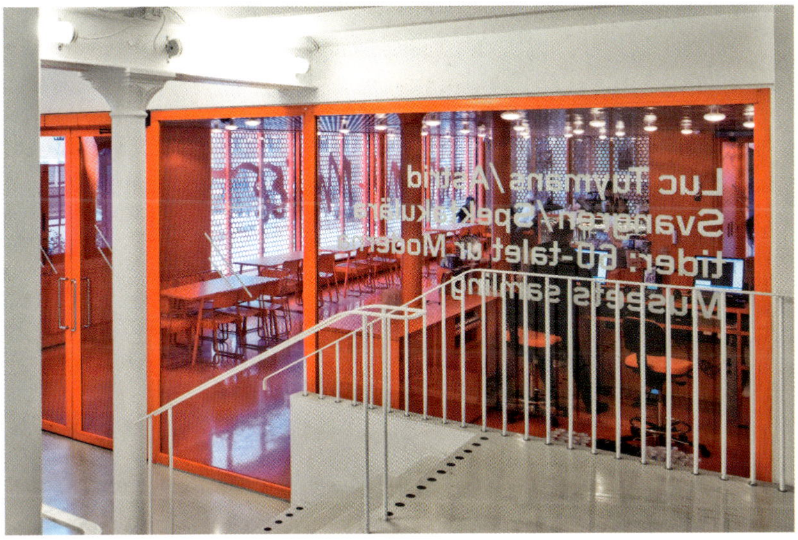

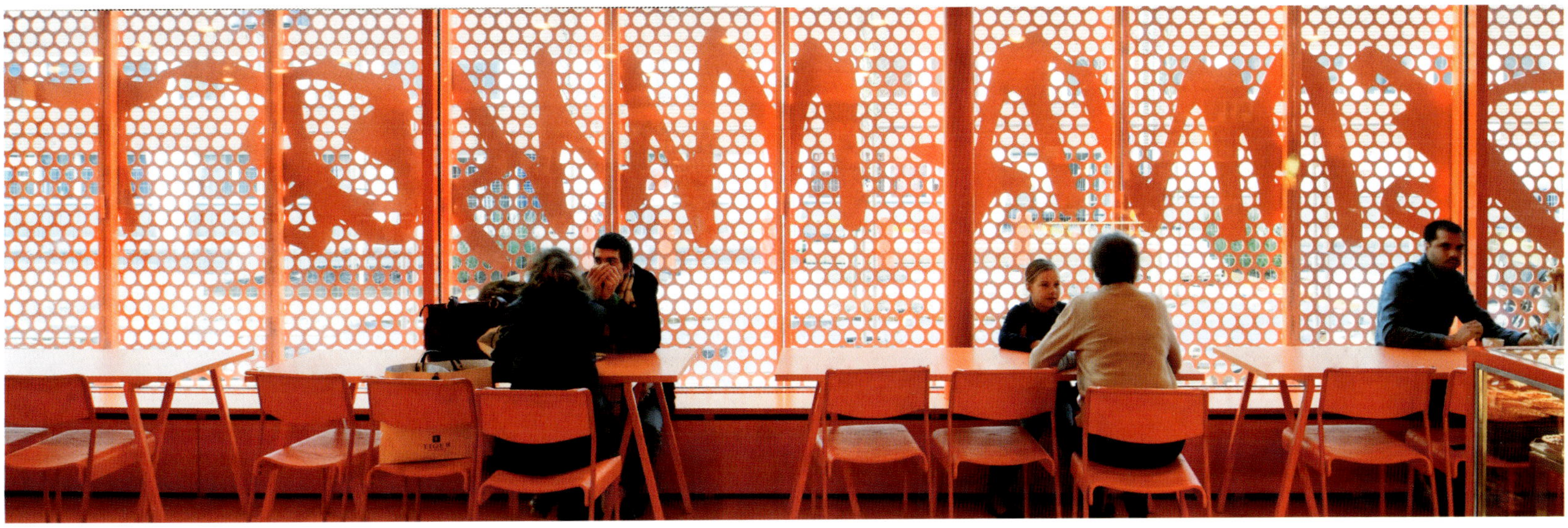

SWITZERLAND_BASEL **KUNSTHALLE BASEL**

SCHWEIZ_SUISSE_SUIZA
MILLER & MARANTA
2004
KUNSTMUSEUM_MUSÉE D'ART_MUSEO DE ARTE
1,680 M²
PHOTOS COURTESY OF THE ARCHITECTS (399 B.), KUNSTHALLE BASEL (398, 398 A.)

Im Auftrag des Basler Kunstvereins wurde der Gebäudekomplex von 1872 saniert und den Bedürfnissen eines aktuellen Kunstbetriebs angepasst. Die Sanierung umfasste die Ausstellungsräume, das Restaurant und den Kunsthallengarten im Herzen der Anlage. Für den Ausstellungsbetrieb wurden die raumklimatischen und sicherheitstechnischen Bedingungen verbessert. Gleichzeitig wurden Holzböden und Beleuchtung ersetzt. Im Innern des Restaurants wurde das erste Obergeschoss renoviert. Unionssaal und Bar bilden nun wieder eine Einheit. Im Garten wurden die Verbindung zum hinteren Flügel mit dem Stadtkino verbessert und die Freiluft-Bar ersetzt.

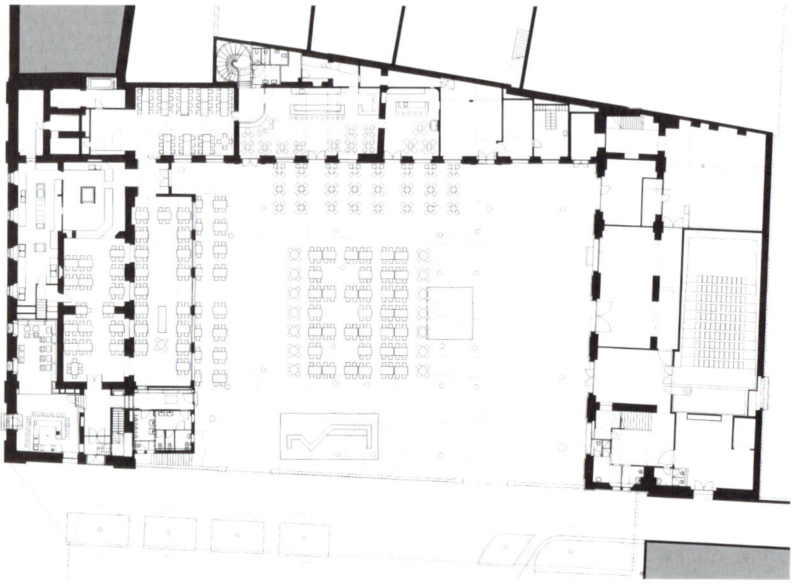

Sur mandat de l'association Basler Kunstverein, le complexe du bâtiment datant de 1872 a été restauré et adapté à l'état de l'art. La rénovation comprend les espaces d'exposition, de restauration et d'arts de Kunsthalleng au cœur du site. Les conditions techniques en matière de sécurité et de climatisation ont été améliorées pour l'exploitation des espaces d'exposition. Les planchers et l'éclairage ont été remplacés simultanément. Le premier étage supérieur a été rénové à l'intérieur de l'espace restauration. La salle de réunion et le bar forment désormais une unité. Dans le jardin, la jonction de l'aile arrière au cinéma de la ville a été améliorée avant d'être remplacée par un bar en plein air.

Por encargo de la Asociación de Artistas de Basilea, se renovó el complejo edilicio de 1872 y se lo adaptó a las necesidades actuales de la actividad artística. La renovación abarcó las salas de exhibición, los servicios gastronómicos y el jardín del museo como corazón de las instalaciones. Para las actividades de exhibición se mejoraron las condiciones de climatización y la tecnología de seguridad. Al mismo tiempo, se reemplazaron los suelos de madera y la iluminación. En el interior del establecimiento gastronómico se renovó el primer piso. Ahora, la Unionssaal y el bar constituyen nuevamente una unidad. En el jardín se mejoró la vinculación del ala trasera con el cine y se sustituyó el bar al aire libre.

links: Grundriss Erdgeschoss_Außenbau_Ausstellungssaal. rechts: Ausstellungssaal_Bar_Sitzgruppe in der Bar.
gauche: Plan du rez-de-chaussée_Construction extérieure_Salle d'exposition. droite: Salle d'exposition_Bar_Places assises dans le bar.
izquierda: Plano de planta baja_Vista exterior_Sala de exhibiciones. derecha: Sala de exhibiciones_Bar_Rincón con sillones en el bar.

SWITZERLAND_BERNE **ZENTRUM PAUL KLEE**

SCHWEIZ_SUISSE_SUIZA
RENZO PIANO BUILDING WORKSHOP, ARCHITECTS WITH ARB, ARCHITECTS
2005
KUNSTMUSEUM_MUSÉE D'ART_MUSEO DE ARTE
16,000 M²
PHOTOS ENRICO CANO (400 B. R.), MICHEL DENANCÉ (400 B. L., 401)

Das Leben und Werk des Künstlers Paul Klee (1879–1940) stehen im Zentrum dieses neuen Kulturinstituts. Mit rund 4000 Kunstwerken gilt die Sammlung des Zentrums Paul Klee als größte Kollektion eines Künstlers von Weltrang. Die Architekten schufen eine großzügige grüne Insel, aus der sich das Gebäude in drei geschwungenen Wellen erhebt. Die drei Hügel aus Glas und Stahl sind Spiegel des Programms und stehen für einen interdisziplinären Ansatz. Neben dem großzügigen Ausstellungsraum gibt es in dem Zentrum auch eine hochwertige Musik- und Aufführungshalle, ein Kindermuseum, eine Mehrzweckpromenade und Seminarräume.

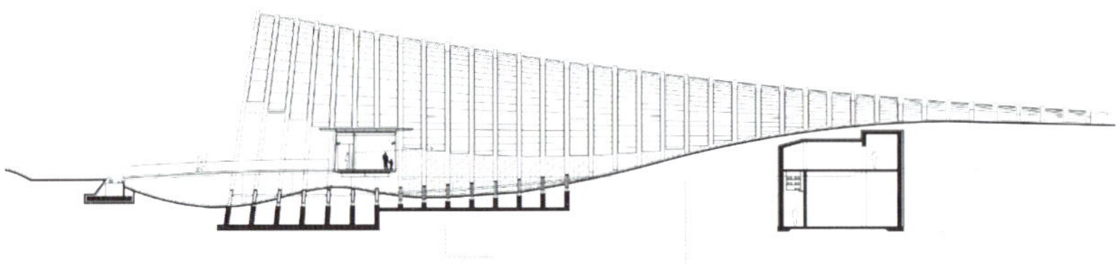

La vie et l'œuvre de l'artiste Paul Klee (1879–1940) est au centre de ce nouveau institut dédié à la culture. La collection du centre regroupant environ 4 000 œuvres d'art est considérée comme la plus importante collection réalisée par un artiste d'envergure internationale. Les architectes ont créé une île verte généreuse d'où s'élève le bâtiment en trois vagues ondulées. Les trois collines en verre et acier représentent l'idée du programme et forment une approche interdisciplinaire. Outre l'espace d'exposition généreux, le centre comprend également un hall de représentation et de musique de haute qualité, un musée pour enfants, une promenade multifonctionnelle et des espaces dédiés aux séminaires.

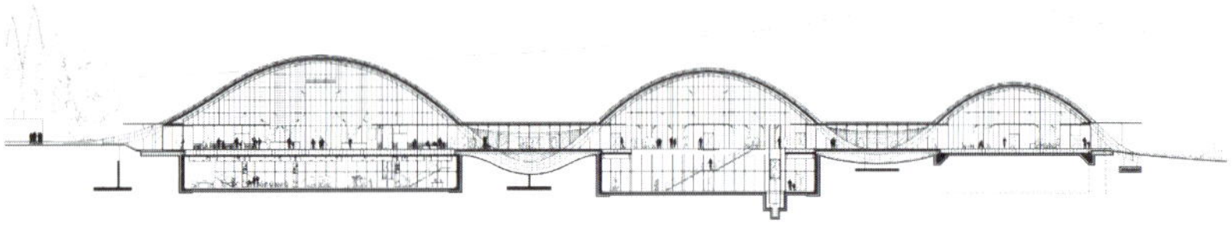

La vida y la obra del artista Paul Klee (1879–1940) constituyen el centro de esta novedosa institución de arte. Con unas 4.000 obras expuestas, la colección de este centro es la mayor dedicada a un artista de fama mundial. Los arquitectos plasmaron una maravillosa isla verde, en la que el edificio se despliega en tres grandes ondas. Las tres colinas acristaladas y aceradas son un espejo del programa, e invitan a un uso interdisciplinario. Además del grandioso espacio para exhibiciones, el centro abarca también una sala de alta calidad para música y actividades, un museo infantil, una explanada multiuso y salas para seminarios.

links: Schnitte_"Creativa" Kinderatelier_Ausstellungsraum. rechts: Achterbahnartiges Profil der Stahlkonstruktion_Ansicht von Osten.
gauche: Coupes_Atelier pour enfants « Creativa »_Espace d'exposition. droite: Profiles de construction en acier comparables à des montagnes russes_Vue à l'est.
izquierda: Cortes_Taller para niños "Creativa"_Sala de exhibiciones. derecha: Perfiles de acero que semejan una montaña rusa_Vista desde el este.

SWITZERLAND_COLOGNY-GENÈVE **FONDATION MARTIN BODMER**

SCHWEIZ_SUISSE_SUIZA
STUDIO ARCHITETTO MARIO BOTTA WITH ARCHILAB
2003
LITERATURMUSEUM_MUSÉE DE LA LITTÉRATURE
MUSEO LITERARIO
NET 1,280 M^2; EXHIBITION AREA: 750 M^2
PHOTOS PINO MUSI, MILAN

Die Erweiterung des Museums besteht aus einem zweistöckigen, unterirdischen Bauteil zwischen zwei klassischen Villen. Die Lichtempfindlichkeit der dort aufbewahrten Dokumente legte es nahe, sie unterirdisch zu präsentieren, so dass draußen nichts sichtbar ist außer fünf gläsernen Kuben, die sich jeweils auf einem quadratischen Sockel aus dem Boden erheben. Sie steigen rund dreieinhalb Meter auf und sind wie eine Reihe von Schirmen perspektivisch auf den Eingang ausgerichtet. Diese gläsernen, vom Boden aufsteigenden Formen dienen als Oberlichter und lassen Tageslicht in die unterirdischen Ausstellungsräume einfallen. Ihre Transparenz und geometrische Form verändern die Wahrnehmung des Innen- und Außenraums.

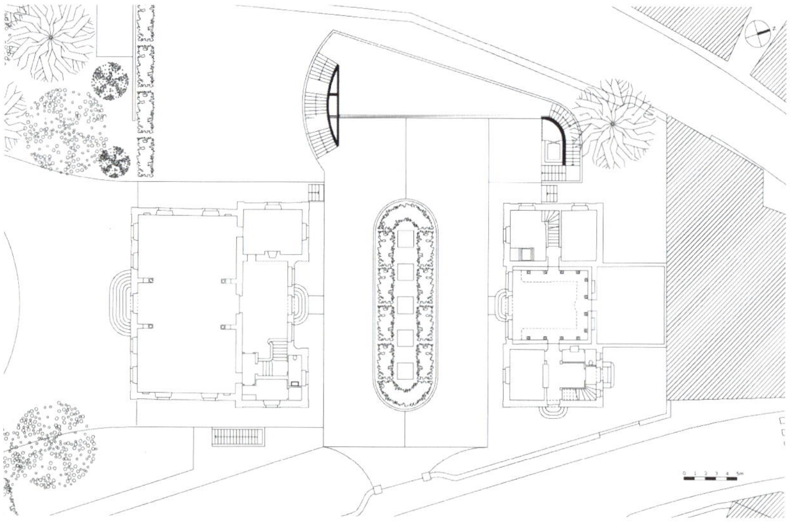

L'extension est constituée d'un bâtiment à deux étages souterrain situé entre les deux villas classiques. Les documents eux-mêmes dictèrent en raison de leur particularité, l'idée d'une présentation souterraine, qui s'élève du sol uniquement grâce à cinq bandes en verre sur un socle carré. Elles s'élèvent de trois mètres et demi environ au-dessus du sol et sont orientées en perspective sur l'entrée comme une série d'écrans. Ces formes en verre s'élevant du sol permettent l'accès de la lumière supérieure et laissent pénétrer la lumière du jour dans les surfaces souterraines d'exposition. Leur forme géométrique et transparente modifie la perception de l'espace.

La ampliación comprende un edificio subterráneo de dos niveles ubicado entre dos villas clásicas. Los propios documentos de la Fundación, por sus características, llevaron a la idea de una presentación subterránea, en la que apenas sobresalen del suelo cinco elementos acristalados sobre un zócalo cuadrado. Se elevan unos tres metros y medio y son como una hilera de pantallas que parecen orientarse en perspectiva hacia el acceso. Estas formas acristaladas que nacen del suelo sirven como lucernarios y permiten que la luz natural penetre hacia las áreas de exhibición subterráneas. Su transparencia y forma geométrica modifican la percepción del espacio.

links: Lageplan_Außenansicht der fünf Lichtstelen_Foyer. rechts: Ständige Ausstellung 1. Untergeschoss_Ständige Ausstellung 2. Untergeschoss.
gauche: Plan de site_Vue extérieure des cinq stèles lumineuses_Foyer. droite: 1er étage inférieur, exposition permanente_2^{ème} étage inférieur, exposition permanente.
izquierda: Ubicación_Vista exterior de las cinco estelas luminosas_Vestíbulo. derecha: Exhibición permanente en el primer subsuelo_Exhibición permanente en el segundo subsuelo.

SWITZERLAND_LUCERNE **VERKEHRSHAUS DER SCHWEIZ**

SCHWEIZ_SUISSE_SUIZA
ANNETTE GIGON / MIKE GUYER, ARCHITEKTEN
2009
KULTURMUSEUM_MUSÉE DE LA CULTURE_MUSEO DE LA CULTURA
10,553 M²
PHOTOS LEONARDO FINOTTI (404 B. L., 406),
HEINRICH HELFENSTEIN, ZURICH (405 A., B. L., 407),
GIGON / GUYER (404 B. R., 405 B. R.)

Der ursprüngliche Wettbewerb sah 1999 eine schrittweise Erneuerung des Verkehrshausareals mit seinen verschiedenen Bauten für die unterschiedlichen Verkehrsträger und ein Neubauprojekt für den Straßenverkehr vor. In der ersten Bauphase wurden die Halle für Straßenverkehr und ein neues Eingangsgebäude erstellt. Das Eingangsgebäude stellt eine brückenartige Verbindung zu den Bestandsgebäuden her, und die Fassaden sind als Vitrinen für Räder, Propeller, Felgen und so weiter ausgebildet. Bei der neuen Halle für Straßenverkehr handelt es sich um eine zweigeschossige, kostengünstige und flexibel nutzbare Black Box mit automatisiertem Parkiersystem und wiederverwendeten Verkehrstafeln als Fassadenblechen.

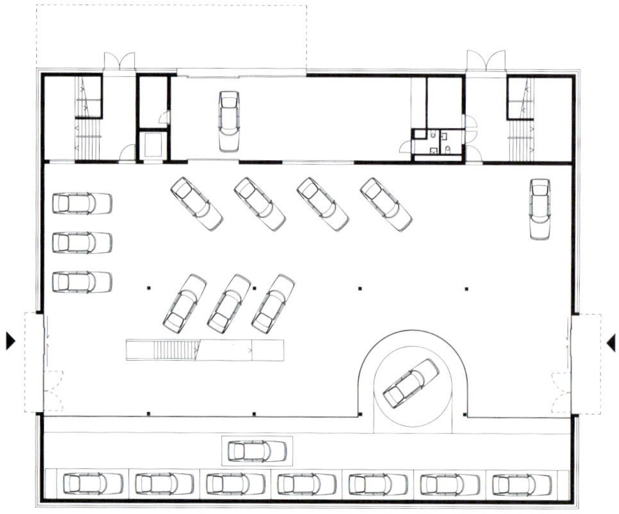

En 1999, l'appel d'offres d'origine prévoit une rénovation successive de l'espace de la halle du transport routier constituée de plusieurs bâtiments consacrés aux différents moyens de transport et un nouveau projet de construction dédié au transport routier. Au cours de la première phase de construction, la halle du transport routier et un nouveau bâtiment furent érigés. Le bâtiment d'entrée permet une jonction en forme de pont vers les bâtiments existants et les façades sont formées de vitrines conçues pour les roues, hélices, jantes, etc. La nouvelle halle pour le transport routier est une boite noire à deux étages, utilisable tout en souplesse et peu onéreuse, équipée d'un système de parking automatique et revêtue de panneaux de signalisation réutilisables servant de tôles pour les façades.

El concurso, originalmente realizado en 1999, preveía una renovación paulatina de las instalaciones de la Casa del Tránsito con sus varias edificaciones para las diversas entidades del tránsito y también un proyecto de obra nueva dedicado al tránsito callejero. En la primera fase se levantaron la sala para el tránsito callejero y un nuevo edificio de acceso. El edificio de acceso constituye una conexión similar a un puente con los edificios existentes; sus fachadas están concebidas como vitrinas para ruedas, hélices, llantas, etc. La nueva sala para tránsito callejero es una "caja negra" de dos plantas, flexible y de bajo coste, con sistema de estacionamiento automatizado y señales de tránsito recicladas a modo de chapas para fachada.

links: Halle für Individual- und Straßenverkehr Erdgeschoss_Blaue Fassade, West_Grüne Fassade und Gebäuderückseite, Südost. rechts: Halle, Nordwest_Zwischenraum zwischen den Gebäuden Ausstellungsregal.
gauche: Halle pour le transport individuel et collectif au rez-de-chaussée_Façade bleue ouest_Façade verte. droite: Halle_Façade blanche_Vitrine d'exposition.
izquierda: Sala para tránsito individual y callejero en planta baja_Fachada azul oeste_Fachada verde y cara trasera de la fachada. derecha: Sala, noroeste_Espacio entre los edificios_Estantería de exhibición.

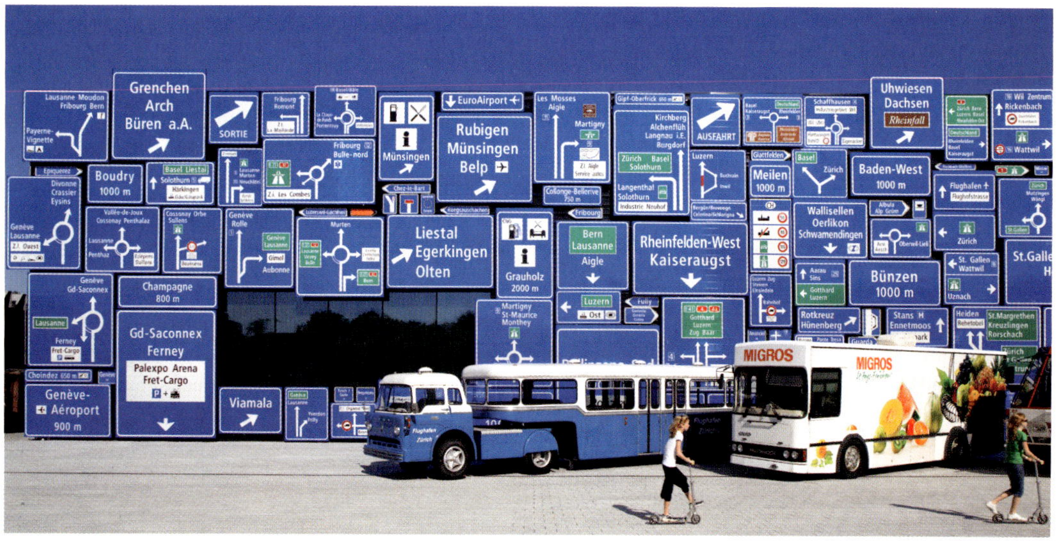

Lausanne Moudon
Fribourg Bern
Payerne-
Vignette
Grenchen
Arch
Büren a.A.
SORTIE
Epiquerez
Divonne
Crassier
Eysins
Genève
Lausanne
Z.I. Ouest
Boudry
1000 m
Basel Liestal
Solothurn
Härkingen
Gäu/Gäupark
Vallée-de-Joux
Cossonay Penthalaz
Lausanne
Penthaz
Eclépens
Daillens
Cossonay Orbe
Sullens
Boussens
Genève
Rolle
Genève
Lausanne
Gimel
Aubonne
Fribourg
Bulle-nord
Z.I. Les Combes
Münsingen
EuroAirport
Rubigen
Münsingen
Belp
Liestal
Egerkingen
Olten
Genève
Gd-Saconnex
Lausanne
Ferney
Fret-Cargo
Champagne
800 m
Gd-Saconnex
Ferney
Palexpo Arena
Fret-Cargo
Choindez 650 m
Genève-
Aéroport
900 m
Viamala
St-Maurice
1000 m
Bellinzona
Locarno
Polizia
Industrie Süd
Industrie Nord
Chur
Luzern
Cher
Bäuler
Lieferwagen
bis 3,5t
Quartier
de la
Sussette
80 Extrafahrt

Bern
Kehrsatz
Beatenberg
Habkern
Solothurn
Cher
Bäuler

RAIFFEISEN

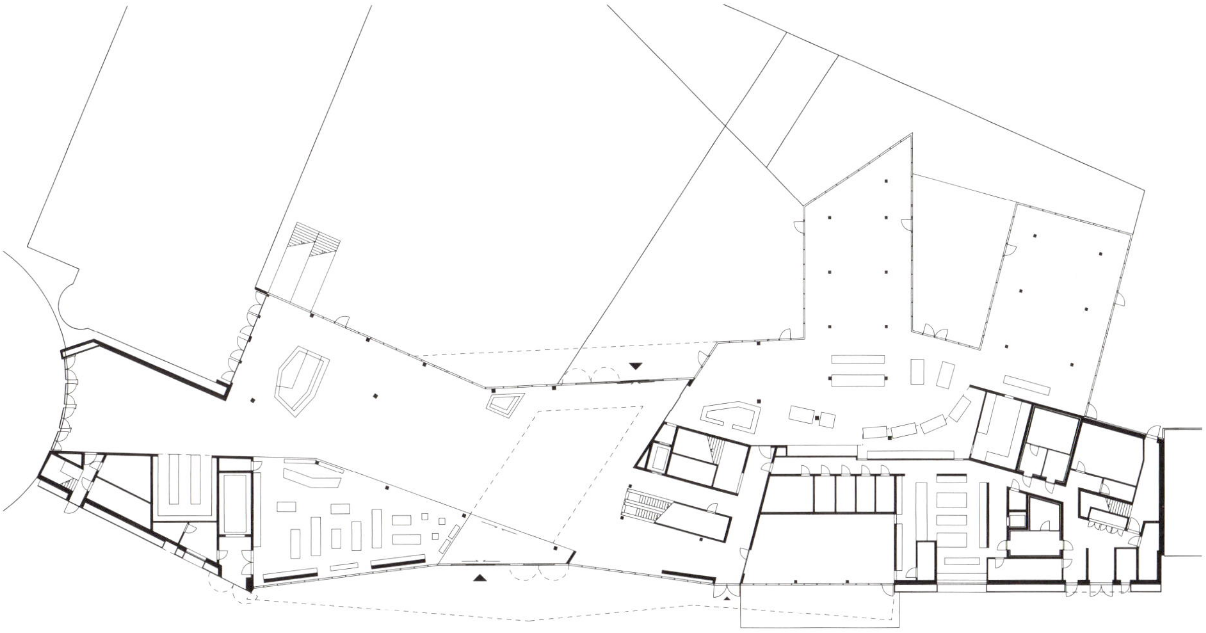

links: Detail der transparenten Fassade des Eingangsgebäudes. rechts: Eingangsgebäude Erdgeschoss_Blick nach draußen_Fassade.
gauche: Détail de la vitrine transparente du bâtiment d'entrée. droite: Bâtiment d'entrée au rez-de-chaussée_Vue sur l'extérieur_Façade.
izquierda: Detalle de la vitrina transparente del edificio del acceso. derecha: Edificio de acceso planta baja_Vista hacia el exterior_Fachada.

SWITZERLAND_ZERNEZ SCHWEIZERISCHES NATIONALPARK-ZENTRUM

SCHWEIZ_SUISSE_SUIZA
VALERIO OLGIATI
2008
NATURKUNDEMUSEUM_MUSEE DE L'HISTOIRE NATURELLE
MUSEO DE HISTORIA NATURAL
1,780 M^2
PHOTOS MIGUEL VERME, CHUR

Von außen erscheint das neue Besucherzentrum mit den beiden ineinander geschobenen Würfeln sehr streng. Der helle Ortbeton des Gebäudes, einziges verwendetes Material, kontrastiert mit der natürlichen Umgebung. Das dreigeschossige Innere entwickelt sich aus Gegensätzen: Verbergen und Zeigen, Schwere und Leichtigkeit, Regelmäßigkeit und Unregelmäßigkeit. Alle Ausstellungsräume sind gleich und über einen versteckten Gang und ein Treppensystem verbunden. Das Format der Fenster ist leicht horizontal und evoziert so einen „beobachtenden Blick" aus allen Räumen in alle Richtungen. Die Ausstellungsräume, je einer pro Stockwerk, können zur Gänze abgedunkelt werden.

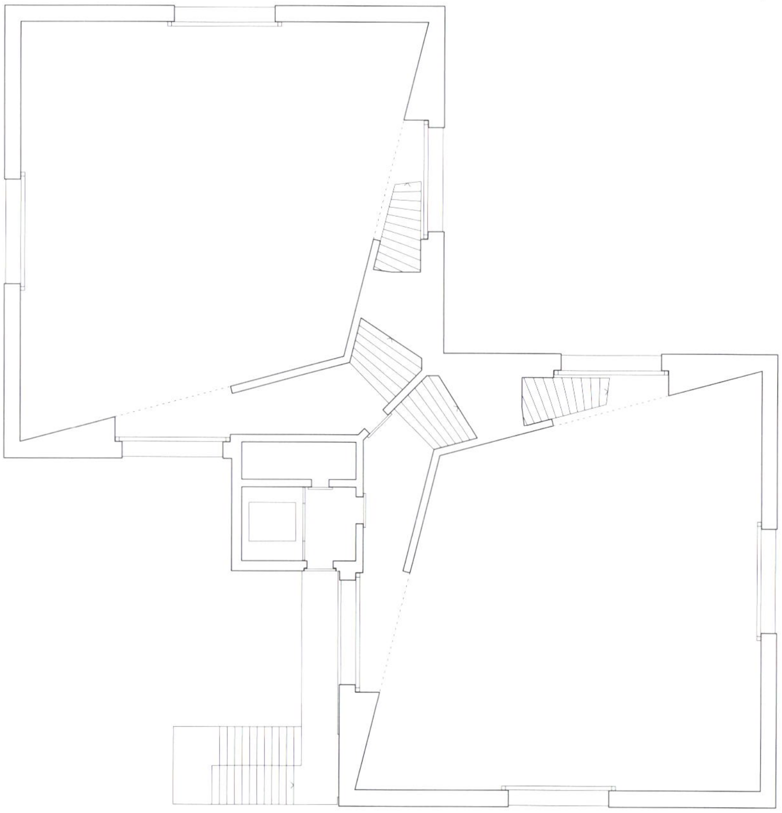

Vu de l'extérieur, le nouveau centre des visiteurs parait très strict avec les deux dés encastrés l'un dans l'autre. Le béton local clair du bâtiment, seul matériau visible, contraste avec l'environnement naturel. L'intérieur sur trois étages est caractérisé par des contradictions : dissimulation / révélation, lourdeur / légèreté et régularité / irrégularité. Tous les espaces d'exposition sont identiques et reliés par un couloir caché et un système d'escaliers. Le format des fenêtres est légèrement horizontal afin d'évoquer une « vue d'observation » à partir de tous les espaces et dans toutes les directions. Les espaces d'exposition, au nombre de un par étage, peuvent être intégralement occultés.

Desde el exterior, el nuevo centro de visitantes parece muy severo con sus dos dados que se penetran entre sí. El claro hormigón visto del edificio, único material visible, contrasta con el entorno natural. El interior, de tres niveles, es rico en contrastes: ocultar y mostrar, masa y liviandad, regularidad e irregularidad. Todas las salas de exhibición son iguales y se conectan con un extenso pasillo y un sistema de escaleras. El formato de las ventanas es levemente horizontal y evoca así una "mirada observadora" en todas las salas y direcciones. Las salas de exhibición, una por piso, pueden oscurecerse por completo.

links: Grundriss 1. Obergeschoss_Gespalteter Treppenlauf_Eingang. rechts: Außenansicht_Fensternische_Ausstellungsraum.
gauche: Plan du 1er étage_Les escaliers scindés_Entrée. droite: Vue extérieure_Niche de fenêtre Espace d'exposition.
izquierda: Plano del primer piso_Escaleras que se separan_Acceso. derecha: Vista exterior_Nicho de ventana_Sala de exhibiciones.

SWITZERLAND_ZURICH **MUSEUM RIETBERG**

SCHWEIZ_SUISSE_SUIZA
GRAZIOLI UND KRISCHANITZ ARCHITEKTEN
2008
KULTURMUSEUM_MUSÉE DE LA CULTURE_MUSEO DE LA CULTURA
5,350 M²
PHOTOS HEINRICH HELFENSTEIN, ZURICH (410 B. L., 411),
MARGHERITA SPILUTTINI, VIENNA (410 B. R.)

Das Glashaus – selbst Zeichen des Schauens an sich – gewährt einen Blick in das Innere der Museumswelt. Das Eingangsgebäude der unterirdischen Erweiterung, die die Grundfläche des Museums nahezu verdoppelt, bietet einen Ausblick auf den Altbau der Villa Wesendonck. Es ist als Vorgebäude zum eigentlichen Ausstellungsbezirk im Zusammenhang mit dem angrenzenden Veranstaltungssaal vielfältig funktional und repräsentativ nutzbar. Sein Name „Baldachine von Smaragd" spielt auf ein Gedicht von Mathilde Wesendonck an, das von Richard Wagner vertont wurde. Dem Glashaus direkt angeschlossen ist eine Raumschicht mit Treppe, Lift und mobilen Elementen wie Kasse, Vitrinen und Garderobe.

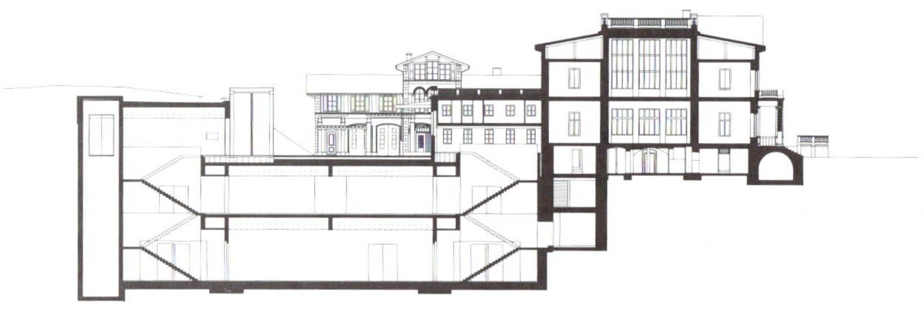

La maison de verre – en soi un signe de la perception visuelle – permet une vue à l'intérieur du monde des musées. Le bâtiment d'entrée de l'extension souterraine double quasiment la superficie du musée et offre une vue sur l'ancien bâtiment de la Villa Wesendonck. En effet, cet espace multifonctionnel et représentatif sert grâce à sa juxtaposition à la salle de manifestations limitrophe. Son nom « Baldachins d'émeraude » fait allusion à un poème de Mathilde Wesendonck adapté par Richard Wagner dans son œuvre musicale. La maison de verre immédiate donne accès à l'escalier, l'ascenseur et les éléments mobiles, notamment, les caisses, vitrines et vestiaires.

La caja de vidrio, todo un símbolo de lo que es "mostrar", facilita la visión hacia el interior del mundo museístico. La ampliación subterránea casi duplica la superficie del museo, y su edificio de acceso permite apreciar la antigua construcción de la Villa Wesendonck. Se ha concebido como un antecuerpo para el área de exhibiciones propiamente dicha; conjuntamente con la sala de actividades anexa, el conjunto tiene una funcionalidad versátil y tiene carácter representativo. El nombre "baldaquines de esmeralda" evoca un poema de Mathilde Wesendonck que fuera musicalizado por Richard Wagner. En conexión directa con la caja de vidrio hay una serie de salas con escaleras, elevador y elementos móviles como vitrinas, cajas y guardarropas.

links: Schnitt_Eingang zum unterirdischen Neubau_Eingangsbereich des Neubaus (Smaragd). rechts: Ausstellungsraum im Neubau_Museumsshop.
gauche: Coupe_Entrée au nouveau bâtiment souterrain_Zone d'entrée du nouveau bâtiment (émeraude). droite: Espace d'exposition dans le nouveau bâtiment_Boutique du musée.
izquierda: Corte_Acceso a la edificación subterránea_Zona de acceso del edificio nuevo (Esmeralda). derecha: Sala de exhibiciones en el edificio nuevo_Tienda del museo.

THE NETHERLANDS_AMSTERDAM **STEDELIJK MUSEUM AMSTERDAM**

NIEDERLANDE_PAYS-BAS_PAÍSES BAJOS
BENTHEM CROUWEL ARCHITECTS
2011
KUNSTMUSEUM_MUSÉE D'ART_MUSEO DE ARTE
26,484 M²
PHOTOS COURTESY OF THE ARCHITECTS

Die charakteristischen Qualitäten des Altbaus – die symmetrische Komposition mit zentralem Treppenhaus und die monumentalen Galerien – bleiben bei der Erweiterung ebenso erhalten wie die Belichtung durch das Dach. Die Verlagerung des Haupteingangs an den Museumsplatz stellt den größten Eingriff dar. Abgesehen vom Eingang selbst wird der neue Gebäudeteil das Informationszentrum, den Museumsshop und das Restaurant umfassen. Zahlreiche neue Räume liegen unterirdisch, darunter der mit 1100 Quadratmetern größte Museumsraum von Amsterdam. Sowohl durch die aufragenden als auch durch die abgesenkten Bauteile bleibt die Originalsubstanz nahezu unverändert erhalten und gänzlich sichtbar. Ein großes weißes, auskragendes Dach markiert den neuen großzügigen und transparenten Eingangsbereich.

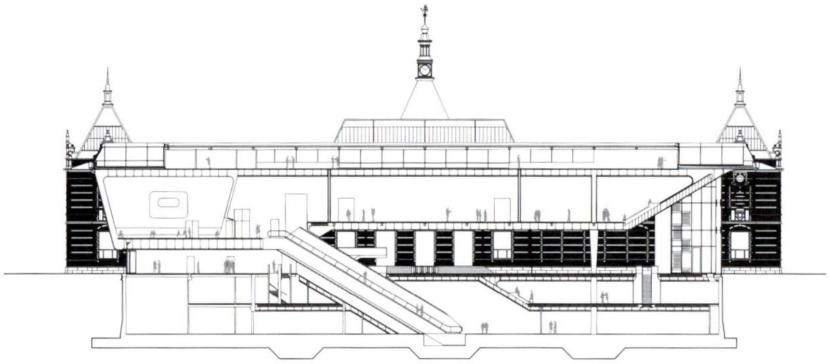

Les qualités caractéristiques de l'ancienne construction – la composition symétrique avec la cage d'escalier centrale et les galeries monumentales – ont été conservées également lors de l'extension, notamment l'éclairage par le toit. Le déplacement de l'entrée principale sur la place du musée représente la transformation la plus spectaculaire. Le nouveau bâtiment comprend outre l'entrée, le centre d'information, la boutique du musée et le restaurant. Plusieurs nouveaux espaces sont construits en souterrain dont le plus grand espace de musées d'Amsterdam avec 1 100 mètres carrés. Le volume bâti d'origine subsiste entièrement visible et sans modification au niveau des éléments architecturaux orientés vers le haut et vers le bas. Un grand toit blanc en saillie caractérise la nouvelle zone d'entrée généreuse et transparente.

Las cualidades características de la construcción original, composición simétrica con escalinata central y galerías monumentales, permanecen inalteradas en el curso de esta ampliación, al igual que la iluminación cenital. El desplazamiento del acceso principal hacia la plaza del museo constituye la mayor intervención en el conjunto. Además del propio acceso, la ampliación alberga el centro de información, la tienda del museo y el restaurante. A nivel subterráneo hay varios salones nuevos, entre ellos el mayor espacio museístico de todo Ámsterdam, de 1.100 metros cuadrados. Tanto los elementos constructivos elevados como los subterráneos preservan la esencia arquitectónica original y plenamente visible. Un gran techo blanco que sobresale marca la magnífica y transparente zona del acceso.

links: Schnitte_Eingangsbereich. rechts: Außenbau_Innenansicht_Situation.
gauche: Coupes_Zone d'entrée. droite: Vue extérieure_Vue intérieure_Situation.
izquierda: Cortes_Zona del acceso. derecha: Exterior_Vista interior_Ubicación.

STEDELIJK MUSEUM

THE NETHERLANDS_AMSTERDAM NIEUW RIJKSMUSEUM AMSTERDAM

NIEDERLANDE_PAYS-BAS_PAÍSES BAJOS
CRUZ Y ORTIZ ARQUITECTOS
2013
KUNSTMUSEUM_MUSÉE D'ART_MUSEO DE ARTE
39,000 M²
PHOTOS CRUZ Y ORTIZ ARQUITECTOS / SEVILLA (414 B. L., 415 A.), DUCCIO MALAGAMBA, BARCELONA (414 B. R., 415 B.)

Das Museum entstand im 19. Jahrhundert als Tor zwischen dem Grachtengürtel und der Stadterweiterung im Süden. Deshalb befindet sich in der Mitte des Gebäudes eine Passage, die den Bau in zwei Teile spaltet. Die Eingriffe für das Nieuwe Rijksmuseum nutzen diese Mittelachse als die natürliche Stelle eines Haupteingangs und strukturieren die alten Innenhöfe neu. Zusätzlicher Raum wird durch verschiedene externe Pavillons gewonnen. Das neue Ateliergebäude des Rijksmuseums in unmittelbarer Nähe zeigt sich mit ebenso funktionalem Programm in einem gleichermaßen funktionalen Stil. Dessen Fassade setzt sich von den umliegenden Villen einerseits ab, greift den städtebaulichen Kontext aber andererseits auf.

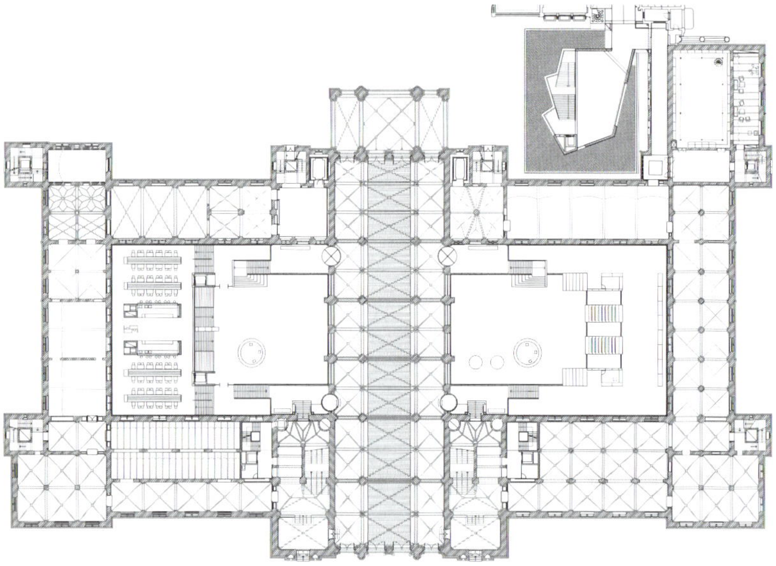

Le bâtiment du musée fut construit au XIX siècle comme une porte entre la ceinture des canaux et l'extension de la ville au Sud. Cette fonction explique la présence d'un passage situé au milieu du bâtiment. Ce passage divisant la construction en deux parties. Les interventions au niveau du Nieuwe Rijksmuseum bénéficient de cet axe central comme position naturelle pour créer une entrée principale et une nouvelle reconstruction des espaces. En outre, les différents pavillons extérieurs permettent de gagner de l'espace supplémentaire. Le nouveau bâtiment d'ateliers du Rijksmuseum se situe à proximité immédiate et se caractérise par son programme fonctionnel ainsi que son style, également fonctionnel. Sa façade se distingue certes par rapport aux villas environnantes, mais reprend néanmoins le contexte de l'environnement urbain.

El edificio del museo surgió en el siglo XIX como arcada entre el cinturón de canales y la ampliación de la ciudad al sur. Así, en el medio de los dos edificios se aprecia un pasaje que divide a la construcción en dos partes. Las intervenciones para el Nuevo Rijksmuseum aprovechan este eje central como sitio natural del acceso principal, estructurando la plaza. Se gana espacio adicional gracias a los diversos pabellones exteriores. En las cercanías, el nuevo edificio-taller del Rijksmuseum se muestra con un programa igualmente funcional, con un estilo homogéneo. Su fachada se despega de las villas circundantes, al tiempo que dialoga con el contexto urbano.

links: Grundriss_Mittelachse_Verbindung Atelierbau mit Villa, Westfassade. rechts: Bereinigter östlicher Hof_Innenansicht Atelierbau_Blick vom Atelierbau zum Altbau.
gauche: Plan_Axe médian_Jonction de l'atelier avec la villa, façade ouest. droite: Cour épurée à l'est_Vue intérieure des ateliers_Vue sur l'ancien bâtiment.
izquierda: Plano_Eje central_Vinculación con el edificio-taller, fachada oeste. derecha: Patio este renovado_Vista interior del edificio-taller_Vista desde el edificio-taller hacia la antigua construcción.

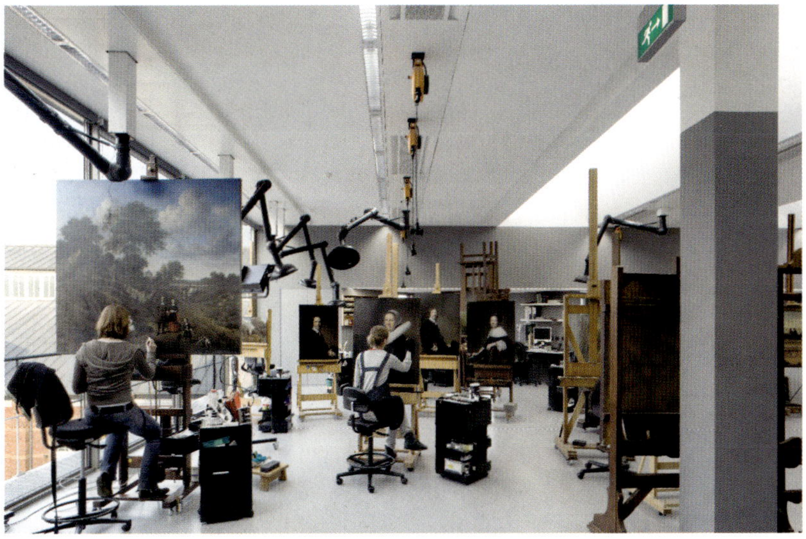

THE NETHERLANDS_APELDOORN **CODA MUSEUM**

NIEDERLANDE_PAYS-BAS_PAÍSES BAJOS
ARCHITECTUURSTUDIO HH
2004
KUNSTMUSEUM_MUSÉE D'ART_MUSEO DE ARTE
9,000 M²
PHOTOS HERMAN HERTZBERGER (416 B. L., 417 B.),
HERMAN VAN DOORN (416 B. R., 417 A.)

Das bestehende „Haus für Bildende Kunst" befindet sich in einer Art geschlossenem Hof. Die Treppe vor diesem Haus der Künste wurde in die sanft geschwungene Innenraumlandschaft des Museums einbezogen. Ohne feste Wände befindet sich der große Museumsraum zum größten Teil unter dem Hof, wo sein geschwungenes Dach als gewellter Boden erscheint. CODA – „Kultur unter Dach" – umfasst neben dem Museum die Erweiterung einer öffentlichen Bücherei, das Stadtarchiv mit einem Lesesaal, Büros, Studienräume und ein Restaurant. All diese Räume sind durch Glasfassaden nach außen gerichtet, was ihre Zugänglichkeit betont und den Blick über den Hof gestattet.

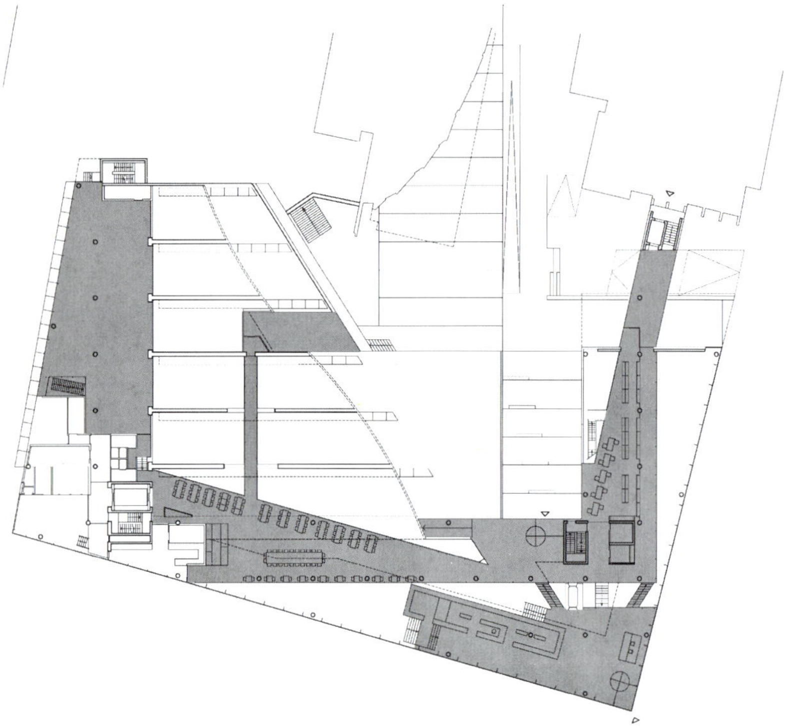

La « maison des Beaux-Arts » se situe dans d'une sorte de cour fermée. Les escaliers devant cette maison dédiée à l'art furent intégrés dans le paysage intérieur tout ondulé du musée. L'espace principal du musée, sans aucun mur fixe, se situe majoritairement sous la cour où son toit ondulé se présente de la même manière. CODA – « culture sous toit » – comprend, outre le musée, l'extension d'une librairie publique, les archives de la ville avec une salle de lecture, les bureaux, les salles d'étude et un restaurant. Tous ces espaces sont orientés vers l'extérieur grâce à des façades en verre qui soulignent l'accessibilité et offre une vue sur la cour.

La "Casa de las Artes Plásticas" existente se levanta en una especie de patio cerrado. La escalera delante de esta casa de arte fue incorporada en el paisaje interior ondulado del museo. Sin muros sólidos, el gran espacio museístico se encuentra en su mayor parte debajo del patio, donde su contorsionado techo semeja un suelo ondulado. CODA, sigla de "cultura bajo techo" en holandés, comprende además del museo la ampliación de una biblioteca pública, el archivo de la ciudad con una sala de lectura, oficinas, salas de estudio y un restaurante. Todos estos ambientes están orientados hacia fuera con fachadas acristaladas, lo que resalta su accesibilidad y permite una vista sobre el patio.

links: Grundriss_Galerie_Hof. rechts: Außenbau_Ausstellungsraum_Erschließungsbrücke.
gauche: Plan_Galerie_Cour. droite: Extérieur_Espace d'exposition_Passerelle d'accès.
izquierda: Plano_Galeria_Patio. derecha: Vista exterior_Sala de exhibiciones_Puente de conexión.

CultuurOnderDakApeldoorn

THE NETHERLANDS_ASSEN **DRENTS MUSEUM**

NIEDERLANDE_PAYS-BAS_PAÍSES BAJOS
ERICK VAN EGERAAT, FRANK HUIBERS
2011
GESCHICHTSMUSEUM_MUSÉE D'HISTOIRE_MUSEO HISTÓRICO
2,000 M²
PHOTOS VIKTOR FRETYÁN, PETER HEAVENS, JORNE JONGSMA

Der neue Eingang und die Erweiterung betten das Museum konsistent in die Struktur der Stadt ein. Aufgrund des Wechselspiels von Gebäude, Landschaft und Wasser entsteht eine neue Identität, die sowohl den malerischen Charakter als auch das historisch-kulturelle Erscheinungsbild des Stadtzentrums aufgreift. Der neue Ausstellungsflügel von 2000 Quadratmetern befindet sich gänzlich unter der Erde, und sein gestaffeltes, organisches Dach bietet einen öffentlichen Garten, der die bestehenden städtischen Parks miteinander verbindet. Das ehemalige Kutschhaus wird zum neuen Haupteingang. Die historische Fassade bleibt unverändert, aber der gesamte Baukörper wird auf einen spektakulären gläsernen Sockel erhoben, der bei Tag den Einfall natürlichen Lichts in die Ausstellung gewährleistet und bei Nacht zum Glanzpunkt der Umgestaltung wird.

La nouvelle entrée et l'extension intègrent le musée de manière cohérente à la structure de la ville. Grâce à l'interaction du bâtiment, du paysage et de l'eau, une nouvelle identité se crée qui conserve le caractère pittoresque et l'image historique et culturelle du centre-ville. La nouvelle aile d'exposition, de 2 000 mètres carrés, se situe entièrement au-dessous du niveau de la terre. Le toit étagé organiquement offre un jardin public qui relie les jardins publics existants. L'ancienne maison des cochers constitue la nouvelle entrée principale. La façade historique, qui a été préservée, et le corps du bâtiment ont été surélevés sur un socle de verre spectaculaire qui permet à la lumière naturelle de pénétrer l'espace d'exposition le jour et qui devient le point d'orgue de la transformation, la nuit.

El nuevo acceso y la ampliación constituyen un vínculo contundente del museo con la estructura urbana. En virtud del contrapunto de la edificación con el paisaje y el agua, nace una nueva identidad que abarca tanto el carácter pintoresco del centro de la ciudad como su imagen histórica y cultural. La novedosa área de exhibiciones de 2.000 metros cuadrados de superficie se encuentra totalmente bajo tierra, y su orgánico techo escalonado presenta un jardín público que vincula a otros jardines preexistentes. La antigua cochera se ha convertido en el acceso principal. La fachada histórica permanece sin cambios; no obstante, en el conjunto se encuentra elevada sobre un espectacular basamento acristalado que, durante el día, permite la penetración de luz natural en la exposición, mientras que por la noche se convierte en un objeto brillante.

links: Schnitte_Unterirdische Ausstellungshalle_Treppenhaus. rechts: Außenanlage_Neuer Eingang Jacob Cramerplein_Landschaftsgestaltung als Dächer.
gauche: Coupes_Salle d'exposition souterraine_Cage d'escalier. droite: Extérieur_Nouvelle entrée Jacob Cramerplein_Aménagement paysagiste des toits.
izquierda: Cortes_Sala de exhibiciones subterránea_Caja de la escalera. derecha: Instalaciones exteriores_Nuevo acceso sobre Jacob Cramerplein_Puentes como techos.

THE NETHERLANDS_HEERENVEEN **MUSEUM BELVÉDÈRE**

NIEDERLANDE_PAYS-BAS_PAÍSES BAJOS
INBO ARCHITECTEN DRACHTEN
2005
KUNSTMUSEUM_MUSÉE D'ART_MUSEO DE ARTE
1,310 M²
PHOTOS GER VAN DER VLUGHT, AMSTERDAM

Das Museum moderner friesischer Kunst überbrückt den großen Kanal des restaurierten klassischen Landschaftsgartens der Villa Oranjewoud. Die rechteckige Hauptform des Gebäudes passt sich in die ebene Landschaft ein, und die Fassaden mit der weitgehend geschlossenen Oberfläche aus Basaltsteinen nehmen abstrahierend auf die Landschaft Bezug. Trotz der geschlossenen Volumen besteht eine Verbindung zwischen Museum und Umgebung: in den Ausstellungsräumen subtil in Form eines gläsernen Sockels, im Museumscafé explizit, indem die Fassade am Kreuzungspunkt von Museum und Kanal wie ein Vorhang aufgezogen wird.

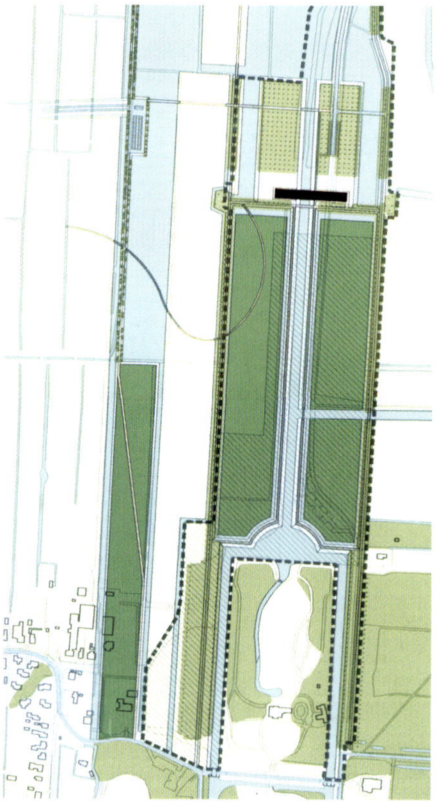

Ce musée d'art moderne orné de frises modernes surplombe le grand canal du jardin paysagiste classique de la Villa Oranjewoud, restauré récemment. La forme rectangulaire du bâtiment s'adapte à un paysage rationnel grâce à ses façades qui présentent des surfaces fermées en pierre basaltique se distinguant du paysage environnant. Ce volume fermé n'empêche pas de conserver les liens qui existent entre le musée et l'environnement : ainsi, de manière subtile, les espaces d'exposition disposent d'un socle de verre, qui sert à l'exposition des tableaux. Le café du musée se distingue par sa façade qui, tel un rideau relevé, se développe à partir du point de croisement entre le musée et le canal.

El museo de arte moderno de Frisia es un puente sobre el gran canal que surca los restaurados jardines paisajísticos de la Villa Oranjewoud. El volumen principal rectangular se adapta a un paisaje racional; las fachadas de piedra basáltica, de superficies mayormente ciegas, abstraen el paisaje. A pesar del volumen cerrado, se logra una vinculación entre el museo y el entorno: sutilmente, en las salas de exhibición con la presencia de un zócalo acristalado, que además colabora con el funcionamiento de las muestras de pintura; o explícitamente en el café del museo donde la fachada se aprecia como una cortina que se alza justo donde el museo cruza el canal.

links: Umgebungsplan_Außenaufnahme Restaurant_Basaltsteinfassade. rechts: Ausstellungsraum_Museum den „Grand Canal" querend_Zugangsbereich.
gauche: Plan de l'environnement_Restaurant vu de l'extérieur_Façade en basalte. droite: Espace d'exposition_Musée situé sur le « Grand Canal »_Zone d'accès.
izquierda: Plano con entorno_Vista exterior del restaurante_Fachada de basalto. derecha: Sala de exhibiciones_El museo cruza el "Grand Canal"_Área del acceso.

THE NETHERLANDS_NIJMEGEN **MUSEUM HET VALKHOF**

NIEDERLANDE_PAYS-BAS_PAÍSES BAJOS
UNSTUDIO
1999
KUNSTMUSEUM_MUSÉE D'ART_MUSEO DE ARTE
39,400 M²
PHOTOS CHRISTIAN RICHTERS

Zwei Bauteile bilden den Kern des Museums: das Treppenhaus und die Decke. Die Treppe ist der struktive Kern des Gebäudes und dessen Verteiler, von dem aus die verschiedenen Bereiche wie Café, Bibliothek und Museum erschlossen werden. Die Decke nimmt die gesamte technische Installation auf und verleiht dem Museum einen einheitlichen Gesamteindruck. Das Gebäude ist in Längsrichtung in parallel verlaufende Gänge mit mehreren seitlichen Öffnungen geteilt und verbindet so im bodennahen Bereich eine streng geordnete mit einer informellen Struktur. Die Decke verdeckt die zahlreichen Beleuchtungs- und Klimaanlagen sowie Leitungen, ohne sie gänzlich zu verbergen. Die Decke hat eine wellenartige Struktur, die sich den Bewegungen der Besucher entsprechend verändert.

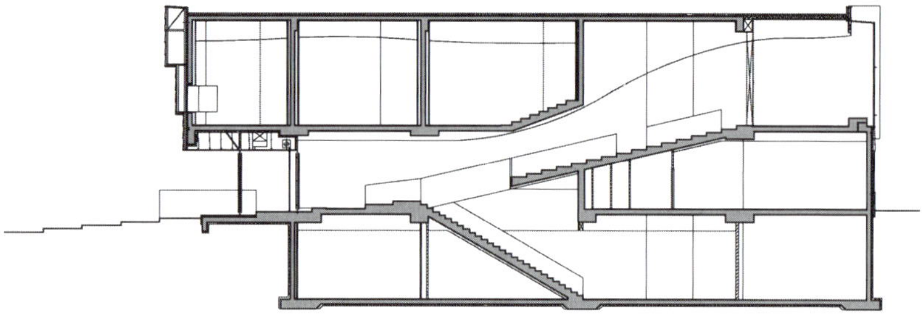

Deux éléments architecturaux forment le centre du musée: la cage d'escalier et le plafond. L'escalier est le centre structuré du bâtiment qui dessert les différentes zones, notamment, le café, la bibliothèque et l'accès au musée. Le plafond comprend l'ensemble de l'installation technique et consolide la cohérence du musée. Au niveau longitudinal, les liens sont réalisés grâce à des lignes parallèles présentant plusieurs ouvertures pour la séparation et la jonction du musée au sein d'une ligne stricte, régulière et néanmoins informelle. Le plafond couvre de nombreuses installations de climatisation, d'éclairage et de canalisations sans les cacher ou les dissimuler. Le plafond ondulé a une structure en forme de vagues qui modifie considérablement les mouvements des visiteurs présents.

Dos elementos constructivos constituyen el corazón del museo: la escalinata y el techo. La escalinata constituye el núcleo estructurador del edificio y es además su distribuidor, al que se conectan múltiples áreas como el café, la biblioteca y el museo. El techo contiene todas las instalaciones técnicas y le otorga coherencia al museo. En dirección longitudinal, en recorridos paralelos con múltiples aberturas laterales, el museo posee una estructura estrictamente regular y otra estructura informal. El techo aberga una multiplicidad de instalaciones de iluminación, climatización y conducciones, pero sin ocultarlas ni disimularlas. El techo ondulado tiene una estructura que semeja oleaje; la misma se modifica en función del movimiento de los visitantes.

links: Schnitt_Treppenhaus_Treppenstufen. rechts: Galerie_Frontfassade.
gauche: Coupe_Cage d'escalier_Escaliers. droite: Galerie_Façade frontale.
izquierda: Corte_Caja de la escalera_Escalones. derecha: Galería_Fachada principal.

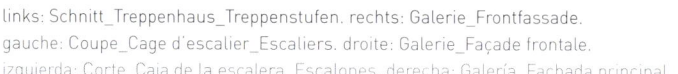

THE NETHERLANDS_ROTTERDAM

MUSEUM BOIJMANS-VAN BEUNINGEN

NIEDERLANDE_PAYS-BAS_PAÍSES BAJOS
ROBBRECHT EN DAEM ARCHITECTEN
2003
KUNSTMUSEUM_MUSÉE D'ART_MUSEO DE ARTE
4,000 M²
PHOTOS KRISTIEN DAEM

Das Museum Boijmans-Van Beuningen in Rotterdam ist ein Konglomerat aus Bauteilen verschiedener Zeiten. Der Neubau fasst diese zu einer Einheit zusammen. Grünfarbige Glasscheiben bringen einen strengen und eleganten Rhythmus in die Fassade, geben aber auch schon in der Schichtung einen Hinweis auf die Komplexität des Baus. Im Inneren überzeugt die Verbindung zwischen Adrianus van der Steurs Backsteingebäude von 1935 und dem Neubau: Altes und Neues verzahnen sich ohne jeden schroffen Übergang und verwandeln das Museum in einen kohärenten und flexiblen Bau. Eine Besonderheit des Museums ist der Bereich der kleinen Ausstellungsräume rund um den Bodon-Flügel, die den Kapellen einer Kathedrale gleichen.

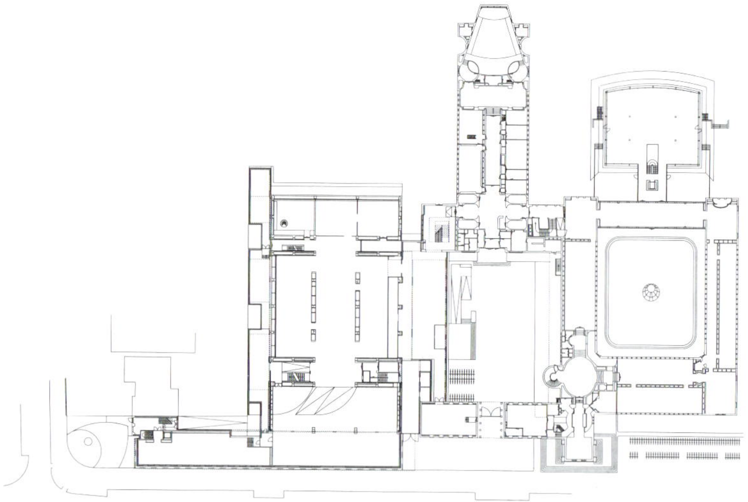

Le musée Boijmans-Van Beuningen à Rotterdam est un conglomérat d'éléments de construction de différentes époques que le nouveau bâtiment réunit. Des vitres de couleur verte apportent un rythme fort et élégant à la façade et donne également une idée sur la complexité de la construction dans sa structure. A l'intérieur, la jonction entre le bâtiment en brique d'Adrianus Van der Steur datant de 1935 et le nouveau bâtiment est séduisante: l'ancien et le nouveau s'associent étroitement sans transition brusque et transforme le musée en une construction souple et cohérente. La particularité de ce musée repose sur la zone composée de petits espaces d'exposition située autour de l'aile Bodon, comparable à la chapelle d'une cathédrale.

El Museo Boijmans-Van Beuningen de Rotterdam es un conglomerado de elementos constructivos de diversas épocas. La obra nueva los resume en una unidad. Cristales verdes aportan un ritmo riguroso y elegante a la fachada, pero también dan una noción de la complejidad de la edificación. En el interior, asombra la conexión entre el edificio de ladrillo de Adrianus van der Steur, que data de 1935, y la edificación nueva: lo nuevo y lo antiguo se conectan en una transición sin fisuras y transforman el museo en una edificación coherente y flexible. Una particularidad del museo es el área de las pequeñas salas de exhibiciones alrededor del ala Bodon, similar a las capillas de una catedral.

links: Grundriss Erdgeschoss_Glasfassade_Hauptansicht. rechts: Ausstellungshalle_Luftaufnahme Ausstellung.
gauche: Plan du rez-de-chaussée_Façade en verre_Vue principale. droite: Hall d'exposition_Prise aérienne_Exposition.
izquierda: Plano de planta baja_Fachada acristalada_Fachada principal. derecha: Sala de exhibiciones_Vista aérea_Exposición.

THE NETHERLANDS_VUGHT

NATIONAL MONUMENT KAMP VUGHT

NIEDERLANDE_PAYS-BAS_PAÍSES BAJOS
CLAUS EN KAAN ARCHITECTEN
2002
GESCHICHTSMUSEUM_MUSÉE D'HISTOIRE_MUSEO HISTÓRICO
1,830 M²
PHOTOS CHRISTIAN RICHTERS

Von dem ehemaligen Konzentrationslager Vught blieb lediglich ein kleiner Bereich mit Resten des Krematoriums erhalten. Die Fassade besteht aus langen römischen Ziegeln. Bänder dieser dünnen Terrakottaschichten wechseln vertikal mit größeren Steinen, die im Mauerverband zurücktreten, so dass der Bereich zwischen den Terrakottaziegeln mit dicken Mörtelbändern gefüllt werden konnte. Durch das Gebäude führen zwei Routen: Die eine empfängt den Besucher beim Betreten des Geländes, die andere entlässt ihn. Die Ausstellung weist eine vormoderne Raumanordnung auf: eine Raumfolge ohne verbindenden Korridor. Jeder Raum hat seine spezifische Länge, Breite und Höhe. Auch dies veranschaulicht den Unterschied zwischen Innen- und Außenwelt.

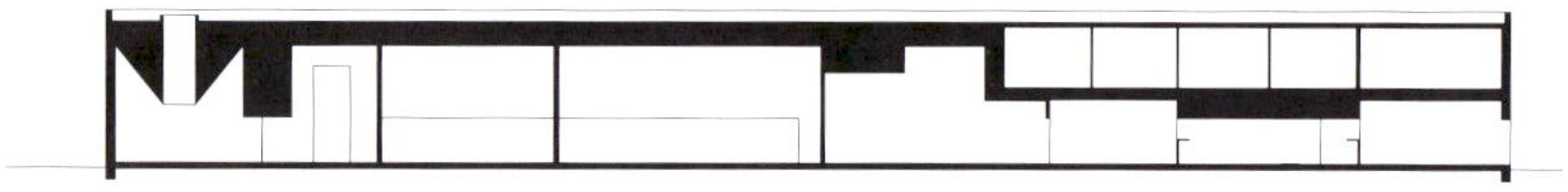

De l'ancien camp de concentration Vught subsiste uniquement une petite zone avec les restes du crématorium. La façade est revêtue en briques romaines longues. Les bandes de ces couches de terre cuite fines sont alternées verticalement à des pierres apparentes plus grosses dans le raccord du mur afin de colmater la zone entre les briques de terre cuite avec d'épaisses bandes de mortier. Deux itinéraires traversent le bâtiment : le premier accueille le visiteur à l'entrée du terrain et l'autre à la sortie. L'agencement de l'espace d'exposition pré-moderne est constitué d'une suite d'espaces sans jonction. Chaque espace a une longueur, largeur et hauteur spécifiques qui représente la différence entre le monde intérieur et extérieur.

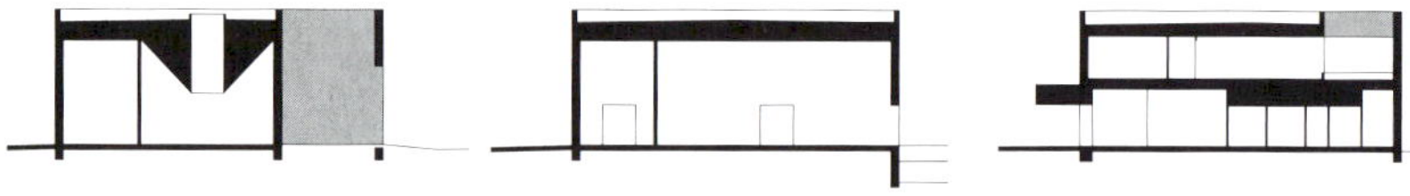

Del antiguo campo de concentración de Vught apenas quedaba una pequeña zona con restos del crematorio. La fachada estaba confeccionada en ladrillos alargados. Franjas de estas delgadas capas de terracota alternan verticalmente con otros elementos de mayores dimensiones en el aparejo de ladrillos, de modo que el hueco entre los ladrillos de terracota se podía rellenar con espesas franjas de mortero. Dos recorridos atraviesan el edificio, uno para recibir a los visitantes, el otro para despedirlos. La exhibición tiene una distribución del espacio premoderna, una secuencia de salas sin pasillo que las conecte. Cada sala tiene su longitud, anchura y altura específicas, que representan la diferencia entre el mundo interior y el exterior.

links: Schnitte_Eingang_Lichtkegel. rechts: Außenbau_Teil des Originalzaunes und Modell des Lagers vor dem Museum.
gauche: Coupes_Entrée_Coupole de lumière. droite: Extérieur_Partie de la clôture d'origine en barbelés et modèle du camp devant le musée.
izquierda: Cortes_Acceso_Cono de luz. derecha: Vista exterior_Parte del cerco original y maqueta del campo frente al museo.

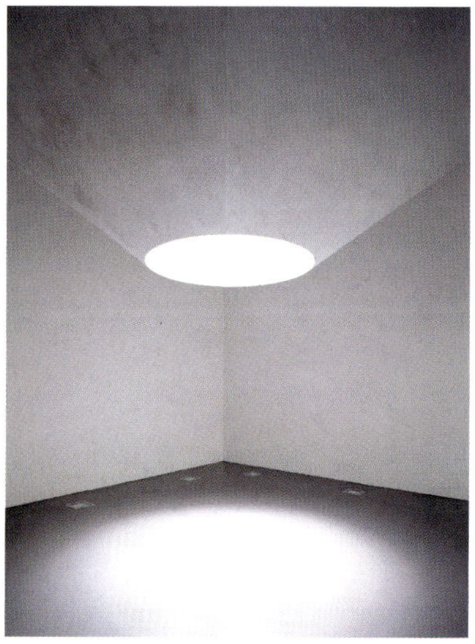

UNITED KINGDOM_CHICHESTER WEALD AND DOWNLAND OPEN AIR MUSEUM

GROSSBRITANNIEN_GRANDE-BRETAGNE_GRAN BRETAÑA
EDWARD CULLINAN ARCHITECTS
2002
KULTURMUSEUM_MUSÉE DE LA CULTURE_MUSEO DE LA CULTURA
1,200 M²
PHOTOS SIMON FENELEY, LONDON (428 B.),
EDWARD CULLINAN ARCHITECTS, LONDON (429 A.),
KEEGAN DUIGENAN, LONDON

Das Gebäude bietet weit mehr als die in der Ausschreibung geforderten Räume für Werkstatt und Lager. Die doppelt gekrümmte Form, die sich sieben Meter über dem Erdboden erhebt, entstand durch das Auslegen eines vierschichtigen Gitters aus grünen Eichenlatten auf einem Gerüst. Nach dem Entfernen der Unterstützung am Rand des Netzes wurden die Seiten herabgezogen und befestigt, so dass sich ein Gewölbe ergab. Der Gewölbescheitel wird von einem zentralen Gerüst angehoben. Der Energieaufwand zur Errichtung des Downland Gridshell lag verglichen mit anderen Bauweisen bei nur 47 Prozent, jener der Gitterstruktur verglichen mit Stahl oder Beton bei nur etwa drei Prozent.

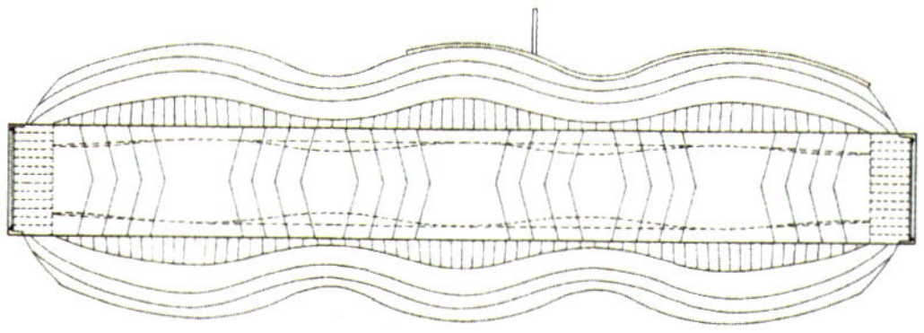

Le bâtiment a davantage à offrir que les exigences de l'appel d'offres concernant les espaces : un atelier et un entrepôt. La forme curviligne doublée d'une hauteur de sept mètres est conçue grâce à un treillis de quatre couches en lattes de chêne vertes sur l'ossature. Après le retrait des supports sur le bord de la trame, les côtés ont été abaissés et fixés afin de former une voute. La clé de voute est rehaussée par une ossature centrale. La consommation d'énergie pour la création de Downland Gridshell se situe en comparaison aux autres constructions de ce type, à uniquement 47 % et, en comparaison avec des structures de treillis en acier ou béton, à uniquement 3 % environ.

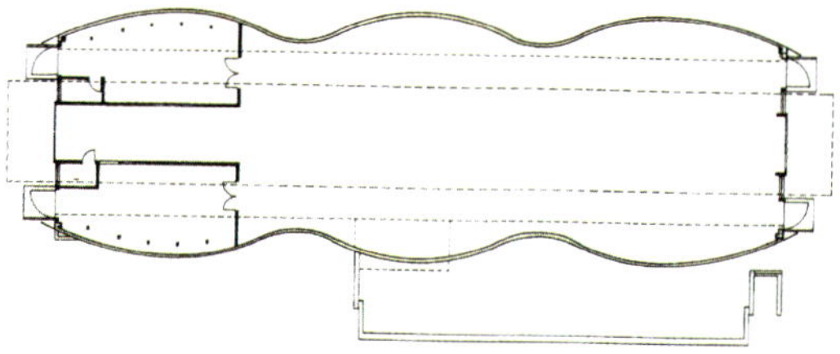

El edificio cubre un área mucho mayor que la estipulada en los pliegos de la licitación para el taller y el depósito. Se logró la forma doblemente curvada que se levanta siete metros sobre el suelo mediante la colocación de una malla de cuatro capas de listones de roble sobre un bastidor. Una vez retirado el apoyo en el borde de la malla, se tensaron y fijaron los lados y, de este modo, se obtuvo esta forma abovedada. La cumbrera de la bóveda está sostenida por un bastidor central. El consumo de energía para levantar el Dowland Gridshell, comparado con el de otros métodos constructivos, fue de un 47 por ciento; en particular, la estructura reticulada consumió apenas un 3 por ciento, si se la compara con el hormigón o el acero.

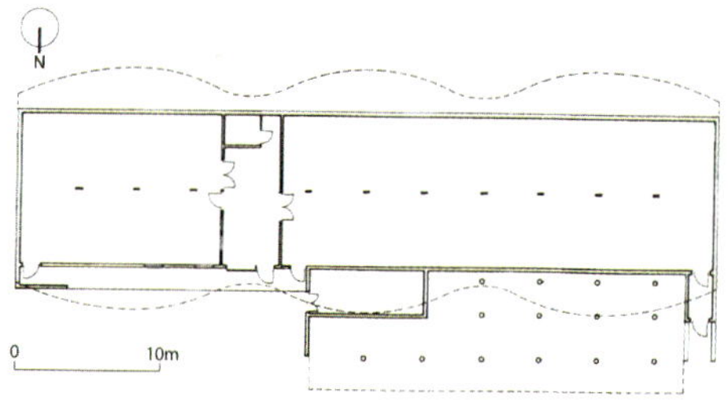

links: Pläne Dach, oberes und unteres Geschoss_Eingang_Atelier. rechts: Verkleidung_Innenraum_Detail.
gauche: Plans de toiture, étage inférieur et supérieur_Entrée_Atelier. droite: Revêtement_Espace intérieur_Détail.
izquierda: Plantas de techo, nivel superior y nivel inferior_Acceso_Taller. derecha: Recubrimiento_Espacio interior_Detalle.

UNITED KINGDOM_LONDON **DARWIN CENTRE**

GROSSBRITANNIEN_GRANDE-BRETAGNE_GRAN BRETAÑA
C. F. MØLLER ARCHITECTS
2009
NATURKUNDEMUSEUM_MUSEE DE L'HISTOIRE NATURELLE
MUSEO DE HISTORIA NATURAL
16,000 M²
PHOTOS TORBEN ESKEROD

Der Anbau an das Natural History Museum hat die Form eines riesigen Kokons aus Beton, der von einer gläsernen Vorhalle umgeben ist. Die Architektur spiegelt die Doppelrolle des Museums als Attraktion und als Wissenschaftszentrum wider. Der Kokon bildet die innere Schutzschicht, und seine Form und Größe vermitteln einen Eindruck vom Umfang der Sammlungen. Die exponierte thermische Masse der einheitlichen Stahlspritzbetonschale hält das Klima im Inneren konstant und minimiert den Energieverbrauch. Der öffentliche Zugang zum wissenschaftlichen Kern des Zentrums erfolgt in Form eines ansteigenden und den Kokon durchdringenden Besucherrundgangs, der einen Blick sowohl auf die Wissenschafts- als auch auf die Sammlungsbereiche erlaubt.

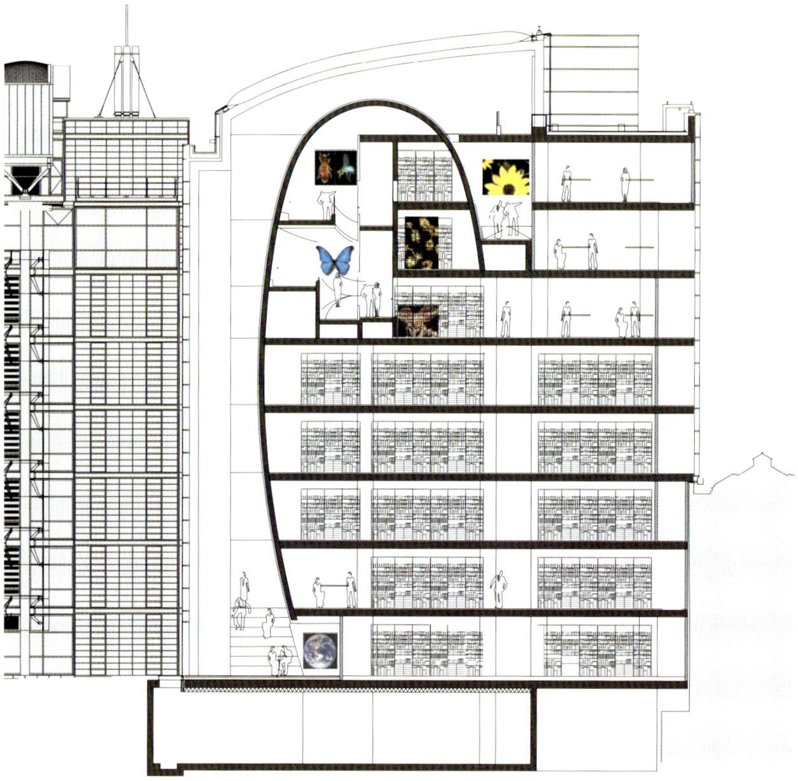

L'aménagement du musée d'histoire naturelle a la forme d'un énorme cocon en béton entouré d'un atrium en verre. L'architecture reflète le double rôle du musée en tant que site d'attractions et centre scientifique. Le cocon forme la couche de protection intérieure alliée à la forme dimensionnée respectant l'importance de la collection. La masse thermique exposée du revêtement en béton projeté / acier homogène maintient une climatisation constante à l'intérieur et minimise ainsi la consommation d'énergie. L'accès public au centre scientifique s'effectue par une galerie permettant aux visiteurs de pénétrer vers le haut dans le cocon et d'admirer du regard les zones dédiées à la recherche et à la collection.

La ampliación del Museo de Historia Natural adopta la forma de un gigantesco capullo de hormigón rodeado por un atrio acristalado. La arquitectura representa el doble papel del museo, como atracción y como centro para las ciencias. El capullo constituye la capa protectora interior; su forma y tamaño permiten apreciar el espectro de las colecciones. La masa térmica expuesta de la cáscara de acero y hormigón proyectado conserva el clima interior y minimiza el consumo energético. El acceso de público al núcleo científico del centro se realiza por una rampa para visitantes que asciende y penetra en el capullo; el mismo permite una vista de las áreas de exhibición y de la investigación.

links: Schnitt_Alt und Neu_Kokon im gläsernen Atrium. rechts: Fassade.
gauche: Coupe_Ancien et nouveau_Cocon dans son atrium en verre. droite: Façade.
izquierda: Corte_Viejo y nuevo_Capullo en el atrio acristalado. derecha: Fachada.

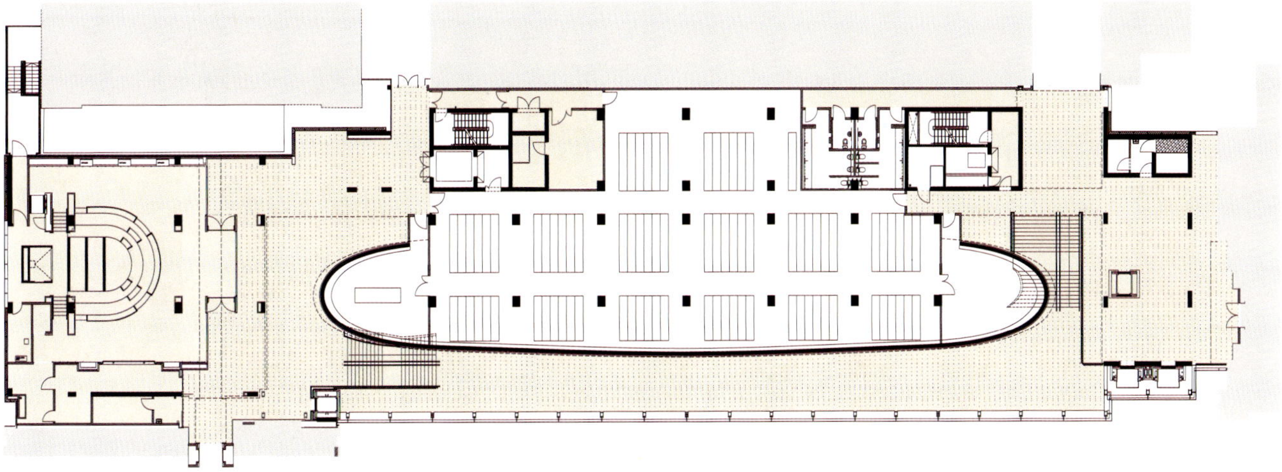

links: Atrium mit Kokon. rechts: Grundriss Hauptgeschoss_Im Kokon_Ausstellungsraum_Blick in die Laboratorien.
gauche: Atrium avec son cocon. droite: Plan de l'étage principal_Dans le cocon_Espace d'exposition_Vue dans les laboratoires.
izquierda: Atrio con capullo. derecha: Plano del piso principal_En el capullo_Sala de exhibiciones_Vista de los laboratorios.

UNITED KINGDOM_LONDON

GARDEN MUSEUM

GROSSBRITANNIEN_GRANDE-BRETAGNE_GRAN BRETAÑA
DOW JONES ARCHITECTS
2008
NATURKUNDEMUSEUM_MUSEE DE L'HISTOIRE NATURELLE
MUSEO DE HISTORIA NATURAL
700 M²
PHOTOS DAVID GRANDORGE, LONDON

Den Wettbewerb zur Umgestaltung des Garden Museums gewannen die Architekten im Oktober 2007. Die Auslobung verlangte einen neuen Raum, in dem wechselnde Ausstellungen sicher und unter kontrollierten Umweltbedingungen untergebracht werden können. Ebenso wichtig war es, einen festen Platz für die Dauerausstellung des Museums zu schaffen, da die Exponate aufgrund von Veranstaltungen bislang häufig bewegt werden mussten. Die Architekten entwickelten eine Lösung für beide Probleme. Ein Belvedere innerhalb des bestehenden Gebäudes beherbergt die neuen Galerien. Von seinem erhöhten Standpunkt aus bietet sich eine neue Aussicht auf den Altbau.

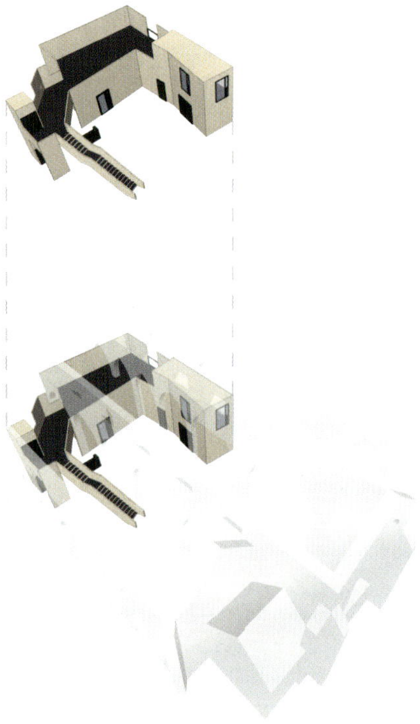

En octobre 2007, les architectes remportèrent l'appel d'offres concernant la transformation du Garden Museum. L'adjudication exigeait un nouvel espace dédié aux expositions tournantes respectant les critères de sécurité et les conditions environnementales contrôlées. L'autre priorité consistait en la création d'un espace propre pour les expositions permanentes du musée étant donné que les objets exposés devaient être fréquemment déplacées pour des manifestations. Les architectes élaborèrent une solution pour résoudre ces deux problématiques. Un belvédère au sein du bâtiment existant héberge désormais les nouvelles galeries qui offrent de son angle élevé de nouvelles perspectives sur l'ancienne construction.

En octubre de 2007 los arquitectos ganaron el concurso para realizar la reforma del Museo de Jardinería. Esta institución requería un espacio nuevo para poder albergar muestras temporarias de manera segura y bajo condiciones ambientales controladas. Todavía más importante era lograr un lugar para la exposición permanente del museo, pues a menudo era necesario mover las colecciones para hacer lugar a actividades diversas. Los arquitectos desarrollaron una solución para los dos problemas. Un belvedere dentro del edificio existente aberga las nuevas galerías; así, desde este punto elevado se logran nuevas vistas de la antigua edificación.

links: Einbau in 3D_Empfang_Unterrichtssaal. rechts: Veranstaltungsraum_Treppe_Ständige Sammlung.
gauche: Montage en 3D_Accueil_Salle d'enseignement. droite: Espace de manifestations_Escalier_Collection permanente.
izquierda: Perspectiva en 3D_Recepción_Sala lectiva. derecha: Sala para actividades_Escalera Colección permanente.

Beth Chatto
Gardens

OUR COLLECTION

UNITED KINGDOM_LONDON **BRITISH MUSEUM**

GROSSBRITANNIEN_GRANDE-BRETAGNE_GRAN BRETAÑA
FOSTER + PARTNERS
2000
KUNST- UND KULTURMUSEUM_MUSÉE D'ART ET DE CULTURE
MUSEO DE ARTE Y CULTURA
15,335 M²
PHOTOS NIGEL YOUNG / FOSTER + PARTNERS

Der Innenhof im Zentrum des British Museum war ursprünglich ein offener Garten, in den kurz nach der Fertigstellung des Museums der runde Leseraum gebaut wurde. Nachdem die British Library eine neue Heimat in St. Pancras gefunden hatte, bot sich die Gelegenheit, den Hof als neues öffentliches Zentrum des Gebäudes zurückzuerobern. Der Great Court verbindet alle umliegenden Galerien. In diesem größten geschlossenen öffentlichen Raum Europas befinden sich Informationsstände, eine Buchhandlung und ein Café. Die verglaste Überdachung verbindet Ingenieurskunst und formale Ökonomie auf höchstem Niveau. Die außergewöhnliche Geometrie des Gewölbes ist auf den unregelmäßigen Abstand zwischen der Trommel des Lesesaals und den Hoffassaden über rechteckigem Grundriss zurückzuführen.

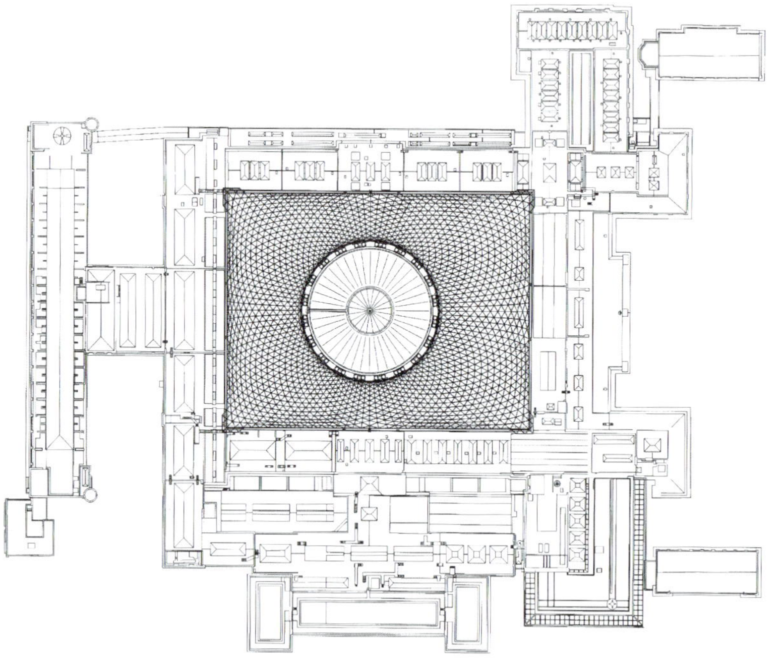

La cour intérieure au centre du British Museum était à l'origine un jardin ouvert qui a été construit peu après la réalisation finale d'une salle de lecture en rotonde. Après la relocalisation de la British Library à St. Pancras, l'opportunité s'est présentée de récupérer la cour afin de la convertir dans le bâtiment en un nouveau centre public. La Great Court relie toutes les galeries environnantes. Dans cet espace public fermé, le plus grand d'Europe, se situent des espaces d'information, une librairie et un café. La couverture en verre fait une jonction entre l'art de l'ingénierie et l'économie formelle à très haut niveau. La géométrie inhabituelle de la voute est due à l'écart irrégulier entre la rotonde de la salle de lecture et les façades de la cour au niveau du plan rectangulaire.

El patio central del Museo Británico era originalmente un jardín abierto; en el mismo se construyó la sala de lectura redonda, poco después de la inauguración. Posteriormente, la Biblioteca Británica encontró su nueva sede en St. Pancras, y se planteó la oportunidad de reconfigurar el patio como un nuevo centro del edificio. El Gran Patio conecta todas las galerías que lo circundan. En este enorme espacio cerrado, el mayor de Europa en su tipo, se encuentran puestos de información, una librería y un café. El techo acristalado combina arte de ingeniería y economía de formas al más alto nivel. Se ha logrado una inusual geometría de la bóveda mediante la separación irregular entre el tambor de la sala de lectura y las fachadas sobre el patio que conforman una planta rectangular.

links: Plan Dach_Glasgewölbe an der Rotunde. rechts: Glasgewölbe im quadratischen Hof.
gauche: Plan du toit_Voute en verre au niveau de la rotonde. droite: Voute en verre dans la cour carrée.
izquierda: Planta de techos_Bóveda de cristal en la rotonda. derecha: Bóveda de cristal en el patio cuadrado.

QUEEN ELIZABETH II AD 2000
Great Court

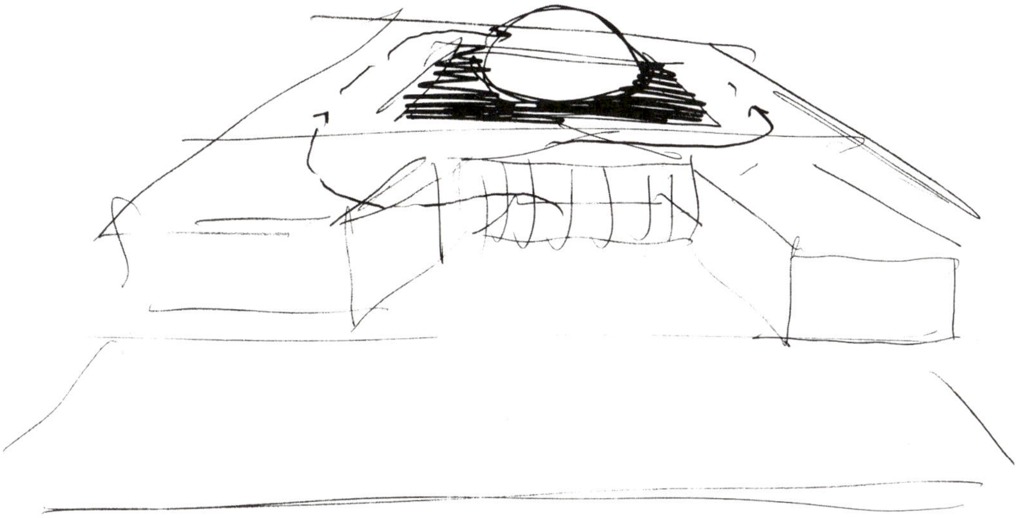

links: Glasgewölbe und Hoffassade. rechts: Skizze_Neuer Raum_Ausstellungsraum_Ausstellung.
gauche: Voute en verre et façade de la cour. droite: Esquisse_Nouvel espace_Espace d'exposition Exposition.
izquierda: Bóveda de cristal y fachada al patio. derecha: Esbozo_Nueva sala_Sala de exhibiciones_Exposición.

UNITED KINGDOM_MANCHESTER IMPERIAL WAR MUSEUM NORTH

GROSSBRITANIEN_GRANDE-BRETAGNE_GRAN BRETAÑA
STUDIO DANIEL LIBESKIND WITH LEACH RHODES WALKER
2001
GESCHICHTSMUSEUM_MUSÉE D'HISTOIRE_MUSEO HISTÓRICO
6,500 M²
PHOTOS BITTER BREDT FOTOGRAFIE, BERLIN (440, 441 B., 442, 443 L.), WEBB AVIATION, GEVELSBERG (441 A.), LEN GRANT, MANCHESTER (443 A. R.), IWMN, MANCHESTER (443 B. R.)

Das Museum erzählt, wie der Krieg das Leben der Bürger Großbritanniens und des Commonwealth seit 1914 beeinflusste. Dem Entwurf liegt das Bild eines zerbrochenen und wieder zusammengefügten Globus zugrunde. Das Gebäude setzt sich aus der Verbindung der drei Fragmente „Erde, Luft und Wasser" zusammen. In ihnen konkretisiert sich, dass die Konflikte des 20. Jahrhunderts nie abstrakt auf einem Stück Papier stattfanden, sondern von Männern und Frauen auf dem Land, im Himmel und auf dem Meer ausgefochten wurden. Die Erdscherbe umfasst den großzügigen, flexiblen Ausstellungsraum und verweist auf den weiten irdischen Bereich von Konflikt und Krieg. Der Luftsplitter bildet den dramatischen Eingang in das Museum. Die Wasserscherbe bietet eine Plattform zum Betrachten des Kanals.

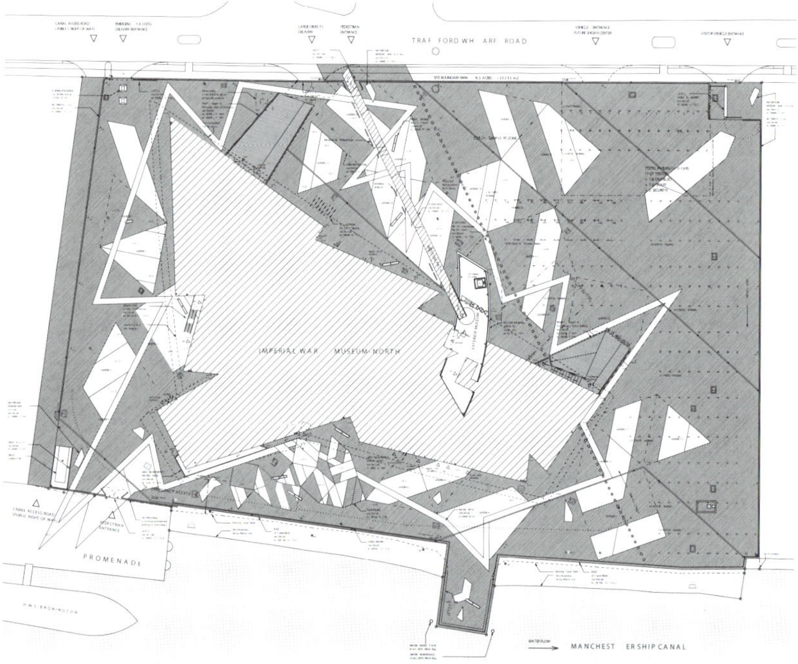

Le musée raconte l'influence de la guerre sur la vie des citoyens de Grande-Bretagne et du Commonwealth depuis 1914. La base du projet repose sur un globe détruit et réassemblé. Le bâtiment est formé en réunissant les trois fragments « terre, air et eau ». Ce site donne la preuve que les conflits du XX siècle n'existent jamais de façon abstraite uniquement sur une feuille de papier, mais qu'ils ont eu réellement lieu sur terre, au ciel et en mer contre des hommes et des femmes. La partie du bâtiment terre comprend un espace d'exposition flexible généreux reflétant la large zone terrestre de conflit et de guerre. La partie air forme l'entrée spectaculaire du musée. La partie du bâtiment maritime forme une plateforme afin de contempler le canal.

El museo ofrece un relato de cómo la guerra influyó en la vida de los ciudadanos de Gran Bretaña y la Mancomunidad de Naciones a partir de 1914. El diseño se basa en la imagen de un globo que se despedaza y después se vuelve a componer. El edificio entrelaza tres fragmentos, que representan la tierra, el aire y el agua. En ellos se concreta la idea de que los conflictos del siglo XX no sucedieron de manera abstracta sobre una hoja de papel, sino que fueron la lucha de hombres y mujeres en la tierra, el cielo y el mar. El fragmento en forma de casquete, que es la tierra, alberga la generosa y adaptable sala de exhibiciones, y remite al amplio ámbito terrestre de los conflictos y las guerras. El fragmento del aire es el acceso al museo, de efecto espectacular. El fragmento del agua forma una plataforma para observar el canal.

links: Lageplan_Ansicht von der Trafford Wharf Road_Ansicht über den Schiffskanal. rechts: Luftaufnahme_Ausstellungsraum mit Projektionen_Ausstellungssilo.
gauche: Plan de site_Vue de la Trafford Wharf Road_Vue sur le chenal. droite: Vue aérienne_Espace d'exposition avec projections_Silo d'exposition.
izquierda: Ubicación_Vista desde la Trafford Wharf Road_Vista sobre el canal de navegación. derecha: Vista del conjunto_Sala de exhibiciones con proyecciones_Salón de exhibiciones.

way out
war
mobilisation

peace?

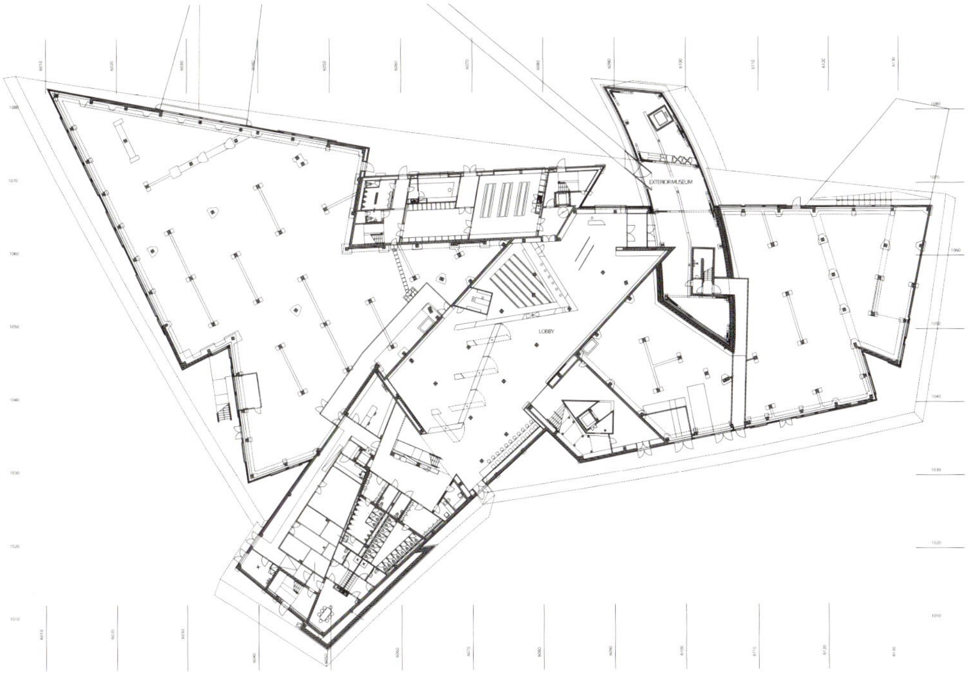

links: Blick über den Kanal. rechts: Grundriss Erdgeschoss_Eingang_Wasser-, Luft- und Erdscherbe In der Luftscherbe.
gauche: Vue sur le canal. droite: Plan du rez-de-chaussée_Entrée_Fragment terre, air et eau_Dans le fragment air.
izquierda: Vista sobre el canal. derecha: Plano de planta baja_Acceso_Fragmentos de agua, aire y tierra_En el fragmento de aire.

UNITED KINGDOM_MIDDLESBROUGH MIMA – INSTITUTE OF MODERN ART

GROSSBRITANNIEN_GRANDE-BRETAGNE_GRAN BRETAÑA
ERICK VAN EGERAAT, ROD ALLAN, ANTONIA INFANGER
2007
KUNSTMUSEUM_MUSÉE D'ART_MUSEO DE ARTE
4,000 M²
PHOTOS CHRISTIAN RICHTERS

Das MIMA ist Teil der laufenden Stadterneuerung in der Innenstadt. In Materialauswahl und Maßstab reagiert es auf das bestehende Umfeld und bindet sich in dieses ein. Ein neuer öffentlicher Platz, integraler Bestandteil des Projekts, wurde in Zusammenarbeit mit West 8 ausgearbeitet. Das gläserne Foyer, der bestimmende Raum innerhalb der Galerie, bildet einen Übergang zwischen diesem öffentlichen Platz und dem Museumsinneren. Mit einer Höhe von mehr als 16 Metern bietet es ein zentrales Treppenhaus, das durch einen abgehängten steinernen Vorhang überfangen wird. Die Wechselbeziehung zwischen Platz und Galerie wird durch die riesige transparente Fassade stimuliert, die die Besucher und Einwohner von Middlesbrough einlädt, die Galerie als Herzstück des neuen Kulturviertels anzunehmen.

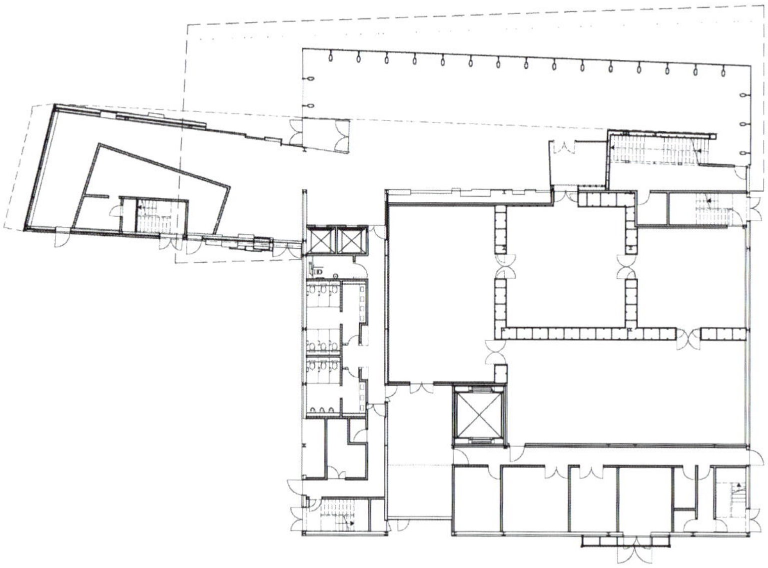

Le MIMA a été conçu dans le cadre du plan de rénovation urbaine réalisé actuellement dans le centre-ville. Le choix des matériaux et les dimensions répondent à l'environnement existant, de manière à l'intégrer. Une nouvelle place publique faisant partie intégrante du projet a été élaborée grâce à la coopération de West 8. Le foyer vitrifié qui définit l'espace dans la galerie crée une transition entre cette place publique et l'intérieur du musée. D'une hauteur supérieure à 16 mètres, il offre un escalier central surplombé par un rideau en pierre suspendu. L'interaction entre la place et la galerie est stimulée par une énorme façade transparente qui invite les visiteurs et les habitants de Middlesbrough à accueillir cette galerie comme le cœur du nouveau quartier culturel.

El MIMA constituye una parte de la renovación urbana a que se está sometiendo la ciudad. En la selección de materiales y dimensiones, este museo reacciona ante el entorno preexistente y se vincula con el mismo. Una nueva plaza pública, parte integral del proyecto, fue diseñada en colaboración con West 8. El vestíbulo acristalado, que define el espacio en la galería, configura una transición entre esa plaza pública y el interior del museo. Con una altura de más de 16 metros, ofrece una escalinata central, disimulada por una pared pétrea suspendida. La interacción entre el sitio y la galería se ve estimulada por la grandiosa fachada transparente que invita a los visitantes y habitantes de Middlesbrough a adoptar la galería como corazón del nuevo distrito cultural.

links: Grundriss Erdgeschoss_Café_Ausstellungsraum. rechts: Foyer bei Nacht.
gauche: Plan du rez-de-chaussée_Cafétéria_Espace d'exposition. droite: Foyer de nuit.
izquierda: Plano de planta baja_Café_Sala de exhibiciones. derecha: Vestíbulo por la noche.

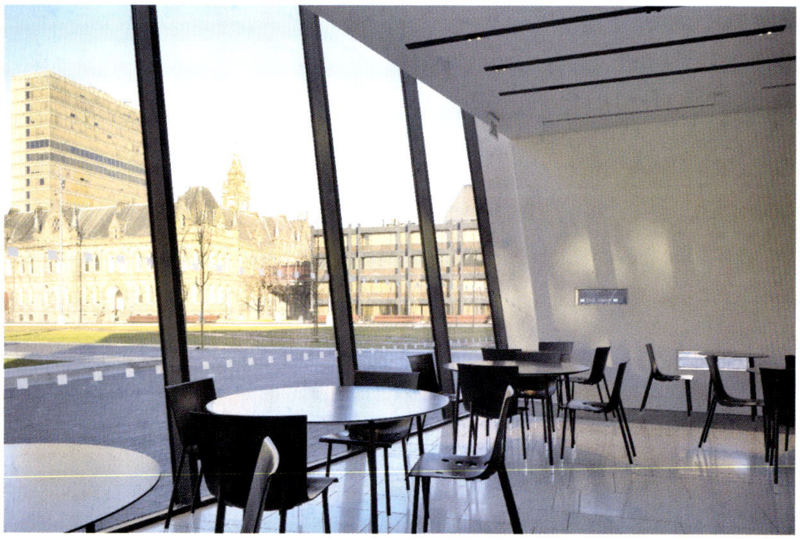

mima

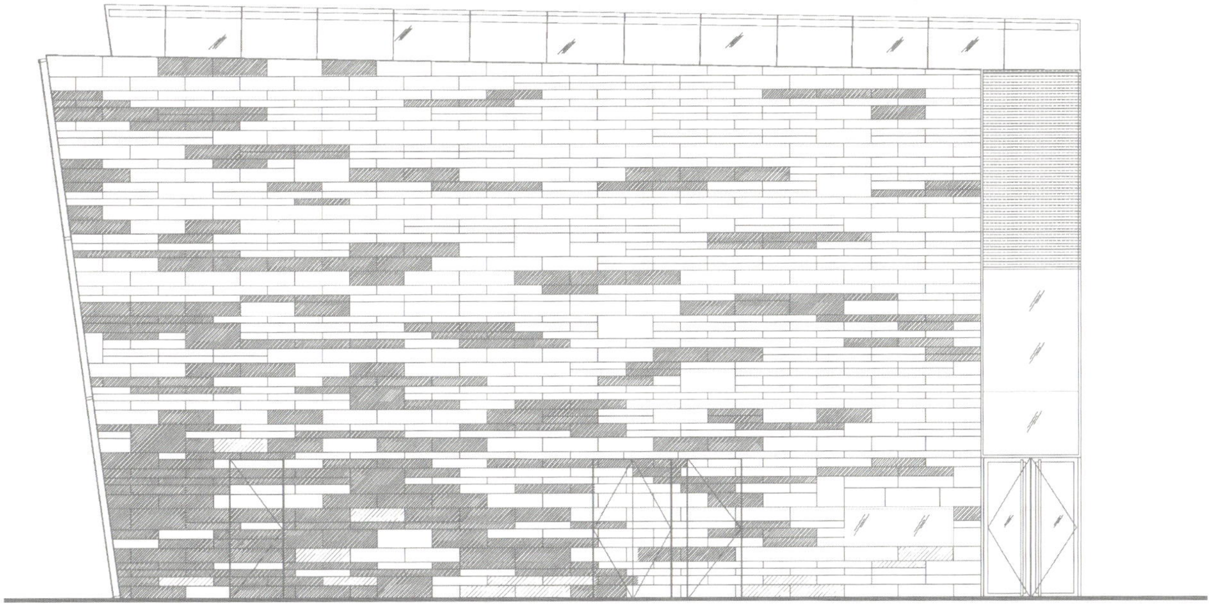

links: Fassadenstruktur. rechts: Aufriss_Treppenlauf_Abgehängte Wandscheibe.
gauche: Structure de façade. droite: Vue en élévation_Système d'escalier_Vitres murales suspendues.
izquierda: Estructura de fachada. derecha: Alzado_Escalera_Muro suspendido.

africa & australia

AND EGYPTIAN MUSEUM (GEM) _EGYPT_GIZA_MUSÉE À VOLUBILIS_MOROC-
_VOLUBILIS_CASULA POWERHOUSE_AUSTRALIA_CASULA (NSW)_ GRAND
YPTIAN MUSEUM (GEM) _EGYPT_GIZA_MUSÉE À VOLUBILIS_MOROCCO_VOL-
ILIS_CASULA POWERHOUSE_AUSTRALIA_CASULA (NSW)_ GRAND EGYPTIAN
SEUM (GEM) _EGYPT_GIZA_MUSÉE À VOLUBILIS_MOROCCO_VOLUBILIS_CA-
LA POWERHOUSE_AUSTRALIA_CASULA (NSW)_ GRAND EGYPTIAN MUSE-
(GEM) _EGYPT_GIZA_MUSÉE À VOLUBILIS_MOROCCO_VOLUBILIS_CASULA
WERHOUSE_AUSTRALIA_CASULA (NSW)_ GRAND EGYPTIAN MUSEUM (GEM
YPT_GIZA_MUSÉE À VOLUBILIS_MOROCCO_VOLUBILIS_CASULA POWER-
USE_AUSTRALIA_CASULA (NSW)_ GRAND EGYPTIAN MUSEUM (GEM) _EGYPT_
A_MUSÉE À VOLUBILIS_MOROCCO_VOLUBILIS_CASULA POWERHOUSE_AUS-
ALIA_CASULA (NSW)_ GRAND EGYPTIAN MUSEUM (GEM) _EGYPT_GIZA_MUSÉE
OLUBILIS_MOROCCO_VOLUBILIS_CASULA POWERHOUSE_AUSTRALIA_CASU-

EGYPT_GIZA **GRAND EGYPTIAN MUSEUM (GEM)**

ÄGYPTEN_EGYPTE_EGIPTO
HENEGHAN.PENG.ARCHITECTS
2014
ARCHÄOLOGIEMUSEUM_MUSÉE DE L'ARCHÉOLOGIE
MUSEO ARQUEOLÓGICO
100,000 M²
PHOTOS COURTESY OF THE ARCHITECTS

Der Siegerentwurf wird auf einem 50 Hektar großen Gelände in der Wüste zwischen den Pyramiden von Gizeh und Kairo errichtet. Er ist als Kulturzentrum mit Aktivitäten zur Ägyptologie geplant und wird zudem Konferenzräume, eine Bibliothek und Multimediaeinrichtungen umfassen. Prämisse des Entwurfs war, dass sich das Schlüsselkunstwerk – die Pyramiden – außerhalb des Gebäudes und in Sichtweite befindet. Die Hauptfassade des Grand Egyptian Museum wird aus einer lichtdurchlässigen Steinwand bestehen. Bei Tag bildet sie mit fein gebrochener und geometrisch strukturierter Oberfläche den Rand eines Plateaus. Nachts greift sie die Präzision und den Glanz der glasartigen, polierten Oberfläche des einst die Pyramiden bedeckenden Fassadensteins auf.

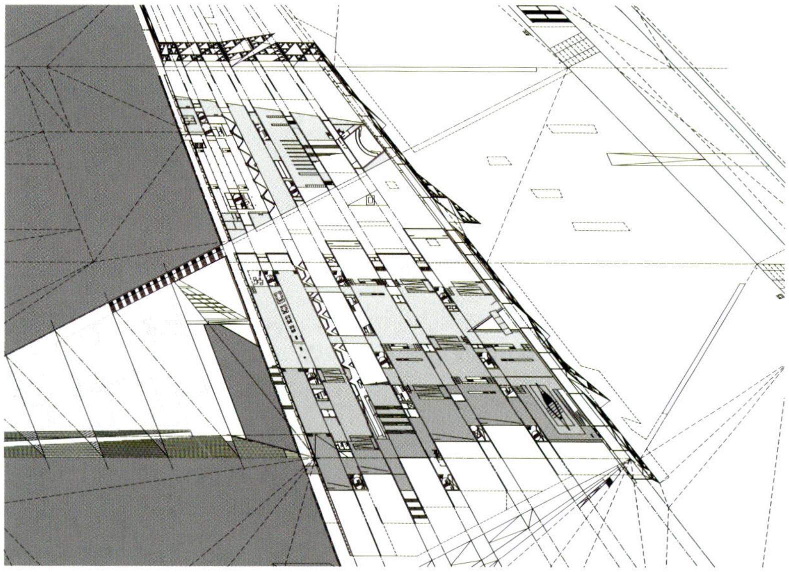

Le projet sélectionné par l'adjudication fut édifié sur un terrain de 50 hectares situé dans le désert entre les pyramides de Gizeh et le Caire. Un centre culturel est prévu avec des activités relatives à l'égyptologie qui comprend en outre des espaces de conférence, une bibliothèque et équipements multimédias. Les conditions sine qua non du projet sont de ne pas rivaliser avec les pyramides visibles au loin à l'extérieur du bâtiment. La façade principale du musée Grand Egyptian consiste en un mur de pierre translucide. Le jour, il forme le bord d'un plateau avec sa surface supérieure structurée géométrique et irrégulière. La nuit, il reprend la précision et la brillance d'une surface polie vitrifiée en pierre ayant recouvert jadis les façades des pyramides.

El proyecto ganador del concurso abarca un terreno de 50 hectáreas de extensión en el desierto entre las pirámides de Giza y la ciudad de El Cairo. Está planificado como centro cultural con actividades relativas a la egiptología, y comprende salas de conferencias, una biblioteca y equipamientos multimedia. La premisa del diseño era que las pirámides, obra de arte clave, debían estar fuera del edificio pero al alcance de la mirada. La fachada principal del Gran Museo Egipcio consta de una pared de piedra translúcida. Durante el día, con su superficie quebrada y geométricamente estructurada, configura el borde de una meseta. Pero, por la noche, evoca la precisión y el brillo de la superficie de las piedras que en otra época recubrían las pirámides, pulida como un espejo.

links: Museum als Fortsetzung der Landschaft_Transluzente Steinwand_Pyramidenfeld als Schlüssel zum Bau. rechts: Wellenförmiges Dach als Erweiterung des Wüstenplateaus_Haupttreppe_Eingangshof.
gauche: Musée en continuité du paysage_Mur en pierre transparent_Champ de pyramides comme attraction clé de la construction. droite: Toit ondulé comme extension du plateau de dunes_Escalier principal_Cour d'entrée.
izquierda: El museo como prolongación del paisaje_Muro de piedra translúcido_El emplazamiento de las pirámides es la clave de la obra. derecha: Techo ondulado que prolonga la planicie desértica Escalinata principal_Patio de acceso.

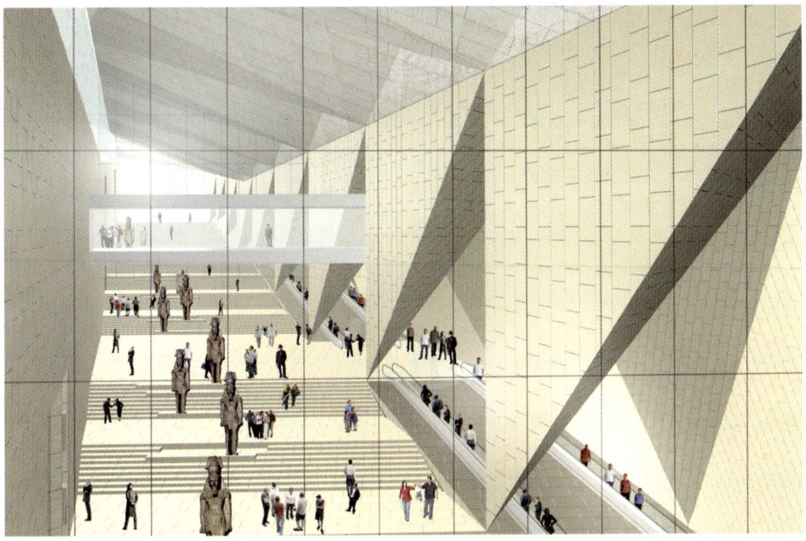

MOROCCO_VOLUBILIS **MUSÉE À VOLUBILIS**

MAROKKO_MAROC_MARRUECOS
KILO
2009
ARCHÄOLOGIEMUSEUM_MUSÉE DE L'ARCHÉOLOGIE
MUSEO ARQUEOLÓGICO
4,200 M²
PHOTOS ELIO GERMANI

Bei der Anlage handelt es sich um ein gut erhaltenes Beispiel einer antiken römischen Kolonialstadt. Das Museum ist in den Hang eingebettet, so dass es von den Besuchern zunächst nicht wahrgenommen wird. Es befindet sich auf einem schmalen Randstreifen des Areals, ist nur acht Meter tief, aber 200 Meter lang. Es besteht aus einer Reihe hölzerner Volumen, die sich entlang einer verlängerten Stützmauer aufreihen und durch die hügelige Landschaft teilweise verborgen und verdeckt werden. Das Projekt verhält sich also ähnlich wie die Ruinen, und in der Tektonik des Baus sowie der zu erwartenden Lebensdauer der verwendeten Materialien ist der künftige Zerfall bereits einkalkuliert.

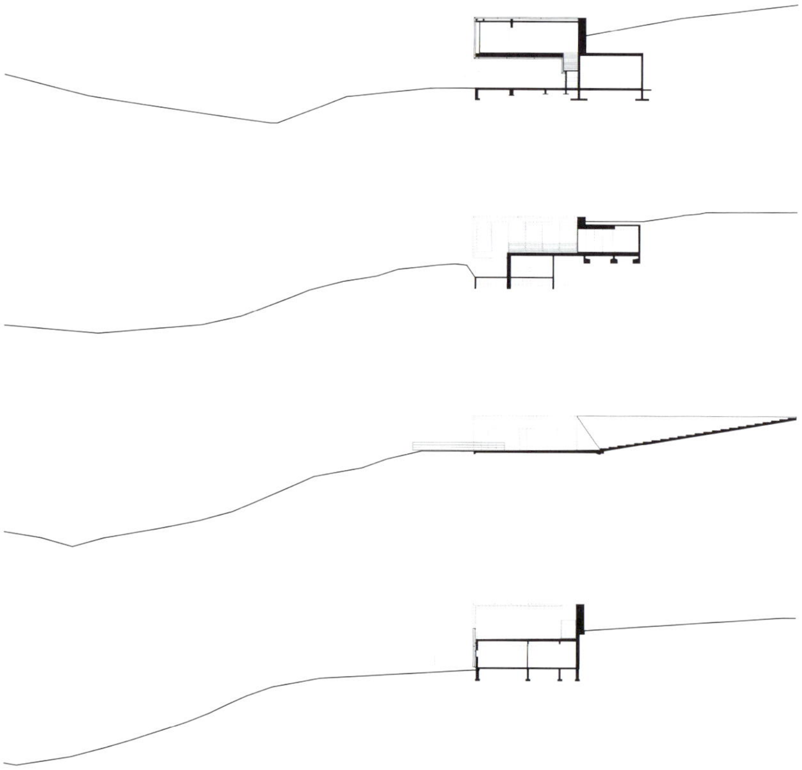

L'installation constitue un exemple bien conservé d'une ville coloniale de l'antiquité romaine. La masse du musée, invisible de prime abord par les visiteurs, est encastrée dans la pente. Le musée se trouve sur une étroite bande située en bordure du terrain et mesure uniquement huit mètres de profondeur sur deux cent mètres de longueur. Il se compose d'une série de volumes en bois alignés le long d'un mur d'appui prolongé, et camouflés, voire cachés partiellement par le paysage vallonné. Ainsi, l'évolution du projet s'assimile également à des ruines au niveau de la tectonique de la construction ainsi qu'au niveau de la durée de vie prévue des matériaux utilisés prenant déjà en calcul l'éventualité du nouveau bâtiment de tomber en ruine.

El sitio se caracteriza por tener un ejemplo de antigua colonia romana muy bien conservada. La masa del museo se inserta en la ladera, de modo que inicialmente los visitantes casi ni lo perciben. Se ubica en una franja angosta de esta superficie, de apenas ocho metros de profundidad, pero con doscientos metros de longitud. Comprende una hilera de volúmenes de madera que se alinean a lo largo de un muro de contención alargado, y que quedan en parte ocultos y disimulados por el paisaje sinuoso. Así, el proyecto se comporta de manera análoga a las ruinas. En la tectónica de la construcción, y también en la vida útil esperable para los materiales utilizados, ya se ha previsto el deterioro futuro de la construcción.

links: Schnitte_Gesamtansicht. rechts: Verbindungsgang_Zwischen den Gebäuden_Innenraum.
gauche: Coupes_Vue d'ensemble. droite: Couloir de jonction_Entre les bâtiments_Espace intérieur.
izquierda: Cortes_Vista del conjunto. derecha: Pasaje de conexión_Entre las edificaciones_Espacio interior.

AUSTRALIA_CASULA (NSW) **CASULA POWERHOUSE**

AUSTRALIEN_AUSTRALIE_AUSTRALIA
TONKIN ZULAIKHA GREER ARCHITECTS
2008
KUNSTMUSEUM_MUSÉE D'ART_MUSEO DE ARTE
2,000 M²
PHOTOS BRETT BOARDMAN, NEWTOWN

Das Casula Powerhouse vereint in einem denkmalgeschützten, stillgelegten Kraftwerk am Georges River eine große regionale Kunstgalerie mit Ateliers und Aufführungsräumen. Die Bausubstanz wurde erhalten, und neue Einrichtungen wurden in die spannenden großen Räume eingebaut. Der Hauptraum, die Turbinenhalle, ist ein Vielzweckraum für raumgreifende Aktivitäten und Ausstellungen und bietet für Aufführungen 750 Sitzplätze. Mit Sonderausstellungen und aufwendigen Ereignissen hat sich das Casula Powerhouse landesweit einen guten Ruf bezüglich Innovation und Exzellenz erworben.

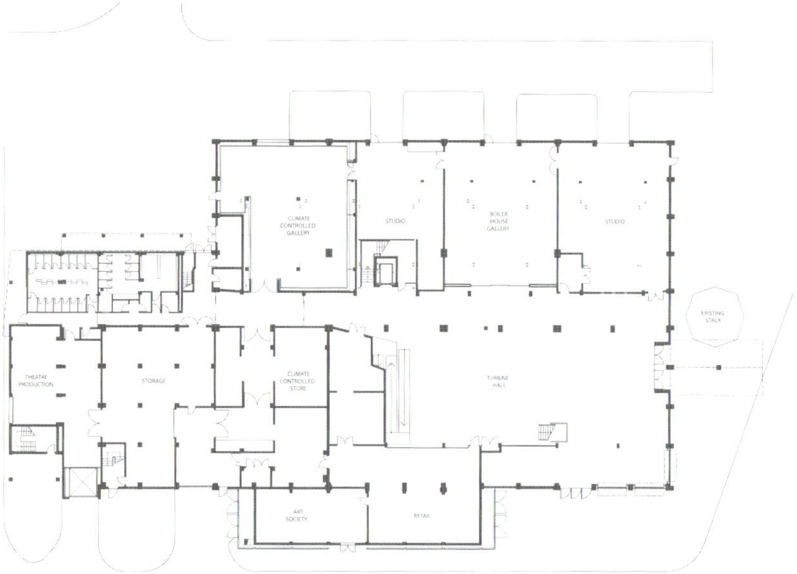

La Casula Powerhouse unit dans une centrale désaffectée, protégée patrimoine de l'humanité sur la rivière Georges, une importante galerie d'art régional dotée d'ateliers et d'espaces de manifestations. La substance bâtie fut préservée et élargie à l'intérieur par de grands espaces existant. L'espace principal, la salle des turbines, est un espace multifonctionnel pour les activités requérant de l'espace et les expositions et propose 750 places pour les manifestations. Grâce aux expositions spécialisées et aux manifestations prestigieuses, Casula Powerhouse a acquis une réputation excellente au niveau de l'innovation et de la qualité à travers le pays entier.

En su antigua usina a orillas del río Georges, actualmente protegida como monumento histórico, Casula Powerhouse aloja una gran galería de arte regional con taller y salas de actividades. Se preservó la sustancia edilicia y se hicieron ampliaciones a su generosa capacidad interior. El espacio principal, la sala de turbinas, es un salón de usos múltiples para todo tipo de exhibiciones y actividades que requieran un ambiente adecuado, y ofrece 750 butacas para espectáculos. Con exposiciones especiales y eventos variados, Casula Powerhouse se ha ganado una gran reputación regional en materia de innovación y excelencia.

links: Grundriss 1. Obergeschoss_Außenansicht_Eingang durch die Turbinenhalle_Originalfenster, darunter die Inschrift „Rollcall" von Nicole Ellis (mit den Namen aller Menschen, die im Kraftwerk gearbeitet haben). rechts: Ausstellungs- und Veranstaltungsfläche in der originalen Turbinenhalle mit einem Bodenkunstwerk von Judy Watson.
gauche: Plan du 1er étage_Extérieur_Entrée par la salle des turbines_Fenêtres d'origine, inscription au-dessous sur un «listel de noms » de Nicole Ellis (en souvenir de toutes les personnes qui ont travaillé dans la centrale). droite: Exposition et espace performance dans la salle des turbines d'origine, motif au sol par Judy Watson.
izquierda: Plano del primer piso_Exterior_Entrada por la sala de turbinas_Ventanas originales con la inscripción llamada "Lista de asistencia" por Nicole Ellis (donde se registran los nombres de las personas que trabajaron en la usina). derecha: Espacio de exposiciones y presentaciones en la sala de turbinas original, con una pintura en el piso por Judy Watson.

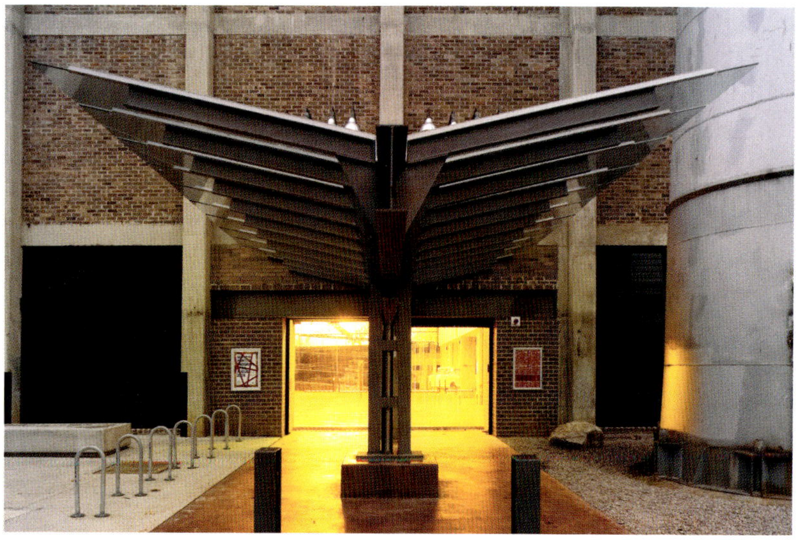

AU

FRANK OLLEY WILLIAM STANTON SYDNEY STEPHENS

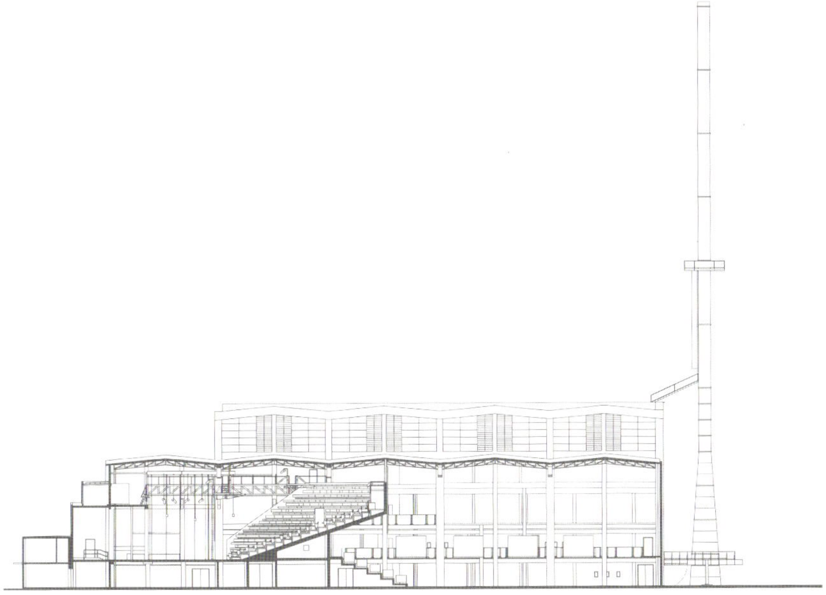

links: Detail der Wechselausstellung „Lap", von Wendy Paramor (2000). rechts: Schnitt_Außenansicht, neue Verkleidung und restaurierte Industrieziegel-Fassade_Fassade_Innenansicht Theater.
gauche: Détail d'une exposition temporaire « recouvrement », 2000 par Wendy Paramor. droite: Coupe_Extérieur montrant le nouveau revêtement entremêlé avec une façade restaurée en brique industrielle_Façade_Intérieur du théâtre.
izquierda: Detalle de una exhibición temporaria "Lap" del año 2000 por Wendy Paramor. derecha: Corte_Exterior con un nuevo revestimiento que se imbrica con la fachada industrial restaurada de ladrillo_Fachada_Interior del teatro.

asia

NE BOXES_CHINA_BEIJING_GUANGZHOU HUADU CULTURE & EXHIBI
ON CENTER_CHINA_GUANGZHOU CITY_XIXI WETLAND ART MUSEUM_CHI
A_HANGZHOU_ERDOS MUSEUM_CHINA_KANG BA SHI CITY_MARITIM MUS
M_CHINA_LINGANG NEW CITY_SHANGHAI-PUDONG MUSEUM_CHINA_SH
IGHAI-PUDONG_EXHIBITION HALL OF NEW 4TH ARMY JIANGNAN HEAD
ARTER_CHINA_SHUIXI VILLAGE_DESIGN MUSEUM HOLON_ISRAEL_HOLON
ST CENTURY MUSEUM OF CONTEMPORARY ART KANAZAWA_JAPAN
HIKAWA_ECHIGO-MATSUNOYAMA MUSEUM OF NATURAL SCIENCE_JAI
_MATSUNOYAMA_TOMIHIRO ART MUSEUM_JAPAN_MIDORI_NATIONAL ART
NTER_JAPAN_MINATO-KU, TOKYO_KANNO MUSEUM_JAPAN_SENDAI_GEN
PAPER SCULPUTURE MUSEUM_JAPAN_TAMA-SHI, TOKYO_MATSUDAI CU
RAL VILLAGE MUSEUM_JAPAN_TOKAMACHI CITY_LEEUM SAMSUNG MUS
M OF ART_KOREA_SEOUL_SEOUL NATIONAL UNIVERSITY MUSEUM_KOREA_S
L_LOUVRE ABU DHABI_UAE_SAADIYAT ISLAND NINE BOXES_CHINA_BEIJING

CHINA_BEIJING **NINE BOXES**

CHINA_CHINE_CHINA
AI WEIWEI / FAKE DESIGN
2004
KUNSTMUSEUM_MUSÉE D'ART_MUSEO DE ARTE
2,751 M²
PHOTOS AI WEIWEI

Der Architekt verwandelte neun spezielle Häuser, jedes in einem anderen und eindeutigen Stil, in Kunstgalerien und Büroflächen und entwarf diese neun Bauten auch individuell mit einer leichten Stahlkonstruktion und einer Haut aus verzinktem Stahl. Im Ergebnis bilden die „Stahlhäuser" einen harmonischen Kontrapunkt zu den grauen Steinbauten des Umfelds. Die „neun Kisten" sind in eine Gras- und Wasserlandschaft eingebettet und bilden, einer autarken kleinen Gartenstadt gleich, einen Kontrast zur wachsenden Großstadt. Die archetypischen Gebäude spiegeln sich auf der Oberfläche des Sees sowie gegenseitig auf den Stahlwänden. Kleine Durchlässe zwischen den Boxen geben Blicke auf die umgebende Landschaft frei und beziehen auch diese in das Ensemble mit ein.

Les architectes ont transformé respectivement neuf maisons spécifiques dans un style individualisé et différent pour devenir des galeries d'art et surfaces de bureaux grâce à la conception de ces neuf bâtiments individualisés, dotés d'ossatures légères en acier, toutes revêtues d'acier galvanisé. Le résultat forme les « maisons d'acier » qui contrastent harmonieusement avec les bâtiments en pierre grise de l'entourage. Les « neuf boites » sont intégrées dans un paysage verdoyant et aquatique, équivalent à une petite ville autarcique située dans un jardin et contrastant avec la grande ville tentaculaire. Les bâtiments emblématiques se reflètent sur la surface du lac ainsi que sur les panneaux en acier et semblent ainsi se multiplier mutuellement. Des petits interstices entre les boites offrent des perspectives libres sur le paysage environnant tout en se référant à l'ensemble uni.

El arquitecto transformó nueve casas específicas, todas ellas de diferentes estilos, en galerías de arte y áreas de oficinas; también le aportó diseño a cada una de estas nueve edificaciones con una construcción liviana en acero y una piel de acero galvanizado. Como resultado, las "casas de acero" constituyen un armónico contraste con las grises y opacas edificaciones del entorno. Los "nueve cajones" están incrustados en un paisaje de césped y agua y, a semejanza de una pequeña ciudad jardín, contrastan bellamente con la gran ciudad que no cesa de crecer. Los edificios arquetípicos se reflejan en la superficie del agua y también recíprocamente en los muros de acero, con lo que parecen multiplicarse. Pequeñas separaciones entre las cajas permiten vistas con perspectivas sobre el paisaje circundante y lo vinculan así con el conjunto.

links: Situation_Außenansicht mit Eingangsbereich. rechts: Zwischen den Bauten_Außenansicht mit Brunnen_Eingangsbereich Box.
gauche: Situation_Vue extérieure avec la zone d'entrée. droite: Entre les constructions_Vue extérieure avec les fontaines_Zone d'entrée de la boîte.
izquierda: Ubicación_Vista exterior con la zona del acceso. derecha: Entre las edificaciones_Vista exterior con fuente_Edificio en la zona del acceso.

艾未未 AI WEI WEI

CHINA_GUANGZHOU CITY

GUANGZHOU HUADU CULTURE & EXHIBITION CENTER

CHINA_CHINE_CHINA
ENDO SHUHEI ARCHITECT INSTITUTE
2011
KULTURMUSEUM_MUSÉE DE LA CULTURE_MUSEO DE LA CULTURA
19,500 M²
PHOTOS COURTESY OF THE ARCHITECTS

Das Grundstück im Norden von Guangzhou City neben der Bezirksregierung von Huadu und Huadu Plaza grenzt an der Ost-, West- und an der Südseite an eine Straße. Der Komplex fasst verschiedene kulturelle Einrichtungen zusammen: ein Kulturzentrum mit einem bis 500 Zuschauer fassenden Theater, ein Tagungszentrum mit digitalen Kinos, einen großen Ausstellungsbereich und den Palast der Jugend. Die Zugänge zu den Bereichen liegen unterirdisch in der Nähe der U-Bahn. Überlegungen zu den Primärfunktionen als Kultur- und Tagungszentrum sowie Ausstellungsraum führten dazu, dass im Süden des Gebäudes an der Quyingbin Ave die Hauptfassade und das Hauptvolumen geplant wurden.

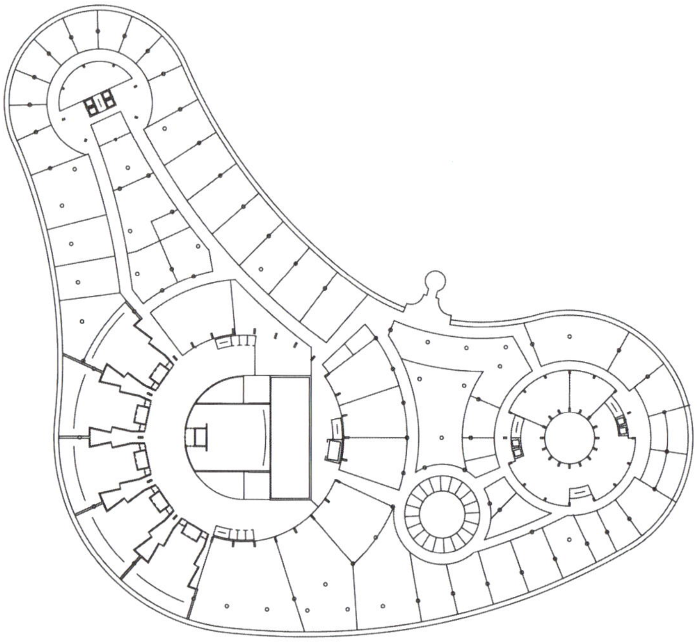

Le terrain au Nord de la ville de Guangzhou à proximité des districts de Huadu et Huadu Plaza est limitrophe à une route à l'Est, l'Ouest et au Sud. Les différentes installations culturelles plutôt complexes englobent un centre culturel doté d'un théâtre de 500 places, un centre de congrès équipé de cinémas numériques, un grand espace d'exposition et un palais de la jeunesse. L'accès aux zones se situe dans le métro sous le niveau de la terre. Les réflexions concernant les fonctions premières du centre des congrès et de la culture ainsi que de l'espace d'exposition ont abouti à la décision de planifier la façade principale et le volume central au Sud du bâtiment au bord de Quyingbin Ave.

El terreno, ubicado en el norte de la ciudad de Cantón junto al distrito de Huadu y la Huadu Plaza, limita con calles en sus lados este, oeste y sur. El complejo reúne muchas instalaciones culturales: un centro cultural con un teatro con capacidad para 500 butacas, un centro de conferencias con cines digitales, una gran área de exhibiciones y el Palacio de la Juventud. Los accesos a estas áreas son subterráneos, ubicados cerca del metro. Las consideraciones relativas a las funciones primarias de centro de conferencias y cultura y área de exhibiciones fueron decisivas en la planificación de la fachada principal y el volumen central en el sur del edificio, junto a la avenida Quyingbin.

links: Grundriss 2. Obergeschoss_Vogelperspektive. rechts: Gesamtansicht_Eingangsbereich Fassade.
gauche: Plan du 2ème étage_Perspective à vol d'oiseau. droite: Vue d'ensemble_Zone d'accès Façade.
izquierda: Plano del segundo piso_Perspectiva a vuelo de pájaro. derecha: Vista del conjunto_Zona del acceso_Fachada.

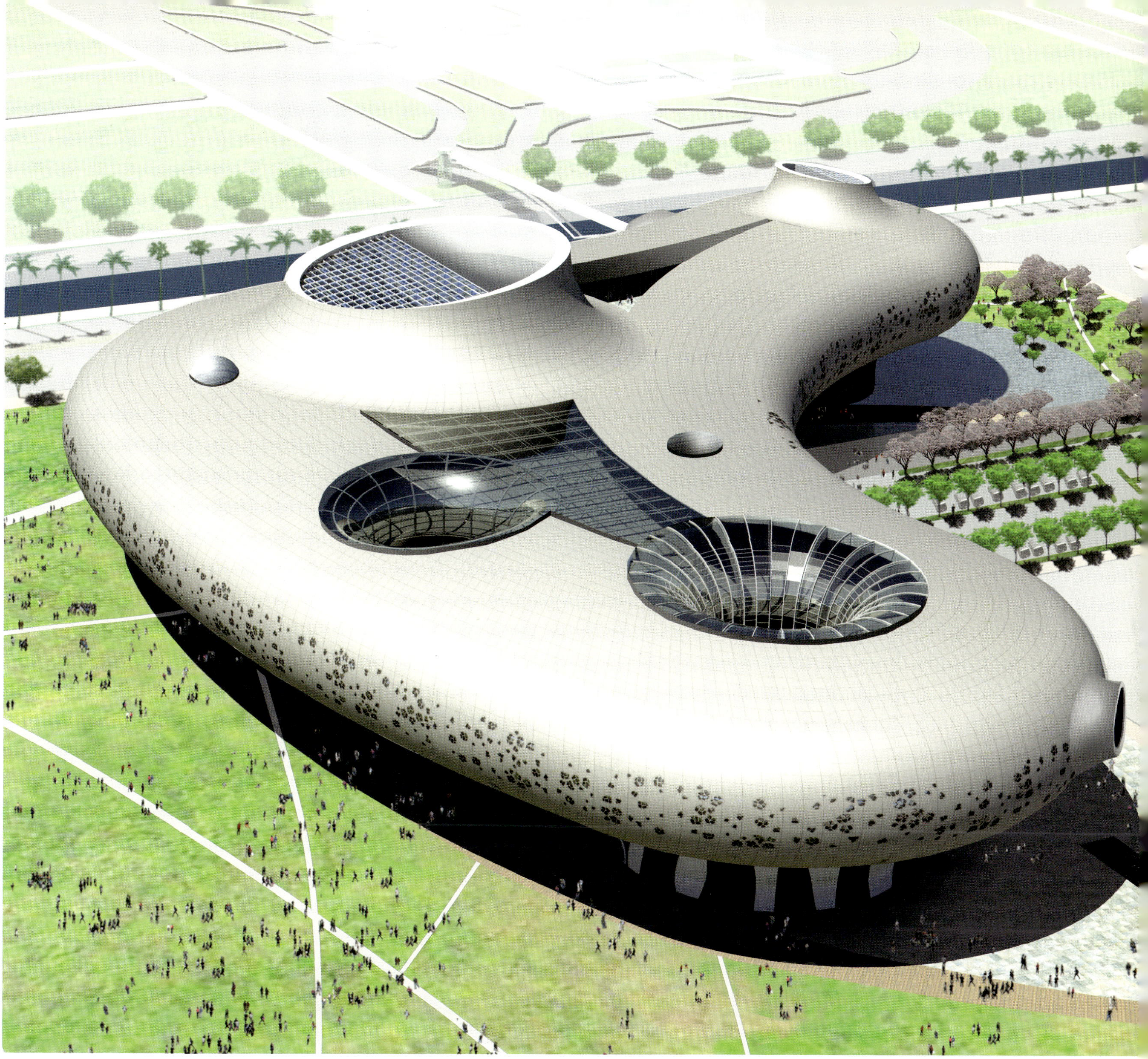

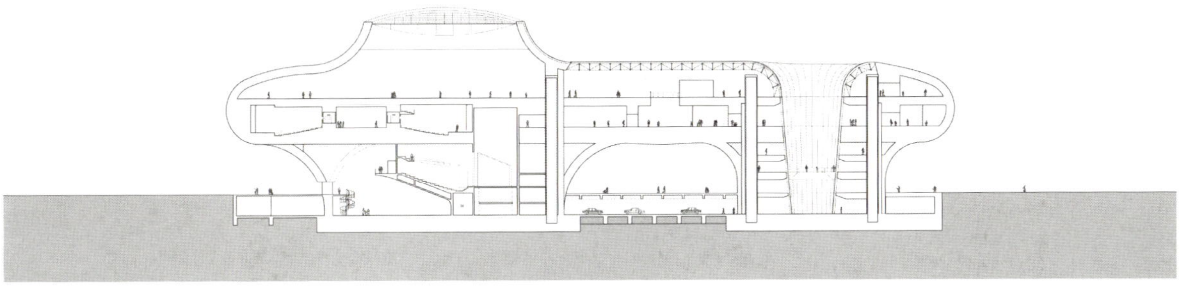

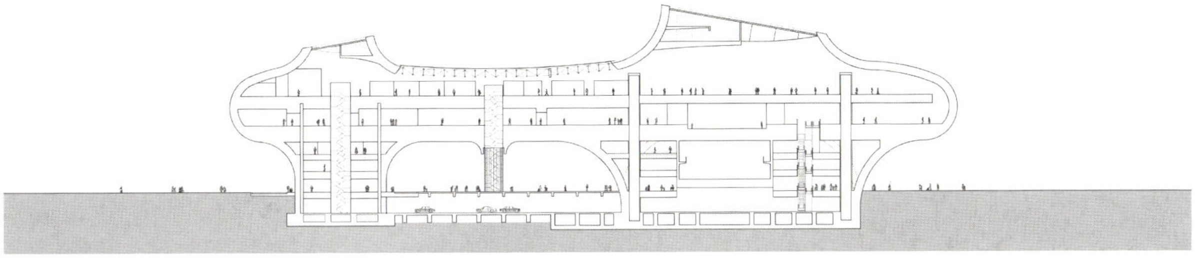

links: Hof. rechts: Schnitte_Oberlicht_Zwei Innenansichten.
gauche: Cour. droite: Coupes_Lumière du jour_Deux vues de l'intérieur.
izquierda: Patio. derecha: Cortes_Lucernario_Dos vistas del interior.

CHINA_HANGZHOU **XIXI WETLAND ART MUSEUM**

CHINA_CHINE_CHINA
STUDIO PEI-ZHU
2010
KUNSTMUSEUM_MUSÉE D'ART_MUSEO DE ARTE
5,793 M^2
PHOTOS COURTESY OF THE ARCHITECTS

Das Konzept des Baus resultiert aus der Wechselwirkung zwischen Gebäude und Natur. Wenn Blätter von Bäumen fallen, landen sie auf dem Boden. Der Entwurf sieht fünf Bauten vor, die wie Blätter auf dem Boden verstreut platziert sind. Da es nie zwei identische Blätter gibt, hat auch jedes Gebäude eine einzigartige und identifizierbare Form. Die Gebäude bleiben niedrig auf dem Boden und wölben sich zum Rand hinauf gegen den Himmel. Helle, reflektierende Zinkpaneele mit gebürsteter Oberfläche bedecken die Bauten. Fenster und Oberlichter sind einem natürlichen Fraktal entsprechend arrangiert und lassen das Sonnenlicht weich schillernd, wie durch ein Blätterdach gefiltert, eindringen.

Cette construction est conçue comme une interaction entre le bâtiment et la nature grâce à sa présentation et sa référence aux feuilles tombées. En effet, quand les feuilles tombent des arbres, elles arrivent au sol. Le projet prévoit cinq bâtiments placés comme des feuilles dispersées sur le sol. Aucune feuille ne ressemble exactement à l'autre. Par conséquent, chaque bâtiment a une forme unique et identifiable. Les bâtiments restent près du sol pour se vouter au niveau des bords vers le ciel. Des panneaux en zinc clair et réfléchissant avec une surface brossée recouvrent les bâtiments. L'arrangement des fenêtres et des ouvrants supérieurs ressemblent à une fractale naturelle qui laisse la lumière du soleil pénétrer avec une douce brillance comme filtrée à travers les couronnes des arbres.

El concepto de la obra es la relación cambiante entre la naturaleza y el edificio, cuya imagen es el reflejo de las hojas que caen de los árboles. Cuando las hojas van cayendo de los árboles, se van acumulando en el suelo. El proyecto prevé cinco edificaciones que parecen extenderse por el suelo cual hojas recién caídas. Así como nunca se encuentran dos hojas iguales, del mismo modo, cada uno de los edificios presenta una forma única e identificable. Los edificios permanecen achatados contra el suelo y se curvan en los bordes, hacia el cielo. Los edificios están recubiertos por paneles de cinc reflectantes de tonalidad clara con superficie rugosa. Las ventanas y lucernarios están dispuestos según un fractal natural y permiten que la luz solar penetre suavemente, como si las copas de los árboles la hubieran filtrado.

links: Lageplan_Außenbau_Innenraum. rechts: Foyer_Außenbau_Außenanlagen.
gauche: Plan de site_Extérieur_Espace intérieur. droite: Foyer_Extérieur_Installation extérieure.
izquierda: Ubicación_Vista exterior_Espacio interior. derecha: Vestíbulo_Vista exterior_Instalaciones exteriores.

CHINA_KANG BA SHI CITY **ERDOS MUSEUM**

CHINA_CHINE_CHINA
MAD ARCHITECTS
2010
KULTURMUSEUM_MUSÉE DE LA CULTURE_MUSEO DE LA CULTURA
41,227 M^2
PHOTOS MAD ARCHITECTS, BEIJING / FANG ZHENNING, BEIJING

Das Museum liegt im Kern des neuen Stadtzentrums, das aufgrund der boomenden Wirtschaft dutzende Kilometer vom alten entfernt entsteht. Der städtebauliche Masterplan sah auf dem zentralen Platz das inhaltlich leere Symbol einer „immer aufgehenden Sonne über dem Grasland" vor. Der Museumsentwurf entstand als Reaktion auf diesen Plan. Er hat im Gegensatz zur strengen Geometrie des Masterplans die Form eines natürlichen, unregelmäßigen Nukleus. Der Bau ist mit polierten Metalljalousien verkleidet, die die künftige Umgebung reflektieren und brechen werden. Das Innere wird von einer fortlaufenden, gekrümmten Wand geprägt und öffnet sich auf einen öffentlichen Platz, der das Museum ganz durchzieht. Das verglaste Dach und leuchtende Wände bringen Licht in diese Innenlandschaft.

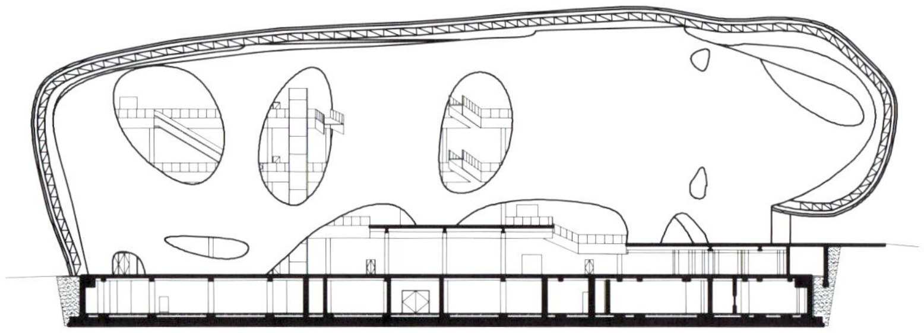

Le musée forme le cœur du nouveau centre-ville construit à des douzaines de kilomètres de l'ancien centre suite à l'essor économique de la ville. À l'origine, le plan d'urbanisme prévoyait d'ériger sur la place centrale le symbole vide de contenu d'un « lever de soleil permanent sur la prairie ». Le projet du musée fut conçu comme une réaction à ce plan. En effet, le bâtiment contraste avec la géométrie stricte du plan d'urbanisme en formant un noyau naturel irrégulier. La construction est revêtue de jalousies en métal poli destinées à refléter et à décomposer le futur paysage environnant. À l'intérieur, un mur curviligne et continu s'ouvre sur une place publique et traverse l'ensemble du musée. Le toit vitrifié et les murs brillants permettent de faire passer la lumière au sein de ce paysage intérieur.

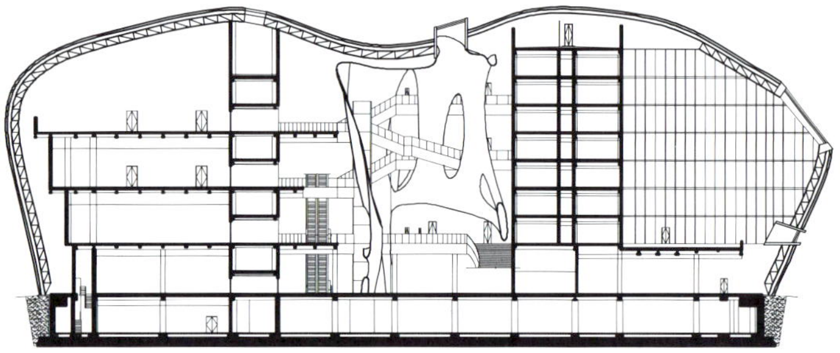

El museo constituye el corazón del nuevo centro cívico que, en virtud de una economía en plena expansión, ha surgido a docenas de kilómetros del antiguo. El plan maestro urbanístico previó en un lugar central el símbolo vacío de contenido de un "sol que siempre sale sobre la pradera". El proyecto del museo surgió como una especie de reacción a ese plan. Al contrario de la estricta geometría del plan maestro, este museo presenta la forma de un núcleo natural e irregular. La construcción está revestida con celosías de metal pulido que habrán de reflejar el futuro paisaje, disgregándolo visualmente. El interior está caracterizado por un muro continuo y curvo, y se abre sobre una plaza pública que traspasa al museo. El techo acristalado y los muros luminosos aportan una nota de luz en el paisaje interior.

links: Schnitt_Modellfotos. rechts: Innenraum_Verkleidung_Baukern.
gauche: Coupe_Photos de maquettes. droite: Espace intérieur_Revêtement_Centre du bâtiment.
izquierda: Corte_Fotos de la maqueta. derecha: Espacio interior_Recubrimiento_Núcleo edilicio.

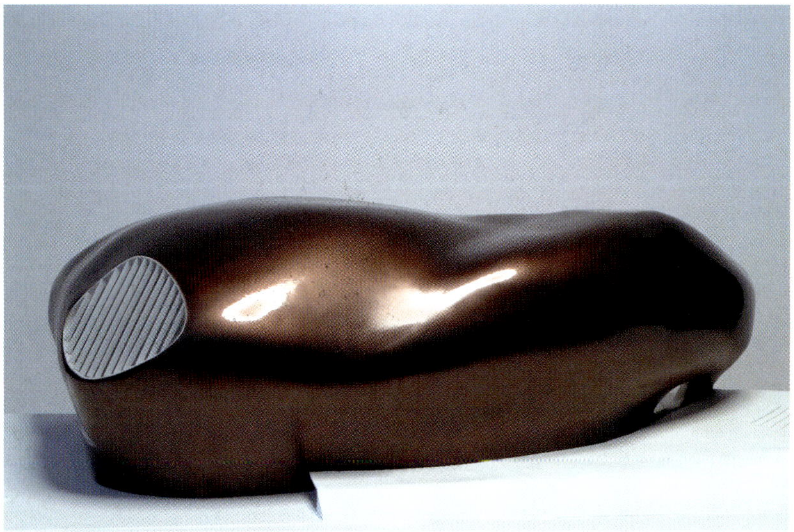

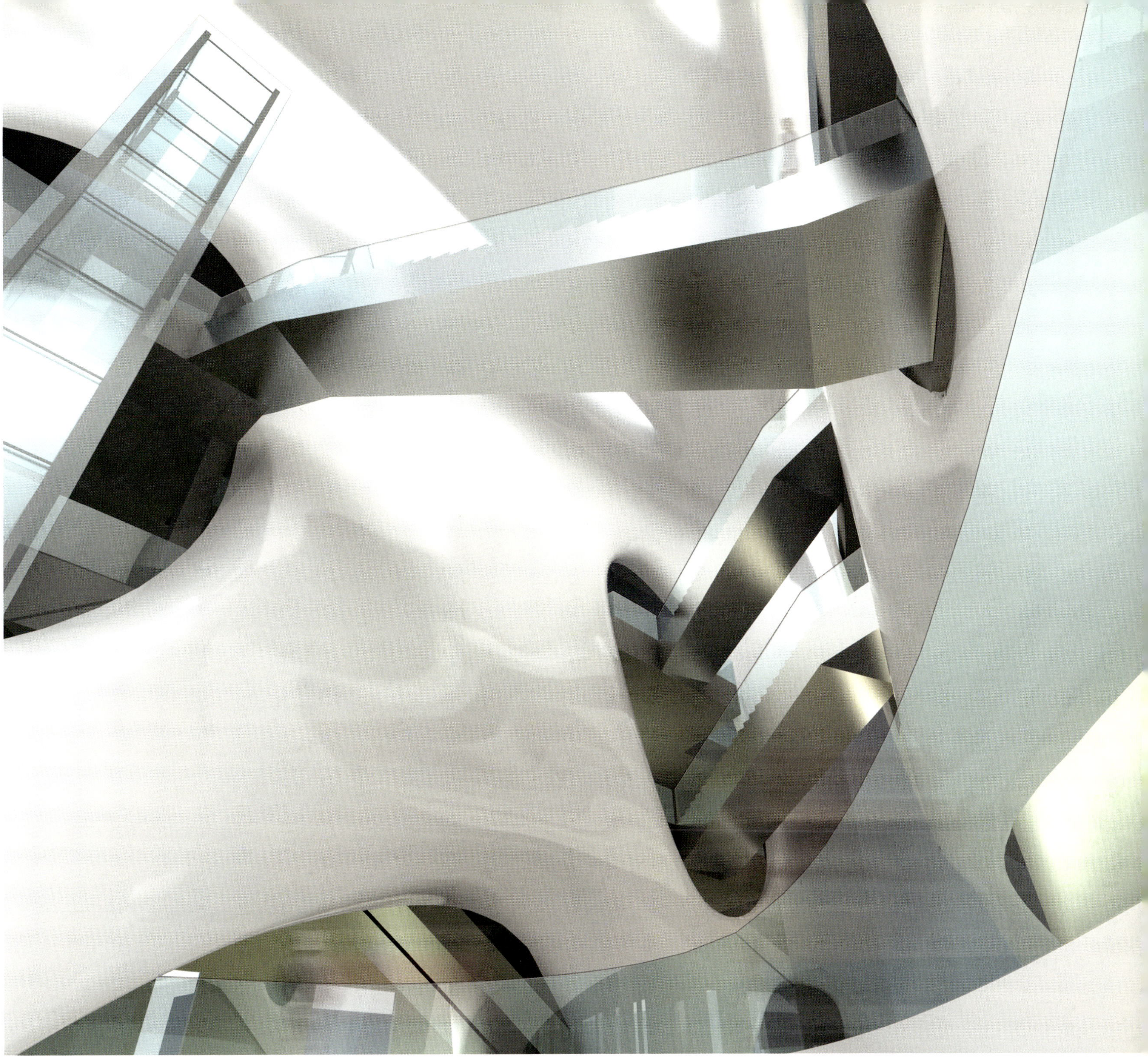

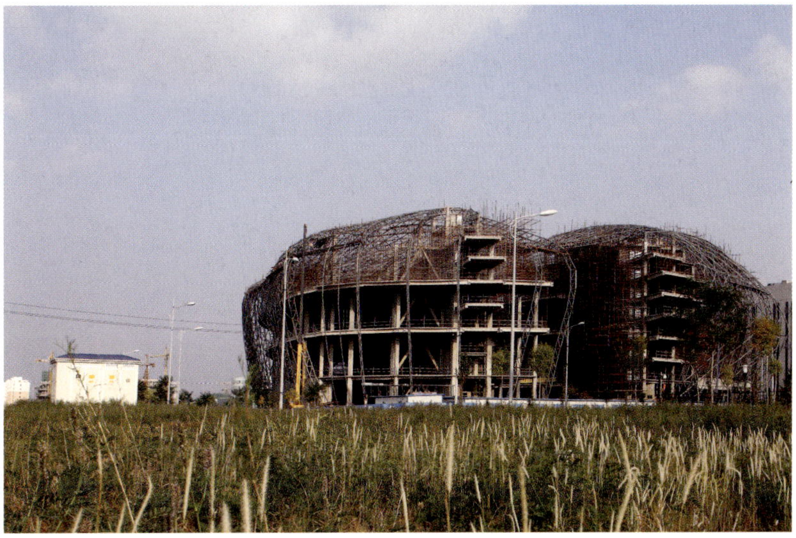

CHINA_LINGANG NEW CITY **MARITIM MUSEUM**

CHINA_CHINE_CHINA
GMP - ARCHITEKTEN VON GERKAN, MARG UND PARTNER
WITH WERNER SOBEK ENGINEER
2009
MARITIMMUSEUM_MUSÉE MARITIME_MUSEO MARÍTIMO
46,400 M^2
PHOTOS HANS GEORG ESCH (470, 471 A., B. R.),
JAN SIEFKE (471 B. L.)

Das Museum, das eine Ausstellung zu Chinas maritimer Geschichte zeigt, liegt im Zentrum von Lingang New City, einer neuen Stadt etwa 60 Kilometer südlich von Shanghai. In perfekter Symmetrie bilden zwei viergeschossige Flügel die rechtwinklige und funktionale Anlage des Museumsquartiers. Das Museum fügt sich um einen angehobenen Hof, dessen eingeschossiger Unterbau alle Funktionsräume aufnimmt. Der ikonische Bezug zu einem im Hafen liegenden Schiff wird mit der abstrakten und symbolhaften Ausbildung zweier „Segel" nahezu im Zentrum des Museumsplatzes weiter fortgeführt. Die 58 Meter hohen konkaven, sphärischen Gewölbe stützen sich gegenseitig an nur einem Berührungspunkt in rund 40 Metern Höhe.

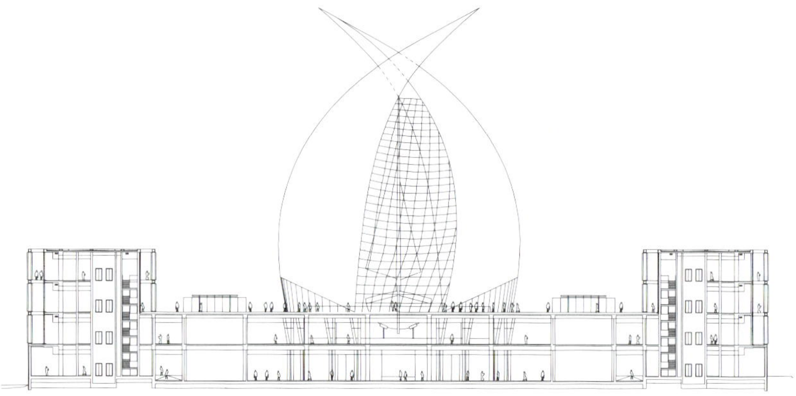

Le musée consacré à une exposition sur l'histoire maritime de la Chine se situe au centre de Lingang New City, une ville nouvelle créée à environ 60 kilomètres au sud de Shanghai. La symétrie parfaite des deux ailes à quatre étages forme la structure rectangulaire et définit la fonctionnalité du quartier des musées. Le musée s'intègre dans une cour élevée dont la fondation à un étage accueille tous les espaces fonctionnels du musée. La référence iconique à un navire appareillé au port est poursuivie grâce à la formation symbolique et abstraite des deux « voiles » quasiment situées au centre de la place du musée. La voute sphérique concave d'une hauteur de 58 mètres repose uniquement sur un point de contact à une hauteur de 40 mètres environ.

El museo exhibe una muestra sobre la historia marítima de China y se levanta en el centro de Lingang New City, una nueva ciudad ubicada a unos 60 kilómetros al sur de Shanghai. La perfecta simetría de dos alas de cuatro plantas configura una edificación rectangular y resalta la funcionalidad de las instalaciones en el barrio. El museo dispone de un patio elevado sobre una amplia construcción de una planta que alberga todas las habitaciones de servicios. La referencia icónica a un barco amarrado en el puerto se ilustra con el diseño abstracto y simbólico de dos "velas", casi en el centro de la plaza del museo. Las bóvedas esféricas cóncavas de 58 metros de altura se apoyan entre sí en tan sólo un punto de contacto a unos 40 metros de altura.

links: Gebäudequerschnitt und Ansicht mit Stahl-Alumnium-Segel_Unterstützungsträger eines Segels_Verglasung zwischen Segeln_Berührungspunkte der Schalen. rechts: Fassade Flussseite Fassade Landseite_Luftaufnahme.
gauche: Coupe longitudinale du bâtiment et vue sur la voile en acier et aluminium_Support d'une voile_Vitrage entre les voiles en béton_Point de contact des coques. droite: Façade côté fleuve_Façade côté terre_Vue aérienne.
izquierda: Corte y vista con vela de aluminio y acero_Vigas de apoyo de una vela_Acristalamiento entre velas de hormigón_Puntos de contacto de las cáscaras. derecha: Fachada sobre el río_Fachada del lado de la tierra_Vista aérea.

CHINA_SHANGHAI-PUDONG **SHANGHAI-PUDONG MUSEUM**

CHINA_CHINE_CHINA
GMP – ARCHITEKTEN VON GERKAN, MARG UND PARTNER WITH SIADR, SHANGHAI INSTITUTE OF ARCHITECTURAL DESIGN & RESEARCH CO., LTD.
2005
KULTURMUSEUM_MUSÉE DE LA CULTURE_MUSEO DE LA CULTURA
41,000 M²
PHOTOS CHRISTIAN GAHL, BERLIN

Das Shanghai-Pudong Museum ist eines der wichtigsten städtebaulichen Projekte in diesem neuen Stadtteil. Es soll die Geschichte und Entwicklung des Stadtteils umfassend dokumentieren und archivieren und umfasst moderne, multifunktionale und offene Ausstellungsflächen, auf denen dem Publikum mit einer Dauerausstellung und Wechselausstellungen ausgewählte Themen präsentiert werden. Der Gebäudekomplex besteht aus drei Teilen: einem horizontal gelagerten, im Grundriss quadratischen Glaskörper mit Ausstellungsräumen, einem breiteren, vier Meter hohen und von Treppen umgebenen Sockelbau für die Archive sowie einem Gebäuderiegel im Osten, der der Verwaltung dient.

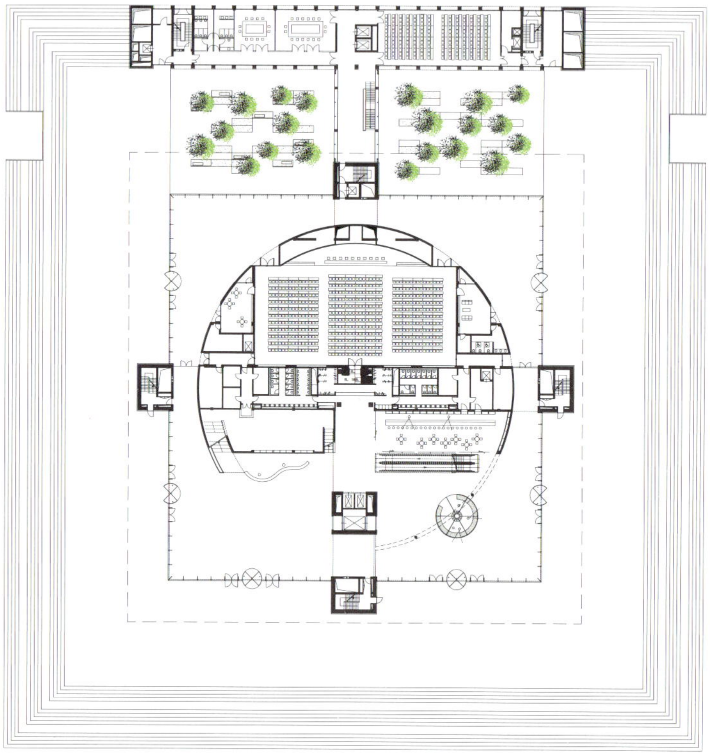

Le musée Shanghai-Pudong compte parmi les principaux projets urbanistiques dans ce nouveau quartier de la ville. En effet, l'objectif de ce musée consiste à documenter et à archiver exhaustivement l'histoire et l'évolution de ce quartier de la ville. Il comprend des surfaces d'exposition modernes, ouvertes et multifonctionnelles qui présentent au public des thématiques sélectionnées dans le cadre d'expositions permanentes et alternantes. Le bâtiment est composé de trois parties : un corps vitré carré installé en position frontale avec des espaces d'exposition, une large base de construction de quatre mètres de hauteur avec des escaliers environnants destinés à l'archivage et une aile de bâtiment à l'est prévu pour l'administration.

El Museo Shanghai-Pudong es uno de los proyectos urbanísticos más importantes de este nuevo barrio. Su finalidad es documentar la historia y el desarrollo de este barrio y abarca superficies de exhibiciones abiertas, modernas y multifuncionales; en las mismas, el público se puede deleitar con una muestra permanente y exhibiciones temporarias de temas seleccionados. El complejo edilicio consta de tres partes: un volumen vidriado de planta cuadrada con salas de exhibiciones; una construcción más ancha en forma de basamento de cuatro metros de altura circundada por escaleras, para albergar los archivos; y un edificio laminar al este, que sirve de área administrativa.

links: Eingangsebene_Komposition aus Sockel, Scheibe, Kubus_Nachtansicht. rechts: Fassade Innenaufnahme.
gauche: Niveau d'entrée_Composition du socle, vitre, cube_Vue de nuit. droite: Façade_Perspective de l'intérieur.
izquierda: Nivel de acceso_Composición de basamento, vidrio y prisma_Vista nocturna. derecha: Fachada_Vista interior.

PUDONG EXPO
上海浦东展览馆

CHINA_SHUIXI VILLAGE

EXHIBITION HALL OF NEW 4TH ARMY JIANGNAN HEADQUARTER

CHINA_CHINE_CHINA
ZHANG LEI / AZL ARCHITECTS
2007
GESCHICHTSMUSEUM_MUSÉE D'HISTOIRE_MUSEO HISTÓRICO
4,200 M^2
PHOTOS AZL ARCHITECTS / LV HENGZHONG (474, 475 A., 477),
AZL ARCHITECTS / JIA FANG (475 B., 476)

In Liyang, einer Stadt 70 Kilometer südöstlich von Nanjing, erinnert die Ausstellungshalle des Jiangnan Hauptquartiers der Neuen vierten Armee an die Geschichte der von der Kommunistischen Partei geführten Neuen vierten Armee in den 1930er Jahren. Granitbruchsteine dienen als Fassadenverkleidung der rein kubischen Volumen, was zu einem monumentalen, der Funktion entsprechenden Gesamteindruck führt. Die Fenster sind dem Mosaik der Steinplatten entsprechend verkantet eingesetzt. Der Innenhof wurde zur Außenfassade gewandelt und zeigt sich in dramatischem Rot, das auf den revolutionären Inhalt verweist.

A Liyang, une ville située à 70 kilomètres au Sud-Est de Nanjing, le hall d'exposition du quartier central Jiangnan de la nouvelle quatrième armée rappelle l'histoire de la nouvelle quatrième armée dirigée par le Parti Communiste dans les années 1930. Les fragments de granit servent à revêtir la façade du volume cubique pur en donnant une expression d'ensemble fonctionnelle de monumentalité. Les fenêtres sont intégrées aux plaques en pierre à l'instar de la mosaïque posée en décalé. La cour intérieure a été transformée comme une façade extérieure et se caractérise par sa couleur rouge marquée évoquant la structure révolutionnaire.

En Liyang, una ciudad ubicada a 70 kilómetros al sudeste de Nankín, la sala de exposiciones del cuartel general del Nuevo Cuarto Ejército de Jiangnan recuerda la historia del Nuevo Cuarto Ejército dirigido por el Partido Comunista en la década de 1930. Piedras graníticas sirven como recubrimiento de fachada del volumen cúbico puro, lo que da por resultado una impresión de conjunto de gran monumentalidad. Las ventanas se han dispuesto inclinadas, según el mosaico de las placas pétreas. El patio interno se transformó en fachada interior y se muestra en un dramático color rojo que dialoga con el contenido revolucionario del museo.

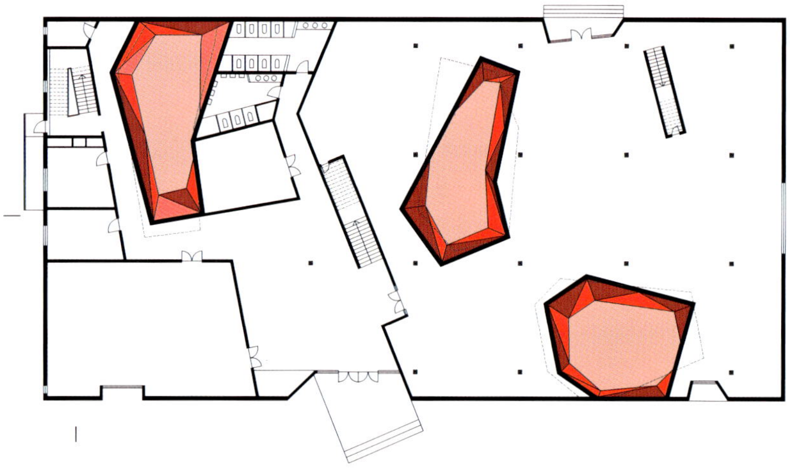

links: Grundriss Erdgeschoss_Südfassade. rechts: Neubau und altes Tor_Nordostseite.
gauche: Plan du rez-de-chaussée_Façade sud. droite: Nouveau bâtiment et porte ancienne_Côté situé au nord-est.
izquierda: Plano de planta baja_Fachada sur. derecha: Vieja puerta de acceso y edificio nuevo_Vista noroeste.

江南革命
N4A

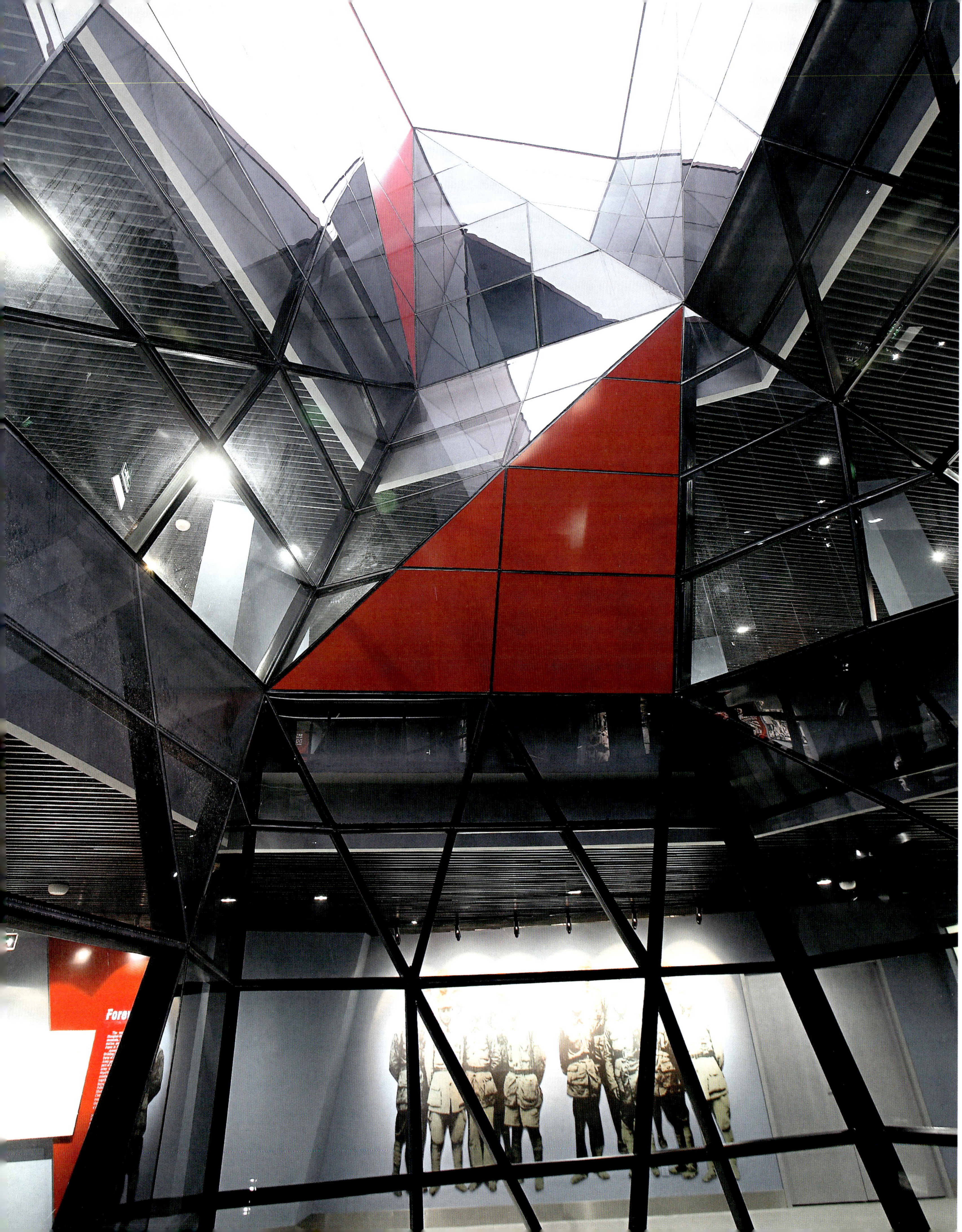

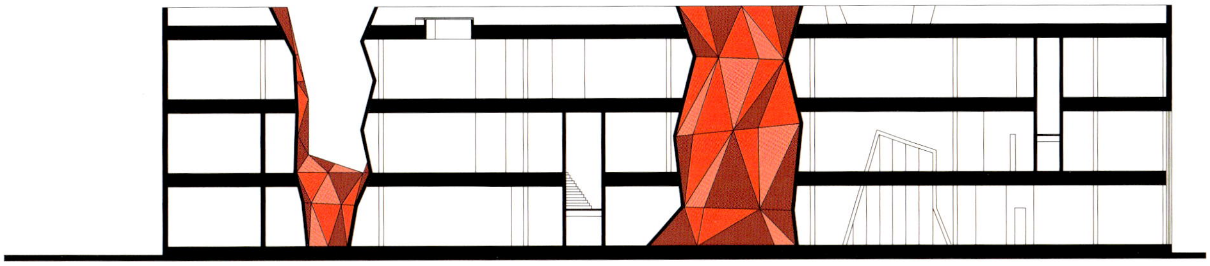

links: Glashof. rechts: Schnitt_Eingangsfassade_Ostfassade_Eingang der Nord-Ost-Seite.
gauche: Cour vitrifiée. droite: Coupe_Façade d'entrée_Façade est_Entrée du côté nord-est.
izquierda: Patio de cristal. derecha: Corte_Fachada de acceso_Fachada este_Acceso del lado nordeste.

ISRAEL_HOLON **DESIGN MUSEUM HOLON**

ISRAEL_ISRAËL_ISRAEL
RON ARAD ARCHITECTS
2010
DESIGN- UND ARCHITEKTURMUSEUM_MUSÉE DE DESIGN ET ARCHITECTURE_MUSEO DE DISEÑO Y ARQUITECTURA
4,100 M²
PHOTOS ASA BRUNO (479, 480, 481 L., B. R.), JAMES FOSTER (478 B. L.), JESSICA LAWRENCE (478 B. R., 481 A. R.)

Das DMH ist das erste nationale Museum für Gestaltung in Israel. Die von öffentlicher Hand finanzierte Anlage befindet sich in einer der größten Städte des Landes südlich von Tel Aviv, einer selbsternannten Kulturhauptstadt. Der Gebäudekomplex umfasst zwei Hauptgalerien, einen Flügel, der Ausbildungszwecken dient, sowie mehrere Außenräume, die aufgrund der klimatischen Bedingungen eine ganzjährige Nutzung erlauben. Fünf gebogene, verwitterte Cortenstahlbänder – mehr als einen Kilometer lang – bilden eine außergewöhnliche Umschließung des Museums. Sie sorgen für eine ikonische Präsenz im urbanen Kontext, bieten gewagt strukturelle Unterstützung und fungieren sowohl als Sonnenschutz als auch als optischer Leitfaden durch das Museum.

Le DMH est le premier musée national dédié au design en Israël. Le site financé par le secteur public se situe dans l'une des principales villes du pays au Sud de Tel Aviv qui se désigne comme une capitale de la culture. Il comprend deux galeries principales et une aile dédiée à la formation ainsi que plusieurs espaces extérieurs adaptés à une utilisation annuelle en raison des conditions climatiques. Cinq bandes en acier corten confusément pliées de plus d'un kilomètre de longueur forment un complexe de musée inhabituel. Elles soulignent le caractère imagé dans un contexte urbain en offrant un soutien structurel osé et une protection contre le rayonnement du soleil ainsi qu'un fil d'Ariane au service du musée.

El DMH es el primer museo israelí dedicado al diseño. Con ayuda financiera estatal, las instalaciones se levantaron en una de las mayores ciudades del país, ubicada al sur de Tel Aviv; esta ciudad es considerada una capital cultural. Incluye dos galerías principales, un ala que sirve para fines didácticos, y varios espacios exteriores que se pueden utilizar durante todo el año gracias a las condiciones climáticas. Cinco cintas curvadas de acero cortén de aspecto corroído, de más de un kilómetro de longitud, constituyen el inesperado envoltorio del museo. Sirven para dar una nota de plasticidad en el contexto urbano, ofrecen un apoyo estructural atrevido y, además, sirven al mismo tiempo de protección solar y de hilo conductor visual por todo el museo.

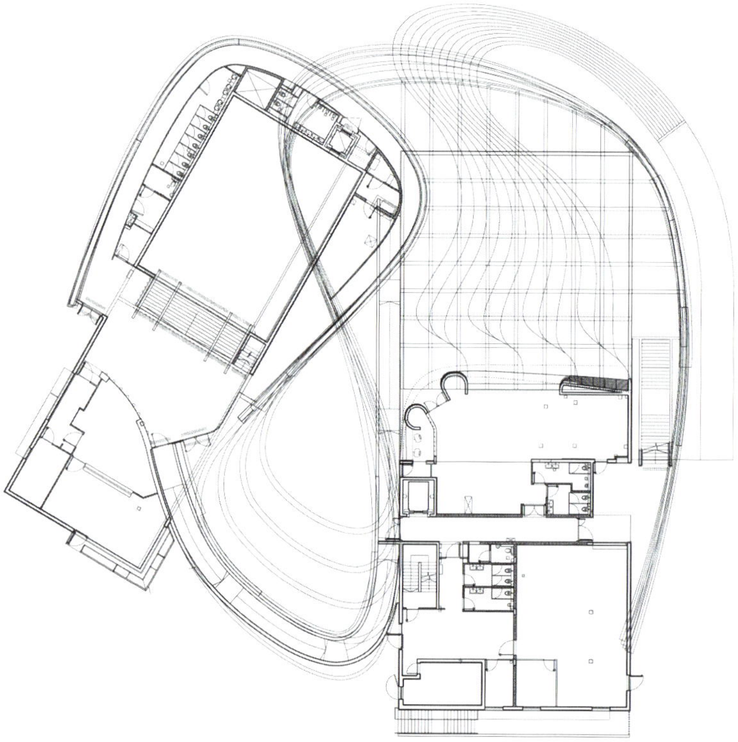

links: Grundriss_Eingangsbereich_Treppen und Bänder. rechts: Luftschlaufe und Fassade.
gauche: Plan_Zone d'entrée_Escalier et bandes. droite: Boucles aérées et façade.
izquierda: Plano de planta_Zona del acceso_Escaleras y cintas. derecha: Lazos en el aire y fachada.

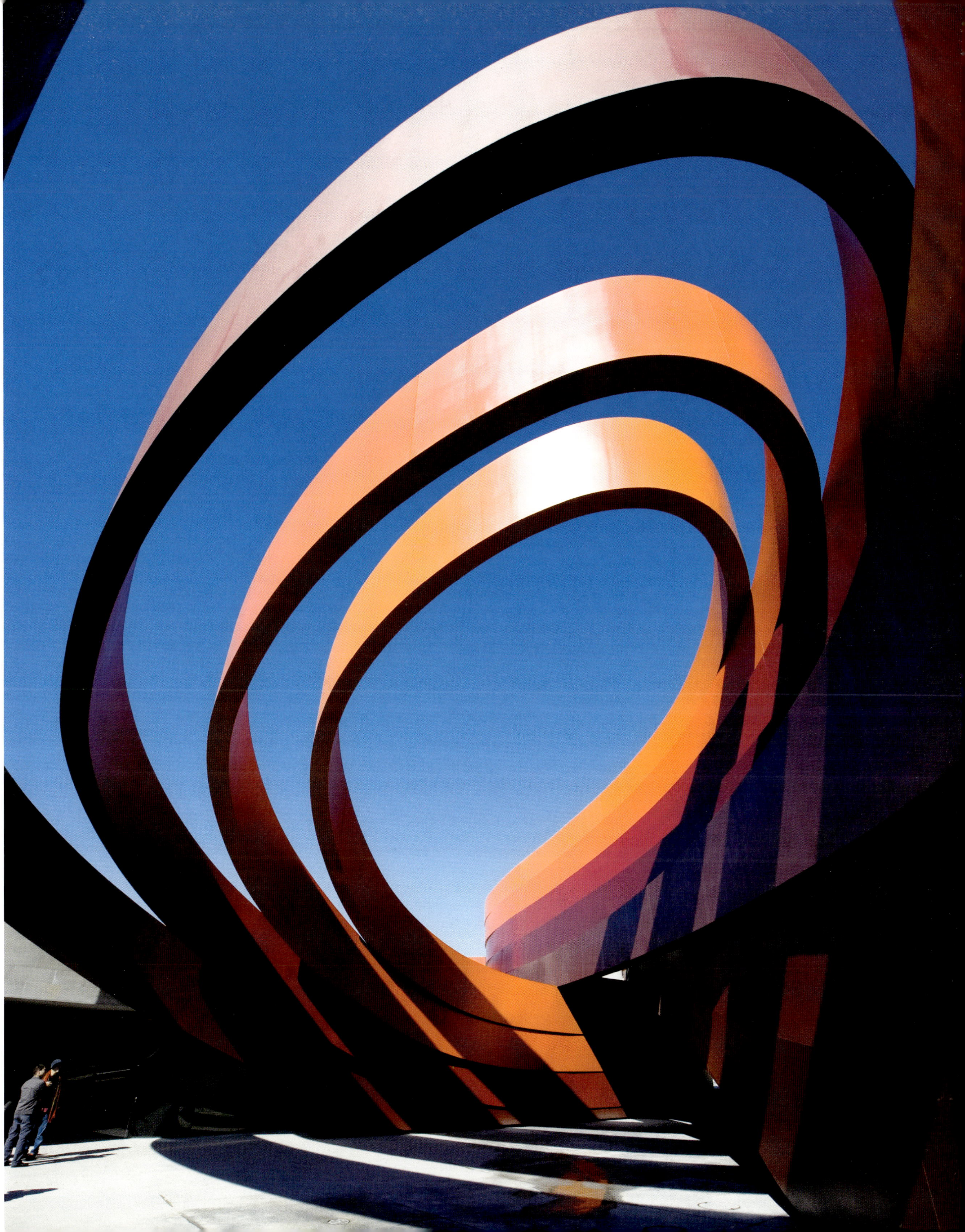

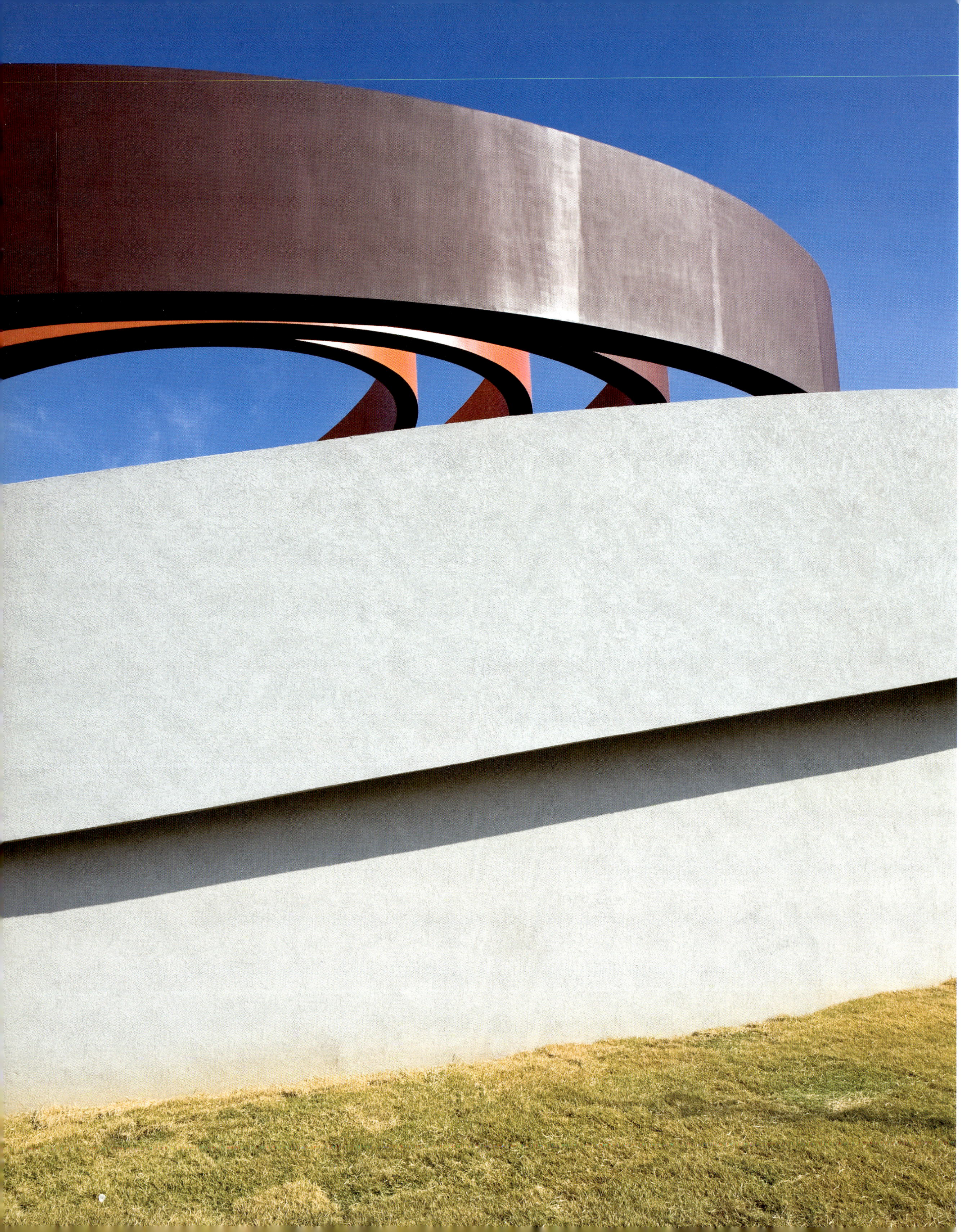

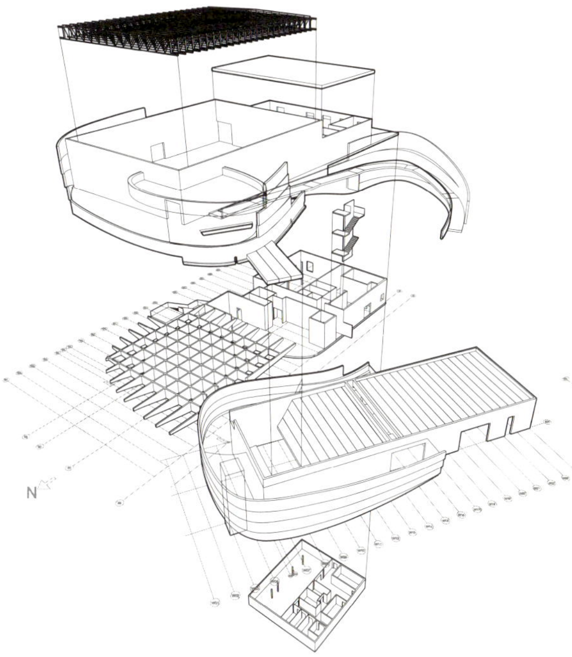

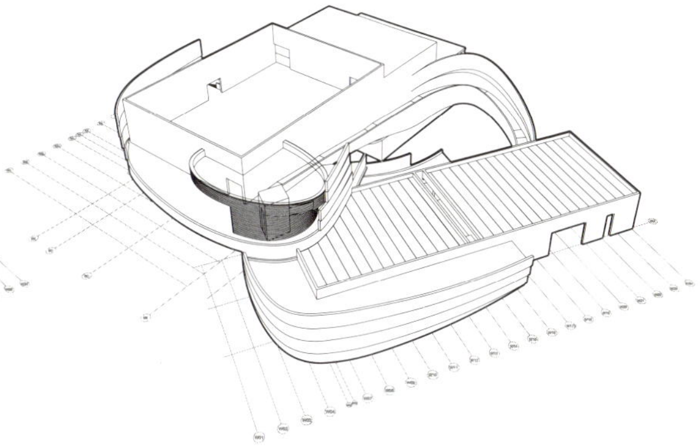

links: Bänder über Beton. rechts: Strukturdiagramm_Ausstellungsraum_Schlaufe über Durchgang_Außenbau.
gauche: Bandes sur béton. droite: Diagramme structurel_Espace d'exposition_Boucles sur le passage_Corps de bâtiment.
izquierda: Cintas sobre hormigón. derecha: Diagrama estructural_Sala de exhibiciones_Cintas sobre pasadizo_Volumen edilicio.

JAPAN_ISHIKAWA 21ST CENTURY MUSEUM OF CONTEMPORARY ART KANAZAWA

JAPAN_JAPON_JAPÓN
SANAA
2004
KUNSTMUSEUM_MUSÉE D'ART_MUSEO DE ARTE
27,920 M²
PHOTOS SANAA

Das Gebäude verfügt neben den Museumsräumen auch über andere öffentliche Räume wie beispielsweise eine Bibliothek, einen Hörsaal und ein Kinderatelier. Die öffentlichen und die Museumsbereiche sind miteinander verflochten, wobei die öffentlichen Räume das Museum umschließen, so dass die potenziellen Nutzergruppen zur Interaktion herausgefordert werden. Das Grundstück verbindet unterschiedliche, wichtige städtische Einrichtungen. Durch die Kreisform hat das Gebäude keine Vorder- oder Rückseite, sondern ist von allen Seiten offen. Ein Spaziergang in der bogenförmigen Glasgalerie entlang der Außenfassade bietet ein 360-Grad-Panorama des Ortes. Die Ausstellungsfläche innerhalb des Erschließungsrunds ist in zahlreiche Galerien unterteilt.

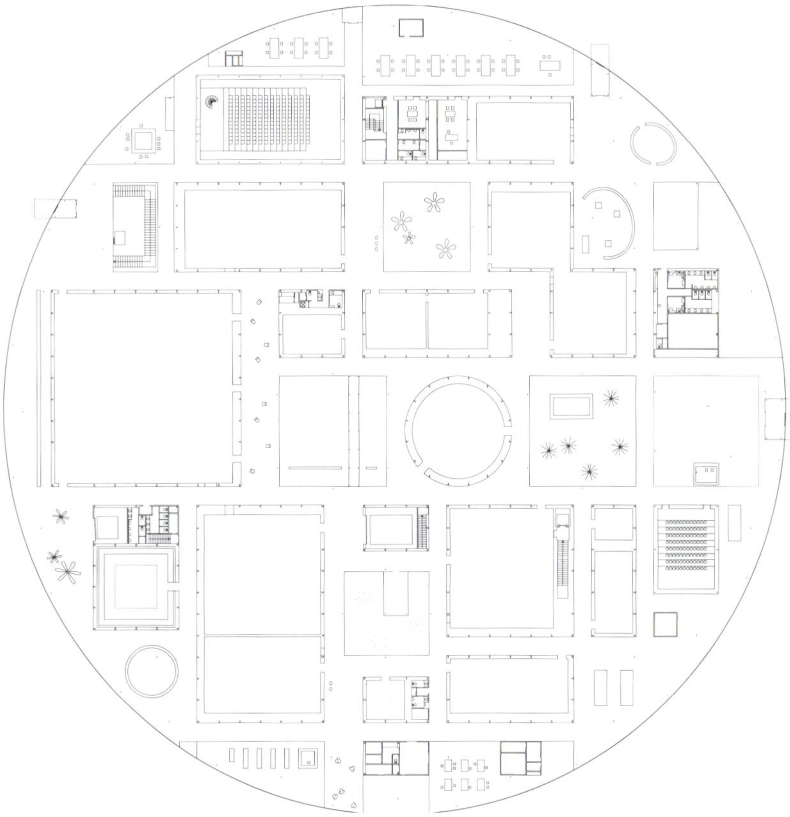

Le bâtiment offre, outre le musée, également des espaces publics divers, notamment une bibliothèque, une salle de conférence et un atelier pour enfants. Les zones consacrées au public et au musée sont très étroitement liées étant donné que les espaces publics entourent le musée afin de favoriser l'interaction entre les groupes d'utilisateurs potentiels. Le terrain relie les différentes installations importantes de la ville. Grâce à sa forme circulaire, le bâtiment n'a aucune partie avant ou arrière : il est ouvert sur tous les côtés. Un passage dans la galerie vitrifiée en arc de cercle de la façade extérieure offre un panorama à 360 degrés du site. La surface d'exposition à l'intérieur de la rotonde d'entrée est divisée en plusieurs galeries.

Además de áreas museísticas, el edificio dispone de otras salas como, por ejemplo, la biblioteca, el auditorio y el taller infantil. Las áreas de museo y público están entrelazadas: los espacios públicos rodean a los museísticos, de modo que los grupos de usuarios potenciales son estimulados a la interacción. En el terreno se conectan diversas instalaciones de uso ciudadano. La forma circular logra que el edificio no tenga frente ni fondo: se puede acceder a él desde todas las direcciones. Un paseo por la galería curva de cristal de la fachada exterior ofrece una panorámica de 360 grados de toda la localidad. La superficie de exhibiciones dentro del círculo se subdivide en numerosas galerías.

links: Grundriss Erdgeschoss_Außenansicht_Glasfassade. rechts: Im Zentrum des Gebäudes_Blick von innen_Innenansicht.
gauche: Plan du rez-de-chaussée_Extérieur_Façade en verre. droite: Au centre du bâtiment_Vue de l'intérieur_Intérieur.
izquierda: Plano de planta baja_Vista exterior_Fachada acristalada. derecha: En el centro del edificio_Vista desde el interior_Vista interior.

JAPAN_MATSUNOYAMA

ECHIGO-MATSUNOYAMA MUSEUM OF NATURAL SCIENCE

JAPAN_JAPON_JAPÓN
TAKAHARU & YUI TEZUKA ARCHITECTS / MIAS
2003
WISSENSCHAFTSMUSEUM_MUSÉE DE LA SCIENCE
MUSEO DE CIENCIAS
1,248 M²
PHOTOS KATSUHISA KIDA

Bei der Konzeption dieser Einrichtung wurde besonderer Nachdruck darauf gelegt, die Natur und die klimatischen Verhältnisse vor Ort einzubeziehen. In den Bergen von Matsunoyama, die für ergiebige Schneefälle bekannt sind, wachsen die japanischen Buchen zunächst horizontal am Boden entlang, bevor sie stark genug sind, um den winterlichen Schneemassen zu widerstehen. Der geneigte Querschnitt des Baus ist durch die Konstruktionen, die die Straßen vor dem Schnee schützen, inspiriert. Der Grundriss hingegen folgt einer Schlange gleich dem Muster der Wege rund um den Ort. Die Außenwände bestehen gänzlich aus 6 Millimeter dicken, geschweißten Cortenstahlplatten, weshalb der Bau aufgrund der winterlichen Kälte um fast 20 Zentimeter in der Länge schrumpft.

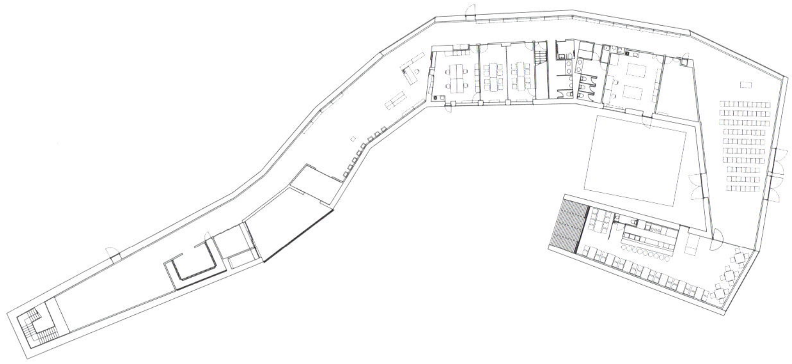

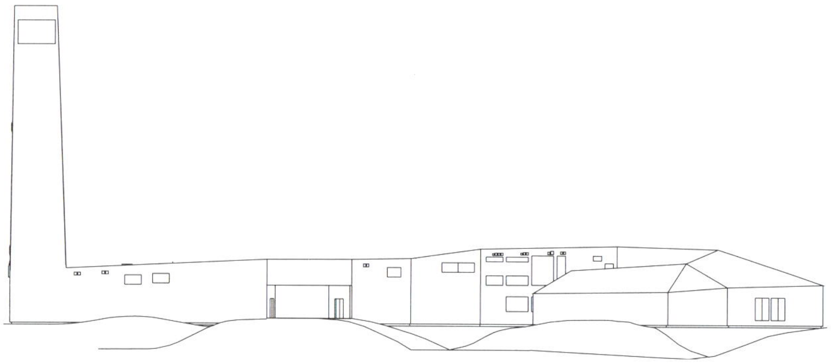

Lors de la conception de l'installation, l'accent particulier a été mis sur l'intégration de la nature et les conditions climatiques sur le site. Dans les montagnes de Matsunoyama, connues pour ses chutes de neige abondantes, les hêtres japonais poussent d'abord à l'horizontale le long du sol avant de se renforcer suffisamment pour résister aux masses de neige hivernales. La coupe transversale inclinée du bâtiment est inspirée par les constructions qui misent à protéger les rues des chutes de neige. Par contre, le plan suit à l'instar d'un serpent le schéma des chemins situés autour du site. Les murs extérieurs sont revêtus intégralement de plaques d'acier corten soudées d'une épaisseur de 6 millimètres et le bâtiment se rétracte sous l'effet du froid hivernal de quasiment 20 centimètres.

En la concepción de las instalaciones se puso especial énfasis en la integración de la naturaleza con las condiciones climáticas del lugar. En las montañas de Matsunoyama, conocidas por sus copiosas nevadas, crecen las hayas japonesas que, al principio, se arrastran horizontalmente por el suelo, hasta que son lo suficientemente fuertes como para soportar las pesadas masas de nieve. La sección inclinada de la edificación se inspira en las construcciones que protegen los caminos de la nieve. La planta, en cambio, se asemeja a una serpiente que se enrosca, de la misma manera que los caminos de la localidad. Las paredes exteriores están completamente hechas en placas de acero corten de 6 milímetros de espesor soldadas entre sí; como consecuencia del frío invernal, el edificio se encoge hasta 20 centímetros.

links: Grundriss Erdgeschoss und Aufriss. Außenbau_Museum im Winter. rechts: Fassade_Ausstellung_Blick ins Café.
gauche: Plan du rez-de-chaussée et vue en élévation_Extérieur_Musée en hiver. droite: Façade Exposition_Vue dans le café.
izquierda: Plano de planta baja y alzado_Vista exterior_El museo en invierno. derecha: Fachada Exposición_Vista hacia el café.

JAPAN_MIDORI **TOMIHIRO ART MUSEUM**

JAPAN_JAPON_JAPÓN
MAKOTO YOKOMIZO / AAT+MAKOTO YOKOMIZO ARCHITECTS, INC.
2005
KUNSTMUSEUM_MUSÉE D'ART_MUSEO DE ARTE
2,463.5 M²
PHOTOS SHIGERU OHNO (486 B. L., 487 B.),
CHRISTOFFER RUDQUIST (486 B. R.),
CHRISTIAN RICHTERS (487 A.)

Das Museum besteht im Grundriss aus 33 Kreisen, deren Größe und Lage dem Bedarf der Kuratoren entspricht. Entsprechend der Ordnung von Seifenblasen ergab sich auch ihre Anordnung als „sich selbst optimierendes" Design. Die ausgeführte Raumgliederung des Museums stellt nur eine unter vielen anderen Möglichkeiten dar. Jeder Kreis hat eine andere Funktion und eine andere Gestaltung. Die Geschlossenheit des Rundraums wird lediglich durch den Durchgang von einem Zylinder zum nächsten gebrochen. Das Museumsinnere bietet viele unterschiedliche Raumerfahrungen. Die Räume zwischen den kreisförmigen Zimmern dienen als Gärten für verschiedene einheimische Pflanzen. Alle Teile der diversen Zylinder wurden in einem Stahlwerk vorgefertigt und anschließend vor Ort montiert.

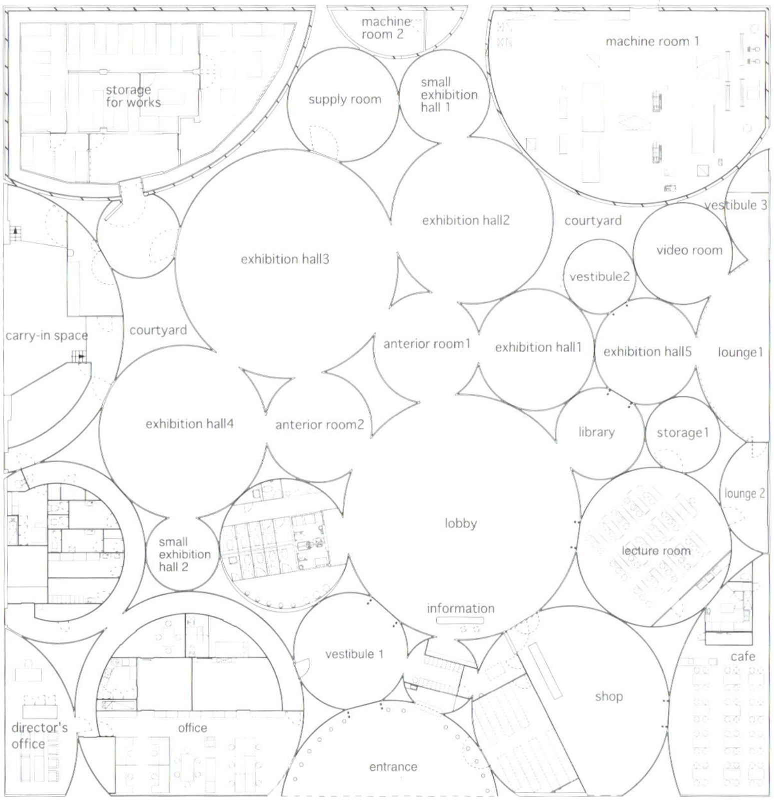

Le plan du musée se compose de 33 cercles dont la dimension et l'emplacement répondent aux exigences des gestionnaires. L'ordre des bulles de savon résulte également de leur disposition à l'instar d'une conception qui s'optimise en soi. La réalisation de la répartition de l'espace du musée est un choix parmi de nombreuses autres options. Chaque cercle a une fonction et une conception différente. La fermeture de l'espace circulaire est uniquement détruite par le passage d'un cylindre à l'autre. L'intérieur du musée offre de nombreuses expériences au niveau spatial. Les espaces intermédiaires entre les pièces en forme circulaire servent de jardins pour les différentes plantes locales. Toutes les parties des différents cylindres sont préfabriquées dans une aciérie et montées ensuite sur place.

La planta del museo consiste de 33 círculos, cuyo tamaño y ubicación corresponde a las necesidades de los curadores. Como si se tratase de pompas de jabón, su disposición se asemeja a un diseño espontáneamente optimizado. La subdivisión del espacio interior del museo fue una opción entre muchas otras posibilidades. Cada círculo posee su propia función y configuración. El espacio redondo es cerrado, y solo se interrumpe en la transición de un cilindro al otro. El interior del museo presenta diversas experiencias de espacialidad. En los espacios intermedios entre las salas redondas hay jardines, donde crecen diversas plantas silvestres. Todas las partes de los diversos cilindros fueron elaboradas en una fundición y se montaron en el sitio.

links: Plan_Museum in Landschaft_Außenbau. rechts: Lounge auf Kusaki-See blickend_Foyer Ausstellungsräume.
gauche: Plan_Musée dans le paysage_Extérieur. droite: Salon avec vue sur le lac Kusaki_Foyer Espaces d'exposition.
izquierda: Planta_Museo en el paisaje_Exterior. derecha: Salón con vista al lago Kusaki_Vestíbulo Salas de exhibiciones.

JAPAN_MINATO-KU, TOKYO **NATIONAL ART CENTER**

JAPAN_JAPON_JAPÓN
KISHO KUROKAWA ARCHITECT & ASSOCIATES
2006
KUNSTMUSEUM_MUSÉE D'ART_MUSEO DE ARTE
49,834 M²
PHOTOS KOJI KOBAYASHI SPIRAL, TOKYO

Das Gebäude umfasst sieben stützenfreie Ausstellungsräume, eine Bibliothek, ein Auditorium, ein Restaurant, Cafés und einen Museumsshop. Die Grundfläche des Kunstzentrums beläuft sich auf rund 50.000 Quadratmeter, was es zur größten Kunstgalerie Japans werden lässt. Das Zentrum ist kein Archiv für Kunst, sondern ein Ausstellungsraum für der Öffentlichkeit zu präsentierende wechselnde Werke und Wanderausstellungen. Im Kontrast zu den technisch geprägten Ausstellungsflächen wurde die Fassade vor dem Atrium als riesige transparente Wellenbewegung gestaltet. Die Bäume, die rund um das Museum wachsen, werden das Atrium in einen umwaldeten öffentlichen Raum verwandeln. Im Atrium befinden sich zwei umgekehrte Kegelstümpfe, deren kreisrunde obere Flächen einem Restaurant und Cafés Raum bieten.

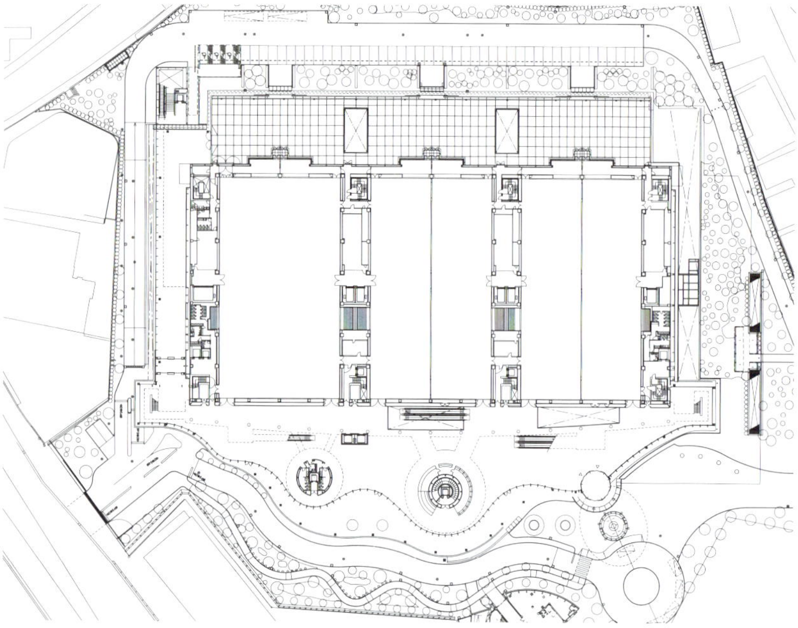

Le bâtiment comprend sept salles d'exposition sans piliers, une bibliothèque, un auditorium, un restaurant, des cafés et la boutique du musée. La superficie du centre d'art s'étend sur environ 50 000 mètres carrés. Par conséquent, c'est la plus grande galerie d'art au Japon. Le centre n'est pas une archive dédiée à l'art, mais un espace d'exposition destiné au public afin de présenter des œuvres en alternance et des expositions itinérantes. Contrairement aux surfaces d'exposition techniques, la conception de la façade située devant l'atrium ressemble à une vague ondulée énorme et transparente. Les arbres plantés tout autour du musée transformeront l'atrium en un espace public boisé. Dans l'atrium, deux cônes renversés offrent des surfaces circulaires où se situent un restaurant et des cafétérias.

El edificio abarca siete salas de exhibiciones sin apoyos intermedios, una biblioteca, un auditorio, un restaurante, cafés y una tienda. La superficie del centro de artes se despliega en 50.000 metros cuadrados, convirtiéndose así en la mayor galería de arte de todo Japón. El centro no constituye un archivo de arte, sino que es un espacio de exhibiciones que se abre al público con presentaciones de exhibiciones temporarias e itinerantes. En contraste con las zonas de exhibición de naturaleza técnica, la fachada delante del atrio está concebida como una enorme superficie en movimiento, ondulante, transparente. Los árboles que crecen alrededor del museo transforman el atrio en un espacio público boscoso. En el atrio se encuentran dos troncos de cono invertidos, cuyas superficies redondeadas ofrecen espacio para un restaurante y cafés.

links: Grundriss 1. Obergeschoss_Gesamtansicht_Perspektive. rechts: Fassadendetail.
gauche: Plan du 1er étage_Vue d'ensemble_Perspective. droite: Façade, détail.
izquierda: Plano del primer piso_Vista del conjunto_Perspectiva. derecha: Detalle de fachada.

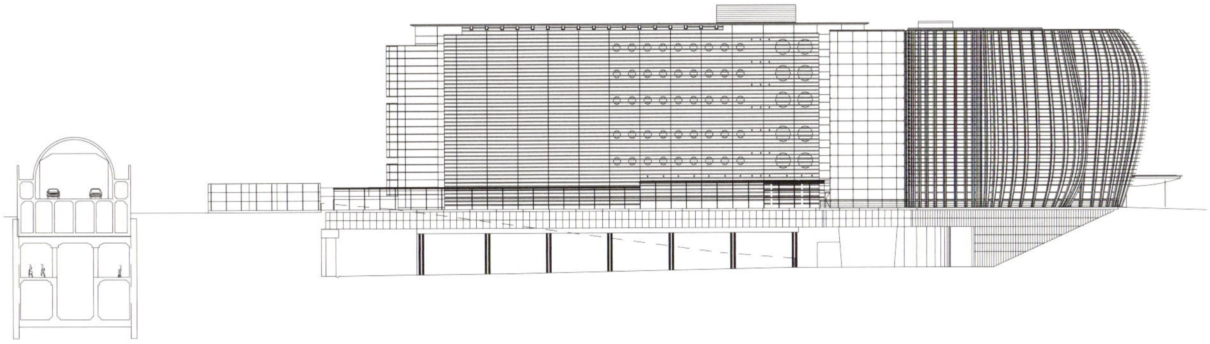

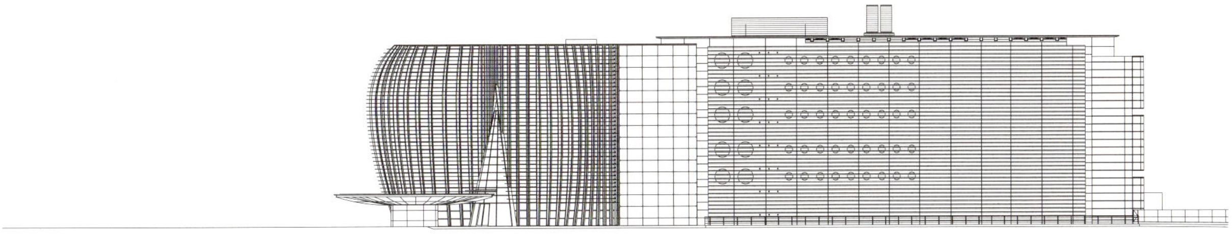

links: Atrium mit Restaurant. rechts: West- und Ostansicht_Fassade_Detail_Fassade.
gauche: Atrium avec le restaurant. droite: Vue côté ouest et est_Façade_Détail_Façade.
izquierda: Atrio con restaurante. derecha: Fachadas oeste y este_Fachada_Detalle_Fachada.

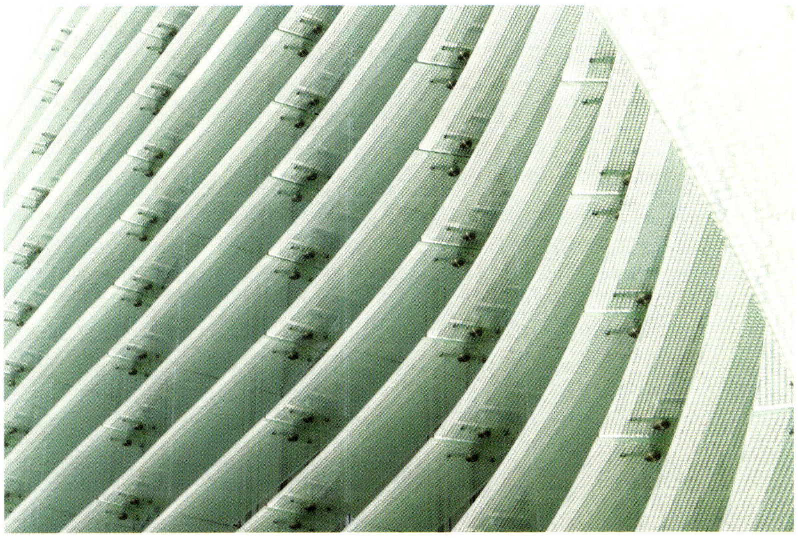

JAPAN_SENDAI **KANNO MUSEUM**

JAPAN_JAPON_JAPÓN
ATELIER HITOSHI ABE
2005
KUNSTMUSEUM_MUSÉE D'ART_MUSEO DE ARTE
220 M²
PHOTOS DAICI ANO, SENDAI

Das Privatmuseum, in dem acht Skulpturen aus der Sammlung des Auftraggebers gezeigt werden, liegt in einem kleinen Ort auf hügeligem Gelände mit Blick auf den Pazifischen Ozean. Ausgehend vom Status Stadt und dem Gebäudeprogramm sollte der Galerieraum selbst wirkungsmächtig genug sein, um lokale künstlerische Aktivitäten zu stimulieren. Statt eines weißen „Kubus", der jedweder Art von Ausstellung Platz bieten würde, wurde eine „Kathedrale" entworfen, eine Ansammlung spezieller Standorte für jede einzelne Skulptur.

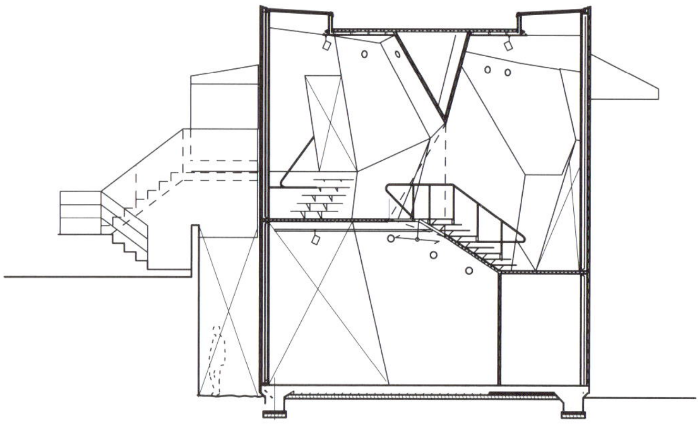

Ce musée privé, qui présente huit sculptures de la collection du mandataire, fait partie d'un petit village situé sur un terrain vallonné qui offre une vue sur l'océan Pacifique. Sur initiative de la ville et conformément au programme du bâtiment, l'espace de la galerie a été doté d'un certain potentiel pour stimuler des activités artistiques au niveau local. À la place d'un « cube » sage pouvant abriter tout type d'exposition, l'édifice a été conçu comme une « cathédrale » composée d'une série de lieux spécifiques dédiés individuellement à chacune des sculptures.

El museo privado, destinado a albergar ocho esculturas de la colección del comitente, se ubica en una pequeña localidad sobre las montañas con vista al Océano Pacífico. Partiendo de la ubicación y del programa del edificio, se decidió que el espacio de la galería debería tener el potencial de estimular diversas actividades artísticas a nivel local. En vez de un "cubo blanco" capaz de albergar cualquier tipo de exhibición, se diseñó una verdadera "catedral", que representa una colección de sitios específicos para cada una de las esculturas.

links: Schnitt_Außenansicht von Osten_Außenansicht von Westen. rechts: Im Erdgeschoss_Im Zwischengeschoss_Eingangsgalerie im Obergeschoss_Innenwand mit geprägter Struktur.
gauche: Coupe_Vue extérieure d'est_Vue extérieure de l'ouest. droite: Au rez-de-chaussée_À l'étage intermédiaire_Galerie d'entrée à l'étage supérieur_Mur intérieur avec structure marquée.
izquierda: Corte_Vista exterior desde el este_Vista exterior desde el oeste. derecha: En planta baja_En el entrepiso_Galería de acceso en el nivel superior_Muro interior esculpido.

JAPAN_TAMA-SHI,TOKYO GENJI PAPER SCULPTURE MUSEUM

JAPAN_JAPON_JAPÓN
CELL SPACE ARCHITECTS, MUTSUE HAYAKUSA
2003
KUNSTMUSEUM_MUSÉE D'ART_MUSEO DE ARTE
1,410 M²
PHOTOS SATOSHI ASAKAWA, TOKYO

Um ein Gleichgewicht zu den Arbeiten des Künstlers herzustellen, wurden für das Museum feinere und zartere Materialien verwendet als bei Architektur im Allgemeinen üblich. Die Architekten experimentierten mit einer Vielzahl von industriellen Geweben, um eine Struktur zu finden, die dem aus Pflanzenfasern hergestellten Japanpapier ähnelt. Schließlich wurde ein Geflecht aus dünnem rostfreiem Stahl gewählt. Die beabsichtigte Wirkung für Fassaden und Raumteilung wurde nur durch die Überlagerung zweier gegenläufiger Effekte von Verbundsicherheitsglas und glänzendem Edelstahlgewebe erreicht: einerseits durch eingeschränkte Sichtbarkeit durch die Edelstahlmaschen und andererseits durch die verstärkte Reflexion auf den Glasflächen.

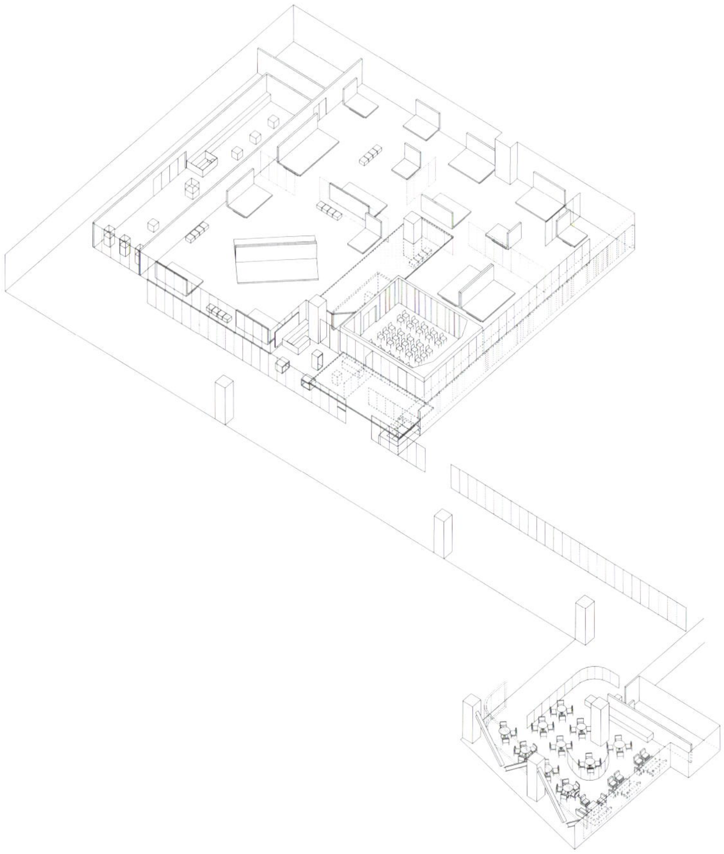

Afin d'établir un équilibre avec les œuvres de l'artiste, des matériaux plus doux et délicats que ceux utilisés habituellement en architecture ont été utilisés lors de la construction de ce musée. Les architectes ont cherché à obtenir une structure similaire au papier japonais fabriqué à partir de fibres de plantes, en expérimentant de multiples textiles industriels. Finalement, leur choix s'est porté sur un treillis en acier inoxydable particulièrement fin. L'effet recherché pour les façades et la répartition des espaces a été atteint grâce à la superposition de deux effets contradictoires entre le verre de sécurité en composite et la structure brillante en acier fin : d'un côté, une image réduite à travers le treillis et, de l'autre, un reflet agrandi sur la surface vitrée.

Para lograr un equilibrio con el trabajo del artista, en este museo se emplearon materiales más delicados y suaves de lo que es habitual en la arquitectura cotidiana. Los arquitectos experimentaron con una multiplicidad de tejidos industriales para obtener una estructura que se asemejase al papel japonés fabricado con fibras vegetales. Finalmente se escogió un tejido de acero inoxidable muy delgado. En las fachadas y las subdivisiones espaciales se logró un efecto deliberado mediante la superposición de los efectos contrapuestos del cristal armado de seguridad y los brillantes tejidos de acero inoxidable: por un lado, una imagen reduccionista con las mallas de acero inoxidable y, por el otro, una reflexión incrementada en las superficies de cristal.

links: Axonometrie_Eingangshalle_Cafe. rechts: Zeittunnel_Museumsshop_Ausstellungshalle.
gauche: Axonométrie_Hall d'entrée_Café. droite: Tunnel temporel_Boutique du musée_Hall d'exposition.
izquierda: Axonométrica_Sala de acceso_Café del museo. derecha: Túnel del tiempo_Tienda del museo_Sala de exhibiciones.

JAPAN_TOKAMACHI CITY **MATSUDAI CULTURAL VILLAGE MUSEUM**

JAPAN_JAPON_JAPÓN
MVRDV
2003
KUNSTMUSEUM_MUSÉE D'ART_MUSEO DE ARTE
2,770 M²
PHOTOS ROB 'T HART

Das Dorf in den Bergen der Präfektur Niigata ist alle drei Jahre das Zentrum der Niigata Kunst-Triennale. Während dieses Festivals ist das Gebäude Hauptveranstaltungsort und dient als Ausstellungsraum. Das Museum erhebt sich auf „Beinen", die im Winter einen schneefreien und trockenen, im Sommer einen schattigen öffentlichen Raum schaffen, wo Veranstaltungen und Konzerte stattfinden können. Diese „Beine" bilden das physische Gerüst des Gebäudes und gewähren Zugang zu ihm. Auf dem Dach formt sich eine steinerne Landschaft aus, die von den strukturellen Anforderungen der beinförmigen Brücken geprägt ist. Die Dachterrasse bietet eine Aussichtsplattform mit Blick auf die Berge und auf die Kunstwerke.

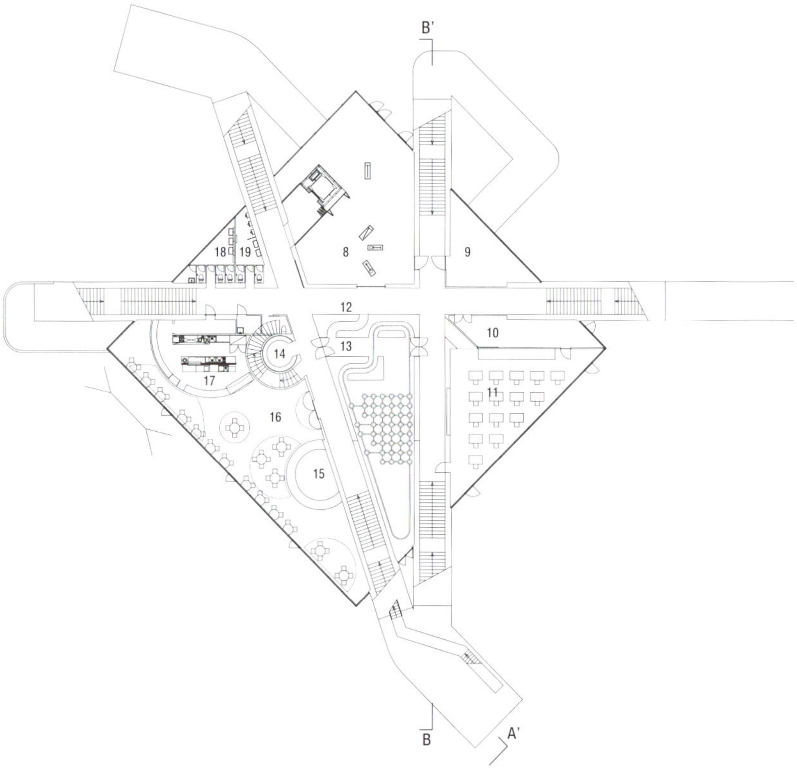

Le village dans les montagnes de la préfecture Niigata accueille tous les trois ans le centre de « Niigata Art Triennal ». Au cours de ce festival, le bâtiment est le lieu de manifestations principales et sert d'espace d'exposition. Le musée s'élève sur des jambes afin d'offrir un espace sec, non enneigé, en hiver et un espace ombragé au public, en été, consacrés aux concerts et manifestations. Ces jambes sont des ossatures physiques permettant l'accès au bâtiment. Sur le toit, un paysage pierreux est marqué par les exigences structurelles des passerelles qui enjambent la structure. La terrasse en toiture offre simultanément une plateforme panoramique sur les montagnes et une perspective sur les œuvres d'art.

Este pueblo, en las montañas de la prefectura de Niigata, alberga cada tres años la "Trienal de Arte de Niigata". Durante este festival, el edificio sirve de centro de actividades y espacio de exhibiciones. El museo se alza sobre pilares y ofrece así un espacio público para conciertos y actividades; en invierno es seco y libre de nieve, en verano ofrece una sombra agradable. Los pilares constituyen el bastidor físico y garantizan el acceso al edificio. En el techo se aprecia un paisaje pétreo, caracterizado por las definiciones estructurales de los puentes en forma de patas. La terraza del techo es a la vez plataforma de observación de las montañas y de las obras de arte.

links: Grundriss 1. Obergeschoss_Außenansicht_Dachterrasse. rechts: Fassade.
gauche: Plan du 1er étage_Vue extérieure_Terrasse de toit. droite: Façade.
izquierda: Plano del primer piso_Vista exterior_Terraza en el techo. derecha: Fachada.

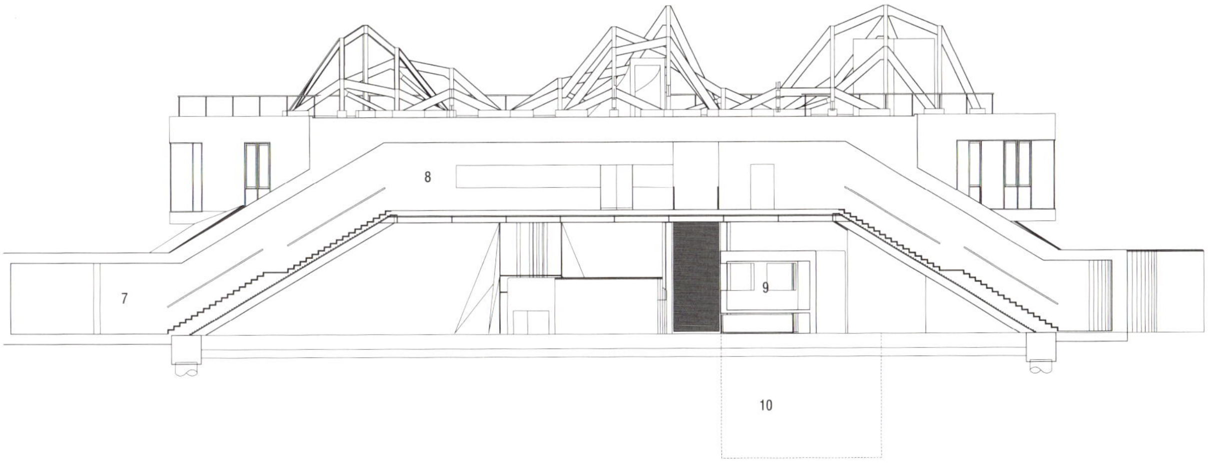

links: Cafeteria. rechts: Schnitt_Aufführungsraum unterhalb des Gebäudes_Ausstellungsbereich Aufgang zum Obergeschoss und WC.
gauche: Cafétéria. droite: Coupe_Espace d'exposition sous le bâtiment_Zone d'exposition_Accès à l'étage supérieur et WC.
izquierda: Cafetería. derecha: Corte_Sala de actividades debajo del edificio_Área de exhibiciones Escalera a la planta alta y sanitario.

KOREA_SEOUL **LEEUM SAMSUNG MUSEUM OF ART**

KOREA_CORÉE_COREA
OFFICE FOR METROPOLITAN ARCHITECTURE (OMA)
2004
KUNSTMUSEUM_MUSÉE D'ART_MUSEO DE ARTE
13,100 M²
PHOTOS OFFICE FOR METROPOLITAN ARCHITECTURE (OMA) (500), PHILIPPE RUAULT (501)

Der Komplex im Wohnviertel Hannam-Dong nahe der Innenstadt Seouls besteht aus drei Bauten von OMA, Mario Botta und Jean Nouvel. Die drei Bauten treffen in einem zentralen Raum zusammen, der Lobby und Information umfasst. Das Gebäude von OMA bietet 13.100 Quadratmeter Ausstellungsfläche für Wechselausstellungen zeitgenössischer Kunst sowie Medien- und Büroräume. Es wird von einer massiven schwarzen Betonbox dominiert, die in einer großen Grabung auf dem bewegten Gelände abgesenkt ist und verschiedene Lichtsituationen innerhalb des Raumes erzeugt. Das Erlebnis der schwarzen Box lenkt den Besucherstrom unter der Box hindurch, in sie hinein und darüber hinweg.

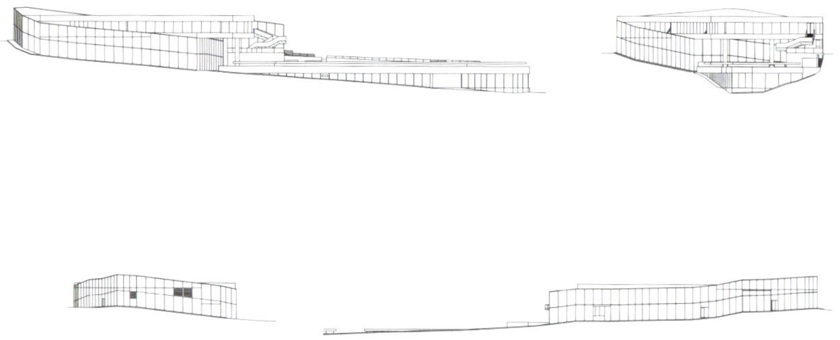

Le complexe situé dans le quartier résidentiel Hannam-Dong à proximité du centre-ville de Séoul est constitué de trois constructions de OMA, Mario Botta et Jean Nouvel. Les trois constructions se rejoignent dans un espace central qui comprend l'entrée et le centre d'information. Le bâtiment OMA offre 13100 mètres carrés d'espaces dédiés aux expositions tournantes d'art contemporain ainsi que des bureaux et espaces audiovisuels. Une boite noire massive domine qui s'allonge vers le bas et domine le terrain animé depuis les hauteurs en produisant des perspectives variées de lumière au sein de l'espace. L'expérience vécue dans la boite noire guide le flux de visiteurs sous la boite, à l'intérieur et au-delà.

El complejo ubicado en el barrio residencial de Hannam-Dong cerca del centro de Seúl comprende tres edificios diseñados por OMA, Mario Botta y Jean Nouvel. Las tres construcciones se encuentran en un espacio central que abarca el vestíbulo y el centro de información. El edificio de OMA ofrece 13.100 metros cuadrados de área de exposiciones para muestras temporarias de arte contemporáneo, además de salas de oficinas y multimedia. Domina una maciza caja negra que se inclina en una excavación sobre el terreno ondulado y genera diversas situaciones luminosas dentro de la sala. La vivencia de la caja negra orienta el flujo de visitantes que pasa bajo la caja, entra en ella y se aleja.

links: Aufrisse_Luftaufnahme_Dachterrasse. rechts: Innenaufnahme_Außenansicht.
gauche: Vue en élévation_Perspective à vol d'oiseau_Terrasse de toit. droite: Vue intérieur_Extérieur.
izquierda: Alzados_Vista aérea_Terraza en el techo. derecha: Vista interior_Vista exterior.

KOREA_SEOUL **SEOUL NATIONAL UNIVERSITY MUSEUM**

KOREA_CORÉE_COREA
OFFICE FOR METROPOLITAN ARCHITECTURE (OMA)
2005
KUNSTMUSEUM_MUSÉE D'ART_MUSEO DE ARTE
4,478 M²
PHOTOS PHILIPPE RUAULT

Das Museum wird durch seine Lage auf einem kleinen Hügel in der Nähe des Eingangs zur Universität bestimmt. Die Form des Baus entstand als rechtwinklige Box, die entsprechend dem Abhang schräg angeschnitten wurde. Diese Form jedoch wurde auf einem kleinen zentralen Kern, dem einzigen Kontakt zum Erdboden, aufgeständert, so dass das Gebäude fast zu schweben scheint und sich hügelauf und -abwärts über das Gelände erstreckt. Die Fassaden des Museums sind lichtdurchlässig und enthüllen das ihm zugrunde liegende tragende Stahlfachwerk. Eine entscheidende Idee war es, sowohl innen wie außen eine freie Bewegung der Besucher zu ermöglichen. Der zwischen erhobenem Bau und Boden vermittelnde Kern dient als Atrium mit rechtwinklig-spiralförmigem Treppenhaus, das die Bereiche Ausstellung, Bildung, Bibliothek und Betrieb miteinander verknüpft.

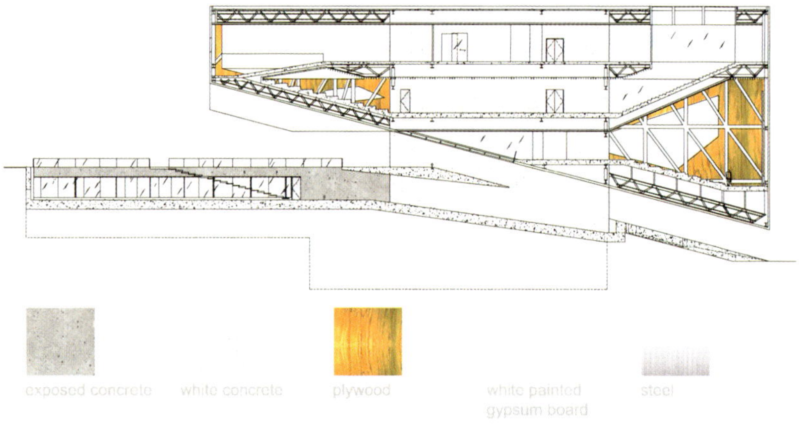

Le musée se caractérise par sa situation sur une petite colline à proximité de l'entrée de l'Université. La forme de la construction apparait découpée comme une boite rectangulaire adaptée à la pente oblique. Cependant, cette forme empilée se concentre sur un petit foyer centralisé comme unique point de contact avec la terre qui contribue à l'aspect presque aérien du bâtiment s'élançant vers les hauteurs et les profondeurs du terrain. Les façades du musée sont translucides et enveloppent la charpente située à la base. L'objectif de l'idée centrale était de favoriser un mouvement libre pour les visiteurs à l'intérieur et à l'extérieur. Le centre communiquant entre la construction élevée et le sol sert d'atrium avec sa cage d'escalier rectangulaire en colimaçon qui relie les zones d'exposition, l'espace formation et opération et la bibliothèque.

El museo está condicionado por su ubicación sobre una pequeña colina cerca del acceso a la universidad. La edificación adoptó una forma de caja ortogonal, recortada según la pendiente. No obstante, esta forma se eleva sobre un pequeño núcleo central que constituye el punto de contacto con el suelo, de modo que el edificio casi parece flotar y se despliega por sobre el terreno. Las fachadas del museo son translúcidas y ocultan el entramado estructural que las sostiene. La idea básica era permitir que el visitante se desplazara libremente, tanto dentro como fuera del museo. El núcleo bajo la construcción sobreelevada sirve de atrio con escalinata ortogonal en espiral, la cual vincula entre sí las áreas de exhibición, educación, biblioteca y empresa.

links: Schnitt_Fassade_Treppenläufe. rechts: Außenbau_Ausstellungsraum_Ausstellung unter dem Dach.
gauche: Coupe_Façade_Système d'escalier. droite: Extérieur_Espace d'exposition_Exposition sous la toiture.
izquierda: Corte_Fachada_Escaleras. derecha: Vista exterior_Sala de exhibiciones_Exhibición bajo techo.

현대미술로의 초대

UAE_SAADIYAT ISLAND **LOUVRE ABU DHABI**

VEREINIGTE ARABISCHE EMIRATE_ÉMIRATS ARABES UNIS
EMIRATOS ÁRABES UNIDOS
ATELIERS JEAN NOUVEL
2012
KUNSTMUSEUM_MUSÉE D'ART_MUSEO DE ARTE
22,500 M²
PHOTOS COURTESY OF THE ARCHITECTS

Der neue Louvre erfindet eine einladende Welt, die Licht und Schatten ebenso in einer gelassenen Atmosphäre vereint wie flirrende und ruhige Plätze. Er ist als im Wasser gebauter und von einem Schirm geschützter Archipel ausgebildet, der von Licht durchdrungen wird. Das Museum ist trockenen Fußes lediglich mit dem Boot oder von der Küste aus über Pontons zu erreichen. Der Entwurf beruht auf einem zentralen Motiv arabischer Architektur: der Kuppel. Dennoch handelt es sich hier – wie die formale Kluft zur Bautradition zeigt – um ganz moderne Architektur. Die doppelte Kuppel ist flach und hat einen Durchmesser von 180 Metern. Sie bietet eine lichtdurchlässige Geometrie, und ihr Schatten wird aufgrund des in zufälliger Anordnung durchbrochenen Gewebes punktuell von Sonnenstrahlen durchstoßen.

Le nouveau Louvre invente un monde accueillant qui réunit dans une atmosphère calme la lumière et l'ombre comme des lieux vibrants et tranquilles. Il est formé tel un archipel construit dans l'eau et protégé par un bouclier qui laisse pénétrer la lumière. Le musée est uniquement accessible par bateau ou par le ponton depuis la côte à pieds secs. Le projet repose sur un thème central issu de l'architecture arabe : la coupole. Cependant, dans ce cas, il s'agit d'une architecture très moderne qui allie un clivage fidèle à la tradition de la construction. La double coupole est plate avec un diamètre de 180 mètres. Elle offre une géométrie perméable à la lumière et son ombre est percée partiellement par les rayons du soleil grâce à la structure nuancée qui permet l'arrivée ponctuelle des rayons de soleil.

El nuevo Louvre inventa un mundo que invita, que aúna luz y sombra en una atmósfera apacible, con rincones tranquilos y resplandores centelleantes. Está conformado como un archipiélago construido en el agua y protegido por un gran paraguas; la luz se tamiza a través del mismo con delicadeza. Solamente se llega al museo por barco, o también desde la costa, a pie, sobre pontones. El proyecto evoca un motivo central de la arquitectura árabe tradicional, la cúpula. No obstante, en este caso se trata de arquitectura netamente moderna, como se aprecia en la brecha formal con la tradición constructiva. La doble cúpula es aplanada y tiene un diámetro de 180 metros. Ofrece una geometría permeable a la luz, y su sombra es proyectada puntualmente por los rayos del sol que atraviesan la aleatoria disposición de su abigarrado entretejido.

links: Lageplan_Flache, zweischalige Kuppel. rechts: Schatten mit Lichtflecken_Ausstellungsbereich.
gauche: Plan de site_Surface, coupole à deux épaisseurs. droite: Parties ombragées avec des tâches lumineuses_Zone d'exposition.
izquierda: Ubicación_Cúpula aplanada de dos capas. derecha: Sombra y manchas de luz_Área de exhibiciones.

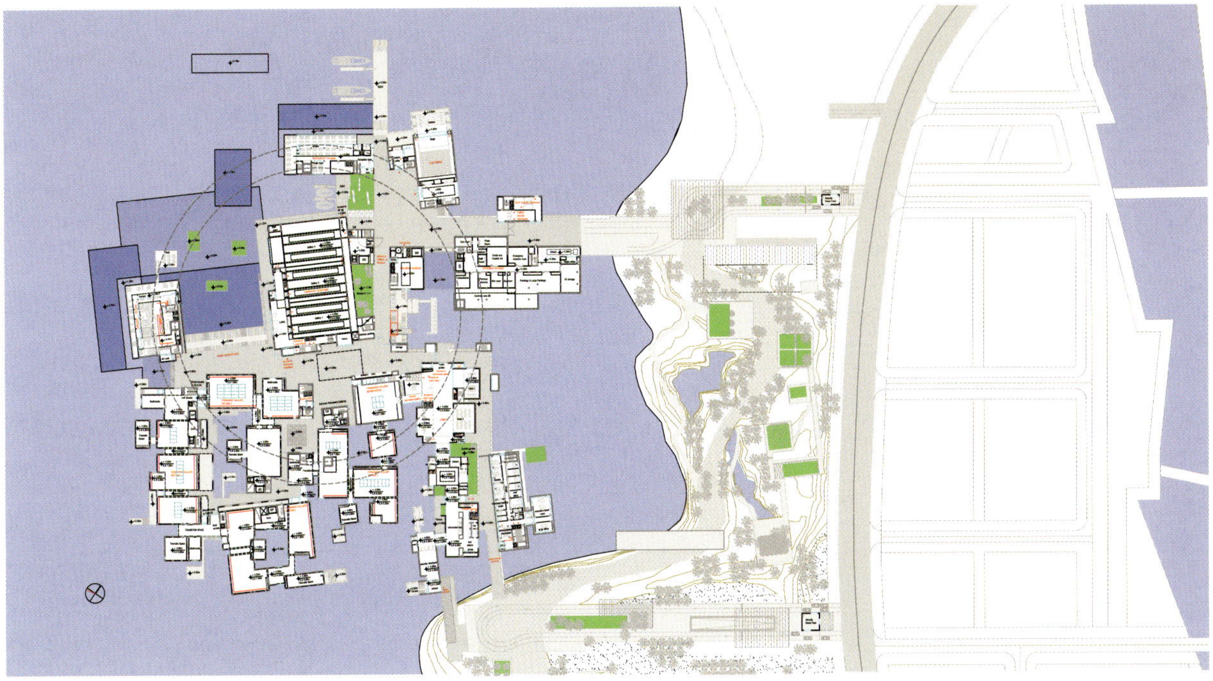

links: Innenraum. rechts: Grundriss Erdgeschoss_Ausstellungsbereich.
gauche: Intérieur. droite: Plan du rez-de-chaussée_Zone d'exposition.
izquierda: Espacio interior. derecha: Plano de planta baja_Área de exhibiciones.

INDEX

ARCHITEKTEN_ARCHITECTES_ARQUITECTOS

PROJEKTE_PROJETS_PROYECTOS